# PAPUA
## NEW GUINEA

# OIL AND GAS SECTOR, ENERGY POLICY, LAWS AND REGULATIONS HANDBOOK

### VOLUME 1
### PRINCIPAL LAWS, REGULATIONS AND POLICIES

International Business Publications, USA
Washington DC, USA - Papua New Guinea

# PAPUA NEW GUINEA

## OIL AND GAS SECTOR, ENERGY POLICY, LAWS AND REGULATIONS HANDBOOK

### VOLUME 1 PRINCIPAL LAWS, REGULATIONS AND POLICIES

*Papua New Guinea Oil & Gas Sector Business and Investment Opportunities Yearbook Volume 1 Regulations and Policies*
*Papua New Guinea Oil & Gas Sector Business and Investment Opportunities Yearbook Volume 2 Exploration, Incentives, Projects*

**UPDATED ANNUALLY**

**We express our sincere appreciation to all government agencies and international organizations which provided information and other materials for this handbook**

**Cover Design: International Business Publications, USA**



**2019 Edition Updated Reprint International Business Publications, USA**
**ISBN 1-43873-798-X**

**For additional analytical, business and investment opportunities information, please contact Global Investment & Business Center, USA at (703) 370-8082. Fax: (703) 370-8083. E-mail: ibpusa3@gmail.com Global Business and Investment Info Databank - www.ibpus.com**

Printed in the USA

**For additional analytical, business and investment opportunities information, please contact Global Investment & Business Center, USA at (703) 370-8082. Fax: (703) 370-8083. E-mail: ibpusa3@gmail.com Global Business and Investment Info Databank - www.ibpus.com**

# PAPUA
## NEW GUINEA

# OIL AND GAS SECTOR, ENERGY POLICY, LAWS AND REGULATIONS HANDBOOK
## VOLUME 1
## PRINCIPAL LAWS, REGULATIONS AND POLICIES

## TABLE OF CONTENTS

# STRATEGIC AND DEVELOPMENT PROFILES

## STRATEGIC PROFILE

| | |
|---|---|
| Capital and largest city | Port Moresby 9°30′S 147°07′E |
| Official languages | • Hiri Motu<br>• Tok Pisin<br>• PNG Sign Language<br>• English |
| Demonym | Papua New Guinean |
| Government | Unitary parliamentary constitutional monarchy |
| • Monarch | Elizabeth II |
| • Governor-General | Bob Dadae |
| • Prime Minister | Peter O'Neill |
| Legislature | National Parliament |
| Independence from Australia | |
| • Papua and New Guinea Act 1949 | 1 July 1949 |
| • Declared and recognised | 16 September 1975 |
| Area | |
| • Total | 462,840 km$^2$ (178,700 sq mi) (54th) |
| • Water (%) | 2 |
| Population | |
| • 2016 census preliminary estimate | 8,084,999 [5] (101st) |
| • 2000 census | 5,190,783 |
| • Density | 15/km$^2$ (38.8/sq mi) (201st) |
| GDP (PPP) | 2017 estimate |
| • Total | $29.481 billion[6] (139th) |
| • Per capita | $3,635[6] |
| GDP (nominal) | 2017 estimate |
| • Total | $21.189 billion[6] (115th) |
| • Per capita | $2,613[6] |
| Gini (1996) | 50.9[7]<br>high |
| HDI | ▲ 0.516[8]<br>low · 154th |
| Currency | Papua New Guinean kina (PGK) |
| Time zone | AEST (UTC+10, +11) |
| Drives on the | left |
| Calling code | +675 |
| ISO 3166 code | PG |
| Internet TLD | .pg |

**Papua New Guinea** officially named the **Independent State of Papua New Guinea**, is a country in Oceania that occupies the eastern half of the island of New Guinea (the western portion of the island is a part of the Indonesian provinces of Papua and West Papua) and numerous offshore islands. It is located in the southwestern Pacific Ocean, in a region described since the early 19th century as Melanesia. The capital is Port Moresby.

Papua New Guinea is one of the most culturally diverse countries in the world. According to recent data, 841 different languages are listed for the country, although 11 of these have no known living speakers. There may be at least as many traditional societies, out of a population of about 6.3 million. It is also one of the most rural, as only 18 percent of its people live in urban centres. The country is one of the world's least explored, culturally and geographically, and many undiscovered species of plants and animals are thought to exist in the interior of Papua New Guinea.

Strong growth in Papua New Guinea's mining and resource sector has led to PNG becoming the sixth fastest-growing economy in the world as of 2011. Despite this, many people live in extreme poverty, with about one-third of the population living on less than US$1.25 per day. The majority of the population still live in traditional societies and practice subsistence-based agriculture. These societies and clans have some explicit acknowledgement within the nation's constitutional framework. The PNG Constitution expresses the wish for "traditional villages and communities to remain as viable units of Papua New Guinean society",and for active steps to be taken in their preservation.

After being ruled by three external powers since 1884, Papua New Guinea acquired self-government in 1973 and independence in 1975. It was not strictly speaking "granted" independence by Australia, which had not been its colonist but only administered British New Guinea after federation in 1901 and German New Guinea after 1914 for the League of Nations and for the United Nations after 1945. It became a separate Commonwealth realm upon independence with Her Majesty Queen Elizabeth II reigning as the Queen of Papua New Guinea.

| | |
|---|---|
| **Background:** | The eastern half of the island of New Guinea - second largest in the world - was divided between Germany (north) and the UK (south) in 1885. The latter area was transferred to Australia in 1902, which occupied the northern portion during World War I and continued to administer the combined areas until independence in 1975. A nine-year secessionist revolt on the island of Bougainville ended in 1997, after claiming some 20,000 lives. |

**GEOGRAPHY**

| | |
|---|---|
| **Location:** | Southeastern Asia, group of islands including the eastern half of the island of New Guinea between the Coral Sea and the South Pacific Ocean, east of Indonesia |
| **Geographic coordinates:** | 6 00 S, 147 00 E |
| **Map references:** | Oceania |
| **Area:** | total: 462,840 sq km<br>land: 452,860 sq km<br>water: 9,980 sq km |
| **Area - comparative:** | slightly larger than California |
| **Land boundaries:** | total: 820 km<br>border countries: Indonesia 820 km |
| **Coastline:** | 5,152 km |
| **Maritime claims:** | measured from claimed archipelagic baselines<br>continental shelf: 200-m depth or to the depth of exploitation<br>exclusive fishing zone: 200 NM<br>territorial sea: 12 NM |
| **Climate:** | tropical; northwest monsoon (December to March), southeast monsoon (May to October); slight seasonal temperature variation |
| **Terrain:** | mostly mountains with coastal lowlands and rolling foothills |
| **Elevation extremes:** | lowest point: Pacific Ocean 0 m |

| | |
|---|---|
| | highest point: Mount Wilhelm 4,509 m |

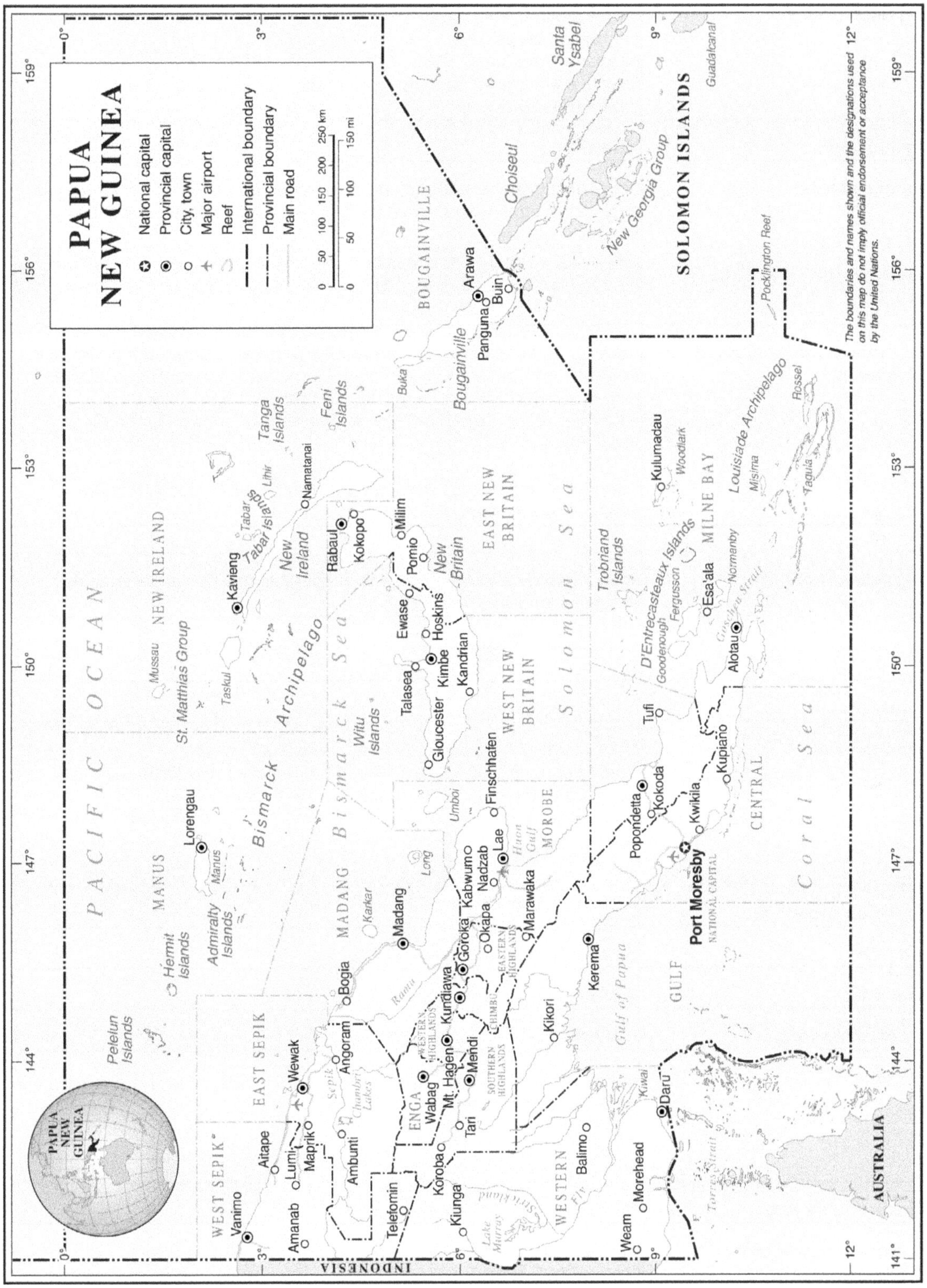

| | |
|---|---|
| **Natural resources:** | gold, copper, silver, natural gas, timber, oil, fisheries |
| **Land use:** | arable land: 0.1%<br>permanent crops: 1%<br>permanent pastures: 0%<br>forests and woodland: 92.9%<br>other: 6% (1993 est.) |
| **Irrigated land:** | NA sq km |
| **Natural hazards:** | active volcanism; situated along the Pacific "Rim of Fire"; the country is subject to frequent and sometimes severe earthquakes; mud slides; tsunamis |
| **ENVIRONMENT - CURRENT ISSUES:** | rain forest subject to deforestation as a result of growing commercial demand for tropical timber; pollution from mining projects; severe drought |
| **Environment - international agreements:** | party to: Antarctic Treaty, Biodiversity, Climate Change, Desertification, Endangered Species, Environmental Modification, Hazardous Wastes, Law of the Sea, Marine Dumping, Nuclear Test Ban, Ozone Layer Protection, Ship Pollution, Tropical Timber 83, Tropical Timber 94, Wetlands<br><br>signed, but not ratified: Antarctic-Environmental Protocol, Climate Change-Kyoto Protocol |

| | |
|---|---|
| **Geography - note:** | shares island of New Guinea with Indonesia; one of world's largest swamps along southwest coast |

**PEOPLE**

| | |
|---|---|
| **Population:** | 5,049,055 |
| **Age structure:** | 0-14 years: 38.7% (male 993,248; female 960,647)<br>15-64 years: 57.63% (male 1,507,064; female 1,402,666)<br>65 years and over: 3.67% (male 87,779; female 97,651) |

| | |
|---|---|
| **Population growth rate:** | 2.43% |
| **Birth rate:** | 32.15 births/1,000 population |
| **Death rate:** | 7.88 deaths/1,000 population |
| **Net migration rate:** | 0 migrant(s)/1,000 population |
| **Sex ratio:** | at birth: 1.05 male(s)/female<br>under 15 years: 1.03 male(s)/female<br>15-64 years: 1.07 male(s)/female<br>65 years and over: 0.9 male(s)/female<br>total population: 1.05 male(s)/female |
| **Infant mortality rate:** | 58.21 deaths/1,000 live births |
| **Life expectancy at birth:** | total population: 63.46 years<br>male: 61.39 years<br>female: 65.64 years |

| | |
|---|---|
| **Total fertility rate:** | 4.3 children born/woman |
| **HIV/AIDS - adult prevalence rate:** | 0.22% |
| **HIV/AIDS - people living with HIV/AIDS:** | 5,400 |
| **HIV/AIDS - deaths:** | 450 |
| **Nationality:** | noun: Papua New Guinean(s)<br>adjective: Papua New Guinean |
| **Ethnic groups:** | Melanesian, Papuan, Negrito, Micronesian, Polynesian |
| **Religions:** | Roman Catholic 22%, Lutheran 16%, Presbyterian/Methodist/London Missionary Society 8%, Anglican 5%, Evangelical Alliance 4%, Seventh-Day Adventist 1%, other Protestant 10%, indigenous beliefs 34% |
| **Languages:** | English spoken by 1%-2%, pidgin English widespread, Motu spoken in Papua region<br>note: 715 indigenous languages |
| **Literacy:** | definition: age 15 and over can read and write<br>total population: 72.2%<br>male: 81%<br>female: 62.7% |

## GOVERNMENT

**Country name:**
**conventional long form:** Independent State of Papua New Guinea
**conventional short form:** Papua New Guinea
**local short form:** Papuaniugini
**former:** Territory of Papua and New Guinea
**abbreviation:** PNG
**etymology:** the word "papua" derives from the Malay "papuah" describing the frizzy hair of the Melanesians; Spanish explorer Ynigo ORTIZ de RETEZ applied the term "Nueva Guinea" to the island of New Guinea in 1545 after noting the resemblance of the locals to the peoples of the Guinea coast of Africa

**Government type:**
parliamentary democracy (National Parliament) under a constitutional monarchy; a Commonwealth realm

**Capital:**
**name:** Port Moresby
**geographic coordinates:** 9 27 S, 147 11 E
**time difference:** UTC+10 (15 hours ahead of Washington, DC, during Standard Time)

**Administrative divisions:**
20 provinces, 1 autonomous region*, and 1 district**; Bougainville*, Central, Chimbu, Eastern Highlands, East New Britain, East Sepik, Enga, Gulf, Hela, Jiwaka, Madang, Manus, Milne Bay, Morobe, National Capital**, New Ireland, Northern, Southern Highlands, Western, Western Highlands, West New Britain, West Sepik

**Independence:**
16 September 1975 (from the Australian-administered UN trusteeship)

**National holiday:**
Independence Day, 16 September (1975)

**Constitution:**
adopted 15 August 1975, effective at independence 16 September 1975; amended many times, last in 2013; note - in September 2015, the Supreme Court nullified the 2013 constitutional amendment that increased the grace period on motions of no confidence (2016)

**Legal system:**
mixed legal system of English common law and customary law

**International law organization participation:**
has not submitted an ICJ jurisdiction declaration; non-party state to the ICCt

**Citizenship:**
**citizenship by birth:** no
**citizenship by descent only:** at least one parent must be a citizen of Papua New Guinea
**dual citizenship recognized:** no
**residency requirement for naturalization:** 8 years

**Suffrage:**
18 years of age; universal

**Executive branch:**

**chief of state:** Queen ELIZABETH II (since 6 February 1952); represented by Governor General Grand Chief Sir Bob DADAE (since 28 February 2017)
**head of government:** Prime Minister Peter Paire O'NEILL (since 2 August 2011); Deputy Prime Minister Charles ABEL (since 4 August 2017)

**cabinet:** National Executive Council appointed by the governor general on the recommendation of the prime minister
**elections/appointments:** the monarchy is hereditary; governor general nominated by the National Parliament and appointed by the chief of state; following legislative elections, the leader of the majority party or majority coalition usually appointed prime minister by the governor general pending the outcome of a National Parliament vote
**election results:** Peter Paire O'NEILL (PNC) reelected prime minister; National Parliament vote - 60 to 46

**Legislative branch:**
**description:** unicameral National Parliament (111 seats; members directly elected in single-seat constituencies - 91 local and 20 provincial - by majority preferential vote; members serve 5-year terms); note - the constitution allows up to 126 seats
**elections:** last held from 24 June 2017 to 8 July 2017 (next to be held in June 2022)
**election results:** results pending as of late October 2017; percent of vote by party - NA; seats by party - NA
**note:** 12 other parties won 2 or fewer seats; association with political parties is fluid

**Judicial branch:**
**highest court(s):** Supreme Court (consists of the chief justice, deputy chief justice, and 28 judges); National Courts (13 courts located in the province capitals, with a total of 19 resident judges)
**judge selection and term of office:** Supreme Court chief justice appointed by the governor-general upon advice of the National Executive Council (cabinet) after consultation with the National Justice Administration Minister; deputy chief justice and other justices appointed by the Judicial and Legal Services Commission, a 5-member body to include the Supreme Court chief and deputy chief justices, the chief ombudsman, and a member of the National Parliament; full-time citizen judges appointed for 10-year renewable terms; non-citizen judges initially appointed for 3-year renewable terms and after first renewal until age 70; appointment and tenure of National Court resident judges NA
**subordinate courts:** district, village, and juvenile courts

**Political parties and leaders:**
National Alliance Party or NAP [Patrick PRUAITCH]

Papua and Niugini Union Party or PANGU [Sam BASIL]
Papua New Guinea Party or PNGP [Belden NAMAH]
People's National Congress Party or PNC [Peter Paire O'NEILL]
People's Party or PP [Peter IPATAS]
People's Progress Party or PPP [Sir Julius CHAN]
Social Democratic Party or SDP [Powes PARKOP]
Triumph Heritage Empowerment Party or THE [Don POLYE]
United Resources Party or URP [William DUMA]
**note:** as of 8 July 2017, 45 political parties were registered

**Political pressure groups and leaders:**
Centre for Environment Law and Community Rights or Celcor [Damien ASE]
Community Coalition Against Corruption
National Council of Women
Transparency International Papau New Guinea or TIPNG (chapter of Transparency International)
**chief of mission:** Ambassador (vacant); Charge D'Affaires Elias Rahuromo WOHENGU (since 30 September 2017)
**International organization participation:**
ACP, ADB, AOSIS, APEC, ARF, ASEAN (observer), C, CD, CP, EITI (candidate country), FAO, G-77, IAEA, IBRD, ICAO, ICRM, IDA, IFAD, IFC, IFRCS, IHO, ILO, IMF, IMO, Interpol, IOC, IOM, IPU, ISO (correspondent), ITSO, ITU, MIGA, NAM, OPCW, PIF, Sparteca, SPC, UN, UNCTAD, UNESCO, UNIDO, UNMISS, UNWTO, UPU, WCO, WFTU (NGOs), WHO, WIPO, WMO, WTO

**Diplomatic representation in the US:**

**chancery:** 1779 Massachusetts Avenue NW, Suite 805, Washington, DC 20036
**telephone:** [1] (202) 745-3680
**FAX:** [1] (202) 745-3679

**Diplomatic representation from the US:**
**chief of mission:** Ambassador Catherine EBERT-GRAY (since 23 February 2016); note - also accredited to the Solomon Islands and Vanuatu
**embassy:** P.O. Box 1492, Port Moresby
**mailing address:** 4240 Port Moresby Place, US Department of State, Washington DC 20521-4240
**telephone:** [675] 321-1455
**FAX:** [675] 321-3423

**Flag description:**
divided diagonally from upper hoist-side corner; the upper triangle is red with a soaring yellow bird of paradise centered; the lower triangle is black with five, white, five-pointed stars of the Southern Cross constellation centered; red, black, and yellow are traditional colors of Papua New Guinea; the bird of paradise - endemic to the island of New Guinea - is an emblem of regional tribal culture and represents the emergence of Papua New Guinea as a nation; the Southern Cross, visible in the night sky, symbolizes Papua New Guinea's connection with Australia and several other countries in the South Pacific

**National symbol(s):**
bird of paradise; national colors: red, black

**National anthem:**
**name:** "O Arise All You Sons"
**lyrics/music:** Thomas SHACKLADY

## ECONOMY

Papua New Guinea (PNG) is richly endowed with natural resources, but exploitation has been hampered by rugged terrain, land tenure issues, and the high cost of developing infrastructure. The economy has a small formal sector, focused mainly on the export of those natural resources, and an informal sector, employing the majority of the population. Agriculture provides a subsistence livelihood for 85% of the people. The global financial crisis had little impact because of continued foreign demand for PNG's commodities.

Mineral deposits, including copper, gold, and oil, account for nearly two-thirds of export earnings. Natural gas reserves amount to an estimated 155 billion cubic meters. Following construction of a $19 billion liquefied natural gas (LNG) project, PNG LNG, a consortium led by ExxonMobil, began exporting liquefied natural gas to Asian markets in May 2014. The project was delivered on time and only slightly above budget. The success of the project has encouraged other companies to look at similar LNG projects. French supermajor Total is expected to begin construction on the Papua LNG project by 2020. Due to lower global commodity prices, resource revenues of all types have fallen dramatically. PNG's government has recently been forced to adjust spending levels downward.

Numerous challenges still face the government of Peter O'NEILL, including providing physical security for foreign investors, regaining investor confidence, restoring integrity to state institutions, promoting economic efficiency by privatizing moribund state institutions, and maintaining good relations with Australia, its former colonial ruler. Other socio-cultural challenges could upend the economy including chronic law and order and land tenure issues.

**GDP (purchasing power parity):**

$28.02 billion (2016 est.)
$27.33 billion (2015 est.)
$25.63 billion (2014 est.)
**note:** data are in 2016 dollars
**country comparison to the world:** 134

**GDP (official exchange rate):**
$19.92 billion (2016 est.)

**GDP - real growth rate:**
2.5% (2016 est.)
6.6% (2015 est.)
7.4% (2014 est.)
**country comparison to the world:** 112

**GDP - per capita (PPP):**
$3,500 (2016 est.)
$3,500 (2015 est.)
$3,400 (2014 est.)
**note:** data are in 2016 dollars
**country comparison to the world:** 183
**Gross national saving:**
38.1% of GDP (2016 est.)
24% of GDP (2015 est.)
-11.7% of GDP (2014 est.)
**country comparison to the world:** 8

**GDP - composition, by end use:**
**household consumption:** 49.4%
**government consumption:** 7.8%
**investment in fixed capital:** 9.9%
**investment in inventories:** 0.4%
**exports of goods and services:** 68.7%
**imports of goods and services:** -36.2% (2016 est.)

**GDP - composition, by sector of origin:**
**agriculture:** 22.3%
**industry:** 37.6%

**services:** 40.1% (2016 est.)

**Agriculture - products:**
coffee, cocoa, copra, palm kernels, tea, sugar, rubber, sweet potatoes, fruit, vegetables, vanilla; poultry, pork; shellfish
**Industries:**
copra crushing, palm oil processing, plywood production, wood chip production; mining (gold, silver, copper); crude oil and petroleum products; construction, tourism

**Industrial production growth rate:**
4.8% (2016 est.)
**country comparison to the world:** 39

**Labor force:**
4.365 million (2016 est.)
**country comparison to the world:** 90

**Labor force - by occupation:**
**agriculture:** 85%
**industry:** NA%
**services:** NA% (2005 est.)
**Unemployment rate:**
2.5% (2014 est.)
2.5% (2013 est.)
**country comparison to the world:** 17

**Population below poverty line:**
37% (est.)

**Household income or consumption by percentage share:**
**lowest 10%:** 1.7%
**highest 10%:** 40.5%

**Distribution of family income - Gini index:**
50.9 (1996)
**country comparison to the world:** 13

**Budget:**
**revenues:** $3.169 billion
**expenditures:** $4.295 billion (2016 est.)

**Taxes and other revenues:**
15.9% of GDP (2016 est.)
**country comparison to the world:** 179

**Budget surplus (+) or deficit (-):**
-5.7% of GDP (2016 est.)
**country comparison to the world:** 171

**Public debt:**
39.4% of GDP (2016 est.)
36.9% of GDP (2015 est.)
**country comparison to the world:** 124

**Fiscal year:**
calendar year

**Inflation rate (consumer prices):**
6.3% (2016 est.)

6% (2015 est.)
**country comparison to the world:** 187

**Central bank discount rate:**
14% (31 December 2010)
6.92% (31 December 2009)
**country comparison to the world:** 13

**Commercial bank prime lending rate:**
8.3% (31 December 2016 est.)
8.73% (31 December 2015 est.)
**country comparison to the world:** 101
**Stock of narrow money:**
$5.282 billion (31 December 2016 est.)
$4.936 billion (31 December 2015 est.)
**country comparison to the world:** 97

**Stock of broad money:**
$8.085 billion (31 December 2014 est.)
$7.477 billion (31 December 2013 est.)
**country comparison to the world:** 115

**Stock of domestic credit:**
$6.36 billion (31 December 2016 est.)
$6.118 billion (31 December 2015 est.)
**country comparison to the world:** 117

**Market value of publicly traded shares:**
$10.71 billion (31 December 2012 est.)
$8.999 billion (31 December 2011 est.)
$9.742 billion (31 December 2010 est.)
**country comparison to the world:** 73

**Current account balance:**
$3.051 billion (2016 est.)
$4.148 billion (2015 est.)
**country comparison to the world:** 28

**Exports:**
$7.886 billion (2016 est.)
$8.377 billion (2015 est.)
**country comparison to the world:** 94

**Exports - commodities:**
oil, gold, copper ore, logs, palm oil, coffee, cocoa, crayfish, prawns

**Exports - partners:**
Japan 17.4%, Australia 15.9%, China 12.1%

**Imports:**
$1.83 billion (2016 est.)
$2.267 billion (2015 est.)
**country comparison to the world:** 165

**Imports - commodities:**
machinery and transport equipment, manufactured goods, food, fuels, chemicals

**Imports - partners:**

Australia 25.9%, China 20%, Singapore 12.6%, Malaysia 7.2%, US 4.2%, Indonesia 4.1%, South Korea 4% (2015)

**Reserves of foreign exchange and gold:**
$1.629 billion (31 December 2016 est.)
$1.738 billion (31 December 2015 est.)
**country comparison to the world:** 121

**Debt - external:**
$22.04 billion (31 December 2016 est.)
$20.41 billion (31 December 2015 est.)
**country comparison to the world:** 85

**Stock of direct foreign investment - at home:**
$NA

**Exchange rates:**
kina (PGK) per US dollar -
3.156 (2016 est.)
2.7684 (2015 est.)
2.7684 (2014 est.)
2.4614 (2013 est.)
2.08 (2012 est.)

## ENERGY

**Electricity access:**
**population without electricity:** 5,568,879
**electrification - total population:** 18%
**electrification - urban areas:** 72%
**electrification - rural areas:** 10%

**Electricity - production:**
3.2 billion kWh (2014 est.)
**country comparison to the world:** 128

**Electricity - consumption:**
3 billion kWh (2014 est.)
**country comparison to the world:** 133

**Electricity - exports:**
0 kWh (2013 est.)
**country comparison to the world:** 186

**Electricity - imports:**
0 kWh (2013 est.)
**country comparison to the world:** 189

**Electricity - installed generating capacity:**
900,000 kW (2014 est.)
**country comparison to the world:** 130

**Electricity - from fossil fuels:**
61.1% of total installed capacity (2012 est.)
**country comparison to the world:** 128

**Electricity - from nuclear fuels:**
0% of total installed capacity (2012 est.)
**country comparison to the world:** 167

**Electricity - from hydroelectric plants:**
30.9% of total installed capacity (2012 est.)
**country comparison to the world:** 75

**Electricity - from other renewable sources:**
8% of total installed capacity (2012 est.)
**country comparison to the world:** 47

**Crude oil - production:**
52,600 bbl/day (2015 est.)
**country comparison to the world:** 55

**Crude oil - exports:**
25,400 bbl/day (2013 est.)
**country comparison to the world:** 54

**Crude oil - imports:**
14,880 bbl/day (2013 est.)
**country comparison to the world:** 70

**Crude oil - proved reserves:**
200 million bbl (1 January 2016 es)
**country comparison to the world:** 62

**Refined petroleum products - production:**
28,340 bbl/day (2013 est.)
**country comparison to the world:** 87

**Refined petroleum products - consumption:**
42,000 bbl/day (2014 est.)
**country comparison to the world:** 109
**Refined petroleum products - exports:**
8,062 bbl/day (2013 est.)
**country comparison to the world:** 86

**Refined petroleum products - imports:**
21,180 bbl/day (2013 est.)
**country comparison to the world:** 115

**Natural gas - production:**
4.75 billion cu m (2014 est.)
**country comparison to the world:** 53

**Natural gas - consumption:**
100 million cu m (2014 est.)
**country comparison to the world:** 109

**Natural gas - exports:**
4.65 billion cu m (2014 est.)
**country comparison to the world:** 33

**Natural gas - imports:**
0 cu m (2013 est.)
**country comparison to the world:** 118

**Natural gas - proved reserves:**
151.3 billion cu m (1 January 2016 es)
**country comparison to the world:** 47

**Carbon dioxide emissions from consumption of energy:**
3.7 million Mt (2013 est.)
**country comparison to the world:** 137

## COMMUNICATIONS

**Telephones - fixed lines:**
**total subscriptions:** 150,000
**subscriptions per 100 inhabitants:** 2 (July 2015 est.)
**country comparison to the world:** 137

**Telephones - mobile cellular:**
**total:** 3.56 million
**subscriptions per 100 inhabitants:** 53 (July 2015 est.)
**country comparison to the world:** 132

**Telephone system:**

**general assessment:** services are minimal; facilities provide radiotelephone and telegraph, coastal radio, aeronautical radio, and international radio communication services

**domestic:** access to telephone services is not widely available although combined fixed-line and mobile-cellular teledensity has increased to roughly 55 per 100 persons

**international:** country code - 675; submarine cables to Australia and Guam; satellite earth station - 1 Intelsat (Pacific Ocean); international radio communication service (2015)

**Broadcast media:**

2 TV stations, 1 commercial station operating since the late 1980s, and 1 state-run station launched in 2008; satellite and cable TV services are available; state-run National Broadcasting Corporation operates 3 radio networks with multiple repeaters and about 20 provincial stations; several commercial radio stations with multiple transmission points as well as several community stations; transmissions of several international broadcasters are accessible

**Internet country code:**

.pg

**Internet users:**
**total:** 527,000
**percent of population:** 7.9% (July 2015 est.)
**country comparison to the world:** 162

## TRANSPORTATION

**National air transport system:**
**number of registered air carriers:** 6
**inventory of registered aircraft operated by air carriers:** 47
**annual passenger traffic on registered air carriers:** 2,062,584

**annual freight traffic on registered air carriers:** 34,827,034 mt-km

**Civil aircraft registration country code prefix:**
P2 (2016)

**Airports:**
561 (2013)

**country comparison to the world:** 12

**Airports - with paved runways:**
**total:** 21
**over 3,047 m:** 1
**2,438 to 3,047 m:** 2
**1,524 to 2,437 m:** 12
**914 to 1,523 m:** 5
**under 914 m:** 1

**Airports - with unpaved runways:**
**total:** 540
**1,524 to 2,437 m:** 11
**914 to 1,523 m:** 53
**under 914 m:** 476

**Heliports:**
2

**Pipelines:**
oil 264 km

**Roadways:**
**total:** 9,349 km
**paved:** 3,000 km
**unpaved:** 6,349 km
**country comparison to the world:** 139

**Waterways:**
11,000 km (2011)
**country comparison to the world:** 11

**Merchant marine:**
**total:** 31
**by type:** bulk carrier 7, cargo 22, petroleum tanker 2
**foreign-owned:** 8 (Germany 1, Malaysia 1, UAE 6)
**country comparison to the world:** 83

**Ports and terminals:**
**major seaport(s):** Kimbe, Lae, Madang, Rabaul, Wewak
**LNG terminal(s) (export):** Port Moresby

## MILITARY

**Military expenditures:**
0.66% of GDP (2014)
0.68% of GDP (2013)
0.72% of GDP (2012)
0.5% of GDP (2011)
**country comparison to the world:** 127

**Military branches:**
Papua New Guinea Defense Force (PNGDF, includes Maritime Operations Element, Air Operations Element) (2013)

**Military service age and obligation:**
16 years of age for voluntary military service (with parental consent); no conscription; graduation from grade 12 required (2013)

## TRANSNATIONAL ISSUES

**Disputes - international:**
relies on assistance from Australia to keep out illegal cross-border activities from primarily Indonesia, including goods smuggling, illegal narcotics trafficking, and squatters and secessionists

**Refugees and internally displaced persons:**
**refugees (country of origin):** 9,368 (Indonesia) (2015)
**IDPs:** 8,400 (natural disasters, tribal conflict, inter-communal violence, development projects)

**Trafficking in persons:**

**current situation:** Papua New Guinea is a source and destination country for men, women, and children subjected to sex trafficking and forced labor; foreign and Papua New Guinean women and children are subjected to sex trafficking, domestic servitude, forced begging, and street vending; parents may sell girls into forced marriages to settle debts or as peace offerings or trade them to another tribe to forge a political alliance, leaving them vulnerable to forced domestic service, or, in urban areas, they may prostitute their children for income or to pay school fees; Chinese, Malaysian, and local men are forced to labor in logging and mining camps through debt bondage schemes; migrant women from Indonesia, Malaysia, Thailand, China, and the Philippines are subjected to sex trafficking and domestic servitude at logging and mining camps, fisheries, and entertainment sites

**tier rating:** Tier 2 Watch List - Papua New Guinea does not fully comply with the minimum standards for the elimination of trafficking; however, it is making significant efforts to do so; the Criminal Code Amendment of 2013, which prohibits all forms of trafficking was brought into force in 2014; the government also formed an anti-trafficking committee, which drafted a national action plan; despite corruption problems, trafficking-related crimes were prosecuted in village courts rather than criminal courts, resulting in restitution to the victim but no prison time for offenders; the government did not investigate, prosecute, or convict any officials or law enforcement personnel complicit in trafficking offenses; the government made no efforts to proactively identify trafficking victims, has no formal victim identification and referral mechanism, and does not provide care facilities to victims or funding to shelters run by NGOs or international organizations (2015)

**Illicit drugs:**

major consumer of cannabis

# IMPORTANT INFORMATION FOR UNDERSTANDING THE COUNTRY

**Official Name: Independent State of Papua New Guinea**

**PROFILE**

**Geography**
Land area: 462,860 sq. km.; about the size of California.
Cities: *Capital*--Port Moresby (254,158). *Other cities*--Lae (78,038), Mt. Hagen (27,789).
Terrain: Mostly mountains with coastal lowlands and rolling foothills. The largest portion of the population lives in fertile highlands valleys that were unknown to the outside world until the 1930s, but that supported agriculture some 10,000 years ago, possibly before agriculture was developed elsewhere.
Climate: Tropical. NW monsoon, Dec.-Mar.; SE monsoon, May-Oct.

**People**
Population: 5.8 million.
Annual growth rate: 3.1%.
Languages: Three official: English, Tok Pisin, and Motu. There are approximately 860 other languages.
Education: *Years compulsory*--0. *Literacy*--57.3%
Health: *Infant mortality rate*--68.4/1,000. *Life expectancy*--56.0 yrs.

**Government**
Type: Constitutional monarchy with parliamentary democracy.
Constitution: September 16, 1975.
Branches: *Executive*--British monarch (chief of state), represented by governor general; prime minister (head of government). *Legislative*--unicameral parliament. *Judicial*--independent; highest is Supreme Court.
Administrative subdivisions: 19 provinces and the national capital district (Port Moresby).
Major political parties: National Alliance (NA), People's Progress Party (PPP), Pangu Pati, People's Democratic Movement (PDM), and Melanesian Alliance (MA).
Suffrage: Universal over 18 years of age.

**Economy**
Natural resources: Gold, copper ore, oil, natural gas, timber, fish.
Agriculture (38% of GDP): *Major products*--coffee, cocoa, coconuts, palm oil, timber, tea, vanilla.
Industry (25% of GDP): *Major sectors*--copra crushing; palm oil processing; plywood production; wood chip production; mining of gold, silver, and copper; construction; tourism; crude oil production.
Trade: *Exports*--66% of GDP: gold, copper ore, oil, timber, palm oil, coffee. *Major markets*--Australia, Japan, China, Germany, U.K., Indonesia. *Imports*--31% of GDP: machinery and transport equipment, manufactured goods, food, fuels, chemicals. *Major suppliers*--Australia, Singapore, New Zealand, China, Japan, Malaysia.

Papua New Guinea is a young, vibrant nation with a great deal to offer foreign investors. Some of the key reasons for taking a closer look at Papua New Guinea include:

***Political stability:*** The country is politically stable with a well-entrenched democratic system of government and institutions;

***Positive attitude to foreign investment:*** The Government of Papua New Guinea recognises the importance of the private sector to the country's development and guarantees the security of foreign investment;

***Investment incentives:*** Generous incentives are available to approved ventures. Impediments to the development of new, worthwhile businesses are being removed;

***Joint venture flexibility:*** The government does not dictate the level of foreign ownership in joint ventures. This is left to mutual agreement between the investor and the local counterpart;

***Preferential market access for certain goods:*** Many products originating in Papua New Guinea are allowed duty-free or preferential entry into a number of important markets;

***No language barriers:*** English is widely spoken and understood, despite the country boasting more than 800 other languages;

***Boundless opportunities:*** The business environment is relatively uncrowded and there are many opportunities for profitable investments;

***Resource-driven potential:*** The country is on the verge of substantial development as large-scale mining and petroleum projects create flow-on activities to many sectors of the economy;

***Abundance of natural, renewable resources:*** The country has an abundance of forest and marine resources; and,

***Agricultural opportunities:*** The climatic conditions of the country are highly-favourable for agricultural activities.

Papua New Guinea genuinely welcomes foreign investment that contributes to the economic development and prosperity of the country.

Investing in Papua New Guinea can be a profitable exercise, irrespective of the size of the project. Some of the world's leading corporate entities already know that Papua New Guinea can be a good place to do business.

## PEOPLE

The indigenous population of Papua New Guinea is one of the most heterogeneous in the world. Papua New Guinea has several thousand separate communities, most with only a few hundred people. Divided by language, customs, and tradition, some of these communities have engaged in low-scale tribal conflict with their neighbors for millennia. The advent of modern weapons and modern migration into urban areas has greatly magnified the impact of this lawlessness.

The isolation created by the mountainous terrain is so great that some groups, until recently, were unaware of the existence of neighboring groups only a few kilometers away. The diversity, reflected in a folk saying, "For each village, a different culture," is perhaps best shown in the local languages. Spoken mainly on the island of New Guinea--composed of Papua New Guinea and the Indonesian province of West Papua--some 800 of these languages have been identified; of these, only 350-450 are related. The remainder seem to be totally unrelated either to each other or to the other major groupings. Most native languages are spoken by a few hundred to a few thousand, although Enga, used in part of the highlands, is spoken by some 130,000 people. However, the Enga people are subdivided into clans that regularly conflict with each other. Many native languages are extremely complex grammatically.

Melanesian Pidgin serves as the lingua franca. English is spoken by educated people and in Milne Bay Province. The overall population density is low, although pockets of overpopulation exist. Papua New Guinea's Western Province averages one person per square kilometer (3 per sq. mi.). The Chimbu Province in the New Guinea highlands averages 20 persons per square kilometer (60 per sq. mi.) and has areas containing up to 200 people farming a square kilometer of land. The highlands are home to 40% of the population.

A considerable urban drift toward Port Moresby and other major centers has occurred in recent years. The trend toward urbanization accelerated in the 1990s, bringing in its wake squatter settlements, ethnic disputes, unemployment, and attendant social problems, especially violent crime.

Approximately 96% of the population is Christian. The churches with the largest number of members are the Roman Catholic Church, the Evangelical Lutheran Church, the United Church, and the Seventh Day

Adventist church. Although the major churches are under indigenous leadership, a large number of missionaries remain in the country. The bulk of the estimated 2,000 Americans resident in Papua New Guinea are missionaries and their families. The non-Christian portion of the indigenous population, as well as a portion of the nominal Christians, practices a wide variety of religions that are an integral part of traditional culture, mainly animism (spirit worship) and ancestor cults.

Foreign residents comprise about 1% of the population. More than half are Australian; others are from the United Kingdom, New Zealand, the Philippines, and the United States, most of whom are missionaries. Since independence, about 900 foreigners have become naturalized citizens.

Though cultures vary widely, traditional Papua New Guinea social structures generally include the following characteristics:

- The practice of subsistence economy;
- Recognition of bonds of kinship with obligations extending beyond the immediate family group;
- Generally egalitarian relationships with an emphasis on acquired, rather than inherited, status; and
- A strong attachment of the people to land, which is held communally. Traditional communities do not recognize a permanent transfer of ownership when land is sold.
- Though land and other possessions may be inherited through the female line in some cultures, women generally are considered and treated as inferiors. Gender violence is endemic.
- Patterns and frequency of sexual activity, though never publicly discussed, contribute to the current rapid spread of HIV.

Most Papua New Guineans still adhere strongly to this traditional social structure, which has its roots in village life.

## HISTORY

Archeological evidence indicates that humans arrived on New Guinea at least 60,000 years ago, probably by sea from Southeast Asia during an Ice Age period when the sea was lower and distances between islands shorter. Although the first arrivals were hunters and gatherers, early evidence shows that people managed the forest environment to provide food. There also are indications of gardening having been practiced at the same time that agriculture was developing in Mesopotamia and Egypt. Early garden crops--many of which are indigenous--included sugarcane, Pacific bananas, yams, and taros, while sago and pandanus were two commonly exploited native forest crops. Today's staples--sweet potatoes and pigs--were later arrivals, but shellfish and fish have long been mainstays of coastal dwellers' diets.

When Europeans first arrived, inhabitants of New Guinea and nearby islands--while still relying on bone, wood, and stone tools--had a productive agricultural system. They traded along the coast, where products mainly were pottery, shell ornaments, and foodstuffs, and in the interior, where forest products were exchanged for shells and other sea products.

The first Europeans to sight New Guinea were probably the Portuguese and Spanish navigators sailing in the South Pacific in the early part of the 16th century. In 1526-27, Don Jorge de Meneses accidentally came upon the principal island and is credited with naming it "Papua," a Malay word for the frizzled quality of Melanesian hair. The term "New Guinea" was applied to the island in 1545 by a Spaniard, Íñigo Ortiz de Retes, because of a fancied resemblance between the islands' inhabitants and those found on the African Guinea coast. Although European navigators visited the islands and explored their coastlines for the next 170 years, little was known of the inhabitants until the late 19th century.

### New Guinea

With Europe's growing need for coconut oil, Godeffroy's of Hamburg, the largest trading firm in the Pacific, began trading for copra in the New Guinea Islands. In 1884, Germany formally took possession of the northeast quarter of the island and put its administration in the hands of a chartered company. In 1899, the German imperial government assumed direct control of the territory, thereafter known as German New Guinea. In 1914, Australian troops occupied German New Guinea, and it remained under Australian military control until 1921. The British Government, on behalf of the Commonwealth of Australia, assumed a mandate from the League of Nations for governing the Territory of New Guinea in 1920. That mandate was administered by the Australian Government until the Japanese invasion in December 1941 brought about its suspension. Following the surrender of the Japanese in 1945, civil administration of Papua as well as New Guinea was restored, and under the Papua New Guinea Provisional Administration Act, 1945-46, Papua and New Guinea were combined in an administrative union.

**Papua**

On November 6, 1884, a British protectorate was proclaimed over the southern coast of New Guinea (the area called Papua) and its adjacent islands. The protectorate, called British New Guinea, was annexed outright on September 4, 1888. The possession was placed under the authority of the Commonwealth of Australia in 1902. Following the passage of the Papua Act of 1905, British New Guinea became the Territory of Papua, and formal Australian administration began in 1906. Papua was administered under the Papua Act until the Japanese invaded the northern parts of the islands in 1941 and began to advance on Port Moresby and civil administration was suspended. During the war, Papua was governed by a military administration from Port Moresby, where Gen. Douglas MacArthur occasionally made his headquarters. As noted, it was later joined in an administrative union with New Guinea during 1945-46 following the surrender of Japan.

**Postwar Developments**

The Papua and New Guinea Act of 1949 formally approved the placing of New Guinea under the international trusteeship system and confirmed the administrative union of New Guinea and Papua under the title of "The Territory of Papua and New Guinea." The act provided for a Legislative Council (established in 1951), a judicial organization, a public service, and a system of local government. A House of Assembly replaced the Legislative Council in 1963, and the first House of Assembly opened on June 8, 1964. In 1972, the name of the territory was changed to Papua New Guinea.

Elections in 1972 resulted in the formation of a ministry headed by Chief Minister Michael Somare, who pledged to lead the country to self-government and then to independence. Papua New Guinea became self-governing in December 1973 and achieved independence on September 16, 1975. The 1977 national elections confirmed Michael Somare as Prime Minister at the head of a coalition led by the Pangu Party. However, his government lost a vote of confidence in 1980 and was replaced by a new cabinet headed by Sir Julius Chan as Prime Minister. The 1982 elections increased Pangu's plurality, and parliament again chose Somare as Prime Minister. In November 1985, the Somare government lost a vote of no confidence, and the parliamentary majority elected Paias Wingti, at the head of a five-party coalition, as Prime Minister. A coalition, headed by Wingti, was victorious in very close elections in July 1987. In July 1988, a no-confidence vote toppled Wingti and brought to power Rabbie Namaliu, who a few weeks earlier had replaced Somare as leader of the Pangu Party.

Such reversals of fortune and a revolving-door succession of prime ministers have characterized Papua New Guinea's national politics. From 1988 to 2002, the country had numerous prime ministers. A plethora of political parties, coalition governments, shifting party loyalties, and motions of no confidence in the leadership all lent an air of instability to political proceedings. For the first 27 years of independence, a "first past the post" electoral system resulted in many parliamentarians elected with less than 15% of their constituency. Fractious politics and a 75% loss rate for incumbents precluded the development of strong political parties or a stable national leadership. Many hope that limited preferential voting, introduced in 2003, and an organic law on political parties will stabilize national politics.

In the 2002 elections, virtually the entire previous cabinet lost their seats. The government was formed by a coalition of several parties, and Sir Michael Somare, the leader of the National Alliance (and the nation's first Prime Minister in 1975), was elected Prime Minister. The 2007 elections returned Somare as Prime Minister. His government was the first to complete a 5-year term since independence.

## GOVERNMENT AND POLITICAL CONDITIONS

Papua New Guinea, a constitutional monarchy, recognizes the Queen of England as head of state. She is represented by a Governor General who is elected by parliament and who performs mainly ceremonial functions. Papua New Guinea has three levels of government--national, provincial, and local. There is a 109-member unicameral parliament, whose members are elected every 5 years. The parliament in turn elects the prime minister, who appoints his cabinet from members of his party or coalition.

Members of parliament are elected from 19 provinces and the national capital district of Port Moresby. Parliament introduced reforms in June 1995 to change the provincial government system, with regional (at-large) members of parliament becoming provincial governors, while retaining their national seats in parliament.

Papua New Guinea's judiciary is independent of the government. It protects constitutional rights and interprets the laws. There are several levels, culminating in the Supreme Court.
Papua New Guinea's politics are highly competitive with most members elected on a personal and ethnic basis within their constituencies rather than as a result of party affiliation. Members of parliament are now elected in a limited preferential voting (LPV) system. There are several parties, but party allegiances are not strong. Winning candidates are usually courted in efforts to forge the majority needed to form a government, and allegiances are fluid. No single party has yet won enough seats to form a government in its own right.

Papua New Guinea has a history of changes in government coalitions and leadership from within parliament during the 5-year intervals between national elections. New governments are protected by law from votes of no confidence for the first 18 months of their incumbency, and no votes of no confidence may be moved in the 12 months preceding a national election. In an effort to create greater stability by reducing incessant votes of no confidence, the Integrity of Political Parties Act was passed in 1999, forbidding members of each party in parliament from shifting loyalty to another party.

In 2003, the electoral system was changed to limited preferential voting, which many hope will encourage politicians to strike alliances and to be responsive to constituent concerns once elected. The new system was first used in a 2004 by-election with modest, but positive results.
On Bougainville Island, a 10-year rebellion was halted by a truce in 1997 and a permanent cease-fire was signed in April 1998. A peace agreement between the Government and ex-combatants was signed in August 2001. Under the eyes of a regional peace-monitoring force and a UN observer mission, the government and provincial leaders established an interim administration and made significant progress toward complete surrender/destruction of weapons. A constitution was drafted in 2004 and provincial government elections were held in May 2005. The elections were deemed to be free and fair by international observers, and Joseph Kabui was elected to serve as the first president of the Autonomous Bougainville Government.

## GOVERNMENT OFFICIALS

The **Cabinet of Papua New Guinea** functions as the policy and decision-making body of the executive branch within the government system of Papua New Guinea. The Prime Minister and Ministers serve as members of the Cabinet.

With Prime Minister Sir Michael Somare having been hospitalised for a serious heart condition, leadership of the nation was vested in Deputy Prime Minister Sam Abal in April 2011. In August, following a Cabinet reshuffle which had led three ministers to join the Opposition, the latter brought a successful motion of no confidence in Abal's government. Parliament chose Peter O'Neill to serve as Prime Minister.

On 27 February 2012, O'Neill removed the Finance portfolio from Don Polye, taking it on himself. He cited "the continuing lack of ability by the department and ministry of finance to contain expenditure overruns outside of the budget appropriations". Polye retained the Treasury portfolio, and gained that of Border Development. O'Neill hinted that the Finance ministry would eventually be returned to him, and also hinted at an imminent major Cabinet reshuffle.

On 9 August 2012, following a general election, O'Neill announced the following cabinet for the 2012-2017 term:

| Portfolio | Minister | Minister's province | Minister's party | Parliamentary secretary | Opposition shadow minister |
|---|---|---|---|---|---|
| Prime Minister | Peter O'Neill | Southern Highlands Province | People's National Congress Party | | |

| Portfolio | Minister | Minister's province | Minister's party | Parliamentary secretary | Opposition shadow minister |
|---|---|---|---|---|---|
| • Deputy Prime Minister<br>• Minister for Inter-Government Relations | Leo Dion | East New Britain Province | Triumph Heritage Empowerment Party | | |
| Minister for Agriculture & Livestock | Tommy Tomscoll | Madang Province | People's Democratic Movement Party | | |
| Minister for Bougainville Affairs | Steven Kamma | Autonomous Region of Bougainville | United Resources Party | | |
| Minister for Civil Aviation | Davis Steven | Milne Bay Province | People's Party | | |
| Minister for Communication & Information Technology | Jimmy Miringtoro | Autonomous Region of Bougainville | People's National Congress Party | | |
| Minister for Community Development, Religion & Youth | Loujaya Toni | Morobe Province | Indigenous People's Party | | |
| Minister for Correctional Services | Jim Simatab | East Sepik Province | National Alliance Party | | |
| Minister for Defence | Fabian Pok | Jiwaka Province | United Resources Party | | |
| Minister for Education | Paru Aihi | Central Province | People's National Congress Party | | |
| Minister for Environment & Conservation | John Pundari | Enga Province | People's Party | | |
| Minister for Finance | James Marape | Hela Province | People's National Congress Party | | |
| Minister for Fisheries & Marine Resources | Mao Zeming | Morobe Province | People's National Congress Party | | |
| Minister for Foreign Affairs & Immigration | Rimbink Pato | Enga Province | United Party | | |
| Minister for Forests & Climate Change | Patrick Pruaitch | West Sepik Province | National Alliance Party | | |
| Minister for Health & HIV/AIDS | Michael Malabag | National Capital District | People's National Congress Party | | |
| Minister for Higher Education, Research, Science, & Technology | [Francis Marus]] | | | | |
| Minister for Housing & Urban Development | Paul Isikiel | Morobe Province | People's National Congress Party | | |
| Minister for Justice & Attorney-General | Kerenga Kua | Chimbu Province | National Alliance Party | | |
| Minister for Labour & Industrial Relations | Mark Maipakai | Gulf Province | Triumph Heritage Empowerment Party | | |

| Portfolio | Minister | Minister's province | Minister's party | Parliamentary secretary | Opposition shadow minister |
|---|---|---|---|---|---|
| Minister for Lands & Physical Planning | Benny Allan | Eastern Highlands Province | People's National Congress Party | | |
| Minister for Mining | Byron Chan | New Ireland Province | People's Progress Party | | |
| Minister for National Planning | Charles Abel | Milne Bay Province | People's National Congress Party | | |
| Minister for Petroleum & Energy | William Duma | Western Highlands Province | United Resources Party | | |
| Minister for Police | Nixon Duban | Madang Province | People's National Congress Party | | |
| Minister for Public Enterprises & State Investment | Ben Micah | New Ireland Province | People's Progress Party | | |
| Minister for Public Service | Sir Puka Temu | Central Province | Our Development Party | | |
| Minister for Sports & Pacific Games | Justin Tkatchenko | National Capital District | Social Democratic Party | | |
| Minister for Tourism, Art & Culture | Boka Kondra | Western Province | People's National Congress Party | | |
| Minister for Trade, Commerce & Industry | Richard Maru | East Sepik Province | Independent | | |
| Minister for Transport & Works | Ano Pala | Central Province | People's National Congress Party | | |
| Minister for Treasury | Don Polye | Enga Province | Triumph Heritage Empowerment Party | | |
| Minister for Works & Implementation | Francis Awesa | Southern Highlands Province | People's National Congress Party | | |

In February 2014, the following reshuffle took place. Police Minister Nixon Duban (MP for Madang, National Congress Party) was reshuffled to the position of Minister of Petroleum and Energy, replacing William Duma (MP for Mount Hagen, United Resources Party), who was dropped from the Cabinet; O'Neill suggested that Duma had not adhered to the principle of Cabinet solidarity. Robert Atiyafa (MP for Henganofi) was appointed as Minister for Police. David Arore (MP for the Northern Province, T.H.E. Party) was replaced as Minister for Higher Education by Delilah Gore (MP for Sohe, T.H.E. Party), while Nick Kuman (MP for Gumine) was appointed Minister for Education. It was the first time ever that the country's Cabinet included two women: Delilah Gore, and Community Development Minister Loujaya Kouza (MP for Lae)

Papua New Guinea maintains an embassy at 1779 Massachusetts Ave. NW, Washington, DC 20036 (tel. 202-745-3680; fax 202-745-3679). The Papua New Guinea mission to the United Nations is at 801 Second Avenue, New York, NY 10017 (tel. 212-682-6447).

## ECONOMY

| | |
|---|---|
| Currency | kina (PGK) |
| Fiscal year | calendar year |
| Trade organisations | WTO, APEC |
| | Statistics |
| GDP | $16.93 billion (2014 World Bank est.) |

| | |
|---|---|
| GDP rank | 115th (nominal) / 130th (PPP) |
| GDP growth | 8.5% (2014 World Bank est.) |
| GDP per capita | $2,800 (2015 CIA World Factbook est.) |
| GDP by sector | Agriculture: 29.9%, industry: 37.6%, services: 32.4% (2011 est.) |
| Inflation (CPI) | 5.2% (2014 World Bank est.) |
| Population below poverty line | 39.9% (2009 World Bank est.) |
| Labour force | 3.896 million (2011 est.) |
| Labour force by occupation | agriculture: 85%, industry: NA%, services: NA% (2005 est.) |
| Unemployment | 1.9% (2008) |
| Main industries | copra crushing, palm oil processing, plywood production, wood chip production; mining (gold, silver, and copper); crude oil production, petroleum refining; construction, tourism |
| Ease-of-doing-business rank | 119th (2017) |
| | External |
| Exports | $6.748 billion (est.) |
| Export goods | oil, gold, copper ore, logs, palm oil, coffee, cocoa, crayfish, prawns |
| Main export partners | Australia 29.0%<br>Japan 9.6%<br>China 4.8% (est.) |
| Imports | $6.106 billion ( est.) |
| Import goods | Machinery and transport equipment, manufactured goods, food, fuels, chemicals |
| Main import partners | Australia 36.3%<br>Singapore 13.8%<br>Malaysia 8.4%<br>China 7.9%<br>Japan 5.8%<br>United States 4.8% |
| | Public finances |
| Public debt | $5.296 billion |
| Revenues | $4.168 billion |
| Expenses | $4.194 billion |
| Economic aid | no data |
| Credit rating | Standard & Poor's:<br>BB- (Domestic)<br>B+ (Foreign)<br>BB (T&C Assessment)<br>Outlook: Stable<br>Moody's:<br>B2<br>Outlook: Stable |

Papua New Guinea's economy is dominated by two sectors: the agricultural, forestry, and fishing sector, where most of the labour force of the country is engaged, and the minerals and energy extraction sector from which most of the export earnings are made. PNG's GDP growth is driven by the extraction industries and real GDP growth per capita has averaged 4% since mid-2000. The country has made significant progress investing proceeds from oil and gas in infrastructure building. As a result, its major cities like Port Moresby and Lae have received increased international investor attention, giving rise to unprecedented building boom to exploit the opportunities presented by the country's rise as a regional economic leader in the South Pacific region. This is well supported by its strategic location as a Pacific's gateway to Asia as well as its comparatively huge landmass and demographic profile (almost 7 times that the rest of smaller Pacific Island nations). International Monetary Fund. Despite this poverty it is richly endowed with natural resources, but exploitation has been hampered by the rugged terrain and the high cost of developing infrastructure.

Agriculture provides a subsistence livelihood for the bulk of the population. Mineral deposits, including oil, copper, and gold, account for 72% of export earnings. Budgetary support from Australia and development aid under World Bank auspices have helped sustain the economy. In 1995, Port Moresby reached an agreement with the International Monetary Fund (IMF) and World Bank on a structural adjustment program, of which the first phase was successfully completed in 1996. In 1997, droughts caused by the El Niño weather pattern wreaked havoc on Papua New Guinea's coffee, cocoa, and coconut production, the mainstays of the agricultural-based economy and major sources of export earnings. The coffee crop was slashed by up to 50% in 1997. Despite problems with drought, the year 1998 saw a small recovery in GDP. Growth increased to 3.6% in 1999 and may be even higher in 2000, say 4.3%.

## MINERAL RESOURCES

Papua New Guinea is richly endowed with gold, copper, oil, natural gas, and other minerals. In 2005 mineral export receipts accounted for 49.7% of GDP. Government revenues and foreign exchange earnings depend heavily on mineral exports. Indigenous landowners in areas affected by minerals projects also receive royalties from those operations. Copper and gold mines are currently in production at Porgera, Ok Tedi, Misima, and Lihir. A consortium led by Exxon/Mobil hopes to begin the commercialization of the country's estimated 22.5 trillion cubic feet of natural gas reserves through the construction of a liquefied natural gas (LNG) production facility. Interoil, an American-owned firm, opened Papua New Guinea's first oil refinery in 2004. It has the capacity to produce 30,000 barrels of product a day.

### Agriculture, Timber, and Fish

Papua New Guinea also produces and exports valuable agricultural, timber, and marine products. Agriculture currently accounts for 30.4% of GDP and supports more than 85% of the population. Cash crops ranked by value are coffee, oil, cocoa, copra, tea, rubber, and sugar. About 40% of the country is covered with exploitable trees, but a domestic woodworking industry has been slow to develop. A number of Southeast Asian companies are active in the timber industry, but World Bank and other donors have withdrawn support from the sector over concern for unregulated deforestation and environmental damage. Recently enacted forestry legislation has exacerbated those concerns. Papua New Guinea has an active tuna industry, but much of the catch is made by boats of other nations fishing in Papua New Guinea waters under license. Papua New Guinea is a signatory to the South Pacific Tuna Treaty (SPTT), under which U.S. purse seiners fish for tuna in the exclusive economic zones (EEZs) of the Pacific Island parties. Locally produced fish exports are confined primarily to shrimp.

### Industry

In general, the Papua New Guinea economy is highly dependent on imports for manufactured goods. Its industrial sector--exclusive of mining--accounts for only 9% of GDP and contributes little to exports. Small-scale industries produce beer, soap, concrete products, clothing, paper products, matches, ice cream, canned meat, fruit juices, furniture, plywood, and paint. The small domestic market, relatively high wages, and high transport costs are constraints to industrial development.

### Trade and Investment

Australia, Singapore, and Japan are the principal exporters to Papua New Guinea. Petroleum and mining machinery and aircraft have been the strongest U.S. exports to Papua New Guinea.
Australia is Papua New Guinea's most important export market, followed by Japan and the European Union. The U.S. imports modest amounts of gold, copper ore, cocoa, coffee, and other agricultural products from Papua New Guinea. Most of those exports take place through third countries.

With the 2003 withdrawal of Chevron/Texaco, Australian companies are the most active in developing Papua New Guinea's mining and petroleum sectors. Exxon/Mobil retains a major share of natural gas reserves and is currently exploring the feasibility of building a liquefied natural gas processing facility. Interoil, an American-owned firm backed by an Overseas Private Investment Corporation (OPIC) loan, operates an oil refinery in Port Moresby. China is increasing its investment in Papua New Guinea, including development of the $1 billion Ramu nickel mine.
Papua New Guinea became a participating economy in the Asia-Pacific Economic Cooperation (APEC) Forum in 1993. It joined the World Trade Organization (WTO) in 1996. It is an observer at ASEAN and a member of the ASEAN Regional Forum.

### Development Programs and Aid

Australia is by far the largest bilateral aid donor to Papua New Guinea, offering about $300 million a year in assistance. Budgetary support, which has been provided in decreasing amounts since independence, was

phased out in 2000, with aid concentrated on project development. In 2004, Australia and Papua New Guinea embarked on the Enhanced Cooperation Program (ECP), under which Australia agreed to provide direct assistance, including 210 line police officers, to the Papua New Guinea constabulary. The ECP met with initial success, but was abruptly ended when Papua New Guinea's Supreme Court stripped Australian police officers of immunity in May 2005. Virtually all ECP personnel left Papua New Guinea following the court's decision. The governments of Papua New Guinea and Australia are now involved in protracted negotiations on a scaled-down version of the ECP.
Other major sources of aid to Papua New Guinea are Japan, the European Union, the People's Republic of China, Taiwan, the United Nations, the Asian Development Bank, the International Monetary Fund, and the World Bank. Volunteers from a number of countries and mission church workers also provide education, health, and development assistance throughout the country. Foreign assistance to Papua New Guinea is approximately $46 per capita. The U.S. funds a $1.5 million-per-year HIV/AIDS project in Papua New Guinea.

**Current Economic Conditions**
After years of decline and government deficit, Papua New Guinea was bolstered in recent years by a general rise in commodity prices and by government steps toward spending control. The economy continues to grow modestly and the government recorded a modest surplus in 2006. However, the economic improvements are based almost entirely on high commodity prices and the nation continues to have serious problems of corruption, a lack of law and order, land tenure concerns stifling investment, political interference in business, and a lack of political will to adopt needed sweeping reforms.

## FOREIGN RELATIONS

Papua New Guinea's foreign policy reflects close ties with Australia and other traditional allies. Papua New Guinea is by far the largest Pacific Island nation and has traditionally viewed itself as part of the Pacific. However, in recent years it has also been cultivating relations with Asian nations. Its views on international political and economic issues are generally moderate. Papua New Guinea has diplomatic relations with 56 countries.

## U.S.-PAPUA NEW GUINEA RELATIONS

The United States and Papua New Guinea established diplomatic relations upon the latter's independence on September 16, 1975. The two nations belong to a variety of regional organizations, including the Asia-Pacific Economic Cooperation (APEC) forum; the ASEAN Regional Forum (ARF); the Secretariat of the Pacific Community (SPC); and the South Pacific Regional Environmental Program (SPREP).

The United States established diplomatic relations with Papua New Guinea in 1975, following its independence from a United Nations trusteeship administered by Australia. As the most populous Pacific Island state (7.8 million: 2013 estimate), Papua New Guinea is important to peace and security in the Asia-Pacific region. The country has experienced recent economic progress and has abundant energy, agricultural, and mineral resources. But it faces challenges including weak governance, corruption, limited capacity to deliver basic services, a deterioration of its health system, and a serious concentrated HIV/AIDS epidemic among key populations and in the Highland provinces.

The United States and Papua New Guinea have enjoyed a close friendship, and the U.S. Government seeks to enhance Papua New Guinea's stability as a U.S. partner. The two countries work together on many issues from improving transparency and good governance, to combating trafficking in persons, curbing the effects of climate change, protecting fisheries, improving public health, and promoting gender equality. Their militaries have had a cooperative security assistance relationship that has focused primarily on joint humanitarian exercises and the training of Papua New Guinean military personnel.

### U.S. Assistance to Papua New Guinea

U.S. bilateral and multilateral assistance funds public health programs in Papua New Guinea including the President's Emergency Plan For AIDS Relief (PEPFAR), TB, and Malaria and Neglected Tropical Diseases and aims to advance the country's public health system. The U.S. Agency for International Development's Pacific Islands Regional Office and the U.S. Centers for Disease Control and Prevention Country Office are both located in Papua New Guinea. The United States builds the capacity and resilience of Papua New

Guinea to adapt to climate change through regional assistance that covers 12 Pacific Island countries. United States assistance supports Papua New Guinea's efforts to protect biodiversity; it contributes to the Coral Triangle Initiative to preserve coral reefs, fisheries, and food security in six countries including Papua New Guinea. The United States also supports efforts to improve the country's disaster preparedness and response. In 2015 and 2016 the United States provided funding for relief efforts in a number of Papua New Guinea's provinces that had suffered from natural disasters caused by continuous heavy rain. U.S. military forces, through Pacific Command in Honolulu, Hawaii, provide training to the Papua New Guinea Defense Force and have held small-scale joint training and engineering exercises. The United States provides police and other education and training courses to national security officials. U.S. companies based in Papua New Guinea have also funded a range of health and development projects.

### Bilateral Economic Relations

Petroleum and mining machinery and aircraft have been the strongest U.S. exports to Papua New Guinea. The United States imports modest amounts of gold, copper ore, cocoa, coffee, and other agricultural products from Papua New Guinea. The ExxonMobil-led liquefied natural gas project has been a success for Papua New Guinea, hailed for its timely and close-to-budget construction and smooth operation. Papua New Guinea is a party to the U.S.-Pacific Islands Multilateral Tuna Fisheries Treaty, which provides access for U.S. fishing vessels in exchange for a license fee from the U.S. industry. Under a separate Economic Assistance Agreement (EAA) associated with the Treaty, the United States Government currently provides $21 million per year to Pacific Island parties. According to U.S. Census Bureau data, in 2016 the United States exported $126.8 million worth of goods to Papua New Guinea and imported $91.8 million worth.

### Papua New Guinea's Membership in International Organizations

Papua New Guinea and the United States belong to a number of the same international organizations, including the United Nations, International Monetary Fund, World Bank, World Trade Organization, Asia-Pacific Economic Cooperation (APEC) forum, ASEAN Regional Forum, the Pacific Community, and Secretariat of the Pacific Regional Environment Programme. Papua New Guinea also belongs to the Pacific Islands Forum, of which the United States is a Dialogue Partner. Papua New Guinea will host APEC in 2018, culminating in a leaders' summit in November 2018.

### Bilateral Representation

The U.S. Ambassador to Papua New Guinea is Catherine EBERT-GRAY (since 23 February 2016)

Papua New Guinea maintains an **embassy** in the United States at 1779 Massachusetts Ave. NW., Washington, DC 20036 (tel. 202-745-3680).

One of the most successful cooperative multilateral efforts linking the U.S. and Papua New Guinea is the U.S.-Pacific Islands Multilateral Tuna Fisheries Treaty, under which the U.S. grants $18 million per year to Pacific Island parties and the latter provide access for U.S. fishing vessels. The United States has provided significant humanitarian assistance to Papua New Guinea and contributed to the rehabilitation of Bougainville. USAID funds a $1.5 million-per-year HIV/AIDS project in Papua New Guinea.

The U.S. also supports Papua New Guinea's efforts to protect biodiversity. The U.S. Government supports the International Coral Reef Initiative aimed at protecting reefs in tropical nations such as Papua New Guinea. U.S. military forces, through Pacific Command (PACOM) in Honolulu, Hawaii, provide training to the Papua New Guinea Defense Force (PNGDF) and have held small-scale joint training exercises. The U.S. provides police and other education and training courses to national security officials. The U.S. also annually sponsors a handful of PNG officials and private citizens to meet and confer with their professional counterparts and to experience the U.S. first-hand through the International Visitor Leadership Program (IVLP).

The U.S. Peace Corps ceased operations in Papua New Guinea in 2001 due to security concerns. About 2,000 U.S. citizens live in Papua New Guinea, with major concentrations at the headquarters of New Tribes Mission and the Summer Institute of Linguistics, both located in the Eastern Highlands Province.

**Principal U.S. Embassy Officials**
Ambassador--Leslie Rowe
Deputy Chief of Mission--Thomas Weinz
Consular Officer--Leslie Livingood

The U.S. Embassy in Papua New Guinea is located on Douglas Street, Port Moresby (tel. 675-321-1455; fax 675-321-3423). The mailing address is 4240 Port Moresby Pl., U.S. Department of State, Washington, DC 20521-4240.

## TRAVEL AND BUSINESS INFORMATION

The U.S. Department of State's Consular Information Program advises Americans traveling and residing abroad through Country Specific Information, Travel Alerts, and Travel Warnings. **Country Specific Information** exists for all countries and includes information on entry and exit requirements, currency regulations, health conditions, safety and security, crime, political disturbances, and the addresses of the U.S. embassies and consulates abroad. **Travel Alerts** are issued to disseminate information quickly about terrorist threats and other relatively short-term conditions overseas that pose significant risks to the security of American travelers. **Travel Warnings** are issued when the State Department recommends that Americans avoid travel to a certain country because the situation is dangerous or unstable.

For the latest security information, Americans living and traveling abroad should regularly monitor the Department's Bureau of Consular Affairs Internet web site at http://www.travel.state.gov, where the current Worldwide Caution, Travel Alerts, and Travel Warnings can be found. Consular Affairs Publications, which contain information on obtaining passports and planning a safe trip abroad, are also available at http://www.travel.state.gov. For additional information on international travel, see http://www.usa.gov/Citizen/Topics/Travel/International.shtml.
The Department of State encourages all U.S citizens traveling or residing abroad to register via the State Department's travel registration website or at the nearest U.S. embassy or consulate abroad. Registration will make your presence and whereabouts known in case it is necessary to contact you in an emergency and will enable you to receive up-to-date information on security conditions.

Emergency information concerning Americans traveling abroad may be obtained by calling 1-888-407-4747 toll free in the U.S. and Canada or the regular toll line 1-202-501-4444 for callers outside the U.S. and Canada.

The National Passport Information Center (NPIC) is the U.S. Department of State's single, centralized public contact center for U.S. passport information. Telephone: 1-877-4USA-PPT (1-877-487-2778). Customer service representatives and operators for TDD/TTY are available Monday-Friday, 7:00 a.m. to 12:00 midnight, Eastern Time, excluding federal holidays.
Travelers can check the latest health information with the U.S. Centers for Disease Control and Prevention in Atlanta, Georgia. A hotline at 877-FYI-TRIP (877-394-8747) and a web site at http://wwwn.cdc.gov/travel/default.aspx give the most recent health advisories, immunization recommendations or requirements, and advice on food and drinking water safety for regions and countries. A booklet entitled "Health Information for International Travel" (HHS publication number CDC-95-8280) is available from the U.S. Government Printing Office, Washington, DC 20402, tel. (202) 512-1800.

## PRINCIPAL U.S. EMBASSY OFFICIALS

### U.S. Ambassador to Papua New Guinea, Solomon Islands and Vanuatu, Catherine Ebert-Gray

Ambassador Catherine Ebert-Gray is a Minister-Counselor in the Senior Foreign Service. She was sworn in as the U.S. Ambassador to Papua New Guinea, Solomon Islands and Vanuatu on January 22, 2016. Between 2011 and 2015 she served as the Deputy Assistant Secretary for Logistics Management and Co-Chair of the Defense – State Executive Steering Group supporting the transitions in Iraq and Afghanistan. Her global division annually managed $7 billion in State Department acquisition in addition to oversight of the Department's global supply chain.

Deputy Chief of Mission--Thomas Weinz
Consular Officer--Leslie Livingood

The U.S. Embassy in Papua New Guinea is located on Douglas Street, Port Moresby (tel. 675-321-1455; fax 675-321-3423). The mailing address is 4240 Port Moresby Pl., U.S. Department of State, Washington, DC 20521-4240.

# PNG ENERGY SECTOR - STRATEGIC INFORMATION

## BASIC INFORMATION

### ENERGY SOURCES

| | |
|---|---|
| **Total installed electricity capacity:** | **582 MW** |
| **Hydro-electric:** | **39.5%** |
| **Diesel:** | **37.3%** |
| **Natural gas:** | **14.1%** |
| **Geothermal:** | **9.1%** |

Total primary energy supply (2009): 2,270 ktoe
Oil and petroleum products: 77%
Natural Gas: 15%
Hydro & others: 8%

PNG generats about 4,000 GWh of electricity (a 9.9% increase from 2008). The sources of generation were thermal at 64% (oil 48%, gas 16%), hydropower at 25%, and geothermal at 11%.The hydropower contribution to electricity generation has remained stable in recent years, with new thermal investments accounting for rising demand.

Electricity is often unreliable, and relatively expensive in PNG. The lack reliable of power constrains growth in urban areas, and contributes to poverty in rural areas. The majority of electricity generation is based on petroleum products, leading to environmental issues, in terms of emissions and lack of sustainability. Baseload generation for the country's transmission network, in particular for the Port Moresby grid, is provided by hydroelectricity. A considerable proportion of the country's hydropower capacity is in excess of 30 years old, and has not been properly maintained, due to financial constraints on the part of PNG Power, the national utility. Transmission and distribution losses are around 20%, and the unreliability and inefficiency of urban power systems discourages further economic development.

In addition, system reliability problems have been observed in the national grid, in particular in the Gazelle network system. Deteriorating transmission lines have led to frequent and often prolonged power outages.

PNG is a net energy exporter. The country had a zero balance net import requirement in 2009, and no electricity was exported that year.

In 2010, oil production fell to 30,360 barrels per day, from three oil fields, a fall of 12.9% from 2009 levels. With the commissioning of its first refinery (Napanapa Oil Refinery, owned by InterOil) in 2004, crude is now refined locally. Around 72% (2313 ktoe) of indigenous crude oil and LNG production is exported. Interoil aims to construct a new LNG production facility by 2012, with a capacity of 32,500 barrels per day. To sustain the economy's export goals, the government allocates an estimated US$20 million of its annual budget to oil and gas exploration. PNG's total proven and probable gas reserves are over 14 trillion cubic feet, half of which constitutes the proven reserve. Much of this reserve is undeveloped, except for the Hides gas field, which supplies around 14–15 million standard cubic feet a day for power generation.

Energy framework

The country's ***Medium Term Development Strategy*** (**MTDS**) **2005–2010** recognises energy and power as critical ingredients for development and poverty reduction. The strategy invites the government to assist the disadvantaged to "lift themselves out of poverty by improving basic services, such as water and electricity." The MTDS places high priority for government spending on non-revenue-generating infrastructure, such as roads and education, without making any financing provisions for electrification, the private sector having been expected to invest in the necessary power infrastructure requirements for development. Unfortunately, progress has been slow, and this has not yet occurred.

The Papua New Guinea Government has initiated The ***National Strategic Plan 2010–2050***, which has seven 'pillars'. Natural resources, climate change and environmental sustainability are among the areas of focus. In March 2010, the Papua New Guinea Government announced the ***Development Strategic Plan (DSP) 2010–2030***, which has five 'pillars'—one of the pillars is 'natural resources and environment'. The DSP 2010–2030 also set this goal: All households have access to a reliable and affordable energy supply, and sufficient power is generated and distributed to meet future energy requirements and demands.

On October 2010, the Papua New Guinea Government announced its Medium Term Development Plan (MTDP) 2011–2015. The MTDP 2011–2015 will focus on increasing access to electricity for all households in the country. New investment from the private sector in solar technology is also expected during the period of the first MTDP. Comprehensive analysis is required into the cost effectiveness of various alternative sources of power.

## NETWORK

In PNG, more than 90% of the population (mostly rural dwellers) have no electricity. There are three grids: one for Port Moresby, the capital; the Gazelle network, covering East New Britain, and the Ramu grid, which covers the cities of Lae and Madang, as well as the Highlands region. PNG Power, the national utility, operates three interconnected distribution systems, plus many provincial power systems. About a hundred small rural electricity systems (called C-centres) are operated by local authorities at government administration centres, powered by diesel generators, small hydropower facilities, and occasionally solar photovoltaics (PV). Responsibility for financing, management and planning rests with provincial authorities, however, many systems are badly managed and are inoperative. In 2008, the Japan Special Fund under the ADB provided a US$ 1.2 million grant to the Government of PNG, matched by US$ 300,000 of the Government's own money, to develop the electricity network of the islands.

## RENEWABLE ENERGY

The technical potential for renewable energy sources in PNG is enormous, but many of these resources are in remote locations with limited demand, and are not readily exploitable.

### Geothermal energy

The Geothermal Energy Association estimates PNG's geothermal potential at 21.92 terawatt-hours; the association also categorises the country as an economy that could, in theory, meet all its electricity needs well into the future from geothermal sources alone. Installed geothermal capacity in 2010 was 56 MW.

### Hydropower

PNG has significant hydroelectric potential. Its land area includes nine large hydrological drainage divisions (basins). The largest river basins are the Serpik (with catchment area of 78,000 sq km), Fly (61,000 sq km), Purari (33,670 sq km), and Markham (12,000 sq km). There are other catchments of less than 5,000 sq km, in areas that are very steep. On the mainland, the mean annual rainfall ranges from less than 2,000 mm to 8,000 mm in some mountainous areas, while the island groups receive a mean annual rainfall of 3,000–7,000 mm. The gross theoretical hydropower potential for PNG is 175 TWh per year. There is little economic potential for the expansion of large hydro, due to the lack of substantive demand near supply sources. However, greater potential exists for developing smaller hydro schemes, with over 10 new small hydropower schemes deemed as feasible in the 2009 Power Development Plan. Combined capacity for these new schemes exceeds 20 MW.

### Ocean Thermal Energy Conversion (OTEC)

There is very limited knowledge of PNG's potential for OTEC, tidal energy or wave energy. Near Port Moresby, the tidal range is 2.7 metres, compared to 1.1–1.6m in much of the country. Reportedly, there is a 6m range in parts of the Torres Strait. There have been very preliminary proposals to tap tidal currents (peaking at 7–11 km/hour) at Buka Passage, near Bougainville.

### Wind energy

There have been no systematic estimates of wind energy potential since the 1970s, when the best potentials were assessed in portions of Central, Western, Milne Bay and New Ireland provinces, and the Port Moresby area. A pilot wind energy project is being installed in the Duke of York islands, jointly funded by the Papua New Guinean and Chinese governments.

**Solar energy**

Solar energy is among the largest potential sources in PNG. Average insolation in much of the country is 400–800 W/m2, with 4.5 to 8 sunshine hours a day. Of 23 locations assessed, Port Moresby has the largest resource, with 2,478 sunshine hours per year. The lowest is Tambul, Western Highlands, with 1,292 hours. The best locations for solar PV are the offshore islands, and in the southern regions of the country. As of 2008, no electricity-producing installations were present in the country, although a solar home systems project for schools is in place, with help from the Sustainable Energy Financing Project from the World Bank/GEF.

**Biomass energy**

Although two thirds of PNG are covered with forest, much of it is inaccessible or unsuited for energy use. 58% of land is subject to strong or severe erosion, and 18% is permanently inundated or regularly flooded. The main practical biomass energy potential is in areas such as logging and agricultural production, using either the crop output or residues. Log exports are roughly 2 million m3 per year, but very little is processed locally, leaving only small amounts of biomass for energy production. There are 18 major wood-processing facilities, but the amount of residue produced and it's availability for energy use is unknown. Traditional rural use of biomass is still relatively high, due to the low level of electricity access for cooking, lighting etc.

## ENERGY EFFICIENCY

In 2007, the total primary energy supply of the country rose 12% in comparison to the previous year. Total final energy consumption was 1055 ktoe (an increase of 2.6% over 2006). The industrial sector accounted for 56% (an increase of 6% over 2006) and was the largest end user, followed by transport (33%) and other sectors, including agriculture and residential/commercial (11%). Petroleum products accounted for 76% of total consumption (an increase of 2.3% over 2006); electricity and others accounted for 24%. Petroleum products such as diesel or petrol are primarily used in the transport and electricity generation sectors.

The predominant method of lighting for much of PNG is kerosene fuel, which is highly inefficient in comparison to incandescent lamps. 90% of the population are estimated to use kerosene lighting. Energy efficiency in buildings has been identified as a potential source of energy savings, and a new building code was adopted in 2009, in line with that of Australia, in an effort to improve building energy efficiency.

## OWNERSHIP

***PNG Power*** (**PNGP**, www.pngpower.com.pg) is wholly government-owned. PNG Power is responsible for the generation, transmission and distribution of electricity in PNG. There are also a large number of IPPs, whose total installed capacity is comparable to that of PNGP. In 2010, IPPs and self-producers managed around 280 MW of capacity, with PNG Power managing approximately 300 MW.

***Oil Search*** (www.oilsearch.com) is PNG's largest oil and natural gas producer, and operates all of the country's oil-producing fields. The company is owned in part by the government of PNG (15%).

PNG Power is responsible for the generation, transmission and distribution of electricity throughout the country, operating three main interconnected systems and 19 smaller provincial systems. The company is entirely owned by the state, and is vertically integrated. PNGP holds the monopoly on the electricity sector in Papua New Guinea.

Oil Search is the sole operator in the oil production sector of the country. Oil exploration activities are carried out by a number of firms, notably the Australian companies Origin Energy and New Guinea Energy. Private companies also hold the capital in the current LNG production facility construction project, including Exxon.

The Asian Development Bank has recently released a Country Partnership Strategy 2011-2015 for Papua New Guinea, which includes recommendations for the development of the power sector, from both a technical and a legislative standpoint, in particular with regards to rural electrification. Technical assistance will also be provided for energy efficiency projects, and new renewable energy projects, particularly micro-hydro for rural electrification.

PNG is a country member of the SPC Applied Geoscience and Technology Division (SOPAC). SOPAC was established in 1972 as a United Nations Development Programme Regional Project for the assessment of deep-sea minerals and hydrocarbon potentials. The work programme of SOPAC has now expanded to include the assessment of oceanic and onshore mineral resource potential, coastal protection and management, and the assessment of potential geological hazards. Over the past decade, its mandate has broadened further, to include water, wastewater, sanitation, energy and disaster risk management.

## GOVERNMENT

The ***Energy Division of the Department of Petroleum and Energy*** (**DPE**) is responsible for energy policies and plans, data collection and analysis, and advice to the government on energy sector issues. In practice, it concentrates on electric power, although PNG Power, the national electricity utility, undertakes the majority power sector planning. The DPE itself reports that extremely limited resources have seriously hampered data collection and analysis. For renewable energy sources, data collection had nearly ceased by the mid 1980s.

The ***Petroleum Division*** of the DPE is responsible for oil and natural gas exploration and development.

### GOVERNMENT AGENCIES

***PNG Sustainable Development Program Limited*** (**PNGSDP**) is the major shareholder of Ok Tedi Mining Limited, and its principal activity is to promote sustainable development of Papua New Guinea, particularly in the Western Province. This activity is undertaken through programs and projects in infrastructure, capacity building, health, education, and community self-reliance. Consistent with its goal, PNGSDP is providing funding to support and facilitate Phase 1 of a rural energy program for the Western Province. Phase 1 projects include the rehabilitation and development of mini grid-power systems and solar home lighting systems.

PNGSDP has appointed PNG Sustainable Energy Limited (PNGSEL) to manage PNGSDP's rural energy projects. PNGSEL is a company incorporated in Papua New Guinea. PNGSDP and the Snowy Mountains Engineering Corporation (SMEC, www.smec.com) equally own PNGSEL, and its principal activity is to participate in the energy and electricity industry in PNG.

*SMEC* has assisted in the preparation of documentation for a number of CDM projects, including the Lihir gold mine geothermal project in PNG. SMEC provides carbon services including project identification, structuring, monitoring and verification, and overseeing CER (Commission for Energy Regulation) issuance and registry account management.

### ENERGY PROCEDURE

The Pacific Islands Greenhouse Gas Abatement through Renewable Energy Project (PIGGAREP) is active in supporting the energy sector of PNG in its development. PNG Sustainable Energy Limited have received technical assistance from the project for use in rural electrification programs, especially with reference to integrated biodiesel systems, and in expanding their renewable energy operations, with wind power feasibility studies for the Hula peninsula, and solar energy system design training. In addition, PNGSEL have secured US$ 673 million to enhance electricity under the electrification program in the economy.

In September 2010, Australia's Province of Queensland and Papua New Guinea agreed to set up a 1,800 MW hydropower plant in PNG, which would supply 1,200 MW of electricity to Queensland through an undersea cable. Origin Energy, which is Australia's 2nd largest energy producer, will submit a feasibility document by 2012. This electricity project is one of the most ambitious International Cooperation Agreements in Energy, as it will involve the construction of 250 km of undersea cable. Electricity produced by the project will also go towards spurring prosperity in PNG, as 600 MW of the plant's capacity would be used locally.

***Promoting Energy Efficiency in the Pacific (Phase 2)***
Under Phase 1 of this $1.4 million regional technical assistance project, the Government of PNG was supported in identifying and piloting demand-side energy-efficiency activities, including the implementation of a pilot Power Factor Correction initiative in Port Moresby. The initiative sought to improve network stability and power quality and, as a result, it reduced energy demand by 180 MWh.

Phase 2 is further supporting the government in expanding the collection of data on power use that will inform future policy decision, and in implementing policies to foster energy efficiency. With $8.75 million funding, this follow on regional technical assistance project is being implemented in PNG, as well as in the Cook Islands, Samoa, Tonga, and Vanuatu. The activities of the project include:

- establishment of database containing baseline data on energy use;
- mainstreaming of energy efficiency practices, such as the Minimum Energy Performance Standards and labelling schemes in government processes, procedures, and policies and regulations;
- evaluation of energy-efficiency pilots undertaken under Phase 1 and scale-up of the most efficient measures; and
- information dissemination and awareness raising.

***Promoting Access to Renewable Energy in the Pacific***
The regional technical assistance is helping the PNG Power prepare the Rouna hydropower cascade development plan, as well as build the capacity of the power utility on system management and maintenance. The project was approved in 2009 for $3.0 million, and is being implemented in PNG, Solomon Islands and Vanuatu.

***Improved Energy Access for Rural Communities***
The ADB's grant will finance the connection of households, schools, and medical clinics in rural communities to the power distribution grid which will be extended by PNG Power to rural communities. It targets 4,500 households, 20 schools, and 20 clinics connected to the grid by 2014. The project will also assist PNG Power to upscale the trials of community-based civil works contracts for distribution powerline construction. A $5 million grant was approved in the first half of 2012, co-financed by the Japan Fund for Poverty Reduction and New Zealand.

## ENERGY REGULATOR

The Electricity Industry Act 2000 authorised the ***Independent Consumer and Competition Commission*** (**ICCC**, www.iccc.gov.pg) as the technical regulator of the electricity sector to determine the standards, perform inspection and control applications on all matters relating to the operations of the supply of electricity. The ICCC became operational in 2002, when the government enacted the ***Independent Consumer and Competition Commission Act 2002*** (**ICCC Act**).

However, because of a lack of technical capacity to perform this regulatory role, the ICCC outsourced this role to PNG Power Limited on a contractual basis for an initial period of two years ending in 2005. The contract was extended for another three-year period ending in 2008. There is no further information on whether this role has been extended.

The Commission consists of a full time Commissioner and two part time Associate Commissioners. One such Associate position is allocated to an overseas competition/regulatory expert. The independence of the Commission from ministerial control is established in law. Funding for the commission is derived from operational revenues and levies, and allocated government funds.

### REGULATORY FRAMEWORK

Sections 21 and 23 of the Electricity Industry Act 2000 outline the functions and powers of PNG Power Limited. Under the Act, PNG Power Limited's function is to plan and coordinate the supply of electricity throughout the economy, especially in urban areas.

No dedicated law or regulation currently exists for the promotion of sustainable energy uptake.

The ICCC regulates the energy sector. It licenses electric power companies, establishes electricity tariffs and controls maximum prices of some petroleum fuels. There is a national power tariff for those served by PNG Power.

The ICCC is the only national regulatory body that acts as a consumer and business watchdog. The provisions of the ICCC Act apply to all businesses in Papua New Guinea, including the government, where it engages in trade. The ICCC Act also applies to conduct outside PNG which affects the PNG market. The objective of the ICCC Act is to enhance the welfare of Papua New Guineans through the promotion of competition and fair trade in the market, the protection of consumer interests and the regulation of prices and service delivery standards in respect of state-owned entities.

Because of a lack of technical capacity to perform a technical regulatory role in the electricity sector, the ICCC has outsourced this role to PNG Power Limited on a contractual basis for an initial period of two years ending 2005, which was extended for another three-year period, ending in 2008. The majority of the responsibility for power sector planning, for example, rests with PNG Power.

The unbundling of PNG Power, followed by the establishment of competition within the electricity market, including the promotion of private-sector involvement, could lead to fairer electricity tariffs, as well as improved standards.

In addition, the creation of policies to promote the utilisation of renewable energy technologies, with particular relevance to financing mechanisms, would facilitate their increased usage. Suitable regulation for the creation of an enabling environment would also be required.

# OIL AND GAS SECTOR DEVELOPMENT

## PETROLEUM EXPLORATION IN PAPUA NEW GUINEA

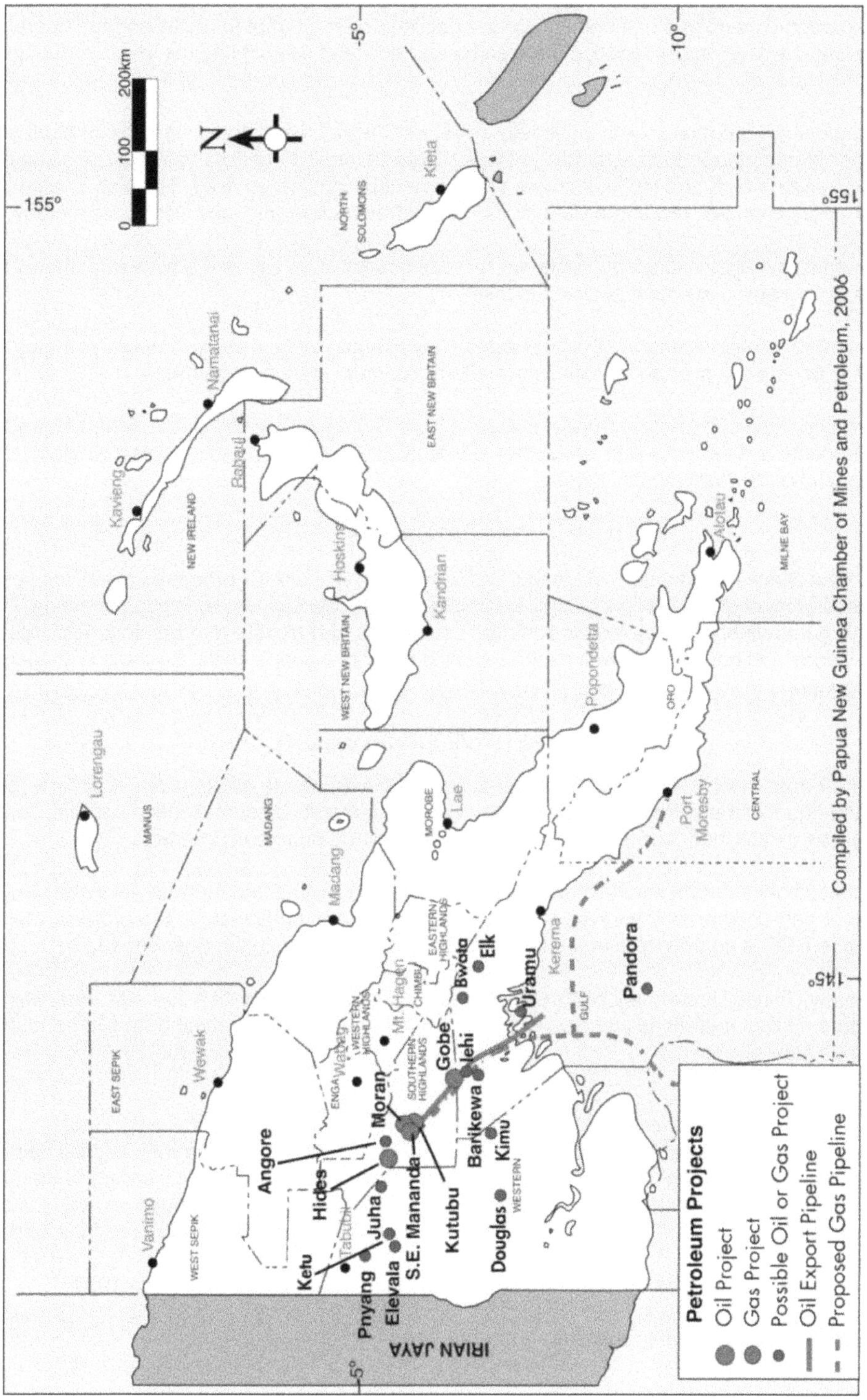

# MINING TO PAPUA NEW GUINEA

## THE MARKET

Australia currently supplies around 65 per cent of total requirements to Papua New Guinea's mining sector.

Mineral exploration expenditure has been in steady decline. In an attempt to revitalise the mineral sector, the Papua New Guinea government reduced the income and dividend withholding tax levels for mining companies.

Investment incentives are available to legitimate investors. This includes duty-free entry of plant and equipment (if not manufactured or available in Papua New Guinea). In general, the cost of doing business in Papua New Guinea is high and the investment environment is considered risky. This risk is associated with government policy changes, law and order issues, poor infrastructure and inefficient bureaucracy.

Australian banks, law firms and accountants are a ready source of investment advice and should be approached before any investment decision is taken.

The Investment Promotion Authority (IPA) of Papua New Guinea, as well as the Papua New Guinea Department of Mining can provide specific information relating to mining investment.

A significant proportion of mining personnel in Papua New Guinea are Australian and therefore use Australian products and services with which they are familiar. Regular air and shipping services, particularly from Queensland ports, facilitate this supply.

## OPPORTUNITIES

The Papua New Guinea Department of Mining, with support from AusAID, promotes initiatives designed to assist the development of small scale alluvial mining in Papua New Guinea, mostly gold mining. Papua New Guinea's only gold refinery (run by Metals Refining Operations Ltd) assists with training, field trips, information videos and booklets, as well as the establishment of a supply outlet for tools and equipment to small scale miners.

## COMPETITIVE ENVIRONMENT

To ensure the Papua New Guinea Government, provincial governments and landowner groups receive maximum and equal benefits from its natural resources; the Mineral Resources Development Company Pty Ltd (MRDC) was established as custodian of national mining and petroleum interests.

MRDC purchases government equity in mining and petroleum projects and then on-sells it to Orogen Minerals Ltd (a part-government, part-privately owned company) to participate in the project or take a shareholding. MRDC is an advocate of the landowners and retains equity on their behalf.

The Papua New Guinea Department of Mining allocates all mineral exploration licences and mining leases. It also monitors mining operations and has an important role in determining mining taxation and investment policy in Papua New Guinea.

## TARIFFS, REGULATIONS AND CUSTOMS

Papua New Guinea has a single rate value added tax (VAT) of 10 per cent. The VAT is collected as part of the normal procedure at the point of entry. The customs valuation is calculated according to the cost, insurance and freight (CIF) value of the imported goods and the VAT is also charged on any customs or excise duty paid.

Papua New Guinea has undertaken a process of steady reduction in tariff rates since 1997.

As of January 2006 the tariff rate regime is:

- 0 per cent for goods if Papua New Guinea doesn't produce that product
- 15 per cent goods used as inputs to businesses

- 25 per cent for final goods competing with Papua New Guinea production
- 40 per cent for goods, competing with Papua New Guinea production and designated as in need special protection

Specific duties, expressed in Kina per measure, are levied on beer, matches, and poultry meat, eggs and tobacco products.

Papua New Guinea Customs use the single column based on the Harmonised system. Most duties are applied ad valorem using the World Trade Organisation (WTO) valuation code guidelines of CIF value (as per Incoterms 1990)

Exporters should ascertain the duty rate that applies to its products, before export. Austrade can assist with this process.

Samples of no commercial value are admitted duty-free although sales tax may still be levied. Valuable samples are admitted, subject to invoice declaration, under a deposit or bond equivalent to normal duty. The deposit is refunded on re-export of the samples. The deposit is refunded on re-export of the samples.

## INDUSTRY STANDARDS

Industry standards in Papua New Guinea are based on Australian standards for the most part.

In Papua New Guinea (PNG), oil has been produced from the onshore Papuan Basin since the early 1990s.

This basin also hosts substantial proven gas accumulations, and PNG may shortly become a regional gas producer with the PNG-Queensland gas pipeline project.

Tertiary limestones and marine clastics were deposited in a passive to foreland basin setting in the Papuan Basin, at the northeast Australian margin. The Pliocene-Recent Papuan Fold Belt forms the northern margin to this basin, and hosts the producing oil and gas fields.

Strontium Isotope Stratigraphy (SIS) has been applied to exploration in PNG for more than a decade now, by analysing the 87Sr/86Sr ratio of Tertiary limestones and calculating the Sr age from the sea-water curve of McArthur et al. (2001) (Version 3: 10/99), Hodell et al. (1991) and Oslick et al. (1994).

CSIRO's application of SIS has been extensive in onshore exploration, primarily in structural mapping in the fold belt within the western Papuan Basin.

The Timeframes Group, a CSIRO specialist consultancy group, has conducted research in parallel with exploration during this time, integrating Sr isotope stratigraphy, limestone microfacies analysis and foraminiferal biostratigraphy in a study of basin sedimentation history. This work has been on surface and well sections in the fold belt and foreland.

SIS has been used extensively in onshore exploration, primarily in structural mapping in the fold belt within the western Papuan Basin.

## CURRENT ACTIVITIES

Over the past three years, the research focus has been in the eastern Papuan Basin, offering an opportunity to examine the problems of reconstructing basin history in an area where massive re-working of biomarkers has occurred through Mesozoic and Tertiary times.
Ongoing research in the Papuan Basin has focused on developing a detailed calibration of the range of the important shallow water index foraminifera to the time scale applying strontium chronostratigraphy.
A long term aim of this research is to investigate the possibility that the stratigraphic range of these neritic faunas, sensitive to sea level change, could be related to major eustatic sea level fluctuations.
Of particular importance is the relationship between the major zonal 'extinctions' and large (3rd order) sea level falls.

### PARTNERS

CSIRO has extensive involvement with companies exploring for hydrocarbons, and have also carried out work for several Australian Universities. Our partners include:

- Oil Search
- InterOil
- Exxon-Mobil
- Chevron
- ConocoPhillips
- Magellan
- Amerada Hess
- Lundin Oil and Gas
- Geoservices
- PT Corelab Indonesia
- Santos
- Woodside
- Institut Français du Pétrole.

### SCIENTISTS

The following scientists were involved:

- Mr Tony Allan
- Dr David Whitford
- Dr Marty Young

# IMPORTANT LAWS AND REGULATIONS

## LEGAL NATURE OF THE PAPUA NEW GUINEA PETROLEUM ARRANGEMENT[1]

Petroleum exploration and development in Papua New Guinea (PNG) are carried out under a policy regime that fixes in advance, conditions under which rights to explore for and produce petroleum are granted. The legal regime is set out primarily in the legislation and complemented by petroleum agreements that are entered into in respect of each exploration licence.

Some countries do not use the legislation to set out the terms and conditions of petroleum development. If there is such a law, it is of a general nature. The government grants exploration and production titles on the basis of individually negotiated agreements.

Other countries take the middle ground by using a hybrid system of fixing the terms of petroleum exploration and production, partly by legislation and partly by agreements. In such cases, certain fundamental terms of petroleum exploration and production are set out in the legislation while the specific terms and conditions are negotiated and settled by agreements.

Petroleum agreements are used in many countries as the main policy instruments, to set the scope of, and govern petroleum exploration and production. These agreements are used exclusively or in association with petroleum legislation.

[1] Melvin Yalapan Law School, University of Papua New Guinea.

The public and private arrangements under which petroleum exploration and production are authorised and undertaken have gone through a variety of phases since the emergence of petroleum as an internationally traded commodity, from the earliest grants of concessions by various sovereigns in the Middle East to the modern concessions, joint venture agreements, service contracts, production sharing contracts or combination of one or more of these traditional forms of petroleum arrangements.

Petroleum arrangements of some countries have the characteristics of more than one formally recognised legal arrangements. This paper will endeavour to identify and consider the salient features of these legal arrangements and apply them to the Papua New Guinea's (PNG) petroleum arrangement. The object of this exercise will be, firstly, to highlight the fundamental features of PNG's petroleum arrangement and, secondly, to classify the PNG's petroleum arrangement under one or more of the recognised forms of petroleum arrangements that are in use in the petroleum industry, globally.

A. Different Petroleum Arrangements

Whilst various legal arrangements are used by different countries to secure and regulate petroleum exploration and production, they deal with common considerations that are essential for petroleum exploration and production. It is the treatment of these features that distinguish the different legal arrangements under which petroleum development is conducted.

(a) Concessions

The history of petroleum agreements begins with the granting of an oil concession by the Persian Government to William D'Arcy in 1901. The original 1901 D'Arcy concession was granted over the whole of the Persian Empire with the exception of 5 provinces, covering 480,000 square miles. Concessions granted by the rulers of Abu Dhabi and Kuwait covered their entire countries. The concessions were granted for very long periods and on modest fiscal terms. Professor Charles Lipton summarised the traditional concession arrangement as follows:

"It was a long term agreement. 99 years was not untypical. It created enclave and give rise to exception to the general law application. Management 'prerogative' were left to the operating company. There was no government participation in the basic decisions such as the rate of operation or marketing. The investor provided all capital typically, and was entitled to all profits, originally paying the government a per ton royalty."

Thus under the traditional concession, the concessionaire was granted, and had, the exclusive right to explore for, produce and deal with petroleum within the concession area. The oil companies therefore made decisions affecting all aspects of the petroleum operation. In terms of petroleum exploration, it meant that the oil companies decided exclusively how much or how little exploration they wished to undertake. Upon discovery, the oil companies decided the rate, extent and level of production.

The companies also had, in a traditional concession, by the grant of the concession, title to the petroleum *in situ*. The host government, or ruler, normally received an initial consideration, roughly amounting to the modern day signature bonus and only the right to receive financial return from the petroleum operation. Originally, this was in the form of royalty payment, and later royalty and taxes.

The scope of the traditional concession is startling when other aspects of a concession are considered. The 1901 Mexican petroleum law, for example, authorised, granting of liberal tax exemption, the right to import machinery, equipment and materials duty free and other special privileges, which included the right to expropriate land necessary to conduct petroleum operations.

The situation existed until the late 1950's when governments with the aid of progress in technology, considerable discovery of new oil fields and worldwide dependence on oil, broke the shackle that underpinned the traditional concession arrangement. These enabled governments to demand and secure improved terms under which the petroleum resources located within their territories could be developed.

The post 1950's concessions provided significant new terms. The financial return to the host country increased significantly with provisions for equitable profit sharing. The petroleum acreages were reduced, and provisions for relinquishment of the concession areas or part of the concession areas, driven by work program and budget were introduced. It was during this period that governments began to take direct equity participation in petroleum projects. In addition, host governments also enacted legislation that dealt specifically with petroleum exploration and production, thus establishing uniformity the basic terms under which petroleum exploration and production were undertaken within the country.

The increased concerns of governments with regard to ownership and control of the natural resources led to the assertion of permanent sovereignty over the natural resources within the states' territories. The 1962 *UN Resolution on the Permanent Sovereignty over Natural Resources* is the reflection of the assertion of sovereignty, particularly by the newly independent third world governments, to natural resources within their territories.

The *UN Resolution on the Permanent Sovereignty over Natural Resources* also provided further impetus for the creation of alternative legal arrangements for petroleum development. These were structured not only to enable host states to retain ownership of the resources *in situ* in their national boundaries but at the same time, to allow oil companies to conduct petroleum operation in the country. Old concession arrangements were revised and new concession arrangements were established.

The modern concessions differ in important respect from the traditional form of concession. Under the new concession arrangements:

"...ownership of petroleum in the ground remains with the State, and at best provision is made for 'sharing' of petroleum at the well-head between governments and companies. Power of management and control over operations are vested in the government. Duration is shorter and the size of the area covered by the agreement considerably smaller than under the traditional concession".

Provisions for relinquishment of, and reduction in, the concession areas were introduced. Minimum work and expenditure commitments were established. Requirements for training of national work force and procurement of local goods and services were also introduced. In some instances, provisions were made for crude oil to be made available for local consumption and host states also participated in the petroleum development either directly or through a state enterprise. Generally, greater powers of management and control of petroleum development shifted from the oil companies to the host states. One can say that the entire bundle of rights that governed petroleum development changed hands, from the oil companies to the host governments.

New legal arrangements for petroleum development were also developed and introduced. Such arrangements included joint venture agreements, service contracts and production sharing contracts.

(b) Joint Ventures

The oil companies traditionally prefer partnership with the host government in the petroleum exploration and production to be limited to *profit sharing*. As host governments become conscious of the need to actively participate in petroleum development, they began pressing for greater control over the resources in their territories.

Under the traditional concessions, the near total control exercised by the companies was based on its ownership of the petroleum resources. However, the exclusive ownership of the petroleum resources by the concessionaire naturally militated against the desire by governments to own the petroleum resources located in their territory and to develop these resources to pursue national development objectives. The joint venture arrangement was therefore developed to realise these national goals and aspirations.

The joint venture agreement was pioneered as a new form of petroleum arrangement by Italian State Oil Company – ENI. The first of such agreement was entered into between ENI through its subsidiary Agip Mineraria and the National Iranian Oil Company (NIOC). The Agip-NIOC Joint Venture was established under a joint stock company, and a joint Board of Directors managed the company.

Under the joint venture arrangement, the entire petroleum operation is a joint activity. A joint operation company is formed between the host country (more usually the host country's national oil company), and the company to develop the petroleum reserves. The acreage is jointly licensed and the petroleum operation is

jointly conducted, consistent with the joint ownership of the venture. However, the entire exploration expenditure is financed solely by the oil company. In the event of a commercial discovery, the oil company is fully reimbursed either in kind or out of revenue earned either directly by the state or through the allocation of part of the state's share of the petroleum produced. *[18]* The joint venture arrangement is therefore a partnership arrangement between the state through its national oil company and the non-state oil company, under an arrangement of share equity, ownership rights and interest in the project. Martin Olisa summarised the arrangement as follows:
"The structure and content of various joint ventures vary considerably...(On) the national side you have private, or government controlled enterprises. The foreign enterprise supplies the risk capital for, and carries out, exploration. Explorations expenses in whole or in part are recoverable from production, if obtained. If commercial production is obtained, an equity joint venture company is established as an operating company. Participation may be on 50:50 basis or one 'partner' may be in a minority position, in which case, a management contract is entered into."*[19]*

The joint venture arrangement was therefore seen as a realisation of host governments' aspirations, not only to take greater management and control over the natural resources within their territories, but also as a realisation of joint ownership of the exploration and production titles.

(c) Production sharing Contract

The "Production Sharing Contract" was pioneered in Indonesia in 1967 and is still used there. Libya, Egypt, India, Ghana, Malaysia and Trinidad and Tobago are some of the countries that also use this contractual arrangement.[20] A. Zen Umar Purba summarised the main features of the Indonesian Production Sharing Contract as follows:

*- management of the oil operations rest with PERTAMINA.[21]*
*- at the time the contract is signed, the contractor pays a bonus to PERTAMINA, which can be treated as a tax credit.*
*- exploration expenses are recoverable if oil is discovered by contractor.*
*- after the exploration cost and expenses are deducted from the oil extracted, the balance (after tax) is divided under a certain formula, mainly 85%:15% in favour of PERTAMINA.*
*- the contractor is required to spare 8.5% of its portion (based on the above formula) to supply the domestic market in Indonesia.*
*- after a certain period of time, the contractor has to relinquish areas of its operations, the area must be re-surrendered if oil is not discovered, or if at the end of the exploration stage, the areas are considered not commercially viable.*
*- title to equipment used in the exploration rest with PERTAMINA as soon as the goods enter Indonesian customs."[22]*

Under the production sharing contract arrangement, the exploration and production of petroleum can be undertaken only by the State, and is exclusively carried out by the State enterprises. The oil company has no proprietary interest in the petroleum exploration and production titles. The company is engaged as a contractor for the state enterprise to undertake services that cannot or yet to be undertaken by the state enterprise.[23]

Although, the oil companies are engaged as contractors to undertake petroleum operations, they however bear all the exploration risk so that if no commercial discovery of petroleum is made, the loss is borne by the contractor. In the event of a commercial discovery, the contractor is entitled to be reimbursed by a percentage of the oil produced. This is achieved by applying portions of petroleum produced as *"cost oil,"* to defray the pre-development expenditure. Once all the authorised expenses have been deducted up to the maximum percentage of "cost oil" set out in the agreement, the remaining oil, usually called the *"profit oil,"* (less *"cost oil,"*) is shared between the contractor and the national oil company in accordance with an agreed formula.[24]

Ownership of the petroleum, either in the ground or as produced, rest with the state until it reaches the point of export. This differs from the traditional concession arrangement where title in petroleum rest in the oil company, and under the new concession arrangement where the petroleum companies acquire title to the petroleum at the wellhead.

The legal rational for using the production sharing contract is that from the host government's standpoint, it does not involve surrender of the host country's sovereignty in the title to the resource. In entering into a production sharing contract, the company receives less than title or interest to the oil.[25]

(d) Service Contracts

The final form of petroleum exploration and production arrangement that require specific consideration for the purpose of this paper is the service contract. Under this contractual arrangement, the foreign oil company is engaged by the national oil company to conduct petroleum exploration for a fee or a share of production. The oil company also provides the host country and its national oil company with technical services and information relating to the development of the petroleum resources.

Upon discovery of petroleum in the area, the national oil company engages the foreign oil company as its agent to produce the oil, and if it so agrees, also to market the oil produced on behalf of the national oil company. The feature of a service contract is summarised as follows:
"The national oil company is by law the sole titular holder of the area under the agreement. All petroleum deposit and oil and/or gas produced are the property of the national oil company at the wellhead. The foreign company either directly or through a subsidiary, acts as general contractor for the national oil company and as such carries out, in the name and on behalf the latter, all operations necessary for exploration and development of oil deposits. Thus the contractor is not a concession holder or partner, but merely a hired agent."*[26]*

In a pure service contract, the host country's national oil company would contract the oil company to perform a specified service for a flat fee. However, in view of the difficulties that countries face in obtaining capital to finance the payment of service fees, some agreements provide that the contractor may be paid in kind with a certain specified amount of production from the acreage, the subject of the service contract. Thus service contracts can be arranged as *Risk-Service Contract* or *Service Contract (Non-Risk)*. Under a Risk-Service Contract arrangement, the host government pays for the services of the oil companies in cash and not in kind. On the other hand, under the Service Contract (Non-Risk) arrangement, the oil company is paid a flat rate for its services usually by applying a percentage of the oil produced.[27]

Generally, the oil company provides all the risk capital. If oil is found, the amount spent in exploration is "deemed" as loan to the national oil company to be debited from the national oil company's accounts. The oil company may also sell for the national oil company, if agreed, the oil produced. From the revenue earned by the national oil company, a percentage is applied towards the repayment of the "deemed loan" until the loan is reduced to zero.[28]

The title in the petroleum *in situ* rests in the state and upon production is transferred at the wellhead to the national oil company. The oil company does not acquire exploration or production title nor does it acquire ownership to the petroleum produced at any stage of the production chain. It is engaged simply as an agent to the national oil company and is paid a fee either in cash or in kind from the oil produced, in consideration for the services rendered.

Service contracts are used in countries like Venezuela, Brazil and Iran as a form of legal arrangement for the development of petroleum located within the territories of these countries.[29]

(e) Petroleum Arrangements

Petroleum arrangements developed post 1950's also included contracts under names such as Operations Agreement[30] and Works and Technical Services Agreement.[31]

The post 1950's contractual arrangements have different *"labels"* but they have common objectives and hence share common features. For instance, the production sharing contract petroleum arrangement is similar in terms to the service contract arrangement. The arrangements differ from each other on the consideration as to who bears the exploration risk. In a service contract, the title to petroleum *in situ* rests with the host state through its national oil company and the oil company is engaged by the national oil company as a contractor to conduct petroleum operations for consideration either in cash or in kind from petroleum produced from the petroleum operations. The exploration and production risk rest with the national oil company or the host government. However, under the production sharing contract, the oil company undertakes the petroleum exploration and production at its risk. It then takes the share of production as *"cost oil."* The balance of the production, which is normally termed *"profit oil,"* is shared between the host government or its national oil company and the oil company. On the other hand, under the joint venture structure, title to the licence and the means of production are jointly held between the state and the oil companies, and petroleum is jointly produced and sold. The following features are common in the post-1950 petroleum arrangements.[32]

(i) The risk of exploration is borne by the oil company and the cost of exploration is not recoverable unless a commercial discovery is made.

(ii) The exploration phase is distinguished from the production phase. Accordingly, if no significant discovery of petroleum is made within the stipulated period, the company must surrender the acreage.

(iii) The oil company is subjected to minimum work and expenditure program.

(iv) The oil company is subject to obligations to provide information and data to the host government.

(v) Provisions are made for division of revenue generated by the projects which feature increased financial take by governments in the form of income tax and revenue from equity in the projects.

(vi) Provisions are made for procurement of local goods and services and for the training and employment of nationals.

There are variances in the treatment of different considerations under different petroleum arrangements. Notable among these is the treatment of title in the oil produced, whether title in the oil is acquired by the oil company either at the point of export or at the wellhead. The second consideration relates to exploration and production risk – whether the exploration and production risk is borne by the oil company or the host government. The third consideration relates to the fiscal arrangement under which governments take active participation in the management and control over the project; in essence, equity participation in the project.

The key features of the petroleum titular system, the arrangement for State equity participation under the petroleum arrangements and the fiscal regime applicable to petroleum exploration and development will be considered in some details with particular reference to the PNG's petroleum arrangement.

B. PNG's Petroleum Exploration and Production Licencing Regime

The PNG legal and fiscal regime that governs petroleum development could be described as that which is governed primarily by legislation. The terms for the granting of petroleum exploration and production licences are set out in the legislation[33] and these are supplemented by details set out in the petroleum licence.

The basic considerations in dealing with natural resources development is firstly, the question of who has the title to the resources and secondly, who has right to exclusive use, control or management of the resources. Generally, the owner of the resources would have the right to use, control and manage the exploitation of these resources. Ownership therefore underpins property rights and provides the basis to manage the exploitation of the resources.[34]

The English Common Law presumes that the owner of the land is entitled to all that is located above and below the land; *cujus est solum ejus est usque ad colum et usque ad inferos*. Under common law, minerals naturally occurring form part of the land on which they are situated unless these minerals are specifically severed from the crown land grant. The only exceptions are the royal metals; gold and silver, which remain subject to crown ownership, notwithstanding the crown grant of the land on which minerals are naturally occurring.[35]

PNG's natural resources laws adopted the practice of reserving title to mineral and petroleum *in situ* exclusively to the State.[36] Ownership in resources *in situ* therefore rests with the State. The vesting of ownership of mineral and petroleum resources *in situ* together with the vesting of the prerogative to licence the exploration and production of these resources, and the prerogative to manage the exploration and development of same, provides the foundation of resources law. It underpins the legal arrangement under which the resources are developed. The prerogative to manage the exploitation of these resources is a significant factor that one would need to examine in the quest to identify the contractual arrangement of the PNG's petroleum regime. This is underlined by the fact that despite State ownership of the petroleum naturally occurring, the resources will be developed by private enterprise and hence the petroleum policy regime is geared towards encouraging private sector investment in petroleum development.

The licensing system governing petroleum exploration and production is therefore the ultimate exercise of the host state's ownership of these resources and the exercise of the management prerogative is the ultimate exercise of sovereignty over the exploration and production of the resources that lay within its national boundaries.

(a) Exploration Licence

The PNG's petroleum exploration and development licensing system is primarily a two-tier system. A Petroleum Prospecting Licence (PPL) is an exploration licence issued to an oil company pursuant to which the oil company undertakes petroleum exploration.[37] The Petroleum Development Licence (PDL) is a production licence[38] issued to the holder of a PPL upon commercial discovery of petroleum, to produce and deal with the petroleum produced within the acreage.

The process of granting a PPL commences on application for or upon invitation by the Minister, for a PPL.[39] For the purpose of granting an exploration or a production licence, the earth's surface is divided up into gratucular sections called-blocks, comprising five minutes longitudes and five minutes latitude.[40] An application for a PPL would be made in respect of not more than 60 blocks[41]and in special circumstances the minimum acreage could be increased to 200 blocks.[42]

The conditions under which petroleum exploration and production will be undertaken are prescribed by legislation.[43] A PPL is granted for a term not exceeding 6 years[44]and renewable for a further term of 5 years but for a reduced area,[45] and is also subject to work and expenditure requirements.[46]

A licence sets out the basic terms and conditions under which petroleum exploration will be undertaken.[47]

Where petroleum discovery is made in a exploration acreage, a declaration would be made of a location, within the exploration acreage, of a petroleum discovery. [48] Subsequent to the declaration of a location, the oil company may apply for and be granted a further extension of the exploration licence for a further period of not more than 3 years.[49]

A PPL confers on the licensee the exclusive right to explore for petroleum, to carry out appraisal work in respect of the petroleum discovery, and to undertake such task as are necessary to otherwise explore for, produce and sell or otherwise disposed of petroleum produced. The legislation provides the scope of a PPL as follows:

"A petroleum prospecting licence, while it remains in force, confers on the licensee, subject to this Act, and to the conditions specified in the licence, the exclusive right to explore for petroleum, and to carry out appraisal of a petroleum discovery, and to carry on such operations and execute such works as are necessary for those purposes, in the licence area, including the construction and operations of water lines, tests for appraisal of a petroleum pool (including the construction in accordance with the authorization and disposal), and the recovery and sale or other disposal of all petroleum so produced."*[50]*

As noted, the legislation gives sufficient scope and rights, in exclusivity, to the holder of an exploration licence to explore for, produce and sell or dispose of petroleum produced within the exploration acreage. The scope of a PPL is therefore as wide as a PDL. The case on point is the Moran Petroleum Project.[51] In September 1996, oil was discovered in Moran IX sidetrack well in PDL 2.[52] In early 1997, the State approved the PDL 2 (Kutubu Joint Venture) to carry out an Extended Well Test Program (EWT)[53] within PDL 2 pursuant to which the PDL 2 licensee produced oil within the block under the EWT program.[54]

Moreover, the State proceeded to approve the licence holders of PPL 138[55] to conduct EWT program using Moran 4 well and the PPL 138 licensees produced oil within the exploration licence area from Moran 4 exploration well under a EWT program. Hence, oil was produced at PPL 138 under the EWT program prior to carving out the area and grant of PDL.[56] The production of petroleum at Moran 4 well within Moran PPL 138 is a case on point to demonstrate that the scope of a PPL - an exploration licence, includes exclusive rights not only to explore for, but also to produce and sell or dispose of, petroleum produced within the exploration acreage. A PPL could also contain incidental features as are necessary to undertake and facilitate production of oil within the PPL, including construction of flow-lines and gathering lines, roads and bridges, and other infrastructure.

Technical justifications can be advanced to justify oil production within the exploration acreage under an EWT program but consideration of the same is not within the scope of this paper. The fact that petroleum production is undertaken within the exploration acreage is, for the purposes of this paper, sufficient endorsement of the view that petroleum production can be undertaken under an exploration licence in the PNG's petroleum arrangement.
(b) Petroleum Retention Licence

An exploration licensee may also exclusively apply for a Petroleum Retention Licence (retention licence) in respect of blocks within the exploration acreage in which petroleum is located.[57] This may be done within 2 years from the date on which the blocks were declared as a location.[58]

A retention licence can be issued over *"... a gas field or, a part of the gas field or, for better administration of petroleum activities."* [59] The provision is designed primarily to allow holders of an exploration licence to retain and hold natural gas discoveries within the acreage pending commercial extraction of the same. However, provisions are also made for retention licence to be issued in respect of oil discoveries within the acreage "... *for better administration of petroleum activities."* The proviso creates scope for retention licences to be issued in respect of marginal oil fields where the reserves cannot be commercially produced.[60] That is, where a discovery is over a marginal field and it is not commercially viable to produce the petroleum discovered within the location, a retention licence may be issued over the respective blocks in the exploration acreage, which would allow the exploration licensee to retain the discovery pending further appraisal, further and additional discovery and commercial production of the petroleum discovered within the acreage.[61]

A retention licence may be granted for 5 years[62]and may be extended for further terms of 5 years at each extension.[63] Accordingly, a retention licence can be further extended over number of 5 years extension periods before commercial production can be realised. It therefore allows a holder of an exploration licence to hold onto the acreage pending commercial production of the discovery.[64]

(c) Petroleum Development Licence

If significant petroleum discovery is made that can sustain commercial production, a PDL, which is the production licence, will be issued to the holder of the PPL.[65] The basic requirement of a PDL is fixed by legislation.[66] A PDL is issued to the holder of an exploration or retention licence for a period not exceeding 25 years, renewable for a term not exceeding 20 years.[67]

A PDL confers on the licensee the exclusive rights to explore for petroleum within the licence area, to produce petroleum within the licence area, to sell or otherwise disposed of petroleum so produced and to carry out such other works in the licence area as are necessary to conduct petroleum operations in accordance with the terms of the licence.[68] The works necessary to carry out petroleum operations include construction of flow lines and gathering lines, roads, bridges and other civil works, airports, seaports and related facilities.[69]

In the case of the Kutubu project, the PDL 2 licensees also own and operate the only oil pipeline in PNG that transport oil from the oil fields to the offshore loading terminal.

The development licensee is therefore licensed not only to produce and sell or disposed of petroleum produced, but also the added right to *"...carry on such operations and execute such work as are necessary for or in connection..."* with carrying out petroleum operations.[70]

C. Charecteristics of Petroleum Agreements

The PNG petroleum agreements deal with matters, which include State equity participation, foreign currency management, local business development and procurement of local goods and services. For the purpose of this paper, particular consideration is given to those provisions dealing with State equity participation.

The State takes its share of the revenue from production and sale of petroleum, primarily from petroleum taxation computed and collected under the *Income Tax Act*,[71] petroleum royalty and from direct equity participation in the project. In computing the State's share of the petroleum produced or the revenue derived from sale of petroleum produced within the acreage, and the oil companies' share of the petroleum produced, the amount taken up by the State pursuant to the exercise of its rights to take equity participation in the petroleum project within a license area is regarded and treated by oil companies as the State's share of the oil or revenue. Accordingly, the State equity participation policy regime is an important element of the State's petroleum policy regime, and that which forms the core of the petroleum agreement.

The terms under which the State may take equity participation in the petroleum project are set out in the petroleum agreements entered into in respect of each PPL. The petroleum agreements are entered into pursuant to the petroleum legislation.[72] The respective petroleum agreements, as a matter of policy, are entered into prior to discovery of petroleum. Therefore the subsequent PDL incorporates provisions of both the negotiated agreement and legislation, which form the conditions of the PDL.[73] Both instruments are therefore needed to undertake petroleum development.

The detailed features of State equity participation in a petroleum project are not covered by the legislation[74] but are set out in the respective petroleum agreements. This is a major feature of the PNG's petroleum arrangement that can be termed as *the heart* of the petroleum agreement. It is therefore the fiscal arrangement and the arrangement for the State's equity participation in the projects that distinguish the PNG's petroleum agreement from other recognised forms of petroleum agreements.

The basis of the State's equity participation in petroleum projects is legislatively framed[75] and forms part and parcel of the State's petroleum policy regime. The genesis of the State equity participation policy can be traced backed to the 1976 petroleum policy white paper which provides that the government's *"total financial take"* from oil produced in any production licence area follows:

"(I) 11/4 percent royalty on well-head value of production;
(II) a percentage income tax at a rate of 50 per cent of taxable income;
(III) an additional profits tax at rate 50 per cent of after tax cash flow after total investment has been recouped with a money returned of 25 per cent;
(IV) State participation in development of commercial fields on 'carried interest' principles"[76] (My emphasis).

The State's equity participation in petroleum projects is, therefore, on the basis of *"carried interest principles."*

As a matter of practice, the holder of a PPL is advised to enter into a petroleum agreement with the State before any well is drilled in the exploration acreage. The agreement defines, *inter alia,* the State's equity participation in the subsequent petroleum discovery. [77] The agreements state that the State has an option to take equity participation in the project, up to the nominated percentage.[78] It can also elect not to take equity participation in a particular project. For instance, the *PPL 100 (Kutubu) Petroleum Agreement*, provides that:
"...the State may acquire for a Nominee of the State from the Oil Companies constituting the Development Licensee in the Development License Area, an unencumbered ... interest in the venture interest attributable to the Development Licence Area... up to nominated percentage not exceeding twenty – two and one-half percent (22 ½%) and where the State has acquired such a Joint Venture Interest for a Nominee of the State, the Nominee of the State shall have the right to share... production from that Development Licence Area equal to the nominated percentage,..."*[79]*

The provisions of the petroleum agreement[80] set out the terms under which the State will take equity participation in the project.[81] The State upon electing to take equity participation in the project acquires equity through its Nominee,[82] to the value of the nominated percentage.[83] It also enters into joint venture arrangement with the oil companies that are holders of the PDL. In entering into a joint venture agreement with the oil companies, the State's Nominee becomes a joint participant under the joint venture arrangement,[84] effectively a tenant in common of the PDL under the joint venture structure with the other joint participants. In this respect it also subscribes to all licences, permits and authorisations necessary for the conduct of project development as a joint venturer and holds the petroleum titles jointly and severally with the oil companies in the joint venture as a tenant in common.

The State in taking up equity in the project, through its Nominee, also becomes a joint venturer and a joint licensee of the PDL. The non-State joint venturers finance the Nominee's *pro rata* percentage of exploration, development and other cost and expenditures under the *"carried interest"* arrangement. Under the arrangement, the amount owed to the oil companies by the Nominee is "deemed" as a loan from the oil companies to the Nominee at a commercial interest rate, to be debited from the Nominee's revenue from its proportionate share of the petroleum produced within that PDL.[85]

The production titleholders acquire title to the petroleum, upon production, at the wellhead. Similarly, the State, through the Nominee, as joint licensee and tenant in common, acquires title to petroleum produced at the wellhead. However, the Nominee does not lift the petroleum produced and deal with oil produced during the period it has outstanding liability to the oil companies under the *carried interest* arrangement. Instead, the oil companies lift the State's proportionate share of the petroleum produced, sell same and apply the revenue derived to defray the liability of the State under the *carried interest* arrangement. When the aggregate of the exploration, development and operation expenditures, proportionately owed to the respective oil companies, is reduced to zero, the *carried interest* arrangement is discharged and the State, through the Nominee, is able to take petroleum, unencumbered, at the well-head and sell or dispose of same as a joint licensee and a member of the joint venture.

The liability to the oil companies is computed, applying a pre-agreed formula.[86] This is ascertained, at any given time, by deducting from the State's proportionate share of the revenue earned, the *pro rata* share of exploration and capital expenditures, and amount spent by the oil companies attributable to the oil production. The arrangement remains in place for the duration of the period when income from the share of oil produced, attributable to the State's equity participation, is insufficient to discharge its liability to the oil companies.

The legal arrangement under which the State equity participation is accommodated and facilitated by the oil companies constituting the relevant licence is similar to the arrangement under the joint venture agreement.[87]

D. Income Tax Treatment of the "Carried Interest Arrangement"

The treatment of the petroleum exploration and production titles in the petroleum legislation and the petroleum agreements is followed through in the taxation regime.[88] Under the taxation regime, a petroleum project is *"re-fenced"* for taxation purposes and taxed on project basis.[89] That is, each oil company as a taxpayer (taxpayer) is assessed in relation to each project as if the assessable income of the taxpayer from petroleum operations attributable to the petroleum project was the only assessable income derived by that taxpayer, and conversely, all allowable deductions are deducted against future income from the petroleum project.[90]

For petroleum tax purposes, the pre-PDL exploration expenditures incurred by the taxpayer within the relevant exploration licence area in relation to a petroleum project are carried forward and accumulated for 20 years.[91] Upon commencement of petroleum production, the exploration expenditure is deducted from the income derived by the taxpayer from sale of petroleum produced from petroleum operations conducted within the PDL area. The exploration expenditure incurred in relation to the PDL is reduced; firstly in paying for the exploration expenditure incurred by the taxpayer in relation to the PDL in the relevant year of income; and secondly, any excess amount is applied to reduce the exploration expenditure incurred by the taxpayer in relation the PDL against the expenses earliest incurred within the 20 years period to the year of income, until the amount is fully recovered. [92] This has the effect of accelerating the recovery of exploration expenditures by applying all the available income derived from sale of petroleum produced from the petroleum project.

The *Income Tax Act's* treatment of allowable capital expenditures is similar to treatment of allowable exploration expenditure under income tax principles.[93] In substance, the capital expenditures are carried forward and depreciated against future income derived by the taxpayer from sale of petroleum produced from petroleum operations conducted within the PDL area until the amount is fully depreciated by applying the relevant rate of depreciation.[94]

As to the nature of the petroleum titles, the *Income Tax Act* recognises that interest in the petroleum title is proprietary in nature, which can be sold or transferred for valuable consideration by the titleholders. In such transaction, the vendor and the purchaser can agree to treat the exploration expenditures as exploration expenditure *per se*, or capital expenditures, or partly capital and partly exploration expenditures, at their discretion, with minimum requirement to inform the Commissioner General of the Internal Revenue Commission of the arrangement as between the parties.[95] The holder of a petroleum title can therefore deal with the petroleum titles as a property right.[96]

The State, through its Nominee, is also treated as a purchaser of petroleum title, from the oil companies constituting the relevant petroleum title, as a tenant in common. The interest in the petroleum title, acquired by the State through its Nominee, is treated by the *Income Tax Act* as a sale of petroleum interest between oil companies. The tax treatment of the State's equity in the petroleum projects also endorses the proprietary nature of the PDL. The *Income Tax Act* treatment of the petroleum title held by the State, through its Nominee, is also consistent with the treatment of the same under the petroleum legislation and the petroleum agreements.

Upon becoming a joint licensee and a member of the relevant joint venture, the Nominee, as a joint licensee, produces petroleum and acquires title to same at the well-head[97] together with other joint licensees, as tenant in common,[98] and pay royalty, for the petroleum produced, which is also computed and paid using the well head value. The Nominee, for the purpose of petroleum operations, is treated as a joint licensee of the PDL. This is the arrangement under which states or their nominee take an active participation in petroleum operations conducted within the country under the new concession arrangement.

In addition to the concession based tax regime, the petroleum agreements guarantee the holder of a production licence, the right to export petroleum free of export tax.[99] The oil company is also given a degree of comfort in relation to import duties in that the petroleum agreement guarantees non-discriminatory rates, taxes, duties, levies and other impost.[100] The concessions accorded in export duty exemptions for the petroleum exported and the degree of comfort given in relation to rate, taxes, import duties, levies and other impost are incidence of a concession based contract.

The PNG petroleum taxation regime is, without doubt, a concession based taxation regime.

E. Conclusion, The Nature of Petroleum Arrangement

The question to be considered at this juncture is; what is the legal nature of the PNG's petroleum arrangement if one has to classify the arrangement under one or more of the internationally recognised petroleum arrangements.

(a) The Legal Nature of the Licensing Regime

As observed in this paper, there is little doubt that the PNG's petroleum licensing regime is concession based. It can also be noted that the general emphasis in the petroleum licensing or titular system has always been to create and give certainty as to petroleum title. The petroleum titular regime therefore guarantees the holder of an exploration licence the exclusive right to be given a retention licence[101]where an application for such a licence can be sustained. An exploration licence also gives the holder of the licence exclusive right to explore for, produce petroleum and sell or dispose of the petroleum produced within the exploration acreage and to undertake works that are necessary to explore for and produce petroleum within the exploration acreage.[102] The exploration licence is also issued over a relatively large area. These are incidents of a concession-based licensing system.

The introduction of retention licence to the licensing regime underlines the concession nature of the licensing regime.[103] Upon petroleum discovery, the holder of the exploration licence is guaranteed a production licence. In addition, the exploration licensee is guaranteed the right to produce marginal fields in future by utilising the provisions for retention licences, which can be issued exclusively to the holder of a PPL, where the discovery is not sufficient to undertake commercial production of the discovery. Further, the scope of the production licence is such that it guarantees exclusive rights to produce and sell or disposed of petroleum.[104] Upon production of the petroleum, title to the petroleum produced transfers from the State to the holder of the production licence at the wellhead.[105] The holder of a production licence may also undertake such work as are necessary to produce petroleum.[106] These are features of the new concession arrangement.

The terms of the petroleum exploration, retention and production licences are relatively longer compared to petroleum titular regimes where petroleum exploration and production is conducted under the joint venture, service contract and the production sharing contract petroleum arrangements. The comparatively longer terms of the petroleum exploration licences, retention licences and production licences give the PNG petroleum titular regime the nature of a petroleum concession arrangement. Further, the tenants of the PNG's petroleum regime are closely related to the concession arrangement where the concessionaire has the exclusive right to explore for, produce and deal with petroleum produced within the concession for relative long title period.[107]

Title to petroleum *in situ* is vested in the State and passes to the production licensee at the wellhead.[108] This is an incident of the modern concession arrangement as opposed to the traditional oil concession arrangement where title to petroleum *in situ* is granted to and held by the concessionaire. The treatment of title to petroleum *in situ* is consistent with the new concession arrangement, where title to petroleum is owned by the State, but upon production, the title in the petroleum produced shifts from the State to production licensees.

The petroleum titular regime is without doubt a concession-based licensing regime.

(b) Legal Nature of the Petroleum Agreements

Several matters can be considered as distinguishing features of the PNG's petroleum agreements.

Firstly, petroleum title is acquired and exclusively held by the oil companies and not by the State enterprise. In this respect, the oil companies own the petroleum titles and operate the projects as opposed to the production sharing contract, and service contract arrangements where the host state holds the petroleum title, either directly or through its national oil company, and the oil company is engaged as a service provider. Further, under the PNG's petroleum arrangement, title to the petroleum produced passes from the State to the oil company at the wellhead. This is opposed to the production sharing contract and service contract arrangements where title to petroleum always rest with the host state.

Secondly, the State's share of revenue from the project is appropriated, primarily through petroleum taxation and by modest royalty rate of 2%, applied at the wellhead. [109] This can be contrasted with the production sharing contract arrangements where the petroleum produced is apportioned as cost oil and profit oil, and under the service contract arrangement where the oil company is engaged as a contractor and hence the issue of royalty payment for the oil produced is not a relevant consideration. These place the PNG's petroleum arrangement away from the production sharing contract and service contract petroleum arrangements and align the arrangement with the new concession arrangement and joint venture arrangement.

Thirdly, oil companies are granted exploration title, exclusively of the State, with the State retaining the right to participate in petroleum production. Upon successful petroleum exploration and discovery, the State may elect to take up an equity position in the ensuing petroleum project. In such case, the State, through its Nominee, is assigned a portion of the petroleum production licence and other titles, leases, licences, permits and authorisations proportionate to its participating interest. It also enters into a joint operating agreement with the oil companies, and hold the petroleum title and the project assets and liabilities, jointly and severally with the oil companies as a tenant in common. These are features of joint venture contractual arrangements.

Fourthly, the State's equity participation, as set out under the relevant petroleum agreements, is paid for under a carried interest arrangement. Under this arrangement, the *pro rata* amount on account of exploration, capital and operation expenditure is represented as a debt from the State to the oil companies. The debt is classified as a loan to the State from the oil companies, from the issuance of the production licence. The amount owed to the oil companies accrues interest at a commercial rate and the debt or the "deemed loan" is defrayed by the revenue earned from sale of "oil foregone" in favour of the oil companies during the period the liability remains outstanding. The financial arrangement under which the State pays for its participation in the project reflects features of a service contract and joint venture arrangement. However, the treatment of the title to petroleum produced under the PNG's petroleum arrangement is not analogous to the arrangements under the service contract arrangements[110] but is more aligned with the treatment of title to oil produced and owned under a joint venture agreement, where title to the petroleum passes at the wellhead upon production. The petroleum titles, under the PNG's petroleum arrangement rest with the oil companies, which are granted the same under the petroleum legislation. This is unlike the service contract arrangement or the production sharing contract where the petroleum title rest with the state enterprise, and the oil company is engaged as a contractor and its services are paid for either in cash or from portion of the oil produced. Further, the State equity participation is carried by the oil companies and defrayed through the allocation of the State's share of petroleum produced. This incident is consistent with that of a joint venture petroleum arrangement.

Fifthly, title in the petroleum *in situ* rests with the State and is acquired upon production at the wellhead. Accordingly, it can be argued that the petroleum title is of proprietary nature.[111] This is confirmed by the taxation treatment of the titles, which gives the petroleum titles proprietary nature. The acquisition of title to petroleum by the companies from the State at the wellhead, upon production, is a feature of the concession arrangement.

In summation, the PNG's petroleum arrangement cannot be exclusively classified under one of the established petroleum arrangements. However, it contains basic features, primarily of the joint venture and the new concession arrangements. The bundle of legal incidences governing petroleum exploration and production and the fiscal regime is a concession-based regime. However, the State equity participation arrangement, established under the petroleum agreement, is primarily a joint venture agreement.

Generally, the PNG's petroleum arrangement is a *unique hybrid* with features of different established petroleum arrangements, fixed partly by legislation and partly by agreement. The salient features of the arrangement that distinguish it from other petroleum arrangement are the legal incidences of the petroleum titles set out under the legislation,[112] the arrangement for the State's equity participation in the projects as set out under the petroleum agreements[113] and the tax treatment of title to petroleum produced as set out under the *Income Tax Act.*[114]

The titular regime established by legislation and the income tax regime are concession based, and the petroleum agreement shows elements of arrangements under joint venture agreement. Consistently therefore, the PNG petroleum agreements can be *labeled* as a *Concession Based Joint Venture Agreement.*

**AL=SVI (E+D+OC)+S-F-W-Z-R.** Where-

**AL=** total amount owing to the PDL licensee at any time by the State Nominee.
**SVI=** State Nominee's interest expressed in percentage.
**E=** Pre-PDL exploration expenditures.
**D=** PDL Capital Expenditures
**OC=** Any amount spent by the oil companies in the PDL area attributable to the State's equity participation, during the period in which income from pro rata share of the oil production is insufficient to finance project cost that is not specifically included under E&D.
**S=** Amount spent on behalf of the State Nominee during the shortfall period when its pro rata share of the revenue from the petroleum produced an sold is in-sufficient to meet project costs.

**F=** Aggregate revenue from sale of oil attributable to the State Nominee's equity interest.

**W=** Amounts attributable to money spent by the State in funding any project facility or amount spent in connection with project development.
**Z=** Amount contributed by the Nominee of the State or the State in reduction of the AL.
**R=** Amounts foregone by the State Nominee (share of insurance proceeds, etc.) that is credited to the oil companies towards payment and discharge of the AL.

## OIL AND GAS ACT 1998

Being an Act to enact comprehensive legislation governing the exploration for and production of petroleum (including oil and gas) in Papua New Guinea, including the offshore area, and the grant to traditional landowners and Provincial Governments and Local-level Governments of benefits arising from projects for the production of petroleum (including oil and gas), and the processing and transportation in Papua New Guinea of petroleum and petroleum products, and to repeal various Acts, and for related purposes.

### PART I. – PRELIMINARY.

### 1. COMPLIANCE WITH CONSTITUTIONAL REQUIREMENTS, ETC.

(1) This Act, to the extent that it regulates or restricts a right or freedom referred to in Subdivision III.3.C (*qualified rights*) of the *Constitution*, namely–

(*a*) Section 44 (*the freedom from arbitrary search and entry*); and
(*b*) Section 48 (*the right to freedom of employment*); and
(*c*) Section 49 (*the right to privacy*); and
(*d*) Section 51 (*the right to freedom of information*),

is a law made for that purpose, taking into account the National Goals and Directive Principles and the Basic Social Obligations, in particular the National Goals and Directive Principles entitled–

(*e*) national sovereignty and self reliance; and
(*f*) natural resources and environment,

for the purpose of giving effect to the public interest in public order and public welfare.
(2) For the purposes of Section 53(1) (*protection from unjust deprivation of property*) of the *Constitution* and the *Land Act 1996*, and any other relevant law, the purpose and reason for which this Act permits possession to be compulsorily taken of any property and permits any interest in or rights over property to be compulsorily acquired are set out below and are declared and described to be a public purpose, whether pursued by a licensee, the State or any other person exercising rights under this Act, and to be a reason that is reasonably justified in a democratic society that has a proper regard for the rights and dignity of mankind–

(*a*) the conducting of geological surveys, seismic tests, test drilling and other prospecting operations for petroleum in a licence area; and
(*b*) the drilling for and the recovery of petroleum in a licence area; and
(*c*) the storage of petroleum or petroleum products in connection with the operations of a licensee; and
(*d*) the processing of petroleum or petroleum products by a licensee; and
(*e*) the conveyance of petroleum or petroleum products by a licensee, whether by pipeline, land transport, sea transport or air transport, including the pumping, loading, unloading and discharging of petroleum or petroleum products; and
(*f*) the accommodation of the officers, agents and employees of a licensee or any contractor or sub-contractor of a licensee in connection with the prospecting for, recovery or conveyance or processing of petroleum or petroleum products; and
(*g*) the disposal of waste material from operations for, or associated with prospecting for, recovery or conveyance or processing of petroleum or petroleum products; and
(*h*) the establishing of a town to service an industry for the recovery, conveyance or processing of petroleum or petroleum products including civic, cultural and social facilities in the town; and
(*ha*) the construction, maintenance or operation of facilities (including, without limitation, access roads, docks, ports, airports, marinas and accommodation) to be used by a licensee in connection with the prospecting for, recovery, conveyance or processing of petroleum or petroleum products; and
(*i*) the acquisition of land or other property for activities in connection with the above purposes; and
(*j*) the acquisition of a participating interest in a petroleum project in accordance with Part IV.

(3) For the purposes of Section 53(2) of the *Constitution*, this Act is expressed to be made and each of the activities described above in Subsection (2) is expressed to be in the national interest.
(4) For the purposes of–

(*a*) Section 29 of the *Organic Law on Provincial Government*; and
(*b*) Section 41 of the *Organic Law on Provincial Governments and Local-level Governments*,

it is declared that this Act relates to a matter of national interest.

**2. APPLICATION OF PROVISIONS OF ORGANIC LAW ON PROVINCIAL GOVERNMENTS AND LOCAL-LEVEL GOVERNMENTS.**

(1) For the purpose of Section 98 of the *Organic Law on Provincial Governments and Local-level Governments* it is hereby declared that this Act–

(*a*) establishes the benefits and levies which are payable pursuant to Subsection (2) of that section in respect of petroleum projects; and
(*b*) provides for the rates, management, sharing arrangement and application of such development levies; and
(*c*) establishes the trust funds referred to in Subsection (3) of that section for the controlling and distribution of development levies.

(2) For the purpose of Section 99 of the *Organic Law on Provincial Governments and Local-level Governments* it is hereby declared that this Act establishes the principles by which the National Government and its statutory agencies will share with applicable Provincial Governments and Local-level Governments the revenues of the National Government generated from petroleum projects.
(3) For the purpose of Section 116 of the *Organic Law on Provincial Governments and Local-level Governments* it is hereby declared that this Act establishes–

(*a*) the consultation process amongst stakeholders, including the establishment and procedures for development forums, for petroleum projects; and
(*b*) the extent to which the parties may participate in petroleum projects.

**3. INTERPRETATION.**

(1) In this Act, unless the contrary intention appears–

**"access arrangements"** means the access arrangements applying to strategic pipelines which are referred to in Section 75, or the access arrangements applying to strategic petroleum processing facilities which are referred to in Section 89, as the case may be;
**"affected Local-level Government"** means, in relation to a petroleum project, a Local-level Government within whose geographic jurisdiction lies a dedicated project facility of that petroleum project or any part of a petroleum development licence the production of petroleum from which is part of that petroleum project;
**"affected Provincial Government"** means, in relation to a petroleum project, a Provincial Government within whose geographic jurisdiction lies a dedicated project facility of that petroleum project or any part of a petroleum development licence the production of petroleum from which is part of that petroleum project;
**"annual fee"** means a fee prescribed by Subsection 157(2);
**"approved"** means approved by the Minister;
**"arbitration"** means arbitration under the *Arbitration Act 1951* or, where the Minister or the State and a licensee have agreed to substitute some other form of arbitration for that Act, that other form of arbitration;
**"authorized officer"** in relation to–

(*a*) the doing of any act; or
(*b*) the exercise of any power or function; or
(*c*) the performance of any duty,

means the officer authorized in writing by the Minister for that purpose;
**"block"** means a block constituted as provided by Section 17;
**"the Board"** means the Petroleum Advisory Board established under Section 13;
**"buffer zone"** means, in relation to a petroleum project, the area around the dedicated project facilities of that petroleum project determined by the Minister to be the buffer zone for that petroleum project, but does not include land within a petroleum development licence pursuant to which the petroleum project is conducted or any land not within five kilometres of a dedicated project facility;
**"the Chief Inspector"** means the Chief Inspector appointed under Section 151(1);
**"the Chief Warden"** means the Chief Warden appointed under Section 119(1)(a);
**"commence to construct"** means any clearing of land, excavation, construction or other action at the site for the purpose of constructing any petroleum processing facility, but does not include temporary use of sites for less than 90 days, conducting tests, taking samples or borings, preparing plans and designs, contracting for the fabrication of equipment and improvements, or the legal occupation of land;
**"commencement date"** means the date of coming into operation of this Act;
**"the Company"** means Orogen Minerals Limited;
**"Customary land"** means the land that is owned or posssed by an automatic citizen or community of automatic citizens by virtue of rights of proprietary or possessory kind that belonged to that citizen or community and arise from and are regulated by custom;
**"customary land owner"** means a person who has an interest in customary land.
**"dedicated project facility"** means, in relation to a petroleum project–

(*a*) a pipeline; or
(*b*) a pipe or system of pipes referred to in Paragraphs (a) to (d) inclusive of the definition of "pipeline"; or
(*c*) a petroleum processing facility; or
(*d*) any other facility used exclusively by the tenement holder or other person in carrying on that petroleum project,

the operations of which are part of the same "petroleum project" or "designated gas project" as those terms are defined in the *Income Tax Act 1959*, but does not include a facility which is excluded as a dedicated project facility by an instrument signed by the Minister;

**"Department"** means the Department responsible for petroleum matters;
**"development agreement"** means, in relation to a petroleum project, a written agreement between–

(*a*) the State; and
(*b*) the project area landowners, affected Local-level Governments or affected Provincial Governments of the petroleum project, or any of them, as the case may be;

**"development forum"** means, in relation to a petroleum project or a proposed petroleum project, a meeting or combination of meetings convened in accordance with Section 48;
**"the Director"** means the Director appointed under Section 11;
**"document"** includes any map, book, record, or writing;
**"domestic gas operator"** means a person who connects, installs or repairs equipment and appliances for the purpose of the combustion of gas for domestic utilisation, other than a portable gas appliance that is designed to have within it, or attached to it, its own source of gas;
**"domestic gas supplier"** means a person who supplies in Papua New Guinea by pipeline or in cylinders or other containers natural gas or liquefied petroleum gas for domestic utilisation;
**"domestic utilisation"** means the consumption or distribution of petroleum or petroleum products as a fuel or feedstock within Papua New Guinea;
**"drilling"** means the perforation of the earth's surface whether the hole is vertical, inclined, or horizontal and includes–

(*a*) all operations for preventing the collapse of the sides of the hole or for preventing the hole from becoming filled by extraneous materials (including water); and
(*b*) the fitting of wellheads, coring, and logging;

**"equity benefit"** means, in relation to a petroleum project, a 2% participating interest in that petroleum project, free of encumbrances or liabilities as at the commencement of commercial production of petroleum from that petroleum project;
**"Expenditure Implementation Committee"** means a committee established in accordance with Subsection 178(2);
**"flow lines or gathering lines"** means pipes or a system of pipes for one of the uses referred to in Paragraphs (a), (b) and (c) of the definition of "pipeline";
**"former Act"** means the Acts repealed by Section 186;
**"gas agreement"** means an agreement referred to in Section 184;
**"gas field"** means a petroleum pool consisting, in some part, of petroleum recoverable as natural gas at the surface where oil recovery is not, or is not expected to be, the primary object of petroleum recovery;
**"gas operations"** means petroleum operations relating to the recovery from a gas field;
**"gas project"** means–

(*a*) where a gas agreement does not apply to a project–a petroleum project having the purpose of recovering natural gas (other than recovery of natural gas which is incidental to the recovery of other petroleum); and
(*b*) where a gas agreement applies to the project – a petroleum project, as and to the extent defined in such gas agreement, having the purpose of recovering: –

(i) natural gas; and
(ii) other petroleum which is incidental to the recovery of natural gas or which is otherwise dealt with in or the subject of that gas agreement;

**"good oilfield practice"** means practice which is generally accepted within the petroleum industry as good and safe–

(*a*) in the carrying on of exploration for petroleum; or
(*b*) in operations for the recovery of petroleum,

as the case may be;
**"graticular section"** means a section referred to in Section 17(1);
**"improvements"** means–

(*a*) any building or structure; or
(*b*) any yard, fence, wall or other erection, construction or appliance affixed to land–

(i) for the working or management of the land or of stock depastured on the land; or
(ii) for maintaining or increasing the natural capacity of the land to produce or to give shelter or enjoyment to humans or animals; or

(*c*) any planted crop or trees, whether planted for commercial or domestic purposes,

and includes–

(*d*) any well, bore, reservoir, spring, dam or other artificial water course or watering place; or
(*e*) any road, track, footpath, railway, tramway, culvert, bridge or crossing; or
(*f*) the site of any sports ground, recreation area, sing sing ground, village or community meeting place, burial place or sacred ground;

**"incorporated land group"** has the meaning given in the *Land Groups Incorporation Act 1974*;
**"in-plant piping"** means pipes or a system of pipes referred to in Paragraph (d) of the definition of "pipeline";
**"inspector"** means a person appointed under Section 151, and includes the Chief Inspector;
**"land"** includes the offshore area and the bed of any river, stream, estuary, lake or swamp;
**"licence"** means–

(*a*) a petroleum prospecting licence issued under Section 23; or
(*b*) a petroleum retention licence issued under Section 40; or
(*c*) a petroleum development licence issued under Section 57; or
(*d*) a pipeline licence issued under Section 74; or
(*e*) a petroleum processing facility licence issued under Section 88,

or any of them, as the context requires, and includes any extension of those licences;
**"licence area"** means the area constituted by the blocks that are the subject of a tenement;
**"licensee"** means the registered holder of a licence;
**"location"** means the blocks in respect of which a declaration under Section 34 is in force;
**"low water line"** means–

(*a*) the low water line on a coast of Papua New Guinea at mean low water springs; or
(*b*) any line declared by the Minister to be a low water line under Section 4;

**"major modification"** means, in relation to a petroleum processing facility–

(*a*) installation of new processing units or debottlenecking of existing processing units which results in an increase of the rated capacity of the petroleum processing facility to more than one hundred and twenty five percent of its original design capacity; or
(*b*) the installation of new facilities or modification of existing facilities costing in excess of 30% of the replacement cost of the petroleum processing facility; or
(*c*) any other modification to the petroleum processing facility involving a fundamental change to the process or the petroleum products produced by the petroleum processing facility;

**"month"** means the period from and including a day in one calendar month to and excluding the corresponding day in the next calendar month and including the last day in the next calendar month if there is no corresponding day;
**"MRDC"** means Mineral Resources Development Company Pty Limited;
**"natural gas"** means fluid obtained from a well which is a gas at standard temperature and pressure and which consists primarily of hydrocarbons;
**"NGC"** means a company called or to be called National Gas Corporation Limited to be incorporated in accordance with Section 179;
**"offshore area"** means the area that comprises–

(*a*) the seabed underlying the waters (if any) between the low water line and the baseline; and
(*b*) the seabed underlying the territorial sea; and
(*c*) the seabed adjacent to the coast of Papua New Guinea that underlies the offshore seas to a depth not exceeding 200 m or, beyond that limit, to a depth where the superjacent waters admit of the exploitation of the natural resources in the subsurface or on the seabed of that area;

[13]**"operator"** means, in relation to a license –

(*a*) where there is only one registered holder of that license –that registered holder; and
(*b*) in all other cases –the person, who shall be a licensee, for the time being designated by the operating agreement, in respect of that license as the operator of operations conducted in relation to that licence;

**"operating agreement"** means, in respect of a license, the agreement executed between the holders of that license and provided to the Director pursuant to Section 123A in relation to that licence.
**"option"** has the meaning given to it in the option agreement;
**"option agreement"** has the meaning given to it in the *Mineral Resources Development Company Pty Limited (Privatisation) Act 1996*;
**"Orogen option project"** means a petroleum project which is also a Project as defined in the option agreement;
**"participating interest"** means, in relation to a petroleum project an undivided beneficial interest in all of the project assets of that petroleum project;
**"petroleum"** means–

(*a*) any naturally occurring hydrocarbons, whether in a gaseous, liquid, or solid state; or
(*b*) any naturally occurring mixture of hydrocarbons, whether in a gaseous, liquid, or solid state; or
(*c*) any naturally occurring mixture of one or more hydrocarbons, (whether in a gaseous, liquid, or solid state) and any other substance,

and includes any processed petroleum, and any petroleum as defined by Paragraph (a), (b) or (c) that has been returned to a natural reservoir, but does not include coal, shale, or any substance that may be extracted from coal, shale, or other rock;
**"petroleum development licence"** means a licence issued under Division III.7;
**"petroleum development licensee"** means the registered holder of a petroleum development licence;
**"petroleum pool"** means a naturally occurring discrete accumulation of petroleum;
**"petroleum processing"** means refining, separating, stabilising, liquefying, storing, reclaiming, treating, fractionation, cracking, polymerisation, reforming or re-refining of petroleum, or the conversion of petroleum to other petroleum derivates, and all related operations; and "processed", in relation to petroleum or petroleum products, has the corresponding meaning;
**"petroleum processing facility"** means a facility, whether onshore or offshore, for petroleum processing, and includes tanks for bulk storage of petroleum or petroleum products and in-plant piping;
**"petroleum processing facility licence"** means a licence granted under Division III.10;
**"petroleum processing facility licensee"** means the registered holder of a petroleum processing facility licence;
**"petroleum product"** means a distillate of petroleum or a reformate or derivate of petroleum;
**"petroleum project"** means a project in Papua New Guinea for the production of petroleum, and includes, if they are part of the same project or developed in conjunction with the petroleum production development, the construction and operation pursuant to a licence of facilities for the recovery, processing or transportation of petroleum, and a project which is the subject of a licence and over which the Company has the right to exercise an option under the option agreement;
**"petroleum prospecting licence"** means a licence issued under Division III.2;
**"petroleum prospecting licensee"** means the registered holder of a petroleum prospecting licence;
**"petroleum retention licence"** means a licence issued under Division III.4;
**"petroleum retention licensee"** means the registered holder of a petroleum retention licence;
**"pipeline"** means pipes and other interconnected facilities operated as an integrated system (including pumping stations, metering stations, valve stations, storage tanks and pig launching and receiving stations) for transporting petroleum or petroleum products from receipt points to delivery points either for petroleum processing within the country or for further processing or export, but does not include pipes and facilities for–

(*a*) returning petroleum to a reservoir for pressure maintenance or storage or conservation; or
(*b*) transporting petroleum that is to be flared or vented, or recovered for test purposes under a tenement (including drill stem or extended production tests) and transported to facilities for testing or measurement or disposal; or
(*c*) gathering petroleum for transportation to petroleum processing facilities within a licence area where all such pipes and transportation facilities are within a licence area; or
(*d*) transporting petroleum or petroleum products between receipt points and delivery points in a petroleum processing facility;

**"pipeline licence"** means a licence to construct and operate a pipeline issued under Division III.9;
**"pipeline licensee"** means the registered holder of a pipeline licence;
**"private land"** means land other than Government land as defined in Section 2 of the *Mining Act 1992*;
**"processed petroleum"** means stabilised crude oil, condensate, processed natural gas that conforms to a quality specification prescribed in a sales contract or elsewhere, liquefied petroleum gas, or liquefied natural gas, or any other petroleum which has been processed but which is not a petroleum product;
[15]**"project area landowners"** means, in relation to a petroleum project, the persons who are customary land owners or who have registered title to–

(*a*) any part of the licence area of a petroleum development licence the operations under which are part of that petroleum project; or
(*b*) any land within the buffer zone of that petroleum project;

**"project assets"** means, in relation to a petroleum project–

(*a*) the licence or licences pursuant to which the petroleum project or any part of it is conducted; and
(*b*) the property, real or personal, present or future, owned or acquired or held for use by or on behalf of the licensee or licensees or other persons affiliated with the licensee or licensees who are carrying out the petroleum project, which is held for the purposes of the petroleum project or any part of it, including all property in dedicated project facilities of the petroleum project; and
(*c*) the right to receive in kind and to dispose of all petroleum recovered in the course of the petroleum project,

in each case to the extent that such petroleum project is an entire or more than one entire "petroleum projects" or "designated gas projects" as defined in the *Income Tax Act 1959*;
**"project pipeline"** means a pipeline which is not a strategic pipeline;
**"pumping station"** means equipment for pumping petroleum or petroleum products or water and includes any structure associated with that equipment;
**"Register"** means a Register kept under Division III.11;
**"registered holder"**, in relation to a licence, means the person whose name is for the time being shown in the Register as being the holder of the licence;
**"royalty benefit"** means, in relation to a petroleum project, a sum of money each month equal to the amount of royalty payable in the previous month pursuant to Section 159 by a licensee in respect of that petroleum project, less any tax or withholding payable to the State in respect of such royalty upon payment to third persons;
**"royalty period"**, in relation to a tenement means–

(*a*) the period commencing on the date on which the tenement comes into effect to the end of that month; and
(*b*) each month afterwards;

**"State equity entitlement"** means the entitlement of the State, pursuant to Section 165, to acquire, directly or through a nominee, a participating interest in a petroleum project;
**"storage"** means the accumulation of petroleum or petroleum products pending transportation to a petroleum processing facility or loading for transportation or sale;
**"strategic petroleum processing facility"** means a petroleum processing facility directly connected to or directly integrated with a strategic pipeline, either upstream or downstream, but does not include a petroleum processing facility which is exempted under Section 89(7);
**"strategic pipeline"** means a pipeline referred to in Section 75(1);

**"tank station"** means a tank or system of tanks for holding or storing petroleum, and includes any structure associated with that tank or system of tanks;
**"temporary operations"** means any of the following operations:–

(*a*) geological, geochemical and geophysical surveying;
(*b*) taking samples by hand or hand held methods;
(*c*) aerial and land surveying;
(*d*) transportation of crews and equipment by haul roads, navigable waterways or aircraft;
(*e*) any activity prescribed by regulation as a preliminary survey,

and any lawful act incidental to any activity to which Paragraphs (a) to (e) relate to the extent that it does not involve any activity that results in surveys of greater than minimum scale and in no circumstances shall include activities involving–

(*f*) exploring for petroleum; or
(*g*) the cutting, destroying, removing or injury of any vegetation on greater than a minimum scale; or
(*h*) the use of explosives, other than for geophysical survey; or

(i) damage to improvements, stock or chattels on any land; or

(*j*) any breach of the provisions of this or any other Act, including provisions relating to protected native plants, water, noise and historic sites; or
(*k*) the use of more persons for any particular activity than is reasonably necessary; or
(*l*) any survey prescribed as a prohibited survey; or
(*m*) entry on land prescribed as prohibited land;

**"tenement"** means–

(*a*) a petroleum prospecting licence issued under Section 23; or
(*b*) a petroleum retention licence issued under Section 40; or
(*c*) a petroleum development licence issued under Section 57,

or any of them, as the context requires, and includes any extension of those licences;
**"tenement holder"** means the registered holder of a tenement;
**"this Act"** includes the regulations;
**"transportation"** means the act of delivering petroleum or petroleum products, whether by barge, pipeline, road tanker, ship, drums or other container or otherwise, from a receipt point to a destination point including back hauls, displacement, exchange and in-transit storage;
**"valve station"** means equipment for regulating the flow of petroleum, and includes any structure associated with that equipment;
**"vessel"** means a vessel used in navigation, other than air navigation, and includes a barge, lighter or other floating vessel;
[16]**"Warden"** means a Warden appointed under Section 119(1)(b);
**"water line"** means a pipe or system of pipes for conveying water to be used in connection with prospecting for, or the recovery of, petroleum;
**"well"** means a hole in land or the subsoil of land, made by drilling, boring or any other means–

(*a*) in connection with exploration for petroleum; or
(*b*) in operations for the recovery of petroleum,

but does not include a seismic shot hole.

(2) In this Act, a reference–

(*a*) to the term of a licence, is a reference to the period during which the licence remains in force and includes the period of any extension of such licence; and
(*b*) to the date of expiration of a licence, is a reference to the day on which the licence ceases to have effect.

(3) In this Act, a reference to a year of the term of a licence is a reference to a period of one year commencing on the date from and including which the licence has effect or on any anniversary of that date.
(4) In this Act, a reference to a licence is a reference to the licence as varied from time to time under this Act.
(5) For the purposes of this Act, **"Papua New Guinea"** includes the offshore area.

**4. DECLARATION OF LOW WATER LINE.**

In any case where he considers there is doubt as to the location of a low water line, the Minister may, by notice in the National Gazette, declare the location of the line by whatever method appears to him to be appropriate, and the line so declared shall be the low water line.

**5. APPLICATION.**

This Act applies–

(*a*) to all natural persons, whether resident in the country or not; and
(*b*) to all corporations, whether incorporated or carrying on business in the country or not.

**6. PETROLEUM THE PROPERTY OF THE STATE.**

(1) Subject to this Act, but notwithstanding anything contained in any other law or in any grant, instrument of title or other document, all petroleum and helium at or below the surface of any land is, and shall be deemed at all times to have been, the property of the State.
(2) Nothing in Subsection (1) shall be construed as an additional acquisition of property in relation to Section 53 of the *Constitution* beyond that which prevailed under the former Act and all previous Acts.
(3) Petroleum and helium shall not be removed from the land from which it has been obtained, or disposed of in any manner, except–

(*a*) subject to Subsection (4), by a tenement holder, for the purpose of sampling or analysis; or
(*b*) by a tenement holder in accordance with the terms of his tenement or a written agreement with the State; or
(*c*) as otherwise permitted by this Act.

(4) A licensee shall not take or send out of the country any samples of petroleum or helium without the written consent of the Director.

**7. THE DIRECTOR MAY CARRY ON OPERATIONS.**

(1) The Director may, on behalf of the State, carry on prospecting for, and the recovery and conveyance of, petroleum and helium, and activities incidental to those operations.
(2) Where the Director carries on any operations under this section, he has the same rights, benefits, and privileges as a licensee.
(3) Where the Director carries on any operations under this section, he shall to the extent that they can be practicably applied to him, be subject to the same duties and obligations under this Act as apply to a licensee.

**8. EXPLORATION FOR AND RECOVERY OF PETROLEUM.**

A person who–

(*a*) explores for petroleum otherwise than under and in accordance with a tenement or an instrument of consent issued under this Act; or
(*b*) carries on operations for the recovery of petroleum otherwise than under and in accordance with a tenement,

is guilty of an offence.
Penalty: A fine not exceeding K50,000.00.
Default penalty: A fine not exceeding K50,000.00.

**PART II. – APPLICATION OF LAWS AND ADMINISTRATION.**

**9. LAWS OF PAPUA NEW GUINEA TO APPLY.**

(1) Subject to this Act, the provisions of all laws for the time being in force in Papua New Guinea, and the provisions of any instrument having effect under any of those laws, apply in the offshore area.
(2) The provisions referred to in Subsection (1) apply to and in relation to–

(*a*) all acts, omissions, matters, circumstances and things touching, concerning, arising out of, or connected with the exploration for petroleum of the sea, seabed or subsoil of the offshore area; and
(*b*) the exploitation of the natural resources, being petroleum, of the sea, seabed or subsoil of the offshore area.

(3) Without limiting the generality of Subsection (2), the provisions that apply in accordance with this section in the offshore area apply–

(*a*) to and in relation to–

(i) an act or omission that takes place in, on, above, below, or in the vicinity of the sea, seabed or subsoil of that area; and
(ii) a matter, circumstance, or thing that exists or arises with respect to or in connection with a vessel, aircraft, structure or installation or equipment or other property that is in that area for any reason touching, concerning, arising out of or connected with–

(A) the exploration for petroleum; or
(B) the exploitation of the natural resources, being petroleum,
of the sea, seabed or subsoil of that area; and

(*b*) to and in relation to a person who–

(i) is in that area; or
(ii) is in, on, above, below, or in the vicinity of a vessel, aircraft, structure or installation, or equipment or other property that is in that area,

for any reason of the kind referred to in Paragraph (a); and

(*c*) to and in relation to a person in respect of his carrying on any operation or doing any work in that area for any reason of the kind referred to in Paragraph (a).

(4) The regulations may provide that such of the provisions that apply in accordance with this section in the offshore area that are specified in the regulations do not apply, or apply with such modifications as are specified in the regulations.
(5) For the purposes of Subsection (4), **"modifications"** includes the omission or addition of a provision or the substitution of a provision for another provision.

**10. JURISDICTION OF COURTS.**

(1) The National Court of Papua New Guinea is vested with jurisdiction in all matters arising under this Act, including all matters arising under the provisions applied by Section 9, and shall have jurisdiction to hear and determine all actions, suits, claims, demands, disputes, prosecutions and questions which may arise under this Act or those provisions.
(2) Subject to this Act, the laws with respect to the arrest and custody of offenders or persons charged with offences, and the procedure for–

(*a*) their summary conviction; and
(*b*) their examination and committal for trial on indictment; and
(*c*) their trial and conviction on indictment; and
(*d*) the hearing and determination of appeals arising out of any such trial or conviction or out of any proceedings connected with t,

and for holding accused persons to bail apply, so far as they are applicable, to a person who is charged with an offence against any of the provisions applied by Section 9.

**11. APPOINTMENT OF DIRECTOR.**

The Minister may, by notice in the National Gazette, appoint a person to be the Director for the purposes of this Act.

**12. DELEGATION.**

The Director may, by notice in the National Gazette, delegate to an officer all or any of his powers and functions under this Act (except this power of delegation).

**13. PETROLEUM ADVISORY BOARD.**

(1) There shall be a Petroleum Advisory Board.
(2)[17] [18]Subject to Subsection (3), the Board shall consist of –

(*a*) the Director, who shall be the Chairman, or his delegate; and
(*b*) the Secretary of the Department responsible for national planning matters or his delegate appointment in writing and furnished to the Director; and
(*c*) the Secretary of the Department responsible for treasury matters or his delegate appointed in writing and furnished to the Director; and
(*d*) the Secretary of the Department responsible for provincial and Local government matters or his delegate appointed in writing and furnished to the Director; and
(*e*) the Director of Petroleum Division of the Department, who shall be the Deputy Chairman, or his delegate appointed in writing; and
(*f*) the Chief Inspector appointed pursuant to Section 151 or his delegate appointed in writing and furnished to the Director; and
(*g*) the Director of the Investment Promotion Authority or his delegate appointed in writing and furnished to the Director.

(3) If a member of the Board, other than the Chairman or Deputy Chairman is, for any reason, unable to perform his duties as a member, that member may, in writing, appoint a person to act as his substitute for the period of that member's inability, and a person so appointed shall, while so appointed, be a member of the Board.

(3A)[19] [20]In the absence of the Chairman, the Deputy Chairman appointed pursuant to Section 12(2)(e) shall act as Chairman and exercise all powers and responsibilities of the Chairman.
(4)[21] [22]For the purposes of this section, a delegate appointed under this section shall be a senior officer at the Assistant Secretary level or above.

**14. MEETINGS OF THE BOARD.**

(1) The Board shall meet as often as is necessary to carry out its functions and at such times and places as the Chairman, or in his absence the Deputy Chairman, directs.
(2) At a meeting of the Board–

(*a*)[23] the Chairman or in his absence the Deputy Chairman, and three other persons specified in Section 13(2) are a quorum.
(*b*) all matters shall be decided by a majority of votes and the Chairman, or in his absence the Deputy Chairman, has a deliberative, and, in the event of an equality of votes, also a casting vote.

**15. POWERS AND DUTIES OF BOARD.**

(1) The Minister may refer to the Board for advice any question or matter relating to the administration of this Act.
(2) The Board shall inquire into and advise the Minister on any question or matter referred to it under Subsection (1) or as required by this Act.
(3) The referral of a question or matter under Subsection (1) shall be deemed to be a Commission issued under the *Commissions of Inquiry Act 1951*, and the provisions of that Act, including the provisions relating to penalties, apply to and in respect of an inquiry under this section as if the Minister were the Head of State, acting on advice, and the members of the Board were Commissioners within the meaning of that Act.

**16. NO PERSONAL LIABILITY FOR BOARD, MINISTER OR DIRECTOR.**

A member of the Board, the Minister, the Director, or a servant or agent of the State acting under the direction of one of them or an authority delegated to him under this Act, or an inspector, shall not be personally liable to an action, suit or proceeding or claim for damages for or in respect of an act or matter done or omitted to be done in good faith in exercise or purported exercise of any power or authority conferred by this Act.

**PART III. – PETROLEUM EXPLORATION AND DEVELOPMENT.**

**DIVISION 1. PRELIMINARY.**

**17. GRATICULATION OF EARTH'S SURFACE AND CONSTITUTION OF BLOCKS.**

(1) For the purposes of this Act, the surface of the Earth shall be deemed to be divided into sections–

(*a*) by the meridian of Greenwich and by meridians that are at a distance from that meridian of five minutes, or a multiple of five minutes, of longitude; and
(*b*) by the equator and by parallels of latitude that are at a distance from the equator of five minutes, or a multiple of five minutes, of latitude,

each of which is bounded–

(*c*) by portions of two of those meridians that are at a distance from each other of five minutes of longitude; and
(*d*) by portions of two of those parallels of latitude that are at a distance from each other of five minutes of latitude.

(2) Subject to Subsection (3), all or so much of a graticular section that is contained in the area of the country and the offshore area constitutes a block.
(3) Where the area in respect of which a tenement is in force includes one or more portions of a block constituted as provided by Subsection (1)–

(*a*) the area of that portion or those portions constitutes a block; and
(*b*) the area of the remaining portion or portions of the first-mentioned block (but not including any part of that area in respect of which a tenement is in force) constitutes a block.

(4) Where a tenement ceases to be in force in respect of an area referred to in Subsection (3)(a), the Minister may, by instrument determine that the area shall be amalgamated with another block or blocks, being a block or blocks–

(*a*) constituted as provided by this section; and
(*b*) forming part of the graticular section of which the area forms part; and
(*c*) that is or are either–

(i) a block or blocks in respect of which a tenement is in force; or
(ii) a block or blocks constituted under Subsection (3)(b).

(5) Where a determination is made under Subsection (4)–

(*a*) the area and blocks both the subject of the determination, cease to constitute separate blocks and their areas together constitute a single block; and
(*b*) in respect of the area and a block in respect of which there is a tenement in force–the block constituted by the determination is a block for the remainder of the term of that tenement.

(6) In this Act–

(*a*) a reference to a block that is constituted by a graticular section includes a reference to a block that is constituted by the area of a part of a graticular section; and
(*b*) a reference to a graticular section that constitutes a block includes a reference to a graticular section part only of which constitutes a block.

**18. PROSPECTING LICENCES UNDER TORRES STRAIT TREATY.**

(1) This Part, other than this section and Divisions 3, 10, 13 and 14 does not apply to licences issued under this section.
(2) In Divisions 3, 10, 13 and 14 **"licence"** and **"tenement"** shall, where applicable, include a licence granted under this section.
(3) In this section **"the Treaty"** means the Treaty between the Independent State of Papua New Guinea and Australia concerning Sovereignty and Maritime Boundaries in the area between the two countries, including the area known as Torres Strait and related matters signed at Sydney 18 December 1978.
(4) Where, under Article 5 of the Treaty, a person entitled to apply for a petroleum prospecting licence, so applies, the Minister shall grant to him a petroleum prospecting licence.
(5) A licence granted under Subsection (4) shall be granted on terms that are not less favourable than a tenement granted under Division 2.

**19. ISSUE OF LICENCES.**

(1) Subject to this Act, a tenement may be issued to a person in respect of any block except a block that is–

(*a*) comprised in a tenement; or
(*b*) reserved by declaration under Section 20.

(2) A licence may be held by–

(*a*) a natural person; or
(*b*) a body corporate that is incorporated in Papua New Guinea or registered as an overseas company under the *Companies Act 1997*; or
(*c*) an unincorporated combination of–

(i) natural persons; or
(ii) corporations to which Paragraph (b) applies; or
(iii) a natural person or natural persons and a corporation or corporations to which Paragraph (b) applies.

(3) A notification of the issue of a licence shall be published in the National Gazette.

**20. RESERVATION OF BLOCKS.**

(1) The Minister may, by notice in the National Gazette, declare that a block or blocks specified in the notice (not being a block or blocks in respect of which a tenement is in force) shall not be the subject of a tenement, and may in the same manner revoke or vary such notice.
(2) While a declaration under Subsection (1) remains in force in respect of a block or blocks, a tenement shall not be granted in respect of that block or those blocks.

**DIVISION 2. PETROLEUM PROSPECTING LICENCES.**

**21. APPLICATIONS FOR PETROLEUM PROSPECTING LICENCE.**

(1) A person may make an application to the Director for the grant of a petroleum prospecting licence in respect of any block or blocks.
(2) The Minister may, by notice in the National Gazette–

(*a*) invite applications for the grant of a petroleum prospecting licence in respect of the block or blocks specified in the notice; and
(*b*) specify the period during which an application may be made.

**22. FORM OF APPLICATION FOR PETROLEUM PROSPECTING LICENCE.**

(1) An application made under, or as a result of an invitation under, Section 21–

(*a*) shall be in an approved form; and
(*b*) shall be made in an approved manner; and
(*c*) subject to Subsection (2)–shall be in respect of not more than 60 blocks; and
(*d*) shall be accompanied by particulars of–

(i) the detailed proposals of the applicant for work and expenditure in respect of the block or blocks specified in the application during the first two years of the term of the licence and an outline of proposals for work and expenditure during the remaining four years of the licence; and
(ii) the technical qualifications of the applicant and of his employees; and
(iii) the technical advice available to the applicant; and
(iv) the financial resources available to the applicant; and

(*e*) may set out any other matters that the applicant wishes the Minister to consider; and
(*f*) shall be accompanied by the fee prescribed by Section 157.

(2) The Minister may consider an application in respect of more than 60 but not more than 200 blocks where he is satisfied that special circumstances exist for his doing so.
(3) The blocks specified in the application referred to in Subsections (1) and (2) shall be constituted by graticular sections that–

(*a*) form a single area; and
(*b*) are such that each graticular section in that area has a side in common with at least one other graticular section in that area.

(4) The Director may, at any time, by instrument served on the applicant, require him to furnish, within the time specified in the instrument, such further written information in connection with his application as the Director considers necessary.
(5) Where an application is received under, or as a result of an invitation under, Section 21–

(*a*) notice of the application shall be published by the Director in the National Gazette; and
(*b*) any person who claims to be affected by the application may file notice of his objection to that application with the Director within one month after the date of publication of the notice of application and all objections shall be considered by the Board before the Board reports on the application.

(6) As soon as practicable after the granting of a licence in respect of any block or blocks specified in an application made under, or as a result of an invitation under, Section 21, the Minister shall cause to be published in the National Gazette, particulars of any licence so granted.

**23. GRANT OR REFUSAL OF PETROLEUM PROSPECTING LICENCE.**

(1) Where an application has been made under, or as a result of an invitation under, Section 21, the Minister may, after consideration of a report from the Board and after having regard to physical planning considerations–

(*a*) by instrument served on the applicant, inform the applicant–

(i) that he is prepared to grant to the applicant a petroleum prospecting licence in respect of any or all of the blocks specified in the instrument, being blocks to which the application relates; and
(ii) that the applicant will be required to lodge a security for compliance with the conditions to which the licence, if granted, will be subject, and with the provisions of this Act, and to pay the first annual fee; or

(*b*) refuse to grant a licence to the applicant.

(2) An instrument under Subsection (1)(a) shall contain–

(*a*) the conditions subject to which the licence is to be granted; and
(*b*) a statement to the effect that the application will lapse if the applicant does not make a request under Subsection (3) in respect of the grant of the licence and lodge with the Director the security specified in the instrument and the first annual fee.

(3) An applicant who has been served with an instrument under Subsection (1) may, within a period of one month after the date of service of the instrument on him, or within such further period, not exceeding three months, as the Minister may allow–

(*a*) by instrument served on the Minister request the Minister to grant him the licence; and
(*b*) lodge with the Director the security referred to in Subsection (1)(a) and the first annual fee referred to in that subsection.

(4) Where an applicant has complied with the requirements of Subsection (3), the Minister shall grant to him a petroleum prospecting licence in respect of the block or blocks specified in the instrument, subject to the conditions specified in the instrument or such other conditions as are agreed on by the Minister and the applicant, but in any other case the application lapses.

**24. VARIATION OF PETROLEUM PROSPECTING LICENCE.**

(1) The holder of a petroleum prospecting licence may, at any time, make an application to the Minister for a variation of the petroleum prospecting licence.
(2) An application under Subsection (1) shall–

(*a*) specify the reasons for proposed variation; and
(*b*) be made in an approved form and contain the information specified in Section 22.

(3) The Director may require the applicant to furnish such further information in connection with his application as the Director considers necessary.

(4) Following receipt of an application under Subsection (1) the Minister may, after considering a report of the Board and any matters submitted to him under this section–

(*a*) amend the terms of the petroleum prospecting licence to provide as stipulated in the application or as otherwise agreed with the petroleum prospecting licensee; or
(*b*) refuse the application, in which case the existing petroleum prospecting licence shall remain in full force and effect.

**25. RIGHTS CONFERRED BY PETROLEUM PROSPECTING LICENCE.**

A petroleum prospecting licence, while it remains in force, confers on the licensee, subject to this Act, and to the conditions specified in the licence, the exclusive right to explore for petroleum, and to carry out appraisal of a petroleum discovery, and to carry on such operations and execute such works as are necessary for those purposes, in the licence area, including the construction and operation of water lines, and, if authorized by the Director, the completion of wells, the conduct of drill stem or extended production tests for appraisal of a petroleum pool (including the construction in accordance with the authorization and the operation of pipes and facilities to gather and transport petroleum to a point of testing or treatment or disposal), and the recovery and sale or other disposal of all petroleum so produced.

**26. TERM OF PETROLEUM PROSPECTING LICENCE.**

Subject to this Act and to any condition in the licence, a petroleum prospecting licence remains in force–

(*a*) for a period of six years commencing on the day the licence takes effect; and
(*b*) where the licence is extended under Section 29–for a further period of five years; and
(*c*) where the licence is extended under Section 30–for the further period specified by the Minister on the grant of the extension.

**27. APPLICATION FOR EXTENSION OF PETROLEUM PROSPECTING LICENCE.**

(1) Subject to Section 28, the holder of a petroleum prospecting licence may make an application to the Director for the extension of the petroleum prospecting licence in respect of any block or blocks in the licence area.
(2) An application under this section may be made once only in respect of any petroleum prospecting licence.
(3) An application under this section–

(*a*) shall be in an approved form; and
(*b*) shall be made in an approved manner; and
(*c*) shall be made not less than three months before the day on which the licence is due to expire; and
(*d*) shall be accompanied by particulars of–

(i) the work carried out in, and the amounts expended in respect of, the licence area during the term of the licence up to and including the date of the application; and
(ii) the proposals of the applicant for work and expenditure in respect of the blocks specified in the application; and

(*e*) may set out any other matters that the applicant requires the Minister to consider; and
(*f*) shall be accompanied by the fee prescribed by Section 157.

(4) The Minister may, after considering a report from the Board, accept an application for the extension of a petroleum prospecting licence less than three months before, but not in any case after, the date of expiry of the licence.

**28. APPLICATION FOR EXTENSION TO BE IN RESPECT OF REDUCED AREA.**

(1) The number of blocks in respect of which an application for the extension of a petroleum prospecting licence may be made shall not exceed the number that is the sum of–

(*a*) the number of blocks (if any) the subject of the petroleum prospecting licence that, at the date of expiration of the petroleum prospecting licence, were a location not subject to a petroleum retention licence or an application for a petroleum retention licence; and
(*b*) the number of blocks (if any) the subject of the petroleum prospecting licence that, at the date of expiration of the petroleum prospecting licence, are contained within a petroleum retention licence or the subject of an application for a petroleum retention licence; and
(*c*) half the number of blocks in respect of which the petroleum prospecting licence was issued.

(2) The blocks specified in an application for the extension of a petroleum prospecting licence shall be blocks that relate to graticular sections that–

(*a*) constitute a single area or not more than three discrete areas; and
(*b*) are such that each graticular section in each area has a side in common with at least one other graticular section in that area.

**29. GRANT OR REFUSAL OF EXTENSION OF PETROLEUM PROSPECTING LICENCE.**

(1) Where a licensee has made an application under Section 27 for an extension of a petroleum prospecting licence and has furnished any additional information in connection with the application required by the Director, the Minister–

(*a*) shall, if the licensee has complied with the conditions to which the licence is subject and the provisions of this Act; or
(*b*) may, if the licensee has not complied with the conditions to which the licence is subject or the provisions of this Act and the Minister after considering a report from the Board is satisfied that although the licensee has not so complied, special circumstances exist that justify the granting of the extension of the licence,

inform the licensee, by instrument served on the licensee–

(*c*) that he is prepared to grant to the licensee the extension of the licence; and
(*d*) that the licensee will be required to lodge a security, or extend a security already lodged, for compliance with–

(i) the conditions to which the licence, if the extension is granted, will from time to time be subject; and
(ii) with the provisions of this Act; and

(*e*) of the amount of the next annual fee.

(2) If the licensee has not complied with the conditions to which the licence is subject or with the provisions of this Act, and if the Minister is not satisfied that special circumstances exist that justify the granting of the extension of the licence, the Minister shall, subject to Subsection (3), by instrument served on the licensee, refuse to grant the extension of the licence.
(3) The Minister shall not refuse to grant the extension of a petroleum prospecting licence under this section unless–

(*a*) he has, by instrument served on the licensee, given not less than one month's notice of his intention to refuse to grant the extension of the licence; and
(*b*) he has caused a copy of the instrument to be served on such other persons (if any) as he thinks fit; and
(*c*) he has, in the instrument–

(i) given particulars of the reasons for the intention; and
(ii) specified a date on or before which written submissions may be served on the Minister in connection with the proposed refusal; and

(*d*) after–

(i) taking into account any matters submitted to him under Paragraph (c)(ii) on or before the specified date; and
(ii) considering a report from the Board on those matters,

he is not satisfied that special conditions exist that justify the granting of the extension of the licence.
(4) An instrument under Subsection (1) shall–

(*a*) specify the conditions to which the licence, on the grant of the extension, is to be subject; and
(*b*) contain a statement to the effect that the application will lapse if the applicant does not–

(i) make a request under Subsection (5) in respect of the grant of the extension of the licence; and
(ii) lodge with the Director the security specified in the instrument and the annual fee.

(5) A licensee who has been served with an instrument under Subsection (1) may, within a period of one month after the date of service of the instrument on him–

(*a*) by instrument served on the Minister request the Minister to grant to him the extension of the licence; and
(*b*) lodge with the Director the security specified in the instrument and pay the annual fee.

(6) Where a licensee who has been served with an instrument under Subsection (1) has, within the period specified in Subsection (5)–

(*a*) made a request under Subsection (5); and
(*b*) lodged with the Director the security specified in the instrument referred to in Subsection (1) and paid the next annual fee,

the Minister shall grant to the licensee the extension of the licence.
(7) Where a licensee who has been served with an instrument under Subsection (1) has not, within the period specified in Subsection (5)–

(*a*) made a request under Subsection (5); or
(*b*) lodged with the Director the security specified in the instrument and paid the annual fee,

the application lapses at the end of that period.
(8) Where–

(*a*) an application for the extension of a licence has been made; and
(*b*) the licence expires–

(i) before the Minister grants, or refuses to grant, the extension of the licence; or
(ii) before the application lapses under Subsection (7),

the licence shall be deemed to continue in force until the Minister grants or refuses to grant the extension of the licence, or the application lapses under Subsection (7), whichever first occurs.
(9) As soon as practicable after the grant or refusal of an extension of a licence under this section, the Minister shall cause to be published in the National Gazette particulars of any extension so granted or, in the case of a refusal, a statement to that effect.
(10) Where a petroleum prospecting licence is not extended on an application under this section, 90% of the fee referred to in Section 27(3)(f) shall be refunded to the applicant.

**30. EXTENSION OF PETROLEUM PROSPECTING LICENCE IN RESPECT OF LOCATION.**

(1) Where–

(*a*) petroleum is discovered in a petroleum prospecting licence area within the period of two years before the date of expiration of a petroleum prospecting licence that has been extended under Section 29; and
(*b*) the Minister has made a declaration of a location under Section 34, or the licensee has nominated a block or blocks under that section for the purpose of a declaration of a location,

the Minister may grant a further extension of the licence in respect of the block or blocks to which Paragraph (b) applies.
(2) A further extension granted under Subsection (1)–

(*a*) shall be for a period not exceeding three years; and
(*b*) shall be subject to any conditions that the Minister, after considering a report of the Board, thinks fit and specifies in the licence.

(3) Where, before the expiration of a petroleum prospecting licence that includes blocks that constitute a location, the licensee–

(*a*) makes written application to the Minister for an extension or a further extension of the licence in respect of some or all of those blocks; and
(*b*) satisfies the Minister that–

(iii) the blocks contain all or part of a petroleum pool or are otherwise properly included in a location; and
(iv) the construction, establishment and operation of facilities for the recovery of petroleum is not economically feasible,

the Minister may grant an extension or a further extension of the petroleum prospecting licence in respect of those blocks.
(4) An extension under Subsection (3) shall be for a period not exceeding one year.

**31. CONDITIONS OF GRANT OF PETROLEUM PROSPECTING LICENCE.**

(1) A petroleum prospecting licence may be granted subject to such conditions as the Minister, after considering the advice of the Board, thinks fit and specifies in the licence.
(2) In addition to conditions included in a petroleum prospecting licence under Subsection (1) or on an extension of that licence under Section 29, the licence is subject to the conditions–

(*a*) that acceptable proposals for work and expenditure in the third, fourth, fifth, and sixth years, if applicable, of the licence or that extension shall be submitted to the Minister for approval not later than two months before the expiration of the second and fourth years of the licence or that extension, as the case requires; and
(*b*) that in, or in relation to, the licence area, the licensee will, during the first two years of the licence, carry out the work and expend the amounts specified in the licence conditions for those years; and
(*c*) that at the end of the period of six months after the date of grant of the licence and at the end of every subsequent period of six months of the term of the licence, the licensee shall forward to the Director, in duplicate, a report showing the nature and results of prospecting operations conducted during the immediately preceding period of six months, with a plan of the area prospected, showing all available information together with a programme of his operations for the next succeeding six months; and
(*d*) that, at the end of the period of six months after the date of grant, and at the end of every subsequent period of six months, the licensee shall forward to the Director a statement, in duplicate, showing the amounts expended in relation to the licence during the immediately preceding period of six months; and
(*e*) that the licensee will provide to the Director reports on the activities of the licensee in respect of the licence containing such information and at such frequency as are specified in and will otherwise comply with any direction given under Section 148; and
(*f*) that the licensee will carry out social mapping and landowner identification studies in accordance with Section 47; and
(*g*) that, in addition to complying with Paragraph (f), at the end of each year of the licence, the licensee shall present to the Director a report on prospecting operations in the previous year and proposed operations for the following year.

(3) The conditions to which a licence or an extension of that licence under Section 29 is subject, including the conditions specified in Subsection (2), may be varied in the third, fourth, fifth and sixth years, if applicable, insofar as they relate to the work programme and in accordance with proposals submitted under Subsection (2)(a).

## DIVISION 3. DISCOVERY OF PETROLEUM IN LICENCE AREA.

### 32. DISCOVERY OF PETROLEUM TO BE NOTIFIED.

(1) Where petroleum is discovered in a licence area, the tenement holder–

(*a*) shall immediately inform the Director of the discovery; and
(*b*) shall, within a period of three days after the date of the discovery, furnish to the Minister written particulars of the discovery.

(2) Where petroleum is discovered in a licence area, the Director may, from time to time, by instrument served on the tenement holder, direct the tenement holder to furnish to him, within the period specified in the instrument, written particulars of–

(*a*) the chemical composition and physical properties of the petroleum; and
(*b*) the nature of the subsoil in which the petroleum occurs; and
(*c*) any other matters relating to the discovery that are specified by the Director in the instrument.

(3) A person to whom a direction is given under Subsection (2) who fails or refuses to comply with the direction is guilty of an offence.
Penalty: A fine not exceeding K5,000.00.

### 33. DIRECTIONS BY MINISTER ON DISCOVERY OF PETROLEUM.

(1) Where petroleum is discovered in a licence area, the Minister may, by instrument served on the tenement holder, direct the tenement holder to do, within the period specified in the instrument, such things as the Minister thinks necessary and specifies in the instrument, including the completion of wells, the conduct of drill stem or extended production tests for appraisal of the petroleum pool to which the discovery relates (including the construction in accordance with the direction and the operation of pipes and facilities to gather and transport petroleum to a point of testing or treatment or disposal), and the recovery and sale or other disposal of all petroleum so produced, to determine–

(*a*) the chemical composition and physical properties of the petroleum; and
(*b*) the quantity of petroleum in the petroleum pool to which the discovery relates, or if part only of that petroleum pool is within the licence area, in the part of the petroleum pool that is within the licence area.

(2) A person to whom a direction is given under Subsection (1) who fails or refuses to comply with the direction is guilty of an offence.
Penalty: A fine not exceeding K5,000.00.

### 34. DECLARATION OF LOCATION.

(1) In this section, **"discovery block"** means a block in which petroleum has been discovered.
(2) Where petroleum has been discovered in a block within a tenement (not being a block that is or is included in a location) the Minister–

(*a*) shall, on receipt of a request from the licensee; and
(*b*) may in any case,

declare by notice in the National Gazette–

(*c*) in a case referred to in Paragraph (a)–the discovery block and not more than eight adjoining blocks within the licence area that are nominated by the licensee; or
(*d*) in any other case–the discovery block and such adjoining blocks as the Minister thinks proper,

to be a location for the purposes of this Act.
(3) At the request of the tenement holder or of his own volition the Minister may, by notice in the National Gazette–

(*a*) include in a location additional adjoining blocks; or
(*b*) revoke the declaration of a location in respect of one or more blocks,

but a location may not at any time include more than nine blocks.
(4) For the purposes of this section, a block adjoins a discovery block, if the graticular section that constitutes or includes the first-mentioned block has a side in common with, or touches–

(*a*) the discovery block; or
(*b*) any block that has a side in common with, or touches, the discovery block.

**35. INVESTIGATION, ETC., OF LOCATION.**

(1) Where a location has been declared under Section 34, the Minister may, by written notice served on the tenement holder, direct that the tenement holder carry out, within a period specified in the notice of not less than two years, such investigations and studies as the Minister thinks proper to assess the feasibility of the construction, establishment and operation of an industry for the recovery of petroleum from the location.
(2) The investigations and studies referred to in Subsection (1) may include–
(*a*) technical and economic feasibility studies relating to the recovery and transport of petroleum from the location and processing of the petroleum; and
(*b*) studies of proposed sites for facilities that would be required by the industry referred to in Subsection (1); and
(*c*) studies of port or berthing facilities, and roads, pipelines or other transportation facilities; and
(*d*) investigations into–

(i) suitable water facilities and reticulation systems for industrial and town purposes; and
(ii) the location and design of a suitable airstrip and associated landing and terminal facilities, if required; and
(iii) the generation and transmission of electricity as required; and

(*e*) investigations into the development, if required, of a suitable town for the industry referred to in Subsection (1), including the design of housing facilities and associated civic, cultural and social facilities; and
(*f*) investigations of any other works, services or facilities that may be required by that industry in relation to the location; and
(*g*) studies of future labour requirements for that industry; and
(*h*) physical impact studies into the possible effects of that industry on the environment.

(3) The tenement holder shall furnish to the Minister, within the period specified in the notice under Subsection (1), such reports, analyses and data resulting from the investigations and studies carried out under this section as the Minister, by written notice served on the tenement holder, may require.

**36. REVOCATION OF DECLARATION OF LOCATION.**

(1) Where, in respect of a block included in a location, the licensee does not within–

(*a*) a period of two years following the declaration of the location under Section 34(2); or
(*b*) any further period that the Minister allows under Section 53(1),

apply–

(*c*) in the case of a location declared in a petroleum prospecting licence, for a petroleum retention licence or petroleum development licence in respect of the blocks included in the location; or
(*d*) in the case of a location declared in a petroleum retention licence, for a petroleum development licence in respect of the blocks included in the location or a variation of the petroleum retention licence to cover the specific petroleum pool in respect of which the location was declared; or
(*e*) in the case of a location declared in a petroleum development licence, for a variation of the petroleum development licence to provide for the development of the specific petroleum pool in respect of which the location was declared,

the Minister shall, by notice in the National Gazette, revoke the declaration of the location.
(2) Where all applications made under Section 53(1) for a petroleum development licence or Section 37(1) for a petroleum retention licence in respect of a block that is included in a location have lapsed, the petroleum prospecting licence or petroleum retention licence, as the case may be, is revoked in respect of that block.
(3) Where a petroleum prospecting licence is revoked in respect of a block under Subsection (2), the Minister shall, by notice in the National Gazette, revoke the declaration of the location so far as it includes that block.

**DIVISION 4. PETROLEUM RETENTION LICENCES.**

**37. APPLICATION FOR PETROLEUM RETENTION LICENCE.**

(1) A licensee whose petroleum prospecting licence is in force in respect of the blocks that constitute a location may, within two years after the date on which the blocks were declared to be a location, or such further period as the Minister allows, make application to the Director for the grant of a petroleum retention licence in respect of such of the blocks as the licensee satisfies the Minister contain a gas field or a part of a gas field or, for the better administration of petroleum activities, should be included in a petroleum retention licence.
(2) A licensee may, during the term of a petroleum prospecting licence, make application to the Director for a petroleum retention licence in respect of any block or blocks within the licence area–

(*a*) that he satisfies the Minister contains or contain a gas field or part of a gas field, or, for the better administration of petroleum activities, should be included in a petroleum retention licence; and
(*b*) that do not at the time of making the application constitute a location.

(3) A person who is not the holder of a tenement in respect of a block or blocks may make application to the Director for a petroleum retention licence in respect of that block or those blocks where–

(*a*) he satisfies the Minister that such block or blocks contains or contain a gas field or part of a gas field; and
(*b*) that block is not a block or those blocks are not blocks in respect of which a tenement is in force at the time of the application.

**38. FORM OF APPLICATION FOR PETROLEUM RETENTION LICENCE.**

(1) An application under Section 37–

(*a*) shall be in an approved form; and
(*b*) shall be made in an approved manner; and
(*c*) shall be accompanied by particulars of–

(i) the proposals of the applicant for work and expenditure in respect of the area comprised in the block or blocks specified in the application; and
(ii) the commercial viability of the recovery of petroleum from the area comprised in the block or blocks specified in the application at the time of the application, and of the possible future commercial viability of the recovery of petroleum from that area; and

(*d*) may set out any other matters that the applicant wishes the Minister to consider; and
(*e*) shall be accompanied by the fee prescribed by Section 157.

(2) The Director may, by instrument served on the applicant, require him to furnish, within a period specified in the instrument–

(*a*) such further written information in connection with his application as the Director specifies in the instrument; and
(*b*) such proposals, in addition to or by way of alteration to any proposals that have already been furnished under Subsection (1) as the Director specifies in the instrument, including proposals relating to any of the matters referred to in Section 35(2).

**39. NOTIFICATION OF GRANT OF PETROLEUM RETENTION LICENCE.**

(1) Where an application for the grant of a petroleum retention licence has been made–

(*a*) under Section 37(1) or (2); and
(*b*) the applicant has furnished proposals and any further information required by the Director under Section 38; and
(*c*) the Minister, after considering a report from the Board, is satisfied as to the matters set out in Section 37(1) or (2) and with the proposals and other information provided under Section 38 and that recovery of petroleum from the area comprised in the blocks specified in the application–

(i) is not at the time of application commercially viable; and
(ii) could become commercially viable within the period of time ending at the expiration of a petroleum retention licence if extended for the maximum permitted period,

the Minister shall, by instrument served on the applicant, inform the applicant–

(*d*) that–

(i) he is prepared to approve the proposals wholly or in part, and to grant to the applicant, on the basis of the approved proposals, a petroleum retention licence in respect of the blocks specified in the application; and
(ii)[24] the applicant will be required to lodge a security for compliance with the conditions to which the licence, if granted, will be subject, and with the provisions of this Act, and to pay the first annual fee; or

(*e*) that he will defer consideration of a decision on the licence application until the applicant furnishes such proposals, in addition to or by way of alteration to the proposals furnished under Section 38 as the Minister specifies in the instrument, including proposals relating to any of the matters referred to in Section 35(2); or
(*e*) that he is prepared to approve the proposals and to grant to the applicant a petroleum retention licence in respect of the blocks specified in the application, subject to the applicant–

(i) making such alterations to the proposals; or
(ii) complying with such conditions in relation to the proposals,

as the Minister thinks reasonable.
(2) Where an application is made under Section 37(3), the Minister may–

(*a*) refuse to grant the application and advise the applicant accordingly; or
(*b*) treat the application as an application made under Section 37(1) or (2).

(3) Where, under Subsection (2), the Minister elects to treat an application as an application made under Section 37(1) or (2), that application shall, for the purposes of this section and Section 40, be deemed to be an application so made.
(4) In the case of an instrument to which Subsection (1)(f) applies, the Minister shall give to the applicant details of his reasons for requiring the alterations or imposing the conditions referred to in the instrument.

(5) An instrument under Subsection (1)(d), (e) or (f) shall contain a statement to the effect that the application will lapse if–

(*a*) the applicant does not furnish any further proposals that the Minister requires within such period as the Minister specifies in the instrument, being a period of not less than two months nor more than one year; or
(*b*) the applicant does not make a request under Section 40(1) in respect of the grant of the licence; or
(*c*)[25] the applicant does not lodge with the Director the security referred to in Subsection (1)(d)(ii), and does not pay the first annual fee referred to in that Subsection.

(6) In determining whether recovery of petroleum is commercially viable for the purposes of Subsection (1)(c) and Section 45(1)(b), the Minister shall invite and consider submissions from the applicant and shall take into account all relevant matters including technical assessment of the petroleum situated within the blocks constituting the area at the time and the estimated development costs and likelihood that a development would earn a reasonable rate consistent with international petroleum industry anticipated returns on gas projects.

**40. GRANT OR REFUSAL OF PETROLEUM RETENTION LICENCE.**

(1) An applicant who has been served with an instrument under Section 39(1) may, before the expiration of–

(*a*) the period of three months after the date of service of the instrument on him or such further period, not exceeding three months, as the Minister allows; or
(*b*) the period specified by the Minister under Section 39(5)(a),

whichever is the later,

(*c*) by instrument served on the Minister–

(i) request the Minister to grant to him the licence to which the first-mentioned instrument relates; or
(ii) furnish the Minister with any further particulars required under Section 39(1)(e); and
(iii) pay the first annual fee to the Director.

(*d*)[26] lodged with the Director the security and the first annual fee referred to in Section 39(1)(d)(ii).

(2) Where–

(*a*) an applicant has, within the period specified in Subsection (1)–

(i) made a request under Subsection (1)(c); and
(ii)[27] lodge with the Director the security and the first annual fee referred to in Section 39(1)(d)(ii); and
(iii) furnished the Minister with any further proposals required under Section 39(1)(e); and

(*b*) the Minister is satisfied that the applicant's proposals and further proposals adequately provide for such market and technical studies as may reasonably be expected to provide sufficient information to enable the gas field to be brought to timely economic development,

the Minister shall approve the proposals and grant to the applicant a petroleum retention licence in respect of the blocks referred to in Section 39(1)(c), but in any other case the Minister may, by instrument, refuse to grant the licence.
(3) The Minister shall not refuse under Subsection (2) to grant the licence unless–

(*a*) he has, by the instrument referred to in Subsection (2) served on the applicant, given not less than one month's notice of his intention to do so; and
(*b*) he has, in that instrument–

(i) given the reasons for his intention; and
(ii) specified a date on or before which the applicant may, by instrument served on the Minister, submit any matter that the applicant requires the Minister to consider including new proposals generally or in respect of some particular matter; and

(*c*) he has given to the applicant, and to any persons whom the applicant thinks fit to consult, a full opportunity to consult with the Minister concerning the Minister's intention to refuse the licence; and
(*d*) he has taken into account, after considering a report from the Board, any matters raised in the course of such consultations by the applicant or by any other person referred to in Paragraph (c).

(4) Where the holder of a petroleum prospecting licence applies for a petroleum retention licence in respect of all or part of the area of that petroleum prospecting licence, then notwithstanding the provisions of Division 2 as to expiry of the petroleum prospecting licence that petroleum prospecting licence shall not expire in respect of the area for which a petroleum retention licence is sought until the Minister has granted or refused to grant, as the case may be, a petroleum retention licence under Subsection (2).
(5) Where the holder of a petroleum prospecting licence applies for a petroleum retention licence in respect of all or part of the area of that petroleum prospecting licence and the Minister refuses to grant a petroleum retention licence on the ground that he is not satisfied as to the matter referred to in Section 39(1)(c)(i), then notwithstanding the provisions of Division 2 as to expiry of the petroleum prospecting licence that petroleum prospecting licence shall not expire in respect of the area for which a petroleum retention licence was sought until one year after the date of the instrument referred to in Subsection (2).

**41. VARIATION OF PETROLEUM RETENTION LICENCE.**

(1) The holder of a petroleum retention licence may make application to the Minister for a variation of the licence by the inclusion of an additional block or group of blocks–

(*a*) having a side or sides in common, or touching, a block the subject of the petroleum retention licence; and
(*b*) not being the subject of a tenement held by a person other than the applicant or the subject of a petroleum development licence held by the applicant.

(2) Where an application is made under Subsection (1), the Minister may, by instrument served on the licensee, vary the petroleum retention licence to include in the licence area the block or blocks to which the application relates.
(3) From and including the day on which a variation of a licence under this section takes effect–

(*a*) the blocks included in the licence area by reason of the variation are, subject to this Act, for the remainder of the term of the licence, blocks in respect of which the petroleum retention licence is in force; and
(*b*) any petroleum prospecting licence that is in force in respect of the blocks so included is revoked in respect of those blocks.

(4) The holder of a petroleum retention licence may, at any time, make an application to the Minister for any other variation of the petroleum retention licence.
(5) An application under Subsection (4) shall–

(*a*) specify the reasons for proposed variation; and
(*b*) be made in an approved form and contain the information specified in Section 38.

(6) The Director may require the applicant to furnish such further information in connection with his application as the Director considers necessary.
(7) Following receipt of an application under Subsection (4) the Minister may, after considering a report of the Board and any matters submitted to him under this section–

(*a*) amend the terms of the petroleum retention licence to provide as stipulated in the application or as otherwise agreed with the petroleum retention licensee; or

(*b*) refuse the application, in which case the existing petroleum retention licence shall remain in full force and effect.

**42. RIGHTS CONFERRED BY PETROLEUM RETENTION LICENCE.**

A petroleum retention licence, while it remains in force, confers on the licensee, subject to this Act and to the conditions specified in the licence, exclusive rights–

(*a*) to explore for petroleum in the petroleum retention licence area; and
(*b*) to carry on field studies to obtain information to ensure timely economic development of the gas field in the petroleum retention licence area; and
(*c*)[28] to carry on such operations and execute such works in the petroleum retention licence area as are necessary for or in connection with the purposes specified in Paragraphs (a) and (b), including the construction and operation of water lines; and.
(*d*)[29] if authorized by the Director, to complete wells, carry out drill stem tests or extended production tests for appraisal of a petroleum pool (including the construction and the operation of pipes and facilities to gather and transport petroleum to a point of testing or treatment or disposal), and to recover ans sell or otherwise dispose of all petroleum do produced.

**43. TERM OF PETROLEUM RETENTION LICENCE.**

Subject to this Act and to any condition in the licence, a petroleum retention licence remains in force–

(*a*) for a period of five years commencing on the day on which the licence takes effect; and
(*b*) where the licence is extended under Section 45–for a further period of five years at each extension.

**44. APPLICATION FOR EXTENSION OF PETROLEUM RETENTION LICENCE.**

(1) The holder of a petroleum retention licence may make application to the Minister for an extension of the licence.
(2) An application under this section may be made twice only in respect of a licence.
(3) An application for an extension of a petroleum retention licence–

(*a*) shall be in an approved form; and
(*b*) subject to Subsection (4), shall be made in an approved manner not later than six months before the day on which the licence is due to expire; and
(*c*) shall be accompanied by particulars of–

(i) the blocks in respect of which the extension is sought; and
(ii) the work carried out and the amounts expended in respect of the licence area up to and including a date not earlier than one month immediately preceding the date of application; and
(iii) the proposals of the licensee for work and expenditure in respect of the area; and

(*d*) shall be accompanied by the applicant's submissions in respect of the matters set out in Paragraphs 45(1)(a), (b) and (c); and
(*e*) shall be accompanied by the fee prescribed by Section 157.

(4) The Minister may, after considering a report from the Board, accept an application for the extension of a petroleum retention licence later than six months before the licence is due to expire, but in any case not after the licence has expired.

**45. GRANT OR REFUSAL OF EXTENSION OF PETROLEUM RETENTION LICENCE.**

(1) Where a petroleum retention licensee who has complied with the conditions specified in the petroleum retention licence and with the provisions of this Act, makes an application under Section 44 for the extension of the licence, the Minister shall, if he is satisfied–

(*a*) that–

(i) the blocks in respect of which the extension is sought contain a gas field or part thereof; or
(ii) it is appropriate for the proper administration of petroleum activities that the blocks in respect of which the extension is sought are included in the licence; and

(*b*) that the recovery of petroleum from the area comprised in the blocks specified in the application–

(i) is not at the time of application commercially viable; and
(ii) could become commercially viable within the period of time ending at the expiration of the petroleum retention licence if extended for the maximum permitted time; and

(*c*) that the applicant's proposals provide adequately for such market and technical studies and other work as may reasonably be expected to provide sufficient information to enable the gas field to be brought to timely economic development,

inform the licensee, by instrument served on the licensee, that he is prepared to grant to the licensee the extension of the licence.
(2) Where a petroleum retention licensee who has not complied with the conditions specified in the licence or with the provisions of this Act, makes an application under Section 44 for the extension of the licence, the Minister may, if, after considering a report from the Board, he is satisfied as to the matters set out in Subsection (1) and further satisfied that, although the licensee has not so complied, special circumstances exists that justify the granting of the extension of the licence, inform the licensee, by instrument served on the licensee, that he is prepared to grant to him an extension of the licence.
(3) Where a petroleum retention licensee has not complied with the conditions specified in the licence or with the provisions of this Act, and the Minister is not satisfied that special circumstances exist that justify the granting of the extension of the licence, the Minister shall, subject to Subsection (5), by instrument served on the licensee, refuse to grant the extension of the licence.
(4) Where the Minister is not satisfied as to the matters set out in Subsection (1), the Minister shall, subject to Subsection (5), by instrument served on the licensee, refuse to grant the extension of the licence.
(5) The Minister shall not refuse to grant the extension of a petroleum retention licence unless–

(*a*) he has, by instrument served on the licensee, given not less than one month's notice of his intention to refuse to grant the extension of the licence; and
(*b*) he has served a copy of the instrument on such other persons (if any) as he thinks fit; and
(*c*) he has, in the instrument–

(i) given the reasons for his intention to refuse; and
(ii) specified a date on or before which the licensee or a person on whom a copy of the instrument is served may, by instrument served on the Minister, submit any matters that he requires the Minister to consider; and

(*d*) he has taken into account, after considering a report from the Board, any matters so submitted to him, on or before the specified date, by the licensee or a person on whom a copy of the instrument has been served.

(6) An instrument under Subsection (1) or (2) shall contain–

(*a*) a summary of the conditions to which the grant of the extension is to be subject; and
(*b*) a statement to the effect that the application will lapse if the licensee–

(i) does not make a request under Subsection (7); or
(ii) does not pay the annual fee.

(7) A licensee who has been served with an instrument under Subsection (1) or (2) may, within a period of one month after the date of service of the instrument on him–

(*a*) by instrument served on the Minister, request the Minister to grant to him the extension of the licence; and
(*b*) pay the next annual fee.

(8) Where a licensee who has been served with an instrument under Subsection (1) or (2) has, within the period specified in Subsection (7)–

(*a*) made a request under Subsection (7); and
(*b*) paid the next annual fee,

the Minister shall approve the proposals and grant to the licensee the extension of the licence.
(9) Where a licensee who has been served with an instrument under Subsection (1) or (2) has not, within the period specified in Subsection (7)–

(*a*) made a request under Subsection (7); or
(*b*) paid the next annual fee,

the application lapses at the end of that period.
(10) Subject to Subsection (11), where–

(*a*) an application for the extension of a licence is made under Section 44; and
(*b*) the licence expires–

(i) before the Minister grants, or refuses to grant, the extension of the licence; or
(ii) before the application lapses under Subsection (9),

the licence shall be deemed to continue in force in all respects–

(*c*) until the Minister refuses to grant the extension of the licence; or
(*d*) until the application lapses under Subsection (9),

whichever first occurs.
(11) Where the Minister refuses to grant an extension under this section on the ground that he is not satisfied as to the matter referred to in Subsection (1)(b)(i), then notwithstanding the provisions of this Division as to expiry of the petroleum retention licence that petroleum retention licence shall not expire until one year after the date of service of the instrument referred to in Subsection (4).

**46. CONDITIONS OF PETROLEUM RETENTION LICENCE.**

A petroleum retention licence and any extension of a petroleum retention licence–

(*a*) is subject to conditions that–

(i) the licensee will carry out the proposals approved under Section 40(2) or 45(8); and
(ii) the licensee will provide to the Director reports on the activities of the licensee in respect of the licence containing such information and at such frequency as are specified in and will otherwise comply with any direction given under Section 148; and
(iii) the licensee will carry out social mapping and landowner identification studies in accordance with Section 47; and

(*b*) may be made subject to such other conditions not inconsistent with this Act–

(i) as the Minister thinks proper and as are specified in the licence or extension of the licence; or
(ii) in respect of any matter or matters arising out of the applicant's proposals referred to in Section 38(1)(c) that are not administered under this Act, as the Minister, after consultation with the Minister responsible for

administering that matter or those matters, thinks proper and specifies in the licence or extension of the licence; and

(*c*) may require the licensee to enter into a gas agreement.

## DIVISION 5. SOCIAL MAPPING AND LANDOWNER IDENTIFICATION STUDIES.

### 47. SOCIAL MAPPING AND LANDOWNER IDENTIFICATION STUDIES.

(1) It shall be a condition of every petroleum prospecting licence that the licensee undertake social mapping studies and landowner identification studies in accordance with this section.
(2) It shall be a condition of every petroleum retention licence that the licensee undertake social mapping studies and landowner identification studies in accordance with this section, to the extent that such studies have not been undertaken pursuant to a petroleum prospecting licence out of which the petroleum retention licence was granted.
(3) It shall be a condition of every petroleum development licence that the licensee undertake social mapping studies and landowner identification studies in accordance with this section, to the extent that such studies have not been undertaken pursuant to a petroleum prospecting licence or petroleum retention licence out of which the petroleum development licence was granted.
(4)[30] [31]Prior to first entry on to the licence area for the purposes of exploration pursuant to a petroleum prospecting licence or a petroleum retention licence, the licensee shall undertake–

(*a*) a preliminary social mapping study; and
(*b*) a preliminary landowner identification study,

of the customary land owners comprised in the licence area, with particular reference to that part of the licence area where the licensee's exploration activities are to be concentrated.
(5)[32] [33]If a licensee or a person makes an application for a petroleum development licence under Section 53, the licensee shall submit with that application a full-scale social mapping study and landowner identification study of customary land owners in –

(*a*) the licence area of that petroleum development licence; and
(*b*) other licence areas, including pipeline areas, which pertain to that petroleum development licence; and
(*c*) the land within five kilometres of any facility which would be a dedicated project facility (other than a facility which would be situated on such a petroleum development licence) of the petroleum project; and
(*d*) other areas which would be affected by the petroleum project if developed.

(5A)[34] [35]If a licensee makes an application for a variation of the licence under Section 85(1), to include an additional block or blocks in a petroleum development licence, the licensee shall submit with that application a full-scale social mapping study and landowner identification study os customary land owners in –

(*a*) the additional block or blocks that will form part of that petroleum development licence; and
(*b*) other licence areas, including pipeline easements, which are associated with the petroleum development licence upon variation of such licence; and
(*c*) the land within five kilometres of any facility which would be a dedicated project facility (other than a facility which would be situated on such a petroleum development licence) of the petroleum project; and
(*d*) other areas which would be affected by the development of the additional block or blocks.

(6) The Minister may by regulation prescribe the scope and method of a social mapping study or landowner identification study conducted in accordance with this section, and requirements as to reports of such studies.
(7) Copies of any social mapping or landowner identification studies undertaken in accordance with this section (excluding any information which is confidential to the licensee or to the local groups of landowners) shall be provided to the Director.

## DIVISION 6. PROJECT CONSULTATION.

**48. DEVELOPMENT FORUM.**

[36](1) Subject to Section 169(8), prior to the first grant of a licence or licences in respect of a petroleum project, the Minister shall convene a development forum at a place close to the proposed licence area to provide ease of access, being a meeting to which are invited persons who, in the view of the Minister, will be affected by that petroleum project, including –

(*a*) the applicant or intending applicant for the licence or licences; and
(*b*) the project area landowners determined under Section 169(2) or their duly appointed or elected respresentatives; and
(*c*) the Local-level Government or Governments who would be affected Local-level Governments of the project if the application is granted; and
(*d*) the Provincial Government or Governments who would be affected Provincial Governments of the project if the application is granted; and
(*e*) the State.

(2) If subsequent to the first grant of a licence or licences in respect of a petroleum project there is an application for a further licence or licences or the variation under Section 58(1) of a petroleum development licence in respect of that petroleum project, the Minister shall convene a further development forum in respect of that petroleum project to which are invited persons who, as a result of social mapping and landowner identification studies, in the view of the Minister, fairly represent those parties defined in Section 48(1)(a) to (e) inclusive.
(3) The purpose of a development forum is to endeavour to reach agreement on matters on which agreement among those present is desirable, including the matters referred to in Part IV.

**49. MATTERS REQUIRED BEFORE DEVELOPMENT FORUM.**

A development forum shall not be convened in respect of a proposed petroleum project until–

(*a*) the applicant or intending applicant for a licence or licences has completed and presented to the Minister full-scale social mapping and landowner identification studies in accordance with Subsection 47(5); and
(*b*) the Minister is satisfied, on the basis of the results of those studies, that the people who would be project area landowners of the petroleum project are truly represented by the persons who are to be invited to the development forum as their representatives; and
(*c*) the applicant or intending applicant has submitted to the Minister, and to the Minister responsible for environmental matters, a socio-economic impact study as part of the environmental plan required under the *Environmental Planning Act 1978*; and
(*d*) the Director has prepared a proposal, after giving due consideration to the results of the full-scale social mapping and landowner identification studies and the socio-economic impact study and the principle set out in Section 170(3), for the equitable sharing of the equity benefit and the royalty benefit amongst project area landowners, and has provided that proposal to representatives of those future project area landowners.

**50. DEVELOPMENT AGREEMENT.**

(1) An agreement between the State and any of the project area landowners, the affected Local-level Governments and the affected Provincial Government of a petroleum project governing the matters subject to agreement which are referred to in Part IV shall be contained in a development agreement.
(2) In addition to the matters referred to in Subsection (1), a development agreement may contain any other matter agreed between the parties.

**50A. COORDINATION OF BENEFITS FOR GAS PROJECTS.**

[37](1) Where –

(*a*) licensees enter into aunit development under Section 64 or co-ordinated petroleum development under Section 65; or
(*b*) a gas agreement defines the extend of a particular gas project to include more than one licence,

the State and the project area landowners, the affected Local level-Governments and affected Provincial Governments may enter into a co-ordinated development agreement which may vary or replace an agreement or agreements in relation to petroleum projects under the former Act or a development agreement or agreements under this Act.
(2) A co-ordinated development agreement shall govern the matters subject to agreement referred to in Part IV of this Act and any other matter agreed to between parties.

### 51. POWER TO SIGN DEVELOPMENT AGREEMENT.

[38]The Minister, acting with the approval of the National Executive Council, has the power to execute on behalf of the State a development agreement or a co-ordinated development agreement and any amendment of such agreements.

### 52. CONSULTATION WITH AFFECTED LOCAL-LEVEL GOVERNMENTS AND AFFECTED PROVINCIAL GOVERNMENTS.

(1)[39] [40]The Minister shall, following notification to tenement holder under Section 35(1), notify each Local-level Government and Provincial Government which would likely be an affected Local-level Government or affected Provincial Government of the petroleum project if developed, of the details of the notice served on the tenement holder.
(2) The Minister shall, in relation to any proposed petroleum project, consult with each Local-level Government and Provincial Government which would likely be an affected Local-level Government or affected Provincial Government of the petroleum project if developed, on the terms of–

(*a*) any written agreement to be entered into by the State in relation to the proposed petroleum project; and
(*b*) any licence to be granted in respect of the proposed petroleum project.

### 52A. COORDINATION OF DEVELOPMENT FORUM.

[41](1) Where a licensee makes application under Section 53, or applies to vary a licence by the inclusion of additional blocks under Section 58, or where the State enters into a gas agreement under Section 184 with a licensee which defines the extent of the gas project to include all or part of the licence areas of a petroleum prospecting licence, a petroleum development licence or a petroleum retention licence, the licensee of any licence of any licence affected by such application, variation or gas agreement and the State shall upon a plan to coordinate convening a development forum pursuant to the provisions of Section 48.
(2) An applicant shall pay a prescribed amount, not exceeding K250,000.00, as its contribution towards the cost of the development forum, if a development forum is required under Section 48.
(3) Where a coordinated development pursuant to a gas agreement requires the grant of additional licences or the variation of licences, then that coordinated development will require only a development forum to be held in respect of that gas agreement as part of the coordinated development represented in that gas agreement unless the Minister considers that those factors mentioned in Section 48(2) requires more than one development forum to be held in respect of that coordinated development.

## DIVISION 7. PETROLEUM DEVELOPMENT LICENCES.

### 53. APPLICATION FOR PETROLEUM DEVELOPMENT LICENCE.

(1) A licensee whose petroleum prospecting licence or petroleum retention licence is in force in respect of the blocks that constitute a location may, within two years after the date on which the blocks were declared to be a location, or such further period as the Minister allows, make application to the Director for the grant of a petroleum development licence in respect of such of the blocks as the licensee satisfies the Minister contain a petroleum pool or a part of a petroleum pool.
(2) A licensee may, during the term of a petroleum prospecting licence or petroleum retention licence, make application to the Director for a petroleum development licence in respect of any block or blocks within the licence area–

(*a*) that he satisfies the Minister contains or contain a petroleum pool or part of a petroleum pool; and
(*b*) that do not at the time of making the application constitute a location.

(3) A person who is not the holder of a tenement in respect of that block or those blocks may make application to the Director for a petroleum development licence in respect of a block or blocks–

(*a*) that he satisfies the Minister contains or contain a petroleum pool or part of a petroleum pool; and
(*b*) that is not a block or are not blocks in respect of which a tenement is in force at the time of the application.

**54. FORM OF APPLICATION FOR PETROLEUM DEVELOPMENT LICENCE.**

(1) An application under Section 53–

(*a*) shall be in an approved form; and
(*b*) shall be made in an approved manner; and
(*c*) shall be accompanied by detailed proposals by the applicant for the construction, establishment and operation of all facilities and services for and incidental to the recovery, processing, storage and transportation of petroleum from the licence area; and
(*d*) may set out any other matters that the applicant wishes the Minister to consider; and
(*e*) shall be accompanied by the fee prescribed by Section 157.

(2) The Director may, by instrument served on the applicant, require him to furnish, within a period specified in the instrument–

(*a*) such further written information in connection with his application as the Director specifies in the instrument; and
(*b*) such proposals, in addition to or by way of alteration to any proposals that have already been furnished under Subsection (1) as the Director specifies in the instrument, including proposals relating to any of the matters referred to in Section 35(2); and
(*c*) such information and proposals, or information and proposals in addition to or by way of alteration to information and proposals already supplied, relating to–

(i) the acquisition by the State or its nominee of a participating interest in the petroleum project in respect of which the application is made; and
(ii) the transfer of some or all of the participating interest in an Orogen option project to the Company in accordance with the option agreement and other matters and transactions contemplated by the option agreement.

**55. NOTICE OF APPLICATION TO BE PROVIDED TO THE COMPANY, ETC.**

(1)[42] [43]On receipt of an application under Section 53 or 73 or 86 in relation to an Orogen option project, the Director or the Minister, as the case may be, shall give written notice to the Company of the receipt of the application.
(2) At any time after receipt of a notice under Subsection (1), the Company may request the applicant to provide to the Company, or to allow the Company access to, such information concerning the application and the applicant's proposals as the Company may reasonably require for the purpose of determining whether it will exercise its option under the option agreement in respect of the Orogen option project.
(3) On receipt of a request under Subsection (2), the applicant shall provide to the Company or allow the Company access to the information requested within such reasonable period as the Company may specify in its request on the condition that the Company–

(*a*) pays the reasonable costs of the applicant incurred in providing or allowing the Company access to the information requested; and
(*b*) subject to Subsection (4), keeps the information confidential on such terms and conditions as the applicant may reasonably require.

(4) The Company shall be permitted to disclose the information referred to in Subsection (2) to–

(*a*) such of its employees, officers or agents whose duties in connection with the exercise of the option require the disclosure of the information; and
(*b*) any adviser or other expert retained in connection with a proposal by the Company to exercise the option,

who undertakes to keep the information confidential on such terms and conditions as the applicant may reasonably require.
(5) A person who discloses the information referred to in Subsection (2) in contravention of the terms and conditions required by the applicant in accordance with Subsections (3)(b) or (4) is guilty of an offence.
Penalty: A fine not exceeding K10,000.00 or imprisonment for a term not exceeding four years or both.

**56. NOTIFICATION OF GRANT OF PETROLEUM DEVELOPMENT LICENCE.**

(1) Where an application for the grant of a petroleum development licence has been made under Section 53(1) or (2) and the applicant has furnished proposals and any further information required by the Director under Section 54, the Minister, after having regard to physical planning considerations shall, by instrument served on the applicant, inform the applicant–

(*a*) that–

(i) he is prepared to approve the proposals wholly or in part, and to grant to the applicant on the basis of the approved proposals, a petroleum development licence in respect of the blocks specified in the application; and
(ii) the applicant will be required to lodge a security deposit for compliance with–

(A) the conditions relating to the protection and restoration of the environment; and
(B) the provisions of this Act; and
(C) any requirement in any law relating to the protection and restoration of the environment, or any condition imposed on the licensee under any such law; and
(D) any condition relating to the physical planning of the area; and

(iii) the applicant will be required to pay the first annual fee as a condition of the grant of the licence; or

(*b*) that he will defer consideration of a decision on the proposals until the applicant furnishes such proposals, in addition to or by way of alteration to the proposals furnished under Section 54 as the Minister specifies in the instrument, including proposals relating to any of the matters referred to in Section 35(2) or 54(2)(c); or
(*c*) that he is prepared to approve the proposals and to grant to the applicant a petroleum development licence in respect of the blocks specified in the application, subject to the applicant–

(i) making such alterations to the proposals; or
(ii) complying with such conditions in relation to the proposals,

as the Minister thinks reasonable.
(2) Where an application is made under Section 53(3), the Minister may–

(*a*) refuse to grant the application and advise the applicant accordingly; or
(*b*) treat the application as an application made under Section 53(1) or (2).

(3) Where, under Subsection (2), the Minister elects to treat an application as an application made under Section 53(1) or (2), that application shall, for the purposes of this section and Section 57, be deemed to be an application so made.
(4) In the case of an instrument to which Subsection (1)(c) applies, the Minister shall give to the applicant details of his reasons for requiring the alterations or imposing the conditions referred to in the instrument.

(5) An instrument under Subsection (1)(a), (b) or (c) shall contain a statement to the effect that the application will lapse if–

(*a*) the applicant does not furnish any further proposals that the Minister requires within such period as the Minister specifies in the instrument, being a period of not less than two months nor more than one year; or
(*b*) the applicant does not make a request under Section 57(1) in respect of the grant of the licence; or
(*c*) the applicant does not pay to the Director the first annual fee; or
(*d*) the applicant does not lodge with the Director the security specified in the instrument.

**57. GRANT OR REFUSAL OF PETROLEUM DEVELOPMENT LICENCE.**

(1) An applicant who has been served with an instrument under Section 56(1) may, before the expiration of–

(*a*) the period of three months after the date of service of the instrument on him or such further period or periods as the Minister allows; or
(*b*) the period specified by the Minister under Section 56(5)(a),

whichever is the later, by instrument served on the Minister–

(*c*) request the Minister to grant to him the licence to which the first-mentioned instrument relates; and
(*d*) furnish the Minister with any further proposals required under Section 56(1)(b); and
(*e*) pay the first annual fee to the Director; and
(*f*) lodge with the Director the security deposit referred to in the instrument issued under Section 56(1)(a).

(2) Where–

(*a*) an applicant has, within the period specified in Subsection (1)–

(i) made a request under Subsection (1)(c); and
(ii) paid the first annual fee to the Director; and
(iii) furnished the Minister with any further proposals required under Section 56(1)(b); and
(iv) lodged with the Director the security deposit referred to in the instrument issued under Section 56(1)(a); and

(*b*) the Minister is satisfied, having considered the applicant's proposals and any further submissions of information, and a report from the Board and where it is available the relevant cost-benefit analysis carried out and made available to the National Executive Council by the National Economic and Fiscal Commission under Section 117(8)(a)(v) of the *Organic Law on Provincial Governments and Local-level Governments*, that the proposals for development–

(i) will achieve maximum efficient recovery and prevention of resource waste by applying good oilfield practice; and
(ii) do not interfere with the rights of licensees of adjacent tenements covering common petroleum pools; and
(iii) comply with the State's policy on non-discriminatory access for other persons to any strategic pipelines or strategic petroleum processing facilities involved in the proposals; and
(iv) provide adequately for the protection of the environment and the welfare of the people of the area; and
(v)[44] demonstrate that the applicant has adequately identified the persons who are customary land owners in areas specified under Section 47(5); and
(vi) have duly considered co-ordinated development of any adjacent petroleum discoveries which studies and investigations conducted pursuant to a direction given under Section 65 reveal to be in the interest of the State; and
(vii) promote viable domestic utilisation of petroleum and petroleum products to the extent reasonably possible; and
(viii) will otherwise be in the best interests of the Independent State of Papua New Guinea,

the Minister shall approve the proposals and grant to the applicant a petroleum development licence in respect of the blocks referred to in Section 56(1)(c), but in any other case the Minister may, by instrument, refuse to grant the licence.
(3) The Minister shall not refuse under Subsection (2) to grant a petroleum development licence unless–

(*a*) he has, by the instrument referred to in Subsection (2) served on the applicant, given not less than one month's notice of his intention to do so; and
(*b*) he has, in that instrument–

(i) given particulars of the reasons for his intention; and
(ii) specified a date on or before which the applicant may, by instrument served on the Minister, submit any matters that the applicant requires the Minister to consider, including new proposals generally or in respect of some particular matter; and

(*c*) he has given to the applicant, and to any persons whom the applicant thinks fit to consult, a full opportunity to consult with the Minister concerning the Minister's intention to refuse to grant the licence; and
(*d*) he has taken into account, after considering a report from the Board, any matters raised in the course of such consultations by the applicant or by any other person referred to in Paragraph (c).

(4) Where the grounds for the Minister's refusal, under this section, of an application is that the applicant's proposals or further proposals do not satisfy the requirements of Subsection (2)(b), the applicant may, by written notice to the Minister before the date referred to in Subsection (3)(b)(ii), require that the question be referred to arbitration.
(5) The method of arbitration for the purpose of Subsection (4) may be the subject of a written agreement between the State and the applicant, and the method so agreed will be binding on the Minister.
(6) Where the method of arbitration is not the subject of an agreement referred to in Subsection (5), the matter stands referred to arbitration in accordance with the *Arbitration Act 1951* on receipt by the Minister of the requirement.
(7) Where a matter is referred to arbitration under this section, the application does not lapse until the arbitrator has made his award and, where the award is made in the applicant's favour, the Minister has granted the petroleum development licence.
(8) Subject to Subsection (7), where an applicant has been served with an instrument under Subsection (2) refusing to grant an application, the application lapses at the end of the period referred to in Subsection (3)(b)(ii) unless the Minister withdraws his refusal.
(9) Where a licensee makes application under Section 53(1) or (2) for a petroleum development licence and the petroleum prospecting licence or petroleum retention licence would but for this subsection expire before the application has been dealt with in accordance with this section, the petroleum prospecting licence or petroleum retention licence, as the case may be, shall, notwithstanding the provisions of Division 2 or 4 as to the expiry thereof, continue in force in respect of the block or blocks until the first-mentioned application has been dealt with.
(10) The Minister shall not grant a petroleum development licence under this section in relation to an Orogen option project unless the Minister has first given to the Company written notice.

**58. VARIATION OF PETROLEUM DEVELOPMENT LICENCE.**

[45](1) The holder of a petroleum development licence may make application to the Minister for a variation of the licence by the inclusion of an additional block or group of blocks –

(*a*) having a side or sides in common, or touching, block the subject of the petroleum development licence; and
(*b*) subject to Subsection (2), not being the subject of a tenement held by a person other than the applicant.

(2) The holder of a petroleum development licence may make an application under Subsection (1) for the inclusion of an additional block or group of blocks even they are the subject of a tenement held by a person other than the applicant if –

(*a*) the holder of the tenement in respect of the additional block or groups of blocks has entered into an agreement in writing with the holder of the petroleum development licence consenting to the variation; and
(*b*) the State or Company pursuant to Section 165 and 166 and the applicable petroleum agreement have an entitlement to acquire a participating interest in the additional blocks or group of blocks, and all of the affected tenement holders including the holder of the petroleum development licence, have entered into an agreement concerning the terms of the State or Company participation in the enlarged petroleum licence; and
(*c*) a copy of any such agreement is provided to the Minister with the application for the variation; and
(*d*) any such agreement provided to the Minister shall have been lodged and registered in accordance with Section 100.

(3) The Minister shall not approve an application under Subsection (1) unless he is satisfied, after considering a report of the Board, that the additional block or group of blocks proposed to be included in the licence contain a petroleum pool or part of a petroleum pool.
(4) Where an application is made under Subsection (1), the Minister shall, after considering a report of the Board and having used all reasonable efforts, by instrument served on the applicant within one month from having received the application either –

(*a*) inform the applicant that the variation of the licence by the inclusion of the additional block or group of blocks as the case may be will be approved; or
(*b*) refuse the application in which case the existing licences remain in full force and effect.

(5) An applicant who has been served with an instrument under Subsection (4)(a) may, within one month after the date of service of the instrument on him or such further period as the Minister allows, by instrument served on the Director accept the variation and upon service of such instrument or the Director, the petroleum development licence shall be varied to include in the licence area the block or group of blocks to which the application relates.
(6) From and including the day on which the variation of a licence takes effect under Subsection (5), the blocks included in the licence area by reason of the variation are –

(*a*) subject to this Act, for the remainder of the term of the licence, blocks in respect of which an applicant's petroleum development licence is in force; and
(*b*) any other licence that is in force in respect of the blocks so included is revoked in respect of those blocks.

(7) The holders of a petroleum development licence may, at any time, make an application to the Minister for any other variation of the petroleum development licence.
(8) An application under Subsection (7) shall –

(*a*) specify the reason for the proposed variation; and
(*b*) be made in an approved form and contain the information specified in Section 54.

(9) The Director may require the applicant to furnish such information in connection with his application as the Director considers necessary.
(10) Following receipt of an application under Subsection (7) the Minister shall, after considering a report of the Board and any matters submitted to him under this section and having used all reasonable efforts, by instrument served on the applicant within two months from the date of receiving the application –

(*a*) inform the applicant that he is prepared to approve the variation of the licence as stipulated in the application or as otherwise agreed with the applicant; or
(*b*) refuse the application, in which case the existing petroleum development licence will remain in full force and effect.

(11) An applicant who has been served with an instrument under Subsection (10)(a) may, within one month after the date of service of the instrument on him or such further periods as the Minister allows, by instrument served on the Director accept the variation and upon service of such instrument on the Director

the petroleum development licence shall be varied as stipulated in the application or as otherwise agreed with the applicant.

**59. RIGHTS CONFERRED BY PETROLEUM DEVELOPMENT LICENCE.**

A petroleum development licence, while it remains in force confers on the licensee, subject to this Act and to the conditions specified in the licence, exclusive rights–

(*a*) to explore for petroleum in the licence area; and
(*b*) to carry on operations for the recovery of petroleum in the licence area; and
(*c*) to sell or otherwise dispose of the petroleum so recovered; and
(*d*) to carry on such operations and execute such works in the licence area as are necessary for or in connection with the purposes specified in Paragraphs (a), (b), and (c) including the construction and operation of flow lines or gathering lines and water lines.

**60. TERM OF PETROLEUM DEVELOPMENT LICENCE.**

[46]Subject to this Act and to any condition in the licence, a petroleum development licence remains in force –

(*a*) for a period of 25 years commencing on the day on which the licence takes effect; and
(*b*)[47] where the licence has been extended under Section 62–for such further period or periods not exceeding 20 years as the Minister determines is reasonably required to recover from the licence area the maximum amount of petroleum the recovery of which is consistent with good oil field practice.

**61. APPLICATION FOR EXTENSION OF PETROLEUM DEVELOPMENT LICENCE.**

(1) The holder of a petroleum development licence may make an application to the Minister for an extension of the licence.
(2)[48] [49]Unless otherwise provided in a written agreement entered into between the holder of the petroleum development licence and the State, an application under this section may be made once only in respect of a licence.
(3) An application for an extension of a petroleum development licence–

(*a*) shall be in an approved form; and
(*b*) subject to Subsection (4), shall be made in an approved manner not later than six months before the day on which the licence is due to expire; and
(*c*) shall be accompanied by–

(i) a detailed assessment of the field life and the economically recoverable and economically unrecoverable petroleum within the pool or pools which are the subject of the licence, providing a justification for the assessment of petroleum as economically recoverable or unrecoverable, as the case may be; and
(ii) a detailed statement of anticipated future operations under the licence; and
(iii) the fee prescribed by Section 157.

(4)[50] [51]The Minister may, after considering a report of the Board, accept an application at any time prior to the last year of the current term of the licence where that application also relates to a variation of a petroleum development licence pursuant to Section 58(7) and the applicant can demonstrate that the remaining period of current term of licence is insufficient to permit the maximum recovery of the petroleum from the licence area.

**62. GRANT OR REFUSAL OF EXTENSION OF PETROLEUM DEVELOPMENT LICENCE.**

(1) Where a licensee who has complied with the conditions specified in the licence and with the provisions of this Act, makes an application under Section 61 for the extension of a licence, the Minister shall inform the licensee, by instrument served on the licensee, that he is prepared to grant to the licensee the extension of the licence.

(2) Where a licensee who has not complied with the conditions specified in the licence or with the provisions of this Act, makes an application under Section 61 for the extension of a licence, the Minister may, if after considering a report from the Board, he is satisfied that, although the licensee has not so complied, special circumstances exist that justify the granting of the extension of the licence, inform the licensee, by instrument served on the licensee, that he is prepared to grant to him an extension of the licence.
(3) If a licensee has not complied with the conditions specified in the licence or with the provisions of this Act, and the Minister is not satisfied that special circumstances exist that justify the granting of the extension of the licence, the Minister shall, subject to Subsection (4), by instrument served on the licensee, refuse to grant the extension of the licence.
(4) The Minister shall not refuse to grant the extension of a licence under this section unless–

(*a*) he has, by instrument served on the licensee, given not less than one month's notice of his intention to refuse to grant the extension of the licence; and
(*b*) he has served a copy of the instrument on such other persons (if any) as he thinks fit; and
(*c*) he has, in the instrument–

(i) given particulars of the reasons for his intention to refuse; and
(ii) specified a date on or before which the licensee or a person on whom a copy of the instrument is served may, by instrument served on the Minister, submit any matters that he requires the Minister to consider; and

(*d*) he has taken into account, after considering a report from the Board, any matters so submitted to him, on or before the specified date, by the licensee or a person on whom a copy of the instrument has been served.

(5) An instrument under Subsection (1) or (2) shall contain–

(*a*) a summary of the conditions to which the grant of the extension is to be subject; and
(*b*) a statement to the effect that the application will lapse if the licensee–

(i) does not make a request under Subsection (6); and
(ii) does not pay the annual fee.

(6) A licensee who has been served with an instrument under Subsection (1) or (2) may, within a period of one month after the date of service of the instrument on him–

(*a*) by instrument served on the Minister, request the Minister to grant to him the extension of the licence; and
(*b*) pay the next annual fee.

(7) Where a licensee who has been served with an instrument under Subsection (1) or (2) has, within the period specified in Subsection (6)–

(*a*) made a request under Subsection (6); and
(*b*) paid the next annual fee,

the Minister shall grant to him the extension of the licence.
(8) Where a licensee who has been served with an instrument under Subsection (1) or (2) has not, within the period specified in Subsection (6)–

(*a*) made a request under Subsection (6); or
(*b*) paid the next annual fee,

the application lapses at the end of that period.
(9) Where–

(*a*) an application for the extension of a licence is made under Section 61; and
(*b*) the licence expires–

(i) before the Minister grants, or refuses to grant, the extension of the licence; or
(ii) before the application lapses under Subsection (8),

the licence shall be deemed to continue in force in all respects–

(*c*) until the Minister refuses to grant the extension of the licence; or
(*d*) until the application lapses under Subsection (8),

whichever first occurs.

**63. CONDITIONS OF PETROLEUM DEVELOPMENT LICENCE.**

[52]A petroleum development licence and any extension or variation of a petroleum development licence–

(*a*) is subject to conditions that–

(i) the licensee will carry out the proposals approved under Section 57(2); and
(i) the licensee will provide to the Director reports on the activities of the licensee in respect of the licence containing such information and at such frequency as are specified in and will otherwise comply with any direction given under Section 148; and
(iii)[53] the licensee will carry out social mapping and landowner identification studies as directed by the Minister in accordance with Section 47; and

(*b*) may be made subject to such other conditions not inconsistent with this Act–

(i) as the Minister thinks proper and specifies in the licence or extension of the licence; or
(ii) in respect of any matter or matters arising out of the applicant's proposals referred to in Section 54(1)(c) that are not administered under this Act, as the Minister, after consultation with the Minister responsible for administering that matter or those matters, thinks proper and specifies in the licence or extension of the licence.

**64. UNIT DEVELOPMENT.**

(1) In this section, **"unit development"** means, in relation to a petroleum pool, the co-ordination of operations for the recovery of petroleum being carried on or to be carried on in a licence area in which there is part of the pool, with other operations for the recovery of petroleum being carried on or to be carried on in any other licence area in which there is part of the same pool.
(2) The Minister may of his own motion or on written application made to him by a licensee in whose licence area there is a part of a particular petroleum pool, after receiving the advice of the Board, for the purpose of securing the more effective recovery of petroleum from that petroleum pool, direct any licensee whose licence area includes part of that petroleum pool to enter into a written agreement within the period specified by the Minister for or in relation to the unit development of the petroleum pool, and to lodge the agreement with the Minister immediately for approval and registration in accordance with Section 100.
(3) Where–

(*a*) a licensee who is directed under Subsection (2) to enter into an agreement for or in relation to the unit development of a petroleum pool does not enter into such an agreement within the specified period; or
(*b*) a licensee enters into such an agreement but the agreement is not lodged with the Minister in accordance with Subsection (2), or if so lodged is not approved under Section 100,

the Minister may, by instrument served on the licensee, direct the licensee to submit to him, within the period specified in the instrument, a scheme for or in relation to the unit development of the petroleum pool.
(4) An agreement under this section is an instrument to which Section 100 applies.

**65. CO-ORDINATED PETROLEUM DEVELOPMENTS.**

(1) Where the Director considers that, in order to prevent waste, avoid unnecessary competitive drilling, protect the correlative rights of licensees of adjacent tenements, secure the maximum ultimate recovery of petroleum or achieve the optimum economic development of petroleum resources, the interests of the State might best be furthered through two or more licensees developing a co-ordinated petroleum development with each other, the Director may give a licensee a direction under this section.
(2) A licensee given a direction under this section shall, within the period, if any, and in accordance with any other directions specified in the instrument, conduct such studies and investigations into the possibilities and merits of a co-ordinated petroleum development as are specified in the direction.

**66. DIRECTIONS AS TO RECOVERY OF PETROLEUM.**

(1) Where petroleum is not being recovered in a licence area and the Minister, with the advice of the Board, is satisfied that there is recoverable petroleum in that licence area, he may, by instrument served on the licensee, direct the licensee to take all necessary and practicable steps to recover that petroleum.
(2) Where the Director is not satisfied with the steps taken or being taken by a licensee to whom a direction has been given under Subsection (1), the Director may, by instrument served on the licensee, give to the licensee such directions as the Director thinks necessary for or in relation to the recovery of petroleum in the licence area.
(3) Where petroleum is being recovered in a licence area, the Minister may, with the advice of the Board, by instrument served on the licensee, direct the licensee to take all necessary and practical steps to increase or reduce the rate at which the petroleum is being recovered to such rate, not exceeding the capacity of existing production facilities, as the Minister specifies in the instrument.
(4) Where the Director is not satisfied with the steps taken or being taken by a licensee to whom a direction has been given under Subsection (3), the Director may, by instrument served on the licensee, give to the licensee such directions as the Director thinks necessary for or in relation to the increase or reduction of the rate at which petroleum is being recovered in the licence area.

**67. DOMESTIC MARKET OBLIGATION.**

(1)[54] [55]A person shall, in disposing of processed petroleum produced in Papua New Guinea which is owned by him, comply with this section.
(2) A person referred to in Subsection (1) shall–

(*a*) if approached by a *bona fide* prospective purchaser wishing to purchase processed petroleum from that person, negotiate in good faith with that *bona fide* purchaser for the sale and supply of such processed petroleum; and
(*b*) if offered by a *bona fide* prospective purchaser equivalent export terms for a quantity of his processed petroleum, sell and supply that quantity of processed petroleum to that *bona fide* prospective purchaser on those equivalent export terms.

(3) In this section, **"equivalent export terms"** means a purchase price and terms which are no less favourable to the seller than the price and terms which he could obtain at that same time as such offer by selling and exporting that processed petroleum, adjusted for such differences as quality, quantity, delivery, transportation, and other terms, but excluding government-to-government sales, barter, swaps, sales between related corporations, and similar non-arms-length transactions.
(4) A person referred to in Subsection (1) shall, if offered equivalent export terms, accommodate the reasonable requirements of the offer or for adjustments from the normal practices of that person in selling and delivering processed petroleum in relation to quantities sold, delivery arrangements and transportation requirements.
(5) The obligations of a person under this section are subject to–

(*a*) the purchaser within a reasonable time offering to enter into an agreement containing commercial sale and purchase terms which are standard in the international petroleum industry, including payment in a currency appropriate for that processed petroleum having regard to normal international industry standards at a place acceptable to the seller within a reasonable time after delivery; and
(*b*) prior *bona fide* contractual commitments of the seller in respect of the sale or consumption of such processed petroleum; and
(*c*) the reasonable requirements of the seller as to the timing of the disposal of his processed petroleum and

the creditworthiness of the purchaser; and
(*d*) the seller being at liberty to sell his processed petroleum in Papua New Guinea for a higher price or on terms which objectively are preferable, and for that purpose to retain in Papua New Guinea that quantity of processed petroleum; and
(*e*) the seller being at liberty to use any processed petroleum required for his own operations; and
(*f*) the provisions of any written agreement between the State and that person; and
(*g*) the requirements of all laws for the time being in force in Papua New Guinea.

(6) A *bona fide* prospective purchaser aggrieved at the failure of another person to comply with his obligations under this section shall have standing to seek injunctive relief and damages from a person who has failed to comply with his obligations under this section.

## DIVISION 8. PROCESSING AND EXPORT OF NATURAL GAS.

### 68. PROCESSING OF NATURAL GAS.

(1) This section applies to all natural gas recovered in a petroleum project, other than natural gas which is–

(*a*) reinjected; or
(*b*) flared in accordance with this Act; or
(*c*) consumed in Papua New Guinea in operations under a licence.

(2) All natural gas produced in a petroleum project shall be processed in a petroleum processing facility in Papua New Guinea.

### 69. EXPORT OF NATURAL GAS.

(1) Natural gas shall only be exported from Papua New Guinea if permitted by–

(*a*) the terms of a written agreement to which the State is a party; or
(*b*) a licence; or
(*c*) the Minister, by instrument.

(2) Subject to Subsection (3), any natural gas which is exported from Papua New Guinea shall conform with quality specifications prescribed by the Minister, by instrument.
(3) In the event of an emergency affecting the operation of a petroleum processing facility which processes natural gas which is permitted to be exported in accordance with Subsection (1), natural gas which does not conform with the quality specifications stipulated by Subsection (2) may be exported, but–

(*a*) within 24 hours of the emergency occurring, the exporter shall file a report with the Director setting out the details of the emergency, the steps being taken to deal with it and the reason why natural gas conforming with the quality specifications stipulated by Subsection (2) is not being produced; and
(*b*) the exporter shall not continue to export natural gas not conforming with the specifications for more than 72 hours after first doing so, without written permission from the Director or the Minister.

(4) An exporter relying upon a written permission granted under Subsection (3) shall, whilst the emergency continues, only export natural gas in accordance with the terms of the written permission.
(5) A written permission granted under Subsection (3) may be varied or revoked by the author.

## DIVISION 9. PIPELINE LICENCES.

### 70. PIPELINE LICENCE REQUIRED.

(1) No person shall commence to construct or continue the construction of or operate or alter or reconstruct a pipeline except under and in accordance with a pipeline licence.

(2) A person who commences to construct or continues the construction of or operates or alters or reconstructs a pipeline otherwise than pursuant to a pipeline licence is guilty of an offence.
Penalty: A fine not exceeding K10,000.00 for each day of the offence.

**71. ACTS DONE IN AN EMERGENCY.**

It is not an offence against Section 70–

(*a*) if, in an emergency, a person does an act to avoid loss or injury or to maintain the pipeline in good order and repair and notifies an inspector as soon as practicable of the act done; or
(*b*) if a person does an act in compliance with a direction given under this Act.

**72. REMOVAL OF PIPELINE.**

(1) Where the construction of a pipeline is commenced, continued, completed, altered or reconstructed in contravention of this Act, the Director may, by instrument served on the appropriate person, direct him–

(*a*) to make such alterations to the pipeline as are specified in the instrument; or
(*b*) to move the pipeline to a specified area or to remove it entirely,

within the period specified in the instrument.
(2) For the purpose of Subsection (1), the appropriate person is–

(*a*) where construction of the pipeline has been completed–its owner; or
(*b*) where the construction of the pipeline has not been completed–the persons for whom it is being constructed.

(3) Where a person who has been served with an instrument under Subsection (1) does not, within the period specified in the instrument, comply with the direction, the Director may do all or any of the things required by the direction to be done.
(4) Any costs and expenses incurred by the Director under Subsection (3) are a debt due from the person referred to in that subsection to the State.

**73. APPLICATION FOR PIPELINE LICENCE.**

(1)[56] [57]A person may make an application to the Minister for the grant of a pipeline licence and the Minister shall cause a notice for an application for a pipeline licence and the Minister shall cause a notice for an application for a pipeline licence under this section to be published in the National Gazette.
(2) An application for a pipeline licence–

(*a*) shall be in an approved form; and
(*b*) shall be made in an approved manner; and
(*c*) shall be accompanied by particulars of–

(i) the proposed design and construction of the pipeline; and
(ii) the proposed size and capacity of the pipeline; and
(iii) the proposals of the applicant for work and expenditure in respect of the construction of the pipeline; and
(iv) the technical qualifications of the applicant and his employees; and
(v) the technical advice available to the applicant; and
(vi) the financial resources available to the applicant; and
(vii) any agreement entered into, or proposed to be entered into, by the applicant for or in relation to the supply or conveyance of petroleum by means of the pipeline; and

(*d*) shall be accompanied by a plan, drawn to an approved scale, showing–

(i) the route to be followed by the pipeline; and
(ii) the sites of pumping stations, tank stations, and valve stations to be part of or used in connection with the pipeline; and

(*e*) may set out any matter that the applicant wishes the Minister to consider; and
(*f*) shall be accompanied by the fee prescribed by Section 157.

(3) Where a proposed pipeline is in any part of a physical planning area under the *Physical Planning Act 1989*, the applicant for the pipeline licence shall–

(*a*) notify the National Physical Planning Board; and
(*b*) notify any Physical Planning Board under the *Physical Planning Act 1989* within whose jurisdiction the proposed pipeline lies; and
(*c*) provide these Physical Planning Boards with a copy of the plan referred to in Subsection (2)(d),

and these Physical Planning Boards may, within 28 days of the receipt of such notification, give their views on the application to the Minister.
(4) Where a notice under Subsection (1) of an application by a person for a pipeline licence in respect of the construction of a project pipeline for the conveyance of petroleum recovered or to be recovered from a petroleum development licence is published in the National Gazette, the registered holder of that petroleum development licence may, within a period of two months after the date of publication, make an application to the Minister for such a pipeline licence and, in the application, request that the application referred to in the notice be rejected.
(5) Where a pipeline licence is granted to a registered holder of a petroleum development licence on an application under Subsection (4), the Minister shall, by instrument served on the original applicant, reject the application referred to in the notice under Subsection (1).
(6) The Director may, at any time, by instrument served on a person who has made an application under this section, require him to furnish such written information in connection with his application as the Minister considers necessary.
(7) An application for a pipeline licence in respect of a strategic pipeline shall, in addition to the matters set out in Subsection (2), be accompanied by–

(*a*) draft access arrangements which the applicant proposes should be the access arrangements applying to that strategic pipeline; and
(*b*) pro forma accounts for the pipeline and the other petroleum processing facilities referred to in Section 75(7), and an explanation of how the financial records for the pipeline will be maintained separately from other operations of the pipeline licensee.

(8) Prior to submitting an application for a pipeline licence in respect of a strategic pipeline, the applicant shall make all reasonable efforts to consult with existing and potential third party users of the pipeline, and shall furnish to the Minister a report on the possible third party users and their possible requirements in using the pipeline and their views on the contents of the access arrangements to apply to the pipeline.
(9)[58] [59]Where an application for a pipeline licence relates to a strategic pipeline, the notice referred to in Subsection (1) shall invite potential third party users of the pipeline to make submissions to the Minister within the period stipulated in the notice as to their potential requirements in using the pipeline and the contents of the access arrangements to apply to the pipeline.
(10) The draft access arrangements submitted by the applicant shall be a public document, and any person may inspect that document or those documents at the office of the Director.
(11) The Minister shall notify the applicant of any submissions received in response to invitations made in accordance with Subsection (9) and provide the applicant with a copy of all such submissions if requested.

**74. GRANT OR REFUSAL OF PIPELINE LICENCE.**

(1) Where a person makes an application in accordance with Section 73 for a pipeline licence in respect of the construction of a project pipeline for the conveyance of petroleum recovered or to be recovered from a petroleum development licence, the Minister, after having regard to physical planning considerations–

(*a*) shall, if that person–

(i) is the registered holder of that petroleum development licence; and
(ii)[60] has complied with the conditions specified in the licence and with the provisions of this Act; or

(*b*) may, if that person is not the registered holder of that petroleum development licence and the application has not been rejected under Section 73(5),

inform that person, by instrument served on him, that the Minister is prepared to grant a pipeline licence to him.
(2) Where–

(*a*) an application is made in accordance with Section 73 for a pipeline licence in respect of the construction of a project pipeline for the conveyance of petroleum recovered or to be recovered from a petroleum development licence, by a person who is the registered holder of that petroleum development licence; and
(*b*) that person has not complied with the conditions specified in that licence or with the provisions of this Act,

the Minister may inform that person, by instrument served on him, that–

(*c*) he is prepared to grant a pipeline licence to that person; or
(*d*) he has refused to grant a pipeline licence to that person.

(3) The Minister shall not, under Subsection (2), refuse to grant a pipeline licence unless–

(*a*) he has, by instrument served on the person who made the application, given to that person not less than one month's notice of his intention to refuse to grant the pipeline licence; and
(*b*) he has served a copy of the instrument on such other persons as he thinks fit; and
(*c*) he has, in the instrument–

(i) given particulars of the reasons for his intention; or
(ii) specified a date on or before which the person who made the application or a person on whom a copy of the instrument is served may, by instrument served on the Director, submit any matters that he wishes the Minister to consider; and

(*d*) he has taken into account any matters so submitted to him on or before the specified date by the person who made the application, or by a person on whom a copy of the instrument has been served.

(4) Where an application is made in accordance with Section 73 for a pipeline licence in respect of the construction of a pipeline for the conveyance of petroleum recovered or to be recovered from a petroleum development licence by a person other than the registered holder of that petroleum development licence, the Minister may, by instrument served on the applicant, refuse to grant a pipeline licence.
(5) Where the Minister is required, or proposes, to serve on a person an instrument under Subsection (1) or (2)(c), he shall, by the instrument, inform that person that he will be required to lodge a security for compliance with the conditions to which the pipeline licence, if granted, will from time to time be subject, and with the provisions of this Act.
(6) An instrument under Subsection (1) or (2)(c)–

(*a*) shall specify the route to be followed by the pipeline; and
(*b*) shall contain a summary of the conditions to be specified in the pipeline licence to be granted; and
(*c*) shall contain a statement to the effect that the application will lapse if the applicant does not–

(i) make a request under Subsection (8); and
(ii) lodge with the Director the security referred to in the instrument.

(7) The route to be specified in an instrument under Subsection (1) or (2)(c) shall be–

(*a*) the route shown in the plan accompanying the application; or
(*b*) if the Minister is of the opinion that, for any reason, that route is not appropriate–a route that, in the opinion of the Minister, is appropriate.

(8) A person who has been served with an instrument under Subsection (1) or (2)(c) may, within a period of three months after the date of service of the instrument on him or such further period or periods as the Minister allows–

(*a*) by instrument served on the Director, request the Minister to grant to him the pipeline licence; and
(*b*) lodge with the Director the security referred to in the instrument served on him under that subsection.

(9) Where a person who has been served with an instrument under Subsection (1) or (2)(c) has, within the period specified in Subsection (8)–

(*a*) made a request under Subsection (8); and
(*b*) lodged with the Director the security referred to in the instrument,

the Minister shall grant to that person a licence to construct and operate a pipeline specified in the instrument.
(10) Where a person who has been served with an instrument under Subsection (1) or (2)(c) has not, within the period specified in Subsection (8)–

(*a*) made a request under Subsection (8); or
(*b*) lodged with the Director the security referred to in the instrument,

the application lapses at the end of that period.
(11) Where a pipeline licence is not granted on an application, 90% of the fee under Section 157 shall be refunded to the applicant.
(12) Where a person makes application in accordance with Section 73 for a pipeline licence in respect of a strategic pipeline, the Minister, after having regard to physical planning considerations, may inform that person, by instrument served on him, that–

(*a*) the Minister is prepared to grant a pipeline licence to that person; or
(*b*) the Minister has refused to grant a pipeline licence to that person.

(13) The Minister shall only refuse under Subsection (12) to grant a pipeline licence after considering the advice of the Board.
(14) Where the Minister proposes to serve an instrument under Subsection (12)(a), he shall, by the instrument, inform that person that he will be required to lodge a security for compliance with the conditions to which the pipeline licence, if granted, will from time to time be subject, and with the provisions of this Act.
(15) An instrument under Subsection (12)(a)–

(*a*) shall specify the route to be followed by the pipeline; and
(*b*) shall contain the conditions to be specified in the pipeline licence to be granted; and
(*c*) shall specify the terms of the access arrangements, complying with Section 75, that will be approved by the Minister and apply to the pipeline in accordance with Section 75; and
(*d*) shall contain a statement to the effect that the application will lapse if the applicant does not–

(i) make a request under Subsection (17); and
(ii) lodge with the Director the security referred to in the instrument.

(16) The route to be specified in the instrument under Subsection (12)(a) shall be–

(*a*) the route shown in the plan accompanying the application; or
(*b*) if the Minister, in accordance with the advice of the Board, considers for any reason that that route is not appropriate–a route that the Minister, in accordance with the advice of the Board, considers appropriate.

(17) A person who has been served with an instrument under Subsection (12)(a) may, within a period of three months after the date of service of the instrument on him, or such longer period as may be specified in the instrument–

(*a*) by instrument served on the Director, request the Minister to grant to him the pipeline licence; and
(*b*) lodge with the Director the security referred to in the instrument served on him under Subsection (12)(a).

(18) Where a person who has been served with an instrument under Subsection (12)(a) has, within the period specified in Subsection (17) or such longer period or periods as the Minister allows–

(*a*) made a request under Subsection (17); and
(*b*) lodged with the Director the security referred to in the instrument,

the Minister shall approve the access arrangements specified in the instrument and grant to that person a pipeline licence conforming with the instrument.
(19) Where a person who has been served with an instrument under Subsection (12)(a) has not, within the period specified in Subsection (17)–

(*a*) made a request under Subsection (17); and
(*b*) lodged with the Director the security referred to in the instrument,

the application lapses at the end of that period.
(20) A pipeline licence shall not be granted under this section in respect of a strategic pipeline unless the Minister has approved access arrangements complying with Section 75 and the applicant has accepted those access arrangements in accordance with Subsection(17).

**75. STRATEGIC PIPELINES.**

(1) Pipeline licences in respect of the following pipelines shall contain a licence condition designating the pipeline to be a strategic pipeline:–

(*a*) pipelines constructed for the transportation of petroleum from two or more petroleum projects, or for the transportation of petroleum products from two or more petroleum processing facilities; and
(*b*) pipelines constructed for the transport of petroleum or petroleum products across an international boundary; and
(*c*) pipelines constructed for the transportation of petroleum or petroleum products from a strategic petroleum processing facility; and
(*d*) pipelines in respect of which the applicant for a pipeline licence elects that this section will apply; and
(*e*) pipelines which become strategic pipelines in accordance with Subsections 81(10) or 82(12).

(2) The pipeline licensee under a pipeline licence applying to a strategic pipeline shall adopt and comply with access arrangements approved by the Minister, whereby third parties may have petroleum or petroleum products transported by the pipeline licensee through that strategic pipeline.
(3) The access arrangements applying to a strategic pipeline shall be registered and the pipeline licensee shall make copies available to all prospective third party users requesting a copy of them.
(4) Subject to any written agreement between the State and the pipeline licensee, access arrangements applying to strategic pipelines–

(*a*) shall comply with the requirements of regulations on the operation of strategic pipelines; and
(*b*) shall comply with the following principles:–

(i) the arrangements should encourage third party use of the pipeline, without requiring reduced tariffs for marginally economic petroleum fields or petroleum processing facilities;
(ii) the arrangements should achieve the lowest sustainable tariffs for users which provide a reasonable return on investment for the pipeline licensee, having regard to the circumstances of the investment, including due consideration of risk;

(iii) the arrangements should provide commercial incentives for investors and foundation shippers in respect of risks assumed, improved efficiency and increased throughputs;
(iv) the arrangements should provide certainty of tariff methodology for the term of the transportation contract;
(v) the arrangements should constitute an open dissemination of information regarding the pipeline and the service available, so as to enable prospective third party users to evaluate the technical and economic feasibility of transporting petroleum or petroleum products using any spare capacity or developable capacity;
(vi) the arrangements should recognise the entitlement of the pipeline licensee to be assured as to the creditworthiness of third party users of the pipeline prior to entering into contracts for service;
(vii) the arrangements should recognise the legitimate business interests of the pipeline licensee and existing and potential third party users; and

(*c*) shall include–

(i) the route of the pipeline and the location and ownership of receipt and delivery facilities; and
(ii) reasonable definitions of total capacity, excess capacity, and developable capacity of the pipeline; and
(iii) a process for identifying the need for, and implementing, expansion to take up the pipeline's developable capacity; and
(iv) reasonable processes that may lead to the extension or expansion of the pipeline if demonstrated to be commercially, technically, and operationally viable; and
(v) a procedure for requesting service and concluding transportation arrangements within a reasonable period of time; and
(vi) the classes of transportation service offered to third parties by the pipeline licensee, separating the charges and tariffs to be charged in respect of each class of service; and
(vii) the terms and conditions of the agreement to be offered by the pipeline licensee and third-party users for the transportation of petroleum or petroleum products; and
(viii) tariff methodology, with sample calculations; and
(ix) billing and payment arrangements; and
(x) processes for the inclusion of additional receipt and delivery points on the system; and
(xi) procedures for nominations for deliveries under a transportation agreement; and
(xii) a queuing policy in respect of competing proposals for use of the pipeline; and
(xiii) a mechanism for inter-shipper trading of service entitlements under transportation agreements, without derogating from the safety or integrity of pipeline operations; and
(xiv) a policy for allocation of pipeline capacity in the event of capacity restrictions from time to time; and
(xv) a dispute resolution procedure; and
(xvi) reasonable pipeline entry quality specifications which are not unfairly discriminatory to third party users, and where necessary intended procedures for system balancing and adjustments for differences in quality of petroleum or petroleum products entering the pipeline; and
(xvii) the expected pipeline operating pressure regime; and

(*d*) may include–

(i) different terms and conditions for foundation users of the pipeline which are commensurate with the different obligations undertaken and risks assumed by those users; and
(ii) any other provisions consistent with the normal international practice for open access pipelines which are approved by the Minister.

(5) Access arrangements approved by the Minister under Subsections 74(18), 81(8), 82(8) or 82(11) shall, for as long as the pipeline licence remains in force, be binding on the pipeline licensee and compliance with those access arrangements shall be a condition of the pipeline licence.
(6) The access arrangements referred to in Subsection (5) shall have legal effect and shall be enforceable according to their terms in a court of law by any person having a *bona fide* interest in the terms of the access arrangements.
(7) The pipeline licensee of a strategic pipeline shall maintain separate financial records and accounts for the operation of the pipeline, together with such other petroleum processing facilities as are agreed in writing between the Director and the pipeline licensee, and shall if requested by the Director lodge with the Director by the end of April in each calendar year a set of audited accounts for the strategic pipeline operations which accord with international generally accepted accounting practice setting out the financial results of the strategic pipeline and those other petroleum processing facilities.

(8) Nothing in this section limits the terms and conditions which a pipeline licensee may agree with a third party user as the terms of an access arrangement.
(9)[61] [62]Where a strategic pipeline is constructed as part of a petroleum project or a gas project and is linked to a strategic petroleum processing facility, which is also processing facility licensee may submit to the Minister for approval one access arrangement for such strategic pipeline and strategic petroleum processing facility, which may include a single published tariff for integrated processing and transportation.

**76. RIGHTS CONFERRED BY PIPELINE LICENCE.**

A pipeline licence, while it remains in force, authorizes the licensee, subject to this Act and in accordance with the conditions specified in the pipeline licence–

(*a*) to construct and operate a pipeline (including the pumping stations, tank stations and valve stations specified in the licence) of the design, construction, size and capacity specified in the licence, along the route specified in the licence; and
(*b*) to carry on all operations, to execute all works and to do all other things that are necessary for or incidental to the construction and operation of the pipeline.

**77. TERM OF PIPELINE LICENCE.**

(1) Subject to this Act and to any condition in the licence, a pipeline licence remains in force–

(*a*) for a period of 25 years commencing on the day on which the licence takes effect; and
(*b*)[63] where the licence is extended under Section 79–for consecutive period or periods, not exceeding 20 years, as the pipeline licensee requires.

(2) Where the Minister is of the opinion that, having regard to the dates of expiration of the petroleum development licences that relate to the licence area from which the petroleum is, or is to be, conveyed by means of the pipeline it is not necessary for the pipeline licence to remain in force for the relevant period referred to in Subsection (1), the Minister may specify in the licence such lesser period as he thinks fit, and the pipeline licence shall remain in force for that lesser period so specified.

**78. APPLICATION FOR EXTENSION OF PIPELINE LICENCE.**

(1)[64] [65]A pipeline licensee may make an application to the Minister for extension of that licence on the following number of occassions –

(*a*) in the case of a pipeline licence for a project pipeline where no written agreement has been entered into between the holder of the pipeline licence and the State allowing for multiple extensions – once only; and
(*b*) in the case of a pipeline licence for a project pipeline where a written agreement has been entered into between the holder of the pipeline licence and the State allowing for multiple extensions – that number of times provided for in that agreement; and
(*c*) in the case of a pipeline licence for a strategic pipeline – unlimited number of occasions.

(2) An application for the extension of a pipeline licence–

(*a*) shall be in an approved form; and
(*b*) shall be made in an approved manner not later than six months before the day on which the pipeline licence is due to expire; and
(*c*) shall be accompanied by the fee prescribed by Section 157; and
(*d*) shall specify the period, not exceeding 20 years, for which the extension is sought.

(3)[66] [67]The Minister may, after considering a report of the Board, accept an application at any time prior to the last year of the current term of the licence where that application also relates to a variation of a pipeline licence pursuant to Section 58(7) or an application for a new pipeline licence and the applicant can demonstrate that the remaining period of the current term of the licence is insufficient to permit the transportation of petroleum from the one or more petroleum development licence areas.

**79. GRANT OR REFUSAL OF EXTENSION OF PIPELINE LICENCE.**

(1) Where a pipeline licensee makes an application for the extension of the pipeline licence under Section 78, the Minister–

(*a*) shall, if the pipeline licensee has complied with the conditions specified in the pipeline licence and with the provisions of this Act; or
(*b*) may, if the pipeline licensee has not complied with the conditions specified in the licence and with the provisions of this Act, and the Minister is satisfied that, although the pipeline licensee has not so complied, special circumstances exist that justify the granting of the extension of the pipeline licence,

inform the licensee, by instrument served on the licensee–

(*c*) that he is prepared to grant to the licensee the extension of the pipeline licence; and
(*d*) that the licensee will be required to lodge a security for compliance with the conditions to be specified in the pipeline licence, if the extension is granted, and with the provisions of this Act.

(2) The Minister shall not, under Subsection (1), refuse to grant a pipeline licence to a licensee unless–

(*a*) he has, by instrument served on the licensee, given not less than one month's notice of his intention to refuse to grant the pipeline licence; and
(*b*) he has served a copy of the instrument on such other persons as he thinks fit; and
(*c*) he has, in the instrument–

(i) given particulars of the reasons for his intention to refuse; and
(ii) specified a date on or before which the licensee or a person on whom a copy of the instrument has been served may, by instrument served on the Minister, submit any matters that he wishes the Minister to consider; and

(*d*) he has taken into account any matters so submitted to him, on or before the specified date, by the licensee, or by a person on whom a copy of the instrument has been served.

(3) Where an application for the extension of a pipeline licence is made under Section 78 and the pipeline licence otherwise expires before the Minister grants or refuses to grant the extension of the pipeline licence, the pipeline licence shall be deemed to continue in force in all respects until the Minister refuses to grant the extension of the pipeline licence.

**80. CONDITIONS OF PIPELINE LICENCE.**

A pipeline licence may be granted subject to such conditions as the Minister thinks fit and specifies in the licence.

**81. VARIATION OF PIPELINE LICENCE ON APPLICATION BY LICENSEE.**

(1) The holder of a pipeline licence may at any time make an application to the Minister for a variation of the pipeline licence to–

(*a*) extend the specified route of the pipeline; or
(*b*) include additional receipt and delivery points; or
(*c*) construct additional pipelines using the same route specified in the pipeline licence; or
(*d*) install pumping stations, compressors, valve stations, measurement stations, storage tanks or other improvements for the safety and operation of the pipeline or to increase its capacity; or

(*e*) convert a pipeline to transport a different form of petroleum or petroleum product from the petroleum or petroleum products described in the initial licence application; or
(*f*) make any other change which would improve the operating efficiency of the pipeline; or
(*g*) in the case of a project pipeline, change its designation to a strategic pipeline; or
(*h*) in the case of a strategic pipeline, vary the access arrangements applicable thereto.

(2) An application under this section shall–

(*a*) be in an approved form; and
(*b*) be made in an approved manner; and
(*c*) be accompanied by particulars of the proposed variation; and
(*d*) specify the reason for the proposed variation; and
(*e*) in the case of an application to convert a project pipeline to a strategic pipeline, be accompanied by–

(i) draft access arrangements which the applicant proposes should be the access arrangements applying to that pipeline; and
(ii) pro forma accounts for the pipeline and the other petroleum processing facilities referred to in Subsection 75(7), and an explanation of how the financial records for the pipeline will be maintained separately from other operations of the pipeline licensee; and

(*f*) in the case of an application to vary the access arrangements applicable to a strategic pipeline, be accompanied by draft modified access arrangements.

(3) The Minister may require the pipeline licensee to furnish such further information in connection with the application as the Minister considers necessary.
(4) In the case of an application to convert a project pipeline to a strategic pipeline or an application to vary the access arrangements applying to a strategic pipeline–

(*a*) the applicant shall, prior to submitting its application, consult with existing and potential third party users of the pipeline, and shall furnish to the Minister a report on the possible third party users and their possible requirements in using the pipeline and their views on the contents of the access arrangements to apply to the pipeline; and
(*b*) upon receipt of the application the Minister shall cause a notice to be published in the National Gazette advising of the application and particulars of the pipeline, and inviting existing and potential third party users of the pipeline to make submissions to the Minister within the period specified in the notice as to their potential requirements in using the pipeline and the contents of the access arrangements to apply to the pipeline; and
(*c*) the draft access arrangements submitted by the applicant shall be a public document, and any person may inspect that document or those documents at the office of the Director; and
(*d*) the Minister shall notify the applicant of any submissions received in accordance with Subsection (4)(b) and provide the applicant with a copy of all such submissions if requested.

(5) In the case of any application under this section other than an application to convert a project pipeline to a strategic pipeline or an application to vary the access arrangements applying to a strategic pipeline, the Minister may, after considering a report from the Board and any matter submitted to him under this section–

(*a*) vary the pipeline licence in accordance with the application or otherwise as he may agree with the pipeline licensee; or
(*b*) reject the application.

(6) In the case of an application to convert a project pipeline to a strategic pipeline or an application to vary the access arrangements applying to a strategic pipeline, the Minister may, after considering a report from the Board and any matter submitted to him under this section–

(*a*) serve on the pipeline licensee an instrument–

(i) advising the pipeline licensee that the Minister is prepared to vary the pipeline licence to convert the pipeline to a strategic pipeline or vary the access arrangements, as the case may be; and
(ii) specifying the terms of the access arrangements or varied access arrangements, complying with Section 75, to be approved by the Minister and apply to the pipeline in accordance with Section 75; or

(*b*) reject the application.

(7) A pipeline licensee who has been served with an instrument under Subsection (6)(a) may, within a period of three months after the date of service of the instrument on him, by instrument served on the Director, request the Minister to vary the pipeline licence in accordance with the instrument referred to in that subsection.
(8) Where a pipeline licensee who has been served with an instrument under Subsection (6)(a) has, within the period specified in Subsection (7), made a request under Subsection (7), the Minister shall approve the access arrangements or varied access arrangements specified in the instrument and vary the pipeline licence in accordance with the instrument.
(9) A pipeline licence shall not be varied under this section to convert the pipeline to a strategic pipeline or to vary the access arrangements applying to a strategic pipeline unless the Minister has approved access arrangements or varied access arrangements complying with Section 75 and the applicant has accepted those access arrangements or varied access arrangements in accordance with Subsection (7).
(10) Where the Minister varies a pipeline licence under this section, he shall cause to be published in the National Gazette a notice of the variation.
(11) A project pipeline which is converted to a strategic pipeline under this section shall be a strategic pipeline with effect from the date the variation of the licence for that purpose takes effect, and thereafter those approved access arrangements shall apply to that pipeline in accordance with Section 75.
(12) Where the access arrangements applying to a strategic pipeline are varied under this section, the varied access arrangements shall apply to that pipeline in accordance with Section 75 with effect from the date the variation of the licence for that purpose takes effect.
(13) Notwithstanding Subsections (11) and (12), the establishment or variation under this section of the access arrangements applying to a strategic pipeline shall not affect the validity of agreements previously entered into by the pipeline licensee for transportation of petroleum.

**82. VARIATION OF PIPELINE LICENCE BY MINISTER.**

(1) The Minister may, if in his opinion it is necessary–

(*a*) for the protection of health and safety; or
(*b*) to avoid obstruction of, or interference with, the rights of other persons,

by instrument served on a pipeline licensee, direct the licensee to make such changes in the design, construction and route or position of the pipeline (including pumping stations, tank stations or valve stations) to which the pipeline licence relates as are specified in the instrument, within the period specified in the instrument.
(2) A person to whom a direction is given under Subsection (1) who fails or refuses to comply with the direction is guilty of an offence.
Penalty: A fine not exceeding K25,000.00.
Default penalty: A fine not exceeding K25,000.00.
(3) Where the Minister gives a direction under Subsection (1) and the person to whom the direction is given complies with the direction, the Minister may grant to that person such sum as he considers reasonable in the circumstances.
(4) Where the Minister gives a direction under Subsection (1), any pipeline licence affected by the direction shall be deemed to be varied to the extent reasonably necessary to enable the direction to be complied with.
(5) If, in the opinion of the Minister, acting in accordance with the advice of the Board–

(*a*) it is desirable that a project pipeline be used by third parties for transportation of their petroleum or petroleum products, and that such third parties will have petroleum or petroleum products to be transported in that pipeline, he may by instrument served on the pipeline licensee direct that a project pipeline be converted to a strategic pipeline; or
(*b*) it is desirable that the terms of access arrangements applying to a strategic pipeline be varied, he may by

instrument served on the pipeline licensee direct that the access arrangements applying to that strategic pipeline be varied.

(6) If the Minister gives a direction under Subsection (5), he shall publish in the National Gazette notice advising of that direction and particulars of the pipeline, and inviting existing and potential third party users of the pipeline to make submissions to the Minister as to their potential requirements in using the pipeline and the contents of the access arrangements to apply to the pipeline.
(7) Within three months of receipt of a direction under Subsection (5), a pipeline licensee shall lodge with the Minister–

(*a*) draft access arrangements complying with Section 75, which the applicant proposes should be the access arrangements or varied access arrangements applying to that pipeline; and
(*b*) in the case of a direction to convert from a project pipeline to a strategic pipeline, pro forma accounts for the pipeline and the other petroleum processing facilities referred to in Subsection 75(7), and an explanation of how the financial records for the pipeline will be maintained separately from other operations of the pipeline licensee.

(8) Prior to submitting draft access arrangements, the applicant shall make all reasonable efforts to consult with existing and potential third party users of the pipeline, and shall furnish to the Minister a report on the possible third party users and their possible requirements in using the pipeline and their views on the contents of the access arrangements to apply to the pipeline.
(9) A notice referred to in Subsection (6) shall invite existing and potential third party users of the pipeline to make submissions to the Minister within the period stipulated in the notice as to their potential requirements in using the pipeline and the contents of the access arrangements to apply to the pipeline.
(10) The draft access arrangements submitted by the pipeline licensee shall be a public document, and any person may inspect that document or those documents at the office of the Director.
(11) The Minister shall notify the applicant of any submissions received in response to invitations made in accordance with Subsection (6) and provide the applicant with a copy of all such submissions if requested.
(12) If the draft access arrangements or varied access arrangements proposed by the pipeline licensee, as they may be amended by agreement between the Minister and the pipeline licensee, are acceptable to the Minister, the Minister shall approve those access arrangements, and vary the pipeline licence to convert the project pipeline to be a strategic pipeline or adopt the new access arrangements, as the case may be.
(13) If the draft access arrangements or varied access arrangements proposed by the pipeline licensee are not acceptable to the Minister and the pipeline licensee and the Minister are not able to reach agreement on amendments to the draft, the Minister may refer the question of the terms of the access arrangements or varied access arrangements to apply to the pipeline for expert determination in accordance with Subsection (14).
(14) If the Minister makes a reference under Subsection (13), then the terms of the access arrangements or varied access arrangements shall be determined by an expert appointed by the Minister for that purpose and paid for by the State, who shall–

(*a*) be independent of the State and the pipeline licensee; and
(*b*) be qualified by experience in dealing with open access arrangements for pipelines; and
(*c*) prior to making his decision, consult with the Minister and the pipeline licensee and any person who has made a submission under Subsection (6); and
(*d*) in making his decision have regard to the reasonable requirements of those persons making such submissions; and
(*e*) determine terms of access arrangements which comply with Section 75.

(15) When the access arrangements are determined by expert determination under Subsection (14), the Minister may–

(*a*) approve the access arrangements or varied access arrangements so determined; and
(*b*) vary the pipeline licence to convert the project pipeline to be a strategic pipeline or adopt the varied access arrangements, as the case may be.

(16) Where the Minister varies a pipeline licence under this section, he shall cause to be published in the National Gazette a notice of the variation.

(17) A project pipeline which is converted to a strategic pipeline under this section shall be a strategic pipeline with effect from the date the variation of the licence for that purpose takes effect, and thereafter those approved access arrangements shall apply to that pipeline in accordance with Section 75.
(18) Where the access arrangements applying to a strategic pipeline are varied under this section, the varied access arrangements shall apply to that pipeline in accordance with Section 75 with effect from the date the variation of the licence for that purpose takes effect.
(19) Notwithstanding Subsections (17) and (18), the establishment or variation under this section of the access arrangements applying to a strategic pipeline shall not affect the validity of agreements previously entered into by the pipeline licensee for transportation of petroleum.

**83. COMMON CARRIER.**

(1) Subject to the terms of a written agreement between the State and the pipeline licensee, the Minister, acting in accordance with a report of the Board, may by instrument served on the pipeline licensee of a project pipeline direct the pipeline licensee to be a common carrier in respect of that project pipeline.
(2) Where a pipeline licensee is given a direction under this section, that pipeline licensee shall thereafter be a common carrier in respect of that pipeline, and the provisions of this section and of any regulations prescribed under Subsection (3) shall apply to the pipeline operations conducted under that pipeline licence.
(3) Subject to Subsection (4), regulations may prescribe the manner of the operation of a pipeline in respect of which a direction has been given under this section.
(4) Any regulation made under Subsection (3) shall give priority to–

(*a*) *bona fide* prior contractual commitments of the pipeline licensee with unrelated parties; and
(*b*) the *bona fide* requirements of the pipeline licensee to transport petroleum or petroleum products produced from a petroleum project in respect of which the pipeline licensee holds a petroleum development licence.

(5) A pipeline licensee which has been given a direction under this section in respect of a pipeline may, notwithstanding that direction, make an application under Subsection 81(1)(g) in respect of that pipeline.
(6) If, on an application under Subsection 81(1)(g) in relation to a pipeline by a pipeline licensee which has been given a direction under this section in respect of that pipeline, the Minister grants a variation to that pipeline licence to convert the pipeline to a strategic pipeline, the provisions of this section and the regulations in relation to common carriage shall cease to apply to that pipeline.

**84. CEASING TO OPERATE PIPELINE.**

(1) Except with the written consent of the Minister, and subject to compliance with such conditions (if any) as are specified in the instrument of consent, a pipeline licensee who ceases to operate the pipeline is guilty of an offence.
Penalty: A fine not exceeding K50,000.00.
(2) It is not an offence against Subsection (1) if the failure to operate the pipeline–

(*a*) was in the ordinary course of the operation of the pipeline; or
(*b*) was for the purpose of repairing or maintaining the pipeline; or
(*c*) was in an emergency in which there was a likelihood of loss or injury; or
(*d*) was as a result of an industrial strike or picket.

**DIVISION 10. PETROLEUM PROCESSING FACILITY LICENCES.**

**85. PETROLEUM PROCESSING FACILITY LICENCE REQUIRED.**

(1) Subject to this section, no person shall commence to construct or continue the construction of or make major modifications to or operate a petroleum processing facility without a petroleum processing facility licence in respect of that petroleum processing facility.
(2) The provisions of Subsection (1) shall not apply to the holder of a petroleum development licence in respect of a petroleum processing facility which is part of the proposals for development approved for that petroleum development licence by the Minister under Section 57(2) as varied from time to time, but the

licensee thereof shall comply with all regulations prescribed for securing, regulating, controlling or restricting petroleum processing facilities and the facilities shall be subject to inspection under Section 152.
(3) The provisions of Subsection (1) shall not apply in relation to–

(*a*) storage and transportation facilities for domestic utilisation that are designated by regulation to be exempt; or
(*b*) pipelines in respect of which a pipeline licence is in force,

but the operator thereof shall comply with all regulations prescribed for securing, regulating, controlling or restricting petroleum processing facilities and the facilities shall be subject to inspection under Section 152.

**86. APPLICATION FOR PETROLEUM PROCESSING FACILITY LICENCE.**

(1) A person may make an application to the Minister for the grant of a petroleum processing facility licence.
(2) The Minister may, by notice in the National Gazette–

(*a*) invite application for the grant of a petroleum processing facility licence; and
(*b*) specify the period during which such an application should be made.

**87. FORM OF APPLICATION FOR PETROLEUM PROCESSING FACILITY LICENCE.**

(1) An application made under Section 86 shall–

(*a*) be made in an approved form; and
(*b*) be made in an approved manner; and
(*c*) be accompanied by particulars of–

(i) the names and address of the persons who will construct, operate and own the petroleum processing facility; and
(ii) the proposed site for the petroleum processing facility and arrangements for the legal occupation of the site; and
(iii) the design of the petroleum processing facility; and
(iv) the technical qualifications of the applicant and his contractors; and
(v) the financial capacity of the applicant to construct and operate the petroleum processing facility; and
(vi) environmental monitoring systems, waste disposal procedures and the results of environmental studies; and
(vii) the intended date for commencement of construction and estimated dates for commissioning and full operation; and
(viii) the intended output of petroleum or petroleum products; and

(*d*) be accompanied by payment of the application fee prescribed by Section 157.

(2) Where an application is received under Subsection (1)–

(*a*) notice of the application shall be published in the National Gazette; and
(*b*) any person who claims to be affected by the application may file notice of his objection to that application with the Director within one month after the date of publication of the notice of application and all objections shall be considered by the Board before it reports to the Minister on the application.

(3) An application for a petroleum processing facility licence in respect of a strategic petroleum processing facility shall, in addition to the matters set out in Subsection (1), be accompanied by draft access arrangements which the applicant proposes should be access arrangements applying to that strategic petroleum processing facility.
(4) Prior to submitting an application for a petroleum processing facility licence in respect of a strategic petroleum processing facility, the applicant shall make all reasonable efforts to consult with existing and potential third party users of the petroleum processing facility, and shall furnish to the Minister a report on

the possible third party users and their possible requirements in using the petroleum processing facility and their views on the contents of the access arrangements to apply to the petroleum processing facility.
(5) Where an application for a petroleum processing facility licence relates to a strategic petroleum processing facility, the notice referred to in Subsection (2) shall invite potential third party users of the petroleum processing facility to make submissions to the Minister as to their potential requirements in using the petroleum processing facility and the contents of the access arrangements to apply to the petroleum processing facility.
(6) The draft access arrangements submitted by the applicant shall be a public document, and any person may inspect that document or those documents at the office of the Director.
(7) The Minister shall notify the applicant of any submissions received in accordance with Subsection (5), and provide the applicant with a copy of all such submissions if requested.

**88. GRANT OR REFUSAL OF PETROLEUM PROCESSING FACILITY LICENCE.**

(1) Where an application has been made under Section 86 in respect of a petroleum processing facility which is not a strategic petroleum processing facility, the Minister may, after considering a report of the Board–

(*a*) by instrument served on the applicant, inform the applicant–

(i) that he is prepared to grant to the applicant a petroleum processing facility licence in respect of the site and for construction of the petroleum processing facility specified in the application; and
(ii) that the applicant will be required to lodge a security for compliance with the conditions to which the petroleum processing facility licence, if granted, will be subject and the provisions of this Act, and to pay the annual fee; or

(*b*) refuse to grant a petroleum processing facility licence to the applicant.

(2) An instrument under Subsection (1)(a) shall contain–

(*a*) the conditions subject to which the petroleum processing facility licence is to be granted; and
(*b*) a statement to the effect that the application will lapse if the applicant does not make a request under Subsection (3) in respect of the grant of the petroleum processing facility licence and lodge with the Director the security specified in the instrument and the first annual fee as prescribed by Section 157.

(3) An applicant who has been served with an instrument under Subsection (1) may, within a period of one month after the date of service of the instrument, or within such further period or periods as the Minister may allow–

(*a*) by instrument served on the Minister request the Minister to grant him the petroleum processing facility licence; and
(*b*) lodge with the Director the security referred to in Subsection (1)(a) and the first annual fee referred to in that subsection.

(4) Where an applicant has complied with the requirements of Subsection (3), the Minister shall grant a petroleum processing facility licence for the site and the petroleum processing facility specified in the instrument, subject to the conditions specified in the instrument or such other conditions as are agreed by the Minister and the applicant, but in any other case the application lapses.
(5) Where an application has been made under Section 86 in respect of a strategic petroleum processing facility, the Minister may, after considering a report of the Board–

(*a*) by instrument served on the applicant, inform the applicant–

(i) that he is prepared to grant to the applicant a petroleum processing facility licence in respect of the site and for construction and operation of the petroleum processing facility specified in the application; and
(ii) that the applicant will be required to lodge a security for compliance with the conditions to which the

petroleum processing facility licence, if granted, will be subject and the provisions of this Act, and to pay the annual fee; or

(*b*) refuse to grant a petroleum processing facility licence to the applicant.

(6) The Minister shall not refuse under Subsections (1) or (5) to grant a petroleum processing facility licence unless–

(*a*) he has, by the instrument referred to in those subsections served on the applicant, given not less than one month's notice of his intention to do so; and
(*b*) he has, in that instrument–

(i) given particulars of the reason for his intention; and
(ii) specified a date on or before which the applicant may, by instrument served on the Minister, submit any matters that the applicant requires the Minister to consider, including new proposals generally or in respect of some particular matter; and

(*c*) he has given to the applicant, and to any persons whom the applicant thinks fit to consult, a full opportunity to consult with the Minister concerning the Minister's intention to refuse to grant a petroleum processing facility licence; and
(*d*) he has taken into account, after considering a report from the Board, any matters raised in the course of such consultations by the applicant or by any other person referred to in Paragraph (c).

(7) An instrument under Subsection (5)(a) shall contain–

(*a*) the conditions subject to which the petroleum processing facility licence is to be granted; and
(*b*) the terms of the access arrangements, complying with Section 89, to be approved by the Minister and apply to the petroleum processing facility in accordance with Section 89; and
(*c*) a statement to the effect that the application will lapse if the applicant does not make a request under Subsection (8) in respect of the grant of the petroleum processing facility licence and lodge with the Director the security specified in the instrument and the first annual fee as prescribed by Section 157.

(8) An applicant who has been served with an instrument under Subsection (5)(a) may, within a period of one month after the date of service of the instrument, or within such further period or periods as the Minister may allow–

(*a*) by instrument served on the Minister request the Minister to grant him the petroleum processing facility licence; and
(*b*) lodge with the Director the security referred to in Subsection (5)(a) and the first annual fee as prescribed by Section 157.

(9) Where an applicant has complied with the requirements of Subsection (8), the Minister shall approve the access arrangements specified in the instrument and grant a petroleum processing facility licence for the site and the petroleum processing facility specified in the instrument, subject to the conditions specified in the instrument or such other conditions as are agreed by the Minister and the applicant, but in any other case the application lapses.
(10) A petroleum processing facility licence shall not be granted under this section in respect of a strategic petroleum processing facility unless the Minister has approved access arrangements complying with Section 89 and the applicant has accepted those access arrangements in accordance with Subsection (8).

**89. STRATEGIC PETROLEUM PROCESSING FACILITIES.**

(1) A petroleum processing facility licence in respect of a strategic petroleum processing facility shall contain a licence condition designating the petroleum processing facility to be a strategic petroleum processing facility.

(2) A petroleum processing facility licensee in respect of a strategic petroleum processing facility shall adopt and comply with access arrangements approved by the Minister, whereby third parties may have petroleum or petroleum products processed by the petroleum processing facility licensee through that strategic petroleum processing facility.
(3) The access arrangements applying to a strategic petroleum processing facility shall be registered and the petroleum processing facility licensee shall make copies available to all prospective third party users requesting a copy of them.
(4) Subject to any written agreement between the State and the petroleum processing facility licensee, access arrangements applying to strategic petroleum processing facilities–

(*a*) shall comply with the requirements of regulations on the operation of strategic petroleum processing facilities; and
(*b*) shall comply with the following principles:–

(i) the arrangements should encourage third party use of the facility, without requiring reduced tariffs for otherwise marginally economic use of the petroleum processing facilities;
(ii) the arrangements should achieve the lowest sustainable tariffs for users which provide a reasonable return on investment for the petroleum processing facility licensee, having regard to the circumstances of the investment, including due consideration of risk;
(iii) the arrangements should provide commercial incentives for investors in respect of risks assumed, improved efficiency and increased throughputs;
(iv) the arrangements should provide certainty of tariff methodology for the term of the processing contract;
(v) the arrangements should constitute an open dissemination of information regarding the facility and the service available, so as to enable prospective third party users to evaluate the technical and economic feasibility of processing petroleum or petroleum products using any spare capacity or developable capacity;
(vi) the arrangements should recognise the entitlement of the petroleum processing facility licensee to be assured as to the creditworthiness of third party users of the petroleum processing facility prior to entering into contracts for processing;
(vii) the arrangements should recognise the legitimate business interests of the petroleum processing facility licensee and existing and potential third party users; and

(*c*) shall include–

(i) the location and ownership of receipt and delivery facilities; and
(ii) reasonable definitions of total capacity, excess capacity, and developable capacity of the petroleum processing facility for specified conditions; and
(iii) a process for identifying the need for, and implementing, expansion to take up the petroleum processing facility's capacity or other modification of the petroleum processing facility; and
(iv) reasonable processes that may lead to the extension or expansion or modification of the petroleum processing facility if demonstrated to be commercially, technically, and operationally viable; and
(v) a procedure for requesting service and concluding processing arrangements within a reasonable period of time; and
(vi) the classes of processing service offered to third parties by the petroleum processing facility licensee, separating the charges and tariffs to be charged in respect of each class of service; and
(vii) the terms and conditions of the agreement to be offered by the petroleum processing facility licensee to third-party users for the processing of petroleum or petroleum products; and
(viii) tariff methodology, with sample calculations; and
(ix) billing and payment arrangements; and
(x) a queuing policy in respect of competing proposals for processing; and
(xi) a policy for allocation of petroleum processing facility capacity in the event of capacity restrictions from time to time; and
(xii) a dispute resolution procedure; and
(xiii) acceptable quality specifications for petroleum or petroleum products which are not unfairly discriminatory to third party users, measurement requirements, and balancing and adjustments for differences in quality of petroleum or petroleum products entering the petroleum processing facility; and

(*d*) may include–

(i) different terms and conditions for foundation users of the petroleum processing facility which are commensurate with the different obligations undertaken and risks assumed by those users; and
(ii) any other provisions consistent with the normal international practice for open access petroleum processing facilities which are approved by the Minister.

(5) Access arrangements approved by the Minister under Sections 88(9), 92(8), 93(9) or 93(12) shall, for as long as the petroleum processing facility licence remains in force, be binding on the petroleum processing facility licensee and compliance with those access arrangements shall be a condition of the petroleum processing facility licence.
(6) The access arrangements referred to in Subsection (5) shall have legal effect and shall be enforceable according to their terms in a court of law by any person having a *bona fide* interest in the terms of the access arrangements.
(7) A petroleum processing facility shall not be a strategic petroleum processing facility if it is exempted by a written agreement between the State and the holder of the petroleum processing facility licence or by a condition of the petroleum processing facility licence or by an instrument signed by the Minister.
(8) Where by an instrument the Minister exempts a petroleum processing facility under Subsection (7), that exemption may be revoked by the Minister by instrument.
(9) Nothing in this section limits the terms and conditions which a petroleum processing facility licensee may agree with a third party user as the terms of an access arrangement.
(10)[68] [69]Where a strategic petroleum processing facility is constructed as part of a petroleum project or a gas project and is linked to a strategic pipeline, which is also part of such a petroleum project or gas project, the petroleum processing facility licensee and the pipeline licensee may submit to the Minister for approval one access arrangement for such strategic petroleum processing facility and strategic pipeline, which may include a single published tariff for integrated processing and transportation.

**90. RIGHTS CONFERRED BY PETROLEUM PROCESSING FACILITY LICENCE.**

(1) Subject to Subsection (2), a petroleum processing facility licence, while it remains in force, confers on the petroleum processing facility licensee, subject to this Act and to the conditions specified in the petroleum processing facility licence, exclusive rights to–

(*a*) construct the petroleum processing facility at the site for which the petroleum processing facility licence was granted; and
(*b*) conduct operations for petroleum processing through the petroleum processing facility; and
(*c*) carry on such operations and execute such works at the site of the petroleum processing facility, other than a major modification, as are necessary and reasonable for or in connection with the purposes specified in Paragraphs (a) and (b).

(2) A petroleum processing facility licensee shall not make a major modification to his petroleum processing facility except pursuant to a variation of the petroleum processing facility licence under Section 92 or 93.
(3) Nothing in this section shall affect the rights conferred on the holder of a petroleum development licence under Section 59 or on a pipeline licensee under Section 76.

**91. TERM OF PETROLEUM PROCESSING FACILITY LICENCE.**

Subject to this Division, and to any condition in the petroleum processing facility licence, a petroleum processing facility licence remains in force until cancelled by the Minister under Section 138 or surrendered by the petroleum processing facility licensee under Section 137.

**92. VARIATION OF PETROLEUM PROCESSING FACILITY LICENCE ON APPLICATION BY LICENSEE.**

(1) The holder of a petroleum processing facility licence may, at any time, make an application to the Minister for a variation of the petroleum processing facility licence.
(2) An application under this section shall–

(*a*) specify the reasons for proposed variation; and
(*b*) be made in an approved form and contain the information specified in Section 87; and

(*c*) in the case of an application to vary a petroleum processing facility licence to vary the access arrangements applying to a strategic petroleum processing facility, be accompanied by draft access arrangements which the applicant proposes should be the access arrangements applying to the strategic petroleum processing facility.

(3) The Minister may require the applicant to furnish such further information in connection with his application as the Minister considers necessary.
(4) In the case of an application to vary a petroleum processing facility licence other than to vary the access arrangements applying to a strategic petroleum processing facility, the Minister may, after considering a report of the Board and any matters submitted to him under this section–

(*a*) amend the terms of the petroleum processing facility licence to provide as stipulated in the application or as otherwise agreed with the petroleum processing facility licensee; or
(*b*) refuse the application, in which case the existing petroleum processing facility licence shall remain in full force and effect.

(5) In the case of an application to vary a petroleum processing facility licence to vary the access arrangements applying to a strategic petroleum processing facility–

(*a*) the applicant shall, prior to submitting his application, make all reasonable efforts to consult with existing and potential third party users of the petroleum processing facility, and shall furnish to the Minister a report on the possible third party users and their possible requirements in using the petroleum processing facility and their views on the contents of the access arrangements to apply to the petroleum processing facility; and
(*b*) upon receipt of the application the Minister shall cause a notice to be published in the National Gazette advising of the application and particulars of the petroleum processing facility, and inviting existing and potential third party users of the petroleum processing facility to make submissions to the Minister as to their potential requirements in using the petroleum processing facility and the contents of the access arrangements to apply to the petroleum processing facility; and
(*c*) the draft access arrangements submitted by the applicant shall be a public document, and any person may inspect that document or those documents at the office of the Director; and
(*d*) the Minister shall notify the applicant of any submissions received in accordance with Subsection (5)(b) and provide the applicant with a copy of all such submissions if requested.

(6) In the case of an application to vary a petroleum processing facility licence to vary the access arrangements applying to a strategic petroleum processing facility, the Minister may, after considering a report from the Board and any matter submitted to him under this section–

(*a*) serve on the petroleum processing facility licensee an instrument–

(i) advising the petroleum processing facility licensee that the Minister is prepared to vary the petroleum processing facility licence to vary the access arrangements; and
(ii) specifying the terms of the varied access arrangements, complying with Section 89, to be approved by the Minister and apply to the petroleum processing facility in accordance with Section 89; or

(*b*) reject the application.

(7) A petroleum processing facility licensee who has been served with an instrument under Subsection (6)(a) may, within a period of three months after the date of service of the instrument on him, by instrument served on the Director, request the Minister to vary the petroleum processing facility licence in accordance with the instrument referred to in that Subsection.
(8) Where a petroleum processing facility licensee who has been served with an instrument under Subsection (6)(a) has, within the period specified in Subsection (7), made a request under Subsection (7), the Minister shall approve the varied access arrangements specified in the instrument and vary the petroleum processing facility licence in accordance with the instrument.

(9) A petroleum processing facility licence shall not be varied under this section to vary the access arrangements unless the Minister has approved varied access arrangements complying with Section 89 and the applicant has accepted those varied access arrangements in accordance with Subsection (7).
(10) Where the Minister varies a petroleum processing facility licence under this section, he shall cause to be published in the National Gazette a notice of the variation.
(11) Where access arrangements are established or varied under this section, the varied access arrangements shall apply to that petroleum processing facility in accordance with Section 89 with effect from the date the variation of the licence for that purpose takes effect.
(13) Notwithstanding Subsection (11), the establishment or variation under this section of the access arrangements applying to a strategic petroleum processing facility shall not affect the validity of agreements previously entered into by the petroleum processing facility licensee for processing of petroleum.

**93. VARIATION OF PETROLEUM PROCESSING FACILITY LICENCE BY MINISTER.**

(1) If the Minister gives to a pipeline licensee a direction under Section 82(5)(a) and as a consequence of the pipeline to which that direction relates becoming a strategic pipeline a petroleum processing facility would become a strategic petroleum processing facility, the Minister shall give to the petroleum processing facility licensee in respect of that petroleum processing facility a direction under this Section.
(2) If the Minister, acting in accordance with the advice of the Board, considers that it is desirable that the terms of access arrangements applying to a strategic petroleum processing facility be varied, the Minister may by instrument served on the petroleum processing facility licensee direct that the access arrangements applying to that strategic petroleum processing facility be varied.
(3) If the Minister gives a direction under Subsections (1) or (2) he shall publish in the National Gazette a notice advising of that direction and particulars of the petroleum processing facility, and inviting existing and potential third party users of the petroleum processing facility to make submissions to the Minister as to their potential requirements in using the petroleum processing facility and the contents of the access arrangements to apply to the petroleum processing facility.
(4) Within three months of receipt of a direction under Subsections (1) or (2), a petroleum processing facility licensee shall lodge with the Minister draft access arrangements complying with Section 89, which the applicant proposes should be the access arrangements or varied access arrangements applying to that petroleum processing facility.
(5) Prior to submitting draft access arrangements, the petroleum processing facility licensee shall make all reasonable efforts to consult with existing and potential third party users of the petroleum processing facility, and shall furnish to the Minister a report on the possible third party users and their possible requirements in using the petroleum processing facility and their views on the contents of the access arrangements to apply to the petroleum processing facility.
(6) A notice referred to in Subsection (3) shall invite existing and potential third party users of the petroleum processing facility to make submissions to the Minister within the period stipulated in the notice as to their potential requirements in using the petroleum processing facility and the contents of the access arrangements to apply to the petroleum processing facility.
(7) The draft access arrangements submitted by the petroleum processing facility licensee shall be a public document, and any person may inspect that document or those documents at the office of the Director.
(8) The Minister shall notify the petroleum processing facility licensee of any submissions received in response to invitations made in accordance with Subsection (3) and provide the petroleum processing facility licensee with a copy of all such submissions if requested.
(9) If the draft access arrangements or varied access arrangements proposed by the petroleum processing facility licensee, as they may be amended by agreement between the Minister and the petroleum processing facility licensee, are acceptable to the Minister, the Minister shall approve those access arrangements, and vary the petroleum processing facility licence to convert the petroleum processing facility to be a strategic petroleum processing facility or adopt the new access arrangements, as the case may be.
(10) If the draft access arrangements or varied access arrangements proposed by the petroleum processing facility licensee is not acceptable to the Minister and the petroleum processing facility licensee and the Minister are not able to reach agreement on amendments to the draft, the Minister may refer the question of the terms of the access arrangements or varied access arrangements to apply to the petroleum processing facility for expert determination in accordance with Subsection (11).
(11) If the Minister makes a reference under Subsection (10), then the terms of the access arrangements or varied access arrangements shall be determined by an expert appointed by the Minister for that purpose and paid for by the State, who shall–

(*a*) be independent of the State and the petroleum processing facility licensee; and
(*b*) be qualified by experience in dealing with open access arrangements for petroleum processing facilities; and
(*c*) prior to making his decision, consult with the Minister and the petroleum processing facility licensee and any person who has made a submission under Subsection (3); and
(*d*) in making his decision have regard to the reasonable requirements of those persons making such submissions; and
(*e*) determine terms of access arrangements which comply with Section 89.

(12) When the access arrangements are determined by expert determination under Subsection (11), the Minister may–

(*a*) approve the access arrangements or varied access arrangements so determined; and
(*b*) vary the petroleum processing facility licence to convert the petroleum processing facility to be a strategic petroleum processing facility or adopt the varied access arrangements, as the case may be.

(13) Where the Minister varies a petroleum processing facility licence under this section, he shall cause to be published in the National Gazette a notice of the variation.
(14) A petroleum processing facility which is converted to a strategic petroleum processing facility under this section shall be a strategic petroleum processing facility with effect from the date upon which the variation of the licence for that purpose takes effect, and thereafter those approved access arrangements shall apply to that petroleum processing facility in accordance with Section 89.
(15)[70] [71]Where the access arrangements applying to a strategic petroleum processing facility are varied under this section, the varied access arrangements shall apply to that petroleum processing facilty in accordance with Section 89 with effect from the date the variation of the licence for that purpose takes effect.
(16) Notwithstanding Subsection (15), the establishment or variation under this section of the access arrangements applying to a strategic petroleum processing facility shall not affect the validity of agreements previously entered into by the petroleum processing facility licensee for processing of petroleum or petroleum products.

**94. CONDITIONS OF PETROLEUM PROCESSING FACILITY LICENCE.**

A petroleum processing facility licence may be granted, or an application for a variation approved, subject to such conditions as the Minister, after considering a report of the Board, thinks fit and specifies in his grant or approval and which may include, but are not limited to, conditions for–

(*a*) the construction, conduct, control, management and operation of the petroleum processing facility; and
(*b*) furnishing reports and information to the Director concerning in-put, out-put and sales volumes; and
(*c*) the removal of the petroleum processing facility and restoration of the site upon termination of the petroleum processing facility licence.

**95. REGULATIONS FOR DOMESTIC UTILISATION BUSINESS.**

(1) The Head of State, acting on advice, may make regulations prescribing the activities of–

(*a*) a domestic gas supplier; or
(*b*) a domestic gas operator; or
(*c*) the owner of a facility for the storage or transportation of cylinders containing compressed natural gas or liquefied petroleum gas.

(2) Nothing contained in regulations under Subsection (1) applies in respect of petroleum processing facilities licensed under this Act, or the activities of a petroleum development licensee, pipeline licensee or petroleum processing facility licensee in respect of the subject matter of his licence.

**DIVISION 11. REGISTRATION OF INSTRUMENTS.**

**96. REGISTER TO BE KEPT.**

(1) The Minister shall cause to be kept a Register of applications, grants, extensions, transfers and dealings in licences.
(2) The Register shall contain such details as are prescribed or as the Minister directs.
(3) A copy of any entry in the Register may be obtained on payment of the prescribed fee.

**97. APPROVAL AND REGISTRATION OF TRANSFERS.**

(1) Subject to this section, the Minister may approve the transfer of a licence from one person to another and such approval may be subject to such conditions (if any) as the Minister thinks fit.
(2) In addition to any other condition that the Minister may impose under Subsection (1), the Minister may require the transferee to lodge with him such security as the Minister thinks fit for the transferee's compliance with the conditions to which the licence is from time to time subject.
(3) The transfer of a licence shall have no effect until it is approved and registered in accordance with this section.
(4) Where the Minister approves the transfer of a licence from a company to a company that is a related corporation within the meaning of the *Companies Act 1997*, he shall impose no new conditions on the licence as a condition of that approval.
(5) A licensee who desires to transfer his licence to another person, or to himself and another person jointly, may lodge with the Director an application for approval of the transfer of the licence.
(6) The application shall be accompanied by an instrument of transfer of the licence duly executed by the transferor and transferee, together with a copy of that instrument of transfer.
(7) If the Minister approves the application, the Director shall–

(*a*) immediately endorse on the instrument of transfer and on the copy a memorandum of approval; and
(*b*) on payment of the prescribed fee enter in the Register a memorandum of the transfer and the name of the transferee.

(8) The transfer shall be deemed to be registered as soon as a memorandum of the transfer and the name of the transferee has been entered in the Register and, on that memorandum being so entered, the transferee becomes the registered holder of the licence to which the instrument of transfer relates.
(9) The copy of the instrument of transfer endorsed with the memorandum of approval shall be retained by the Director and is subject to inspection in accordance with this Division.
(10) The instrument of transfer endorsed with the memorandum of approval shall be returned to the person who lodged the application.
(11) The Minister shall not approve a transfer of a licence unless it is an absolute transfer of the whole of the transferor's interest in the licence.

**98. ENTRIES IN REGISTER OF DEVOLUTION OF TITLE.**

(1) A person on whom the rights of a licensee have devolved by operation of law may apply in writing to the Director to have his name entered in the Register as the registered holder of the licence.
(2) The Director shall, if he is satisfied that the rights of the holder have devolved on the applicant by operation of law, and on payment of the prescribed fee, enter the name of the applicant in the Register as the holder of the licence and, on that entry being so made, the applicant becomes the registered holder of the licence.

**99. INTERESTS NOT TO BE CREATED, ETC., EXCEPT BY INSTRUMENT.**

A legal or equitable interest in or affecting an existing or future licence is not capable of being created, assigned, affected or dealt with, whether directly or indirectly, except by an instrument.

**100. APPROVAL OF INSTRUMENTS CREATING, ETC., INTERESTS.**

(1) This section applies to an instrument by which a legal or equitable interest in, or affecting, an existing or future licence is or may be created, assigned, affected or dealt with, whether directly or indirectly, not being an instrument of transfer to which Section 97 applies.
(2) An instrument to which this section applies is of no force or effect until–

(*a*) the instrument has been approved by the Minister either unconditionally or subject to such conditions as he thinks fit; and
(*b*) an entry has been made in the Register by the Director in accordance with Subsection (5).

(3) A party to an instrument to which this section applies, or a person having an interest in or in relation to a licence by reason of such an instrument, may lodge with the Director an application for approval of the instrument.
(4) An application under Subsection (3) shall be accompanied by the instrument and by a copy of the instrument.
(5) If the Minister approves the instrument, the Director shall, on payment of the prescribed fee, immediately endorse on the original instrument and the copy of the instrument a memorandum of approval.
(6) The copy of the instrument endorsed with the memorandum of approval shall be retained in the Register by the Director and is subject to inspection in accordance with this Division.
(7) The original instrument endorsed with the memorandum of approval shall be returned to the person who lodged the application for approval.
(8) If the Minister refuses the application, the Director shall cause a notation of the refusal to be made in the Register.

**101. TRUE CONSIDERATION TO BE SHOWN.**

A party to a transfer referred to in Section 97 or to an instrument to which Section 100 applies who, with intent to defraud, executes the transfer or instrument if the transfer or instrument does not fully and truly set forth the true consideration for the transfer or instrument is guilty of an offence.
Penalty: A fine not exceeding K5,000.00.

**102. MINISTER NOT CONCERNED WITH CERTAIN MATTERS.**

The Minister or a person acting under his direction or authority shall not be concerned with the effect in law of any instrument lodged in accordance with this Division, nor does the approval of such an instrument give to it any force, effect or validity that it would not have had if this Division had not been enacted.

**103. POWER OF MINISTER TO REQUIRE INFORMATION AS TO PROPOSED DEALINGS.**

(1) The Minister or Director may require the person lodging an instrument for approval under this Division to furnish to him such written information concerning the instrument, or the transaction to which the instrument relates, as the Minister or Director thinks fit.
(2) A person who, when required under Subsection (1) to furnish information, furnishes information that is false or misleading in a material particular is guilty of an offence.
Penalty: A fine not exceeding K2,000.00.

**104. PRODUCTION AND INSPECTION OF DOCUMENTS.**

(1) The Minister or Director may require any person to produce to him, or to make available for inspection by him, any document in the possession or under the control of that person and relating–

(*a*) to an instrument lodged for approval under this Division; or
(*b*) to the transaction to which such an instrument relates.

(2) A person who refuses or fails within a reasonable time to comply with a requirement under Subsection (1) is guilty of an offence.
Penalty: A fine not exceeding K2,000.00.

### 105. INSPECTION OF REGISTER AND DOCUMENTS.

(1) The Register shall, at all reasonable times, be open for inspection by any person on payment of the prescribed fee.
(2) Any person may take copies of any licence or entry in the Register on payment of the prescribed fee.

### 106. EVIDENTIARY PROVISIONS.

(1) The Register shall be received by all courts as evidence of all matters required or authorized by this Division to be entered in the Register.
(2) The Director may, on payment of the prescribed fee, supply copies of or extracts from the Register certified by writing under his hand, and a document purporting to be a copy or extract so certified is admissible in evidence in all courts and proceedings without further proof or production of the original.
(3) The Director may, on payment of the prescribed fee, by instrument under his hand, certify that an entry, matter or thing required or permitted by or under this Division to be made or done or not to be made or done has or has not, as the case may be, been made or done and a document purporting to be such a certificate is evidence in all courts and proceedings of the statements contained in the certificate.

### 107. REGISTER MAY BE RECTIFIED.

Where the Minister is satisfied that there has been a mistake made in, or that some matter has been incorrectly entered in, the Register, he shall rectify the Register by correcting that mistake or incorrect entry.

### 108. MINISTER OR DIRECTOR NOT LIABLE FOR CERTAIN ACTIONS.

The Minister, the Director, or a person acting under the direction or authority of the Minister or the Director shall not be liable to an action, suit or proceeding for or in respect of an act or matter done or omitted to be done in good faith in the exercise or purported exercise of any power or authority conferred by this Division.

### 109. OFFENCES.

A person who wilfully–

(*a*) makes, causes to be made or concurs in making, a false entry in the Register; or
(*b*) produces or tenders in evidence a document falsely purporting to be a copy of or extract from an entry in the Register of or from an instrument lodged with the Minister under this Division,

is guilty of an offence.
Penalty: Imprisonment for a term not exceeding two years.

## DIVISION 12. RIGHTS IN RESPECT OF LAND AND PROPERTY.

### 110. RIGHTS OF TENEMENT HOLDERS IN RESPECT OF LAND AND PROPERTY.

(1) Subject to this Division, the rights conferred on a tenement holder by Section 25, 42 or 59 are, by virtue of this Act, exercisable on any land within the licence area and, for the purpose of exercising those rights, a tenement holder, by himself or his agents or workmen, may to the extent reasonably necessary for the tenement holder's operations or proposed operations in the licence area–

(*a*) enter on any land in the licence area; and
(*b*) subject to Sections 117 and 118, occupy any land in the licence area that is from time to time required for–

(i) effectively carrying on the operations he is entitled under the tenement to carry on; and
(ii) adequately protecting those operations and the improvements and equipment on or under the land; and

(*c*) erect buildings on land occupied under Paragraph (b) and at any time remove any building so erected and, subject to Section 118, remove any other building from land so occupied; and
(*d*) bring any machinery or other equipment into the licence area and erect or install it on land occupied under Paragraph (b) or in any building erected under Paragraph (c), and at any time remove any such machinery or equipment; and
(*e*) request the Minister to acquire any land required by the tenement holder for a purpose specified in Section 120; and
(*f*) subject to the *Water Resources Act 1982*, take and divert water from any lake, stream or watercourse in the licence area; and
(*g*) construct in the licence area roads, airstrips or helicopter pads; and
(*h*) cut and use the timber in the licence area (other than timber forming part of any improvements) for building or construction work within the licence area; and
(*i*) remove any stone, clay or gravel in the licence area (other than that forming part of any improvements) for or in connection with building or construction work within the licence area.

(2) For the purposes of Section 20 of the *Water Resources Act 1982*, the rights conferred under this Act on a tenement holder shall be deemed to be rights in land to which that section applies.

**111. RIGHTS OF PIPELINE LICENSEES IN RESPECT OF LAND AND PROPERTY.**

Subject to this Division, the rights conferred on a pipeline licensee by Section 76 are, by virtue of this Act, exercisable on any land–

(*a*) that is occupied or to be occupied by the pipeline and other improvements required for safety of operations; or
(*b*) that is at a distance not exceeding 10m on either side of the pipeline,

and within that area of land and for the purpose of exercising those rights, the pipeline licensee, by himself or his agents or workmen, may to the extent reasonably necessary for the pipeline licensee's operations or proposed operations in that area–

(*c*) enter on any land; and
(*d*) subject to Sections 117 and 118, occupy with his pipeline land substantially along the route and on the sites specified in the pipeline licence; and
(*e*) erect buildings on land occupied under Paragraph (d) and at any time remove any building so erected and, subject to Section 118 remove any other building from any land so occupied; and
(*f*) bring any machinery or equipment on land occupied under Paragraph (d) and erect or install it on such land or in any building erected under Paragraph (e), and at any time remove any such machinery or equipment; and
(*g*) request the Minister to acquire any land required by the pipeline licensee for a purpose specified in Section 120; and
(*h*) construct roads to give adequate access to the pipeline; and
(*i*) cut and use the timber (other than timber forming part of any improvements) for building or construction work related to the pipeline; and
(*j*) remove any stone, clay or gravel (other than that forming part of any improvements) for or in connection with building or construction work related to the pipeline.

**112. RIGHTS OF PETROLEUM PROCESSING FACILITY LICENSEES IN RESPECT OF LAND AND PROPERTY.**

Subject to this Division, the rights conferred on a petroleum processing facility licensee by Section 90 are, by virtue of this Act, exercisable on any land–

(*a*) that is occupied or to be occupied by the petroleum processing facility and other improvements required for safety of operations; or
(*b*) that is at a distance not exceeding 100m of such petroleum processing facility and other improvements,

and within that area of land and for the purpose of exercising those rights, the petroleum processing facility licensee, by himself or his agents or workmen, may to the extent reasonably necessary for the petroleum processing facility licensee's operations or proposed operations in that area–

(*c*) enter on any land; and
(*d*) subject to Sections 117 and 118, occupy with his petroleum processing facility land at the sites specified in the petroleum processing facility licence; and
(*e*) erect buildings on land occupied under Paragraph (d) and at any time remove any building so erected and, subject to Section 118 remove any other building from any land so occupied; and
(*f*) bring any machinery or equipment on land occupied under Paragraph (d) and erect or install it on such land or in any building erected under Paragraph (e), and at any time remove any such machinery or equipment; and
(*g*) request the Minister to acquire any land required by the petroleum processing facility licensee for a purpose specified in Section 120; and
(*h*) construct roads to give adequate access to the petroleum processing facility; and
(*i*) cut and use the timber (other than timber forming part of any improvements) for building or construction work related to the petroleum processing facility; and
(*j*) remove any stone, clay or gravel (other than that forming part of any improvements) for or in connection with building or construction work related to the petroleum processing facility.

**113. RIGHTS OF LANDOWNERS.**

(1) The owner, occupier or other person having an interest in any private land in a licence area or occupied or to be occupied by a pipeline or petroleum processing facility or any part thereof may continue to use, occupy and enjoy the land, with the exception of any part of that land reasonably required from time to time by the licensee for the exercise of his rights under his licence.
(2) Where a dispute arises as to interests in customary land or the position of boundaries of customary land, such dispute shall not affect–

(*a*) the right of a person to make application for and be granted a licence under this Act; or
(*b*) the validity of a licence granted under this Act.

(3) A dispute referred to in Subsection (2) shall be settled as provided for in the *Land Disputes Settlement Act 1975.*

**114. INTERFERENCE WITH OTHER RIGHTS.**

(1) A person carrying on operations under a licence or instrument of consent under Section 150 shall carry on those operations in a manner that does not interfere with the existing use of the land to any greater extent than is reasonably necessary for the exercise of the rights, and performance of the duties, of that person.
(2) Without limiting the generality of Subsection (1), a person carrying on operations under a licence or instrument of consent under Section 150 shall not take any action that in any way interferes with–

(*a*) fishing; or
(*b*) navigation; or
(*c*) any other operation being lawfully carried on by way of–

(i) prospecting for, recovery of or conveyance or processing of petroleum, petroleum products, helium, minerals or gold; or
(ii) construction of a pipeline or petroleum processing facility,

unless he gives prior written notice to the Director of the expected nature and duration of such interference.
(3) A person who fails to comply with the provisions of this section is guilty of an offence.
Penalty: A fine not exceeding K5,000.00.

**115. RESPONSIBILITY TO REPAIR DAMAGE.**

(1) Subject to Sections 110 and 111, a licensee shall, as soon as and to the extent practicable having regard to his operations, repair any damage–

(*a*) to any improvements; or
(*b*) to any land capable of being used for any agricultural purposes; or
(*c*) to the water supply to such improvements or land,

resulting from his operations or from the flow of petroleum, petroleum products, water or waste from any of those operations.
(2) Where a licensee fails to comply with Subsection (1), the Minister may repair the damage, and any costs or expenses incurred are a debt due from the licensee to the State.

**116. ADDITIONAL RIGHTS OF ENTRY.**

(1) Where, in the opinion of the Minister, it is necessary for an applicant or intending applicant for a licence–

(*a*) to enter on to land to survey the proposed route of a pipeline or the proposed site of an exploration or appraisal or development activity or facility or a pipeline or petroleum processing facility; or
(*b*) to conduct tests or to obtain information in relation to any such route or site; or
(*c*) to conduct temporary operations,

the Minister may, on the application of that person and subject to Section 118, by instrument authorize that person to enter on the land for that purpose.
(1A)[72] [73]Where, in the opinion of the Minister, it is necessary or expedient for an applicant or an intending applicant for a licence to conduct activities in relation to or in preparation for construction works which are or will be proposed in the licence application of the applicant or intending applicant, the Minister may, on the application of that person and subject to Section 118, by instrument, authorize that person to enter or any land for that purpose for such period as may be reasonably required for the conduct of those activities as are specified in the instrument.
(2) Where, in the opinion of the Minister, it is necessary for the effective exercise of a licensee's rights or the performance of his duties under this Act for the licensee to enter on any land not held by him under a tenement in order to obtain geological information for use in relation to his licence area, the Minister may, on application by the licensee and subject to Section 118, authorize that licensee to enter on that land and there carry out such acts as are necessary to obtain that information.
(3) An authorization under Subsection (2) shall not entitle a licensee to prospect for petroleum by the drilling of wells on the land.
(4) Where, in the opinion of the Minister, it is necessary for the effective exercise of the rights or the performance of obligations under a licence or under this Act, or to enable the licensee to carry out other activities in the course of a project including business development activities, the provision of community services and incurring expenditure in accordance with Section 219C of the *Income Tax Act 1959*, for a licensee to enter on any land not held by him under a tenement, the Minister may by instrument authorize the licensee to enter on such other lands–

(*a*) in order to obtain access to any part of his tenement or to the site or proposed site of the pipeline or petroleum processing facility or any part thereof; or
(*b*) for the transport of personnel, equipment or materials for operational and construction activities approved under the licence; or
(*c*) in order to carry out specified activities or expenditure on such other lands.

(5) Where an applicant for a licence, a person intending to apply for a licence or a licensee is granted rights of entry under this section, he shall before entering the land serve a copy of the authorization on the licensee of any licence covering or pertaining to any land to which entry is so granted.
(6) If in the *bona fide* opinion of a licensee an emergency exists in his operations which threatens–

(*a*) the safety, health or welfare of persons engaged in those operations or in the licence area or the vicinity of the pipeline or petroleum processing facility; or

(*b*) the environment; or
(*c*) the State's petroleum resource in the licence area,

the licensee may, without first obtaining an authorization under this section, enter onto lands not held by him under a licence in order to obtain access to any part of the licence area or the site or proposed site of the pipeline or petroleum processing facility or to transport personnel, equipment or materials to deal with the emergency, but–

(*d*) within 24 hours of first entering onto that land, the licensee shall file a report with the Director setting out the details of the emergency, the steps being taken to deal with it and the reason why such access was needed; and
(*e*) the licensee shall not without obtaining a further authorization under this section continue to enter onto or occupy such land for more than 72 hours after first entering that land.

**117. LAND OCCUPIED TO BE SURVEYED.**

The licensee shall cause to be surveyed and, if so required by the Director, securely fenced, any part of the land in a licence area which the licensee requires in order effectively to carry on drilling operations.

**118. COMPENSATION.**

(1)[74] [75]A licensee shall be liable to pay compensation in accordance with this section to the lawful owners and rightful occupiers of, and any persons interested in, any private land in relation to their several interests, in respect of the entry on or occupation of the land by the licensee under this Division.
(2) Subject to this section, compensation shall be paid for–

(*a*) the deprivation of the use and enjoyment of the surface of the land or any part of it or of any rights customarily associated with it, except where there has been a reservation in favour of the State of the right to such use and enjoyment; and
(*b*) damage–

(i) to the surface of the land or any part of it, or any improvements on it; or
(ii) to any trees, fish or animals,

caused by the carrying on of operations by the licensee; and

(*c*) severance of the land from other land of any owner, occupier or person interested in the land; and
(*b*) rights of way and easements; and
(*c*) any other damage consequential on the licensee's use or occupation of the land.

(3) If any private land adjoining or in the vicinity of land comprised in any licence area or occupied under any pipeline licence or petroleum processing facility licence or any improvements on the land is or are damaged or depreciated in value–

(*a*) by any operations carried on by or on behalf of a licensee; or
(*b*) by reason of any right of way acquired by the licensee,

the owners and occupiers of, and any persons interested in, that private land or those improvements shall be entitled in respect of their several interests to compensation for all loss and damage sustained under Paragraph (a) or (b) and the amount of compensation shall be ascertained in accordance with this section.
(4) A licensee may agree with any person entitled to compensation under this section as to the amount of compensation.
(5) An agreement under Subsection (4) shall not be valid unless it is in writing and signed by the parties to it, or their agents, and is lodged with the Director.

(6) Where applicable, compensation payable under this section shall be determined with reference to the values for economic trees published by the Valuer-General, and any other values published by the Valuer-General.
(7) No compensation shall be payable and no claim for compensation shall lie, whether under this Act or otherwise, and compensation under this Section shall not be determined, by reference to any petroleum, helium or minerals known or supposed to be in, on or under the land.
(8) If the licensee and a person claiming compensation under this section are unable to agree on the compensation payable, either may, by notice to the Chief Warden, request that the Chief Warden or a Warden determine the amount payable.
(9) On receipt of a notice under Subsection (8), the Chief Warden shall–

(*a*) fix a place and date for conducting a determination of the amount of compensation to be paid; and
(*b*) notify the licensee and the person claiming compensation of the place and date so fixed; and
(*c*) at that place and on that date conduct a determination of the amount of compensation to be paid.

(10) In conducting a determination under this section the Warden shall allow the parties to present their evidence and arguments to him in such manner as he thinks fit, but shall at all times have regard to the principles of natural justice.
(11) The Warden shall–

(*a*) make a determination on the basis of the evidence presented to him and arguments submitted to him and in accordance with the principles of compensation contained in this section; and
(*b*) record his decision in writing; and
(*c*) give a copy of his decision to each of the parties.

(12) Where the Warden considers it impractical or inexpedient to assess the full amount of compensation to be paid in satisfaction of the loss or damage, he may make a determination of the amount of compensation payable in respect of a particular period or item of loss or damage and defer his determination of the remainder of the claim until a later time.
(13) The Warden may, at any stage of the determination process, make an order against the person from whom compensation is sought, restricting that person from commencing or continuing any operations under this Act until he has given such security as the Warden thinks fit for payment of any compensation for which he is or may become liable.
(14) If, after a Warden has determined any amount of compensation under this section, it is proved that further loss or damage, not being loss or damage in respect of which compensation has already been determined, has been sustained, the Warden may determine compensation for the further loss or damage and order that further compensation be paid by the licensee to the person entitled to that further compensation.
(15) Where a Warden has made an order for compensation or further compensation under this section, the amount of compensation stated in that order is an amount payable by the licensee for the purposes of Section 138(1)(d).
(16) In determining the amount of compensation payable under this section the Warden shall–

(*a*) take into consideration the amount of any compensation which the owners or occupiers of, or the persons interested in, the land or any of them or their predecessors in title have or has already received for the damage or loss for which compensation is being determined; and
(*b*) deduct that amount from the amount to which they or any of them respectively would otherwise be entitled.

(17) A party to a determination of a Warden under this section who is aggrieved as to the amount of compensation to which he is entitled or which he is obliged to pay, may appeal to the National Court.
(18) Where a dispute, as defined in the *Land Disputes Settlement Act 1975*, concerning the land the subject of a licence or petroleum processing facility licence or crossed by a pipeline licence makes agreement on compensation impracticable, the amount of compensation to be paid shall be determined by a Warden under this section, and the amount of such compensation shall be payable into a trust account established for that purpose by the Director to be held therein until the dispute has been finally resolved.
(19) Following final resolution of a dispute as provided in Subsection (18), compensation shall be paid out of the trust account in accordance with a compensation agreement or a further determination by a Warden

under this section, and in making such a further determination the Warden shall be empowered, if he considers on the basis of the evidence and arguments then presented to him that the amount of compensation payable should be greater than the amount in the trust account, to order payment of amounts in addition to the amount in the trust account.

**119. WARDENS.**

[76](1) The Director shall appoint –

(*a*) a senior officer of the Department or the public service to be Chief Warden; and
(*b*) such other number of officers as considered necessary to be appointed as Warden,

for the purposes of the Act.
(2) The functions, powers and duties of a Warden are as specified in this Act or regulations.
(3) The Chief Warden shall undertake –

(*a*) the duties of a Warden; and
(*b*) such additional functions as are specifically allocated under this Act or regulations or as the Director may confer.

(4) The Chief Warden may, by instrument in writing, delegate all or any powers (except this power of delegation) to a Warden.

**120. ACQUISITION OF LAND.**

(1)[77] [78]Notwithstanding any provision of the *Land Act 1996* in determining the compensation payable for land compulsorily acquired for a purpose specified in Section 1(2)–

(*a*) no allowance shall be made for any petroleum, helium, minerals or gold known or supposed to be in, on or under the land acquired; and
(*b*) no compensation shall be payable in respect of improvements made to the land by a licensee.

(2) Whenever it is proved, to the satisfaction of a court of competent jurisdiction, under the *Land Act 1996* that damage has been sustained by a claimant by reason of the severance of the land acquired from other adjoining land of the claimant, or land in which he is interested, the court may order that such adjoining land or some portion of it shall also be acquired.
(3)[79] [80]Where land has been acquired for a purpose specified in Section 1(2) and has been made available to a licensee for the purposes of his operations under his licence, the amount of any compensation that the State has paid in respect of that land is a debt due and payable by the licensee to the State.
(4) An amount payable under Subsection (3), on written demand being served on the licensee, is an amount payable by him under this Act for the purposes of Section 138(1)(d).

**121. DETERMINATION OF CUSTOMARY LAND.**

(1) Where for the purposes of this Act it is necessary to determine the rightful owners or occupiers of, or persons having an interest in, any customary land, or any improvements on it other than in circumstances where Section 9 of the *Land Act 1996* applies, the determination may be made under the provisions of the *Land Disputes Settlement Act 1975* and for the purposes, and within the meaning, of that Act, there shall be deemed to be a dispute between such persons or groups as the court, within the meaning of that Act, may direct.
(2) Where the Director considers that a dispute of the type referred to in Subsection (1) exists, he may–

(*a*) refer that dispute to the Provincial Land Disputes Committee for the Province in question as a dispute under the *Land Disputes Settlement Act 1975*; or
(*b*) make an application in respect of the dispute to the applicable Local Land Court under Section 27 of that Act.

(3) Where the Director makes a referral or application under Subsection (2)–

(*a*) the dispute shall be deemed for the purpose of the *Land Disputes Settlement Act 1975* to be a dispute relating to land; and
(*b*) the Director shall be deemed to be a party to the dispute for all procedural matters under that Act, and he or his representative shall be entitled to participate in any mediation or court hearing in relation to the dispute.

(4) Where the Director makes a referral under Subsection (2)(a)–

(*a*) the reference to the Provincial Land Disputes Committee shall be deemed to be a request by a Local-level Government under Section 9(1) of the *Land Disputes Settlement Act 1975*; and
(*b*) the Committee shall declare the area which is the subject of the dispute to be a Land Mediation Area and a single Land Mediation Division, and forthwith appoint a Land Mediator for that Land Mediation Division.

(5) Where the Director makes an application under Subsection (2)(b), the dispute shall be deemed to have been the subject of a certificate given by a Land Mediator under Section 27(1) of the *Land Disputes Settlement Act 1975* and a certificate given by a Magistrate under Subsection 27(2) of that Act.

**122. TRESPASS ON LAND HELD UNDER A LICENCE.**

(1) A person (including the owner or occupier of, or any person interested in, private land) shall not enter on, occupy or interfere with–

(*a*) any land in a licence area which is being used by the licensee for or in connection with prospecting operations or operations for the recovery of petroleum, including land required to be kept vacant for the purpose of compliance with the licensee's obligations under this Act or any other law; or
(*b*) any pipeline or any land permanently occupied by a pipeline licensee under his pipeline licence or being lawfully used by the pipeline licensee for or in connection with pipeline operations or the construction of the pipeline or required to be kept vacant for the purpose of compliance with the licensee's obligations under this Act or any other law; or
(*c*) any petroleum processing facility or any land permanently occupied by the petroleum processing facility licensee under his petroleum processing facility licence or being lawfully used by the petroleum processing facility licensee for or in connection with petroleum processing facility operations or the construction of the petroleum processing facility, or required to be kept vacant for the purpose of compliance with the licensee's obligations under this Act or any other law,

unless authorized or permitted by or under this Act or any other law of the State, or by the licensee.
(2) Every entry, occupation or interference in contravention of Subsection (1) shall, in addition to constituting an offence under this Act, be deemed to be a trespass.
(3) A licensee may proceed in the National Court for trespass under this section and for damages in respect of the trespass.
(4) This section shall not be construed as depriving a licensee of any other right he might have under a law in force in the country in respect of his occupation and use of the land.

## DIVISION 13. GENERAL.

**123. DATE OF EFFECT OF LICENCES, ETC.**

(1) A licence takes effect from and including the day specified for the purpose in the licence.
(2) A variation of a licence takes effect from and including the day on which notice of the variation is published in the National Gazette.

**123A. DESIGNATION OF OPERATOR AND OPERATING AGREEMENT.**

[81](1) Subject to Subsection (3), where there is more than one holder of a licence, the holders shall, as soon as reasonably practicable after the date of grant of the licence, provide to the Director a copy of an agreement between holders, relating to designation of operator and the conduct of operations in relation to that licence.
(2) Where an agreement has been provided to the Director under Subsection (1), the holders shall, within one month after any amendment, variation or replacement of that agreement, provide to the Director a copy of the agreement (if any) effecting the amendment, variation or replacement.
(3) The holders shall, upon providing a copy of an agreement to the Director under Subsections (1) or (2), and upon any change to the identity of the operator under the provisions of the agreement, give notice in writing to the Director of the name and address of the new operator appointed under the agreement.
(4) An agreement lodged for registration under Division 11 or previously registered under that Division in respect of a licence shall be deemed to have been provided under Subsection (1).

**124. WORK PRACTICES FOR TENEMENT HOLDER.**

(1) A tenement holder must–

(*a*) carry out all petroleum exploration operations and operations for the recovery of petroleum in the licence area in a proper and workman like manner and in accordance with good oilfield practice; and
(*b*) secure the safety, health and welfare of persons engaged in those operations in or about the licence area; and
(*c*) act in accordance with–

(i) this Act, including the regulations, and any direction given under this Act; and
(ii) any restriction imposed or requirement made by an inspector under this Act.

(2) In particular, and without limiting the generality of Subsection (1), a tenement holder must–

(*a*) control the flow and prevent the escape in the licence area of petroleum or water, except in accordance with a permit or licence issued under a law regulating the discharge or release of petroleum, petroleum products or water; and
(*b*) prevent the escape in the licence area of any mixture of water or drilling fluid and petroleum or any other matter; and
(*c*) prevent damage to petroleum-bearing strata in an area in respect of which the tenement is not in force; and
(*d*) keep separate–

(i) each petroleum pool discovered in the licence area; and
(ii) such of the sources of water (if any) discovered in that area,

as the Minister, by instrument served on the licensee, directs; and

(*e*) prevent water or any other matter entering any petroleum pool through wells in the licence area except when required by, and in accordance with, good oilfield practice; and
(*f*) prevent the pollution of any water-well, spring, stream, river, lake, reservoir, estuary, harbour or area of sea by the escape of petroleum, salt water, drilling fluid, chemical additive or any other waste product or effluent; and
(*g*) furnish to the Director, prior to the drilling of any well, a detailed report on the technique to be employed, the material to be used and the safety measures to be employed, in the drilling of the well.

(3) This section shall not prevent a tenement holder from flaring natural gas–

(*a*) where the written consent of the Director has been obtained; or
(*b*) where, in an emergency, flaring is required–

(i) to safeguard the health and safety of persons in the licence area; or
(ii) to prevent damage to the property of any person in the licence area.

**125. WORK PRACTICES FOR PIPELINE LICENSEE.**

(1) A pipeline licensee must operate the pipeline in a proper and workmanlike manner and must secure the safety, health and welfare of persons engaged in operations in connection with the pipeline.
(2) In particular and without limiting the generality of Subsection (1), a pipeline licensee must prevent the escape of petroleum or petroleum products or water from the pipeline, except in accordance with a permit or licence issued under a law regulating the discharge or release of petroleum, petroleum products or water.

**126. WORK PRACTICES FOR PETROLEUM PROCESSING FACILITY LICENSEE.**

(1) A petroleum processing facility licensee shall operate the petroleum processing facility in a proper and workmanlike manner and shall secure the safety, health and welfare of persons engaged in operations in connection with the petroleum processing facility.
(2) In particular and without limiting the generality of Subsection (1), a petroleum processing facility licensee shall prevent the escape of petroleum or petroleum products or water from the petroleum processing facility, except in accordance with a permit or licence issued under a law regulating the discharge or release of petroleum, petroleum products or water.
(3) The Head of State, acting on advice, may make regulations prescribing the conduct of petroleum processing facility operations, including the qualifications of persons in charge of those operations.

**127. WORK PRACTICES FOR HOLDERS OF INSTRUMENTS OF CONSENT.**

A person who is the holder of an instrument of consent under Section 150 must–

(*a*) carry out all petroleum exploration operations in the area in respect of which the instrument of consent is in force in a proper and workmanlike manner and in accordance with good oilfield practice; and
(*b*) secure the safety, health and welfare of persons engaged in those operations in or about that area.

**128. PENALTY FOR BREACH OF SECTION 124, 125, 126 OR 127.**

(1) A licensee or holder of an instrument of consent who contravenes or fails to comply with a requirement of Section 124, 125, 126 or 127, as the case may be, is guilty of an offence.
Penalty: A fine not exceeding K5,000.00.
(2) It is a defence to a charge for an offence under this section, if the person charged proves that he took all reasonable steps to comply with the requirements of the relevant section applicable to him.

**129. LOCAL PURCHASE OBLIGATION.**

(1) Subject to the provisions of this section, a licensee shall, in its operations in Papua New Guinea and in the construction and development of a project–

(*a*) use and purchase goods and services supplied, produced or manufactured in Papua New Guinea whenever the same can be obtained at equivalent terms, including prices, conditions and delivery or performance dates and are in all respects of a quality comparable with those available from outside Papua New Guinea; and
(*b*) encourage and assist citizens of Papua New Guinea who are desirous of establishing businesses providing goods and services for the operations or the project and for any town constructed primarily for the purposes of the project and the residents thereof; and
(*c*) make maximum use of Papua New Guinea contractors and subcontractors where services of a standard comparable with those which the licensee would obtain but for the operation of this section are available from such Papua New Guinea contractors or subcontractors at equivalent prices, and on equivalent terms, conditions and delivery or performance dates.

(2) A licensee which, for the purpose of its operations in Papua New Guinea or the construction and development of its project, requires imported vehicles, machinery, plant or equipment, and does not purchase such items direct from the manufacturer, shall effect the purchase of such items through traders based in Papua New Guinea or the Papua New Guinea operations of traders based elsewhere but having operations in Papua New Guinea.
(3) Subsection (2) does not apply to a licensee in respect of a particular purchase if–

(*a*) such items are not available through such traders or trading operations at an equivalent price, and on equivalent terms, conditions and delivery dates; or
(*b*) compliance would adversely affect the financing of the licensee's operations or the development of the licensee's project.

(4) Nothing contained in this section obliges a licensee to grant or lend money to any person or any local enterprise.
(5) Where a licensee seeks to grant to persons who are landowners in the area of the licensee's operations a contract for the supply of labour or services and a dispute which delays the grant of such a contract arises amongst persons claiming to be such landowners, the licensee may refer the dispute to the Director who may determine the dispute.

**130. MEASUREMENT AND METERING.**

(1) At such intervals as the Director determines, licensees shall measure and report to the Director the following, as applicable:–

(*a*) the continuous volume of petroleum produced (including separate recording of associated natural gas which is either flared or injected) where–

(i) the volume of oil shall be calculated on the basis of acceptable meter readings or tank measurements with such accuracy as is required by the Director; and
(ii) the volume of natural gas shall be measured by a meter approved for the purposes of Section 161; and
(iii) unless otherwise authorized by the Director, with all volumes produced, sold, injected or flared adjusted to a standard temperature and pressure base as determined by the Director;

(*b*) the continuous volume of petroleum or petroleum products transported by pipeline as measured at the meters for sale or transfer of custody;
(*c*) the continuous volume of the output of petroleum or petroleum products at a petroleum processing facility in units and in a manner acceptable to the Director,

in each case in accordance with internationally accepted measurement standards.
(2) Except as prescribed by regulation, a person shall not install in any facility or use any measuring device to measure the volume of petroleum or petroleum products unless such measuring device is approved by the Minister.

**131. MAINTENANCE, ETC., OF PROPERTY.**

(1) A tenement holder shall–

(*a*) maintain in good condition and keep in good repair all structures, equipment and other property in the licence area which are used by him in connection with the operations in which he is engaged; and
(*b*) remove from the licence area all structures, equipment and other property owned by him which is not being, or intended to be, so used.

(2) A pipeline licensee or petroleum processing facility licensee shall–

(*a*) maintain in good condition and repair all structures, equipment and other property in the area in which the pipeline or petroleum processing facility is constructed and which are used by him in connection with the

operations in which he is engaged; and
(*b*) subject to Section 139, remove from the area all structures, equipment and other property owned by him which is not being, or intended to be, so used.

**132. DRILLING NEAR BOUNDARIES.**

(1) A tenement holder shall not make a well any part of which is less than 300 m from a boundary of a licence area, except with the written consent of the Director and in accordance with such conditions (if any) as are specified in the instrument of consent.
(2) Where a tenement holder fails to comply with Subsection (1), the Director may, by instrument served on the tenement holder, direct him–

(*a*) to plug the well; or
(*b*) to close off the well; or
(*c*) to comply with the directions relating to the making or maintenance of the well specified in the instrument,

within the period specified in the instrument and the tenement holder shall comply with the direction within that period.

**133. DIRECTIONS.**

(1) The Minister, the Director or an inspector may, by instrument served on a person, give to that person such directions as are prescribed.
(2) A direction under Subsection (1) has effect and shall be complied with notwithstanding anything in the regulations and, to the extent to which the regulations are inconsistent with the directions, the person to whom the direction is given is not obliged to comply with the regulations.
(3) A person who refuses or fails to comply with a direction given under Subsection (1) is guilty of an offence.
Penalty: A fine not exceeding K2,000.00.

**134. COMPLIANCE WITH DIRECTIONS.**

(1) Where a person fails to comply with a direction given to him under this Act or under the regulations, the Minister may do all or any of the things required by the directions to be done.
(2) Any costs or expenses incurred by the Minister under Subsection (1) in relation to a direction are a debt due by the person to whom the direction was given to the State.
(3) It is a defence to a charge of failing to comply with a direction given under this Act or under the regulations if the person charged proves that he took all reasonable steps to comply with the direction.

**135. EXEMPTIONS, VARIATIONS, ETC.**

(1) Where–

(*a*) under this Part, a licence is deemed to continue in force; or
(*b*) a licence is varied under Section 24 or 41 or 58 or 81 or 82 or 92 or 93; or
(*c*) a licensee enters into an agreement under Section 66 or a direction is given to the licensee under that section; or
(*d*) a tenement is partly cancelled, partly determined or surrendered as to one or more, but not all of the blocks in respect of which it is in force; or
(*e*) the term of a petroleum prospecting licence is extended under Section 29 or 30; or
(*f*) the term of a petroleum retention licence is extended under Section 45; or
(*g*) a licensee, by instrument served on the Director, applies–

(i) for a variation or suspension of the licence; or
(ii) for exemption from compliance with any of the conditions specified in the licence; or

(*h*) under this Act or the regulations the Minister gives a direction or consent to a licensee; or
(*i*) a direction is given to the pipeline licensee under Section 83,

the Minister may, at any time, by instrument served on the licensee–

(*j*) vary or suspend; or
(*k*) exempt the licensee from compliance with,

any of the conditions specified in the licence, on such conditions (if any) as the Minister determines and specifies in the instrument.
(2) Subsection (1) does not authorize the making of an instrument to the extent–

(*a*) that it would affect the term of a licence; or
(*b*) that it would be inconsistent with the terms of a petroleum agreement or gas agreement applying to the licence in question; or
(*c*) in the case of an instrument relating to an application referred to in Subsection (1)(f)–that it would not be in accordance with the application, or the application as varied by agreement, before the making of the instrument.

**136. PREVENTION FROM CARRYING ON PROSPECTING OPERATIONS.**

(1) A petroleum prospecting licensee or petroleum retention licensee who has been, or is being, prevented from carrying on in the licence area any operations authorized by the licence, may make an application to the Minister for a direction under this section.
(2) An application under Subsection (1)–

(*a*) shall be made not more than one month after the date of commencement of the circumstances causing the prevention, or such longer period as the Minister may allow, but in any event before the licence concerned ceases to have effect; and
(*b*) shall specify the operations that the licensee has been or is being prevented from carrying on; and
(*c*) shall set out the circumstances by reason of which the licensee has been or is being prevented from carrying on those operations; and
(*d*) may set out any other matters that the licensee wishes the Minister to consider.

(3) Where a licensee has made an application under Subsection (1), the Minister shall, after considering a report from the Board, by instrument served on the licensee–

(*a*) if he is satisfied that the licensee has been by reason of circumstances beyond the control of the licensee, prevented from carrying on in the licence area, during any period during which the licence was in force, any of the operations specified in the application–direct that the term of the licence be extended for the period specified in the instrument being a period not greater than the period for which the licensee was prevented from carrying on operations, subject to such conditions (if any) as the Minister determines and specifies in the instrument; or
(*b*) in any other case–refuse the application.

(4) Where the Minister makes a direction under Subsection (3)(a), the licence continues in force for the period directed.
(5) Where a licensee has made an application under Subsection (1) and an instrument under Subsection (3) has not been served on the licensee before the licence would, but for this subsection, cease to have effect–

(*a*) any application under Section 27, 30 or 44 for the extension of the licence lapses; and
(*b*) the licensee may, notwithstanding anything contained in that section, make an application or further application under that section for the extension of the licence–

(i) if the Minister, by instrument under Subsection (3) directs that the term of the licence be extended for a specified period–within a period of one month after the expiration of the specified period; or

(ii) if the Minister, by instrument under Subsection (3), refuses the application under Subsection (1)–within a period of one month after the day on which the instrument is served on the licensee; and

(*c*) the licence continues in force by reason of this subsection until the expiration of that period of one month, or until an application is made under Section 27, 30 or 44 for the extension of the licence, whichever first occurs.

**137. SURRENDER OF LICENCES.**

(1) In this section, **"the area to which the surrender relates"** means–

(*a*) in relation to a surrender of a tenement–the area constituted by the blocks in relation to which the tenement is proposed to be surrendered; and
(*b*) in relation to a surrender of a pipeline licence or petroleum processing facility licence–the area in which the pipeline or petroleum processing facility or part thereof, in relation to which the licence is proposed to be surrendered, is constructed.

(2) A licensee may, at any time, by written notice served on the Director, apply to the Minister for consent to surrender the licence–

(*a*) in the case of a tenement–as to all or any of the blocks in respect of which it is in force; and
(*b*) in the case of a pipeline licence or petroleum processing facility licence–as to the whole or part of the pipeline or petroleum processing facility in respect of which it is in force.

(2A)[82] [83]A licensee may state in its application under Subsection (2) that the surrender is, if consented to by the Minister, to take effect on a date or upon the occurrence of a particular event specified in the application in which case the surrender shall, if so consented to and if implemented by the applicant in accordance with Subsection (6), take effect on that date or upon the occurrence of that event, as the case maybe.
(3) Subject to Subsection (5), the Minister shall not give his consent to a surrender of a licence under Subsection (2) unless the licensee–

(*a*) has paid all fees and amounts payable by him under this Act or has made arrangements that are satisfactory to the Minister for the payment of those fees and amounts; and
(*b*) has, subject to Subsection (4), complied with the conditions specified in the licence and with the provisions of this Act; and
(*c*) has, to the satisfaction of the Minister, plugged or closed off all wells made in that area by any person engaged or concerned in the operations authorized by the licence or made arrangements with respect to the termination of operations of the pipeline or petroleum processing facility to which the surrender relates; and
(*d*) has to the satisfaction of the Minister–

(i) removed or caused to be removed from the area to which the surrender relates all property brought into that area by any person and any wastes deposited in that area by the licensee or any person on his behalf; or
(ii) made arrangements with respect to that property or waste; and

(*e*) has made provision, to the satisfaction of the Minister, for the reclamation of the site of the pipeline or petroleum processing facility in the area to which the surrender relates and the conservation and protection of the natural resources in that area.

(4) For the purpose of Subsection (3)(b), the holder of a petroleum prospecting licence or a petroleum retention licence who has otherwise complied with the conditions referred to in Section 31(2) or 46, as the case may be, shall not be taken to have failed to comply with the conditions specified in the licence for the reason only that he has failed to complete any work or expend any amount referred to, or specified, in the licence so far as it relates to any period subsequent to the date on which an application under this section, to which the Minister subsequently consents, is made.

(5) Where a licensee has not complied with the conditions specified in the licence, or with the provisions of this Act, the Minister may give his consent to a surrender of the licence under Subsection (2) if he is satisfied that, although the licensee has not so complied, special circumstances exist that justify the giving of consent to the surrender.
(6) Where the Minister consents to an application under Subsection (2), the applicant may, by instrument served on the Director, surrender the licence.
(7) The surrender of a licence under this section shall not release the licensee from any liability in respect of–

(*a*) the licence up to the date of surrender; or
(*b*) any act or omission under the licence up to the date of surrender giving rise to cause of action; or
(*c*) compliance with other obligations under the laws of Papua New Guinea.

(8) A licensee who permanently ceases operations under his licence shall–

(*a*) do all of the things specified in Subsection (3), unless the Minister, after considering a report of the Board, approves otherwise; and
(*b*) apply to the Minister under Subsection (2) to surrender the licence.

**138. SUSPENSION AND CANCELLATION OF LICENCES.**

(1) Where a licensee has not–

(*a*) in the opinion of the Minister, complied with a condition specified in the licence; or
(*b*) in the opinion of the Minister, complied with a direction given to him under this Act by the Minister, the Director or an inspector; or
(*c*) complied with a provision of this Act; or
(*d*) paid any amount payable by him under this Act within a period of three months after the date on which the amount became payable,

the Minister may, by instrument served on the licensee–

(*e*) in the case of a tenement–suspend for such period as the Minister thinks fit or cancel the licence as to all or any of the blocks in respect of which it is in force; or
(*f*) in the case of a pipeline licence or petroleum processing facility licence–suspend for such period as the Minister thinks fit or cancel the licence as to the whole or a part of the pipeline or petroleum processing facility in respect of which it is in force.

(2) The Minister shall not, under Subsection (1), suspend or cancel a licence as to all or any of the blocks, or as to the whole or part of the pipeline or petroleum processing facility, unless–

(*a*) he has, by instrument served on the licensee, given not less than one month's notice of his intention to suspend or cancel the licence, specifying the grounds upon which the suspension or cancellation is based; and
(*b*) he has caused a copy of the instrument to be served on such other persons (if any) as he thinks fit; and
(*c*) he has, in the instrument, specified a date, being not less than 14 days prior to the end of the period specified in the instrument referred to in Paragraph (a), on or before which written submissions may be served on the Minister in connection with the proposed suspension or cancellation; and
(*d*) after taking into account–

(i) any action taken by the licensee to remove that ground or to prevent the recurrence of similar grounds; and
(ii) any matters so submitted to him on or before the specified date; and
(iii) a report on those matters from the Board,

he considers that special circumstances exist that justify a decision to suspend or cancel the licence.

(3) The suspension or cancellation of a licence by the Minister pursuant to this section shall not release the licensee from any liability in respect of the licence incurred before the date of cancellation or before or during the period of suspension.

**139. REMOVAL OF PROPERTY, ETC., BY LICENSEE, ETC.**

(1) Prior to abandonment of a well a tenement holder shall–

(*a*) furnish the Director with notice of his intention to abandon the well together with a request for the Director to approve a program for abandonment which includes removal of equipment, plugging the well bore, and reclaiming the well site; and
(*b*) complete logging and testing and submission of such information and relevant evaluations which have not previously been submitted to the Director with the tenement holder's notice under Paragraph (a); and
(*c*) conduct abandonment operations according to the manner prescribed by regulations.

(2) Where any licence has been wholly determined, partly determined, wholly cancelled or partly cancelled or has expired, the Minister may by instrument served on the person who was, or is, the licensee, direct that person to–

(*a*) make arrangements, to the satisfaction of the Minister, with respect to the complete or partial abandonment of any pipeline or petroleum processing facility or other plant and equipment which is or was the subject of the licence; and
(*b*) remove or cause to be removed from the area in respect of which the tenement has been determined or cancelled or has expired or the area in which the pipeline or petroleum processing facility or part thereof, in relation to which the licence is determined or cancelled or has expired, is constructed, all property brought into that area by any person engaged or concerned in the operations authorized by the licence, or to make arrangements that are satisfactory to the Minister with respect to that property; and
(*c*) plug or close off, to the satisfaction of the Minister, all wells made in that area by any person engaged or concerned in those operations; and
(*d*) make provision, to the satisfaction of the Minister, for the conservation and protection of the natural resources in that area.

(3) Notwithstanding Subsection (2), if agreed by the Minister by instrument or as a condition of a licence or by the State in a written agreement, buried pipelines, or pipes or facilities referred to in Paragraphs (a) to (d) inclusive of the definition of "pipeline", may be abandoned in place, subject to the terms of the licence condition or instrument or written agreement.
(4) The holder of any licence shall–

(*a*) at the time of surrender of the licence or cancellation by the Minister; and
(*b*) five years prior to the expiration of the term of the licence or in the case of a petroleum processing facility licence five years prior to the expected date of abandonment of the petroleum processing facility,

demonstrate to the satisfaction of the Minister that it is able to meet has or will have sufficient financial resources to meet its obligations under this section upon surrender, cancellation or expiry of the licence.
(5) The licensee shall demonstrate such financial resources–

(*a*) by establishing a reserve account for abandonment costs in accordance with the report of a certified independent auditor; or
(*b*) by providing, in a form acceptable to the Minister, a financial undertaking (or in the case of a licensee which is a joint venture, several undertakings) in the form of a bond, letter of credit or guarantee or other instrument acceptable to the Minister; or
(*c*) by granting the Minister a charge or similar security over its assets and income.

(6) A person to whom a direction under Subsection (2) is given who refuses, or fails, to comply with the direction within the period specified in the instrument by which the direction was given is guilty of an offence. Penalty: A fine not exceeding K25,000.00.

**140. REMOVAL AND SALE OF PROPERTY.**

(1) Where a direction under Section 139 has not been complied with, the Minister may–

(*a*) do or cause to be done all or any of the things required by the direction to be done; and
(*b*) remove or cause to be removed, in such manner as he thinks fit, all or any of the property from the relinquished area concerned; and
(*c*) dispose of, in such manner as he thinks fit, all or any of the property referred to in Paragraph (b); and
(*d*) if he has served a copy of the instrument by which the direction was given on a person who he believed to be an owner of the property or part of the property–sell or cause to be sold by public auction or otherwise as he thinks fit, all or any of the property referred to in Paragraph (b) that belongs, or that he believes to belong, to that person.

(2) The Minister may deduct from the proceeds of a sale of property under Subsection (1) that belongs, or that he believes to belong, to a particular person–

(*a*) all or any part of any costs and expenses incurred by him under that subsection in relation to that property; and
(*b*) all or any part of any costs and expenses incurred by him in relation to the doing of anything required by a direction under Section 139 to be done by the person; and
(*c*) all or any part of any fees or amounts due and payable under this Act by the person.

(3) The costs and expenses incurred by the Minister under Subsection (1)–

(*a*) if incurred in relation to the removal, disposal or sale of property–are a debt due by the owner of the property to the State; or
(*b*) if incurred in relation to the doing of anything required by a direction under Section 139 to be done by a person who is or was a licensee–are a debt due by that person to the State,

and to the extent to which they are not recovered under Subsection (2) are recoverable by the State as a debt.
(4) Subject to Subsection (3), no action lies in respect of the removal, disposal or sale of property under this section.

**141. PENALTY FOR LATE PAYMENTS.**

(1) Where the liability of a person under this Act to pay an amount is not discharged on or before the time when the amount is payable, there is payable by that person an additional amount calculated at the rate of % per day on so much of that amount as from time to time remains unpaid, to be computed from the time that the amount became payable until it is paid.
(2) The Minister may, in a particular case, for reasons that in his opinion are sufficient, remit the whole or part of an amount payable under this section.

**142. SECURITIES.**

(1)[84] [85]A security referred to in Division 2, 4, 7, 9 or 10–

(*a*) shall be in such amount not exceeding K1,000,000.00 as the Minister thinks reasonable; and
(*b*) shall be by way of a bond to pay the amount, executed by the licensee, in an approved form, and be supported by–

(i) a cash deposit from the licensee; or
(ii) a guarantee of a bank acceptable to the Minister and in an approved form; or
(ii) some other approved form of security,

or any combination of the alternatives specified in sub-paragraph (i), (ii) or (iii).

(2) A bond, guarantee or other security document given in an approved form, although it is not sealed, shall bind the person subscribing to it as if it were sealed.
(3) Whenever a security under this Act is the subject of legal proceedings, the production of the security, without further proof, entitles the Minister to judgement against the person appearing to have executed the security, for the amount of his stated liability or for such lesser amount as is claimed, unless that person proves–

(*a*) compliance with the conditions of the security; or
(*b*) that the security was not executed by him; or
(*c*) release or satisfaction.

(4) For the purposes of Subsection (3)(a), the holder of a petroleum prospecting licence who has complied with a condition referred to in Section 31(2) shall not be taken to have failed to comply with the conditions of the security for the reason only that he has failed to complete any work referred to, or expend any amount specified, in the licence so far as it relates to any period subsequent to the date on which an application under Section 137(2), to which the Minister subsequently consents, is made.
(5) If it appears to the court that a condition of a security under this Act has not been complied with, the security shall not be deemed to have been discharged or invalidated, and the subscriber shall not be deemed to have been released or discharged from liability by reason of–

(*a*) any extension of time or other concession; or
(*b*) any consent to, or acquiescence in, a previous non-compliance with a condition; or
(*c*) any failure to bring legal proceedings against the subscriber on the occurrence of a previous non-compliance with the condition.

(6) If there is more than one subscriber to the security, each is bound, unless the security otherwise provides, jointly and severally and for the full amount.

**143. FURTHER INFORMATION TO BE FURNISHED, ETC.**

(1) Where the Minister, the Director or an inspector has reason to believe that a person is capable of giving information or producing documents relating to petroleum exploration operations, or operations for the recovery of petroleum, he may, by instrument served on that person, require that person–

(*a*) to furnish that information to him in writing within the period and in the manner specified in the instrument; or
(*b*) to attend before him or a person specified in the instrument, at such time and place as is so specified, and there to answer questions relating to those operations and to produce such documents relating to those operations as are specified in the instrument.

(2) A person is not excused from furnishing information, answering a question or producing a document when required to do so under this section, on the grounds that the information so furnished, the answer to the question or the production of the document might tend to incriminate him or make him liable to a penalty, but the information so furnished or his answer to the question is not admissible in evidence against him in proceedings other than proceedings for an offence against Section 144.

**144. FAILING TO FURNISH INFORMATION, ETC.**

A person who–

(*a*) refuses or fails to comply with a requirement in an instrument under Section 143 to the extent to which he is capable of complying with it; or
(*b*) in purported compliance with a requirement referred to in Paragraph (a)–knowingly furnishes information that is false or misleading in a material particular; or
(*c*) when attending before the Minister, the Director or an inspector under a requirement referred to in Paragraph (a)–knowingly makes a statement or produces a document that is false or misleading in a material particular,

is guilty of an offence.
Penalty: A fine not exceeding K5,000.00.

**145. DRILLING FOR AND DISCOVERY OF WATER.**

A person shall not, except in accordance with such conditions as are determined by the Minister, or in accordance with the provisions of the *Water Resources Act 1982*, drill for water in any licence area.

**146. SURVEY OF WELLS, ETC.**

(1) The Minister or the Director may, at any time, by instrument served on a tenement holder, direct the tenement holder–

(*a*) to carry out a survey of the position of the well, structure or equipment specified in the instrument; and
(*b*) to furnish to the Minister or Director, as the case may be, a written report of the survey.

(2) Where the Minister or the Director is not satisfied with a report of a survey furnished to him under Subsection (1) by a tenement holder, he may, by instrument served on the tenement holder, direct the tenement holder to furnish further written information in connection with the survey.
(3) A person to whom a direction is given under Subsection (1) or (2) who fails to comply with the direction is guilty of an offence.
Penalty: A fine not exceeding K5,000.00.

**147. RECORDS, ETC., TO BE KEPT.**

The Minister or the Director may, by instrument served on a person carrying on operations under a licence or an instrument of consent under Section 150, direct that person–

(*a*) to keep such accounts, records and other documents in connection with those operations as are specified in the instrument; and
(*b*) to collect and retain such cores, cuttings and samples in connection with those operations as are specified in the instrument; and
(*c*) to furnish to the Minister in the manner specified in the instrument such reports, returns, other documents, cores, cuttings and samples in connection with those operations,

as are specified in the instrument.

**148. REPORTING BY LICENSEES.**

(1) The Minister or the Director may give directions to a licensee as to reports to be provided to the Director by the licensee on the activities of the licensee in respect of the licence, and as to the frequency of and information to be contained in such reports, and such other matters by way of reports in respect of the licence, including the production, sale, processing or transportation of petroleum or petroleum products, as the Minister or Director sees fit.
(2) A licensee to whom a direction is given under Subsection (1) shall provide such reports containing such information and at such frequency as is specified in the direction, and shall otherwise comply with the direction given.
(3) A person to whom a direction is given under Subsection (2) who fails or refuses to comply with the direction is guilty of an offence.
Penalty: A fine not exceeding K5,000.00.

**149. CONFIDENTIALITY, ETC., OF INFORMATION.**

(1) All information supplied to the Minister, the Director or an inspector under this Act shall, if the Minister so directs, be verified by statutory declaration in a prescribed form.

(2) The following information furnished to the Board, the Minister, the Director or an inspector under this or the former Acts, or to any other representative of the State, shall be treated as confidential:–

(*a*) all geological and geophysical information (including information concerning cores or cuttings from, or samples of, the land surface, sea bed or subsoil in a block);
(*b*) all intellectual property including, without limitation, industrial processes;
(*c*) all information related to the business of the licensee to which the information relates including sales forecasts, market projections or marketing information;
(*d*) all applications for licences, commercial and economic evaluations, marketing information, and other information which the person furnishing the information may designate as being commercially sensitive,

except where the licensee or person furnishing the information has given his consent for disclosure or the information is otherwise available in the public domain or is disclosed in accordance with Subsection (3).
(3) Information referred to in Subsection (2)(a) may be disclosed, and cores, cuttings or samples made available–

(*a*) to an officer or other representative of the State expressly authorized by the Minister or Director to receive that information or to examine those cores, cuttings or samples; and
(*b*) in respect of a block or part of a block that was previously the subject of a licence under this Act or a licence under the former Act and is not the subject of a current licence under this Act–to the public; and
(*c*) in respect of a block the subject of a current petroleum prospecting licence or petroleum retention licence that is not, or is not included in, a location–to the public not earlier than two years after that information was, or those cores, cuttings or samples were, required to be supplied to the Minister, the Director, or an inspector, as the case may be; and
(*d*) in respect of a block the subject of a current petroleum development licence–to the public not earlier than one year after that information was, or those cores, cuttings or samples were, required to be supplied to the Minister, the Director, or an inspector, as the case may be.

(4) Information referred to in Subsection (2)(a) to (d) inclusive may be disclosed to an officer or other representative of the State expressly authorized by the Minister or Director to receive that information.
(5) The Minister may at any time make use of any information or matter supplied by a licensee for the purpose of preparing and publishing aggregate returns and general reports with respect to operations under this Act.
(6) A person who acts in the execution of any duty under this Act shall not, except in the performance of that duty, divulge any information supplied to the Minister or to the Director in pursuance of this Act.
(7) A person who has been an officer or who has performed a duty under this Act shall not communicate any information acquired by him in the performance of that duty to any person other than a person authorized by law or by the Minister or the Director to receive that information.

**150. SCIENTIFIC INVESTIGATIONS: INSTRUMENTS OF CONSENT.**

(1) The Minister may, by instrument, consent to the carrying on by any person of petroleum exploration operations in the course of a scientific investigation.
(2) An instrument of consent shall be subject to such conditions (if any) as are specified in the instrument.
(3) An instrument of consent under this section authorizes the person to whom it is issued to carry out the petroleum exploration operation specified in the instrument–

(*a*) in the area; and
(*b*) subject to the conditions (if any),

specified in the instrument, in the course of scientific investigation.

**151. INSPECTORS.**

(1) The Minister may, by notice in the National Gazette, appoint–

(*a*) a person to be the Chief Inspector; and
(*b*) such other persons to be inspectors as he thinks necessary,

for the purposes of this Act.
(2) The Minister shall issue to the Chief Inspector and to each inspector a certificate stating that he is an inspector.
(3) Where the appointment of a person under this section expires or is revoked, that person shall immediately surrender to the Minister the certificate issued to him under this section.

**152. POWERS OF INSPECTORS.**

(1) For the purposes of this Act, an inspector, at all reasonable times may–

(*a*) enter any area, structure, vehicle, vessel, aircraft or building that, in his opinion, has been, is being or is to be, used in connection with–

(i) petroleum exploration operations; or
(ii) operations for the recovery of petroleum; or
(iii) operations connected with the construction or operation of a pipeline or a petroleum processing facility; and

(*b*) inspect and test any machinery or equipment that, in his opinion, has been, is being or is to be, used in connection with any of the operations referred to in Paragraph (a); and
(*c*) take or remove for the purpose of analysis or testing, or for use in evidence in connection with an offence against this Act, samples of petroleum, water or other substances from a well or samples of petroleum or petroleum products or other substances from a pipeline or a petroleum processing facility; and
(*d*) inspect, take extracts from, and make copies of, any document relating to any of the operations referred to in Paragraph (a); and
(*e*) with respect to the health and safety of persons employed by a licensee in or in connection with any of the operations referred to in Paragraph (a)–by instrument, issue directions to and impose restrictions on the licensee, or any person so employed; and
(*f*) order, by instrument–

(i) the cessation of operations on or in, and the withdrawal of all persons from, any structure or building that is being used in connection with any of the operations referred to in Paragraph (a); or
(ii) the discontinuance of the use of any machinery or equipment,

which he considers unsafe after taking into account the following matters:–

(iii) good oilfield practice or generally accepted petroleum processing operations practice, as the case may be;
(iv) consultation with the person referred to in Subsection (2);
(v) consultation with the Chief Inspector or the Director,

unless and until such action as is necessary for safety and specified in the instrument is taken and completed; and

(*g*) make such examinations and inquiries as are necessary to ensure that the provisions of this Act, and any directions issued, restrictions imposed or orders made under this Act, are being complied with; and
(*h*) obtain and record statements from witnesses, and appear at or conduct inquiries held regarding accidents occurring in the course of any of the operations referred to in Paragraph (a), and appear at inquests, and call and examine witnesses, and cross-examine witnesses, and conduct or assist in conducting a prosecution for any offence against this Act.

(2) Before exercising any of his powers under Subsection (1), if there is any person present who is or appears to be in charge of the area, structure, vehicle, vessel, aircraft, building, machinery, equipment or

matter or thing in respect of which the power is about to be exercised, the inspector shall produce his certificate referred to in Section 151(2) to that person and to any person to whom he is about to give an order or a direction.
(3) Any person who is aggrieved by a decision, direction or order of an inspector made under this section may appeal in writing to the Chief Inspector who shall, as soon as practicable, hear and dispose of the appeal, but the bringing of the appeal does not affect the operation of the decision, direction or order appealed from pending disposition of the appeal.
(4) On appeal under Subsection (3), the Chief Inspector may–

(*a*) rescind or affirm the decision, direction or order appealed from; or
(*b*) substitute a new decision, direction or order.

(5) In exercising his powers under Subsection (1), an inspector may be accompanied by any person who the inspector believes has special or expert knowledge of any matter being inspected, tested or examined.
(6) A person who is an occupier or person in charge of any building, structure or place, or the person in charge of any vehicle, vessel, aircraft, machinery or equipment referred to in Subsection (1), must provide an inspector with all reasonable facilities and assistance for the effective exercise of the inspector's powers under this section.
Penalty: A fine not exceeding K5,000.00.
(7) A person who–

(*a*) without reasonable excuse, obstructs, molests or hinders an inspector in the exercise of his powers under this section; or
(*b*) knowingly makes a statement or produces a document that is false or misleading in a material particular to an inspector engaged in carrying out his duties and functions under this Act,

is guilty of an offence.
Penalty: A fine not exceeding K5,000.00.

**153. GENERAL PENALTY.**

A person who contravenes or fails to comply with–

(*a*) a provision of this Act applicable to him and for which no other penalty is provided; or
(*b*) a requirement, direction, order or instruction lawfully given or made under this Act, other than a direction under Section 133,

is guilty of an offence.
Penalty: A fine not exceeding K1,000.00.

**154. CONTINUING OFFENCES.**

(1) Where an offence is committed by a person by reason of his failure to comply, within the period specified in a direction given to him under this Act, with the requirements specified in the direction, the offence, for the purposes of Subsection (3), shall be deemed to continue so long as any requirement specified in the direction remains undone, notwithstanding that the period has elapsed.
(2) Where an offence is committed by a person by reason of his failure to comply with a requirement made by this Act, the offence, for the purposes of Subsection (3), shall be deemed to continue so long as that failure continues, notwithstanding that any period within which the requirement was to be complied with has elapsed.
(3) Where, under Subsection (1) or (2), an offence is deemed to continue, the person who committed the offence commits an additional offence against this Act on each day during which the offence is deemed to continue and is liable, on conviction for such an additional offence, to a fine not exceeding K5,000.00.

**155. ORDERS FOR FORFEITURE IN RESPECT OF CERTAIN OFFENCES.**

(1) Where a person is convicted of an offence against this Act a court may, in addition to imposing a fine, make–

(*a*) an order for the forfeiture of any vehicle, aircraft, vessel or equipment used in the commission of the offence; and
(*b*) an order–

(i) for the forfeiture of petroleum recovered, or conveyed through a pipeline, as the case may be, in the course of the commission of the offence; or
(ii) for the payment by that person to the State of an amount equal to the proceeds of the sale of petroleum so recovered or conveyed; or
(iii) for the payment by that person to the State of the value at the wellhead, assessed by the court in respect of the quantity so assessed, of petroleum so recovered or conveyed or for the payment of such a part of that amount as the court, having regard to all the circumstances, thinks fit.

(2) Where the court is satisfied that an order made under Subsection (1)(b)(i) cannot for any reason be enforced, the court may, on the application of the person by whom the proceedings were brought, set aside the order and make an order referred to in Subsection (1)(b)(ii) or (iii).
(3) The court may, before making an order under this section require notice to be given to, and hear, such persons as the court thinks fit.

**156. SERVICE.**

(1) A document required or permitted by this Act to be served on a person, other than the Minister or the Director, shall be deemed to be duly served if sent by registered post addressed to the usual postal address last known to the Director of that person.
(2) A document required or permitted by this Act to be served on the Minister or the Director may be served by registered post addressed to the Director.
(3) Where a document to be served is served by post in accordance with this section, service shall be deemed to have been effected at the time at which the letter would have been delivered in the ordinary course of post.

**156A. PRE-SUBMISSION OF INFORMATION.**

[86]In this Act, where a section provides for information, particulars, proposals, studies, investigations, reports, accounts, documents or other like material to be furnished or provided to an inspector, the Director or the Minister for consideration in connection with that section, such information, particulars, proposals, studies, investigations, reports, accounts, documents or other like material may be submitted in a complete draft form for discussion purposes without prejudice to the rights of the submitting party or the State arising under the relevant section, to assist in the preparation and submission of a complete formal submission of that information, particulars, proposals, studies, investigations, reports, accounts, documents or other like material in due course and in accordance with the Act.

**DIVISION 14. FEES AND ROYALTIES.**

**157. FEES.**

(1) An applicant shall pay a fee of–

(*a*) K10,000.00 at the time of making application for a petroleum prospecting licence or an extension thereof; and
(*b*) K10,000.00 at the time of making application for a petroleum retention licence or an extension thereof; and
(*c*) K50,000.00 at the time of making application for a petroleum development licence or an extension thereof; and
(*d*) K50,000.00 at the time of making application for a pipeline licence or an extension thereof; and
(*e*) K50,000.00 at the time of making application for a petroleum processing facility licence.

(2) A licensee shall pay an annual fee on the anniversary of the licence at the rate of–

(*a*) in the case of a petroleum prospecting licence granted otherwise than by way of extension, K500.00 for each block in the licence area; and
(*b*) in the case of a petroleum prospecting licence granted by way of extension–for each block in the licence area–

(i) K1,000.00 in the first year of the term of extension; and
(ii) K1,500.00 in the second year of the term of the extension; and
(iii) K2,000.00 in the third year of the term of the extension; and
(iv) K3,000.00 in the fourth year of the term of the extension; and
(v) K4,000.00 in the fifth year of the term of the extension; and

(*c*) K30,000.00 in the case of a petroleum retention licence; and
(*d*) K100,000.00 in the case of a petroleum development licence; and
(*e*) in the case of a pipeline licence, the greater of–

(i) K10,000; and
(ii) the lesser of–

(A) K100,000; and
(B) K1,000 multiplied by the number of entire kilometres in the length of the pipeline; and

(*f*) K100,000.00 in the case of a petroleum processing facility licence.

(3) Subject to this Act, an annual fee referred to in Subsection (2) is payable–

(*a*) in the case of the first year of the term of a licence–before the licence is granted; and
(*b*) in the case of each subsequent year of the term of a licence–on the anniversary date of the day the licence took effect.

(4) Where a licence is surrendered or cancelled during a year of its term, no refund shall be made of any part of the annual fee paid for that year.
(5) A person who fails to pay the fees referred to in this section by the date they are payable is guilty of an offence.
Penalty: A fine not exceeding K10,000.00.

**158. DETERMINATION OF VALUE OF PETROLEUM.**

[87]Except as otherwise provided in the Schedule, the Minister shall, from time to time, after considering any information furnished by the tenement holder and any other information that the Minister thinks relevant, determine in accordance with Schedule 1 the value, for the purposes of this Act, of petroleum produced from a licence area–

(*a*) in the case of petroleum intended for export–as at the point of export; or
(*b*) in the case of petroleum not intended for export–as at the point of delivery to a refinery or processing facility in Papua New Guinea; or
(*c*) where a gas agreement applies, at the point specified in the gas agreement.

**159. ROYALTY.**

(1) Subject to Subsection (2), a tenement holder shall pay to the State royalty at a rate of 2.00% of the wellhead value of all petroleum produced from the licence area.
(2)[88] [89]For the purposes of Subsection (1), the wellhead value of any petroleum is the value of the petroleum determined in accordance with Section 158 less any deductions prescribed in the regulations to the extent and in the manner prescribed.

(3)[90] [*Repealed.*]
(4)[91] [92]Notwithstanding the provisions of the *Income Tax Act 1959*, where, in a financial year, in relation to the same licence area, a person has paid–

(*a*) royalty under this section; and
(*b*) development levy under Section 160,

the royalty paid by that person under this section shall be deemed to be income tax paid by that person in respect of its liability to income tax under the *Income Tax Act 1959* on its assessable income from petroleum operations derived from the petroleum project to which the royalty relates.

**160. DEVELOPMENT LEVIES.**

(1)[93] [94]Subject to this section, a petroleum development licensee shall pay in accordance with Section 98 of the *Organic Law on Provincial Governments and Local-level Governments* to the affected Provincial or Local-level Governments of a petroleum project development levies at a rate of 2.00% of the wellhead value of all petroleum product from the licence area, calculated in the same manner as provided for in Section 159.
(2) Subject to Subsection (3), this section shall not apply to production of petroleum from a petroleum development licence where the petroleum development licence was granted prior to the commencement date.
(3) Subsection (2) does not apply to production of petroleum from a petroleum project where a petroleum development licence granted prior to the commencement date is varied after the commencement date to permit the construction and operation of that petroleum project.
(4)[95] [96]Development levies payable under this section shall be payable directly by a petroleum development licensee to a trust fund in accordance with the *Public Finances (Management) Act 1995*, annually in arrears on or before 31 January in the year following the year of production to which the development levy relates.
(5) No other development levies pursuant to Section 98 of the *Organic Law on Provincial Governments and Local-level Governments* shall be applied to petroleum projects.
(6)[97] [98]Development levies which has been paid in accordance with this section shall be disbursed from the trust account only in accordance with an appropriation approved by Parliament.

**161. ASCERTAINING QUANTITY OF PETROLEUM RECOVERED.**

For the purposes of this Act, the quantity of petroleum recovered by a licensee during a period is–

(*a*) the quantity measured during that period by an approved measuring device installed at the wellhead or some other approved place; or
(*b*) where no such measuring device is installed, or the Minister is not satisfied that the quantity of petroleum recovered by the licensee has been properly or accurately measured by such a device–the quantity determined by the Minister as being the quantity so recovered during that period.

**162. PAYMENT OF ROYALTY AND PENALTY FOR LATE PAYMENT.**

(1)[99] [100]Royalty under this Act in respect of petroleum recovered during a royalty period is payable not later than the last day of the next succeeding royalty period except where a gas agreement applies, royalty is payable no later than one month after the last day of the next succeeding royalty period.
(2) Where the amount of royalty under this Act is not paid as provided by Subsection (1), there is payable to the Director by the licensee an additional amount calculated at the rate of % per day on the amount of royalty from time to time remaining unpaid, to be computed from the time when the royalty became payable until it is paid.
(3) An additional amount is not payable under Subsection (2) in respect of any period before the expiration of seven days after the value of the petroleum was determined under Section 158.

**163. REGISTRATION FEES.**

There is payable to the Director in respect of all instruments required to be registered under this Act such fees as are prescribed.

## PART IV. – STATE EQUITY ENTITLEMENT AND PROJECT BENEFITS.

### 164. NO EFFECT ON COMPENSATION ENTITLEMENT.

Nothing contained in this Part affects the entitlement of a person to be compensated pursuant to Section 118.

### 165. STATE EQUITY ENTITLEMENT.

(1) The State has the right (but not the obligation) to acquire, directly or through a nominee, all or any part of a participating interest not exceeding 22.5% in each petroleum project.
(2)[101] [102]The right referred to in Subsection (1) may be exercised by the State–

(*a*) in the case of a petroleum project which is an Orogen option project–

(i) at the time of the grant of the licence or licences pursuant to which the petroleum project is conducted; or
(ii) if the Company has exercised its option under the option agreement in respect of that Orogen option project, at any time prior to the date upon which MRDC is required under the terms of the option agreement to complete the transfer to the Company of a participating interest in the Orogen option project; and

(*b*) in the case of any other petroleum project, at the time of the grant of the licence or licences pursuant to which the petroleum project is conducted.

(3) Subject to Subsection (4), the consideration payable by the State for an acquisition under Subsection (1) shall be a percentage of the unrecouped sunk costs of the vendor attributable to the vendor's interest in the petroleum project, equal to the percentage participating interest in the petroleum project being acquired by the State.
(4)[103] [104]Any interest acquired under Subsection (1) shall be acquired on and any consideration payable under Subsection (3) shall be calculated in accordance with specific terms and conditions contained in an agreement entered into in accordance with Section 183 or 184.
(5) The State shall exercise its right under Subsection (1) in respect of a petroleum project–

(*a*) if the Company has an option under the option agreement in respect of that petroleum project and has exercised that option, to the extent necessary to ensure that MRDC can complete the transfer of a participating interest in the petroleum project to the Company under the option agreement; and
(*b*) to the extent necessary to ensure that any equity benefit required to be granted under Section 167 can be granted in accordance with that section.

(6) Subject to–

(*a*) Section 167; and
(*b*) the terms of the option agreement; and
(*c*) the terms of any written agreement between the State and the vendor of the participating interest in a petroleum project acquired by the State pursuant to the State equity entitlement,

the State or the nominee of the State which acquires a participating interest in a petroleum project in accordance with this section shall be free to deal with that participating interest as it sees fit.

### 166. ACQUISITION OF PARTICIPATING INTEREST BY THE COMPANY.

(1)[105] [106]Notwithstanding any other provision of this Act or the terms of any agreement made by the State,–

(*a*) the Company shall have the right to acquire, and the State or MRDC, as the case may be, shall have the right to transfer to the Company, out of the State equity entitlement, a participating interest in an Orogen option project in accordance with the option agreement; and
(*b*) without limitation–

(i) any petroleum prospecting licence or petroleum retention licence; and
(ii) the terms of any agreement made by the State in relation to a petroleum prospecting licence or petroleum retention licence; and
(iii) any petroleum development licence or pipeline licence or petroleum processing facility licence granted in relation to an Orogen option project or any part thereof,

granted or made after the coming into operation of Parts II and III of the *Mineral Resources Development Company Pty Limited (Privatisation) Act 1996* shall be subject to the exercise of those rights.
(2)[107] [108]The State shall, subject to and in accordance with the option agreement, nominate MRDC or the Company to acquire a participating interest referred to in Subsection (1).

**167. EQUITY BENEFIT.**

(1) Out of the State equity entitlement referred to in Section 165, there is reserved an equity benefit to be dealt with in accordance with this section.
(2) The cost of–

(*a*) acquiring the participating interest in the petroleum project for the purposes of the equity benefit; and
(*b*) development attributable to that participating interest up until the commencement of commercial production of petroleum from that petroleum project,

shall be borne by the State.
(3) Subject to this section and Section 169, the State grants to the project area landowners and the affected Local-level Governments of a petroleum project, if any, an equity benefit in that petroleum project.
(4) The equity benefit granted under this section shall be shared between the project area landowners and affected Local-level Governments of the project in proportions agreed by them in a development agreement, but in default of such agreement in the proportions determined by the Minister, by instrument.
(5) The equity benefit granted under this section shall be held on trust for the grantees in accordance with Section 176.
(6) The participating interest in a petroleum project which comprises the equity benefit granted under this section shall be subject to the obligations applying thereto by law or by agreements to which the licensee is party, save that the State and not the grantee of the benefit shall be responsible for liabilities attributable to that participating interest until the commencement of commercial production of petroleum from that petroleum project.
(7) If in respect of a petroleum project there are no project area landowners or affected Local-level Governments, the State shall not be required to exercise its State equity entitlement to provide an equity benefit, but if it does so it shall be at liberty to grant that equity benefit to such organisations for such public purposes as it sees fit.
(8) This section shall only apply in respect of petroleum projects which commence development subsequent to the commencement date, and shall not affect arrangements in existence on the commencement date in relation to petroleum projects which on the commencement date are in production or have commenced development.

**168. ROYALTY BENEFIT.**

(1) Subject to this section and Section 169, the State grants to the project area landowners, the affected Local-level Governments and the affected Provincial Governments of a petroleum project, if any, a royalty benefit in respect of that petroleum project.
(2) The royalty benefit granted under this section shall be shared between the project area landowners the affected Local-level Governments and the affected Provincial Governments of the project in proportions agreed by them in a development agreement, but in default of such agreement in the proportions determined by the Minister, by instrument.

(3) The royalty benefit granted under this section shall be payable monthly, by the Minister, out of royalties payable to the Minister pursuant to Section 159.
(4) The royalty benefit granted under this section shall be paid to the trustee and held on trust for the grantees in accordance with Section 176.
(5) If in respect of a petroleum project there are no project area landowners or affected Local-level Governments or affected Provincial Governments, no royalty benefit shall be payable, and all royalties received pursuant to Section 159 shall be paid over to consolidated revenue.
(6) This section shall only apply in respect of petroleum projects which commence development pursuant to licences granted subsequent to the commencement date, and shall not affect arrangements in existence on the commencement date in relation to petroleum projects which on the commencement date are in production or have commenced development.

**169. IDENTIFICATION OF LANDOWNER BENEFICIARIES.**

(1) Notwithstanding any other provision of this Act, the persons (other than affected Local-level Governments or affected Provincial Governments) who shall receive the benefits granted by Sections 167 and 168 shall be identified in accordance with this section.
(2)[109] [110]Prior to convening or during a development forum under Section 48, the Minister shall determine, by instrument–

(*a*) the persons (other than affected Local-level Governments or affected Provincial Governments) who shall receive the benefits granted by Sections 167 and 168; and
(*b*) the incorporated land groups or, if permitted in accordance with Section 176(3)(f), any other persons or entities who shall represent and receive the benefit on behalf of the grantees of the benefit.

(3) An instrument under Subsection (2) shall only be valid if also signed by the Director and the Secretary of the Department of Treasury or other National Government Department responsible for financial matters.
(4)[111] [112]In making a determination under Subsection (2), the Minister shall consider any agreements by persons who are or claim to be project area landowners, the decisions of courts of Papua New Guinea as to ownership of land or rights in relation to land in the vicinity of the petroleum project in question, the results of social mapping and landowner identification studies carried out in accordance with this Act, and submissions from affected Local-level Governments or affected Provincial Governments of the petroleum project in question or from any other person claiming an interest or to be affected by the decision of the Minister.
(5) A petroleum development licensee or applicant for a petroleum development licence may, at any time after an application for the grant or variation of a petroleum development licence in respect of a petroleum project, apply to the Minister for a determination under Subsection (2).
(6) Where a licensee or an applicant for a licence applies to the Minister for a determination under Subsection (5), the Minister shall allow a period of 30 days, or such longer period as the Minister may allow, for persons referred to in Subsection (4) to make submissions or in the case of persons claiming to be project area landowners to advise him of agreements reached by them on the determination.
(7) Where a dispute exists as to which persons or incorporated land groups or other entities should be identified to receive benefits in accordance with this section, the Minister may make a determination under Subsection (2) or may direct that monies or other benefits which are the subject of the dispute shall be held in abeyance pending a resolution of that dispute by other means, and where such a direction is given by the Minister the trustee referred to in Section 176 shall hold such monies or other benefits in accordance with that direction.
(8)[113] [114]Where the minister directs that monies or other benefits are to be held in abeyance under Subsection (7) or where the Minister's determination under Subsection (2) is subject to judicial review, the Minister may grant the licence or licences in respect of the petroleum project.
(9)[115] [116]Where the Minister has granted the licence or licences under Subsection (8) and the dispute is resolved the Minister shall make a determination under Subsection (2) and convene a development forum under Section 48.
(10)[117] [118]A ministerial determination made pursuant to the section shall not be reviewable before any court unless an application for review is made within 28 days of the Ministerial determination.

**169A. IDENTIFICATION OF LANDOWNERS BENEFICIARIES AND SHARING OF BENEFITS IN RELATION TO EXISTING PETROLEUM PROJECTS.**

[119](1) If in respect of petroleum projects which on the commencement date are in production or have commenced development, persons, or incorporated land groups or other entities, who should be receiving benefits from such petroleum projects, have not been identified or where a dispute exists as to which persons or incorporated land groups or other entities should be identified to receive such benefits, the Minister may make a determination as to the persons or incorporated land groups or other entities who should receive the benefits arising from such petroleum project.
(2) In making a determination under Subsection (1), the Minister shall consider any agreements by persons who are or claim to be project area landowners, the decisions of courts of Papua New Guinea as to ownership of land or rights in relation to land in the vicinity of the petroleum project in question, the results of social mapping and landowner identification studies that have been carried out in accordance with this Act, and submissions from affected Local-level Governments or affected Provincial Governments of the petroleum project in question or from any other person claiming an interest or to be affected by the decision of the Minister.
(3) Where, in the opinion of the Minister, having considered any agreements by persons who are or claim to be project area landowners, the decisions of the courts of Papua New Guinea as to ownership of land or rights in relation to land in the vicinity of the petroleum project in question, the results of any social mapping and landowner identification studies that have been carried out in accordance with Section 47, some project area landowners have a greater or more substantial occupation or right of occupation of the land referred to in the definition of "project area landowners" or are more adversely impacted by the petroleum project than other project area landowners, the Minister may, by instrument, determine that the sharing amongst project area landowners of equity benefits or royalty benefits in accordance with this section shall favour, on a per capita basis, those project area landowners who have that greater or more substantial occupation or right of occupation or are more adversely impacted by the petroleum project.

**170. SHARING OF BENEFITS AMONGST PROJECT AREA LANDOWNERS.**

(1) Any equity benefit or royalty benefit granted to project area landowners shall be shared amongst project area landowners in accordance with this section.
(2) Equity benefits and royalty benefits granted to project area landowners under this Act shall be shared among project area landowners or groups of project area landowners in proportions to be agreed by them in a development agreement, but in default of such agreement in the proportions determined by the Minister, by instrument.
(3) Where, in the opinion of the Minister, having considered the results of social mapping and landowner identification studies conducted in accordance with Section 47, some project area landowners have a greater or more substantial occupation or right of occupation of the land referred to in the definition of "project area landowners" or are more adversely impacted by the petroleum project that other project area landowners, the Minister may, by instrument, determine that the sharing amongst project area landowners of equity benefits or royalty benefits in accordance with this section shall favour, on a per capita basis, those project area landowners who have that greater or more substantial occupation or right of occupation or are more adversely impacted by the petroleum project.
(4) A trust deed implemented in accordance with Subsections 176(3) shall provide for the distribution of equity benefits and royalty benefits in accordance with this section.

**171. OTHER PROJECT AREA LANDOWNER BENEFITS.**

(1) Subject to Section 174 the State may, in a development agreement, reach agreement with project area landowners to provide and may provide to or for the benefit of project area landowners or the people of the project area or the people of the region, by way of grants out of consolidated revenue or otherwise, such other benefits in addition to those specified in this Part as the State sees fit.
(2) Nothing contained in this Part affects any agreement which might be reached between project area landowners and the developers of a petroleum project as to benefits to be provided or other commitments made to those project area landowners by those developers.

**172. SHARING OF BENEFITS AMONGST AFFECTED LOCAL-LEVEL GOVERNMENTS AND AFFECTED PROVINCIAL GOVERNMENTS.**

(1) If in respect of a petroleum project there is more than one affected Local-level Government, the equity benefit and royalty benefit granted to affected Local-level Governments by this Part shall, unless otherwise

agreed in writing by the affected Local-level Governments and the State, be shared between those affected Local-level Governments in proportion to the number of project area landowners who receive those benefits in respect of that project who reside within the jurisdiction of each affected Local-level Government.
(2) If in respect of a petroleum project there is more than one affected Provincial Government, the royalty benefit granted to affected Local-level Governments by this Part shall, unless otherwise agreed in writing by the affected Local-level Governments and the State, be shared between those affected Provincial Governments in proportion to the number of project area landowners who receive a royalty benefit in respect of that project who reside within the jurisdiction of each affected Provincial Government.

**173. PROJECT GRANTS.**

(1) In addition to the other benefits granted to affected Local-level Governments and affected Provincial Governments under this Part, the State shall make grants to affected Local-level Governments and affected Provincial Governments of a petroleum project in accordance with this section.
(2) The State shall in a development agreement and may in any other agreement agree with the affected Local-level Governments and affected Provincial Governments of a petroleum project upon the amount and nature and timing of grants to be made by the State to those affected Local-level Governments and affected Provincial Governments in relation to the petroleum project.
(3) Grants made in accordance with this section may be in the form of monetary payments or in the form of provision of infrastructure or services or other benefits.
(4) The provision to an affected Local-level Government or an affected Provincial Government of a benefit in the form of infrastructure (or any other benefit) which is funded by the licensee in respect of the petroleum project pursuant to Section 219C of the *Income Tax Act 1959* shall be taken to be a grant made in accordance with this section.
(5) The State may, in addition to grants made to affected Local-level Governments or affected Provincial Governments under this section, make grants to project area landowners or customary owners of land in a petroleum project area.

**174. LIMITATION ON PROJECT BENEFITS.**

(1) The total benefits granted in accordance with this Act to project area landowners and affected Local-level Governments and affected Provincial Governments and any other persons or organisations shall not, when added to other costs incurred by the State in the course of the development or operation of a petroleum project, exceed 20% of the total net benefit to the State from that petroleum project as determined in a cost-benefit analysis under Section 116 of the *Organic Law on Provincial Governments and Local-level Governments*.
(2) No commitment shall be made by the State pursuant to Section 171 or 173 unless the Minister is satisfied that, following the provision of any benefits or grants which might be agreed under those sections, Subsection (1) is complied with.

**175. ADDITIONAL INTERESTS IN PETROLEUM PROJECTS.**

(1) Affected Provincial Governments, affected Local-level Governments and project area landowners of a petroleum project are at liberty to negotiate with a licensee to acquire from the licensee, on freely negotiated commercial terms, a participating interest in a petroleum project, in addition to the participating interest in that project granted under Section 167.
(2) Where an affected Provincial Government or an affected Local-level Government or project area landowners seeks or seek to acquire an additional participating interest in accordance with Subsection (1), the State, through MRDC, shall assist that process by providing, to the extent permitted by law, information and technical advice to the affected Provincial Government, affected Local-level Government or project area landowners, as the case may be.
(3) Nothing contained in this section obliges–

(*a*) a licensee to sell a participating interest in a petroleum project, or an interest in any other asset; or
(*b*) the State to provide or procure finance for an acquisition in accordance with this section or to procure any agreement with a licensee.

**176. PROJECT BENEFITS TRUSTS.**

(1)[120] [121]The equity benefit granted by the State in accordance with Section 167 and royalty benefit granted by the State in accordance with Section 168 to project area landowners, and any additional participating interest in a petroleum project acquired by project area landowners in accordance with Section 175, shall be received and held upon trust for those project area landowners by a corporate trustee which is wholly owned by MRDC.
(2)[122] [123]Where by an act or agreement the State grants to project area landowners or other customary land owners any other benefit in relation to the petroleum project, whether by way of a beneficial interest in a licence or assets attributable to a licence, or payments based on production or profits of the petroleum project, or otherwise, that benefit shall be received and held upon trust for those persons by a corporate trustee which is wholly owned by MRDC.
(3) Where a benefit referred to in Subsection (1) or (2) is held by a trustee upon trust pursuant to Subsection (1) or (2)–

(*a*) the terms of the trust shall be set out in a deed approved by the Minister; and
(*b*) the board of directors of the trustee shall be comprised in the majority by representatives of the State (including the managing director of MRDC) and in the minority by representatives of the grantees of the benefit; and
(*c*) any equity interest or equivalent in a petroleum project held by the trustee shall not without the consent of the State be sold or transferred or charged, mortgaged or otherwise encumbered other than for the purpose of financing the activities of the trustee in that petroleum project or securing its joint venture obligations in that petroleum project; and
(*d*) the trustee and the trust funds and any assets held by the trustee shall be managed by MRDC; and
(*e*) the trustee and MRDC shall enter into a management agreement on terms approved by the Minister which agreement shall govern the management of the trustee and its assets and the amounts charged to the trustee for those management services; and
(*f*) unless otherwise agreed between the State and the grantees of the benefit or prescribed by law, the beneficiaries of the trust shall be incorporated land groups on behalf of the grantees; and
(*g*) where project area landowners entitled to an equity benefit in accordance with this section and who are equally entitled amongst themselves to share in that benefit are represented by more than one incorporated land group (or other representative if permitted in accordance with Paragraph (f)) the incorporated land groups or other representatives shall be allocated the benefit in proportion to the number of project area landowners each represents; and
(*h*) the terms of the trust shall prescribe:

(i) that 30%, or such greater proportion as may be agreed between the State and the project area landowners, of the net income of the trust fund after payment of all costs and expenses shall be held upon trust for future generations of project area landowners; and
(ii) subject to the terms of any agreement between the State and project area landowners in force at the commencement of this section, that 30%, or such greater proportion as may be agreed between the State and the project area landowners, of the net income of the trust fund after payment of all costs and expenses shall be accumulated in investments in accordance with the terms of the trust and, together with the income from those investments, applied by the trustee for the benefit of project area landowners existing during the term of the trust for any one or more of the following purposes:–

(A) the general health, welfare, education and well being of the project area landowners;
(B) the provision or maintenance of community projects in the area of the petroleum project;
(C) such other purpose for the benefit of the project area landowners as is approved by the Minister; and

(*i*)[124] the grantees of the benefit shall be at liberty to share or distribute income received by them from the trust in accordance with any customary arrangements or agreements they have entered into with the customary land owners outside of the area of the petroleum project, but such other customary land owners shall have no entitlement to or claim upon any part of the trust funds.

(4) The equity benefit granted by the State in accordance with Section 167 of this Act to affected Local-level Governments or affected Provincial Governments, and any additional participating interest in a petroleum project acquired by an affected Local-level Government or an affected Provincial Government in accordance with Section 175, shall be received and held upon trust for those grantees by a corporate trustee which is wholly owned by MRDC.

(5) Subject to Subsection (6), where by an act or by agreement the State grants to a Local-level Government or Provincial Government any other benefit in relation to the petroleum project, whether by way of a beneficial interest in a licence or assets attributable to a licence, or payments based on production or profits of the petroleum project, or otherwise, that benefit shall be received and held upon trust for that government by a corporate trustee which is wholly owned by MRDC.
(6) Subsection (5) shall not apply to–

(*a*) monetary grants made by the State to a Local-level Government or Provincial Government; or
(*b*) any interest in buildings or other infrastructure provided to a Local-level Government or Provincial Government where the buildings or infrastructure are not dedicated project facilities of the petroleum project.

(7) Where a benefit referred to in Subsection (4) or (5) is held by a trustee upon trust pursuant to Subsection (4) or (5)–

(*a*) the terms of the trust shall be set out in a deed approved by the Minister; and
(*b*) the board of directors of the trustee shall be comprised in the majority by representatives of the State (including the managing director of MRDC) and in the minority by representatives of that government; and
(*c*) any equity interest or equivalent in a petroleum project held by the trustee shall not without the consent of the State be sold or transferred or charged, mortgaged or otherwise encumbered other than for the purpose of financing the activities of the trustee in that petroleum project or securing its joint venture obligations in that petroleum project; and
(*d*) the trustee and the trust funds and any assets held by the trustee shall be managed by MRDC; and
(*e*) the trustee and MRDC shall enter into a management agreement on terms approved by the Minister which agreement shall govern the management of the trustee and its assets and the amounts charged to the trustee for those management services.

(8)[125] [126]Notwithstanding any other provision of this Act, the royalty and equity benefits granted b ythe State to project area land owners who have been identified as grantees of such benefits in petroleum projects which were at the commencement date of this Act are in production or have commenced development, shall be received and held upon trust for those project area landowners by a corporate trustee which is wholly owned by MRDC in accordance with this section.

**177. BENEFITS WHERE PIPELINE OR PETROLEUM PROCESSING FACILITY NOT PART OF PETROLEUM PROJECT.**

[127]Where a pipeline or petroleum processing facility is constructed otherwise than as part of a petroleum project, customary land owners in the area in which the pipeline or petroleum processing facility is constructed shall be entitled only to such benefits as may be agreed between the licensee of the pipeline or petroleum processing facility and those customary land owners or between that licensee and the State.

**178. EXPENDITURE ON BEHALF OF AFFECTED LOCAL-LEVEL GOVERNMENTS AND AFFECTED PROVINCIAL GOVERNMENTS.**

(1) All grants made in accordance with Section 173, and all monies held on behalf of an affected Local-level Government or affected Provincial Government in accordance with Section 176 and available to be spent by the affected Local-level Government or affected Provincial Government, shall be administered in accordance with this section.
(2)[128] [129]The Minister shall establish, in respect of each petroleum project, an Expenditure Implementation Committee comprising –

(*a*) the Secretary of the Department of National Planning or the department responsible for national planning matters, who shall be the Chairman; and
(*b*) the Director; and
(*c*) the Secretary of the Department of Treasury or the department responsible for national government finances; and
(*d*) the Secretary of the Department of Works and Transport; and
(*e*) the Secretary of the Department of Provincial and Local level Government Affairs; and

(*f*) the Administrator responsible of each affected Provincial Government or District Administrator responsible for an affected Local level Government; and
(*g*) the chief executive of the Operator who shall respect the licensees of the petroleum project,

or their respresentatives.
(3) Expenditure of monies referred to in Subsection (1) by or on behalf of an affected Local-level Government or affected Provincial Government and the implementation of grants referred to in that subsection shall be made only–

(*a*) in accordance with development plans submitted by the relevant Local-level Government or Provincial Government; and
(*b*) in accordance with the approval of the Expenditure Implementation Committee for the petroleum project in question.

(4) The Expenditure Implementation Committee shall be responsible for–

(*a*) monitoring budgets and timetables for construction and implementation of grant and benefit expenditure on behalf of affected Local-level Governments and affected Provincial Governments, and approving such expenditure; and
(*b*) monitoring expenditure made pursuant to Section 219C of the *Income Tax Act 1959* to ensure that project funded pursuant to that section comply with the development plans submitted by the relevant Local-level Government or Provincial Government; and
(*c*) monitoring the program of ongoing projects for expenditure of monies in accordance with this section.

(5) Notwithstanding the provisions of Section 219C of the *Income Tax Act 1959*, no expenditure by a licensee in respect of a petroleum project shall fulfil the requirements of that section unless approved by the Expenditure Implementation Committee of the petroleum project in question.

**179. NATIONAL GAS CORPORATION.**

(1) The Provincial Governments of Papua New Guinea, acting jointly, shall be at liberty to incorporate under the *Companies Act 1997* a company to be called National Gas Corporation Limited.
(2) If National Gas Corporation is formed in accordance with Subsection (1)–

(*a*) each of the Provincial Governments shall be entitled to a shareholding in NGC in accordance with a shareholders' agreement, which they may enter into; and
(*b*) NGC shall act as a corporate trustee for the Provincial Governments or any of them and any project area landowners on whose behalf it holds assets, and it shall hold its assets upon the trusts for which they were acquired and it and its office holders shall be subject to the fiduciary obligations of a trustee in favour of those beneficiaries; and
(*c*) NGC shall have the purpose of managing participating interests of Provincial Governments and project area landowners in gas projects (including downstream processing of natural gas) in Papua New Guinea conducted pursuant to licences granted after the commencement date, whether such participating interests are granted under this Act or acquired on commercial terms; and
(*d*)[130] NGC shall have the legal capacity–

(i) to do all things necessary to implement the purpose referred to in Paragraph (a); and
(ii) to obtain petroleum processing facility licences for processing of natural gas and any permits required for NGC to be a domestic gas operator or a domestic gas supplier or an owner or operator of facilities for the storage or transportation of cylinders containing compressed natural gas or liquefied petroleum gas; and
(iii)[131] to hold and enter into agreements with licensees to acquire by agreement on commercial terms participating interests in gas projects; and
(iv)[132] to acquire by agreement on commercial terms, a participating interest in the Hides petroleum project conducted pursuant to Petroleum Development Licence 1, irrespective of whether the State exercistes its rights under Section 165 or any other law; and
(v)[133] to acquire by agreement or commercial terms processed petroleum including all liquefied petroleum gas; and

(vi)[134] to acquire by agreement by agreement on commercial terms an interest in a gas project at such time as any participant in a gas project wishes to sell such an interest; and
(vii) to borrow money for the purpose of acquiring or developing assets held by it in accordance with this section, and for that purpose to charge its assets; and

(*e*) NGC shall for the purposes of this Part be deemed to be a corporate trustee referred to in Section 176, and the provisions of this Part applying to corporate trustees referred to in Section 176 shall apply to NGC; and
(*f*) NGC shall obtain competent and professional management and shall provide to the Minister fully detailed quarterly reports on all of its activities and half yearly audited financial statements; and
(*g*) NGC shall not engage in any activities other than those referred to in this subsection or activities incidental thereto.

(3) Provincial Governments and project area landowners shall not be liable for the debts of NGC, notwithstanding that they may be a beneficiary of a trust referred to in Subsection (2).
(4) Nothing contained in this section obliges–

(*a*) a licensee to sell a participating interest in a gas project, or an interest in any other property; or
(*b*) the State to provide or procure finance for an acquisition in accordance with this section or to procure any agreement with a licensee.

(5)[135] [136]Notwithstanding in this Section 179 affects, restricts or limits, or will be taken to affect, restrict or limit, in any way, any right or entitlement of any person (regardless of that source of that right or entitlement), including, without limitation, the rights and entitlements of the State under Section 165 and the rights and entitlements of the Company under this Act or the option agreement,

## PART V. – MISCELLANEOUS.

### 180. INSPECTORS NOT TO HAVE ANY INTERESTS IN LICENCES, ETC.

The Minister, the Director, an inspector or an authorized officer appointed under this Act must not hold, or have any interest in, any licence, or hold shares in any company holding, or having any interest in, any licence under this Act.
Penalty: A fine not exceeding K1,000.00 or imprisonment for a term not exceeding two years or both.

### 181. POINTS, ETC., TO BE ASCERTAINED BY REFERENCE TO GEODETIC DATUM.

(1) Where for the purposes of this Act, or for the purpose of an instrument under this Act, it is necessary to determine the position on the surface of the Earth at a point, line or area, that position shall be determined by reference to a spheroid having its centre at the centre of the Earth and a major (equatorial) radius of 6,378,160 m and a flattening of 100/29825 and by reference to the position of the Bevan Rapids (AA 070) Geodetic Station in the Gulf Province of Papua New Guinea.
(2) The Bevan Rapids Geodetic Station shall be taken to be situated at 7 degrees 21 minutes 34.7974 seconds of south latitude and at 145 degrees 15 minutes 52.9878 seconds of east longitude and to have a ground level of 406.30 m above mean sea level.

### 182. REGULATIONS.

(1) The Head of State, acting on advice, may make regulations not inconsistent with this Act, prescribing all matters that by this Act are required or permitted to be prescribed or are necessary or convenient to be prescribed for carrying out or giving effect to this Act or for securing, regulating, controlling or restricting–

(*a*) the exploration for petroleum and the carrying on of operations, and the execution of works, for that purpose; and
(*b*) the recovery of petroleum and the carrying on of operations, and the execution of works, for that purpose; and
(*c*) the construction and operation of pipelines and any of the pipes or facilities referred to in Paragraphs (a) to (d) inclusive of the definition of "pipeline"; and

(*d*)[137] the construction and operation of petroleum processing facilities; and
(*e*)[138] limitation of project benefits granted in accordance with this Act.

(2) Without limiting the generality of Subsection (1), the regulations may–

(*a*) prescribe work practices and safety measures to–

(i) control the flow and prevent the escape of petroleum or water; and
(ii) prevent the escape of water or drilling fluid or the mixture of water or drilling fluid with petroleum or any other matter; and
(iii) prevent damage to petroleum-bearing strata in an area in respect of which a licence is not in force; and
(iv) keep separate each petroleum pool and each source of water discovered in a licence area; and
(v) prevent water or other matter entering a petroleum pool through wells; and
(vi) prevent the pollution of any water-well, spring, stream, river, lake, reservoir, estuary, harbour or area of sea by the escape of petroleum, salt water, drilling fluid, chemical additive or any other waste product or effluent; and

(*b*) prescribe areas where drilling for petroleum is prohibited; and
(*c*) regulate the location and spacing of wells, and for this purpose provide for the establishment and designation of spacing units; and
(*d*) prescribe the methods, equipment and materials to be used in boring, drilling completing, plugging or operating wells; and
(*e*) regulate the construction, erection, maintenance, operation or use of installations or equipment; and
(*f*) prescribe measures to prevent the escape of petroleum or petroleum products or water from a pipeline, water line, flow lines or gathering lines, pumping station, tank station or valve station; and
(*g*) require a licensee to maintain in good condition and repair all structures, equipment and other property used or intended to be used for or in connection with exploration for, or the recovery or conveyance or processing of, petroleum or petroleum products; and
(*h*) provide for the removal of structures, equipment and other property, brought into the country in connection with exploration for, or the recovery or conveyance or processing of, petroleum or petroleum products, that are not used or intended to be used in connection with that exploration, recovery or conveyance or processing; and
(*i*) regulate the pressure maintenance in, or the repressuring of, a petroleum pool and the recycling of petroleum; and
(*j*) regulate the secondary or tertiary recovery of petroleum from a petroleum pool and provide for the methods to be used in such recovery; and
(*k*) regulate the use of wells and the use of the subsurface for the disposal of petroleum, water and other substances produced in association with the exploration for or the recovery of petroleum; and
(*l*) prescribe the rates, or the method of setting the rates, at which petroleum and water may be recovered from any well or petroleum pool; and
(*m*) prescribe the methods to be used for the measurement of petroleum, water and other substances from a well; and
(*n*)[139] regulate or control the tariffs charged by pipeline licensees or petroleum processing licensees and the conditions of use of pipelines or petroleum processing facilities; and
(*o*) prescribe safety standards and provide for the health and safety of persons employed in or in connection with the exploration for or the recovery or conveyance of petroleum; and
(*p*) require licensees to take, preserve and furnish to the Director cores, cuttings and samples from wells and samples of petroleum and water; and
(*q*) require licensees to give to the Director reports, returns and other information; and
(*r*) require a tenement holder to take logs or directional surveys or make other down-hole investigations; and
(*s*) prescribe forms and other documents to be used in the administration of this Act, other than approved forms; and
(*t*) prescribe penalties of fines not exceeding K5,000.00 and default penalties of fines not exceeding K500.00 for offences against the regulations; and
(*u*) prescribe fees; and
(*v*) prescribe work practices and safety measures, including qualifications for persons in control of petroleum processing facilities; and
(*w*) regulate the siting of petroleum processing facilities; and
(*x*) prescribe the methods, equipment and materials to be used in the operation of petroleum processing

facilities; and
(*y*) prescribe the methods, equipment and materials to be used in the operation of domestic utilisation facilities; and
(*z*) regulate the construction, erection, maintenance, operation or use of installations or equipment; and
(*aa*) require a petroleum processing facility licensee to maintain in good condition and repair all structures, equipment and other property used or intended to be used for or in connection with the processing of petroleum; and
(*bb*) provide for the removal of structures, equipment and other property, brought into the country in connection with the processing of petroleum that are not used or intended to be used in connection with that processing; and
(*cc*) prescribe standards for construction, maintenance, calibration and listing of metering and measurement devices; and
(*dd*) prescribe standards for pressure, purity and uniformity of calorific value of petroleum or petroleum products that is, or is intended to be, supplied for domestic utilisation or export; and
(*ee*) prescribe other standards with respect to the properties, condition and composition of petroleum or petroleum products that is, or is intended to be, supplied for domestic utilisation or export; and
(*ff*) prescribe safety standards and provide for the health and safety of persons employed in or in connection with the processing or supply of petroleum or petroleum products for domestic utilisation; and
(*gg*) require petroleum processing facility licensees and domestic gas suppliers who are not petroleum processing facility licensees to give to the Director reports, returns and other information; and
(*hh*) prescribe requirements for access arrangements for third-party use of strategic pipelines or strategic petroleum processing facilities; and
(*ii*) prescribe the manner in which the State acquires interests in petroleum development licences, pipeline licences, and petroleum processing facility licences and the assets that are related to those licences.
(*jj*)[140] prescribe the powers, functions and duties of the Chief Warden and the Wardens; and
(*kk*)[141] prescribe the manner and scope of agreement between a licensee and the State in relation to the co-ordination of a development forum, and the amount of money that a licensee can contribute for purposes of co-ordinating a development forum, and how payment of such monies will be made.

**183. PETROLEUM AGREEMENT.**

[142]The Minister may, on behalf of the State, execute an agreement with a licensee, providing for–

(*a*) the definition of the extent of a particular petroleum project and operations for that petroleum project, for the purposes of this Act and any other law; and
(*b*) the transfer and assignment of State equity interest in that petroleum project to MRDC; and
(*c*) any other matters relating to that petroleum project or those operations, which are agreed to by the parties to such agreement, which, without limiting the generality of the foregoing, may include –

(i) the application of particular provisions of this Act to that petroleum project and those operations; and
(ii) where permitted by other Acts, the application of particular provisions of those other Acts to that petroleum project and those operations,

and such agreement will, once so executed, have effect in accordance with its terms and notwithstanding any other provision of this Act.

**184. GAS AGREEMENT.**

[143]The Minister may, on behalf of the State, execute an agreement with a licensee, providing for–

(*a*) the definition of the extent of a particular gas project and gas operation for the gas project, for the purposes of this Act and any other law; and
(*b*) the transfer and assignment of a State equity interest in that gas project to MRDC; and
(*c*) any other matters relating to that gas project or those operations, which are agreed to by the parties to such agreement, which, without limiting the generality of the foregoing, may include:

(i) the application of particular provisions of this Act to that gas project and those operations; and
(ii) where permitted by other Acts, the application of particular provision of those other Acts to that gas project and those operations,

and such agreement will, once so executed, have effect in accordance with its terms and notwithstanding any other provision of this Act.

**185. AGREEMENTS BY THE STATE.**

[144]Notwithstanding any other provision of this Act, or any other Act (but without limiting Sections 183 or 184) where in a written agreement with a licensee, whether entered into before or after the commencement of this Act, the State agrees that a discretion under this Act or any other Act or any regulations under this Act or any other Act will be exercised in a certain way, or that certain rights or consents or authorisations or licences under this Act or any other Act or any regulation under this Act or any other Act will be granted to the licensee, then that discretion shall be exercised and those rights or consents or authorisations or licences shall be granted in accordance with that written agreement.

**186. REPEAL.**

The following Acts are repealed:–

(*a*) *Petroleum Act* (Chapter 198); and
(*b*) *Petroleum (Amendment) Act* 1987; and
(*c*) *Petroleum (Amendment No. 2) Act* 1987.

**PART VI. – TRANSITIONAL PROVISIONS.**

**187. LICENCES UNDER FORMER ACT.**

(1) Where, on the commencement date–

(*a*) a petroleum prospecting licence issued under Division III.2 of the former Act; or
(*b*) a petroleum retention licence issued under Division III.3B of the former Act; or
(*c*) a petroleum development licence issued under Division III.4 of the former Act,

was in force, that licence shall continue in force and shall be deemed for all purposes under this Act to be a tenement issued under Division III.2, III.4 or III.7 of this Act, as applicable, commencing on the date on which such licence was issued under the former Act.
(2)[145] [146]A licence referred to in Subsection (1) shall be subject–

(*a*) in the case of a petroleum prospecting licence issued under Division III.2 of the former Act, to the conditions referred to in Section 31(2); or
(*b*) in the case of a petroleum retention licence issued under Division III.3B of the former Act, to the conditions referred to in Section 46(a)(ii) and (iii) and to the condition that the licensee will, if he has not already done so, carry out the proposals approved in respect of that licence under Sections 31E(2) or 31J(8) of the former Act; or
(*c*) in the case of a petroleum development licence issued under Division III.4 of the former Act, to the conditions referred to in Section 63(a)(ii) and (iii) and to the condition that the licensee will, if he has not already done so, carry out the proposals approved in respect of that licence under Subsection 35(2) of the former Act,

and, to the extent consistent with this Act, to the conditions to which it was subject immediately prior to the commencement date.

**188. PIPELINE LICENCES UNDER FORMER ACT.**

(1) Where, on the commencement date a pipeline licence issued under Division III.5 of the former Act was in force, that pipeline licence shall continue in force and shall be deemed for all purposes under this Act to be a pipeline licence issued under Division III.9 of this Act, commencing on the date on which such licence was issued under the former Act.
(2) A licence referred to in Subsection (1) shall be subject, to the extent consistent with this Act, to the conditions to which it was subject immediately prior to the commencement date.
(3) Where construction or operation of a pipeline has commenced under a pipeline licence issued under the former Act and in force on the commencement date, the pipeline in question shall for the purposes of this Act be a project pipeline, unless converted to a strategic pipeline under Section 81 or 82.

**189. EXISTING OR PROPOSED PETROLEUM PROCESSING FACILITIES.**

(1) Where prior to the commencement date a person has commenced construction of a petroleum processing facility which was not previously required to be licensed under the former Act, or the State has entered into an agreement with a person which provides for the construction of a petroleum processing facility or has granted to a person a licence or pipeline licence under the former Act which provides for the construction of a petroleum processing facility in circumstances where a separate petroleum processing facility licence is required under this Act, the Minister shall, upon request by that person and without the requirement for a formal application or an application fee, grant to that person a petroleum processing facility licence under this Act on terms consistent with any applicable existing agreement with or licence or pipeline licence granted under the former Act which is held by that person.
(2) Where a person referred to in Subsection (1) requests the Minister to grant a petroleum processing facility licence within six months of the commencement date, until that person is granted a petroleum processing facility licence as required by Subsection (1) the petroleum processing facility in question shall be deemed to be licensed under this Act and the person shall not be in breach of this Act only by reason of the fact that he is continuing to construct or is operating a petroleum processing facility without a petroleum processing facility licence in respect thereof.

**190. REFERENCES TO FORMER ACT, ETC.**

A reference in any law or in any instrument made under or in relation to the former Act or a provision of the former Act shall, on and after the commencement date, unless the context otherwise requires, be read and construed as a reference to this Act or to the corresponding provision of this Act.

**SCHEDULE 1 – DETERMINATION OF VALUE OF PETROLEUM UNDER SECTION 158.**

Sec. 158.

**PART 1. – PRELIMINARY.**

**1. INTERPRETATION OF SCHEDULE.**

In this Schedule–

**"adjusted price"** means net realisable price with any appropriate adjustment for sales margins or commissions;
**"appropriate adjustment"**, in relation to any provision of this Schedule, means such adjustment for the purposes of the provision as is agreed on between the Minister and the licensee, or in default of agreement, as is reasonably determined by the Minister;
**"domestic value"** means a value to be determined under Section 158 for petroleum not intended for export;
**"export value"** means a value to be determined under Section 158 for petroleum intended for export;
**"the guidelines"** means the guidelines adopted under Part 3 of this Schedule;
**"the licensee"** means the holder of the licence from which the petroleum which is to be given a value under Section 158 is produced;
**"relevant contract"** means an agreement for the sale at an arms' length price of petroleum for delivery–

(*a*) by more than one shipment; and
(*b*) over a period of more than three months,

that was in force during the relevant period;
**"the relevant period"**, in relation to the determination of a value for any petroleum, means the period of three months, or such longer period as in special circumstances is agreed on between the Minister and the licensee, before the date as at which the value is to be determined.

**2. "SALE AT ARMS' LENGTH".**

For the purposes of this Schedule, a sale is at arms' length where–

(*a*) the consideration expressed in the agreement for the sale is the sole consideration for the sale; and
(*b*) the terms of the sale are not affected by any commercial relationship (other than the relationship created by the agreement or sale) between the seller and the buyer or any person connected with the buyer; and
(*c*) neither the seller nor any person connected with him has any direct or indirect interest in the subsequent re-sale or disposal of the petroleum or of any product of it,

and no other sale shall be taken to be at arms' length.

**3. "ARMS' LENGTH PRICE".**

(1) In this Schedule, **"arms' length price"**, in relation to a sale or an agreement for the sale of any petroleum, means–

(*a*) where the sale was, or was to be, at arms' length–the sale price; and
(*b*) where the sale was not, or was not to be, at arms' length–the price that, in the opinion of the Minister, the petroleum would have brought had the sale been at arms' length.

(2) Subject to Subsection (3), where in the opinion of the Minister it is not practicable in the circumstances of a particular sale that was not at arms' length, or of a particular agreement for such a sale, to determine what would have been the price referred to in Subsection (1)(b), the sale shall be disregarded for the purposes of any provision of this Schedule that relates to arms' length prices.
(3) For the purposes of any provision of this Schedule that refers to an average price based on sales at arms' length or arms' length prices, a sale that is not a sale at arms' length, or a price that is not an arms' length price, may be taken into account where the Minister is satisfied that a series of sales, or a number of related sales, of which the sale concerned was one, was or were such that the total of the prices paid amounted to, or was the equivalent of, an arms' length price for all the petroleum sold.

**4. COMPARISON OF PETROLEUM.**

Where it is necessary for the purposes of this Schedule to compare–

(*a*) petroleum of different qualities or grades; or
(*b*) prices of–

(i) petroleum of different qualities or grades; or
(ii) petroleum sold, or agreed to be sold, in significantly different quantities,

appropriate adjustments shall be made to reconcile or compensate for the difference.

**5. COMPARISON OF PRICES.**

Where it is necessary for the purposes of this Schedule to compare prices, appropriate adjustments shall be made for differences in any relevant costs, including the terms of any credit allowed and transport costs, in addition to any adjustments to be made in accordance with Schedule Section 4 to enable the prices to be related to comparable qualities, grades or quantities of petroleum.

**PART 2. – NORM VALUES.**

### 6. DETERMINATION OF VALUE BY REFERENCE TO RELEVANT CONTRACTS.

If the Minister is satisfied that there has been a sufficient number of relevant contracts for the sale–

(*a*) where the value to be determined is an export value–of locally produced petroleum for export; or
(*b*) where the value to be determined is a domestic value–of locally produced petroleum for refining or processing in Papua New Guinea,

to allow a norm price to be satisfactorily determined, the export value or the domestic value, as the case may be, shall be determined having regard to the weighted average of the comparable adjusted prices per barrel under the contracts to which Paragraph (a) or (b), as the case may be, relates.

### 7. DETERMINATION OF VALUE IN OTHER CASES.

In a case to which Schedule Section 6 does not apply, the Minister shall determine an export value or a domestic value, as the case requires, that in his opinion represents a fair arms' length price for the petroleum concerned, and in so doing he shall have regard to any appropriate marker price adopted under Schedule Section 9.

## PART 3. – GUIDELINES.

### 8. REGULATIONS AS TO GUIDELINES.

Subject to Section 158 and to this Schedule, the regulations may make provision in respect of the adoption of guidelines to be followed in, and in relation to, the determination of the value of petroleum under that section.

### 9. MARKER PRICES.

(1) The guidelines may adopt or provide for the adoption of marker prices for the purposes of the guidelines and of this Schedule.
(2) In arriving at any decision or opinion, and in making any calculation or estimation, for the purposes of this Schedule the Minister shall, to the extent and in the manner provided in this Schedule and the guidelines, have regard to any appropriate marker price adopted under Subsection (1).

## PART 4. – ARBITRATION.

### 10. REFERENCES TO ARBITRATION.

(1) Subject to Subsection (3), where there is a dispute between the Minister and the licensee as to the value that should, in accordance with this Schedule, be determined for any petroleum, the licensee may, by written notice to the Minister, require that any matter relating to the determination of the value, being a matter of a kind specified in Schedule Section 11, be referred to arbitration.
(2) Where a licensee makes a requirement under Subsection (1), the matter stands referred to arbitration in accordance with the *Arbitration Act*, and pending a decision on the reference, the determination by the Minister stands.
(3) This section does not apply unless the difference between the value determined by the Minister and the value claimed by the licensee exceeds 0.5% of the former.

### 11. MATTERS REFERABLE TO ARBITRATION.

The matters that may be referred to arbitration under Schedule Section 10 are–

(*a*) any question, whether the Minister has had proper regard to the matters to which, under this Schedule or the guidelines, regard is to be had; and
(*b*) any question, whether the Minister has properly followed the guidelines; and

(*c*) any question as to the comparability of petroleum or of sales or prices, or as to the appropriate adjustments to be made in any case; and
(*d*) any question as to the sufficiency, for any purpose of this Schedule or of the guidelines, of a number of sales or contracts; and
(*e*) any question, whether a sale was an arms' length sale, or a price was an arms' length price; and
(*f*) any question, whether an export value or a domestic value determined under Schedule Section 7 represents a fair arms' length price; and
(*g*) any relevant scientific or technical matter, or any relevant factual matter; and
(*h*) any other matter that is prescribed, or that is agreed on by the Minister and the licensee, for the purpose.

Office of Legislative Counsel, PNG

## PNG ENERGY SECTOR - BASIC INFORMATION AND POLOICY DEVELOPMENT[2]

Historical energy balances have been produced for each of the five years 2007-11 as well as forecasts for the period 2012-20. This section presents the historical estimates. Table 2.1 sets out the detailed estimates for 2011 and Table 4.2 summarises the annual estimates for 2007-11. PNG does not currently produce energy balances but it does publish some statistics which can be used to produce annual energy balances. Data has also been collected directly from PNG energy companies.

The format of the International Energy Agency (IEA), who produce energy balances and others statistics for many countries in the world, but not those for the countries in the South Pacific, has been used. Other bodies, such as the Asian Development Bank (ADB), use slightly different formats for energy balances but it is not believed those differences are significant for the study.

| Supply and Consumption | Coal and Peat | Crude Oil | Oil Products | Natural Gas | Nuclear | Hydro | Wind | Solar | Geothermal | Biofuel | Biomass | Electricity | Heat | Total |
|---|---|---|---|---|---|---|---|---|---|---|---|---|---|---|
| Production | | 1,460,000 | | 49,500 | | 104,100 | | | 46,300 | | 1,289,000 | | | 2,948,900 |
| Imports | | 1,708,600 | 300,900 | | | | | | | | | | | 2,009,500 |
| Exports | | -1,460,000 | | | | | | | | | | | | -1,460,000 |
| International Marine Bunkers | | | | | | | | | | | | | | |
| International Aviation Bunkers | | | | | | | | | | | | | | |
| **TPES** | | | **2,009,500** | **49,500** | | **104,100** | | | **46,300** | | **1,289,000** | | | **3,498,400** |
| Transfers | | | | | | | | | | | | | | |
| Statistical Differences | | | | | | | | | | | | | | |
| Electricity Plants | | | -1,438,000 | -49,500 | | -104,100 | | | -46,300 | | | 322,400 | | |
| CHP Plants | | | | | | | | | | | | | | |
| Heat Plants | | | | | | | | | | | | | | |
| Gas Works | | | | | | | | | | | | | | |
| Oil Refineries | | -1,708,600 | | | | | | | | | | | | |
| Coal Transformation | | | | | | | | | | | | | | |
| Energy Industry Own Use | | | | | | | | | | | | | | |
| Losses | | | | | | | | | | | | | | |
| **TFC** | | **0** | **571,500** | **0** | | **0** | | | **0** | | **1,289,000** | **322,400** | | **2,182,900** |
| **Industry** | | | **388,600** | | | | | | | | | **257,900** | | **646,500** |
| **Transport** | | | **134,700** | | | | | | | | | | | **134,700** |
| **Other** | | | **48,200** | | | | | | | | **1,289,000** | **64,500** | | **1,401,700** |
| Residential | | | 5,100 | | | | | | | | 1,289,000 | 31,900 | | 1,326,000 |
| Commercial and Public Services | | | 6,100 | | | | | | | | | 25,700 | | 31,800 |
| Agriculture/Forestry | | | 23,600 | | | | | | | | | 1,200 | | 24,800 |
| Fishing | | | 8,800 | | | | | | | | | 400 | | 9,200 |
| Non-specified | | | 4,600 | | | | | | | | | 5,300 | | 9,900 |

**Table 2.1: Energy balance for Papua New Guinea 2011,tonnes oil equivalent** Source: Experts' estimates

Some years ago the ADB published a detailed report entitled Energy Statistics in Asia and the Pacific 1990-2006 which gave energy balances for PNG and the other countries in the region. The estimates for 2006 appear to be the latest available and have been used as the starting point for the historical calculation estimates. Updated energy supply and demand estimates for the years 2007-2011, have been produced with the assistance of the Secretariat of the Pacific Community (SPC).

[2] Based on research materials of the European Union and the Secretariat of the Pacific Community.

**Table 2.2: Papua New Guinea summary energy balances 2007-11 tonnes oil equivalent**

| | 2007 | 2008 | 2009 | 2010 | 2011 |
|---|---|---|---|---|---|
| **Indigenious Production (TOE)** | | | | | |
| Coal and Peat | | | | | |
| Crude Oil | 2,043,500 | 1,853,200 | 1,695,100 | 1,477,300 | 1,460,000 |
| Oil Products | | | | | |
| Natural Gas | 48,200 | 47,800 | 46,800 | 47,100 | 49,500 |
| Nuclear | | | | | |
| Hydro | 88,100 | 90,100 | 96,500 | 99,200 | 104,100 |
| Wind | | | | | |
| Solar | | | | | |
| Geothermal | 48,800 | 46,100 | 44,500 | 44,100 | 46,300 |
| Biofuel | | | | | |
| Biomass | 1,145,000 | 1,180,000 | 1,215,000 | 1,252,000 | 1,289,000 |
| Electricity | | | | | |
| Heat | | | | | |
| **Total** | **3,373,600** | **3,217,200** | **3,097,900** | **2,919,700** | **2,948,900** |
| **Primary Energy Supply (TOE)** | | | | | |
| Coal and Peat | | | | | |
| Crude Oil | | | | | |
| Oil Products | 1,286,700 | 1,508,700 | 1,639,600 | 1,814,300 | 2,009,500 |
| Natural Gas | 48,200 | 47,800 | 46,800 | 47,100 | 49,500 |
| Nuclear | | | | | |
| Hydro | 88,100 | 90,100 | 96,500 | 99,200 | 104,100 |
| Wind | | | | | |
| Solar | | | | | |
| Geothermal | 48,800 | 46,100 | 44,500 | 44,100 | 46,300 |
| Biofuel | | | | | |
| Biomass | 1,145,000 | 1,180,000 | 1,215,000 | 1,252,000 | 1,289,000 |
| Electricity | | | | | |
| Heat | | | | | |
| **Total** | **2,616,800** | **2,872,700** | **3,042,400** | **3,256,700** | **3,498,400** |
| **Final Energy Consumption (TOE) by sector** | | | | | |
| Industry | 436,000 | 479,100 | 517,400 | 583,800 | 647,500 |
| Transport | 103,900 | 109,400 | 115,200 | 121,200 | 134,700 |
| Other | 1,259,700 | 1,310,000 | 1,344,300 | 1,368,600 | 1,401,700 |
| Residential | 1,197,000 | 1,245,100 | 1,276,400 | 1,297,100 | 1,326,000 |
| Commercial and Public Services | 25,300 | 26,300 | 27,700 | 29,400 | 31,800 |
| Agriculture/Forestry | 22,100 | 22,500 | 23,200 | 24,000 | 24,800 |
| Fishing | 7,800 | 8,200 | 8,500 | 8,900 | 9,200 |
| Non-specified | 7,500 | 7,900 | 8,500 | 9,200 | 9,900 |
| Non-Energy Use | | | | | |
| - of which Petrochemical Feedstocks | | | | | |
| | **1,799,600** | **1,898,500** | **1,976,900** | **2,073,600** | **2,182,900** |
| **by type** | | | | | |
| Coal and Peat | | | | | |
| Crude Oil | | | | | |
| Oil Products | 365,900 | 428,500 | 465,600 | 515,300 | 571,500 |
| Natural Gas | | | | | |
| Biofuel | | | | | |
| Biomass | 1,145,000 | 1,180,000 | 1,215,000 | 1,252,000 | 1,289,000 |
| Electricity | 288,700 | 290,000 | 296,300 | 306,300 | 322,400 |
| Heat | | | | | |
| **Total** | **1,799,600** | **1,898,500** | **1,976,900** | **2,073,600** | **2,182,900** |

Source: Expert's estimates

PNG is unusual in the region because it has its own oil and gas production. The other two countries in the study are 100% dependent on imports of oil products.

Table 2.1 presents estimates of the 2011 energy balances. The two main indicators are TPES and TFC. It is estimated that TPES in PNG in 2011 was just below 3.5 million tonnes oil equivalent (toe). Oil products accounted for 57.4% of that and biomass (primarily wood) 36.8%, with a combined share of 94.2%. The other supply sources – hydro, natural gas and geothermal – accounted for just 5.8% of the total, as illustrated in Figure 2.1.

The oil balances for PNG are complicated, as explained in Section 6. Virtually all the crude oil production is exported, although there is an oil refinery in Port Moresby. However, the refinery mainly uses imported crude to refine its products rather than the domestic production. The crude oil exports are not included in the TPES but are included in the domestic energy production shown in Tables 2.1 and 2.2. Domestic oil production has declined significantly in recent years whilst consumption has continued to increase.

**Figure 2.1: TPES in Papua New Guinea, 2011**

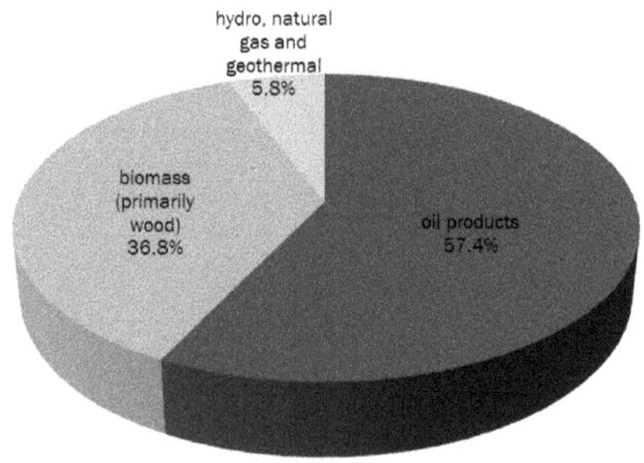


Source: Expert's estimates

It is estimated that consumption of oil products totalled just over 2 million tonnes in 2011. Production was just below 1.5 million tonnes so there was a net import deficit of about -550,000 tonnes or 27% of the consumption.

Most of the population of PNG are dependent on biomass – primarily wood - for their energy needs.

However, it is very difficult to get accurate statistics on biomass consumption. For example, the ADB 2006 energy balances for PNG show no biomass consumption. The SPC have undertaken a detailed analysis of biomass consumption in Vanuatu, which is referred to in the Vanuatu country review that forms part of this study. It refers to data from a 1990 PREA study which is believed to be still relevant. That study gave an estimate of 693,300 biomass consumption in PNG in 1990. An annual growth rate of +3% has been applied to that figure to give the estimates in Tables 2.1 and 2.2. On that basis biomass consumption in PNG in 2011 was just below 1.3 million tonnes. That was 36.8% of the country's TPES energy supply.

It is possible to produce much higher estimates. For example, the SPC estimates for Vanuatu assume average per person consumption of 6.95 kilograms per day for rural households and 4.93 kg per day for urban households, which are equivalent to 2.6 tonnes per year for rural people and 1.8 tonnes for urban people. The recent census in PNG put the country's population at just over 7 million. If it is assumed that about 6 million of those people live in rural areas and 1 million in urban areas and apply the Vanuatu averages, then an estimate as high as 17.4 million tonnes biomass consumption in 2011 may be derived. That is more than ten times greater than the estimate included in Table

**Figure 2.2: Estimates of TFC in Papua New Guinea, 2011**

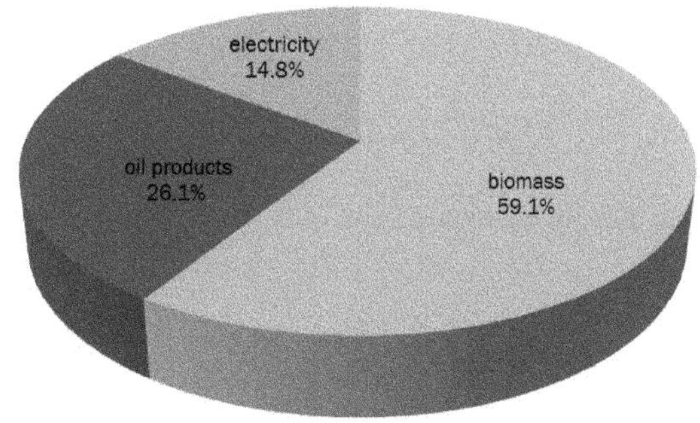


Source: Expert's estimates

These differences require further analysis, which perhaps the SPC can undertake. However, biomass is not an important part of this study insofar as ascertaining the potential for private sector engagement in RE development.

Table 2.1 also sets out the estimates of TFC in 2011. It was just below 2.2 million tonnes, of which biomass accounted for 59.1%, oil products 26.1% and electricity 14.8%, as illustrated in Figure 2.2.

The difference between the 2.2 million tonnes TFC and the 3.5 million tonnes TPES is explained by the conversion of the oil products into electricity.

**Figure 2.3: Breakdown of 2011 consumption in PNG**

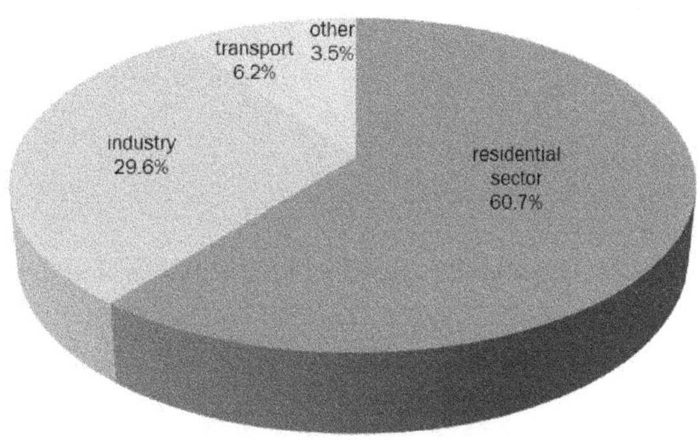


Source: Expert's estimates

Table 2.1 also gives a breakdown of the consumption. It is estimated that the residential sector accounted for 60.7% of the 2011 total, industry 29.6%, transport 6.2% and others 3.5%, as illustrated in Figure 2.3. Most of the residential consumption was biomass, of course, with a much smaller quantity of electricity.

The historical trends 2007-11 are shown in Table 2.2. The country's TPES is estimated to have increased by +35% over the five years, with average annual growth of about +6%. The rate of growth in oil products supply has averaged nearly +10% per year because of the development of the LNG project, various mining projects and an associated boom in the capital Port Moresby. The assumed rate of growth in biomass supply and consumption is +3% per year.

Oil's share of TPES rose from 49.2% in 2007 to 57.4% in 2011. The biomass share fell from 43.8% to 36.8%. The share of the other energy sources – hydro, natural gas and geothermal - also fell from 7.0% to

5.8%. TFC increased by +27% over the five years, with average annual growth of about +5%. Oil consumption increased by +5%, electricity by +22% and biomass by just less than +13%.

## ELECTRICITY SECTOR

### PNG TOTALAverage Rates Across All Systems

Average Consumption Growth 5.0%
Average Loss Level 5.1%
Average Load Factor 83%

| | 2007 | 2008 | 2009 | 2010 | 2011 | 2012 | 2013 |
|---|---|---|---|---|---|---|---|
| Consumption (MWh) | 3,140,100 | 3,163,360 | 3,174,990 | 3,406,468 | 3,585,500 | 3,774,099 | 3,994,576 |
| Gross Generation (MWh) | 3,357,000 | 3,372,000 | 3,445,000 | 3,561,604 | 3,749,046 | 3,946,521 | 4,178,002 |
| Peak Demand (MW) | 426.81 | 430.40 | 444.44 | 462.81 | 487.38 | 555.34 | 588.31 |
| Capacity Requirement (MW) | 426.81 | 430.40 | 444.44 | 462.81 | 487.38 | 564.98 | 598.47 |
| Total Capacity (MW) | 551.06 | 551.06 | 551.06 | 526.06 | 529.56 | 618.56 | 636.56 |
| Total Hydro | 232.20 | 232.20 | 232.20 | 207.20 | 207.20 | 232.20 | 250.20 |
| Total Diesel | 194.06 | 194.06 | 194.06 | 194.06 | 197.56 | 261.56 | 261.56 |
| Total Gas | 72.00 | 72.00 | 72.00 | 72.00 | 72.00 | 72.00 | 72.00 |
| Total Geothermal | 52.80 | 52.80 | 52.80 | 52.80 | 52.80 | 52.80 | 52.80 |
| Total Solar | 0.004 | 0.004 | 0.004 | 0.004 | 0.004 | 0.004 | 0.004 |
| Total Wind | - | - | - | - | - | - | - |
| Total Biomass | - | - | - | - | - | - | - |
| Total Biogas | - | - | - | - | - | - | - |
| Total Coal | - | - | - | - | - | - | - |
| Capacity Balance (MW) | 124.25 | 120.66 | 106.62 | 63.25 | 42.18 | 53.58 | 38.09 |

| | 2014 | 2015 | 2016 | 2017 | 2018 | 2019 | 202 |
|---|---|---|---|---|---|---|---|
| Consumption (MWh) | 4,228,950 | 4,478,170 | 4,728,080 | 4,942,226 | 5,166,287 | 5,400,732 | 5,646,047 |
| Gross Generation (MWh) | 4,424,146 | 4,685,959 | 4,948,209 | 5,171,692 | 5,405,498 | 5,650,112 | 5,906,043 |
| Peak Demand (MW) | 623.39 | 660.74 | 698.03 | 729.29 | 761.99 | 796.18 | 831.95 |
| Capacity Requirement (MW) | 634.11 | 672.05 | 726.50 | 758.82 | 792.61 | 827.95 | 864.89 |
| Total Capacity (MW) | 636.56 | 768.60 | 832.60 | 962.30 | 1,005.80 | 1,105.80 | 1,327.80 |
| Total Hydro | 250.20 | 461.80 | 525.80 | 655.50 | 699.00 | 799.00 | 823.00 |
| Total Diesel | 261.56 | 103.80 | 103.80 | 103.80 | 103.80 | 103.80 | 63.80 |
| Total Gas | 72.00 | 130.00 | 130.00 | 130.00 | 130.00 | 130.00 | 280.00 |
| Total Geothermal | 52.80 | 63.00 | 63.00 | 63.00 | 63.00 | 63.00 | 112.00 |
| Total Solar | 0.004 | 2.000 | 2.000 | 2.000 | 2.000 | 2.000 | 4.0 |
| Total Wind | - | 3.00 | 3.00 | 3.00 | 3.00 | 3.00 | 6.00 |
| Total Biomass | - | 3.00 | 3.00 | 3.00 | 3.00 | 3.00 | 6.00 |
| Total Biogas | - | 2.00 | 2.00 | 2.00 | 2.00 | 2.00 | 3.00 |
| Total Coal | - | - | - | - | - | - | 30.00 |
| Capacity Balance (MW) | 2.45 | 96.55 | 106.10 | 203.48 | 213.19 | 277.86 | 462.91 |

### Current Status of the Electricity Sector

Some headline figures for the sector as a whole for 2012 include:

A total of 618.56 MW generating capacity, of which 232.20 MW (38%) is from hydro sources, 261.556 MW (42%) from diesel, 72 MW (11%) from gas, 52.8 MW (8%) from geothermal and 0.004 MW (less than 1%) from solar.
Electricity generation was 3.445 GWh in 2009.
Electricity consumption was 3,175 GWh in 2009.
Capacity balance was 106 MW in 2009.
Average peak demand was 444 MW in 2009.
12.4% of households have access to electricity.[3]
Tariff for domestic usage is US$0.12/kWh.[4]
Average annual historical electricity consumption growth rate from 2007-2009 was less than 1%.

Only just over 12% of PNG's 6.2 million population has access to electricity services which is one of the lowest electrification rates in the region. As described below, there are some mitigating factors for this situation (i.e. dispersed communities and difficult topographical conditions). However, it is also a reflection of a lack of government investment and commitment, particularly in relation to rural electrification.

In the public sector, the electricity sector is presently dominated by PPL. The Government Power Stations Act (1970) allocated responsibility to Provincial governments for maintaining a number of stand-alone rural generation facilities known as C-centres. However, the majority of these are no longer operational and where they do presently exist they are operated by PPL.

PPL operates through three main interconnected systems as well as nineteen smaller provincial systems and holds the exclusive rights to retail electricity in areas in which it supplies power together with a 10 km surrounding zone. As such, PPL has a monopoly in the transmission sector whilst the generation, distribution and retail sectors are all potentially contestable. PPL generates electricity using both

[3] PNG Development Strategic Plan 2010-2030

[4] PNG Power Ltd Renewable Energy Workshop Brief Presentation, 2005

hydroelectric and thermal generation (generally diesel powered) plant. PPL has a generation capacity of 72 MW for gas, 164.3 MW for hydro, 167.7 MW for diesel generation. The grid systems of Port Moresby, Ramu (Lae, Madang and the Highlands) and Gazelle in East New Britain each feature hydro generation that supplies the bulk of the power produced. Overall, hydro supplies about 57.5% of PPL's requirements. The regional centres that are not connected to these power grids rely on diesel powered thermal generating plant.

There is at present no national grid system due mainly to challenges posed by PNG's difficult topography as well as vast distances between various towns or load centres. PPL nonetheless has plans to interconnect the Ramu and the Port Moresby systems. The project however depends entirely on the planned construction of a trans-island road to link the New Guinea Highlands to Papua.

PPL has bilateral power purchasing arrangements with two IPPs – namely Baiune Hydro in Morobe Province and Kanudi Power Plant in Port Moresby (owned by a Korean company called Hanjung Power Ltd). The company is also a partner in a joint-venture with the Hides petroleum development in relation to a gas fired generation facility. The Kanudi agreement – a 15 year build-operate-transfer (BOT) arrangement signed in 1999 – is nearing the end of its term. Although details of the power purchasing agreement (PPA) are confidential, it is understood that they are quite onerous on PPL which may perhaps reflect the fact that the deal was not subject to a competitive bidding process.

Another significant body that is involved in the electricity industry is Western Power (WP). WP is responsible for operating power plants of up to 10 MW in Western Province and is the only company other than PPL to have been granted (in 2007) energy generation, transmission, distribution and retail licences in Papua New Guinea. . In 2011, WP owned 3,660 kW of capacity (all diesel except for 4 kW of solar) which was used to supply approximately 19,000 customers. WP also recently completed a two-stage project to build small power plants in second tier population centres such as Balimo and Lake Murray and also 31 village communities along the Tutuwe Corridor that connects Ok Menga to Kiunga. A transmission line is being considered to connect Ok Tedi's power plants with Kiunga, at which point some of the community-based diesel plants located in the Tutuwe Corridor may be decommissioned. The goal is to turn WP into a genuine commercial utility and a rollout of prepayment electricity metres in Kiunga is part of this plan.

## ELECTRICITY BALANCE FORECAST

The Base Case forecast (which may also be considered to be a fairly Optimistic Scenario) is based on the assumption that the government will use its best endeavours to achieve the targets it has set out for itself in the Development Strategic Plan 2010-2030. As discuss below, many of the targets set out in this Plan are considered to be over-ambitious. However, in the Base Case scenario it is assumed that reasonable progress is made in achieving many of the proposed capacity additions in order to meet firm (but not a significant) increase in electricity demand as overall economic growth remains firm and new customers (both grid and off-grid) are connected.

More specifically, in the Base Case scenario it is assumed that the average annual growth in demand across the entire country will be 5.0% which is roughly in line with government forecasts of relatively fast growth in the near term and then a slowdown after 2013/14 as the PNG LNG construction phase winds down.

This demand growth assumption is a little more pessimistic than that underling the Power Sector Development Plan (2009) which forecast that Port Moresby demand would grow by 9.87% in 2010 and continue high growth until 2015 before settling down to a 3.8% growth from 2016 – 2030. In the assumptions for the three existing grid networks, relatively strong demand growth (~9%) is forecast for the Port Moresby System from 2012 – 2015 but thereafter historical growth levels (~4%) are expected to resume. Firm demand growth (~ 6%) is expected from 2012 to 2015 for the Ramu system falling to 3.5% thereafter whilst relatively low demand growth (~2%) is forecast from 2012 – 2020 for the Gazelle system. Finally, the Other / Western Province will exhibit consistent, strong growth (~5%) until 2020.

This demand growth will require an additional 400 MW of new capacity by 2020. This capacity development will principally be derived from RE infrastructure development as described in the Sections below but also from some gas fired capacity (also described below). The overall capacity balance remains positive throughout the forecast period thanks to this increase in capacity.

An important assumption underlying the Base Case capacity development forecast is that all schemes presently in the planning stage will come to fruition by 2020. In addition to this, it is expected that at least a portion of the planned "electricity super-corridor" is built, that at least one new gas fired plant is developed in the next three years and that some limited biomass, solar and wind projects will also be developed (in non-grid areas).

These assumptions are somewhat different from the government's DSP which simply assumes that new capacity development will materialise. The result of this difference is that negative electricity balances feature across much of the entire forecast period as capacity development is unable to keep pace with demand.

***PNG Government's DSP 2010 – 2030 – Electricity Forecasts***

| DSP sector goal | Indicator | Source | Baseline | 2015 target | 2020 target | 2025 target | 2030 DSP target |
|---|---|---|---|---|---|---|---|
| All households have access to reliable and affordable energy supply and sufficient power is generated and distributed to meet current and future energy requirements and demands. | Access to electricity | PNG Power, DPE-ADB Power Sector Report | 12.4% of households | 27 % of households | 41% of households | 55% of households | At least 70% of households |
| | Capacity of gas generation | PPL | 70 MW | 130 MW | 280 MW | 390 MW | 390 MW |
| | Capacity of hydro generation | PPL | 215 MW | 430 MW | 580 MW | 750 MW | 1020 MW |
| | Capacity of geothermal generation | DPE | 56 MW | 63 MW | 112 MW | 196 MW | 350 MW |
| | Capacity of solar installations | DPE | 0 MW | 4 MW | 8 MW | 14 MW | 25 MW |
| | Capacity of wind power technologies | DPE | 0 MW | 7 MW | 13 MW | 22 MW | 40 MW |
| | Capacity of biomass generation | DPE | 0 MW | 14 MW | 24 MW | 42 MW | 75 MW |
| | Capacity of biogas generation | DPE | 0 MW | 2 MW | 3 MW | 6 MW | 10 MW |
| | Capacity of diesel- generation | PPL | 160 MW | 100 MW | 60 MW | 40 MW | 30 MW |
| | Capacity of coal-generation | DPE | 0 MW | 30 MW | 30 MW | 30 MW | 30 MW |
| | Existence of a national grid | DPE | NIL | nil | nil | nil | exists |
| | Percentage of households installed with easipay (pre-paid) system | PPL | 4% | 9% | 18% | 23% | >50% |
| Lead government department | Department of Petroleum and Energy (DPE) | | | | | | |

***Base Case – Key Assumptions***

| Criteria | Assumption |
|---|---|
| Consumption | Pt Moresby: 9% to 2015 and then 4% thereafter<br><br>Ramu: 6% from 2012 to 2015 and then 3.5% thereafter<br><br>Gazelle: 2% from 2012 to 2020<br><br>Other / Western province: 5% from 2012 to 2020 |
| Capacity | Hydro –significant capacity additions largely in accordance with the government's 2010 – 2030 DSP.<br><br>Diesel – reasonably significant replacement is forecast (a reduction of approximately 150 MW from 2015)<br><br>Gas – one plant to be developed by 2015 and a second by the end of the forecast period<br><br>Coal – investment as set out in the Strategic Plan<br><br>Other – some limited renewable energy capacity development principally to serve |

| | |
|---|---|
| | demand in off-grid areas |
| Load Factor | As more hydro capacity is built (and to a limited extent replaces some diesel) so the capacity load factor will be expected to fall slightly |
| Energy Efficiency | Expected to be negligible across the forecast period |

A Pessimistic scenario has also been produced. Its assumptions and key outputs are described in an Annex to this Report.

# RENEWABLE ENERGY DEVELOPMENT

PNG's primary source of electricity is derived from hydroelectric schemes which provide a little over 38% of the country's 618 MW of electricity generation capacity. Much of the remainder is provided by diesel generators but there is some small amount of geothermal generation.

The PNG Government's DSP 2010-2030 has set some very ambitious targets for RE development, as set out in the table below. In short, hydroelectric capacity is expected to provide over half and other renewable energy sources (encompassing geothermal, solar, wind, biomass and biofuel) a quarter of total generation capacity (i.e. a total of 75% compared to 54% today).

**Table 5.1: PNG Development Strategic Plan 2010-2030**

| Generation Source | 2012 (MW) | % Total | 2030 (MW) | % Total | Change |
|---|---|---|---|---|---|
| Hydro | 232.20 | 38% | 1,020 | 52% | 344% |
| Gas | 72.00 | 12% | 390 | 20% | 375% |
| Other Renewables | 52.8 | 8% | 500 | 25% | 847% |
| Diesel / Coal | 261.56 | 42% | 70 | 4% | -61% |
| Total | 618.56 | | 1,980 | | 204% |

*Source: PNG Government*

## HYDROELECTRICITY

As indicated above, hydroelectric power already accounts for 38% of PNG's generation capacity portfolio and is expected to account for 52% of total capacity by 2030. This translates into an additional 788 MW of hydro capacity to be developed over a twenty year period which is a major undertaking but definitely feasible.

In general, there is a lot of interest from both the private sector and the donor community (especially the ADB, WB and EIB) to finance large hydro projects. There is also some interest from bilateral donors, predominantly Japan.

Following on from this previous point, there are a number of rehabilitation and new construction activities already underway. The Base Case forecast assumes that 230 MW of new hydro capacity could be installed by the end of 2015. These development activities are discussed in the following paragraphs along with details of other schemes that are less likely to come to fruition.

The Rouna hydropower complex near Port Moresby owned and operated by PPL is being upgraded to increase its capacity to 66 MW (including 1.5 MW at the Sirinumu plant)[5].

[5] ADB Power Sector Development Plan, 2009

In May 2012, PNG's National Executive Council authorised the creation of a special-purpose company within PPL, called Yonki Hydro Limited, to rehabilitate the Yonki power assets and expand the scheme. A three stage programme is envisaged for rehabilitating and expanding the site:

The first step involves the refurbishment and upgrade of Ramu 1 power station (costing K58 million) in order to restore the station to full operational capacity (75 MW) by the end of 2012.

The second stage involves the completion and commissioning of the Toe of Dam (Yonki Toe) generation system. The Toe of Dam project is designed to generate 18 MW of power from water flowing down the dam spillway that would otherwise be wasted. Construction on this project began in 2009 but was suspended because of problems with the contractors. PNG Power has now resumed construction work with support from two Japanese companies — Nippon Koei and Daiho – and expects the plant to be commissioned by the middle of 2013.

The third stage involves the construction of a new powerhouse, Ramu 2, which will generate an additional 60 - 120 MW bringing the total power generated at Yonki from 45 MW to at least 110 MW.

The Naoro Brown Hydro scheme, a 60 MW run of river plant, is presently being developed by PPL in partnership with the World Bank. The development is estimated to cost approximately K600m and is expected to deliver up to 270GWhr/yr annually to the Port Moresby system by the time commercial operation begins (tentatively scheduled for 2017).

Also linked to the Port Moresby system is the proposed Udava Hydro Project. This scheme would have a capacity of 70 MW and is planned to be developed immediately after Naoro Brown is completed (i.e. around 2017 – 2018).

A 50:50 joint venture between Origin Energy and PNG Sustainable Development Program Ltd is undertaking a feasibility study to investigate the potential of developing a hydroelectric plant on the Purari River in Gulf Province (also known as the "Wabo" scheme). Under the plan, electricity from the project (which is estimated to have a potential capacity of 1,800 MW and be completed in 2018/19) would be used to power villages in PNG (potentially up to 600 MW) and the remainder would be transmitted to Australia via Weipa to join the national electricity grid at Townsville. This project has been mooted for over thirty years and remains highly unlikely to come to fruition not least because of the need to construct a 250 km underwater cable from Wabo to Weipa in Queensland and a further 1,100 km HV link from Weipa to Townsville and the landowner issues that would need to be overcome.

A 120 MW hydro scheme is being considered being developed by Talisman Energy in the Southern Highlands.

Some other, smaller schemes that are presently in planning stage include: Gowar (21.6MW); Mongi (69.7MW); Bulum (43.5MW).

## SOLAR

PNG Government's DSP 2010-2030 forecasts that installed solar capacity will increase from 0 MW in 2010 to 30 MW by 2030. The Base Case forecast is not quite so optimistic – some 4 MW by the end of 2020 – because the vast majority of these schemes will be small scale which translates into many thousands of installations that will be logistically (and financially) challenging for the purchasers.

Being practically on the equator, PNG is in a favourable geographical location for year-round solar energy applications. Average insolation in most parts of the country is in the range of 400-800 W/m2, with mean sunshine ranging from 4.5 to 8 hours a day. On a regional basis, the Southern, Momase and Islands Regions are estimated to have a mean annual sunshine duration of more than 2000 hours while the Highlands Region has durations of less than 1500 hours.

The Pacific Islands Greenhouse Gas Abatement through Renewable Energy Project (PIGGAREP) did engage in some solar development activities funded through the Government of Italy and the PIC Cooperation Programme. These proposals included:

Baiteta solar PV project (Madang Province).

Buakap solar PV project (Huon, Morobe).

Bago solar PV project (Pomio, ENB).

It is not clear whether or not these projects were successful. The fact that very few PV installations appear to have been installed in the country would suggest not. This, presumably, is a consequence of their relatively high cost and the difficulties associated with supplying and installing solar panels to rural regions. One might expect, however, that the infrastructure supply problem will improve over time particularly as solar component prices fall. The 30 MW target, therefore, appears potentially achievable.

## BIOFUEL AND BIOMASS

PNG Government's DSP 2010-2030 forecasts that biofuel capacity will increase from 0 MW to 10 MW and biomass capacity will increase from 0 MW to 75 MW between 2010 and 2030. The forecast total for the two categories is 27 MW by the end of 2020 – as discussed below there is potential for more capacity but experience to date suggests that take-up will be slow

There are certainly multiple potential applications for biofuel and biomass in PNG including:

Forestry waste material.

Agricultural waste from the final processing of crops such as coffee husks.

Large-scale biogas production from pig farms.

Cassava, sago palm and nipa palm for fuel alcohol.

Coconut oil.

Again, within the context of the aforementioned PIGGAREP, PNG Sustainable Energy Ltd (PNGSEL) was reportedly looking to use straight coconut oil/biodiesel to provide power supply to remote rural communities where the cost of petroleum diesel is very high. Specifically, the Pomio Coconut and Biodiesel Rural Electrification Project sought to utilise coconuts that had been left unattended because of the high cost of transport. The aim was to promote coconut tree rehabilitation and to develop a local market for coconut oil. This would grow the local economy as well as improve education and health programs through the availability of power supply.

PNGSEL was also involved in implementing a trial bio-diesel project at Aroma. This trial involved the use of small scale biofuel production to provide power to 480 people (80 households). Under the model, PNGSEL would provide a local coconut plantation owner with oil extraction machinery and arrange a purchase agreement of buy straight coconut oil (SCO) at a set price. SCO will be used to power the adjacent villages.

Other biofuel trialling schemes are also underway. For example, Innovative Agro Industry Ltd (an Israeli company) in partnership with SDPPNG has produced a short business plan for Jatropha bean oil development in Balimo.

However, the development targets are relatively ambitious objectives, particularly in regards to biomass, because such generators are typically small scale and also most suited for rural electrification purposes.

Reaching 75 MW of such capacity, therefore, requires a large number of such facilities to be developed. Consequently, the Base Case forecast is for just 9 MW to be developed.

## GEOTHERMAL

PNG Government's DSP 2010-2030 forecasts that geothermal capacity will increase from 52.8 MW in 2010 to 112 MW by 2020 and 350 MW by 2030. The Base Case forecast for 2020 matches the DSP target as it implies the construction of perhaps one new plant in 2015 with a capacity of 10 MW and another new plant in 2020 with a capacity of 49 MW.

The country's only existing geothermal facility is owned and operated by Lihir Gold Ltd. to support its mine operations. Other companies are reportedly looking to develop geothermal resources. For example, a company called Reykjavik Geothermal has apparently completed desk studies covering Kairiru Island, Talasea, Rabaul, Fergusson Island and Madilogo and have commenced surface exploration activities in Rabaul. Another firm, Bismarck Energy, is looking at a site near Lae. However, such investment is high risk in and of itself but the problems are compounded if there is no major anchor customer committed to off-take the bulk of the electricity supply and if third party access to SIEA's grid network is required. Furthermore, the absence of geothermal sector legislation in PNG produces a very uncertain development environment.

## WIND

PNG Government's DSP 2010-2030 forecasts that wind capacity will increase from 0 MW in 2010 to 40 MW by 2030. The Base Case forecast is for just 6 MW by the end of 2020 (and even this is rather optimistic) because no significant wind capacity exists today which suggests that there are significant barriers to take-up.

An SPREP study conducted in 2004 indicated that the annual average power generation potential in PNG could be up to 2,600 kWh/kW of efficiently installed capacity. The potential sites for wind power generation are Manus, Central, Western, Milne Bay, New Ireland and NCD with high potential, whereas medium potential sites include North Solomons, Gulf, East New Britain, Morobe and Oro.

PNGSEL is also reportedly interested in investigating the potential for wind power generation in Hula Peninsula. This would aim to cater for the local population of approximately 11,970 people (1,855 households). Load is estimated at 820kW or 3.5 GWh/a and would entail installing around 900kW of wind capacity and a similar amount of diesel generation in a hybrid setup.

However, with the exception of this one project, no other feasibility studies relating to the development of commercial scale wind farms are evident which suggest that the DSP capacity target may be a little ambitious.

## HYDROCARBON SECTOR

PNG is unusual within the context of this study as it has significant fossil fuel reserves and gas resources in particular. The upstream energy sector in PNG is dominated by several, large, private energy companies including ExxonMobil and Oil Search. It is reported that other 'oil majors' such as Shell are also interested in entering the industry. However, the incentives / barriers associated with market entry by such private entities are of limited interest to this study simply because these corporations are of such size and influence that they can easily influence policy directly.

One area of significance, however, relates to how the country's gas resources are being utilised. Significant quantities of gas reserves mean that there is also potential for gas-fired Independent Power Producer (IPPs) to be developed. Gas fired generation is potentially attractive for several reasons – the gas can easily replace imported diesel fuel[6], gas is a cleaner fossil fuel than diesel and the resulting diversity of supply is

[6] Developers tend to prefer thermal plants over large scale hydro because hydro construction costs are 150-200% higher than thermal and hydro is riskier from both a technical point of view and because of higher soft costs (e.g. land access issues, settlement relocation, etc.).

valuable in dry years when hydro capacity is impacted. Two further benefits are that gas fired power plants are reasonably quick and simple to construct and have a relatively small footprint (unlike hydro power) which means they should also be easier to develop.

It is perhaps for these reasons that the PNG Government's DSP 2010-2030 forecasts that gas generation capacity will increase from 72 MW today to 390 MW by 2030.

However, gas fired IPP development depends on there being sufficient quantities of fuel to be sourced. For the time being all the gas being extracted by ExxonMobil is apparently earmarked for export. As discussed earlier, the absence of any significant DMO associated with gas field development means that until such time as alternative gas resources become available (e.g. through successful exploration and extraction by other energy firms such as InterOil and Talisman Energy) then the potential for gas fired capacity development appears limited.

If one assumes that gas does become available, then a number of alternative models may be adopted for utilising the supply for electricity generation purposes. These include:

Shipping LNG to load centres and using re-gasification barges to send gas to the generation plant (as practised in Norway and Singapore and planned for Indonesia).

A power generator could potentially be constructed near to a gas field and then the power transmitted to load centres (e.g. Lae or Madang). Alternatively a gas plant could be constructed near the LNG terminal and the electricity transmitted to Port Moresby.

The gas could be piped to a power generator located near a load centre.

Irrespective of the approach, proximity to a load centre is clearly important and locating near a mining operation (e.g. Bougainville, Newcress, Wafe near Lei) is a particularly attractive concept because mines tend to be better customers than government which reduces the off-take risk for developers.

The Government's DSP 2010-2030 also forecasts that there will be some 30 MW of new coal fired capacity by 2015. This development has been included in the Base Case forecast as it represents just one relatively small scale plant. However, there are some doubts as to whether this facility will indeed materialise by 2015 (if at all).

# ENERGY POLICIES OVERVIEW

The Government via the Department for National Planning and Monitoring recently produced:

Development Strategic Plan 2010-30.

Medium Term Development Plan 2011-15.

Both of these reports have sections on the energy sector. The MTDP is intended to be the first of four rolling plans to implement the longer term DSP.

The plans identify Energy Development – and electricity in particular – as a Key Sector and Petroleum as an Economic Sector.

The PNG government's main policy goal for the oil / gas sector is to "build a world leading petroleum industry that maximises benefits to PNG and landowners, minimises impacts on the environment and social welfare and provides PNG with energy security."

The MTDP states that "achieving the goal for petroleum requires a strengthening of the state institutions responsible for policy making, administration and enforcement of regulations within the first MTDP. An important strategy is to have an efficient and effective delivery mechanism established to achieve the targets."

Those targets include:

Maintaining oil production at or above the 2009 level.

Three LNG plants by 2030 and one petrochemical plant.

85+ petroleum licences in 2020 and 120+ in 2030, compared with 75 in 2009.

The Government's policies for the oil and gas industry are discussed in more detail in Annexes to this Report.

Considerably more policy attention and focus is placed on the electricity sector (as discussed below). The MTDP states that "electricity is a crucial input to production and modern society cannot function without it. Electricity is essential for improving living standards by supporting economic growth and providing access to technology and services that would not otherwise be available. Approximately 88% of the population do not have access to electricity and the progress in providing electricity to rural PNG has been slow. In some cases the level of electricity services has been deteriorating because of insufficient funds for maintenance."

**POLICY FRAMEWORK**

The DSP forms the heart of PNG's policy framework, particularly with regards to (renewable) electricity infrastructure development. Specific development targets to be achieved by 2030 have been set (as presented in the table below) and a range of relevant policies are being drafted or amended.

| Key indicators | Baseline information | 2030 target / objective |
|---|---|---|
| Access to electricity | 12.4% of households | At least 70% of households |
| Gas, hydro and other renewable generation capacity | Gas: 72 MW Hydro: 232 MW Other: 53 MW | Gas: 390 MW Hydro: 1,020 MW Other renewables: 500 MW |
| Diesel and coal generation capacity | 158 MW grid connected diesel generation | Less than 40 MW capacity diesel generation and 30 MW coal generation |
| National grid | Does not exist | All major towns and cities to be in the national grid which will feed off an electricity super-corridor |
| Easipay domestic customers (prepaid power) | 4% of households (51,000 households) | Most households have access to Easipay |

Of central importance to this plan is the development of an electricity super-corridor that passes through areas where electricity can be generated at lowest cost with a national grid feeding off it and transmission lines passing through each of the economic corridors. This will allow the towns, cities and rural economies to access electricity where it can be generated at lowest cost. It also allows electricity to be allocated efficiently across the country and even allows the possibility of interconnection to a regional grid where electricity can be exported. However, building this super-corridor will incur significant cost and is expected to rely heavily on private sector participation through public private partnerships. This applies both to the construction of transmission lines and to the building of electricity generation capacity.

Further to the previous point, there are a number of important pieces of legislation and sector specific policy documents that will impact upon energy sector infrastructure development and the role the private sector is expected to play within this framework. The most important of these are described in the paragraphs below.

The government's MTDP 2011 – 2015 represents the first of four steps in realising the ambitions of the 2010-2030 DSP. Key elements relating to energy sector development during this initial period include:

Conducting a feasibility study for the development of a national grid. While this study is underway, major maintenance work will be undertaken on the existing regional grids — the Port Moresby Rouna grid, the Ramu grid and the Gazelle grid. Priority will be give to Rouna, followed by Ramu and then Gazelle. The maintenance work will help prepare the grids for national connection.

Pending the outcome of the feasibility study and available resources, work may commence on the national interconnection in the first MTDP, but will otherwise commence in the second MTDP period.

The viability of the national grid will be boosted with the prospect of exporting electricity, particularly to Australia. Planning for export will commence during the first MTDP.

Comprehensive analysis of the cost effectiveness of various alternative sources of power will take place during the first MTDP. This analysis will then form the basis for investment planning in generation and distribution capacity. The emphasis will be establishing hydroelectric, geothermal and other renewable energy technologies to replace diesel. For the transport sector, biofuel will be assessed as a low cost alternative to diesel.

Inefficiencies in the electricity systems will also be addressed in the first MTDP. In particular, 50% of technical losses in electricity systems will be rectified and a framework will be established for eradicating non-technical losses.

The tables below (copied from the MTDP 2011–2015 document) sets out how PNG Government's Development Strategic Plan 2010-2030 relating to the energy sector is expected to be accomplished over the course of four MTDPs. Highlights of this plan include:

Development of multiple forms of renewable energy including wind, solar, biomass and biofuel none of which exist today.

Considerable engagement by the private sector both in relation to IPP developments feeding into the national grid and in off-grid locations.

The government undertaking investment in rural electrification where it is not deemed commercially viable.

By 2015, the following will have been achieved:

200 rural schools and 200 rural health posts will have been electrified through renewable energy systems.

130 MW of gas fired generation capacity will be installed.

430 MW of hydroelectric generation capacity will be installed.

90 MW of other renewable energy generation capacity will be installed.

It is perhaps telling that the DSP and MTDP plans for the energy sector were finalised and published in advance of the country's National Energy Policy (NEP), Electricity Industry Policy (EIP) and Rural Electrification Policy (REP). Of these documents only the EIP document has been finalised. The other two Reports remain in draft form.

The draft NEP covers indigenous energy resources in PNG that includes oil, gas, hydropower and other renewable. The stated economic agenda in the NEP encompasses increasing technical and financial development assistance from international and domestic development partners including the private sector, promoting corporatisation and commercialisation, expanding private sector participation, and establishing and enabling as well a competitive environment as possible for the introduction of IPPs. The principles outlined for achieving the proposed agenda include promoting adequate, safe, reliable, and affordable supplies of oil, gas and other non-renewable energy sources, ensuring that all sectors of the economy have access to adequate, safe, reliable and affordable electricity supplies, promoting a ten percent renewable energy target, ensuring cost effective and wise utilisation of energy in national development, and encouraging involvement of the private sector in the development and provision of energy services. In order to guide the development of energy sector as per the outlined principles, the policy spells out a multitude of strategies.

The EIP (published in 2012) is focused on improving the reliability, accessibility and affordability of electricity services to the majority of PNG's population. The EIP is significant because it is the first of the energy sector specific policy documents to have been published and, as such, it should contain some specific linkages to the DSP and MTDP plans. In actual fact it does not explicitly do this. Rather it proposes the following:

Establishing an EMC, possibly in 2012, that will be responsible for the coordinated planning of all new electricity infrastructure development. The EMC will have considerable power and influence over the electricity sector as it will review and select new developments. Given that the majority of electricity sector infrastructure development is expected to be financed and implemented by the private sector (perhaps under some form of PPP arrangement), the EMC is expected to be the principal counterparty in negotiating such development. The creation of the EMC is, therefore, potentially very positive if decision making is better coordinated and development momentum created. However, given that the EMC will include among its members a variety of sectoral and policy representatives, there is also the possibility that the EMC will be hamstrung by countervailing political interests.

The EIP proposes several models for competition based on three market segments. These are: PPL exclusive supply areas (where it operates grid networks as well as a 10km zone surrounding these networks), large loads (defined as >= 10 MW) and small loads (< 10 MW) located outside of PPL's exclusive area (and most located in rural areas.

Within PPL's exclusive zone, IPPs can choose to sign bilateral PPA contracts incorporating feed-in-tariffs with PPL or may enter into private contracts with large loads (> 10 MW) utilising PPL's network (as necessary). This proposal for third party supply to customers is potentially an important facilitating step to encourage IPP development. However, it is contingent on establishing a credible regime of third party access rules, technical codes and charges.

An ETF is to be established (funded from the national budget) to provide capital expenditure subsidies for small load (< 10 MW) developments. The electricity tariff for such subsidised projects will be subject to a price cap determined by the ICCC. Again, the ETF is potentially a good concept but the challenge will be in making sufficient funding available and accessible.

Tax incentives (e.g. accelerated / flexible depreciation, income tax exemptions) may be made available to developers although these policies have yet to be finalised.

Competitive tendering will be utilised for all new projects. PPL will be entitled to bid for projects, which is positive in the sense that it is an important and experienced player in the sector. However, the presence of an incumbent party in the bidding process could potentially cause distortion if the company is able to exploit economic advantages or political links. This dilemma could possible lead to the crowding out of private sector interests and thus impede development.

Technical regulation for the electricity sector is to be handed over to the Department of Energy (DoE) whilst economic regulation responsibilities will remain with the ICCC. There is potentially a major conflict here as, clearly, there are strong linkages and overlaps between the two forms of regulation. That said, the ICCC has been delegating this role to the DoE for some time already and so this move simply formalises the arrangement.

The Draft REP focuses on establishing mechanisms for the scaling-up of rural electrification through the development of renewable energy resources with the objective of enhancing the living standards of the rural population through the sustainable provision of electricity. In a background note to the REP, the availability of renewable energy resources in the country, such as solar, hydro, wind, marine, biomass, geothermal and bio energy are identified. The REP seeks to capitalise upon the availability of these resources to enhance the livelihood of the rural population. Chapter One of the draft REP provides an overview of the rural electrification with a note on the history and performance of C Centres and the current status of rural electrification services encompassing PPL's three hydro grid networks in Rouna, Ramu and Gazelle. The REP also sets out grid extension options and the linking of RE policy with other sectoral development policies promulgated by the PNG government.

A Geothermal Policy document is presently was ready by late 2012.

Key pieces of legislation that impact upon the energy sector include:

Electricity Supply (Government Power Stations) Act (amended in 2006) which deals with powers of the Minister for Petroleum and Energy for generation, supply and extension of electricity from power facilities built with government funds.

Electricity Industry Act (2002) that specifies the functions and powers of PPL.

Independent Public Business Corporation Act (2002) that governs the arrangement under which the government holds all shares on PPL.

Independent Consumer and Competition Act (2000) that establishes the regulation regime for the electricity and petroleum sectors.

Environment Act (2000) that compels project developers to conduct detailed studies (biological, social and cultural) of the environmental implication of proposed development projects with the finding presented to the Minister for Environment for public scrutiny and debate. The final decision regarding the commencement of any development project lies with the State through the National Executive Council (NEC).

Organic Law on Provincial Government and Local Level Government Law (1995) which grants authority to 19 provincial and 299 local governments town, manage and regulate their local electricity operations.

Public Finance (Management) Act (1995) sets out rules relating to the state financing of electricity projects.

Oil & Gas Act (1998) that governs the exploration for as well as the production, processing and transportation of petroleum (including oil and gas) in PNG, including the offshore area.

The Land Act (1996) that sets out the procedures for the State to attain customary land for public purposes. This includes the State acquiring land by agreement with landowners and, under some circumstances, for the Minister for Lands to make compulsory purchase when land is required for a public purpose as defined in the Act.

Land Disputes Settlement Act (2000) sets out the legal process for the resolution of disputes involving customary land and provides for a land disputes committee to be established at local, district or provincial level to mediate grievances on land issues.

Lands Groups Incorporation Act (1974) was developed in recognition of the need for indigenous peoples to participate in the formal economy whilst at the same time protecting their customary land interests. A customary group can register with the Register of Incorporated Land Group and, once registered, the rights and liabilities of the customary group become the rights and liabilities of the Incorporated Land Group (ILG).

The ILG then becomes the representative of the tribe in the formal legal system and is able to enter into agreements and make decisions on behalf of the customary group.

Through funding from the ADB, a PPP Policy was developed in 2010 for PNG and efforts are being made to create a PPP Unit. However, there is concern over insufficient treasury resources to man both the Unit and undertake other structural policy activities. This factor, combined with the energy sector-specific PPP initiatives being undertaken (as described above), is likely to mean that a PPP Unit, if one should be established, is unlikely to have much influence over private sector engagement in the energy sector.

The International Finance Institutions (IFIs) play (and have played) an important role in PNG's energy sector development plans. Three of the region's main donors – the ADB, World Bank (WB) and Japan International cooperation Agency (JICA) – are all engaged in some important energy sector development projects. These include:

World Bank – Rural Electricity Policy and Rural Strategy Plan. The project expected to commence in 2012.

World Bank – National Electrification Rollout Plan. To commence in late 2012.

ADB – PEEP Phase 1 is completed and Phase 2 is underway.

ADB – Town Electrification Programme. Three projects are underway (two hydro schemes in Bougainville and Northern Province and one transmission project in Kimbe). Two further projects to come.

JICA – Funding of the electricity transmission link from Port Moresby to Lae.

## OTHER POLICY ISSUES

**Domestic Market Obligations.**

There are reportedly some limited DMOs associated with gas development and, specifically, the allocation of some extracted gas for electricity generation purposes. However, all such DMOs are apparently utilised through self-generation activities suggesting they are very limited. The application (or not) of DMOs is an important government policy decision. There is obviously a trade-off between permitting gas companies to export as much of their production as possible with the government benefitting from royalties and duties applied to such sales versus requiring these same gas companies to allocate at least some portion of its gas sales for domestic generation purposes. This allocation could be made available just to PPL or, ideally, to any eligible generator. The gas sales price need not be discounted or subsidised (although this would be another government policy decision) but it would be expected to be less than (or equal to) the export sales price and would be expected to be below the imported diesel price. The fact that such DMOs do not presently exist in any significant form suggests that the government's priority is not to promote energy security but to maximise its income from gas export sales.

**Strategic Plan viability.**

Whilst the PNG government should be applauded for developing its ambitious energy sector development plan, many of its goals and objectives are unlikely to be realised. For example, gas fired generation capacity is expected to reach 130 MW (an additional 60 MW of capacity) by 2015 but there is no domestic gas presently available to fuel such plants. This suggests that either more gas will have to be imported or the plans will be delayed. Similarly, seven IPPs (two linked to the grid and five to supply off-grid local loads) are expected to be operational by 2015 but, as far as is known, no such projects are presently underway which makes it unlikely that the target will be met. Lastly, a feed-in tariff and network access regime is also supposed to be established by 2015 (and such arrangements will be necessary to deal with the new IPPs) and work has yet to start on this task as well.

**Land ownership.**

As across much of the region, land ownership and access problems act as a major deterrent to development. To its credit, the PNG government has proposed ways of trying to deal with the issue. Specifically, it is proposing to "develop a framework for landowner participation as private equity partners" and also to "encourage the employment of landowner companies in the development and construction phase by acting as preferred providers of services." Both appear to be sensible strategies. The question is whether they will be successful particularly as the country attempts to scale up its hydroelectric capacity.

**Energy demand**.

There is an inherent trade-off between the economic motivation to construct large scale generation facilities in order to benefit from the economies of scale that ensue and the problem that, with the exception of a few urban communities, there is insufficient demand to warrant such investment. Most commercial and domestic loads are insufficient to warrant major generation investment. The possible exception are hotels and tourist resorts but even here, increasing demand may potentially be offset by reduced demand from energy efficiency initiatives (e.g. installing more efficient air conditioning units).

The ideal solution is for larger scale power development to be anchored by an industrial or large commercial enterprise such as a mine, canning facility, marina development, etc. When such businesses are located near to population centres then a potentially opportune mix of a guaranteed minimum off-take from the generation facility is combined with service provision to smaller commercial and residential customers. However, in many instances (especially in the case of mines), these potential anchor tenants are located far from other load centres. The only solution under these circumstances is for multiple small scale, distributed generation facilities to be constructed which is costly and therefore unaffordable for many of the customers who wish to be served. In off-grid rural areas, stand alone household solar systems are probably the best option as each household can manage its own energy supply, there are no land issues to deal with and benefits in the form of reduced kerosene / wood usage can be enjoyed.

**Subsidies**.

Following on from the previous point, if affordable energy services are to be provided to (rural) communities then subsidies will be required and it is the PNG government who will have to fund these directly or through financial support to a third party. These subsidies will almost certainly take the form of paying some (or all) of the upfront capital costs associated with electricity infrastructure development. Even then there is every likelihood that ongoing energy payments to cover operating and maintenance costs will become intermittent or cease altogether if tight management control is not in place. However, where such controls do exist and where income producing activities can be identified (e.g. phone charging stations, produce cooling/freezing, etc.) then poverty can be alleviated and communities made considerably better off.

**Community access**.

Associated with the previous point is the fundamental problem of inaccessible rural communities. The costs associated with extending grid networks to rural villages (which will usually mean getting a road built first) or transporting fuel / materials to such locations is prohibitive and will likely always remain the case. Consequently, there is probably a ceiling to the level of rural electrification possible in the country. This does not mean that all communities cannot be provided with some form of alternative energy supply to wood and kerosene (e.g. solar lanterns) but even small scale RE infrastructure development is unlikely to be viable for the reasons set out in the paragraphs above.

**Sustainability**.

Appendix G of the Power Development Plan developed by PPL notes that most locally based and community managed power systems in PNG have not been sustained in the long term to provide reliable and efficient power systems. There are some exceptions to this general rule – some mini-hydro systems operated by missionaries are still functioning, even after 30-40 years (e.g. Kairiru Island in East Sepik Province and FANE in Goilala, Central province, operated by the Catholic Church). However, these are the exceptions to the rule. As the Power Development Plan makes clear, there are a number of reasons for this including:

Lack of management skills for an introduced foreign technology that most indigenous people find difficult to manage. For example, the rural electricity co-operative at Lese Kavora in Gulf province simply could not be adequately managed, even as the power infrastructure remains functional to-date.

Cultural system of the community is not impacted by the introduction of a power supply. For instance, people are not used to paying regular fees for services within a village and enforcement is difficult for a family relative having various traditional obligations /relationships that are also very important.

A perception that the government ought to provide electricity infrastructure and services for free which translates into an unwillingness to pay for a publically provided electricity scheme. The perception may be different, however, for privately provided infrastructure.

The solution proposed by PPL is for training in appropriate management skills to be delivered to the affected communities to ensure that a power project is sustainably managed and, appropriate to the cultural expectations of the indigenous people. Also, PPL suggests that a separate entity should probably be set up to deal with rural electrification management issues affecting locally based power supply. This could be a group within PPL or the Electricity Division of the Department of Petroleum and Energy.

**Unbundling and privatisation**.

Given the scale of private (generation) investment that is envisaged in PNG, unbundling PPL into its constituent generation, transmission and distribution components may be an appropriate way forward. Under such circumstances, IPP developers will likely have more faith in being treated fairly by the network operator(s) and this would especially be the case if PPL's generation assets were privatised thereby delivering a potentially fully competitive generation sector. Furthermore, the need for large scale investment in transmission assets to accommodate the expected increase in generation capacity may also mean that PPL's transmission business will have to be subject to some kind of PPP arrangement (e.g. a long term concession as adopted in the Philippines).

**Financing**.

Significant RE system dissemination usually needs to be supported by the simultaneous development of small and micro scale financing infrastructure. Larger commercial banks can also get involved (as has successfully been achieved in Fiji through ANZ) but a learning process, often supported by a major donor funded initiative, is required in order that both customers and the financing institutions understand how loans, collateral and payment terms can be structured to suit all parties. The donors also have a role to play with respect to offering guarantee facilities, establishing revolving funds (or other forms of loan finance) and providing subsidy support mechanisms.

**Project development support**.

Just as important as the provision of 'hard support' in the form of direct funding for electricity infrastructure development is the provision of 'soft support'. This takes many forms such as providing feasibility studies, compiling and sharing data on accredited equipment manufacturers and installers, providing skills training, etc.

## INSTITUTIONAL FRAMEWORK OF THE ELECTRICITY SECTOR

There are four key 'operational' actors in PNG's electricity sector: the DPE, PPL and the ICCC. In addition there is the IPBC which was established in 2002 to hold and manage the majority of state-owned commercial assets in trust including those of PPL.

The DPE is mandated by the Government to oversee and manage the sector. Within the DPE, the Electricity Division is responsible for formulating and implementing policy for the electricity sector. However, the Division claims to presently be under-resourced (the unit has 24 staff, 18 of whom are technical officers) which means they do not have the capacity to carry out energy planning studies, etc. A total of 51 new positions have been identified through the EP initiative and the expectation is most of these roles will be filled by the end of 2012.

The major operators in PNG's electricity industry include PPL and a number of IPPs most of which are associated with mining operations. PPL is a vertically integrated government-owned body vested with the power to plan, develop, generate, transmit, distribute and sell electricity throughout PNG. The company was established pursuant to the provisions of the Electricity Industry Act 2002.

The IPBC is PPL's shareholder and manages the state's assets in a General Business Trust.

The ICCC is the authority responsible for regulating the energy sector which includes licensing operators, approving tariffs and ensuring service standards are met.

**Key Policy, Legislative & Institutional Framework Summary**

| Name | Summary | Status |
|---|---|---|
| Policy | | |
| Development Strategic Plan 2010-2030 | Overarching plan for PNG development that includes some ambitious electricity capacity development targets | Key document underlying electricity sector development |
| Medium Term Development Strategy 2011 – 2015 | Enabling document for key medium term activities (e.g. Least Cost Development Plan and Electricity Super Corridor Feasibility Study) that will help achieve DSP objectives | Main driving force behind near term electricity sector development |
| Electricity Industry Policy | Specific policy initiatives for the sector including: establishment of an Electricity Management Committee to plan / procure new electricity infrastructure and strong focus on PSP for development | Needs 'operationalisation' of EMC to become effective |
| Rural Electrification Policy | Focuses on establishing mechanisms for the scaling-up of rural electrification principally through renewable energy development | Subsumed into DSP |
| Legislation | | |
| Electricity Supply Act | Specifies the powers of the Minister for Petroleum and Energy in relation to electricity infrastructure built with government funds | Needs updating |
| Electricity Industry Act | Specifies the functions and powers of PPL | Needs updating |
| Independent Consumer and Competition Act | Establishes the ICCC and associated regulation regime for the electricity and petroleum sectors | Needs updating |
| Geothermal Act | Will be an important enabler for geothermal capacity development | In development |
| Institution | | |
| Department of Petroleum and Energy | Electricity Division is responsible for formulating and implementing policy for the sector but provides only limited output and influence | Under-resourced |
| PNG Power Limited | State-owned electricity utility with some monopoly rights | Needs reforming if PSP is to be enabled |
| Independent Consumer and Competition Commission | Regulator for the electricity sector | Under-resourced |
| Independent Public Business Corporation of PNG | PPL shareholder and so influential with respect to reform decisions | Appears fine |

# ENERGY EFFICIENCY - POLICIES AND TRENDS

EE does feature as part of PNG's energy policy but only to a limited extent. On the supply side, the country's public utility PPL has integrated a few energy efficiency measure into its supply chain whist the utility's main (commercial) customers have registered interest in adopting EE initiatives but lack the knowledge them This would suggest that there is potential for EE product / service providers to fill this gap. Furthermore, the significant (and ambitious) electrification plans contained in the DSP would stand a greater chance of being fulfilled if they were accompanied by a formal EE programme. However, as described below, there are some significant barriers to EE adoption.

Some efforts have, historically, been made to implement EE initiatives in Port Moresby. Specifically, a pilot project undertaken by the Promoting Energy Efficiency in the Pacific (PEEP[7]) assisted PPL in running two EE programmes focused on street lighting and Power Factor Correction (PFC). However, only the PFC programme was selected for implementation as it linked in with an ongoing project being carried out by PPL in relation to its key customers.

The PFC programme commenced by targeting customers using the Kone feeder in Port Moresby because that feeder was overloaded. Thereafter, the customer base was expanded to include those with a high load demand. These customers were ranked according to the size of their loads and the level of their power factor and those deemed to have the greatest potential savings through PFC installation had PFC units designed and installed for them. However, only 10 of the 250 customers have completed the installations to date. The remaining installations are still pending the customer's approval for their facilities to be shut down and reconnected after PPL has installed the PFC units.

In addition, although installing the PFC units can result in energy savings as less energy is lost during the electricity distribution process, total energy savings are still relatively small as line losses are generally low in percentage terms. For example, if the power factor were improved from 80% to 95% with line loss percent savings of about 29%, total power savings would be around 0.58% as technical losses are 2% of the total power draw.

The PEEP Phase One study proposed focusing EE efforts in seven key areas. The table below presents the forecast energy and cost savings associated with these Energy Conservation Measures (ECMs). The total potential annual savings that can be attained with implementation of the ECMs is forecast to be 4.1% of total energy consumption (translating into 29,500 MWh), USD 9.9 million and emission reductions of 53,600 TCO2 (see table below).

| | Baseline Energy Use | Savings Potential (Sector) | Savings Potential (Country) | Peak Road Reduction | Savings Potential | | Estimated Investment | Simple Payback | Annual Emission Reduction | Investment per saved kWh |
|---|---|---|---|---|---|---|---|---|---|---|
| | MWh | % | % | kW | MWh | USD (M) | USD (M) | Years | $TCO_2$ | USD/kWh |
| Energy Efficiency in Government Buildings | 47,781 | 8.4 | 0.6 | 691 | 4,035 | 0.99 | 3.28 | 3.3 | 2,623 | 0.102 |
| Implementation of LED for Street Lighting | 2,573 | 71.7 | 0.3 | 375 | 1,844 | 0.46 | 2.74 | 6.0 | 1,199 | 0.185 |
| Energy Efficiency in the Hotel Sector | 17,905 | 21.1 | 0.5 | 527 | 3,771 | 1.08 | 4.33 | 4.0 | 2,451 | 0.143 |
| Energy Efficiency in | 131,828 | 4.1 | 0.8 | 2,570 | 5,401 | 0.96 | 0.40 | 0.4 | 3,511 | 0.008 |

[7] This programme took place under Phase One of PEEP. Phase Two is now underway.

| | | | | | | | | | | |
|---|---|---|---|---|---|---|---|---|---|---|
| the Residential Sector | | | | | | | | | | |
| Energy Efficiency in the Industrial Sector | 156,093 | 2.4 | 0.5 | 435 | 3,814 | 3.77 | 8.94 | 2.4 | 36,874 | 0.043 |
| Energy Labelling and MEPS | 713,016 | 1.5 | 1.5 | 951 | 10,419 | 2.57 | 1.90 | 0.7 | 6,772 | 0.022 |
| Power Factor Correction Systems | 39,113 | 0.5 | 0.0 | - | 208 | 0.06 | 0.40 | 6.8 | 135 | 0.216 |
| Total | | | 4.1 | 5,550 | 29,500 | 9.9 | 22.0 | 2.2 | 53,600 | |

Source: Table 14, TA 6485-REG: Promoting Energy Efficiency in the Pacific

A paper entitled "Regulatory and Financing Mechanisms for Scaling-up Energy Efficiency" produced in January 2012 discusses barriers to scaling up EE investments globally. These are summarised in the Table below and most, if not nearly all, of these are applicable to PNG. Therefore, significant progress in delivering the EE initiatives described in the paragraphs below is only likely to be made when most, if not all, of these barriers are overcome.

**Barriers to Energy Efficiency**

| Policy & Regulatory Barriers | End-Use Barriers | Barriers related to Equipment & Service Providers | Institutional Barriers | Financing Barriers |
|---|---|---|---|---|
| Low or subsidized energy prices | High cost of energy efficient products | Limited development of EE services market | Lack of formal institutional framework for developing and implementing energy efficiency strategies, policies and programs | Small project size |
| Distorted fiscal and regulatory policies | Consumer preferences for non-EE attributes | High project development and transaction costs | | High transaction costs |
| Rigid procurement and budgeting procedures | Split incentives | Limited risk management skills | Emphasis on increasing energy supplies; not on reducing consumption | Limited availability of funds |
| Limitations of public financing | Low management priority on EE | Limited access to equity capital | Lack of confidence in EE improvements to deliver savings | High perceived risks |
| Ad hoc planning | Limited technical knowledge of EE | Lack of credibility with consumers and financial institutions | Lack of "champions" for promoting EE | Lack of interest on the part of banks and financial institutions |
| Limited data availability & quality | Lack of internal funds for EE investments | limited monitoring and validation capacity | Limited knowledge and understanding of EE by consumers | Limited development of targeted financial products for EE |

Source: Regulatory and Financing Mechanisms for Scaling-up Energy Efficiency, 2012

# PROPOSED IMPROVEMENTS

**Energy Efficiency in Government Buildings.**

A number of government buildings, such as offices and hospitals, have been selected (based on their electricity consumption) for an energy efficiency study carried out under PEEP. Energy saving potential is calculated, based on average energy usage, and then several energy efficiency measures – typically targeting lighting and cooling functions – were then proposed to be implemented. These measures include optimization of operating hours for centralized systems, installation efficient lighting fixtures and LCD monitors, air-leak reduction and using efficient fans and motors. However, only 367 of the largest energy using buildings have been considered to be included in the study as the rest of PNG's buildings have an average monthly consumption of less than 100 kWh which is considered to be too low to be worthwhile including in an energy efficiency project.

**Street Lighting**. Most of PNG's 6,092 street lamps are old and inefficient whilst many others need to be replaced as they are no longer functioning. The PEEP report therefore proposes replacing energy inefficient mercury lamps with more energy efficient Light-Emitting Diode (LED) lamps. LED lamps have the dual advantage of increasing the lighting level and reducing energy costs.

**Energy Efficiency in the Hotel Sector**. Energy efficiency measures targeted at the hotel sector are not expected to have a substantial impact as total consumption for this group stands at just 17.90 GWh which represents less than 5% of PNG's total electricity consumption. The main energy efficiency measures proposed for the hotel sector are :

Efficient lighting, mainly CFLs, for interior and exterior lighting

Solar Water Heaters (SWHs)

Reduced flow for shower heads, sinks and toilet flush

Key tag switches for room electrical system

Efficient air conditioning units

Cooling setting point adjustments

Pool pump operation optimization

High-efficiency pumps and motors

Installation of timers for equipment operation optimization

Air curtain installation

**Energy Efficiency in the Residential Sector.**

In order to improve energy efficiency in homes, PEEP recommends the replacement of incandescent lamps (averaging 60 W) with compact fluorescent lamps (CFLs) that have an average load of13 W. PEEP estimates that a 10% savings on electricity bills would generate total savings of up to USD 975 million.

**Energy Efficiency in the Industrial Sector.** The industrial sector constitutes a significant percentage (approximately a quarter) of total electricity consumed in PNG. Based on previous studies, the potential energy savings derived from the adoption of energy efficient measure in the industrial sector are estimated by PEEP to be about 26%. These energy efficiency measures include:

Boiler Efficiency Improvements (combustion and insulation)

Heat Recovery Systems

High Efficiency Motors

Cogeneration - Exhaust Gas

Preheating Systems

Improvement of Lighting Systems

Solar Water Heaters

Improvement of Cooling Systems

**Energy Labelling and MEPS.**

In the early stages of project implementation, the PEEP Report suggests that the government set up a laboratory for equipment testing and validation as well as seek to develop support for Minimum Energy Performance Standards (MEPS) development and implementation. The second part of the project implementation entails carrying out detailed studies of the equipment and appliance markets to estimate the likely costs of MEPS and labelling requirements on imported appliances. A similar, previous study carried out in Fiji estimated the costs to be between 10% and 25% of the value of the benefits.

**Power Factor Correction Systems.**

Power factor improvement on the demand side would increase PPL transmission and distribution capacity, reduce technical losses, and provide customers with a more stable voltage supply. As mentioned previously, most of PPL's customers have yet to install the PFC units into their systems resulting in their power factor being well below the new minimum requirement. In a study conducted on 50 customers in Port Moresby to establish the energy saving potential for PFCS implementation, the calculated PFCS needed range between 10 kVAR and 310 kVAR. Therefore, PPL should target these customers in order to derive power savings along with additional transmission and distribution capacity of 2,416 kVA.

These EE activity recommendations need to be supported by the adoption of strong energy efficiency policies and actions. In order for these to materialise, PEEP proposes that a series of policy, legal, structural and educational adjustments will have to be made. They are as follows:

**PNG Government Energy Efficiency Programme Management.**

An energy efficiency division could be established in the Energy Department to better manage the EE activities organised by the Energy Department.

**PPL Energy Efficiency Unit.**

PPL's senior management is supportive of EE initiatives and so therefore may consider creating their own Energy Efficiency Unit in the organisation to better manage their EE efforts.

**General Information / Awareness Programs.**

The public is generally unaware of the concept of energy efficiency and its associated activities and it is the responsibility of the government and the Energy Division to help address this issue. Activities that this awareness raising programme might undertake include distributing books and leaflets, advertising energy efficiency measures that could be adopted and supplying educational materials for schools.

**Education and Training.**

Education and training programmes are crucial in supporting EE promotion and implementation activities. Education and training activities that may be considered include conducting training sessions on energy audits including financial analysis and reporting to customers and conducting training sessions on energy-efficient building construction practices for large building developers.

**Energy Labelling and Minimum Energy Performance Standards.** International assistance may be required to design and initiate a programme tailored specifically to the needs of PNG. However, although implementation of such a programme may be a costly operation, several more practical options could be carried out instead such as requesting from importers/retailers proof of compliance with energy labelling and MEPS for material displayed on the shelves and accepting existing labelling schemes (from Australia-New Zealand and perhaps other countries as well) as a starting point for the development and implementation of a domestic labelling programme.

**Energy Efficiency Provisions in Building Code.**

Building codes in PNG do not make provision for EE at present. It is important, therefore, to enforce compliance on EE practices in order to minimize energy wastage and lower costs. As well as possibly revising the code to include EE regulations other measures such as informing / training architects and contractors on implementing EE approaches could also be implemented.

**Setting up an Energy Efficiency Centre.**

The government might consider setting up a non-profit centre to focus on energy efficiency activities. The role of the Energy Efficiency Centre could include conducting energy efficiency applied research and analysis, raising energy efficiency awareness and recommending / implementing energy efficiency policies.

**Legal Framework Development.**

A supporting legal framework needs to be put in place to help ensure that energy efficiency programmes can be carried out effectively. Such a framework might include establishing appropriate rules to enforce technical energy efficiency specifications for new buildings, implementing energy efficiency appliance and equipment standards, developing an energy efficiency fund which could provide subsidies for appropriate energy efficiency projects in all sectors and organising professional energy efficiency accreditation and define terms of reference for energy auditing.

**Nomination of Energy Managers in Government Buildings.**

Government buildings in PNG could assign energy managers to monitor and analyse energy consumption levels and improve energy efficiency. These managers could also prepare monthly reports detailing energy usage in order to identify all energy consumption anomalies.

**Development of an Energy Efficiency Fund.**

An energy efficiency fund could be established and financed through taxing high energy-consuming equipment such as electrical water heaters, low-performance air conditioning units, incandescent lamps and large fuel inefficient vehicles used in the transportation sector. This fund could be useful in promoting investments and encouraging financial institutions to participate in energy efficiency initiatives development.

**Public Sector Procurement.**

An effort could be made by the government to introduce energy efficiency regulations in procurement procedures which can in turn provide significant energy savings. Furthermore, such a step would send a clear signal to the community that the energy efficiency policy is being taken seriously by the government.

**PPL Interruptible tariff.**

PPL can establish a formal agreement with large customers to introduce an interruptible tariff to reduce peak demand load. No evidence has been found of EE initiatives targeted at the transport sector. There are likely to be a number of reasons for this including the fact that the topographical nature of the country means that larger, less efficient vehicles (that are often poorly maintained) tend to be used. Also, limited road access means that a significant proportion of travel around the country needs to take place via shipping or aviation both of which are major petroleum product users. Finally, it is also an easier option to target EE initiatives at government and industry.

In summary, therefore, there exists much untapped potential for implementing energy savings in PNG. Significant economic benefits could potentially ensue from adopting such initiatives as well as tangential rewards such as institutional and human capital development. However, a major challenge to adopting EE initiatives in PNG is the lack of accurate information on energy consumption by sector, sub-sector and energy type. In order to develop a detailed EE programme and prioritise specific energy efficiency strategies, it is essential to gather comprehensive data on sector energy consumption and demand profiles.

# FORECAST ENERGY BALANCES 2010-2020

Table 7.1 presents the forecast energy balances for each year to 2020. The detailed assumptions for each of the sectors were explained in the preceding sections.

**Table 7.1: Forecast energy balances for Papua New Guinea, 2011-20**

| | 2011 | 2012 | 2013 | 2014 | 2015 | 2016 | 2017 | 2018 | 2019 | 2020 |
|---|---|---|---|---|---|---|---|---|---|---|
| **Domestic production (TOE)** | | | | | | | | | | |
| Coal and Peat | | | | | | | | | | |
| Crude Oil | 1,460,000 | 1,460,000 | 1,460,000 | 1,460,000 | 1,950,000 | 2,450,000 | 2,450,000 | 2,450,000 | 2,450,000 | 2,450,000 |
| Oil Products | | | | | | | | | | |
| Natural Gas | 49,500 | 44,000 | 46,400 | 48,900 | 92,700 | 96,000 | 99,900 | 104,800 | 110,000 | 164,800 |
| Nuclear | | | | | | | | | | |
| Hydro | 104,100 | 104,400 | 113,000 | 120,200 | 173,400 | 190,200 | 203,400 | 212,500 | 222,400 | 211,500 |
| Wind | | | | | 1,300 | 1,300 | 1,300 | 1,300 | 1,300 | 1,900 |
| Solar | | | | | 700 | 700 | 700 | 700 | 800 | 1,100 |
| Geothermal | 46,300 | 46,100 | 44,500 | 44,400 | 56,300 | 59,100 | 62,100 | 65,200 | 68,500 | 82,100 |
| Biofuel | | | | | 2,500 | 2,500 | 2,500 | 2,600 | 2,600 | 3,400 |
| Biomass | 1,289,000 | 1,328,000 | 1,368,000 | 1,409,000 | 1,451,000 | 1,495,000 | 1,540,000 | 1,586,000 | 1,633,000 | 1,682,000 |
| Electricity | | | | | | | | | | |
| Heat | | | | | | | | | | |
| **Total** | 2,948,900 | 2,982,500 | 3,031,900 | 3,082,500 | 3,727,900 | 4,294,800 | 4,359,900 | 4,423,100 | 4,488,600 | 4,596,800 |
| | | | | | | | | | | |
| **Primary energy supply (TOE)** | | | | | | | | | | |
| Coal and Peat | | | | | | | | | | |
| Crude Oil | | | | | | | | | | |
| Oil Products | 2,009,500 | 2,210,400 | 2,321,000 | 2,437,100 | 2,558,900 | 2,686,800 | 2,821,200 | 2,962,200 | 3,110,400 | 3,265,900 |
| Natural Gas | 49,500 | 44,000 | 46,400 | 48,900 | 73,900 | 76,200 | 79,100 | 83,000 | 87,100 | 140,600 |
| Nuclear | | | | | | | | | | |
| Hydro | 104,100 | 104,400 | 113,000 | 120,200 | 173,400 | 190,200 | 203,400 | 212,500 | 222,400 | 211,500 |
| Wind | | | | | 1,300 | 1,300 | 1,300 | 1,300 | 1,300 | 1,900 |
| Solar | | | | | 700 | 700 | 700 | 700 | 800 | 1,100 |
| Geothermal | 46,300 | 46,100 | 44,500 | 44,400 | 56,300 | 59,100 | 62,100 | 65,200 | 68,500 | 82,100 |
| Biofuel | | | | | 2,500 | 2,500 | 2,500 | 2,600 | 2,600 | 3,400 |
| Biomass | 1,289,000 | 1,328,000 | 1,368,000 | 1,409,000 | 1,451,000 | 1,495,000 | 1,540,000 | 1,586,000 | 1,633,000 | 1,682,000 |
| Electricity | | | | | | | | | | |
| Heat | | | | | | | | | | |
| **Total** | 3,498,400 | 3,732,900 | 3,892,900 | 4,059,600 | 4,318,000 | 4,511,800 | 4,710,300 | 4,913,500 | 5,126,100 | 5,388,500 |
| **Final energy consumption by sector** | | | | | | | | | | |
| | | | | | | | | | | |
| Industry | 647,500 | 689,600 | 741,300 | 785,800 | 844,700 | 902,100 | 965,300 | 1,023,200 | 1,084,800 | 1,159,700 |
| Transport | 134,700 | 144,800 | 156,400 | 168,100 | 183,200 | 201,300 | 213,400 | 226,200 | 243,200 | 262,600 |
| Other | 1,401,700 | 1,462,900 | 1,514,300 | 1,554,500 | 1,598,800 | 1,623,300 | 1,652,500 | 1,690,200 | 1,724,000 | 1,747,400 |
| Residential | 1,326,000 | 1,382,700 | 1,430,900 | 1,468,500 | 1,508,900 | 1,529,900 | 1,555,300 | 1,589,300 | 1,619,900 | 1,638,600 |
| Commercial and Public Services | 31,800 | 35,000 | 36,800 | 38,600 | 40,500 | 42,500 | 44,700 | 46,900 | 49,200 | 51,700 |
| Agriculture/Forestry | 24,800 | 25,400 | 26,100 | 26,700 | 27,400 | 28,100 | 28,800 | 29,500 | 30,200 | 31,000 |
| Fishing | 9,200 | 9,400 | 9,600 | 9,800 | 10,000 | 10,200 | 10,400 | 10,600 | 10,800 | 11,000 |
| Non-specified | 9,900 | 10,400 | 10,900 | 11,500 | 12,000 | 12,600 | 13,300 | 13,900 | 14,600 | 15,400 |
| Non-Energy Use | | | | | | | | | | |
| - of which Petrochemical Feedstocks | | | | | | | | | | |
| | 2,182,900 | 2,297,300 | 2,412,000 | 2,508,400 | 2,626,700 | 2,726,500 | 2,831,200 | 2,939,600 | 3,052,000 | 3,169,700 |
| | | | | | | | | | | |
| **by type** | | | | | | | | | | |
| Coal and Peat | | | | | | | | | | |
| Crude Oil | | | | | | | | | | |
| Oil Products | 571,500 | 629,900 | 684,700 | 718,900 | 767,700 | 806,000 | 846,400 | 888,700 | 933,100 | 979,800 |
| Natural Gas | | | | | | | | | | |
| Biofuel | | | | | | | | | | |
| Biomass | 1,289,000 | 1,328,000 | 1,368,000 | 1,409,000 | 1,456,000 | 1,495,000 | 1,540,000 | 1,586,000 | 1,633,000 | 1,682,000 |
| **Electricity** | **322,400** | **339,400** | **359,300** | **380,500** | **403,000** | **425,500** | **444,800** | **464,900** | **485,900** | **507,900** |
| Heat | | | | | | | | | | |
| **Total** | 2,182,900 | 2,297,300 | 2,412,000 | 2,508,400 | 2,626,700 | 2,726,500 | 2,831,200 | 2,939,600 | 3,052,000 | 3,169,700 |

PNG's domestic energy supply is predicted to increase massively from just under 3.0 million toe in 2011 to just under 16.7 million in 2020. Most of that increase is attributable to the LNG project, which is expected to produce 4 million toe in 2015, rising to 12.2 million in 2020. Figure 7.1 show the forecast changes over the decade.

**Figure 7.1: Forecast domestic energy supply in Papua New Guinea, 2011-20**

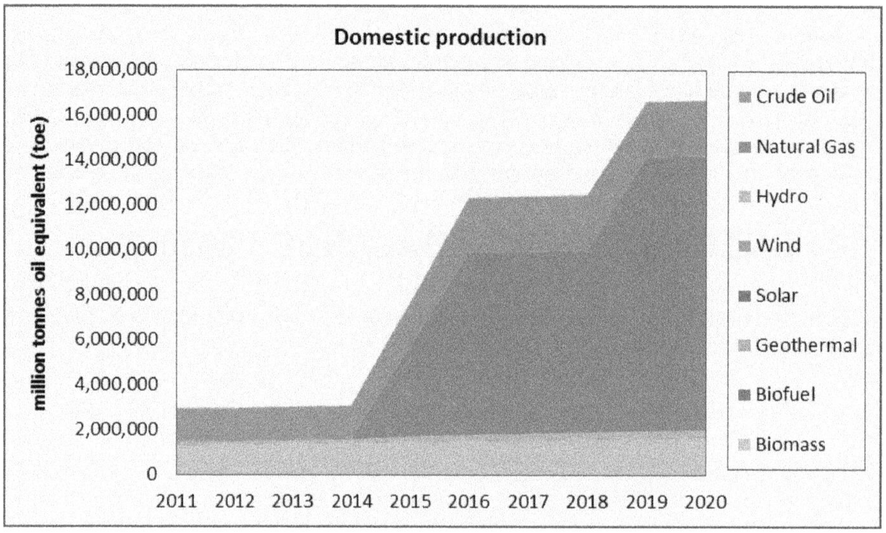


Source: Experts' Estimates

Figure 7.2 gives a breakdown of the forecast production in 2020. The gas/LNG share is predicted to be 73.3% of the total, oil 14.8%, biomass 10%, hydro 1.5% and geothermal 0.4%.

**Figure 7.2: Forecast energy production in Papua New Guinea, 2020**

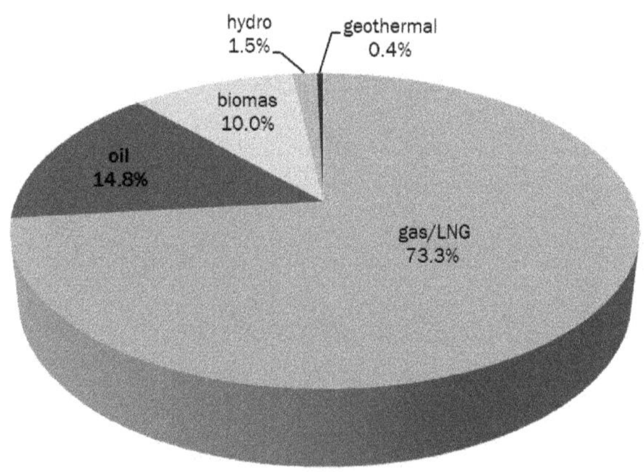


Source: Expert's estimates

PNG's oil production is forecast to increase by about +68% over the decade, in contrast to the declines during the last few years. All of that increase is expected to be condensate production from the LNG project, as explained in Section 6. However, the forecasts show that the country will continue to be a net importer of oil products in each year to 2020 because of rising consumption.

Biomass production and consumption is forecast to continue to increase at +3% per year. However, its share of the total production will fall from 43.7% in 2011 to just 10.1% in 2020.

There are big differences between the domestic production and the domestic energy supply, defined as TPES, however. Table 7.1 shows TPES increasing by +55% from just over 3.5 million tonnes in 2011 to just over 5.4 million in 2020, with average annual growth of nearly +10%. Figure 7.3 illustrates the forecast changes over the decade.

**Figure 7.3: Forecast changes in primary energy supply in Papua New Guinea**

**2011-2020**

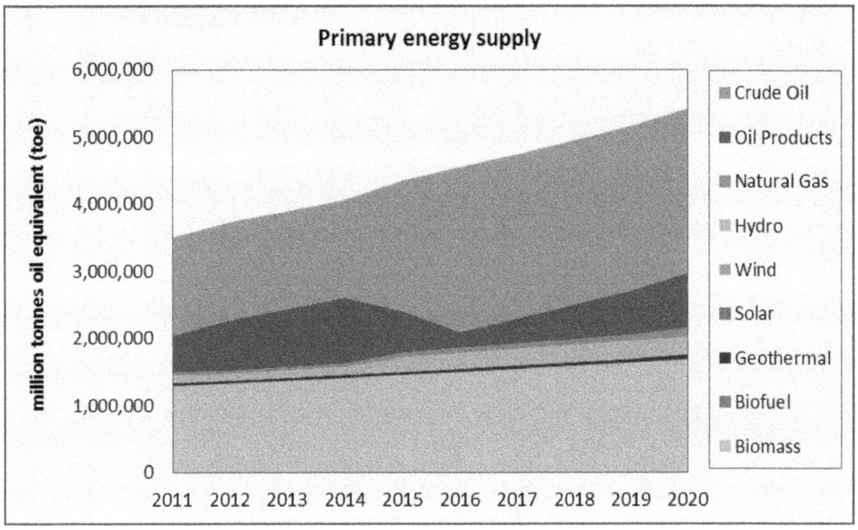


Source: Experts' Estimates

Figure 7.4 shows the actual breakdown of the energy supply in 2011 and the forecast breakdown in 2020. The shares in 2011 were oil 57.4%, biomass 36.8%, hydro 3.1%, gas 1.4% and geothermal 1.3%; and the forecast shares in 2020 are oil 60.3%, biomass 31.1%, hydro 4.6%, gas 2.6%, geothermal 1.3% and other 0.1%.

The forecast changes are relatively small. The most significant for this study is that the renewables share (excluding biomass) is predicted to increase from 5.8% to 8.6%.

The gas share is forecast to rise from just 1.4% in 2011 to 2.6% in 2020. That is based on the expectation of more gas-fired electricity generation, as discussed in Sections 4 and 5.

Only a small volume of gas is currently consumed in PNG and all the gas from the current LNG project is expected to be exported. However, there are other gas reserves and a high priority should be for some of that gas to replace diesel-fired electricity generation.

Similarly, there are important opportunities for more hydro and geothermal generation, as also discussed in Sections 4 and 5.

**Figure 7.4: Breakdowns of energy supply in Papua New Guinea**

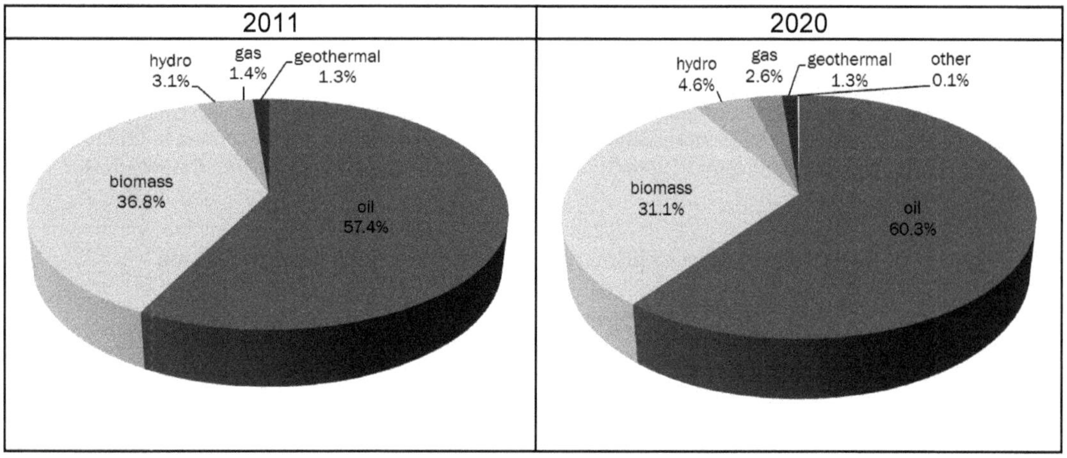


Source: Experts' Estimates

Finally, Table 7.1 also gives the forecasts of energy consumption, defined as TFC. It is predicted to increase by +51% from 3.6 million toe in 2011 to just under 5.5 million in 2020, with average annual growth of just under +5%.

Figure 7.5 illustrates the forecast changes. Oil's share is predicted to increase from 55.5% to 59.9%, the biomass share to fall from 35.6% to 30.8% and electricity's share to rise from 8.9% to 9.3%.

**Figure 7.5: Forecast changes in energy consumption in Papua New Guinea 2011-2020**

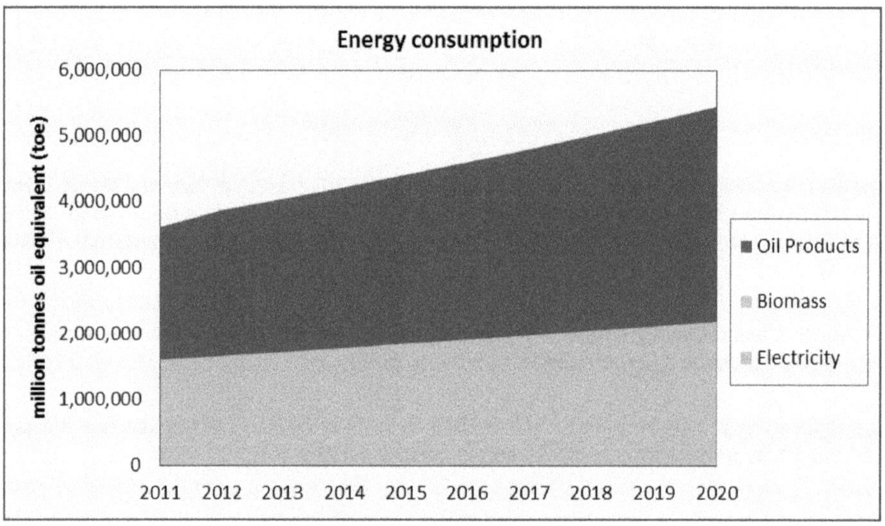


Source: Experts' Estimates

# OPPORTUNITIES FOR PRIVATE INVESTMENTS

The outlook for private investors looking to develop energy infrastructure in PNG is very positive at all levels of the energy value chain and in relation to (renewable) electricity development in particular. Through the DSP, the PNG government has set some very ambitious infrastructure development targets and it also recognises that the private sector has a very important role to play in realising these ambitions.

This Section presents a summary of the potential for private sector engagement in the hydrocarbon and electricity (particularly RE and EE) sectors and, where relevant, an assessment of the enabling conditions required for this potential to be realised.

## HYDROCARBON SECTOR

The oil and gas industry in PNG is already dominated by private sector operators such as ExxonMobil, OilSearch, Talisman Energy and InterOil and this private sector interest will continue into the foreseeable future.

As oil production has tailed off in recent years, so attention has switched to gas development (and the LNG project in particular) where there is considerably more potential. Indeed, the country's proven and probable gas reserves have been estimated to be at least 15 tcf, which is equivalent to approximately 2.7 billion barrels or 360 million tonnes of oil. Thus the gas reserves are probably four times greater than the proven oil reserves and possibly more.

Nonetheless, some private companies (e.g. Oil Search) are reportedly optimistic about finding additional oil reserves in the country whilst ExxonMobil's LNG project will also produce oil liquids, known as condensate, which will be separated from the gas, and are expected to total about 20,000 bpd.

InterOil believe that there are sufficient gas reserves in these fields for a second LNG export plant in PNG. The company's plans were approved by the last PNG government, although the previous Minister of Petroleum and Energy heavily criticised InterOil for lack of progress just before the recent election.

Talisman Energy also have gas in the Stanley field and other discoveries. The company have a Gas Aggregation Project (GAP) which is intended "to aggregate significant discoveries and prospective gas resources" with a view to exporting the gas as LNG.

In summary, therefore, the private sector will continue to develop and operate PNG's hydrocarbon sector and the principal enabling condition is securing exploration and development rights from the PNG government

## ELECTRICITY SECTOR – ON-GRID

As discussed above, the private sector is already engaged in PNG's on-grid electricity sector in a number of ways:

Independent power projects such as the diesel station at Kanudi.

Public-private initiatives such as Yonki Hydro Ltd. and Origin Energy / PNGSDPL.

Looking ahead, the PNG government's DSP 2010-2030 is heavily reliant on the private sector funding and operating much of the country's on-grid energy infrastructure. Consequently there are significant opportunities for private sector engagement, especially in RE deployment in both urban and rural areas.

The success of such development will depend on a number of key factors including:

The EMC quickly developing and implementing an investment plan.

Development of at least part of the electricity super-corridor to which the IPPs will need to connect.

The ICCC (together with PPL) introducing a fit and proper regulatory regime (e.g. third party access rules, contract framework, etc.

There is also a distinct possibility that some or all of PPL will be subject to some kind of private sector participation. One possible scenario would be for one or more PPL generation businesses to be created and then partially or fully privatised, a long term concession applied to the transmission business and the distribution business left as a publically owned corporation.

Resistance to these possible developments is already in evidence, particularly from existing PPL staff who are concerned about the possible impact of these PSP plans upon their employment. Indeed, a strike by PPL workers took place in June 2012 to protest at the creation of the Yonki Hydro company.

## ELECTRICITY SECTOR – OFF-GRID

The private sector already plays a significant role in PNG's off-grid electricity sector through electricity generation in support of industrial and large scale commercial activities. This privately supplied generation for business purposes (and mining in particular) will continue to grow but in most cases the business owner will take responsibility for providing their own power needs and so there will be limited opportunities for pure, private electricity infrastructure developers.

Of greater potential, however, is the off-grid rural sector where there will be considerable opportunity for RE development driven by the DSP's objective of increasing electricity access from approximately 12% in 2010 to 41% by 2020 (and 70% by 2030).

As discussed above, given the highly fragmented and small scale nature of rural electricity infrastructure development, the expectation is that private sector investment will need to be supported by PNG government (or donor) funding. Consequently, a critical enabling factor for such investment to materialise will be the scale of financial resources provided to the ETF and its subsequent success in distributing funds.

**PSP Opportunity Summary – RE Development**

| | Renewable Energy Sector | Other Sectors |
|---|---|---|
| PSP Potential | Considerable potential:<br>Between 200 – 300 MW new hydro capacity by 2015 and 600 MW by 2020<br>Up to 4 MW new solar capacity forecast by 2020<br>Up to 6 MW new wind capacity forecast by 2020<br>Up to 9 MW of biomass / biogas capacity development forecast by 2020<br>59 MW of new geothermal development by 2020 | Significant potential:<br>Forecast of up to 60 MW new gas fired capacity development by 2015 and 210 MW by 2020<br>Forecast of 30 MW new coal fired capacity development by 2020<br>Some (or all) of PPL's generation assets could be subject to partial or outright sale<br>PPL transmission infrastructure could be subject to some form of PSP arrangement (e.g. concession)<br>Off-grid distribution and supply |
| Enabling Factors | A fully capable and functioning EMC<br>Construction of all (or part) of the electricity super-corridor<br>Expanded set of enabling contracting, economic, technical and competition policy regulations<br>Establishment of a fully resourced ETF<br>Unbundling of PPL | |

## ENERGY EFFICIENCY

EE does presently feature as part of PNG's energy policy but only to a limited extent and principally in relation to supply side measures. The EE initiatives that have been carried out to date have been led by donor funded programmes such as PEEP Phase One and now PEEP Phase Two.

In the absence of a comprehensive EE strategy and implementation plan formally adopted by the PNG government, no significant EE activity is forecast despite the fact that considerable untapped potential exists for implementing energy savings and that undertaking EE measures as part of a coordinated plan with the electricity capacity development under DSP would likely save a considerable amount of resources.

The absence of formal policies designing and facilitating EE implementation is largely the consequence of a lack of accurate information on energy consumption by sector, sub-sector and energy type. In order to develop a detailed EE programme and prioritise specific EE strategies, comprehensive data on sector energy consumption and demand profiles needs to be gathered.

## POSSIBLE IMPROVEMENTS

PNG is unique among the South Pacific countries because it produces both oil and gas, and in large quantities. It is therefore much less reliant on imported energy than the other countries in the region, including the Solomon Islands and Vanuatu which are the other two countries in this study.

However, PNG has a very low level of electrification with about 90% of the population having no access to electricity. Most people rely on wood and other biomass for their energy needs.

The country's TPES is predicted to increase by about +55% by 2020 with average annual growth of about +5%. Oil's share of TFC is predicted to increase from 55.5% to 59.9%, the biomass share to fall from 35.6% to 30.8% and electricity's share to rise from 8.9% to 9.3%.

Despite electricity accounting for less than 10% of both the current and forecast energy consumption, it has been the main focus of this study because it offers the best opportunities for further private sector investment in (RE) projects.

The combination of government under-investment, extremely challenging topographical conditions and highly dispersed communities has resulted in PNG having one of the lowest electrification rates in the Pacific region. However, as presented in the tables and graphs above, the government is taking steps to try and rectify the problem by putting forward plans for energy infrastructure development through its DSP 2010-2030. The DSP's main agenda is to increase household access to electricity through increasing (principally renewable) electricity generation capacity, extending the transmission network and increasing usage of Easipay for bill payments.

More specifically, a large part of PNG's energy development plans is focused on expanding renewable energy generation capacity (whilst reducing reliance on diesel power) because of the considerable potential for such resources to be utilized.

Electricity capacity is forecast to increase by +150% during the decade to 2020. Diesel capacity is predicted to fall from 198 MW in 2011 to just 64 MW in 2020. In contrast, hydro capacity is forecast to quadruple from 207 MW in 2011 to 823 MW in 2020. Gas capacity is forecast to increase fourfold from 72 MW to 280 MW and geothermal capacity to double from 53 MW to 112 MW.

Supporting this capacity development is the proposed creation of an electricity superhighway that will provide access to this new generation. However, the significant cost associated with this new capacity and network development means that substantial private sector participation will also be required.

Much smaller increases are forecast for solar and wind energy but nevertheless they will potentially offer important opportunities for small scale (and principally off-grid) private sector engagement.

PNG has produced oil since 1992 and was a net exporter of oil until 2010. However, production has declined substantially in recent years, so the country is now a net importer of oil products. The forecasts show that situation continuing, although the level of imports should fall. Nevertheless, in terms of security of energy supplies PNG is in a much stronger position than the Solomon Islands and Vanuatu.

PNG's gas reserves are believed to be at least five times larger than the original oil reserves. However, gas production to date has been on a tiny scale and limited to a gas-to-electricity project for the Porgera gold mine. The reason for that has been the absence of domestic markets for the gas, with the obvious one being gas for electricity generation, replacing imported diesel and fuel oil.

A massive LNG project is currently under construction by ExxonMobil and partners, involving estimated investment of US$ 15 billion, which will transform the gas industry in PNG and also have a big impact on the national economy. However, all the LNG will be exported to Japan and other countries.

Nevertheless, there are other large gas reserves and one of the main recommendations is that a significant proportion of those be used for electricity generation, replacing imported oil products. That would make a big contribution to improving the security of the country's energy supply.

To date, the private sector has played the lead role in the development of the country's oil and gas sector and has also been engaged in several electricity sector projects. These include electricity generation investment for industrial and large scale commercial activities, independent power projects at Kanudi and joint public-private initiatives such as Yonki Hydro Ltd. and Origin Energy / PNGSDPL.

There are therefore significant opportunities for private sector engagement in the electricity sector, particularly with respect to RE infrastructure development. The private sector is already responding to these opportunities as evidenced by the multiple, ongoing privately financed hydro projects which also typically feature some level of donor support.

In order to help create a more conducive environment for private investment, several important legislation and sector specific policies are either underway or are planned. It is very important that these initiatives proceed as quickly as possible. Specifically, the following activities need to be implemented in the very near term if the targets included in the DSP are to stand any chance of being met:

The ongoing major maintenance work being undertaken on the existing regional grids needs to be concluded in a timely manner whilst the feasibility study for the development of a national grid needs to be rapidly completed and associated construction activities commenced immediately thereafter.

The EMC needs to be established and its work on prioritising and selecting generation investment development has to get underway as soon as possible.

The ETF needs to be resourced and begin providing capital subsidies for small scale generation.

The electricity regulation capacity of the ICCC needs to be enhanced to enable it to rapidly develop the enabling rules, regulations and policies necessary to facilitate private sector generation investment and its integration into the national energy system.

A power purchasing framework and associated contracts (e.g. PPAs) needs to be established.

Energy data collation and analysis systems and protocols need to be enhanced to help enable the creation of viable energy development plans and associated strategies.

Energy efficiency is presently not a main component in PNG's energy development plans. However, as well as generating greater energy savings, EE also leads to significant economic and monetary benefits. Hence, the government and other major players in the energy industry need to step up efforts to integrate EE as part of their response to development of the sector.

In order to sustain a fully functional and expanding energy sector, the Energy Unit may need to employ competent managers that are equipped with the mandatory management skills and technical knowledge on the energy generation. This will also ensure the profitability of the venture as less wastage and mistakes are incurred due to operational deficiencies.

# PAPUA NEW GUINEA'S ELECTRICITY INDUSTRY STRUCTURE AND REGULATORY FRAMEWORK

### PNG'S ELECTRICITY SITUATION AND POLICIES

kutubu oil mine.jpg

In PNG approximately, 87 percent of PNG's 6.2 million population still lack access to electricity services and the progress of rural electrification program has lagged over the years (GoPNG, 2010a). Many factors contribute to this poignant state of affairs however notable amongst all is: the absence of an overarching electricity industry policy, energy policy and rural electrification policy to guide the development of the sector; the high investment cost associated with establishing transmission lines due to PNG's rugged topography; and the lack of investment by PNG Power Ltd (PPL) in maintaining infrastructure and performing operational maintenance on existing generation, transmission and distribution assets (PNG Power Ltd, 2005; ADB, 2008). Conventional wisdom suggests that energy security accelerates rapid economic and social development and stimulates overall economic growth.

However, despite this noble view PNG's energy situation offers a diverging paradigm. PNG is a net energy exporter with oil and gas being the main indigenous energy export product that contributes significantly to PNG's export revenue. The Bank of Papua New Guinea asserts respective crude oil and refined petroleum product export alone account for 18.1 percent of total merchandise exports in 2010

The bulk export revenue is used to import petroleum products such as diesel or petrol to support the transport, manufacturing and electricity generation sectors in PNG (PPL, 2005). At present PNG has about 580 MW of installed generation capacity, which includes hydropower (230 MW), diesel (217 MW), gas-fired (8.2MW) and geothermal (53MW). PNG also has significant underutilized indigenous energy sources such as hydropower with a potential of 15,000MW, natural gas, geothermal and solar yet these remain underdeveloped (ADB, 2008).

## POLICY FRAMEWORK

Since attaining Independence in 1975, PNG has operated its electricity sector without an overarching policy framework to guide the development of the sector. Recent initiative by the Somare – Temu government in 2006 has paved way for the development of three important policy and these are the Electricity Industry Policy, the National Energy Policy and the Rural Electrification Policy. The draft Electricity Industry Policy is in its final stage and awaiting official release by the government in 2011. The National Energy policy and Rural Electrification policy are still in their early draft stages and subject to further consultation and improvisation.

## NATIONAL ENERGY POLICY

The draft National Energy policy covers indigenous energy resources in PNG that includes, oil, gas, hydropower and other renewable. The policy aims to improve to improve the quality of life and sustainable national development of these resources through a robust and vibrant energy sector. The underlying goal of the policy is to ensure that ownership of energy resources is vested with the resource owners and that their development must be accessible, reliable, affordable, efficient and environmentally friendly for the benefit to communities, industries and trade and other development activities. The policy hinges on three basic premises of sustainable development that is social, economic and environmental sustainability, which is an appropriate and recommended approach to comprehend and formulate a sector policy for achieving the desired sustainable development of the sector. The conceived strategies for achieving sustainability are guided by the contemporary global experience drawing relevant experience that can be successfully applied within the context of PNG.

## PETROLEUM (OIL AND GAS)

The Government's main goal is to develop the country's hydrocarbon resources in accordance with the Constitutional pillars, the Fourth National Goal and Directive Principle on natural resources and environment, and the export-driven strategy under the MTDS, whilst incorporating the best industrial practices and standards so as to maximize socio economic benefits and minimize adverse social and environmental impacts to its citizens.

The most important regulatory instruments in the Petroleum Sector are the Oil and Gas Act 1998 and the Oil and Gas Regulation, while the main policy document is the Petroleum Policy Handbook. Other supporting policy documents include Natural Gas Policy, Gas Commercialization Policy, Pipeline Policy, Oil Refinery Policy Guidelines, and Landowner Management Policy.

Additional policy initiatives being embarked on include the Marginal Field Policy, Offshore Operations Policy, Project Abandonment Policy, Downstream Policy, Carbon Tax Policy and National Energy Policy.

To provide an enabling investment environment for development in the hydrocarbon sector, the Government undertook a major fiscal reform in 2003, which saw the reduction of corporate tax rate from 50% to 30% for all petroleum projects developed before 2001, and from 45% to 30% for all petroleum projects developed after 2001, including the abolishment of Additional Profit Tax (APT).

These reforms were necessary amidst the rapid decline in oil and gas exploration and production experienced between 1991 and 2003. The reforms have greatly revamped activities in the Petroleum Sector, expansion of offshore and onshore acreages and commercialization of Papua New Guinea's vast gas resources.

Papua New Guina's real growth in oil and gas exploration and production came in 1990, with commencement of commercial crude export of 1,245 million barrels of crude from the Kutubu oil field in 1990. In 1993, Papua New Guinea recorded its peak crude production totalling 45 million barrels.

Papua New Guinea exports crude oil from Kutubu, Gobe, Moran and South East Mananda to overseas markets and has exported an aggregate of 450,000 million barrels of crude oil since 1990. Export for 2009 alone was 16.4 million barrels of crude oil, while export earnings were PGK 2.6 billion.

Although other producing fields in Gobe, Moran and South East Manada have come on stream, Papua New Guinea continues to experience a gradual decline in total oil production and oil revenues, thus switching the country's focus now from oil production to the commercialization of natural gas reserves.

Since 1990, the overall real GDP from the sector averaged at 4.6% in real terms. This is projected to increase by 3% at the end of 2010 and further consolidated in 2014, when first LNG exports from the US$15 billion PNG LNG Project commences. The positive outlook in overall growth from this sector is also being strengthened by the current overall gas commercialization drives underway, with Papua New Guinea eyeing its second LNG Project in Gulf Province plus gas-based developments, such as petrochemicals and gas to electricity.

Equity Participation

Oil and Gas Projects in Papua New Guinea are developed through equity partnerships. Usually, the Government, under Section 164 of the Oil and Gas Act 1998, can take up to 22.5% participation interests in a development project, which is funded by the State and managed by its nominee company. From the State's 22.5% interests, a negotiable interest of not less than 2% is given to resource area landowners. The remaining interest are taken up by the project proponent and its joint venture partners, which may comprise both foreign and national companies.

The PNG LNG Project

The PNG LNG Project succeeded the initial proposal by Papua New Guinea Government to pipe Natural Gas to Queensland, which was abandoned in 2005. The project is now being undertaken by Exxon Mobil at a total cost of US$15 billion and has a fiscal term of 30 years.

The project is a two train project with a capacity of 6.9 million tonnes per annum and will utilize natural gas from gas fields in Hides, Juha, Angore, Kutubu and Gobe over its 30 years lifespan to produce LNG for exports to customers in China, Japan and Taiwan.

The overall estimated revenue that will be generated over the entire life of the project in taxes, royalties, development levies and equity dividends, is PGK 20 billion or approximately US$6 7 billion.

### ELECTRICITY INDUSTRY POLICY

The draft Electricity Industry Policy identifies the importance and versatility of electricity as an input of production and thus, an essential ingredient to sustain economic and social growth of Papua New Guineans. The policy document identifies problems stemming from the current policy framework and incentives that arise from it and attempts to rectify the situation through developing appropriate mechanisms. The strategic objectives of the EIP are to improve reliability, accessibility and affordability of electricity services to the majority of its population. This is achieved through the following policy strategies; facilitating competition/contestability in the sector, up scaling rural electrification through State financing of consumer service obligations, enhancing technical regulation, creating certainty to investors in the sector by developing a clearly defined access/code access regime and encouraging private sector participation in the sector.

### RURAL ELECTRIFICATION POLICY

The Draft Rural Electrification policy although still in its infant stage, encapsulates the need for up scaling rural electrification through development of renewable energy resources with the vision to enhance livelihood of rural population through sustainable provision of electricity. The policy acknowledges the availability of untapped indigenous renewable energy resources in the country such as solar, hydro, wind, marine, biomass, geothermal and bio energy and aims for the utilisation of these indigenous renewable energy resources for rural communities in PNG. The policy also stipulates grid extension options and the linkages of the Renewable Energy policy with other sectoral development policies of PNG.

## PNG'S ELECTRICITY INDUSTRY STRUCTURE

The PNG Electricity Industry encompasses generation, transmission, distribution and retail activities. The overlying policy body of the sector lies with the Department of Petroleum and Energy which is mandated by the Government to formulate policy for the sector. The current players in PNG's electricity industry include the PNG Power Limited (PPL) plus other Independent power producers (IPPs). The PNG Power Limited (PPL) is a private Government entity established as a regulatory regime vested with the powers to plan, develop, generate, transmit, distribute and sell electricity throughout PNG and is vertically integrated. It is a corporate body, established pursuant to the provisions of the *Electricity Industry Act 2002*. The PNG Independent Public Business Corporation (IPBC) is the repository of PPL and manages the assets of the State in the General Business Trust. Whilst, the PNG Independent Consumer & Competition Commission (ICCC) is the licensing authority responsible for the overall economic regulation of the Industry and ensuring service standards are achieved. The PPL operates through three main interconnected systems and 19 smaller provincial systems and holds the exclusive rights to retail electricity in areas in which it supplied power together with a 10 km surrounding zone at the time of issue of its licence. Accordingly, PPL holds monopoly retail transmission sector while the generation and distribution sector are contestable.

There are also Independent Power Producers (IPP's) that are operating under direct power purchasing agreement whose total installed capacity is comparable to that of PPL, however their activities are limited and within designated locations as indicated in their respective licence. PPL has bilateral power purchasing arrangements with two IPP namely Baiune Hydro in Morobe Province and Kanudi Power Plant in Port Moresby and partners in joint-venture with the Hides petroleum development in gas fired generation (GoPNG, 2010a). Recent players that have entered the electricity market include PNG Sustainable Energy

Limited (now Western Power) which was granted a licence for electricity generation, distribution and supply activities in the Western Province in May 2007 (GoPNG, 2010a). The Kanudi Power Plant in Port Moresby owned by the Korean company Hanjung Power Ltd operates through a negotiated

agreement in 1999 under the 15 year build-operate-transfer (BOT) agreement, where as details of the other IPP's remain vague. According to the draft Electricity industry policy (GoPNG, 2010a);

"The power purchasing arrangements are understood to have been negotiated on a party-and-party basis rather than through open and competitive processes. Consequently, it is not clear whether the terms and conditions of supply and the relative risks borne by the contracting parties are optimal for the State".

Accordingly, while the regulatory framework allows competitors to supply individual customers with power loads of 10MW or more within PPL's exclusivity area and entitles them access to PPL's networks, in reality this has not happened in PNG.

## ELECTRICITY REGULATORY FRAMEWORK

In PNG the relevant Acts of Parliament that deal with energy issues include; the *Electricity Supply Act* which deals with powers of the Minister for Petroleum and Energy for generation, supply and extension of electricity from power facilities built with government funds, the *Electricity Industry Act 2002* that specifies the functions and powers of PPL, the *Independent Public Business Corporation Act 2002* that governs the arrangement under which the government holds all shares on PNG Power Ltd, the *Independent Consumer and Competition Act 2000* that regulates electricity, petroleum and their pricing, the *Environment Act 2000*, which can require environmental impact assessments for prescribed energy investment and the *Organic Law on Provincial Government and Local Level Government 1995* which grants authority to 19 provincial and 299 local governments to regulate their respective electricity.

As stipulated by the ICCC (2011)11 under Chapter IIIB, Section 24C of the *Electricity Industry Act 2002*, the Electricity Supply Industry is declared to be a regulated entity under section 32 of the *ICCC Act 2002*. The PPL is licensed under the *Electricity Industry Act 2002* to generate transmit, distribute and sell electricity in PNG and operates under three main licenses;

* Electricity Generation Licence;
* Electricity Transmission Licence; and,
* Electricity Distribution Licence.

The PPL holds exclusive monopoly in its retail transmission sector while generation and distribution sector are contestable.

Within the framework there is an Electricity Regulatory Contract (Regulatory Contract) that exists which binds the PPL and the ICCC pursuant to the provision of the *ICCC Act 2002* and *Electricity Industry Act 2002*. According to ICCC, (2011);

"This Regulatory Contract regulates the prices the PNG Power may charge for the Supply and Sale of the electricity, the Scheduled Services and the Excluded Services. The Supply and Sale of electricity, the Scheduled Services and the Excluded Services which are the subject of the Regulatory Contract are declared by the Treasurer to be regulated services under section 32 of the ICCC Act 2002. The Commission adjusts tariff in a bundle pricing under the current regulatory arrangement. With respect to the level of service provided, if PNG Power does not meet certain service level requirements stipulated within the regulatory contract, customers must be informed about their eligibility for rebates under clause 6 of the regulatory contract".

PNG Power is regulated under a form of price control mechanism known as the maximum average price („MAP'). Therefore for the individual tariffs PPL charges to different classes of consumers (Industrial, General Supply, Domestic Customers and Public Lighting) the average price of those tariffs must not exceed the MAP that ICCC determines. Whilst, considering tariff submission from PPL, the ICCC incorporates respective regulatory contract requirement and the price path for the regulated period and ensures that charges for each service complement the level of service that is expected to be provided (ICCC, 2011). In essence the tariff setting mechanism considers changes to variables such as local, Australian and US Consumer Price Index (CPI) and the cost of purchased power from the IPP (PPL, 2005).

On a broad perspective the PNG Electricity industry current regulatory framework operates on the following features (GoPNG, 2010a);

* It provides exclusive service (retail) areas for PNG Power Limited (PPL) defined as within 10kilometres of the distribution network operated by PPL as at the date of commencement of the licence) for loads under 10 megawatts(MW).
* It allows for third party producers to generate and supply PPL for the latter's sale to customers. PPL has entered into contracts with IPP's with the term and conditions of these contracts not made public.
* It allows for free entry to serve large customers (i.e. with loads of 10MW or more);
* It provides for regulated third party access to PPL's wires in circumstances where the supplier can lawfully supply, e.g. for supply to customers of loads of 10MW or more;
* It uses a system of postage stamp pricing in the shape of the national single tariff (which charges the same price for customers within a particular category, regardless of location). The inherent cross-subsidies are necessary to maintain the affordability of electricity access in high cost (largely rural) areas; and
* An independent regulator of the electricity industry, the ICCC, established by the Independent Consumer and Competition Commission Act 2002, is responsible for regulating the price and other aspects of electricity supply operation of PPL, under a regulatory contract. The ICCC implements a form of revenue cap price regulation in relation to PPL, and sets licence conditions for PPL and other market participants.

Despite this broad feature the draft Electricity Industry Policy stipulates that this regulatory framework needs further strengthening with regards to the information asymmetry between the regulator and regulated entity. In PNG it is perceived to be exacerbated due to the poor transparency of State owned enterprises (SOE's). In addition, although current market participants have third party access obligation under the law, which is reflected in their licences, the shape and content of this access arrangement remains vague. Even still, the regulatory framework fails to incorporate a detail an explicit and transparent consumer service obligation (CSO) framework that favours for a mutual optimum benefit for all players in the sector (GoPNG, 2010a).

Nonetheless, in terms of the regulator of the sector, the ICCC is the mandated agency that acts as both the economic and technical regulator and has the responsibility for regulating competition, controlling prices and protecting consumers in the electricity industry as well as the monitoring and regulation of safety and technical standard. However due to incapacities associated with the lack of qualified staff and skills to

undertake technical regulatory role, the ICCC has delegated its technical regulatory functions to PPL on a yearly renewable basis as permitted under the Act (PPL, 2010)12. Accordingly, technical regulatory functions are undertaken by PPL and these encompass;

* monitoring and regulation of safety and technical standards relating to the electricity supply industry;
* licensing of electricity generators, networks and retailers, electricians and electrical contractors;
* monitoring and regulation of safety and technical standards with respect to works, electrical installations, electrical appliances and apparatus and associated equipment; and
* any other function conferred by the Act or regulation.

## ELECTRICITY NETWORK

PNG does not operate on a national power grid but instead electricity networks are located around the more populated areas and industrial sites. PNG Power Limited the mandated national electricity utility operates three (3) main power grids the Rouna, Ramu and Gazelle which rely heavily on hydropower. The Rouna serves the National Capital District and surrounding areas in the Central Province, the Ramu serves the Momase Region and Highlands, whilst the Gazelle serves the East New Britain province. Other Provincial centres rely on diesel generators whilst the provincial governments are responsible for maintaining a number of stand-alone rural generation facilities known as C-centres13, but most are nonexistent to date and those that remain are run down mainly due to lack of funding for routine maintenance (Nagai et al, 2010).

Out of the total 580MW installed generation capacity in PNG, PPL capacity is estimated at 300MW, while the additional 280MW is generated by other entities that consume power mainly for their own use, notably the Hides gas field in Southern Highlands, the Porgera gold mine and the Lihir gold mine, Ok Tedi Mine, PNG Forest Products for the township of Wau, and Ramu Sugar Limited. Figure 2.1 below shows the main power grid that is operated by PPL in PNG.

The transmission and distribution systems are also situated around the main power grids at Port Moresby, Ramu and Gazelle, while the distribution networks covers 3,300km – 2800km in Port Moresby, Ramu and Gazelle areas and 500km elsewhere. Table 2.1 below denotes the distribution of PPL generation capacity. Table 2.2 illustrates the current transmission amongst the three (3) major systems. The energy demand for the respective systems are expected to be in line with the level of economic activity and are forecasted by PPL to grow at 1-2% per annum over the next five years (IPBC, 2009)14. Table 2.3 depicts the present energy demand with respect to the three major systems.

Table 2.1 PPL Generating Capacity

| Generating Capacity | | | |
|---|---|---|---|
| System | Hydro | Site Capacity MW Thermal | Total |
| Port Moresby | 62 | 65 | 127 |
| Ramu | 82 | 21 | 103 |
| Gazelle | 9 | 6 | 15 |
| Minor Centres | 2 | 26 | 28 |
| Total | 155 | 118 | 273 |

Source: IPBC, 2009

| Table 2.2 PPL Transmission Systems<br><br>Transmission Systems | | | | |
|---|---|---|---|---|
| System | 132kV | Line length km 66kV | 33kV | Total |
| Port Moresby | - | 151 | 17 | 168 |
| Ramu | 155 | 558 | - | 713 |
| Gazelle | - | 75 | - | 75 |
| Total | 155 | 850 | 17 | 956 |

Source: IPBC, 2009

Table 2.3 PPL Energy sales

| Energy Sales | | | | |
|---|---|---|---|---|
| | | Energy Sales MWh | | |
| System | Demand | General Supply | Domestic | Total |
| Port Moresby | 17,306 | 258,384 | 53,336 | 329,026 |
| Ramu | 40,070 | 139,805 | 41,020 | 220.895 |
| Gazelle | - | 24,336 | 5,922 | 30,258 |
| Minor Centres | - | 42,889 | 17,222 | 60.111 |
| Total | 57,376 | 465,414 | 117,500 | 640,290 |

Source: IPBC, 2009

To conclude, PNG's electricity situation proffers a dynamic challenge, despite great potential from significant underutilized indigenous energy sources such as hydropower, natural gas, geothermal bulk of PNG's population who dwell in rural areas still lack access to electricity. The main issue prevalent within the sector is the lack of an overarching policy to guide and develop the sector. As discussed earlier the three policies that deal with electricity and energy issues are still in their draft stage with the exception of the Electricity Industry Policy which is awaiting endorsement by the government. Nevertheless, PNG's rugged topography also creates a barrier for investment as generation of large scale electricity and extension of grid network would incur significant financial investment. In addition the lack of funding by the government to maintain existing infrastructure has also led to the demise of most electricity generation facilities especially in provincial centres.

In order for the sector to be vibrant and serve its purpose of providing accessible, affordable and reliable power to the bulk of the rural population who at present have no access to electricity it is important that the government prioritise the development of the sector through fast tracking the development of its sectoral policy. In addition the prerogative of the government should be to increase government budget appropriation for the electricity sector and stimulate private sector participation through either open competition or public private partnership mechanism. Nevertheless, the regulatory framework still needs strengthening regarding the information irregularity between the regulator and regulated entity. The power purchasing arrangements within IPP's should be negotiated through open and competitive processes instead of party by party basis. Essentially, the government's prerogative should be on strengthening its regulatory framework and stimulating open competition rather than performing as a monopoly in the sector.

# PNG ENERGY POLICY - STRATEGIC INFORMATION AND DEVELOPMENTS[8]

## NATIONAL RURAL ELECTRIFICATION POLICY

VISION

Improve quality of life and sustainable national development through a robust and vibrant energy sector.

GOAL

Ensure that communities, industries and other development activities have access to reliable, affordable, efficient and environmentally sound energy services and also trade in energy commodities

The above goal will be achieved through the following economic, social and environmental principles and strategies:

A. ECONOMIC

*Principle 1. Promote adequate, safe, reliable, and affordable supplies of oil, gas and other non-renewable energy sources.*

STRATEGIES

1.1 Promote the long-term sustainability of energy supply from oil and gas.

1.2 Promote the development of available energy resources for domestic use and exports.

1.3 Promote petroleum exploration and its sustainable development.

1.4 Improve the competitiveness of petroleum supply options through appropriate regulatory framework.

1.5 Regulate and enforce the collection and dissemination of information on energy trade.

1.6 Encourage conservation and efficiency measures in production and use of petroleum fuels.

1.7 Promote a reliable, cost-efficient supply of petroleum products to communities to meet their demand.

1.8 Ensure security of oil supply through a regulated minimum stock level.

1.9 Promote a national gas grid system for the country.

1.10 Increase access to technical and financial development assistance from international and domestic development partners, including the private sector.

*Principle 2. Ensure that all sectors of the economy have access to adequate, safe, reliable and affordable electricity supplies.*

Strategies

[8] Based on the PNG Government materials

2.1 Promote the long-term sustainability of electricity supply from conventional and renewable resources.

2.2 Ensure appropriate regulatory framework for the generation, supply and retail of electricity.

2.3 Ensure that any power development project, including system expansion, is based on least cost development principle.

2.4 Promote the development of appropriate electricity generation systems.

2.5 Promote energy conservation and efficiency in generation and use of electricity.

2.6 Ensure the provision of electricity to consumers conforms to national and international technical and safety standards.

2.7 Ensure appropriate in-country capacity for managing the electricity sector.

2.8 Promote a national electricity grid system for the country.

*Principle 3. Promote a 10 per cent renewable energy target.* Strategies

3.1 Promote the use and sustainable development of renewable energy source for both process heat and electricity generation.

3.2 Promote the effective management of both grid-connected and stand-alone renewable based power systems.

3.3 Promote a level playing field for the application of renewable energy sources and technologies.

3.4 Promote the provision of electricity based on a least cost development strategy, utilizing proven technologies, with adequate support using local manpower and resources, and are suited to the needs of the user.

3.5 Ensure that renewable energy systems are sustainable.

3.6 Promote renewable electrification systems that are implemented, managed and operated in a manner that empowers rural community involvement.

3.7 Promotion and development of CDM renewable energy projects approved by relevant authority to be developed and administered in partnership with other stakeholders and recipient communities.

*Principle 4. Wise and cost-effective utilization of energy in national development.*

STRATEGIES

4.1 Improve the efficiency of energy production, transmission and distribution through supply side management.

4.2 Promote demand side management programs in all sectors of the economy.

4.3 Promote appropriate incentives to encourage efficient energy use.

4.4 Encourage cooperation in energy efficiency and conservation programs in all sectors.

4.5 Promote public awareness on energy efficiency and CDM projects.

*Principle 5. Encourage involvement of the private sector in the development and provision of energy services.*

STRATEGIES

5.1 Ensure good governance for private sector investment.

5.2 Provide Incentives for private sector investment through appropriate taxation regimes.

5.3 Ensure appropriate legal and financial frameworks are in place for energy sector development.

5.4 Promote public-private participation in provision of energy sector development.

5.5 Promote private sector participation in the provision of energy services.

B. SOCIAL

*Principle 1. Develop and enhance human and institutional capacity to plan and manage the energy sector.*

Strategies

1.1 Strengthen and maintain an energy policy and planning office and regional offices with sufficient resources to independently plan and manage the national energy sector.

1.2 Coordinate national energy sector programs and development partnerships across various stakeholders.

1.3 Promote an interdisciplinary approach to energy training, research and institutional capacity building programs.

1.4 Promote and accelerate human resource development in the power utilities and Independent Power Producers (IPPs) in the areas of production, transmission and distribution.

1.5 Promote and accelerate research and development of energy technologies that are appropriate for adoption within the nation.

1.6 Increase public awareness on alternative and renewable fuels, uses, efficiency and conservation.

1.7 Develop community capacity for project planning and management of conventional and renewable energy projects.

1.8 Promote gender and youth participation in the energy sector.

1.9 Institutionalize cooperative links between the Division of Energy of DPE and other participants in rural renewable energy programs.

1.10 Ensure close cooperation among stakeholders involved in the energy with respect to meeting environmental requirements.

*Principle 2. Develop an integrated planning process for sustainable energy supply and use.*

Strategies

2.1 Promote inter-disciplinary consultations and sharing of information.

2.2 Promote the use of integrated planning tool in energy planning.

2.3 Ensure the setting up of a reliable energy database.

C. ENVIRONMENT

*Principle 1. Ensure the development and use of energy resources are environmentally sustainable.*

STRATEGIES

1.1 Promote Environment Impact Assessment (EIA) in all energy project developments.

1.2 Ensure suppliers meet the minimum quality standards for petroleum products.

1.3 Regulate and enforce energy waste management and oil spills.

1.4 Ensure petroleum storage and handling meet the minimum safety standards.

1.5 Minimize the impact of energy production, distribution and consumption on the environment, and to ensure that these are consumed in an environmentally sustainable manner.

1.6 Ensure minimum energy performance standards for electrical and equipment, and adoption of building energy codes.

1.7 Minimize the adverse impact of energy production, distribution and consumption on the environment.

1.8 Ensure all stakeholders incorporate key energy sector objectives as integral components of the environment management strategy.

# POLICIES AND LAWS REGARDING ENERGY

## ENERGY POLICIES

There are several activities underway in early 2004 within PNG assessing, or touching on, energy-related policy issues: an AusAid-funded Energy Policy Review Project;[12] assistance from the World Bank's (WB's) Gas Technical Assistance Facility to build the capacity of DPE's Petroleum Division; the WB's Rural Electrification Policy and Strategy to Improve Energy Access for Rural Services Delivery; and the ICCC's current review of petroleum product pricing. Accordingly, some policies may well change in the near future.

The most recent policy documents are a draft National Energy Policy Statement (GoPNG, 2001) and National Energy Policy Guidelines of 2001 (GoPNG, 2001a), which have no apparent formal status. Within them, the Energy Division has been allocated a number of responsibilities including the following:

monitor, review and provide recommendations on fuel pricing, electricity tariffs, and government charges and subsidies, to ensure that the full and correct price signals are conveyed to consumers wherever possible;

develop and maintain the capacity to monitor and evaluate the equivalent landed price of petroleum products, the petroleum company cost elements, the pricing formula, and government charges so as to negotiate and maintain equitable pricing;

forecast future energy trends including opportunities for the development of alternative energy sources; and

develop a rural electrification policy, recognising the role of private enterprise in rural electricity supply.

However, according to DPE (GoPNG, 2004), power sector planning is essentially carried out by PNG Power. DPE's Energy Policy and Planning Branch "does not independently undertake research to collect and analyse energy data to complement or corroborate PNG Power's work. In its current state, [it] does very little to assist energy planning. The capacity to plan and undertake surveys, and to analyse data collected is woefully limited."

Rural electrification policy guidelines were developed in 1993 (GoPNG, 1993) to address a number of issues including the low rate of rural electrification (under 10% of households), high costs and high government subsidies to C-centres (over K500 per consumer annually), exorbitant costs of grid connections through ELCOM, and the relative effectiveness of electrification at mission stations compared to GoPNG initiatives. The guidelines advocated decentralised diesel or petrol generators, micromini hydro systems where feasible, and solar photovoltaics (PV). A more recent draft National Rural Electrification Policy (GoPNG, 2001c) noted that rural electrification was a national priority under the GoPNG's development strategy and structural adjustment programme. The draft proposed, among other initiatives: i) a multi-stakeholder approach; ii) priority for renewable energy sources as the preferred option; iii) an incremental approach including demonstration projects and training rural people to operate and manage decentralised rural electrification projects; and iv) priority to community services, in particular education and health.

Despite these initiatives, DPE (GoPNG, 2004) notes that rural electrification remains ad hoc and the C-centres are performing very poorly. The Energy Division of DPE has developed a draft strategic plan for the period 2004-2008 (GoPNG, 2004b) which reintroduces two of the recommendations that were not acted upon in 1993 (or later when again proposed in 1999 and 2001), creation of a Rural Electrification Authority and enactment of enabling legislation for rural electrification.

The strategic plan has a 'vision', 'mission statement', and five tentative priority areas during the five-year period, possibly to be modified within a planned Government White Paper on Energy or new energy policies):

systematic energy market reform and restructuring;

research and information-based energy policy planning and programme coordination;

an equitable and nationally coordinated rural electrification programme;

active renewable energy development and promotion; and

a dedicated and sustainable pooled Rural Energy Fund, with a robust governance system for oversight, funding and management of a national rural electrification programme.

## LEGISLATION

There are several Acts of the Parliament of Papua New Guinea that deal directly or indirectly with energy issues. These are briefly discussed below.

Electricity Supply (Government Power Stations) Act, 1970 (revised 1973 and 2002). The Act deals with the powers of the minister responsible for energy regarding generation, supply and extension of electricity from government power stations (which are not defined) but which DPE understands as "diesel generation assets, mini-hydro schemes and solar and wind energy facilities constructed with national Government funds together with PNG Power's electricity generation assets", which may conflict with the Organic Law (discussed below).

Electricity Industry Act of 2002. Formerly the ELCOM Act, this spells out the functions and powers of the Electricity Commission (now PNG Power Ltd) to "plan and coordinate the supply of electricity throughout the country and determine the standards and inspect and control the application of all matters relating to the operations of the supply of electricity."

Independent Consumer and Competition Act of 2002. Under this Act, its 2003 regulations, and the Electricity Industry Act, the ICCC has granted PNG Power a contract fixing electricity tariffs under a formula. The formula for tariff adjustments includes changes in the consumer price index, the Kina/A$ exchange rate, fuel prices, and certain PNG Power capital investments. Under the Act, ICCC is also responsible for safety standards and technical regulation but has delegated technical regulation to PNG Power for a two-year period from 2004 (GoPNG, 2004). Finally, ICCC has granted PNG Power a series of four exclusive licenses for a 12 year period allowing PNG Power to: i) generate electricity; ii) transmit it through the Moresby, Gazelle and Ramu grids; iii) distribute electricity through existing networks and connect premises with 10 km of the networks; and iv) retail electricity to consumers at premises (with exclusive rights limited to demand of less than 10 MW). There is also an ICCC (Oil Refining Facility State Agreement Exception) Regulation of 2003 regarding pricing issues for the new refinery.

Independent Public Business Corporation of Papua New Guinea Act (2002).

Under this Act, the Independent Public Business Corporation holds all shares of PNG Power on behalf of the GoPNG.

Organic Law on Provincial Government and Local Level Government (1995). The Organic Law grants authority to the 19 provincial governments and 299 local (district/sub-district) governments to pass laws and develop regulations for electricity generation and distribution in their areas of jurisdiction. Under the Law, responsibility for C-centre management and maintenance was transferred to provincial and local level government.

Community Services Trust Act (2002). Under community service obligation (CSO) requirements of this Act, providers of essential community services are required to supply their services at subsidised rates to rural or low-income populations. For example, diesel fuel may be subsidised for electricity generation in C-centres or for use in farm equipment (GoPNG, 2004). There is currently no CSO affecting any electricity provider, whether PNG Power or private. However, this could be imposed in the future.

Environmental Act (2000). The Environment Act, number 64, 2000 came into effect in January 2004. It provides for 'general environmental duty', under which activities causing or likely to cause an environmental harm are prohibited unless all reasonable and practical measures have been taken to minimise harm. Activities are divided into levels 1, 2 and 3. Level 2 activities require permits or plans and may require an environmental impact assessment (EIA). Under Schedule 1 of the Act, Level 2 activities include: i) operation of hydroelectric plants exceeding 2 MW, ii) operation of fuel burning plants exceeding 5 MW, iii) operation of fuel burning facilities such as boilers and furnaces above 20 MW of thermal output; iv) incineration plants exceeding 10 tonnes per year capacity; v) any damming of a river or stream, and vi) electricity transmission lines exceeding 10 km in length. Level 3 activities involve 'matters of national importance' or could have a serious environmental impact and require EIA. These include: i) any project exceeding K50 million in cost; ii) petroleum or gas production and processing; and iii) any hydro reservoir greater than 5 $km^2$ in area.

# ENERGY SUPPLY, DEMAND AND INVENTORY

## ENERGY SUPPLY

Papua New Guinea is the only PIC that produces crude oil and, in 2004, will refine oil products for the local market and export. This section touches briefly on local oil and gas supply and the biomass resource.

### PETROLEUM AND GAS

Since light crude oil production began in 1992, PNG has exported[14] about 340 million barrels, roughly 100,000 bbl/day on average, from an estimated recoverable reserve of 550 million barrels. Exports in 2003 were 15.0 million barrels (worth K1.63 billion in export earnings), a decline of 2.5% by volume from 2002 but an increase of 14% in value due to higher oil prices. It is expected that production will steadily decrease until about 2015 when the resource will be depleted.

The WB and APEC have estimated PNG's gas resource at about 400 billion $m^3$, equivalent to about 2700 million barrels of oil, more than ten times the remaining recoverable oil reserves of 200-250 million barrels. This is believed to be an underestimate[15] but, in any case, PNG's natural gas resource dwarves petroleum, which has itself contributed up to 30% of PNG's export earnings. PNG is investing about US$4.5 billion in the 'Gas to Queensland Project', which will require construction of a pipeline through rugged parts of PNG and under the sea to Australia and is expected to bring over US$11 billion in export earnings over 28 years (GoPNG, 2004). The upper part of Figure 2-2 shows actual and potential oil and gas projects in PNG, all of which are in the remote western part of the mainland.

### PETROLEUM FUEL PRODUCTS

PNG imported about 6700 million litres (ML) of refined petroleum products in 2000 (Table 2-1). In 2003, the approximate wholesale market share of each marketing company was Shell 43%, Mobil 33%, BP 20% and NOC 4%, the last only in the vicinity of Lae (ICCC, 2004).[16] Approximately 160 retailers operating throughout PNG retail petroleum products. As noted in Section 1.6, the market is in the midst of restructuring and a 35,000 to 40,000 barrel-per-day refinery will produce most products by mid 2004, at least for a decade or so.

More recent estimates (GoPNG, 2004) suggest that there are about 25 trillion cubic feet (700 billion $m^3$) of natural gas, about 4,500 million barrels of oil equivalent.

[16] This is very close to the 1990 market share: Shell 42%, Mobil 38% and BP 20% (PREA, WB, 1992).

Recent wholesale prices of gasoline and distillate (i.e. automotive diesel oil, ADO; excluding taxes and duties) are shown in Figure 2-3. Prices in Port Moresby are slightly lower than the PIC average for ADO and somewhat cheaper for gasoline. For kerosene (Figure 2-4), retail prices (again, free of taxes and duties) are average for the region but wholesale prices are below average, suggesting a high mark-up relative to other Pacific island countries.

### COMMERCIAL ENERGY BALANCE

Data from Customs Department are inconsistent. The row in Table 2-1 marked 'Motor Spirit' is listed by Customs as 'Motor spirit (gas) including aviation spirit', The other products may be OK except the row marked 'Distillate fuel' is called 'Spirit type (gasoline) Jet fuel' by Customs, which is bizarre.

summary in Table 2-3.

According to APEC, net primary energy supply was 573 thousand tonnes of oil equivalent (ktoe), down 42.5% from 2000. Light crude oil and petroleum accounted for 61% of the total, gas for 25% and hydro 14%. About 79% of indigenous energy production was exported. The natural gas produced in 2001 (144 ktoe) was used for electricity production at a large gold mine at Porgera (see Figure 2-2).

| Indicator Crude Oil Petroleum Products Mogas Jet Fuel Kero | | | | | | | Diesel Oil Fuel Oil LPG Natural Gas Hydro Electricity Total | | | | | | |
|---|---|---|---|---|---|---|---|---|---|---|---|---|---|
| Indigenous Production | 2532 | - | - | - | - | | - | | - | 144 | 80 | - | 2756 |
| Import | - | 349 | 20 | 29 | 17 | | 1 | 264 | 11 | - | - | - | 349 |
| Export | -2477 | - | - | - | - | | - | | - | - | - | - | -2477 |
| Stock Change | -55 | - | - | - | - | | - | | - | - | - | - | -55 |

| | | | | | | | | | | | | | |
|---|---|---|---|---|---|---|---|---|---|---|---|---|---|
| Total Primary Energy Supply | - | 349 | 20 | 29 | 17 | | 1 | 264 | 11 | 144 | 80 | - | 573 |
| Public Electricity | - | -33 | - | - | - | | - | -33 | - | - | -47 | 96 | 16 |
| Auto producers (Electricity) | - | -169 | - | - | - | | - | -169 | - | -137 | -33 | 131 | -208 |
| Loss and Own Use | - | - | - | - | - | | - | - | - | - | - | -14 | -14 |
| Discrepancy | - | - | - | - | - | | - | | - | - | - | 5 | -2 |
| Total Final Energy Consumption | - | 147 | 20 | 29 | 17 | | 1 | 62 | 11 | - | - | 217 | 364 |
| Industry Sector | - | 58 | - | - | - | | 0 | 49 | 9 | - | - | 160 | 218 |
| Transport Sector | - | 61 | 20 | 29 | - | | 0 | 12 | - | - | - | - | 61 |
| Other Sector | - | 19 | - | - | 17 | | 0 | - | 2 | - | - | 58 | 77 |
| Agriculture | - | 0 | - | - | - | | 0 | - | - | - | - | - | 0 |
| Residential & Commercial | - | 19 | - | - | 17 | | 0 | - | 2 | - | - | 58 | 77 |
| Non-energy | - | 9 | - | - | - | | - | - | - | - | - | - | 9 |
| Source: Adapted from APEC Energy Data and Modelling Centre (Inst | | | | | | | itute of Energy Economics) database: www.ieej.or.jp/egeda/database | | | | | | |

Primary Energy Supply ktoe % Final Energy Consumption ktoe % ElectricityGeneration GWh %

| | | | | | | | | |
|---|---|---|---|---|---|---|---|---|
| Indigenous production | 2,756 | - | Industry Sector | 218 | 60 | Total | 2,638 | 100 |
| Net imports and other | -2,184 | - | Transport Sector | 61 | 17 | Thermal | 1,708 | 65 |
| Total | 573 | 100 | Other Sectors | 86 | 24 | Hydro | 930 | 35 |
| Oil | 349 | 61 | Total | 364 | 100 | Other | - | |
| Gas | 144 | 25 | Coal | - | | | | |
| Other | 80 | 14 | Oil | 147 | 40 | | | |
| | | | Gas | - | | | | |
| Electr & other 217 60 Source: Modified from Energy Overview for Papua New Guinea (APEC, 2003). Totals may ≠100% due to rounding errors | | | | | | | | |

In 2001, installed electric power capacity was 451 MW and generation was 2,638 GWh, nearly double the 2000 output of 1,348 GWh, due to dramatic variation of demand in the mining sector. Hydro provided 35% of generation and thermal 65%, of which natural gas accounted for about 26% and oil thirty nine percent.

### NON-COMMERCIAL ENERGY

In 1990, the PREA (WB, et. al., 1992) estimated that biomass accounted for 693.3 ktoe of gross energy production (and end-use consumption) in PNG as follows: fuelwood, mainly for household use, 540.6 ktoe; agricultural residue, three-fourths for agriculture and the rest for industry and household use, 149.5 ktoe; and ethanol from the sugar industry 3.2 ktoe. Solar energy for water heating and small-scale electricity production was estimated to provide 28 ktoe.

There are no reliable measurements of current non-commercial energy use in PNG. However, the PIREP mission has estimated (see Section 4.6) that about 1,000 ktoe of wood is used for cooking and a small amount of agricultural processing.

## ENERGY DEMAND

The end use consumption of commercial energy was 364 ktoe, a decrease of 58% compared to 2000. Of the total, industry accounted for 60%, transport 17% and agriculture / residential / commercial, 24%. Petroleum accounted for 40% of consumption and other energy forms (mainly electricity) sixty percent.

National Capital District, 77% of households were electrified, 67% had refrigerators and 61% had television. As Table 2-6 shows, over 75% used electric lighting, nearly 40% cooked with kerosene and, surprisingly, nearly 30% reportedly cooked mainly with electricity.

Data available from PNG Power suggest about a 63% electrification rate for the NCD so the survey results should be considered approximate only.

## ELECTRICITY

The mission did not investigate the electric power sector in any depth, did not visit any industrial /mining enclaves, and did not assess any C-centres. The information in this section is indicative only, but does illustrate the huge size and diversity of the PNG power sector compared to other PICs. In 2001 (Table 2-6), there was roughly 600 MW of installed capacity generating about 2,600 GWh of electricity.

PNG Power has over 73,000 customers, and provides electricity to the Port Moresby area and nineteen provincial capitals.It operates three interconnected grid systems (Port Moresby and Ramu on the mainland; and the Gazelle peninsula in East New Britain) in addition to 17 smaller systems.

About half of the PNG power capacity is thermal and half hydro, the main hydro systems being: i) Ramu (Yonki) in the Eastern Highlands, which supplies the highlands and Morobe and Madang provinces; ii) Laloki (Rouna) in Central Province, supplying the Port Moresby area; and Warangoi in the Gazelle Peninsula.

82% of PNG Power's customers are domestic but they accounted for only 11% of sales in 2002, using an average of 166 kWh per month (Table 2-7) or somewhat less, 123 kWh/m, if Port Moresby and Lae are excluded.

It is not possible to calculate the percentage of households in PNG with access to electricity due to large numbers of individual generators and the electrification of houses near mining enclaves (Figure 2-2). However, in 2002, PNG Power supplied electricity to about 5.5% of households nationally, nearly all customers urban or peri-urban, and 55% being in the NCD or Lae. It is likely that well under 10% of the total PNG population, and perhaps 5% of the rural population, are electrified by all means: grid, self-generation, nearby industry, small hydro or solar.

PNG Power expects its sales to grow from 660 GWh in 2003 to 766 GWh in 2012, an AAGR of 1.7%, slightly less than the 1993-2002 growth rate of 1.8%. Aggregate peak demand is expected to increase during the same period from 152 MW to 173 MW, an AAGR of 1.4%. Customer numbers are forecast to grow more rapidly, from 75,557 (2003 estimate) to 102,085, an AAGR of 3.4%, somewhat faster than expected population growth.

#### MAXIMUM DEMAND

This assumes 60,000 PNG domestic customers in 2002 and the total number of households grew from 1,008,969 by 2.7% annually from 2000-2002.

The sales forecast of Table 2-8 is illustrated in Figure 2-6 (bottom thick blue line) along with several earlier ELCOM forecasts of growth. Actual growth since 1982 has been irregular and earlier forecasts have tended to be optimistic. This is not meant to suggest that the latest forecast is too high, merely that estimating growth in a complex system like that of PNG is quite difficult.

PNG Power's generation by source is summarised in Table 2-9. Assuming that all purchases are from thermal facilities, the percentage of generation from hydro is expected to steadily drop.

| Year Hydro Heavy diesel | | | Lightdiesel Gas turbine Power Purchase Total | | | | % hydro | System losses |
|---|---|---|---|---|---|---|---|---|
| 1993 | 428 | 64 | 78 | 44 | 4 | 624 | 69 % | 13.6 % |
| 2002 | 513 | 0 | 99 | 14 | 156 | 781 | 66 % | 16.9 % |
| 2007 | 506 | 0 | 176 | 1 | 157 | 839 | 60 % | 16.0 % |
| 2012 522 0 Source: PNG Power (2003) | | | 222 1 157 901 Note: GWh rounded to nearest whole number | | | | 58 % | 15.0 % |

ELCOM/PNG Power has been under financial distress for some years, and has been unable to undertake sufficient new investment for either expansion or adequate maintenance. One result has been high (and growing) system losses, a substantial amount of generating plant derated, frequent equipment breakdowns, and power outages (GoPNG, 2004). PNG Power, as a commercialised utility with financial problems – and one which may be privatised – is understandably reluctant to undertake rural electrification in unprofitable areas, i.e. most of rural Papua New Guinea.

PNG Power has a complicated tariff structure summarised in Table 2-10. Easipay is a pay-in-advance metering system, which accounted in 2003 for about a third of domestic consumption. In early 2004, domestic credit customers pay a minimum charge of K7 per month, domestic Easipay consumers a minimum of K9/m, and general credit consumers K10/m. Charges have increased considerably since 2000. Domestic consumption above 30 kWh per month has increased by 86% in the past four years. Even before the most recent increases, the ADB (2003) notes that PNG's electricity prices are three times higher than those of neighbouring Indonesia (and labour costs four times higher and urban rents 10 times higher). Charges are, however, not unusually high for the PIC region.

### Commercial Energy Demand

In a relatively small economy dominated by minerals, oil and gas, accurately projecting future patterns of energy demand is difficult. A single mine closure or opening, a new oil discovery, or changes in natural gas prices can have a huge and immediate impact (as evidenced by a doubling of electricity generation between 2000 and 2001). In Section 1.2 it was noted that PNG's population is likely to grow at an AAGR of about 2.7 percent. Section 1.5 showed the highly variable pattern of past economic growth since Independence, with long term real GDP growth from 1975 through 2002 being less than population growth. It is assumed for the purposes of this study that real economic growth over the next 10-15 years will continue at about the same rate as population growth.

PNG Power expects growth in generation to be considerably less than this, only 1.7% per annum, but the Gas to Queensland project and renewed exploration suggest that private industrial power growth could be more robust. Table 2-3 showed the extent to which industry dominates the economy in terms of final energy consumption, 60% of the total compared to 17% for transport and 24% for other (i.e.agriculture, government, households, and commerce.) Accordingly, and considering the paucity of information, no attempt is made to project different growth rates for different economic sectors. PIREP is forecasting economic growth at 2.7% per year, and growth in energy use at 3.0% annually, in order to estimate opportunities for replacing fossil fuels with renewable energy, and thus reduce greenhouse gas (GHG) emissions. For this purpose, it is first assumed as a 'baseline' or business-as-usual case that all growth in commercial energy use is from fossil fuels, in PNG's case, oil and natural gas.

According to PNG's initial communication to the UNFCCC (GoPNG, 2000), in 1994, PNG emitted 947.57 gigagrammes (Gg) of $CO_2$ from petroleum fuels.[20] Table 2-11 provides estimates of commercial energy use and GHG emissions in 2001 (1,470 Gg) and provides baseline estimates for 2016 (2,423 Gg). Assuming commercial energy growth of 3% annually, PNG's GHG emissions from energy use would grow about 3.4% annually. This would not change significantly if different assumptions were made about the relative contributions of petroleum fuels and natural gas.

[20] The report notes that PNG slightly modified the UNFCCC methodology but says this had little effect on the results. The volumes of fuel are not given but the report says that 61% was from diesel fuel, 15% from gasoline, 13% from kerosene, 11% from other oils and less than 1% from LPG. Jet fuel treated as a re-export, was not included.

| | 2001 | | | 2011 | | | | |
|---|---|---|---|---|---|---|---|---|
| Product | Actual Use (ktoe) | Share (%) | GHGs (Gg) | Projected Use (ktoe) | Share (%) | AAGR (%) | | GHGs (Gg) |
| Petroleum products 349 61% 1,040.7 478 62 3.2% Natural gas 144 25% 429.4 211 27 3.9% Hydro 80 14% 0 80 < 11 0 Total 573 100% 1,470 769 100% 3.0 | | | | | | | | 1426.0 629.5 0 2055.5 |
| Source: 2001 use (consumption) from Tables 2.2 and 2.3 based on APC (2003). Notes: 1) $CO_2$ equivalent emissions from Annex 2, petroleum fuels averaging 70 kg of $CO_2$/GJ; natural gas 50 kg/GJ. 2) This estimate does not take into account additional $CO_2$ emissions from the refinery or from gas production. | | | | | | | | |

As discussed in the next chapter, PNG has tremendous potential for further commercial energy production from renewable indigenous resources, including hydropower development, biofuels and geothermal. Ignoring promising technologies that are very unlikely to be commercialised within the next decade or so (such as seawave or ocean thermal energy), Table 2-12 provides very rough, indicative, order-of-magnitude estimates of the potential from renewable resources and their associated GHG reductions.

However, as the assumptions of Box 2–1 show, the assumptions of Table 2-12 are unrealistic and must be adjusted.

1) Large hydro.

Economically viable large hydro conservatively estimated (Section 3.2) as 4,200 MW (36,800 GWh/year). Current installed capacity is only 5% of this. Assume national installed large hydro capacity nearly doubles from 220 MW (Table 4-2) to 400 MW producing 3.3 GWh/MW (PNG Power average, Table 4-1). Assume the additional 180 MW replaces heavy diesel fuel which (Annex 2) saves 666 Gg of CO2

2) Small hydro.

There is vast small hydro potential (section 3.2) including perhaps 45 sites near C-centres. Assume 6 MW of new capacity is developed but with some diesel back up & hydro produces only 2 GWh/MW installed. Assuming ADO and 0.4 litres per /kWh, savings are 12.96 Gg of CO2.

3) Microhydro.

Even for 500 microhydro of 22 kW producing 1,000 useable kWh/kW, and replacing diesel at 0.46 l / kWh (Annex 2), CO2 reduction is only 12.4 Gg.

4) Geothermal.

At Lihir alone (sections 3.1 and 4.1) there is 70 MW of available capacity of which an additional 20 MW or more is already under development. Assume other mines with large demand and nearby geothermal potential. Assume 3.5 GWh/MW replacing fuel oil system using 0.28 l / kWh.

5) Biodiesel.

The GoPNG expects about 30 kilotonnes per year of coconut oil and 350KT of palm oil (at about the same value per tonne) from 2004-2008. This is about 418 ML. Assume only 10% of some vegetable oil is used as diesel replacement. CO2 reduction would be about 113 Gg.

6) Ethanol.

There is vast potential for ethanol from sago and nipa palm (latter part of section 3.6). Conservatively, assume 300 ML of ethanol per year equivalent to about 175 ML of gasoline or diesel fuel. Ignoring CO2 produced during manufacture, savings would be about 430 to 470 Gg depending on the fuel displaced.

7) Other biomass.

Although (section 3.6) every 100 $m^3$ of logs produce about 45 $m^3$ of processed wood and 55 $m^3$ of potential biomass for fuel, nearly all the 2 million $m^3$ of logs produced annually are exported unprocessed. If 10% were processed in PNG, and 5% of that is available as fuel, this would provide 12,000 $m^3$ of fuel. Assuming 400 kg/$m^3$ and 14 MJ/kg, this is equivalent to 67,000 gigajoules (Gj) or only 1.6 ktoe.

8) Solar PV.

There are over one million households in PNG of which at least 300,000 live in areas of high solar insolation. Assume 100,000 rural households receive. PV systems of 100 Wp & 0.25 kWh/day. Assume 300 days/yr operation = 2.55 million kWh/year. At 0.46 l/kWh for small diesel systems, this would displace 3.45 ML of fuel, equivalent to only 9.3 Gg per year.

9) Wind.

Parts of PNG (section 3.4) could reportedly produce well over 2,000 kWh/kW of installed wind turbine capacity. Assuming a more conservative 1,000 kWh/kW and 50 sites of 250 kW each, this would displace

3.8 ML of diesel (assuming it replaced an efficient diesel plant using 0.3 l / kWh) or 10 Gg of CO2 reductions.

10) Energy efficiency (electricity).

It appears from Table 2-2 that about 57% of petroleum products (excluding natural gas used for electricity production at a gold mine) was used for electricity generation. If the same proportion applied in 2011 electricity would account for 0.57 x 478 = 272.5 ktoe. If this is reduced by 5% through end-use efficiency efforts, savings would be 0.05 x 272.7 ktoe = 13.6 ktoe, equivalent tor 40.6 Gg. However, the GHG savings in Table 2-12 from hydro and geothermal energy development for power production add up to 1024 Gg, which is equivalent to 343.2 ktoe of petroleum use. As this is about 26% above the total assumed demand for petroleum fuel for electricity generation in 2011, (i.e. 343.2/272.5), then efficiency measures could save fuel only, not reduce GHGs further.

11) Energy efficiency (transport).

Transport accounts for about 18% of petroleum fuel use or 0.18 x 468 ktoe = 86 ktoe in 2011. If efficiency measures result in a 5% saving, this would reduce petroleum use by 55 x 86 = 4.3 ktoe reducing GHG emissions by 12.8 Gg.

However, transport petroleum use of 86 ktoe is equivalent to about 257 Gg of GHGs. Biodiesel and fuel ethanol production could potentially reduce GHGs by 876 Gg (equivalent to 293.6 ktoe of petroleum fuels) which is more than triple the projected fuel demand in 2011.

As Box 2–1 shows, the potential GHG savings of Table 2-12 assume that PNG can develop renewable energy systems that produce more energy for electricity and transport than the demand assumed in the projections for 2011. About one third of transport fuel is motor spirit. At most (in the short to medium term), ethanol could replace about 20% of this in the form of motor spirit/ethanol blends, reducing the role of biofuels further. Table 2–13 revises the assumed level of renewable energy development downwards to match expected demand.

In principle, PNG could reduce CO2 equivalent GHG emissions through renewable energy investments by over 1,000 Gg per year over the next decade or so, about 70% of total 2001 emissions. Almost all of this would be through renewable energy.

If this level of renewable energy were developed, energy efficiency efforts would reduce fuel consumption, but as this would displace renewable energy, there would be no significant further GHG reductions This indicative and crude estimate is based on proven technologies and more-or-less known resources but does not consider economic, financial, political, social, technical, environmental or other practical constraints. It does not consider emerging applications such as fuel cell technology using some of PNG's vast natural gas resource as fuel. Although this is not renewable energy, natural gas produces only about 60-70% of the emissions of liquid petroleum fuels, depending on the fuel displaced.[23]

Even a fairly large solar PV or wind energy programme would provide very modest GHG reductions. The basis for the above estimates, which are not meant to represent practical or achievable goals, is discussed below.

For transport, assume biofuels can replace 100% of diesel fuel (2/3 of 86 ktoe =57.3 ktoe) and 20% of motor spirit (0.2 x 1/3 x 86 ktoe = 5.7 ktoe. The total is 63 ktoe. 22

Motor spirit, reducing the ethanol blended in, would be 0.8 x 1/3 x 86 ktoe = 22.9 ktoe. 5% saved through efficiency measures is 1.1 ktoe, equivalent to 3.3 Gg. 23

A study by the World Wide Fund for Nature (WWF) and Fuel Cell Europe, looking at life-cycle savings, estimates that "GHG reductions above 50% can be achieved with fuel cells powered by natural gas" (WWF, 2003). The authors expect fairly rapid development of small (under 10 kW) systems.

# POTENTIAL FOR RENEWABLE ENERGY TECHNOLOGIES

The technical potential for energy production from renewable energy technologies (RETs) from local renewable resources in Papua New Guinea is enormous. However, in practice much of this potential is far from locations with significant energy demand and cannot be readily exploited. Many of the resource assessments for hydropower are a decade or two old. Even good knowledge of the national technical potential provides only limited information on practical short-term options. Nonetheless, there is considerable value in estimating the potential resources and associated technologies for geothermal, hydro, ocean based energy, wind, solar and biomass for liquid fuels (coconut oil) and combustion (forest resources). These are discussed below.

PNG's two universities, the University of Papua New Guinea (UPNG in Port Moresby) and the University of Technology (Unitech in Lae), in collaboration with several government departments (Energy and Forestry), organised three national seminars/workshops on 'renewable energy for rural development' in 1987, 1989 and 1994. Some of the information in this chapter is from these meetings. Despite generating enthusiasm and producing a number of reports on RE potential in PNG, very little concrete action followed (Yarka, 1999). Since 1994, very little new information generation and dissemination on RE has taken place through workshops, conferences or seminars (Puy and Sumanasiri, 2003).

### GEOTHERMAL ENERGY

No systematic assessment of PNG's geothermal energy potential has been carried out. However, reconnaissance studies of the country's geothermal potential suggest that the most promising area for investigation is the northern coast of New Britain Island, from the Willaumez Peninsula eastward to the Gazelle Peninsula. There are at least seven geothermal sites in the region: Bamus, Galloseulo, Walo, Kasoli-Hoskins, Garbuna, Pangalu-Talasea and Bola. At Talasea, Pangalu and Kasoli, all on the north coast of New Britain, the thermal fields are associated with a belt of recent volcanic activity. Numerous hot springs, geysers, fumaroles and mud pools are found at temperatures of 90-101°C, reportedly significant H2S and CO2. Geothermometric equilibrium temperatures could be in the 300°C range and a dry steam geothermal reservoir could underlie the region. The fluids in the four geothermal areas to the east of the Willaumez Peninsula have temperatures from 86-100°C and are slightly to moderately acidic, suggesting near surface volcanic heat sources. Apparently AusAID and the Deutsche Gesellschaft für Technische Zusamenarbeit (GTZ, the German Agency for Technical Co-operation) have supported some investigation of geothermal energy resources in PNG but the mission has no details.

There has been only limited commercial geothermal development in PNG (discussed in Section 4.1), because of the small populations, low levels of industrial development and low demand for power in the areas of major volcanic activity. The island of Lihir, off the north coast of New Ireland, is a notable exception. Lihir contains one of the world's largest epithermal gold deposits within an active geothermal system. Geothermal drilling by the Philippine National Oil Company for Lihir Gold Limited, has estimated a geothermal power prospect of up to 70 megawatts.

In 2002 SOPAC, in collaboration with the US Geothermal Industries Corporation (USGIC) prepared a funding proposal for carrying out further assessment of the geothermal resource in five PICs (SOPAC, 2002), including PNG. No funding has thus far been found to implement the project.

### HYDROPOWER

Hydroelectric power potential in PNG is substantial, as a large part of the country is mountainous and receives substantial rainfall. Information on specific sites is limited, due to the absence of systematic hydrological surveys. The WB-funded Hydropower Resources Inventory Study, published in 1994, estimated the gross theoretical hydropower potential of PNG as roughly 175,000 GWh/year (20,000 MW). Defined as the sum of 90% dependable outputs with about 10 MW or larger capacity, the technically feasible potential was estimated at 122,640 GWh/year (14,000 MW). The International Energy Agency (IEA) estimates the economically feasible hydro potential at approximately 36,800 GWh/year (4200 MW) (IEA Small Hydro website, 2004). In November 1980, the GoPNG's DME had estimated gross potential at 25,000 MW (Kalimba, 2004). None of these estimates include small-scale (mini, micro and pico)[24] hydro potential scattered throughout the country, which could be an ideal source of energy for rural communities, and the exploitable potential of which is considerable.

The greatest hydropower potential in the country is in the Gulf Region. The river with the largest potential is the Purari, followed by the Kikori, Fly and Sepik rivers. Sizable potential at a number of medium-size sites is found in and around the large electric demand centres of Port Moresby and Lae, and the moderate demand centres of Madang and the highlands regions. Most estimates are based on run-of-river developments and would greatly increase if dams were constructed for flow regulation (PREA; WB et al, 1992).

A 1985 New Zealand Aid (NZAID) supported a DME assessment of mini hydro potential near 110 load centres in 17 provinces. Investigations were carried out at 31 centres, with the rest examined through desk study. Although the main focus was the power generation potential in the vicinity of C-centres, the study considered the resource potential in the vicinity of the nearby population centres as well. It identified 6 MW of mini hydro potential, more than half of which was concentrated in North Solomons province. Other promising locations were in Madang, Morobe, Eastern Highlands and Southern Highlands provinces. In some locations, the economic viability was judged to be low or uncertain due to low demand and/or cheaper power through grid extension or other renewable energy sources (Beca-Worley International, 1985).

## OCEAN BASED ENERGY TECHNOLOGIES

PNG includes more than 600 islands. Several coastal and island areas, such as Aitape and Kavieng, are renowned for surfing and have wave energy and tidal potential although neither has not been measured (Puy & Sumanasiri, 2003). However, no use is made of ocean based energy technologies (OTEC, tidal or wave energy) and there is limited knowledge of its potential. This is unsurprising as ocean energy technologies, although much hyped, are not commercially available, proven technologies.[25]

A paper presents limited data on tidal energy potential. The tidal range is far greater at Port Moresby (2.7m) than at Anewa Bay, Northern Solomons Province (1.6m); Lae (1.5m); Seeadler Harbour, Manus (1.3m); or Dreger Harbour, Morobe (1.1m). The range is about 6m in parts of the Torres Strait between PNG and Australia (Liu Zhaoxiang, February 2004).

In early 2004, a Chinese renewable energy consultant then at DPE proposed a tidal current system of unknown size for Buka Passage, Bougainville (Liu Zhaoxiang, personal communication (pers.com.), 19 January 2004) with peak currents of about 4-6 knots (7-11 km/hour). It has been suggested that a refurbished boat be moored in the passage and retrofitted with a paddle wheel to extract energy (Figure 3-1), a low efficiency approach which would seem to be insufficiently roust for the conditions. The project, reportedly backed by the local governor, is at a very preliminary stage and requires careful technical and economic confirmation.

As far as the mission could determine, there has been no measurement of deep sea versus surface ocean temperatures to enable estimates of near-shore ocean thermal energy (OTEC) potential. Despite frequent announcements of seawave and OTEC demonstration projects, it is highly unlikely that PNG or other PICs will deploy ocean energy technologies at any scale for the next decade or so.

## WIND ENERGY

The most recent known assessment of

PNG's wind resource was carried out in the late 1970s by the Australian Commonwealth Industrial and Scientific Research Organisation (CSIRO) at the request of the Department of Minerals and Energy (DME). CSIRO (Table 3-1) estimated an annual power generation potential of 607 kWh per kW of installed capacity (J. D Kalma, 1980).

The study ranked the provinces according to wind power potential as follows:

high: Manus, Central, Western, Milne Bay, New Ireland and NCD;

medium: North Solomons, Gulf, East New Britain, Morobe and Oro; and low: Simbu, the Highlands, Enga, Madang, East Sepik, Sandaun and West New Britain.

A prototype seawave system has operated for about a year in Denmark.

If these wind speed estimates are accurate, with improvements in wind energy technology, the annual average potential in PNG could now be considerably higher, up to 2600 kWh/kW for properly sited machines (G Heffner, pers. com., 9 March 2004). However (Mears, 2004), these were mostly model based estimates with very little wind gauging and there is some evidence that weather patterns have since changed significantly, in some cases for the worse.

A Forum Secretariat Southern Pacific Wind and Solar Monitoring Project, which measured wind speeds in a number of PICs in the mid-1990s, did not include Papua New Guinea.

### SOLAR ENERGY

Solar energy represents one of the largest potential sources of energy in PNG. Excepting cloud forest areas, it is in a favourable geographical location for year-round solar energy applications. The average insolation in most parts of the country is in the range of 400-800 $W/m^2$, with a mean sunshine hours ranging from 4.5 - 8 hours a day. Insolation averages 6 $kWh/m^2/day$ with average sunshine hours varying across the country.

Based on measurements from 23 locations (apparently long-term but details unknown), the driest location in PNG is Port Moresby in the NCD with an estimated 2,478 sunshine hours per year and a daily range of 5.8 to 8.2 hours. The lowest sunshine duration is at Tambul in the Western Highlands, with an estimated mean annual of 1292 hours due to frequent fog and mist. On a regional basis, the Southern, Momase and Islands Regions are estimated to have a mean annual sunshine duration of more than 2000 hours, and the Highlands Region less than 1500 hours. Based on climatic conditions, the highest potential provinces for solar PV would be the islands and southern regions. The Momase and Highlands regions have less favourable conditions for solar but relatively high potential for mini hydro (PREA, WB, 1992 and Heffner, 2004).

### BIOMASS ENERGY

Two-thirds of PNG is forested (Table 3-2) but much is inaccessible or unsuited for energy use. The government estimates that 58% of land area is subject to strong or severe erosion and 18% is permanently inundated or regularly flooded. About 200,000 hectares are cleared annually for traditional agriculture (GoPNG, 2000). This section does not attempt to estimate the total biomass resource but confines itself to areas of logging or agricultural production where the output or residues could have potential for energy use.

#### LOGGING

Logging first began in PNG in the early 1920s, mainly in coastal areas. Sawmills were established, mainly by missionaries, to cut timber to build churches, schools, and health centres. The volumes extracted were low and logging was to service local sawn timber needs. Today commercial logging for export is fairly widespread throughout all regions of PNG. After restrictions on round log exports were removed in 1979 (when log exports were just below 0.5 million $m^3$), exports increased substantially.

The logging industry expanded beyond the capacity of regulatory authorities and an official Commission of Inquiry – the Barnett Inquiry – concluded in 1989 that the forest industry was effectively 'out of control'. Several forestry policies were developed to regain control of the sector but log extraction and exports continued to increase throughout much of the 1990s, peaking in 1997 when exports reached about 3m $m^3$. Since then there has been a steady decline: timber extraction is now around 2m $m^3$ per year and exports slightly lower[26] (European Forest Institute website). The best commercial forests have already been lost. As resource rich concessions are logged out, the logging companies shift to less desirable areas with lower densities, explaining the decline in production. The maximum sustainable harvest (from 11 million ha. of forest suitable for large-scale exploitation) is no more than 2m $m^3$ per annum[27] (Shearman & Cannon, 2002). Figure 3-2 shows logging concessions and exports in thousands of $m^3$.

The logging industry is currently dominated by the Malaysian company Rimbunan Hijau, which controls more than 60% of the sector. Of the 1.85 million $m^3$ of declared log exports in 2002, 62% went to China and Hong Kong and 23% to Japan (Greenpeace, 2004). Despite the decline in log export licences granted by the National Forest Authority, declared log exports rose to 2.02 million $m^3$ in 2003, an increase of nearly 10% from 2002 (BPNG, QEB, Dec. 2003).

### Wood processing

Although it has long been GoPNG policy to promote downstream processing of timber, only a very small portion of extracted logs are processed locally. In 1954 PNG's first plywood and veneer mill was established in Bulolo, remaining the only plywood mill until 1998. During the first three decades of operation, production peaked in 1973-1974 at 15,700 $m^3$ of sawn timber and 5000 $m^3$ of veneer. In 1969, production of woodchips started at the Jant mill in Madang, still the sole woodchip mill in PNG, accounting for some 200,000 $m^3$ of logs processed.

[26] Although more precise data are available, sources differ regarding quantities. Therefore indicative data have been used. 27

This is 40% lower than the 3.13m $m^3$/year that FAO estimates for the total potential sustainable production from PNG's forests (source: FAO website; undated).

Processing and exports of timber have increased sharply in the past several years, following the commissioning of the Rimbunan Hijau-owned Panakawa Mill at Kamusie in Western Province. Sawn timber exports grew from 32,000 $m^3$ in 1998 (23,000 $m^3$ in 1999) to 42,348 $m^3$ in 2002. Exports of veneer rose from 1,700 $m^3$ in 1999 to 71,615 $m^3$ in 2002 and plywood exports increased from 7000 $m^3$ in 1999 to 70,083 $m^3$ in 2002 (Greenpeace, 2004).

The wood processing industry produces waste products with potential use for energy production. Table 3-3 lists 18 major industrial facilities, including sawmills, plywood mills, veneer mills, woodchip mills and furniture factories The largest wood processing plants in the country are the PNG Forest Products plywood mill in Bulolo (Morobe); the Rimbunan Hijau veneer mill in Panakawa (Western Province), and the Jant Limited woodchips mill in Madang. Section 4.7 discusses the extent to which wood waste is currently used for energy production.

### Agro-industry

In both production volume and monetary value, the major agricultural products in PNG are palm oil, coffee and cocoa. In terms of value, copra and coconut oil are of much less importance, especially compared with the value of mineral exports. Table 3-4 presents the production of key agricultural commodities and GoPNG projections through 2008. Figure 3-3 shows the value of agricultural exports in 2002.

Coffee was until recently the most important cash crop in terms of foreign exchange. In recent years, levels of coffee production have declined

In 2000, oil palm exports overtook coffee exports for the first time. The volume of oil palm exports rose by almost 80% between 1995 and 2003. Some 100,000 hectares are cultivated for oil palm, almost half of which are managed by smallholders, the rest being estate plantations. There are four major oil palm projects in PNG, in the provinces of West New Britain, Oro, Milne Bay and New Ireland.[28] The leading producer in PNG – and the largest private sector employer – is New Britain Palm Oil Ltd. (NBPOL), which produces approximately 200,000 tonnes of crude palm oil per year, about two-thirds of the total. In 2002, the company built a refinery designed to process about half of its annual capacity. In principle, almost any vegetable oil can be used, sometimes requiring some additional processing, as a fuel.

Sugar cane has been grown in PNG since 1979 when Ramu Sugar Limited (RSL) began operation. RSL can process over 500,000 tonnes of cane per season (April-October). Assuming a yield of 10%, the mill can produce 50,000 tonnes of processed and refined sugar per year. Sugar production exceeded 38,500 tonnes in 2000; 42,400 tonnes in 2001; and 49,100 tonnes in 2002 (IPA website). The main by-product is molasses, part of which is sold locally, primarily as cattle feed. The balance of around 15,000 tonnes per year is converted into alcohol[29] (Vulum, 2003). RSL is diversifying into oil palm, which may account for over 50% of its revenues by 2007 (World Reports website).

Alcohol can also be produced from sago palm or nipa palm, an option which was explored in the early 1980s by DME. Between 200 and 1,100 million litres of fuel alcohol from sago palm could reportedly be available in the Gulf Province alone, with other areas, such as East Sepik, offering further potential. Some 263 million litres of fuel alcohol from nipa palm could potentially be available from the 48,500 ha of palm in the Purari Basin, with much larger areas of nipa palm existing elsewhere in PNG.

Copra has been exported since the 1950s. The total area under coconut cultivation is 260,000 hectares or about 0.6% of PNG's land area. Coconut once accounted for a third of agricultural exports, but its contribution has decreased significantly over the years. Most coastal provinces produce copra but the bulk is from East New Britain, West New Britain, Madang, New Ireland and North Solomons. Smallholders account for 60% of production whereas 40% is from plantations. The Island Provinces combined produce 75% of the total. Madang produces 18,000 tonnes per year, the Southern region 4,000-15,000 tonnes, and Morobe and Sepik Provinces combined 20,000 tonnes. Copra, of course, is used to produce coconut oil (copra oil), which can be, and has been, used successfully as a diesel-fuel replacement.

As a rule of thumb, for each $m^3$ of logs extracted, about the same amount stays in the bush (i.e. is unavailable for productive use); for each $m^3$ of processed timber produced, at least the same amount remains as waste. 200 $m^3$ of logs cut generate about 100 $m^3$ of logs extracted, which generate about 45 $m^3$ of useful processed wood and 55 $m^3$ of waste. In PNG, however, as described above, only a small percentage of the wood extracted is processed locally and much of this goes to the chipmill. The bulk is exported as logs leaving a relatively small amount available in practice for potential energy production.

In principle, PNG could produce a large amount of energy (heat, electricity, liquid fuel) from wood waste, agricultural wastes, molasses, palm oil and copra. These are discussed further in chapter four.

## EXPERIENCES WITH RENEWABLE ENERGY TECHNOLOGIES

### Experience with Geothermal Energy

In April 2003, Lihir Gold Ltd. commissioned a 6 MW geothermal power plant on Lihir Island (see Figures 2-2 and 4-1), the first such system in PNG. Four steam wells, initially drilled for cooling and depressurising the mine, provide the steam for power generation. The power plant requires over 100 tonnes of steam per hour to operate at maximum capacity. The 6 MW capacity is only 10% of total mine power requirements. Lihir Gold is currently installing a further 20-30 MW of geothermal capacity (PREA, 1992; SOPAC, June 2002; Bais, 2004). PNG Power is considering exploring the geothermal potential in both East and West New Britain (Bais, 2004).

### Experience with Hydropower

GoPNG Hydropower Development Programmes

*Small hydropower development*

In the 1980s and 1990s, ELCOM (now PNG Power) considered small hydropower development for the replacement of diesel power plants in isolated systems. Feasibility studies were completed for Divune (3 MW) near Popondetta and Maum-Danop near Wewak, and reconnaissance studies and river gauging were undertaken for potential sites at Alotau (Gumiini), Fischhafen (Butaweng), Kerema (Murua), Lombrum/Lorengau (Lauls), Vanimo (Daundo) and Kimbe. None materialised due to ELCOM's policy to undertake construction of small hydropower stations only if their financial feasibility was confirmed (WB et al, 1992).

*Micro hydropower development*

In 1985 the DME's Energy Division embarked on an ambitious Diesel Power Replacement Programme (DPRP) with the goal of reducing reliance on imported diesel fuel by designing and constructing small hydro schemes to replace the existing diesel generator sets in C-centres in the interior of the highlands. It was hoped that the DPRP would improve the reliability and quality of electric power and reduce overall costs. Forty-five potential sites were identified near existing diesel-powered C-centres. By 1987, feasibility studies at 14 of the sites had been completed, and between 1988 and 1992 three micro-hydro systems were installed. The 300 kW Tari hydro scheme (Southern Highlands Province) was commissioned in 1988 with the European Union (EU) financing 80% of construction costs and the GoPNG the remainder. The 60 kW Woitape hydro scheme (Central Province) and the 100 kW Telefomin project (West Sepik Province) were completed in 1991 and 1992 respectively, both with GoPNG funds. The cost of the Woitape project (including installation, commissioning and site supervision) was approximately US$1.4 million, or US$23,000 per kW. The estimated cost of completing and commissioning the Telefomin system was US$2.4 million, or US$24,000 per kW (Kopi, 2003).

In 1991 the DPRP evolved into the Micro-Hydro Development Programme (MHDP), a five-year initiative encompassing seven additional small hydro projects, and including training of national engineers (WB, et. al., 1992). Funding for the MHDP was sought from the EU (K8.5 million for equipment procurement) and from GTZ (K2.7 million for training). The EU funding apparently never materialised. The GoPNG has reportedly constructed no further small hydro projects since 1992. GTZ funding for training, however, was approved, and a ForSec-managed hydropower training programme started in mid-1993. ForSec contracted a German firm, Projekt-Consult, to train Energy Office staff in the planning, implementation and operation of small-scale hydropower projects and in solar PV systems. As no counterpart was available, and the GoPNG restructured its ministries, affecting the Energy Division, the training programme and its associated funding was transferred from PNG to the Solomon Islands (Fairbairn, 2004).

Installed and planned capacity: government and commercial auto-producers

The installed hydroelectric generating capacity of PNG Power Ltd. (PNG Power) in 2000 was about 162 MW, about 4% of PNG's estimated economically feasible hydro potential. Ok Tedi Mining Ltd. (OTML) operates a 57 MW facility at Ok Menga plus a 2 MW Yuk Creek plant. The installed hydro capacity nation-wide (2000) is about 220 MW, excluding private hydro installations under 2 MW. Nationwide, hydroelectric in 2000 accounted for 32% of installed capacity as shown in Tables 4-1 and 4-2.

Micro-hydro systems have a long history in PNG, with church missions installing them for their own use and sometimes extending supplies to nearby households. Some school and health facilities have installed micro-hydro rather than small diesel or petrol generators. Only three C-centres, the largest consumers of public electricity in rural areas, have hydropower.[30] It is not known how many C-centre hydro schemes are still functioning.

Numerous small and mini hydro installations exist in PNG, but documentation is sketchy, and the various reports discussing them often contain conflicting information. A 1984 study identified 55 micro-hydroelectric schemes installed since 1960, of which 40 were operational at that time (Hothersall, 1984). An earlier estimate suggested that there were about 100 small schemes towards the end of 1976 (Woodward, 1977). Ranatunga noted that more than 45 micro-hydro plants had been installed throughout PNG between 1960 and 1989 but that not many were operational, mainly due to poor maintenance (Ranatunga et. al., 1989). In 2003 Kopi estimated that about 40 mini and micro-hydropower schemes were supplying power to rural communities and institutions, over half of which were established by missions and church organisations, and some of which had been in operation for over 25 years (Kopi, 2003).

This is due mainly to GoPNG policies favouring diesel generators but also because of the limited success of the Diesel Power Replacement Programme and the apparent failure of the Micro-Hydro Development Programme.

This may be due to the different lifestyles (in many areas of PNG people live in geographically sparse hamlets, exceptions being plantations, missions or government stations) and cultural factors (the need for a clan focus to avoid jealousies and land issues) compared to the Solomon Islands.

The estimates by Kopi and Kalimba apparently do not include the community-owned self- built micro- and picohydro schemes in the vicinity of Arawa in Bougainville during the civil war. There are presently (March 2004) reportedly about 30 such schemes in operation, some of which have run for over six years (Mears, 2004).

Combining the various literature sources, the PIREP mission estimates that there may have been as many as 200 pico-, micro- and mini-hydro systems installed in rural PNG between 1960 and 2004.[34] Of these, perhaps 20-25% are still functioning i.e. 2025 systems on Bougainville and roughly the same number throughout the rest of the country.

#### MINI-MICRO HYDRO DEVELOPMENTS

Micro-hydro systems (like solar PV systems) are usually sold (Figure 4-2) to institutions rather than to individual households, although there are signs of an emerging market for the latter. The greatest proponents of small-scale hydro have been missions and agricultural enclaves. Within the resources available for the PIREP study, it has not been possible to compose a complete picture of all mini-hydro initiatives. Some private sector and NGO initiatives are mentioned below. Little data is available on hydro initiatives at churches, schools and health facilities.

#### PRIVATE SECTOR INITIATIVES

Porgera Joint Venture (PJV) at the Porgera mine has assisted local people in the Tari area in the Southern Highlands refurbish a hydro system at Duli. In the Pureni area, PJV is assisting the community to rebuild a dam that was washed away due to floods. When this is completed, a small hydro unit is to be set up using existing equipment and a new alternator. In co-operation with local landowner groups (the Paiam Management and Porgera Development Association), PJV has surveyed the Pongema River where it proposes a 2 MW hydro system to supply Paiam Township, Porgera Station and surrounding areas, if funding can be arranged. The installation would be linked to an existing grid operated by the mine and the company would purchase any excess power generated.

Platypus Power (Australia) has supplied a 30 kW turbine/generating unit to Ok Tedi Mining Limited for the Atemkit village micro hydropower project. The scheme is not yet operational due to design problems, for which OTML is reportedly obtaining expert assistance. By early 2004, Platypus had sold 12 turbine/generating units for community facilities in PNG.

Rainbow Power Company (Australia) has supplied micro hydro systems (300 watt AC units) to several organisations in PNG, including the Appropriate Technology and Community Development Initiative (ATCDI) at Lae, the Australian Baptist Missionary Society, Catholic Health Services, Conservation Melanesia Inc. and many others.

New Britain Palm Oil Limited (NBPOL) is exploring the feasibility of mini hydro potential in the Hala area and is interested in taking over PNG Power's existing mini hydro installations at Kimbe Bay.

The department store ESCO markets solar home systems and micro hydro systems in the Western Highlands. ESCO has sold these to the Kudji Nazarene Hospital and the Ambua Lodge near Tari.

Rural Development Services (RDS) Ltd has helped develop several combined rural water-supply projects and two hydropower schemes (Wakunai and Kieta district) in Central Bougainville (Capon, 2004). Funding came from Community Development Services (CDS, an AusAid assistance program), the National Member of Parliament for Central Bougainville, and his constituency development fund. It is understood (Mears, 2004) that implementation of some of the systems supplied by RDS remain to be completed, or were recently redone by CDS.

Mears (2004) adds that a mini hydro project was commissioned in mid-December 2003 close to the old goldmine near Bwagaoia in Misima. With peak output of 250 kW (average 160 kW), it will, with diesel back-up, replace a much larger 6 MW oil fired power station that was operated by the mine. The Mimisa hydro project will be owned and operated by the landowners. However, arrangements for tariff collection are unclear. The hydro capacity is insufficient to meet present demand, so improved load management and some load shedding will be required. In November 2003 there was reportedly little community awareness of these issues.

### GRASSROOTS INITIATIVES

At least two not-for-profit organisations are involved in hydro-based grassroots electrification in PNG. These are ATCDI, located at Unitech, and the Australian APACE VFEG (Village First Electrification Group).[35]

ATCDI has been a principle focus of grassroots PNG hydro activity, having been founded by some internationally well-known small hydropower experts (Adam Harvey, Allen Inversin, and others) and now carried on by Garaio Gafiye and others. ATCDI has constructed or rehabilitated at least six micro hydro schemes, including (ATCDI, 2004):

Bogo Community School, Simbu Province (design and construction);

Mapos Community School, Morobe Province (design and construction);

Mt Gahavisuka Provincial Park, Eastern Highlands Province (design and construction);

Daulo Pass, Eastern Highlands Province (design and construction but needs upgrading);

Bena SDA School, Eastern Highlands Province (rehabilitation); and

Baindoang, Morobe (rehabilitation).

The 6.4 kW Baindoang community hydro scheme in Morobe province, a joint effort of the local community and ATCDI/Unitech, supplies electricity to a community school and a village. It is running at reduced output due to lack of maintenance because poor management has resulted in failed tariff collection (Mears, 2004).

If funding can be secured, ATCDI plans to install at least one new micro hydro scheme and fix two others, as follows (ATCDI website):

Goglme (Gembogl District, Simbu Province), electrification of a health centre, school and catholic mission (construction);

Daulo Pass Micro Hydro Scheme (upgrading: installation of GI penstock and power poles); and

Rongo Lutheran Mission micro scheme (refurbishing, as it is currently non-operational).

APACE VFEG, with two decades of experience in community-based rural hydro development in the Solomon Islands, has assisted grassroots electrification in PNG. In the 1980s and 1990s, its PNG efforts were limited to a single scheme, in which APACE VFEG helped develop and improve a 5 kW scheme at Agaun village, Milne Bay

APACE VFEG works through local partners to build technical and institutional capacity. Since 2001, it has mentored PNG community groups, reportedly following the communities' wish to establish a PNG Village Electrification Council (PNGVEC). It is understood (Bryce, 2004) that PNGVEC has been formally registered and that a two-year action plan was in place in early2004. However, (Mears, 2004) no hydro systems have yet been realised. Potential micro-hydro schemes for which APACE VFEG has provided some technical and social assistance include (Bryce, 2004):

a combined hydro-water supply system to serve the town of Alotau, for which detailed design work has been completed;

electrification of Arawa township and surrounding settlements of Bougainville, for which a pre-feasibility study was conducted; and

preliminary work at the Chimbu and Maril rivers (Simbu), the Itnonomata river (Oro), the Ramu river (Madang), the Purnine river (Morobe) and several associated with Kandep village (Enga). There has been correspondence with village representatives and several a site visits.

*Micro/pico hydro activities on Bougainville*

Because of its very distinct features, the hydro experience in Bougainville is discussed separately here. From 1988 -1997, Bougainville suffered from civil strife, and the island was blockaded by the GoPNG throughout much of the 1990s. There was considerable resourcefulness during this period. Some communities used coconut oil to fuel vehicles and developed tiny hydro schemes (Figure 4-4) to deliver very limited service (essentially lighting only), due to lack of voltage and frequency control. At the end of hostilities, the new international assistance available to Bougainville included pico-hydro development. In 2001, APACE conducted a two-week training programme in Arawa for village operators of existing micro- and picohydro systems to improve safety and future design. The 55 participants represented some 40 communities, mainly from central Bougainville, which had established micro hydro during the conflict.

In 2002, an Australian renewable energy expert Andrew Mears, in collaboration with Volunteer Service Abroad (VSA of New Zealand) and OXFAM (NZ), and at the invitation of local grass-roots organisations, ran a pico-hydro forum in central Bougainville. This resulted in initiatives to use a pool of skilled labour (pre-crisis mine trained tradesmen) to provide training and local manufacture of robust hydro turbines. The earlier ad-hoc informal hydro schemes on Bougainville had been constructed from components salvaged from the huge copper and gold mine. They were rudimentary, failure-prone and often unsafe. As a result of the training and forum, there is now a mechanical workshop in Arawa which has produced several quality cross flow and Pelton type pico-turbines.

It is likely that a design from the Arawa workshop will be used for a 4 kW installation planned for Paruparu (Avaipa District, Bougainville) which was surveyed in March 2004) for replacement of an earlier non-functioning hydro system. Financed by AusAID's CDS, it will provide power to the school, a health centre, teachers' houses and the Paruparu Education and Development Centre, where the first of the self-built hydro schemes was developed.

#### HYDRO CASE STUDIES

In his April 2003 hydro field survey, Kopi included case studies on the Agaun, Woitape and Fane Catholic mission micro-hydro schemes. Abridged and edited versions are attached as Annex 4 (Kopi, 2003).

### OCEAN BASED ENERGY TECHNOLOGIES

As far as the PIREP mission has determined, there has been no experience in PNG with sea wave, tidal, OTEC or other ocean-based energy demonstrations.

### EXPERIENCE WITH WIND ENERGY

There are very few wind turbines in PNG, and data are sketchy at best. A few wind turbines were installed in farms in the Markham valley, Morobe Province after Independence but it is not known whether any are still functioning (Puy and Sumanasiri, 2003). PNG Power may consider developing a wind farm at the Port Moresby mountain ridge (Bais, 2004), which is believed to have PNG's best wind resource. However, the utility has not begun any wind monitoring at the location. Commercial companies market and sell small wind generators. However, there is little documentation of these systems.

In 2002, the Chinese Government donated 50 small combined wind/solar generators to the GoPNG, the wind component of which is illustrated in Figure 4-5. These are discussed in Section 4.7 below on PNG's experience with hybrid energy technologies.

## SOLAR ENERGY

Solar energy research and utilisation in PNG

Applied research in solar energy applications has been carried out and reported at the RE seminars (see Section 3) held in 1989 and 1994. There have been more than 25 such projects, of which about twenty were undertaken at Unitech (Uppal and Satter, 1985). Unitech's Department of Mechanical Engineering participated in about 15 solar projects from 1980-1993, many of which focused on solar drying of food crops. Research projects underway in 1995 included: i) solar radiation monitoring for Lae; ii) heat pipe solar collectors and thermal storage; iii) Yazaki solar air conditioner; iv) solar drying for cocoa; v) developing a test facility for solar collectors and domestic solar water heaters; vi) PV medicine refrigerator performance monitoring; vii) feasibility study of PV pumping units; and viii) a solar kitchen. Unfortunately, not much of the Unitech solar energy research has progressed towards practical applications (Puy & Sumanasiri, 2003).

Solar energy can be used in a variety of ways. In PNG, the main applications have been solar drying and cooking, solar water heating, and solar PV power generation, each of which is discussed below.

Solar Drying

The most common use of solar energy in PNG has been for copra, cocoa and coffee drying, particularly by small-holders (PREA, 1992). As the mission has no recent data on solar drying practices in PNG, it is not known whether this is practised as much as in 1987, when it was widespread and studied in detail by Gilmour (GoPNG, 1987). AusAID has supported the development of a solar cocoa drier to potentially replace kiln dryers used by smallholders and plantations relying on fuelwood or diesel for process heat.

Solar cooking.

DPE obtained four solar cookers from China in 2002. One of the units was seen by the PIREP mission in the corridors of the DPE Energy Division; it is uncertain whether they have been tested or used. The units were similar to solar cookers tried by DPE's predecessor, DME, during the 1980s but abandoned, as they were unpopular with users.

Solar thermal

In the early 1980s a sizeable solar water heating (SWH) retrofit programme for commercial users, industry and households was implemented by the GoPNG and the private sector. The largest projects were in 1981-1982 by Bougainville Copper Limited (BCL) for about 1700 company houses and the national government for about 1300 government owned houses in Port Moresby (Kopi, 2003). At the time, GoPNG regulations banned the installation of electric water heaters in new homes and provided tax incentives for retrofitting existing electric installations. For a time ELCOM, the forerunner of PNG Power, provided subsidised household SWHs to its customers. As a result of these initiatives, solar water heaters were adopted in many high-income homes. A joint WB/UNDP energy assessment observed that SWH use flourished and estimated that about 7500 units had been installed, of which 90% were in residences (WB/UNDP, 1983). The 1992 PREA estimated SWH use in 1990 to be the equivalent of 28 mtoe, of which 22 mtoe was in the domestic sector and 6 mtoe in the commercial sector (PREA, 1992). The PREA also observed that there were additional opportunities for SWH, particularly for hotels and hospitals.

Since the solar retrofit programme, more than two decades ago, SWH has steadily increased and is now well established for both residential and commercial use. Currently, at least 7000 homes in the Port Moresby area are probably fitted SWHs, plus a considerable number elsewhere (Kopi, 2003). Supply and installation is mainly through commercial suppliers and building contractors (Puy and Sumanasiri, 2003). Liu reports retail prices of K 3000 for a 180 litre unit and K 4000 for 300 litres. He notes that this price is unaffordable by most households and concludes that new systems are bought primarily to replace old ones (Liu, 14 April 2003; Post-Courier). This was confirmed by a local SWH supplier, who sells 50-60 systems per year as replacement units. All are imported, as SWH are not made locally (Associated Plumbing, 2004).

According to Kopi (2003), current suppliers of SWHs include Associated Plumbing Industries, Barlow Industries, Steamship Trading Company, and Brian Bell. Assuming that the other three firms sell on average roughly the same number of systems as Associated Plumbing, some 200 SWH systems are replaced per annum. Considering a lifetime of 20-25 years it seems likely that the total number of operational SHW systems in PNG is decreasing.

Solar Photovoltaics

PV technology was introduced to PNG no later than 1978 with the arrival of an Arco solar module. Over the next 25 years, solar PV use has spread gradually. Nearly all solar PV systems (like mini hydro plants) were initially sold to institutions. However, since 1997 solar PV home systems have been accepted in PNG as attractive sources of electricity for specific applications in remote locations. They are now marketed by a number of private suppliers, and range from small systems of as little as 10 w to larger units of 480 w or more. Their principal use is for lighting, followed by communication (HF/VHF radios) and, less frequently, TVs and other appliances.

The mission has tried to map two and a half decades of solar PV history in PNG and has probably managed to cover the majority of PV systems installed. However, especially for those commissioned before the mid-1990s, data are far from complete. For the period covered (1978-2003), technical, financial, and institutional data could be found for only a few projects. Despite these limitations, a general picture emerges.

From the government side, the departments of energy, health and education and the state-owned telecommunications company have been involved in numerous solar projects, although it has not been always possible to trace which department was involved in a particular project. There was some involvement of the Energy Division of DPE (then called DME) until the mid-1990s, but its role in solar electrification has since been marginal.

Outside government, there are a small number of active companies plus institutions such as the ATCDI in Lae. In the past decade, the largest PV projects have been carried out by the private companies Enertec, TE (PNG) and RDS. The PNG RE/solar industry has designed and installed numerous PV installations throughout the country, and has often benefited from donor funds. A market for individual solar home systems and lighting kits is emerging. Based on interviews with three companies (RDS, EnerTec, and RadTel), Kopi estimates that some 3000 solar home lighting systems were sold to individuals between 1998 and 2002 (Kopi, 2003). Although it is reported that the number of private companies distributing renewable energy systems has decreased in the past several economically-constrained years, interviews by the PIREP mission suggest that PV sales are being maintained or may be increasing, with one thousand or more PV systems being sold per year.[36]

*Chronological listing of solar PV projects*

Solar projects identified by the PIREP mission are listed in the remainder of this section in chronological order to the extent possible.

The first large-scale user of solar PV seems to have been PNG Telecom which uses the technology to power repeater sites. Kalimba (2004) has recently inventoried 173 sites were solar PV systems have been installed. His findings appear as Annex 5 to this report. For 92 sites, the output capacity is available. Extrapolating Kalimba's data, the mission estimates that at the 173 Telecom sites, nearly 5000 solar PV panels have been installed since 1978, with a combined capacity of over 200 kWp. For the period 1998-2002, Kalimba counted 1430 new PV panels of at least a dozen different capacities, nearly 300 panels per year. The mission extrapolation suggesting 5000 Telecom panels correlates well with this number of annual panel additions. The mission has no data on the performance of any of the Telecom solar systems but it is reported that some have been stolen.

Kalimba (2004) also reports nine large PV systems with a total of 606 panels and a total capacity of about 43 kW. Table 4-4 summarises the systems and the locations where they have been installed. The mission has no further data on these systems.

Another early application of PV technology was for water pumping. A range of donors, including the European Community, the Australian High Commission, and a 'Commonwealth Heads of Government Regional Meeting' (CHOGRM, for Asia/Pacific) project financed at least a dozen PV pumping projects in PNG during the 1980s (Table 4-5). It is understood that the DME designed and installed the systems (Wade, 2004). In 1989 the

| Location | Output(Wp) | No. of panels Panel rating (Wp) | |
|---|---|---|---|
| Mt Iusaka | 9900 | 132 | 75 |
| Tsili tsili | 1960 | 56 | 35 |
| Mt Albert Edwards | 5850 | 78 | 75 |
| Gurney | 7200 | 96 | 75 |
| Kiriwina | 5100 | 68 | 75 |
| Mt Konokalang | 2100 | 28 | 75 |
| Mt Mission | 1408 | 22 | 64 |
| Mt Tangi | 3300 | 44 | 75 |
| Kikori | 6150 | 82 | 75 |
| Total | 42968 | 606 | – |

EU was requested to finance another 28 solar PV pumping systems. The mission found no evidence that these eventuated.

In the late 1980s, DME reportedly initiated a small number of PV projects through a GoPNG Rural Energy Development Programme (PREA, 1992). Under the 1984-1994 Lomé II Paciifc regional energy programme, a dozen PV-powered vaccine refrigerators (three 100 litre Alpha FR 160 units and nine 24 litre Electrolux RCW42 units) were installed in 1988. Eleven of these were still functioning in early 1990 (Johnston, 1994). DME also installed solar PV systems for lighting and water pumping at some eight schools and missions (Kopi, 2003).

In 1991 the DME's Energy Division announced a five-year programme to electrify ten coastal villages using PV technology[37]. Funding was sought from the EU national programme for procurement of the equipment procurement. Apparently the funds were not obtained and no village PV systems were installed.

Because of insufficiently developed institutional support mechanisms, the DME's Energy Division did not qualify for full-scale participation in the 1991-1994 PV Follow-Up component of the 1984-1994 EU Lomé II regional energy programme. Instead, it received a single solar PV system for demonstration purposes. The equipment (valued at Fiji $66,962) was to be used for practical technical training for rural electrification staff and to support a facility to demonstrate PV for rural electrification for both government officials and potential users. Due to a change in the location of the demonstration site, the original 20-panel design was too large and was divided into two systems of ten panels each. One system was installed in 1994 at a demonstration house at the DME (now DPE) premises. It included a solar refrigerator, seven fluorescent lights, one 15-watt tube light and a 500 watt 240V 50 Hz inverter for powering a video or other small appliances. The other system that was meant for to PV pumping demonstration had not been installed by late 1995 due to financial and organisational problems at the Energy Division (Wade 1994/5).

As far as the mission has been able to determine, the role of the Energy Division in solar electrification has since been marginal, with a single project (installation of a solar vaccine refrigerator at the Moreguina Sub-Health Centre in the Central Province) since 1995.[38]

A project entitled 'Solar Lighting Kits for Rural Primary Schools' was carried out in 1997 by the Education Department in rural areas throughout the country. With a grant of K15.4 million from the Japan International Cooperation Agency (JICA), the project has electrified 320 schools in all 20 provinces. Each system included solar panels, a controller, a battery, four 40-watt lights and power outlets. In addition to lighting, the systems (320 Wp for lowland sites and 480 Wp for highland sites) could power VHF/HF radios, television sets, video players and low-powered FM/AM broadcast stations.

The JICA project was completed in 1998 (Kopi, 2003) but has never undergone a formal review. However, few of the systems were functioning by early 2004 due (Mears, 2004) to several problems including the following:

lack of access to maintenance and support services. Although they were trained in maintenance, teachers in rural PNG are very mobile. Many who were trained have moved elsewhere so the maintenance capacity was lost. Although maintenance was available on a return-to-base arrangement, the transport costs were prohibitive for rural schools;

poor quality installation. Some systems had PV panels orientated in the wrong direction; and

poor security. Rural teachers rarely work in their home village and students are usually boarders. At the term breaks, schools tend to be empty but schools cannot afford security services. Even with strong mounting brackets, solar PV panels are vulnerable to theft and many have been stolen.

EnerTec was awarded a K2 million project for 296 solar and gas-based vaccine refrigerators in health care facilities in selected parts of rural PNG as part of the GoPNG's Women and Child Health Programme (Kopi, 2003). Later Enertec supplied and installed solar vaccine fridge systems and solar powered medical examination lamps to remote health facilities through two projects funded by AusAid (EnerTec website).

Many of the solar vaccine refrigeration projects (especially those of the International Red Cross) have suffered from inappropriate technical design and panel theft. The Department of Health has reported some success at community run health posts by using panels of distinctive orange colour and combining this with an awareness programme.

Working with the Department of Health, the company TE (PNG) installed 140 vaccine refrigerator units in health centres across the country. TE (PNG) is currently working with the Department of Health on a National Health Services Radio Network

[38] This system, installed in 1999, consisted of two solar panels of 75Wp each with battery storage. The project cost K 15,000 (US$5,883 using the 1999 exchange rate) for a 150 Wp installed system. The high cost was due to high materials and freight charges.

project, installing solar powered HF radios at rural health facilities. Those electrified under the project will be powered by one or two 75 Wp solar PV modules. The project will include a Church Health Services Network to be operated by the Anglican and the Catholic Churches (WB, 2004).

RDS has been involved in the solar electrification of one of the compounds of New Britain Palm Oil Co. Ltd. (NBPOL). The PV systems provide power for homes, schools and clinics, mainly for lighting. The solar electrification of two more such compounds is scheduled for 2004. The company has already received orders for 5,000 solar kits for 2004 (Capon, 2004). RDS in partnership with Courts (PNG) Ltd. Plans to market 50-150 Wp solar PV systems on a retail basis to individual users. The 150 w system costs K 3,000 in cash sales and K 3,444 under a six-month instalment scheme. ESCO outlets have also sold small solar home systems to households in villages.

A number of smaller solar PV projects known to the mission are summarised below:

according to the SPC,[39] the EU funded 12 PV systems, each with five 75 Wp modules. Further details are unknown (SPC, April 2003);

ATCDI installed one pumping and two village lighting/vaccine refrigeration systems in 2000-2002 (ATCDI, January 2004);

Japan funded solar systems at Buin High School in Bougainville and in New Ireland Province. The New Ireland Disaster and Emergency Services will reportedly receive US$70,000 to improve its VHF radio communication;

Rainbow Power (Australia) has supplied PV to several organisations, including ATCDI, the Australian Baptist Missionary Society, Catholic Health Services, Conservation Melanesia Inc. and many others;

Rainbow is also providing sophisticated 'gold-plated' solar home systems to six households on Mali Island in the Lihir group. Financed by Lihir Gold Mines (K164,000), each system will have 8 panels, 12 batteries, 6 fluorescent lights, a 240 volt inverter and a 220 litre refrigerator (LGM, 2003); and

In addition to ESCO, EnerTec, TE (PNG) and RDS, the PNG Yellow Pages and PNG Business Directory (2003) include a few more companies that are understood to sell solar energy equipment but no information is available on their solar business.

installed in PICs

A summary of PV projects identified by the PIREP mission is presented in Table 4-6 below.

| Location | Dept/Agency or Company | No. of systems | No. of PV panels | Capacity per panel | Installed cap (kWp) | Application |
|---|---|---|---|---|---|---|
| Throughout PNG | Energy? | >12 | > 210 | | | water pumping |
| Throughout PNG | Missions? | 9 | 606 | about 70 | 43 | various |
| Throughout PNG | Telecom | 173 | about 5000 | about 53 | 205 | telecom |
| Health care facilities | Energy | 3 | 18 | | | vaccine fridges |
| Health care facilities | Energy | 9 | 54 | | | vaccine fridges |
| Schools, missions, etc | Energy | 8 | | | | lighting, pumping |
| Demonstration | Energy | 2 | 10 | | | urban demo |
| Various | ??? | 12 | 60 | 75 | 4.5 | ??? |
| Primary schools | Education | 320 | about 1600 | 80 | 128 | lighting |
| Health care facilities | Health | 296 | | | | vaccine fridges |
| Health care facilities | Health | 7 | | | | examination lamps |
| Nalogwam | ATCDI | 1 | | | | water pumping |
| Gain aid post | ATCDI | 1 | | | | lighting; vaccine |
| Erop health facility | ATCDI | 1 | | | | lighting; vaccine |
| Health care facilities | TE (PNG) | 140 | ??? | 75 | | vaccine fridges |
| Health care facilities | TE (PNG) | maybe>1000 | maybe>1000 | 75 | | HF radio |
| New Britain | RDS | One | | | | lighting |
| | | compound | | | | |
| New Britain | RDS | two | maybe 5000 | | | lighting |
| | | compounds | | | | |
| Moreguina sub-health | Energy | 1 | 2 | 75 | 0.15 | vaccine fridges |

| | | | | | | |
|---|---|---|---|---|---|---|
| Throughout PNG | Energy | 50 | 50 | small | | focal point electr. |

**BIOMASS ENERGY**

Bio-energy research

Applied research in bio-energy applications has been carried out and reported at several national renewable energy seminars and workshops. Uppal and Satter (1984) reported on four bio-energy research projects twenty year ago: i) charcoal stove-operated refrigeration for vaccine storage; ii) biomass stimulated absorption refrigerator for food storage; iii) fluidised bed burning of coffee husks for the coffee industry; and iv) cassava for ethanol production.

In early 2004, Unitech and the Forest Research Institute (FRI) in Lae are hoping to renew and expand bio-energy research activities. At the initiative of the Agricultural Department, Unitech staff formed a research group in 2003 that is trying to establish a biofuel research and development centre. The initial focus is coconut oil as a biodiesel, perhaps extending to agricultural residues. The group is awaiting a response to a proposal for support submitted to National Planning (DNPRD) in mid-2003 (Puy et. al., 2003 & Komolong, 21 Jan. 2004). In late 2003, Unitech's Civil Engineering Department initiated plans for a Rural Energy Research Group (RERG), whose activities would include research on treatment of wastewater to generate biogas (Fifaia Matainaho, 21 Jan. 2004).

Unitech and FRI plan to collaborate with the Japanese company Nippon Koei Co. Ltd. in a project for reforestation of denuded grasslands and biomass gasification for power generation at Urara village in Eastern Highlands Province (Nippon Koei, 2003; Nalish, 2004).

Solid biofuels

Progress in utilising solid biomass for electricity generation has been restricted mainly to auto production of electricity from oil palm waste in the palm oil industry, and combined heat and power generation from wood waste in the wood processing industry.

Sawmill/logging

Sawmill residues include sawdust, shavings, off-cuts, bark, veneer cores, plywood fines, and condemned timber. According to the 1992 PREA study, none of the timber industries at that time combined generation of heat and power (co-generation). The PIREP mission has been unable to source much information on co-generation in the timber industry. It is understood that PNG Forest Products in Bololo uses biomass to raise process steam but no quantitative data are available.

Agricultural residues

Use of solid biomass to generate heat is common. Agricultural residues from coffee, cocoa and copra processing are used for (smallholder) crop drying, usually supplemented with fuelwood. The final processing of crops, such as coffee husk, in centralised locations offers great potential for energy self-sufficiency in the processing industry, but this potential has apparently not been taken up to any great extent.

The use of heat gasifiers for crop drying was common in the coffee industry in the Eastern Highlands in the 1980s. A New Zealand company, Waterwide, supplied a number of these units to PNG[42]. According to Sanday (1990), there were over 80 Waterwide heat gasifiers in operation in PNG in 1990. The heat gasifiers were generally used to replace diesel fuel burners in the copra, cocoa, coffee and tea industries. While heat gasifiers had significantly penetrated the crop drying market, there were minor problems resulting from improper operation and maintenance reported in 1990. Given the low cost and cost-effectiveness of heat gasifiers, the 1992 PREA mission encouraged their continued use. The PIREP mission is not aware of the current extent of heat gasifier in use in PNG. However, the DME (Kalimba to Laris, 2002) says that "the coffee Industry for example there are at present 52 coffee processors ... currently operating in PNG with an average of two wood burners per coffee processor processing an estimated 300 tonnes of wood per plant per year" The mission has no further details.

In the palm oil industry waste is used to generate electricity. NBPOL generates about 2.5 MWh of electricity annually from palm waste for the factory and workers' quarters. The PIREP mission has no information on palm waste use by other palm oil companies.

Ramu Sugar Mills is establishing a plantation to grow fuelwood to supplement bagasse (sugar cane waste) as a fuel. Currently 50,000 trees (about 50 hectares) are being planted) with plans to expand to one million trees (about 1,000 ha) after five years (Wilmot, 2004).

[42] The Waterwide gasifier is essentially a close-coupled two-stage combustion system. Biomass is first gasified in up-draft conditions and the hot dusty, and tarry fuel gas is immediately burned in a cyclonic combustion system.

Liquid biofuels

The production and use of biofuels from agricultural commodities has been considered in PNG since Independence. Research and implementation projects included the production of bio-ethanol from sugar cane molasses or cassava and the production of bio-diesel from coconuts. The Ramu Sugar Mill produces ethanol for export but currently it is not used in PNG as a fuel. This is also true of industrially produced coconut oil. Except for small experimental or demonstration projects, there has apparently been no recent commercial development in the use of liquid or gaseous biofuels in Papua New Guinea.

Bio-ethanol from molasses

In the early 1980s, the GoPNG considered the production of alcohol (ethanol) from sugar cane molasses at both Ramu and Baiyer River. The Ramu plant was completed in 1983 (UNDP/WB, 1983). Alcohol production at Baiyer River would have required an investment of more than six million Euro's.

THePNG sought co-financing of 714,000 Euro from the Lomé II regional energy programme but this was rejected (Johnston, 1994). The GoPNG also attempted to obtain direct investment by oil companies and others. When no investment funds could be found, the proposed Baiyer River alcohol plant was cancelled.

The 1992 PREA study reported that Ramu Sugar Mill produced four million litres (roughly 3600 tonnes) of ethanol from molasses annually for several years. At the time of the PREA mission (1991), the ethanol was being blended with motor spirit for sale as a fuel, primarily in the Ramu valley. At that time the commercial value of molasses at Ramu was low but the cost of petroleum fuels was high due to poor transportation and roads. The PREA mission anticipated that this situation would not prevail, and that ethanol was unlikely to play a major role in the energy mix in PNG. The PREA prediction has proven to be correct. In 1995 the distillery was upgraded to produce potable-grade alcohol, the bulk of which is currently exported. Alcohol production at Ramu Sugar was 1952 tonnes in 2000, 2042 tonnes in 2001 and 2160 tonnes in 2002 (IPA website). Potable alcohol fetches better prices than fuel grade alcohol; it is unlikely that alcohol produced in Ramu will be used for energy purposes.

Bio-ethanol from cassava

Research in utilising cassava for ethanol production in PNG started in the late 1970s. A GoPNG team, including DME and Agriculture, visited Brazil in the early 1980s to study the Brazilian experience with ethanol from cassava and other feedstock (personal knowledge, P Johnston). A pilot system was built to evaluate the economics of ethanol production but was abandoned due to lack of adequate agronomic data. Subsequent research in agronomic aspects of cassava by the Department of Agriculture at Unitech confirmed the potential of cassava for ethanol production (Puy & Sumanasiri, 2003).

In August 2003, a memorandum of agreement was signed between the GoPNG and a Korean company to develop cassava as an export crop. Initially, cassava will be sent to Korea for ethanol production with subsequent ethanol production in PNG (Puy & Sumanasiri, 2003). The proposed plant, originally planned for Lae, is apparently now to be built at Kwilila, about 100 km from Port Moresby (Oa, 2004). The mission has been unable to obtain further details. As is the case with the molasses-based alcohol, use of cassava-based alcohol as a fuel is unlikely as long as it fetches better prices as potable-grade alcohol.

Biodiesel derived from coconut oil

Coconut oil was used as fuel on a small scale in PNG in the 1980s. A project under the EU Lomé II Pacific regional energy programme was to demonstrate small-scale production of coconut oil for use in diesel engines for electricity generation and vehicle use at a rural site near Wewak. A tender was issued in May 1985 but the sole bidder was 30% over budget and proposed a process different from that specified: esterified (chemically changed) rather than simple coconut oil. However, the project proceeded and reportedly produced "usable" fuel for a year or so until late 1987 when the project closed (Johnston, 1994).

No evidence of any additional research into coconut-oil based biodiesel in the period 1987-2002 in PNG was found. Recently, interest has renewed with coconut-oil based biodiesel reportedly tested by Unitech in late 2002 (Liu, Nov. 2003).

Coconut oil is produced industrially at several locations in PNG. Official statistics issued by the Bank of PNG dating back to 1990 show that at least 30,000 tonnes of coconut oil was produced per year during the 1990s. In 1997, two new copra oil mills, operated by Coconut Products Limited (CPL) and PNG Coconut Commodities (PCC) respectively, came on stream.

CPL has been producing and exporting premium grade coconut oil since 1997. On average CPL crushes 50-60 kilotonnes of copra per year, producing 30-36 kilolitres of coconut oil (IPA website). PCC operates an oil mill in Madang. The Madang Coconut Oil Mill was shipped from Tonga in the mid-1990s and is owned by GoPNG-owned Kokonas Industri Koperesen (KIK). KIK ran into financial problems in 2002 and the Madang oil mill was put up for sale. Local copra farmers mobilised to buy the mill in 2003 but it was sold in early 2004 to Elan Trading Corporation of Australia who plan to operate the mill under a 60%/40% joint venture agreement with local growers, through Madang Commodities Ltd (Mathob, 2003 and 2004).

Small-scale biodiesel from coconut oil

In addition to the two large mills, coconut oil is made in PNG at a much smaller scale, using Tinytech or DME$^{TM}$ technology. Tinytech (of Rajkot, India) produces small ("tiny") expellers that can produce some 300 litres of oil per day, using either a 10 hp electric motor or 12 hp diesel engine. Tinytech has sold more than a thousand units globally, including thirteen units to PICs, where they are used for copra expelling (Tinytech website, undated). Three units have been sold to PNG, all in late 2003 – early 2004 (private communication, Gopal Desai, Tinytech, 19 March 2004).

On both Buka and Bougainville, people fuelled vehicles with coconut oil during the ten-year civil war. Coconut oil was also used for lighting in low-income households to replace kerosene. Buka Copra Mill/Buka Metal Fabricators, based in Tegese village (75 km from Buka town) opened an oil mill in December 2003. Using Tinytech technology, they produce some 600 litres of coconut oil per eight-hour shift on a small commercial scale. The oil is used as fuel in three of their vehicles, initially 80:20 coconut oil / diesel blend, but now pure coconut oil. They are also trying to use coconut oil for cocoa frying. However, recent interest in coconut oil as a fuel has been driven by efforts of the Village Industries Research and Training Unit (VIRTU) of the provincial Department of Commerce, who are proposing distributed small-scale oil production to provide bio-diesel for the Buka town supply.

A second Tinytech plant has been delivered to the Toma/Vunadidir local level government. By March 2004, it had not been put into operation. The third Tinytech unit supplied to PNG is (March 2004) bound for Madang.

Direct Micro Expelling (DME$^{TM}$) technology, invented and promoted by Dan Etherington of Kokonut Pacific Pty Ltd, is designed to produce coconut oil at a very small-scale village level. The oil is squeezed from semi-dried and grated coconuts in a hand-operated press. No electric power is needed. The capacity is some 30 litres per unit per day, about 10% of the capacity of a Tinytech system. The oil produced is very high grade and suitable for use in cosmetics, cooking or as a diesel substitute. DME technology has reportedly been supplied to Misima Island in PNG but the mission has no information on its performance (Kokonut Pacific website, undated).

Biogas

Biogas, a gaseous fuel mixture of methane and carbon dioxide produced as organic matter decays in the absence of air, can be produced from animal dung and vegetable wastes. During the 1970s-1980s, hundreds of biogas systems were built in a dozen PICs. Biogas systems in PNG included the Lae City Council plant at St. John's school and the Wagimek coffee plantation in Hagen. Due to technical problems,[43] both plants became inoperative. Currently there is only one biogas plant known to be operational, set-up by Hombrum piggery about 22 km from Port Moresby (Kalimba to Lari, 2002). A small biogas plant at a twenty-pig piggery was under construction in Central Bougainville in March 2004 (Mears, 2004).

In the opinion of the PNG Energy Division, there is scope for many household biogas systems and they consider this to be an economically feasible renewable energy application in PNG (Veve, 2004). The PIREP mission confirmed the potential or costs for household biogas generation and application.

Waste incineration and recycling

A Chinese renewable energy consultant working with the Energy Division in early 2004 intends seeking Japanese support for garbage recycling for fuel in Port Moresby (Liu, pers. com., 19 Jan. 2004). Despite various attempts, the PIREP mission was unable to obtain information on this and other reported initiatives aimed at generating

[43] Failure of anaerobic digestion (biogas) systems has not been not limited to the developing world. Many of the systems built in Europe in the 1980s period suffered from technical problems too. Solutions to the major technical problems emerged in the 1990s. Current biogas systems are technologically mature, and more than two thousand systems generating heat or power are operational in Germany. In China tens of millions of small household biogas digesters are in use. These typically provide only a small amount of biogas that is used without further treatment for cooking.

power from Port Moresby's waste. The size of the NCD population might suggest that a landfill-based biogas generation project might be economic. A study commissioned by SPREP concluded that waste incineration was not suitable for Port Moresby, as it involved expensive and complex technology, required complex operation and management of ash residues, and produced emissions to the air. Prior incineration in Port Moresby had not been successful (Sinclair Knight Merz, 2000).

**HYBRID WIND / SOLAR ENERGY SYSTEMS**

A hybrid wind-solar energy system of unknown size has reportedly provided power to a highlands school (UNESCO website) but no details are available.

China donated 50 sets of wind generators coupled with PV panels, valued at US$ 236,000, to the GoPNG in June 2002. Each includes a 500 watt wind turbine and two 50 Wp solar PV panels and will be installed at provincial centres at coastal locations. Chinese experts have provided training in installation and maintenance (PNG Post-Courier website). The first six hybrid systems were installed in East New Britain Province in 2002 (Kalimba, 2002). Further units were installed in rural districts in Central Province at Bereina Health Centre in the Kairuku/Hiri District and at Kapari in the Rigo District. The installation costs were K 4500 per system (Tobia, 2004). It is understood by the PIREP mission that the bulk of the systems remain to be installed (March 2004).

The PIREP mission has doubts about the long-term viability of these hybrid systems, which are provided to users for free and for which reportedly no operational or maintenance mechanism has been put in place (Veve, 2004). The electronics of several of the hybrid systems failed shortly after installation, according to a local RE equipment supplier who repaired the units (Capon, 2004).

**PNG'S RENEWABLE ENERGY EXPERIENCE**

It is clear that throughout the country, PNG has enormous resources, which can be tapped for local energy production. There has also been a longstanding interest within the two national universities, particularly Unitech, and several government agencies in tapping this resource, especially for use in rural areas. This chapter demonstrated in some detail the quite considerable and varied experience of PNG over the past twenty years with RETs, primarily hydro, solar and biomass. In the early 1980s, PNG was the PIC's regional leader in the use of biomass energy for agricultural processing, with considerable government support. The GoPNG also supported a wide range of initiatives and studies with biogas, biomass gasification, wood and charcoal cooking, ethanol production, solar PV, and assessments of the hydro and wind resource. These efforts dwindled after about 1985.

Since then, the GoPNG, with donors and NGOs (and ELCOM/PNG Power), has continued some development of micro-hydro and solar PV for schools and health centres but recently the private sector has largely driven RE use. The coffee industry apparently uses about 100 wood-burning driers, the palm oil industry exploits wood waste for electricity, and Ramu Sugar plans to plant 1,000 ha of trees for combustion in its bagasse boilers. At least several thousand new solar home lighting systems are expected to be installed in rural PNG during 2004, overwhelmingly through private initiatives. Yet barriers to the successful long-term use of RETs seem to be considerable. The PIREP mission estimates that three-quarters of the mini/micro hydro systems installed during the past several decades are probably no longer in use.

A very large percentage of PV systems have also failed. This is not an issue limited to RETs; the majority of small C-centre power systems run by provincial and local authorities are not functioning and many others operate poorly and intermittently due to inadequate management and lack of finance. Chapter 5 considers some key barriers that may be associated with, or exacerbated, these failures.

# BARRIERS IDENTIFIED IN THE DEVELOPMENT AND COMMERCIALISATION OF RETS

In the previous chapters, a number of barriers to the development, use and commercialisation of RETs in Papua New Guinea have been raised implicitly or explicitly. This chapter brings together the earlier observations and further barriers. These have been identified through various means:

interviews held by the mission with about 70 people in Port Moresby and Lae, of whom about two thirds were Papua New Guineans, and the rest foreign businessmen, aid workers, diplomatic personnel or NGO workers based in the country;

e-mail and telephone exchanges with people familiar with development and/or energy issues in PNG;

a workshop on "Strengths, Weaknesses, Opportunities and Threats" (SWOT) to RE use and development in PNG attended by a small but vocal group of eight and summarised in Annex 6; and

review of two earlier papers on barriers to rural electrification and rural energy in PNG: a 2003 field study by PNG student Idau Kopi (Annex 7) and the report of a two-day workshop organised by the World Bank in 2003.

This chapter reflects the findings and views of the PIREP mission. All significant barriers found were verified through the SWOT workshop discussions and interviews. However, the writers do not pretend to be experts on PNG development issues and inevitably relied heavily on the views and experiences of local people and others with long experience in PNG.

For convenience, the barriers are categorised into groups. There are numerous overlaps among categories so classifications are to some extent arbitrary. The barriers have not been prioritised and others no doubt exist.

## FISCAL BARRIERS

Fiscal barriers to RETs can include those for which government fiscal policies (import duties, taxes, charges) raised for public finance are biased in favour of conventional energy or biased against renewable energy. Customs officials were unavailable for discussions during our mission. Accordingly, we were unable to ascertain rules for exemptions to import duties or excise taxes for fuels or energy consuming equipment. Fiscal barriers were not often identified by those interviewed. However, several issues did arise:

Exemptions on fuel taxes. PNG Power has received a temporary exemption from the ICCC on excise tax for distillate used to generate electricity. However, at less than US 2 cents per litre, this is unlikely to be a major barrier although it could be a small disincentive against using locally-produced biofuels. Fuel for rural electrification is reportedly not exempt from excise taxes, thus in principle, not giving diesel or petrol generators a fiscal advantage.

Cross-subsidies of urban fuel prices. The tentative decision by the ICCC to maintain the same fuel prices for Port Moresby, Lae, Madang and Rabaul in effect provides a hidden subsidy (of unknown magnitude) for the three outer

centres relative to Port Moresby. It is not known the extent to which this might create, or maintain, a barrier to the use of biofuels.

No incentives for RETs. There is reportedly no fiscal incentive for assembling, manufacturing or importing RETs (e.g. solar water heaters; 1PV systems, 2 volt lights for PV use) rather than conventional systems as import duties and taxes do not differentiate between them.

No incentives or mechanisms for RET loans. There are no incentives to financial institutions, or specific mechanisms, to promote RE investments through 'green' interest rates, or access to foreign capital for RE through government support.

Cross subsidies for PNG Power electrification. Because there is a single national tariff, the customers of the three large interconnected PNG Power grids subsidise the electricity consumption of consumers at the smaller and more costly PNG provincial systems. The subsidy has not been estimated but could be substantial in some locations and form a barrier to the use of RETs where these might be more expensive to construct than diesel systems, but less expensive in the longer term.

## FINANCIAL BARRIERS

In early 2004, the GoPNG's Energy Division had about seven staff in the Policy and Planning Division[44] and a similar number in the Engineering branch. Although this is far more than most PICs, the ED has considerably more responsibility. The lack of access to adequate funds for staff, surveys, travel (especially outside Port Moresby) and communications form a real financial barrier to effectively overseeing national RE developments.

Despite considerable income from the export of minerals and oil, and in some ways a dynamic economy, PNG has been unable to maintain per capita GDP at 1975 (Independence) level, has significant regional inequalities in wealth, and the lowest HDI in the Pacific. Facing serious development issues, GoPNG finance for rural electrification and RETs has not been, and seems unlikely to soon be, a high priority.

Other financial barriers.

Lack of cash in most rural communities. Despite high rural incomes in some enclaves, there is very limited economic activity in most rural areas of PNG with little money circulating in the community. Even where people living at the fringes of a mission or government station could tap into electricity supply, they generally cannot afford even low connection fees and usage charges.

High costs of business. The very high start up and operating costs of establishing businesses in PNG, particularly for small businesses serving rural areas, are daunting to those who might otherwise set up a renewable energy service company (RESCO) or other RE business.

Lack of recent donor support. Except for a few small wind/PV systems from China, there appears to have been very limited financial support from donors for new RET development in PNG in the past five or six years.

High initial costs of RETs. Most rural people cannot afford the high initial costs of RETs (e.g. household or community solar PV; micro-hydro) but there are no formal mechanisms (e.g. accessible rural banks or credit) to help them.

Willingness to pay. In many cases, teachers and public servants at remote locations who receive solar PV or micro-hydro power, and have the ability to pay, are reportedly unwilling to pay for energy services.

Risky investments. Rural landowners have no equity for RE investments that the banks will accept as they do not 'own' the land (i.e. cannot sell it). There is reportedly a perception among financial institutions that RETs and energy service companies are perceived as high risks.

## LEGISLATIVE, REGULATORY AND POLICY BARRIERS

Although there have been numerous drafts over the years, and an issues papers was prepared in early 2004, there is no national energy policy which has been formally endorsed by either the minister responsible for energy or the NEC. There is no clear policy on rural electrification and inconsistent implementation of existing informal policies. In general, there is a lack of transparent policy direction but a widespread belief that the GoPNG does not consider rural electrification as a high priority. The lack of appropriate legislation, approved energy strategies and policies, guidelines and regulations form a significant barrier to the development of renewable energy. Other specific barriers raised in PNG, with which the missions concurs are as follows.

Unclear regulatory framework. The power utility, PNG Power, is monopolist in areas that are close to the grid and could block others from generating electricity. This is not seen a serious barrier today, but rather a potential barrier as PNG Power eventually becomes privatised and the ICCC develops new guidelines on its operations. Some observers feel that future access to the grid (power purchase agreements) is uncertain whereas PNG Power may be reluctant to undertake some investments when the extent of liberalisation of the electricity supply industry is uncertain.

Unclear legislation regarding rural electrification. There may be some concern with DPE, and certainly with its policy adviser, about ambiguities between the Electricity Supply Act, and the Organic Act regarding the respective responsibilities and powers of PNG Power and provincial authorities for C-centre operations. There are uncertainties regarding possible future obligations of PNG Power to provide rural electrification under the Community Services Trust Act.

Lack of legislation for RESCOs. There is no legislation regarding the operation or responsibilities of renewable energy service companies (RESCOs), or their regulatory oversight.

## INSTITUTIONAL BARRIERS

In general, financial governance within the GoPNG is weak. The GoPNG has not been able to effectively tap existing or potential sources of finance (donor and other) for RE. Specific issues, some of which are closely interrelated are outlined below.

National Government: structure of DPE Energy Division. According to DPE's own studies, the Energy Division does little research or planning and little capacity for planning or survey analysis. There is reportedly limited capacity for project planning and economic analysis of proposed projects. A better organisational structure for the Energy Division of DPE has been proposed with additional staff, clear responsibilities and work plans. A clear structure and clear role for the division should be adopted along with additional financial support so its functions can be carried out.

National and provincial governments: lack of support. Since the transfer of the functions of power stations (C-centres) to the provincial government by the national government, there has been little support from the national government (project planning and planning methodology, training, finance, operating guidelines, financial guidelines) or from provincial governments to local communities and local governments (oversight of C-centres, financial arrangements for operators' wages, maintenance support).

Regional organisations: PNG feels left out. A number of those interviewed, officials government and outside government, feel that PNG is treated as a marginal country by regional organisations regarding energy, and energy/environment issues such as climate change and GHGs. Projects and initiatives are seen as having limited relevance or benefit for PNG. Whether justified or not, the perception is strong and may form a barrier to working effectively with the regional organisations.

Lack of institutional development for RE at provincial and community level. In general, the GoPNG (and some private companies) have assisted with hardware for RE in the absence of adequate institutional arrangements for revenue collection, operation, maintenance, technical support, spare parts, financial accountability, etc. In general, there is a lack of access to ongoing support services.

Short-term donor policies. The donor community tends to have a short-range approach to support for RE, often providing hardware but little or no support to assist the GoPNG develop institutional arrangements for RE, discussed immediately above, to be sustainable after the donor departs.

**TECHNICAL BARRIERS**

Most technical barriers in PNG seem to be related with poor knowledge of available RETs and conditions where they are appropriate, rather than technical deficiencies. Key barriers to more use of RE in PNG which are in part technical are listed here.

Limited knowledge of renewable energy resources. Most surveys of the hydro, wind and solar resources are two decades old and were of limited scope even when carried out. Their accuracy and practicality today are questionable. There is little information on the amount of biomass actually available for energy use, its seasonality, geographic locations near areas of energy demand and likely price.

Lack of commercial technologies to exploit all renewable resources. There are no commercially available, proven technologies that can be used to exploit sea waves, ocean current or OTEC resources.

Limited support for increasing local technical knowledge. Unitech had a significant level of financial support and encouragement for its work in RE during the 1980s but very limited support today for its efforts to demonstrate and adapt RETs appropriate for the country.

Limited knowledge of biofuel potential. Although there appears to be considerable potential for displacing a large portion of imported petroleum fuels with biofuels (biodiesel and ethanol), and this potential has been known in PNG for twenty years, there has apparently been limited study since then on practical technical and economic options, for both vegetable oils and ethanol from sag and nipa palm.

**MARKET BARRIERS**

PNG is very rugged with a small communities, many accessible only by air, dispersed over 600 islands. A large percentage of the population is effectively outside the cash market economy. Among the identified market barriers associated with PNG's environment are the following.

Small market size. Although PNG is far bigger than other PICs, nonetheless the local market is too small for local manufacture of most RETs and too small to attract some suppliers who are willing or able to provide back-up or technical services.

Dispersed population, isolation and poor accessibility. Rural communities in PNG are neither compact nor concentrated, with small villages often more than two hours walking distance from each other. In many ways, not just market access, this forms barriers to development of RETs. The cost of project development, technology, spare parts, training, support, etc. are extremely high. The risks to entrepreneurs trying to serve such a market can also be very high.

Lack of productive demand for electricity. The potential market for RETs is also reduced by the lack of easily identifiable or viable economic that could productively use electricity. High freight charges to transport produce to urban markets discourage farmers. There has been a change away from cash cropping in recent years, exacerbated by a current shortage of agricultural field officers in local centres who can advise people on suitable farming methods.

### KNOWLEDGE AND PUBLIC AWARENESS BARRIERS

Key knowledge barriers identified are:

Low level of public awareness of RETs. In PNG, with many hundreds of languages, there is low awareness of RETs and it is difficult to reach much of the population. There have been a number of workshops on energy and climate change issues but was no evidence (in English) of public awareness campaigns on energy or climate change during the mission, although these may well exist.

Low level of technical knowledge regarding RETs. Few people know the practical potential and limitations of specific RETs, e.g. where they are or are not appropriate, what energy demands they can supply economically, how to estimate energy demands in a community, etc. A substantial number of RETs have been poorly installed.

Inadequate training resources. PNG has technical training institutes in most, if not all, provinces and two national universities. Despite some knowledge of RETs, training is inadequate, insufficient numbers of people are trained, and curricula are very weak. There is a lack of management skills needed to plan and manage RETs and the technical skills needed for operation

and maintenance. Those who are trained are highly mobile so training at provincial and community level needs to be regularly repeated and updated.

### PRIVATE SECTOR BARRIERS

There is inadequate experience and knowledge within the private sector regarding technical, institutional, financial and management aspects of RET development.

### ENVIRONMENTAL AND SOCIAL BARRIERS

For those who wish to develop RETs, long-term secure access to land was considered to be a serious barrier. As elsewhere in the region, traditional landowners are very protective of their rights and it can be very difficult to get access to land for RE, especially if it is believed to benefit government, outsiders, or only a few landowners, or others. In some cases, a few dissident landowners (or those who claim to have land rights) have stymied developments. Environmental issues are covered in more detail in Chapter 7. Several environmental and social barriers identified are the following:

vulnerability. PNG is the most vulnerable of all PICs to natural disaster. For a wide range of RETs, equipment or the resource itself (e.g. biomass) can be quickly destroyed;

anti-hydro perceptions. In some communities, there may be a bias against hydropower because of perceptions of extensive downstream damage associated with mining projects, rather than with hydropower per se. The mission saw no evidence that this was likely to be a serious barrier; land access. Access to customary land (i.e. most land in PNG) at a cost fair to both landowner and developer is increasingly difficult. Compensation demands are serious obstacles and can continue for years. Crossing land boundaries with transmission lines requires compensation, possibly reducing opportunities for local grids or grid-connected renewable energy;

little sense of ownership or responsibility. People often perceive government-supported projects as public assets and are unconcerned about their long-term operation. Developers are often alienated from the community; there is little sense within the community of ownership or responsibility for RETs on their land. It can be difficult to determine who is responsible for management of an RET scheme;

high frequency of theft and poor security. Related to the above point, there has been a very high degree of theft of PV modules and associated equipment from schools, health clinics and telecommunications facilities. Rural teachers rarely work in their home village and students are usually boarders. Between school terms, the compounds tend to be empty but schools cannot afford security services. Even with strong mounting brackets, solar PV panels are vulnerable to theft and many have been stolen;

lack of respect for law and order. PNG has suffered from a lack of respect for the rule of law in general, at personal and political levels. It is reportedly not unusual for politicians to undermine the work of predecessors, including rural RE installations. There has reportedly been considerable vandalism of RETs at government facilities;

continuing social instability. Although the Bougainville unrest has ended, there are continuing demands for greater autonomy and secession in several parts of PNG; and

misuse of ethanol. A possible barrier to the use of ethanol as a fuel is a perception among some that it will be used for illicit drinking. This could well be a problem with small-scale rural production but could be more readily controlled at industrial scale where dyes and emetics can be added if necessary. The mission does not know the extent to which this may be a serious barrier.

THE CAPACITY DEVELOPMENT NEEDS FOR REMOVING THE BARRIERS

This chapter examines the capacity development needs of PNG. Addressing these may help to remove or reduce key barriers identified in Chapter 5[45]. These are not prioritised. It is not suggested that those listed are necessarily appropriate for addressing though further GEF support. Many of the suggestions below do not fit exclusively, or even primarily, into one category: issues addressed under, for example, fiscal barriers may be applicable to several others. There is also some repetition with similar issues covered under more than one heading. Finally, it is easier to identify barriers than practical means to remove them (or most would have been removed long ago). The suggestions in this chapter are tentative and incomplete.

6.1 Fiscal Barriers

Section 5.1 identified several possible fiscal barriers to the development and commercialisation of RETs including petroleum fuel pricing and cross-subsidies, electricity tariff policies, and lack of 'green' interest rates or incentives. The following could help to address these issues:

• Import duties and taxes. The capacity within government is limited with regards to analysing the effects of interest rates, import duties, energy prices and taxes on the development of RET and EET measures.

6.2 Financial Barriers

Access to finance is a major barrier to RET development in PNG simply because so many people are largely outside the cash economy. Low government budgets are a serious constraint to rural electrification overall (in a country with perhaps 10% electrification overall and 5% in rural areas) and where rugged terrain in isolated islands means that electrification (and rural services in general) are very expensive to provide. The effective use of available – or potentially available – finance is a constraint. Some of the barriers identified under 'finance' are discussed in this section, others under other headings. Some e.g. the general lack of cash and high cost of doing business in PNG, can't be dealt with by energy interventions in isolation.

Lack of capacity to develop suitable project documents. The increasing competition for limited donor funds has made the preparation of high quality, well developed project requests necessary. The GoPNG and NGO sectors have insufficient capacity to prepare the complex documentation required by multilateral finance organisations such as ADB and GEF and the high quality project proposals needed to be competitive for funds from bi-lateral donors.

Capacity to collect energy payments. There is a lack of capacity for collection of rural service payments even as regards salaried government employees. The GoPNG should develop clear rules for public servants (at least those paid by the national government) serving in rural areas regarding payment for utilities and services such as electricity. Perhaps payments could be deducted from their salaries as is done in some PICs (assuming a

[45] Some of the same or similar recommendations are made in other PIREP reports. In some cases, it may be appropriate to carry out similar studies concurrently in several countries, or through a regional effort. This is discussed in volume 1 of the PIREP analyses, the regional overview.

mechanism exists, or can be developed, for payment into an appropriate account).

• Import duties taxes and energy pricing. The capacity within government is limited with regards to analysing the effects of interest rates, import duties, energy prices and taxes on the development of RET measures.

6.3 Legislative, Regulatory and Policy Barriers

Section 5.3 concluded that the lack of legislation, approved energy policies, guidelines and regulations form a significant barrier to the development of RE. Donors and lending agencies typically expect a clear policy/legislative/regulatory framework to be in place before approving new energy assistance, or sometimes developed as part of this assistance.

Energy Division capacity. Capacity is lacking at the energy division. in many areas of RET development and project management. A clear vision of the responsibilities and authority of the division needs to be established so a focused capacity development programme can be implemented.

Limited capacity to develop policy and legislation. The Energy Division, the Finance Ministry and NGOs do not have the capacity to develop a comprehensive national energy policy or legislation regarding energy that includes the wide range of issues facing Papua New Guinea.

6.4 Institutional Barriers

Some institutional issues have been considered above. Others include the following:

capacity to determine the value of a Rural Electrification Authority. The DPE has proposed, several times, the creation of a Rural Electrification Authority. There should be development of the local capacity to prepare a neutral, disinterested comprehensive study of the costs, benefits, criteria for success (including training, financial needs, technical support), legislative requirements, tariff policy, its relationship with PNG Power (and RESCOs), and its relationship with provincial and local authorities; and regional organisation capacity development. It would be appropriate for the GoPNG, with other PICs, to express in writing to the CROP chair any concerns it may have regarding the Energy Working Group or relationships among CROP agencies that it feels needs development to better provide effective RET implementation in the country and the region.

Technical Barriers

There is an absence of accessible and appropriate technical information on which to make energy choices. Some technical matters relate to the suitability of various technologies for use in PICs in general, and can perhaps best be addressed on a regional level.

Capacity limits for measuring the RE resource. There is a need to develop the local capacity to carry out assessments for wind, biomass and small hydro resources and to clearly understand the processes involved for the assessment of geothermal and oceanic energy resources. There is relatively little information or experience available in PNG regarding the magnitude and accessibility of RE resources. The extensive possibilities for small hydro

development need closer examination. It would also be appropriate to seek funding to monitor promising wind sites for a period of 18 months or more. For geothermal, the high cost of exploration suggests that further drilling should be left to proponents and potential investors (including GEF and IFC). If there are regional efforts to assess ocean energy potential, PNG should participate but not put its own financial resources into this.

Biofuels. There appears to be inadequate capacity within government to enable the development of biofuel as a large scale alternative to petroleum. There is need to develop capacity for technical development, for analysing the effects of large scale (up to 200 ML/year) biofuel production on government revenue and determining other financial issues as well as developing the logistics required for large scale production and delivery of biofuels to urban centres.

Lack of easily understandable reference materials regarding RETs publicly available in PNG. Although the Internet has many technical resources for persons wishing to understand RETs, the access to the Internet in PNG is not wide spread, tends to be slow and computer literacy low. Also, the wide range of information available on the Internet and its highly variable quality makes it is difficult for the novice to be able to determine which is appropriate to PNG. There needs to be developed a local repository of information that can be accessed by anyone wishing to gain knowledge about RETs appropriate to PNG, their cost, applicability, operation, maintenance and opportunities for use. Further, the resource needs to be somehow made available country wide, not just in one urban area.[46]

Market Barriers

Market barriers identified as constraints include the lack of affordable transport to rural communities (generally by air or foot), the small market size, dispersed population, and lack of productive demand for electricity. Incentives for local people to establish businesses to provide RE services have been discussed. Considering that PNG already has a large market for RETs (at least PV systems) by PIC standards, and has installed hundreds of micro/mini hydro systems, a study of the reality and seriousness of market barriers to RETs, and ways to overcome them, is warranted.

Knowledge and Public Awareness Barriers

No studies have been carried out in the region on the effectiveness of awareness campaigns on energy efficiency or renewable energy but studies in developed countries suggest that impacts are generally both very limited and temporary. In PNG, it may be appropriate to include materials on energy efficiency and RETs in school curricula but it is probably not an effective use of public funds to prepare public awareness materials on RE unless focused specifically on the implementation of an RET project..

Training in RETs to date has focused on government officials. There is a large demand for more information and training for NGOs and the private sector.

Private sector Barriers

There is clearly a demand in both the private and public sectors for relevant and practical training for local persons in various aspects of RETs for designing, marketing, installing, operating, maintaining, and repair of RET systems. However, the team had no opportunity to assess the extent and effectiveness of the range of RE training already carried out by regional agencies, donors, NGOs and others. During 2004, the UN's Economic and Social Commission for Asia and the Pacific (ESCAP) is developing a regional RET training programme, in cooperation with regional organisations, specifically for PICs. No specific suggestions are offered here, except that private sector and NGO staff should be included in RE training; thus far it has concentrated overwhelmingly on government officials.

Environmental and Social Barriers

The key barriers to RETs most frequently described as serious in PNG, are: i) access to land with secure arrangements for the long term; and ii) the lack of law and order and associated theft of, and damage to, RETs. There is a need to develop the capacity to deal with landowners in a manner which gives them incentives to allow the use of their land for RETs and to keep them operating over time.

Hardware investments to Remove Barriers

Table 2-12 indicates that large scale hydropower may offer the most opportunity for indigenous energy development in PNG with the potential for substantially reducing GHG emissions from modern sector energy use, followed by biofuels (both biodiesel and ethanol) and geothermal. To the extent that GHG reduction is a priority, investments for these large scale RETs, where environmentally appropriate (see chapter 7) should be considered. However, the team feels that it is not appropriate to make any firm suggestions based on a short time in country and the necessarily somewhat superficial study of PNG's energy sector issues.

Choices regarding RET development in PNG should not be made solely on the basis of their potential impact on GHG emissions, which in any case are nearly inconsequential on either a global or per-capita basis.[47] For PNG, the development impacts of RETs are likely to be greater through a large-scale programme of community scale investment solar PV and micro-hydro, including the development of appropriate institutions for their finance and operation, than large hydro, geothermal or biofuel. A rural energy initiative based on stand-alone PV, micro hydro, and possibly small wind systems in appropriate locations, should be seriously considered if donor funding is available.

[47] Papua New Guinea has no legal obligations to reduce GHGs and is an insignificant producer on a global or even regional scale. The Climate Analysis Indicators Tool (CAIT) of the World Resources Institute (WRI, 2003) calculates national emissions to the nearest 1/100 of 1% of the global total. PNG's emissions, by far the largest of the Pacific Island Countries, are shown as 0.03 percent.

## LARGE SCALE USE OF RENEWABLE ENERGY

For GHG emissions and energy production from RETs, Table 2-12 suggests that the biggest impacts in PNG may come from investments in large hydropower, ethanol as a fuel, geothermal, biodiesel and small hydro respectively. Any of these, if poorly planned, could have significant environmental impacts. Each is discussed briefly below.

### LARGE HYDRO (OVER 10 MW)

The International Rivers Network (IRN), an NGO which lobbies strongly against hydro projects above 10 MW, alleges that major hydro expansion harms: i) efforts to move toward sustainable development, ii) people and ecosystems, and iii) energy security. Among other dangers, they list increased vulnerability to climate change (due to climate and weather changes) and the emission of significant amounts of GHG from large reservoirs (due to rotting organic matter)[48] (IRN, 2003).

While some feel that IRN is alarmist, there has been a history of poorly designed and implemented large hydropower developments throughout they world. There can be significant and irreversible effects on surface water, groundwater and other aspects of water transfer within the hydrological cycle during project construction, project operation and maintenance, and decommissioning. In some cases, there are impacts during the planning phase, probably indirect off-site effects as materials are mined or fabricated in preparation for plant construction. For hydropower, the area of influence is very wide, extending from the upper limits of the watershed catchment to the valley below the dam and as far downstream as the estuary and off-shore zones. The most severe direct hydrological impacts are likely to result from the impoundment of water, flooding of land to form a reservoir, and the reduction of water flow downstream. Potential indirect effects can be caused by construction and operation of work camps, access roads, and power transmission facilities, for example soil erosion affecting surface and ground water. The potential hydrological effects of the environment on the dam depend on land and water use in the watershed area upstream of the reservoir. Often relocations of population from the inundated reservoir area can increase pressures within the watershed resulting in changed land use patterns which increase erosion and subsequently sedimentation in the reservoir. The main hazard risk is a failure of the dam resulting in a sudden and massive flow of water downstream (Johnston, 1994a).

The World Bank (1991) lists the following potential, and often real, hydrological impacts of large hydro dams:

• decomposition of trees in flooded land, causing nutrient enrichment in the reservoir and increased water loss through transpiration;

[48] IRN lists 12 reasons to avoid large hydro in three categories. A) A major expansion of large hydro will harm sustainable development: 1. Large hydro does not have the poverty reduction benefits of decentralized renewables; 2. Including large hydro in renewables; initiatives would crowd out funds for new renewables; 3. Promoters of large hydro regularly underestimate costs and exaggerate benefits; 4. Large hydro will increase vulnerability to climate change; and 5. There is no technology transfer benefit from large hydro. B) A major expansion of large hydro will harm people and ecosystems: 6. Large hydro projects have major negative; social and ecological impacts 7. Efforts to mitigate the impacts of large hydro typically fail; 8. Most large hydro developers and funders oppose measures to prevent the construction of destructive projects and 9. Large reservoirs can emit significant amounts of greenhouse gases. C) A major expansion of large hydro will harm energy security: 10. Large hydro is slow, lumpy, inflexible and getting more expensive; 11. Many countries are already overly dependent on hydropower; and 12. Large hydro reservoirs are often rendered non-renewable by sedimentation. The source is IRN (with Oxfam and other NGOs, 2003).

creation of reservoir dramatically changing water flow (quantity and timing), water quality, and sedimentation within river basin;

disrupted water flow to downstream communities, initially with greatly increased sedimentation and later reduced quantities of water;

loss of wetlands downstream of reservoir;

sedimentation in reservoir reducing storage capacity and lifetime, reducing nutrient-rich silt downstream, increasing riverbed scouring downstream;

altered water table upstream and downstream plus resulting salinisation;

reduced flow of water at times to communities downstream;

reduction in fish production (and catches) downstream;

increased pressure on upstream land due to resettlement followed by poor watershed control (agriculture in steep areas, grazing, deforestation,) causing erosion and increased sedimentation in the reservoir;

deterioration of water quality in reservoir;

sedimentation at reservoir entrance causing waterlogging and flooding upstream;

decrease in water for floodplain agriculture. Floodplain salinisation;

chemical contamination of water during maintenance of transmission lines and towers;

released water from lower portion of reservoir for power is high in pH, low in oxygen, high in hydrogen sulphide and is cold, all affecting animal and plant communities downstream;

seismic events causing catastrophic dam collapse with sudden massive water flow downstream; and

conflicting demands for water uses.

Many potential sites for large hydro development in PNG could, and probably would, be developed as run-of-river systems, greatly reducing potential impacts. In general, any large hydro developments in PNG should be planned, built and operated in accordance with the recommendations of the World Commission on Dams (WCD; guidelines, available from www.dams.org and see a Citizen's Guide to the World Commission on Dams, available from www.irn.org).

**SMALL HYDRO (UNDER 10 MW)**

The International Association for Small Hydro, the European Small Hydro Association and the International Energy Agency's Renewable Energy Working Party all define small hydro as less than 10 megawatts. The IRN says "small hydro can, if responsibly implemented, be environmentally and socially low-impact. ... To ensure that small hydro projects have low impacts and meet community priorities it is imperative that all small hydro schemes are planned, built and operated in line with the recommendations of the World Bank/IUCN-sponsored World Commission on Dams." (IRN, 2003).

**ETHANOL FUEL**

In section 3.6, it was noted that the G0PNG estimates that 58% of land area is subject to strong or severe erosion, 18% is permanently inundated or regularly flooded and about 200,000 hectares are cleared annually for traditional agriculture. Environmental issues regarding the production of ethanol as a fuel in PNG are essentially those of biomass energy use in general: conversion of forests to biomass plantations, encouraging clear cutting, nutrient draining, use of toxic chemicals, increased erosion, and possibly loss of wetlands.

**GEOTHERMAL**

Citizens United for Renewable Energy and Sustainability (CURES), a recently formed international NGO network, has defined new renewable energies as including:

"modern biomass, WCD-compliant small (up to 10MW) hydro, geothermal (emphasis added), wind, all solar, tidal, wave and other marine energy. Modern biomass includes improved use of traditional biomass such as 'smokeless' efficient cook stoves as well as electricity generation, heat production and liquid fuels from carbon neutral and low input, sustainable sources of biomass" (CURES website:www.eenetz.de/cures.html)

Although geothermal has not traditionally always been considered renewable (as reservoirs eventually deplete, at least temporarily) or benign (due to hydrogen sulphide – H2S – and other toxic emissions), it is now considered (Figure 7-1) as an environmentally friendly RET. According to the US Department of Energy "geothermal power plants easily meet the most stringent clean air standards because they emit little carbon dioxide (fossil-fuel power plants produce roughly 1000 to 2000 times as much), no nitrogen oxides, and very low amounts of sulphur dioxide (SO2). Steam and flash plants emit mostly water vapour. Binary power plants run on a closed-loop system, so no gases are emitted." For [plants containing H2S], the sulphur can be "separated, dewatered, and recycled as feedstock for sulphuric acid production. Future technology will use microbial processes to extract metals contained in the sulphur, allowing further reuse. At most geothermal hot-water power plants, H2S is present in such low concentrations that it requires no special controls to comply with environmental regulations. ... A typical geothermal plant requires several wells. Although drilling these wells has an impact on the land, using advanced directional or slant drilling minimizes that impact. Several wells can be drilled from one pad, so less land is needed for access roads and fluid piping." (USDoE website, undated).

## BIODIESEL

The issues indicated in section 7.2 could equally apply here. However, it has been assumed (Table 2-12) that only about 10% of vegetable oil production in PNG might be used for fuel so the impact should be no more severe than current practices.

In terms of use, biodiesel fuels from coconut, oil palm or other vegetable oils are very low in emissions, as they contain almost no sulphur or hazardous materials. In case of spillage to the ground or marine environment, they biodegrade readily and do not cause contamination.

## DEVELOPMENT NEEDS AND CO-FINANCING OPPORTUNITIES

No firm projects were identified as possible co-financing opportunities at this time. The following are recommended as specific studies and co-financing opportunities for capacity development.

Biofuels. A study of the impact of the production of coconut oil-based biofuel in PNG should be carried out at several scales: i) a scale of 20-200 ML per year to replace a large percentage of national distillate imports for power generation and transport; and ii) small-scale production for remote islands and communities to displace distillate for rural electric power and ground transport. The study would consider technical, economic, financial, political, and social issues. It would estimate the effects of various scales of biofuel production on government revenue, including the effect of direct and indirect employment, tax revenues, etc. The report would consider whether it is in the interest of the GoPNG to produce biofuels at various scales and, if so, recommend a strategy to support this development.

Import duties and taxes. A study should be undertaken of the rates of import duties and related taxes, exemption policies, and procedures for establishing duties to determine the extent to which there is a bias for or against the development and use of RETs at small scale (rural, small community) and national scale (grid connected). It would also consider duties and taxes on petroleum fuels and electricity production. The study would recommend changes that encourage the import, possibly manufacture or assembly, and use of RETs, including tools, appliances, and associated monitoring equipment, etc. It would consider the pros and cons (and legality under treaties, conventions and international obligations) of differential import duties on devices that are energy efficient or use indigenous resources.

Development of capacity for effective RET project document creation for donor funding. Though there has been a significant level of support from PNG 's traditional donors for RETs, support has fallen off in recent years and there was no ongoing support found in early 2004. Donor organisations today increasingly require high quality project documents with clear economic analysis components, budgets with realistic justifications, well developed logical frameworks and action plans. In particular, the requirements for preparation of acceptable project documents for GEF and ADB are complex and demanding. The capacity of both the private sector and government to develop clear, logical and adequate project documents is limited and training is needed so donor funding can be accessed on a scale appropriate to the need.

Green interest rates. An assessment should be made of the need for, and practicality of, special interest rates, subsidised by the government, for (majority) locally-owned businesses for the establishment of RE services, including design and installation, operation and maintenance, repair and refurbishing, training local personnel in use of RETs, production of training materials in local languages, etc. If it appears that "green" rates would be a useful incentive, an interest subsidy fund or special government loan arrangements for private RET development should be developed.

Energy policy development. Advisers funded under external development projects and working closely with the GoPNG and the NGO community, should assist in the review of national energy policy and rural energy policy, and prepare practical policy documents for consideration by cabinet. These should include strategic plans with activities, timeframes, priorities, and budgetary requirements. The CROP Energy Working Group's Regional Energy Policy and Plan provides a possible starting point. The DANIDA/UNDP/SOPAC Pacific Islands Energy Policy and Strategic Action Planning project (PIEPSAP), expected to run from about August 2004 for three years, is designed to provide this sort of service but may need cofinancing to meet specific capacity development needs.

Energy Division. The functions, authority, and responsibility of the Energy Division should be clarified. If not already done, an up-to-date staffing structure and job descriptions should be prepared and approved at the appropriate level. Any responsibilities of the Energy Division for coordinating energy sector activities overall, providing information to the public and its relationship to other committees or advisory groups with an energy mandate (e.g. NAACC, PIREP, PIEPSAP, etc.) should be included. Once these functions, authority and responsibilities are clearly defined, a focused capacity building effort needs to be launched.

Development of a public information resource for RETs. Financing to develop a library of RET information materials specifically selected and developed for the PNG government, NGO and private users is needed as is selection of suitable repositories for that library. The recent tendency by the donor community to develop such materials for Internet delivery while ignoring the development of traditional library materials is not suitable for PNG due to the low level of Internet connectivity and the slow data rates generally encountered. Without an information resource covering past experience in PNG, other Pacific experience and general issues of economics, technology, management, etc. organisations wishing to develop RETs in PNG may have difficulty developing the technology without a long trial and error period repeating the costly errors already made in other parts of the Pacific and around the world. Entries could include:

reports on RETs of immediate relevance to PICs. There have been a number of technical reports prepared over the years by donor agencies and others on RETs and their potential suitability for the PICs. Some are out-of-date, inaccessible, biased or too technical or academic in style. It may be useful for a series of short but authoritative technical reports to be prepared (by SOPAC, SPREP or the two jointly) and regularly updated which provide an overview of technical, economic, social, and environmental aspects of RETs of particular relevance to PNG and other PICs. These might initially include solar, wind, and biofuel from coconut oil.[49]

RETs of potential relevance to PICs. There has been considerable hyperbole regarding ocean energy for the Pacific. It would be useful to have a series of short authoritative reports which explain the extent to which ocean energy systems are

[49] SOPAC published a number of technical reports in 2001 and 2002. Issues covered include: hydrogen fuel cells (report MR0416, 2001) OTEC (report MR0417, 2001), space solar power (MR0418, 2001) and geothermal (report MR0452, 2002). No coverage of solar PV, solar thermal, wind, hydro or biomass. It may be worthwhile exploring whether existing materials could be adapted/extended to cover specific PIC needs.

commercially proven and suitable for adoption by PICs in the near future. Perhaps even more useful in the short term would be a critical (in the positive sense) assessment of hybrid energy systems (e.g. wind/solar; RETs/diesel), experience in the Pacific and elsewhere, and their suitability for use in remote areas of PNG and other Pacific islands.

The team notes that in the 1980s, a technical resource library on renewable energy, the 'Commonwealth Regional Renewable Energy Resources Information System' (CRRERIS), was developed by Australia and located in Canberra specifically for the use of the PICs. The effort was somewhat unsuccessful because of inconvenient access, communications problems and the complexity of searching for useful documents. Also the collection was largely academic in nature, all in the English language and not always pertinent to the needs of the PICs. To be useful in PNG, the team believes that it will be necessary for a similar information library to be locally based in several locations around the country, to be carefully fitted to PNG's needs and provided in both print and electronic formats conveniently accessible to public and private users.

Provision of Support for Unitech RET activities. Unitech has a wealth of experience that is not being adequately used. It may be a suitable institution to support for national and regional training on the practical management and use of RETs and can assist in the preparation of a national RET library focused on PNG appropriate technologies and PIC experience.

Assistance in resource assessment capacity development. A programme to assist the Energy Division and other appropriate agencies to develop the capacity to locally perform wind, hydro, biomass and solar resource assessments is needed. Also, assistance in increasing the local capacity to specify and select contractors for geothermal and ocean energy resource assessments is needed.

Development of a local capacity to prepare RET operation and maintenance training and manuals in the local languages. Developing the capacity of rural technicians to install, operate and maintain RET systems requires local language training. This will require external assistance to develop the manuals and training in a metropolitan language then assist local language experts to develop a standard vocabulary for the technical terms and procedures that have to be expressed in the local language as well as translate the documents into the local language.

Assistance in understanding market structures for RETs. Market barriers identified as constraints include the lack of affordable transport to rural communities (generally by air or foot), the small market size, dispersed population, and lack of productive demand for electricity. Considering that PNG already has a relatively large market for RETs (at least PV systems) by PIC standards, and has installed hundreds of micro/mini hydro systems, a study of the reality and seriousness of market barriers to RETs, and ways to overcome them, is warranted if large-scale private sector development is desired.

Vandalism and theft. The extent of this vandalism and theft problem, and the degree of success of the PV panel painting and awareness campaign, should be ascertained. Guidelines for protection of the systems should be prepared and

disseminated (along with appropriate training and awareness) for any new PV systems and similar preventive measures designed for other RETs.

Land Access study. A study with follow-up recommendations for action should be carried out on options and opportunities to involve landowners as potential partners rather than opponents in the development of RETs both small scale (for community, health centre, school, etc. applications) and larger scale (feeding to a grid). This should include case studies of successful and failed approaches in PNG and elsewhere.

Preparation of guidelines for village scale hydro development. Existing international guidelines for hydro development are for much larger scale implementations than useful for village hydro development in the 5-20 kW range for which there are a large number of opportunities in PNG and Melanesia in general. Financing is needed for the development of guidelines for technical assessment, environmental impact assessment, economic analysis, technical design, institutional possibilities, operational requirements and maintenance requirements.

8.1.1 Hardware investments for co-financing

The following investments have the highest short-to-medium term potential for reducing GHG emissions from petroleum energy nationally..

Biofuel. By far the largest potential impact on GHG emissions of new RE investments based on known resources in PNG would be from large scale use of coconut oil as a biofuel. This could eliminate up to two-thirds of the 2003 level of national GHG emissions from petroleum fuel use.

Geothermal. The second largest impact would be from construction of the proposed Efate geothermal plant, which could displace the equivalent of 15% of 2003 emissions initially, more if a second plant were added later. The mission has no information on the likely emissions of sulphur dioxide (SO2), a major pollutant from some geothermal schemes, or other potentially negative environmental effects of geothermal development in PNG.

Hydro. The third largest impact would be from mini and micro hydro, which could displace 13% of current CO2 emissions from petroleum, assuming that the sites identified are all practical and capable of producing the energy estimated during preliminary investigations. (There are also likely to be many more sites not yet assessed, see the resource assessment entry above.)

If finance is available to PNG to develop relatively large scale RETs, all of the above should be seriously considered for support. However, choices regarding RET development should not be made solely on the basis of their potential impact on GHG emissions, which in any case are inconsequential on a global or comparative per-capita basis.

P.O Box 10, Toronto NSW 2283, Australia andrew@majorityworld.com.au

Annex 2 – References

ADB, 2002 Papua New Guinea Country Strategy and Program Update: 2003-2005 (Manila; July)

ADB, 2003 Millennium Development Goals in the Pacific: Relevance and Progress (Manila; March)

ADB, 2003a Papua New Guinea (in 'Asian Development Outlook 2003'; Manila)

ADB, 2003b Papua New Guinea Economic Overview and Key Indicators (Manila) ADB

ADB, undated PNG Country Data (from www.adb.org)

APEC, 2000 Major Energy Indicators of Papua New Guinea (from APEC Energy Statistics 2000)

APEC, undated PNG energy data (APEC Expert Group on Energy Data and Analysis, Institute of Energy Economics, Japan; http://www.ieej.or.jp/egeda/database/)

Associated Plumbing, 2004 pers. com. with national consultant J Wilmot (13 April)

AusAID, 2003 Papua New Guinea and the Pacific – A Development Perspective (canberra; September)

Bais, Chris, 2004 pers. com. (PNG Power; 20 January)

Beca-Worley International, 1985 Mini Hydro Power Resource Inventory (Report for the Department of Minerals and Energy), GoPNG, Port Moresby

Bryce, Paul, 2004 pers. com. (APACE, Sydney, Australia; 24 March)

Capon, Len, 2004 pers. com. (Rural Developments Services; 20 January)

CIA, 2003 World Factbook: PNG chapter (updated August)

CM&P, 2002 Profile: Mining and Petroleum Investment Papua New Guinea, PNG Chamber of Mining and Petroleum, Port Moresby

Fairbairn, Paul, 2004 pers. com. (SOPAC, Suva, Fiji; 26 January)

ForSec, 2001 Foreign Investment Climate in Individual Forum Island Countries: Papua New Guinea

ForSec, 2003 Papua New Guinea Economy and Issues (Suva)

Gafiye, Garaio, 2004 Appropriate Technology and Community Development Institute Energy Programme (description of programme; Lae, January)

Gamser, Matthew, 1980 Household Energy Consumption in Port Moresby (Report for Department of Minerals and Energy, GoPNG, Port Moresby)

Goldthorp, Steve, 2002 Beyond Combustion: A Review of Biomass Gasification Technologies (Forestry Industry Engineering Association Wood Wastes 2002 Conference, Auckland, May 2-3)

GoPNG, 1981 Energy in Papua New Guinea: 1981 (Energy Planning Unit, Department of Minerals and Energy, Government of Papua New Guinea, Port Moresby)

GoPNG, 1987 Wood and Woody Biomass Use in the Agro-Industries: Coffee (technical report 1987/4; prepared by I. A. Gilmour for Energy Planning Unit, Department of Minerals and Energy; GoPNG;

GoPNG, 1993 Rural Electrification in Papua New Guinea: Issues, Options and Development of Policy Guidelines (Department of Energy Development)

GoPNG, 1995/96 National Forest Plan for Papua New Guinea (Draft; PNGFA)

GoPNG, 1997 Industrial / Commercial Energy Use Survey and Household Energy Use Survey (questionnaire formats from Office of Energy Development, Department of Petroleum and Energy)

GoPNG, 1997a Demographic & Health Survey, June 1996-July 1997 (Department of Health and National Statistics Office)

GoPNG, 1999 National Population Policy 2000-2010 (Department of Planning and Monitoring)

GoPNG, 2000 Papua New Guinea Initial Communication Under the United Nations Framework Convention on Climate Change (Department of Environment and Conservation; Port Moresby; November)

GoPNG, 2001 National Energy Policy Statement (Draft, Department of Petroleum and Energy) GoPNG, 2001b National Energy Policy Guidelines (Draft' Department of Petroleum and Energy) GoPNG, 2001c National Rural Electrification Policy (Draft, Department of Petroleum and

Energy)

GoPNG, 2002 Papua New Guinea 2000 Census: Final Figures (National Statistics Office)

GoPNG, 2002a 2002 Energy Survey (industrial energy use questionnaire format from

Department of Petroleum and Energy)

GoPNG, 2003 2004 Budget, Volume 1: Economic and Development Policies (Finance and Treasury Department; Waigani; November)

GoPNG, 2003 National Policy on Downstream Processing of Forest Products (Draft; Ministry of Forest, 28 August)

GoPNG, 2003a Petroleum Production Summary of PNG Since 1991 (from DPE database; prepared by Petroleum Division Engineering Branch; Department of Petroleum and Energy)

GoPNG, 2003b Report of National Symposium on the Clean Development Mechanism & Climate Change (Department of Environment and Conservation with Forsec; Port Moresby, April)

GoPNG, 2003c Report of the National Symposium on the Clean Development Mechanism & Climate Change (Port Moresby, 28-29 April)

GoPNG, 2004 Issues Paper: Energy Sector Review (prepared by Dr Harry Zevon, SAGRIC International for AUSAID & Department of Petroleum and Energy; January)

GoPNG, 2004a Information on New and Renewable Energy in PNG (prepared by Colin Kalimba, Policy & Planning Branch, Energy Division; Report 1/04, Department of Petroleum and Energy)

GoPNG, 2004b Five-Year Strategic Plan for Department of Petroleum and Energy: 2004-2008 (prepared by Dr Harry Zevon, SAGRIC International for AUSAID & Department of Petroleum and Energy; January)

GoPNG, undated Feasibility of Industrial Fuel production from Pyrolysis of Wood Wastes in Papua New Guinea (prepared by J W Tatom for Energy Planning Unit, Department of Minerals and Energy; GoPNG; early 1980s)

Greenpeace, 2004 The Untouchables. Rimbunan Hijau's World of Forest Crime & Political

Patronage (Greenpeace International, January)

Hairai, Peter, 2004 pers. com. (PNG Power Ltd.; 22 January)

Hermescec, Branko, 1981 Forest Energy in Papua New Guinea (Forest Products Research

Centre, Frangipani St Hohola, June)

Horn, Matthias, 2004 pers. com. with national consultant John Wilmot (Buka Metal Fabricators, 11 March)

Hothersall, R.J., 1984 Micro-Hydro Development Study for Papua New Guinea (MPhil Thesis, The Papua New Guinea University of Technology, Lae, June)

IB, 2004 Bougainville's Itch for Independence: Some Secessionists Want it Now (by Matelita Ragogo; in 'Islands Business'; Fiji; April)

IB, 2004a China Reaches for PNG's Nickel (by Rowan Callick; in 'Islands Business'; Fiji;

April)

ICCC, 2004 Petroleum Industry Pricing Review (Draft Report; Port Moresby 24 March)

IMF, 2003 Papua New Guinea: Selected Issues and Statistical Appendix (IMF Country

Report No. 03/176; Washington, DC; June) IRN, 2002 Citizen's Guide to the World Commission on Dams

IRN, 2003 Twelve Reasons to Exclude Large Hydro from Renewables Initiatives (International Rivers Network & twelve other organization; Berkeley; November)

Johnston, Peter, 1994 An Evaluation of the European Community's Lomé II Pacific Regional Energy Programme: Final Report (prepared for South Pacific Forum Secretariat; Suva; August)

Johnston, Peter, 1994a The Potential and Actual Hydrological Effects of A Major Hydroelectric Power Project (MSc paper, University of London, 1994)

Kalimba, Collin, 2002 Minute to Allan Lari of 28 August (DPE; GoPNG)

Kalma J. D, 1980 A Wind Resource Assessment for Papua New Guinea (Land Use Research Division, Institute of Earth Resources, CSIRO, Canberra)

Komolong, Miok, 2004 pers. com. (Unitech, Lae, 21 January)

Kopi, Idau, 2003Field Trip Report on Rural Electrification (prepared for SOPAC, May)

Kuinata, Lastus S., 2004 pers. com with national consultant J Wilmot (14 April)

LGM, 2003 Trial Project Brings Solar Powered Electricity Into Village Homes (Lihir Gold Mines press release; 23 October)

Liu Zhaoxiang Newspaper articles in The National, 14 November 2003:

Liu Zhaoxiang, 2003 Utilise Solar to the Fullest (In Post-Courier, Monday 14 April 2003)

Liu Zhaoxiang, 2004 Harvesting ocean energy in PNG (in The National, 6 February,

www.thenational.com.pg/0206/w3.htm)

Matainaho, Fifaia, 2004 pers. com with national consultant J Wilmot (13 April)

Matainaho, Fifaia, 2004 pers. com. (Unitech, Lae, 21 January)

Matbob, Patrick, 2003 Copra Farmers Unite to Buy Madang Mill: They Want to Turn it into a

Profitable Operation (Available at www.pacificislands.cc/pm12003/pmdefault.php?urlarticleid=0036)

Matbob, Patrick, 2004 New Owner for Madang Mill But Growers Retain 40% (Available at www.pacificislands.cc/pm32004/pmdefault.php?urlarticleid=0030)

Nalish, Sam, 2004 pers. com. (Forest Research Institute; Lae, 21 January))

National, 2004 Shell Inks K4.7 Bln Deal with InterOil (in PNG National; Port Moresby; 19 January)

Nippon Koei, 2003 Community Based Project for the Degraded Land Reforestation and Biomass Power Supply System (Project Brief, December)

Oa, Stanleo, 2004 pers. com. (Department of Agriculture; 22 January)

PNGP, 2003 National & Provincial Ten Year Power Development Plan 2003-2012, March

PNGP, 2003 PNG Power National and Provincial Ten Year Power Development Plan: 20032012 (Port Moresby; March)

Post Courier, 2004 Coconut Oil Mill in Business ( Rural Industries Weekly section, 5 February)

Post Courier, 2004 Rural Industries Weekly section, 11 March

Prime, 2003 InterOil to Drill Again (and other oil news in Prime, Vol. 4 No. 3; Port Moresby; December)

Puy, A and Sumanasiri, K.E.D., 2003 The Potential of Renewable Energy Utilization in Papua New Guinea (Paper presented at 3rd International Conference On Renewable Energy for Sustainable Development; held in Dhaka, Bangladesh; October; PNG University of Technology, Lae)

Puy, A. & K.E.D. Sumanasiri, 2003 The Potential of Renewable Energy Utilisation in Papua New Guinea (Department of Mechanical Engineering, PNG University of Technology, Lae, Papua New Guinea)

Ranatunga, S. et al, 1999 Teptep Micro-hydro plant. Micro-hydro Development Through Community Support (Proceedings of Second National Seminar on Renewable Energy for Rural Development; edited by F. Welt; published by the PNG University of Technology, Lae)

Rannells J, 1990 A Factbook on Modern PNG (Oxford University Press)

Shearman, Phil & Cannon, Jim, 2002 PNG Forest Resources and the Log Export Industry: A Quantitative Analysis of Forest Resources, the Impact of Commercial Logging and the Future for the Log Export Industry (The Papua New Guinea Eco-Forestry Forum, April)

SOPAC, 2002 Pacific Island Regional Geothermal Assessment and Development Initiative -A Funding Proposal (Miscellaneous Report MR463; June).

SPC, 2003 Draft Database on Photovoltaic Systems Installed in Pacific Island Countries (Rural Energy & Development Unit, Noumea, April 2003

Tobia, Brian, 2004 Let There Be Light in Rural PNG. China's Solar and Wind System a Hit (In: Pacific Islands Monthly, February (www.pacificislands.cc/pm22004/pmdefault.php?urlarticleid=0026)

UNCT, 2001 Common Country Assessment: Papua New Guinea (United Nations Country Team, Port Moresby, December)

UNDP, 2003 Human Development Report 2003, Millennium Development Goals: A Compact Among Nations to End Human Poverty (New York)

Uppal A.H. and Satter A.H., 1995 The Current Status of Research in the Utilization of Renewable Energy in Papua New Guinea (Paper presented at the Renewable Energy workshop held in Lae

## BARRIERS TO RURAL ELECTRIFICATION AND RENEWABLE ENERGY IN PNG

This annex summarises the key barriers that hamper rural electrification and the use of renewable energy in PNG that emerged from a study by Idau Kopi 'Field Trip Report on Rural Electrification' (prepared with SOPAC support in May 2003) of three small hydro projects in remote areas of PNG. This has been abridged and substantially edited.

> Isolation (Accessibility): Difficult access to remote rural sites in PNG, maybe accessible only by air, is clearly a significant barrier to project development. Poor access greatly increases costs of technology and spare parts, which have to be transported from main centres. The two related barriers of cost and accessibility were documented in a 1988 PEDP report as the two major constraints to micro- hydro in Papua New Guinea.

Dispersed population. Rural communities in PNG are neither compact nor concentrated, with small villages often more than two hours walking distance from each other. This creates a low level of understanding about choices of locally appropriate possibilities of electricity-based development.

Lack of productive demand for electricity. There were no economic activities at any case study sites that could productively use electricity. Villagers who were once keen farmers of coffee, spices (cardamom) and vegetables have abandoned production for sales in recent years because of high freight charges to transport produce to urban markets. Husking coffee beans and helping dry cash crops are areas where electricity could be put to productive use. The change away from cash cropping has been exacerbated by the lack of agricultural field officers in local centres in recent years to advise people on farming methods.

Lack of cash. There is little economic activity in many rural areas of PNG (including the case study areas) so there is no money circulating in the community. People living at the fringes of a mission or government station can tap into the electricity supply but cannot afford the connection fees and usage charges.

Poor management. The presence of good local government management is important. The absence of an official government representative at one station has resulted in a state of disarray. At other sites, a well-managed mission or government station contributes a great deal to RE project success.

Correct construction procedures ignored. At one site, the original project report revealed that the design did not follow the recommendations of original geological survey and the project has been technically unacceptable.

Lack of follow-up visits. After original operational were resolved, there was no follow-up visit to the hydro plants at any of the sites. The lack of visits creates a feeling of neglect and carelessness on the part of the operator.

Lack of government support. Since the transfer of the functions of power stations (C-centres) to the provincial government by the national government, there has been little support from the provincial government to local communities and local governments, particularly funds for operators' wages and maintenance.

No revenue collection. Only one community hydro committee was successful in collecting revenue from government workers. The wantok system makes revenue collection difficult due to traditional reciprocal exchange of goods and services among the clan members.

Ownership issues. People see government projects as public assets and do not care about their long-term operation. Internal social strains arise from impact of the technology; e.g. government workers at one site do not want to pay for electric services which they feel is their right.

Standards of rural housing. Industry electrical standards and safety codes preclude connection to most forms of customary dwellings (grass huts), based on wiring practices designed for urban areas. In all sites visited, only permanent and semi-permanent dwellings were connected.

Lack of specialist skills. The lack of specialist skills (e.g. electromechanical equipment repair) in PNG created problems for the sites visited. At one site, replacement generator exciter windings had to sent from overseas to restore power. At another site, a voltage control board failed and replacements had to be obtained from Australia. At a third site, a failed governor component had to be sent overseas for repairs, resulting in at least four months with no power from the turbine.

# IMPORTANT LAWS AND REGULATIONS

## ELECTRICITY INDUSTRY ACT

[Electricity Industry Act (Chapter 78) consolidated to No 10 of 2002]

(1) Electricity Industry Act.

(2) Being an Act to to provide for the establishment of an Electricity Commission and to regulate the generation, supply and sale of electricity, and for related purposes.

Being an Act to regulate the generation, supply and sale of electricity, and for related purposes.

**PART I.—PRELIMINARY.**

1. Interpretation.(3)

In this Act, unless the contrary intention appears— "Authorized Officer" means an Authorized Officer appointed under Section 31A;(4)

(5) "the by-laws" . . . [Repealed] "the Chairman" means the Chairman of the Commission appointed under

Section 5(3);(6) "the Chairman" . . . [Repealed] "the Commission" means the Papua New Guinea Electricity Commission established by Section 3;(7) "the Commission" . . . [Repealed] "electrical contractor" includes—

(a) a company, association or body of persons trading as an electrical contractor; and

(b) the holder of an electrical contractor's licence;

"customer" includes (where the context requires) a person seeking the supply or sale of electricity to that person;(8)

(9) "electrical contractor's licence" means an electrical contractor's licence issued under Section 38;

(10) "electrical installation" means any appliances, wires, fittings or other apparatus placed in, on, under or over any premises and used for, or for purposes incidental to, the conveyance, control or use of electricity supplied or intended to be supplied by the State, or an electricity undertaker, whether or not the appliances, wires, fittings or apparatus are supplied by the person contracting or undertaking to supply them or it, and includes additions, alterations and repairs to any such appliances, wires, fittings or apparatus, but does not include—

(11) (a) an electricity supply main or service line of the State, or an (12) (13)

(15) electricity undertaker; or

(b) any appliance, wire, fitting or apparatus—

(i) that is connected to and beyond any electrical outlet socket installed for the purpose of connecting portable electrical appliances, fittings and apparatus; and

(ii) at which fixed wiring terminates; or

(c) any appliance, wire, fitting or apparatus that is placed in, on, under or over any premises owned or occupied by the State, or an electricity undertaker and that—

(i) is not used for the consumption of electricity on those premises; or

(ii) is not used solely for purposes incidental to the conveyance or control of electricity so consumed; or

(d) any electrical installation about a mine; "electrical wiring work" means the actual physical work of installing an electrical installation;

"electrician" means a person, other than an electrical contractor, engaged in electrical wiring work;

"electrician's licence" means an electrician's licence issued under Section 38;

"electricity" includes electric current, electrical energy or any like agency;

"electricity supply industry" means the industry involved in the generation, transmission, distribution, supply and sale of electricity or other operations of a prescribed kind;(14)

"electricity undertaker" means a person, firm or company who or which is licensed under Part IIIB to carry on operations in the electricity supply industry and includes (where the context requires) a person, firm or company who or which has been licensed to carry on operations in the electricity supply industry under that Part whose licence has been suspended or cancelled or has expired;

"electric line" means a wire, conductor or other means used for the purpose of conveying, transmitting or distributing electricity, including—

(a) any casing, coating, covering, tube, pipe, pole, post, frame, bracket or insulator enclosing, surrounding or supporting such a line, or any part of such a line; and

(b) any apparatus connected with such a line for the purpose of conveying, transmitting or distributing electricity; "the General Manager" means the General Manager of the Commission

appointed under Section 9A;(16) "the General Manager" . . . [Repealed] "Inspector" means an Electricity Inspector appointed under Section 32; "member" means a member of the Commission;(17) "member" . . . [Repealed]

"officer of the Regulator" means any person engaged by the Regulator pursuant to Division II.7 of the Independent Consumer and Competition Commission Act 2002;(18)

(19) "Order" . . . [Repealed];

"the Appeals Panel" means the Appeals Panel constituted under Section 42 of the Independent Consumer and Competition Commission Act 2002;(20)

"the Registrar of Titles" means the Registrar of Titles appointed under the Land Registration Act(21) (Chapter 191);

(22) "registered company auditor" means a registered company auditor as

defined in Section 2 of the Accountants Act 1996; "registered company auditor" . . . [Repealed]; "the regulations" means any regulations made under this Act; "Regulator" means the Independent Consumer and Competition

Commission established under the Independent Consumer and

Competition Commission Act 2002;(23) "retail", in relation to electricity, means the sale of electricity;(24) "this Act" includes the regulations;

(25) "works" includes electric lines and any buildings, machinery, equipment (including substations and transformers), engines, works, matters and things used for, or in connection with, the generation or supply of electricity.

2. Saving of other laws.

(1) This Act does not affect the exercise of any right, power or authority under any law relating to Posts and Telegraphs.

(2) This Act shall be read subject to the Electricity Supply (Government Power Stations) Act.

## PART II.—THE PAPUA NEW GUINEA ELECTRICITY COMMISSION.

Division 1.—Establishment and Constitution of the Commission.

3. Establishment of the Commission.(26)

A Papua New Guinea Electricity Commission is hereby established.

Establishment of the Commission. [Repealed] Incorporation of the Commission.(27) The Commission— is a corporation; and has perpetual succession; and shall have a seal; and may acquire, hold and dispose of property; and

is capable of suing and being sued in its corporate name.

All courts, Judges and persons acting judicially shall take judicial notice

of the seal of the Commission affixed to a document, and shall presume that it was duly affixed.

Incorporation of the Commission. [Repealed]

Constitution of the Commission.(28)

(29) (1) The Commission shall consist of three Commissioners appointed by the Minister and who shall hold office during the pleasure of the Minister.

(30)

(1A) . . . [Repealed]

(2) A person shall not, at the same time, be a member of the Commission and the General Manager.(31)

(2) . . . [Repealed]

(32)

(3)

The Minister shall appoint one of the members to be the Chairman of the Commission and who shall hold office during the pleasure of the Minister.

(4) Subject to this Act, the terms and conditions of the members of the Commission are as determined by the Minister responsible for Public Service matters.(33)

(4) . . . [Repealed]

(5) Where a member is—(34)

(a) on leave of absence; or

(b) absent from the country; or

(c) out of speedy and effective communication or otherwise unable to

perform or is not readily available to perform the duties of his office, his alternate has and may exercise all his powers and perform all his functions and duties under this Act.

(5) . . . [Repealed]

(6) [See Note](35)

(36) (6) . . . [Repealed]

Dismissal of members of the Commission. [Repealed](37)

Vacation of office.(38)

The office of a member of the Commission becomes vacant—

(a) if he becomes bankrupt, applies to take the benefit of a law for the relief of bankrupt or insolvent debtors, compounds with his creditors or makes an assignment of his remuneration for their benefit; or

(b) if he resigns his office by writing under his hand addressed to the Minister, and the resignation is accepted; or

(c) if he is absent, except on leave granted by the Minister, from all meetings of the Commission held during a period of three months; or

(d) if in any way, otherwise than with the approval of the Minister or as a

member, and in common with the other members, of an incorporated company consisting of not less than 25 persons, he—

(i) is concerned or interested in a contract or agreement entered into by or on behalf of the Commission; or

(ii) participates or claims to participate in the profit of any such contract or agreement or in a benefit or emolument arising from any such contract or agreement.

Vacation of office. [Repealed]

Leave of absence.(39)

The Minister may grant leave of absence to a member of the Commission on such terms and conditions as the Minister responsible for Public Service matters determines.

Leave of absence. [Repealed]

Meetings of the Commission.(40)

(1) The Commission shall meet at such times and places as the Chairman determines.(41)

(1) . . . [Repealed]

(2) The Minister may at any time convene a meeting of the Commission.(42)

(2) . . . [Repealed]

(3) At a meeting of the Commission—(43)

(44) (a) two members are a quorum; and

(b) the Chairman, or, in his absence, a member elected by the members present from their own number, shall preside; and

(c) all matters shall be decided by a majority of votes of the members present; and

(d) the member presiding has a deliberative and, in the event of an equality of votes on a matter, also a casting vote.

Division 1A.—The General Manager.(46)

9A. Appointment, etc.(47)

(1) There shall be a General Manager for the Commission who—

(a) shall be appointed by the Minister on the recommendation of the Commission; and

(b) shall be appointed for such period as the Minister determines; and

(c) shall be the Chief Executive Officer; and

(d) shall be the head of the Service of the Commission.

(2) The terms and conditions of appointment and service of the General Manager are as determined by the Minister responsible for Public Service matters.

(3) A member of the Commission is not eligible for appointment as the General Manager.

9A. Appointment, etc. [Repealed]

9B. Termination of appointment.(48)

If the General Manager—

(a) becomes permanently incapable of performing his duties; or

(b) resigns his office by writing under his hand to the Minister; or

(c) engages, without the consent of the Commission, in any paid employment outside the duties of his office; or

(d) becomes bankrupt or applies to take the benefit of any law for the relief of bankrupt or insolvent debtors, compounds with his creditors or makes an assignment of his remuneration for their benefit; or

(e) is convicted of an offence punishable under a law by death or by imprisonment for one year or longer, and as a result of the conviction, is sentenced to death or imprisonment,

the Minister shall terminate his appointment.

(2) Subject to Subsection (3), the Minister may, at any time terminate the appointment of the General Manager for inability, inefficiency, incapacity or misbehaviour.

(3) The Minister shall not terminate the appointment of the General Manager, unless he has given, in writing, one month's prior notice of his intention to do so.

9B. Termination of appointment. [Repealed]

9C. Public Service rights.(49)

Where an officer of the Public Service is appointed to be General Manager, his service as General Manager shall be counted as service in the Public Service for the purpose of determining his rights (if any) in respect of—

(a) leave of absence on the grounds of illness; and

(b) furlough or pay instead of furlough (including pay to dependants on the death of the officer).

9C. Public Service rights. [Repealed]

9D. Functions.(50)

(1) The General Manager shall—

(a) manage the Service of the Commission and, in relation to the management of that Service, act in accordance with the policy and directions of the Commission; and

(b) advise the Commission on any matter concerning the Service of the Commission referred to him by the Commission.

(2) The General Manager has such other functions as the Commission from time to time determines.

9D. Functions. [Repealed]

Division 2.—The Service of the Commission.

10. Appointment of officers.(51)

(1) The Commission may appoint to be officers of the Commission such persons as it thinks proper and necessary for the purposes of the Commission.

(2) The General Manager and the officers of the Commission constitute the Service of the Commission.

(3) A person shall not be admitted to the Service of the Commission unless he makes and subscribes an oath or affirmation of office in the prescribed form.

(4) An officer of the Commission holds office for such period and on such terms and conditions as are determined under Section 12.

(5) If a person appointed under this section was, immediately before his appointment, an officer of the Public Service, his service as an officer of the Commission shall be counted as service in the Public Service for the purpose of etermining his existing and accruing rights under the Public Services (Management) Act 1995.

(6)

An office in the service of the Commission is an office to which apply the provisions of the Public Services (Management) Act 1995 relating to leave to serve under another Act.

Appointment of officers. [Repealed]

Temporary and contract appointments.(52)

(1) The Commission may employ—

(a) for a fixed period of service under a formal written contract; or

(b) for a short or indefinite period of service not under a formal written

contract, such persons as it thinks proper and necessary for the purposes of the Commission.

(2) The tenure of office, and the terms and conditions of service of a person employed under this section are as determined under Section 12.

Temporary and contract appointments. [Repealed]

Conditions of appointment.(53)

The Commission shall, in accordance with this section, determine—

the tenure of office and the terms and conditions of service of officers and other employees under this Division; and

other matters relating to the Service of the Commission or other employment with the Commission.

A determination under this section—

shall be in writing under the seal of the Commission; and

shall not be expressed to take effect commencing on a day before the date of the making of the determination where, if it so took effect—

the rights of a person or authority (other than the Commission)

existing at the date of the making of the determination would be affected in a manner prejudicial to him or it; or

liabilities would be imposed on a person or authority (other than the Commission) in respect of anything done or omitted to be done before the date of the making of the determination,

and where in such a determination a provision is made in contravention of this subsection the provision has no effect.

(3) . . . [Repealed]

(4) The Commission shall cause a determination made under this section to be brought as soon as possible to the notice of all officers and other employees of the Commission.

(5) The General Manager may, at the direction of, and on behalf of, the Commission, execute contracts of employment in accordance with a determination under this section.

(6) Every non-citizen employed or to be employed under this Division shall have attached to his contract of employment, and forming part of that contract, a detailed training experience document and a detailed training and localization program for the purpose of training a citizen to replace him, such training program to be supplied by the Commission.

(7) Failure by a non-citizen to comply with the training and localization program referred to in Subsection (6) or any direction that may be issued from time to time by the Commission on training of a citizen shall be sufficient cause for the termination of the contract of employment of that non-citizen.

Conditions of appointment. [Repealed]

Retirement benefits funds.(54)

(1) In this section, "approved retirement benefits fund" means a fund or scheme approved by the Minister responsible for finance matters—

(a) from or under which individual personal benefits, pensions or retiring allowances for, or for dependants of, officers or employees of the Commission are paid; or

(b) in respect of which the rights of the officers and employees, or of the dependants, to receive the benefits, pensions and allowances specified in Paragraph (a) are, to the satisfaction of the Minister responsible for finance matters, fully secured.

(2) The Commission may—

(a) accept contributions from officers and employees for payment to an approved retirement benefits fund; and

(b) advance moneys, on such terms as are agreed on, to an approved retirement benefits fund; and

(c) set apart or pay by way of contributions sums as or to an approved

retirement benefits fund, and may establish, administer and meet the costs of administering an approved retirement benefits fund or funds.

(3) For the purposes of this section, a member of the Commission shall be

deemed to be an officer of the Commission.

13. Retirement benefits funds. [Repealed]

Division 3.—Finance, etc.

14. Capital and profits of the Commission.(55)

(1) In this section—

"the Agreement" means the agreement made on June 1965 between the Administrator of Papua New Guinea and the Commission relating to the acquisition or taking over by the Commission of certain undertakings of the Commonwealth of Australia in its then administration of Papua New Guinea;

"any other agreement" means an agreement entered into between the State and the Commission for the purpose of the consolidation of certain loan moneys and conversion into capital.

(2) The capital of the Commission is, at any time, an amount equal to the sum of—

(a) the amount of K5,764,822.00; and

(b) where before 30 June 1965 the former Administration had transferred or granted to the Commission any interest in land, buildings, plant or equipment (including transmission lines) under or in accordance with any other agreement entered into between that Administration and the Commission after 19 March 1962 (being the date of commencement of the Papua and New Guinea Electricity Commission Act 1961 (Adopted)) such amount as is specified in that agreement for the purposes of this subsection; and

(c) such amount as is specified in any other agreement.

(3) Interest is not payable to the State on the capital of the Commission.

14. Capital and profits of the Commission. [Repealed]

14A. Payment of dividends.(56)

(1) Subject to this section, the Commission shall pay to the State out of the profits of the Commission for a financial year, such amount in relation to that financial year as the Secretary for Finance, with the approval of the Head of State, acting on advice, determines.

(2) In making a determination under Subsection (1), regard shall be had to any advice furnished by the Commission to the Secretary for Finance, in relation to the financial affairs of the Commission.

(3) The Secretary for Finance shall not make a determination under Subsection (1) in respect of a financial year earlier than the financial year commencing on 1 January 1977.

14A. Payment of dividends. [Repealed]

14B. Ex-Gratia payments.(57)

(1) Where, in respect of any land acquired from any person by the State or

by a pre-Independence Administration in Papua New Guinea—

(a) the Commission, for the purposes of this Act, carries out any works; and

(b) the Minister, pursuant to Section 14C, declares such works to be a major civil-engineering project; and

(c) the person, or another person lawfully claiming through the person,

makes application to the Commission, the Commission may, subject to the provisions of this section, make an ex-gratia payment to that person or to that other person lawfully claiming, as the case may be.

(2) The Commission shall not make an ex-gratia payment under Subsection

(1)unless the Commission obtains the prior written approval of the National Executive Council.

(3) The National Executive Council shall not approve an ex-gratia payment under Subsection (2) unless the National Executive Council is satisfied that in the interest of national development it is necessary or expedient so to do.

(4) An ex-gratia payment under this section shall be such amount and shall be paid in such manner as the Commission, with the written approval of the National Executive Council, determines.

(5) For the purposes only of the Rouna 4 Hydro Electric Project this Act is deemed to have come into operation on the first day of January, nineteen hundred and eighty-four.

(6) In this Section— "major civil-engineering project" means any works declared as such

under Section 14C; "pre-Independence Administration in Papua New Guinea" means—

(a) the Administration or Government of a former Territory or the Government of Australia acting in relation to any such Territory; or

(b) the British Military Administration of the former colony of German New Guinea (also known as the Territory of New Guinea); or

(c) the Administration or Government of the former possession of British New Guinea; or

(d) in relation to the former Colony of German New Guinea, the German Imperial Government or the German Government or the Fiscus of that Colony.

14B. Ex-Gratia payments. [Repealed]

14C. Minister may declare works to be major civil-engineering project.(58)

For the purposes of Section 14B the Minister may, after consultation with the Commission, by notice in the National Gazette, declare any works referred to in Section 14B(1)(a) to be a major civil-engineering project.

14C. Minister may declare works to be major civil-engineering project. [Repealed]

15. Moneys of the Commission generally.(59)

(1) The Commission shall open and maintain such bank accounts as are necessary for the exercise and performance of its powers and functions, and shall pay into them—

(a) all moneys received from the Government for the purposes of this Act; and

(b) all moneys appropriated by Act for the purpose of carrying out or giving effect to this Act; and

(c) all moneys received by the Commission for the sale, leasing or hire of property; and

(d) all moneys received by the Commission for the sale or supply of electricity; and

(e) all other moneys received by the Commission in the exercise and performance of its powers, functions and duties.

(2) Out of the moneys standing to the credit of the accounts referred to in Subsection (1), the Commission shall pay—

(a) all moneys payable by it in repayment of advances under this Act, and as interest on such advances; and

(b) the costs, charges and expenses incurred by the Commission in the performance of its functions under this Act; and

(c) the remuneration and allowances of the members of the Commission and of officers and employees of the Commission; and

(d) any other payments that the Commission is authorized or required to make under this Act.

(2) Out of the moneys standing to the credit of the accounts referred to in Subsection (1), the Commission—

(a) shall pay—

(i) all moneys payable by it in repayment of advances under this Act, and as interest on such advances; and

(ii) the costs, charges and expenses incurred by the Commission in the performance of its functions under this Act; and

(iii) the remuneration and allowances of the members of the Commission and of officers and employees of the Commission; and (iv) any other payments that the Commission is authorized or required to make under this Act; and

(b) may—

(i) make loans to officers and employees of the Commission to assist with home ownership; and

(ii) pay the cost of developing as serviced lots land for sale for housing purposes to citizen officers and employees of the Commission; and

(iii) pay the cost of redeveloping or purchasing residential properties initially for the accommodation of non-citizen officers and employees of the Commission and later for sale to citizen officers and employees of the Commission.

(3) In respect of moneys advanced or borrowed under this Act for the purposes of the Commission, the Commission shall maintain a separate account in respect of the moneys that are related to each such purpose, and shall cause proper entries of—

(a) all moneys so advanced or borrowed for a particular purpose of the Commission; and

(b) the purposes to which the moneys have been applied, to be made in the account maintained in respect of the purpose.

Moneys of the Commission generally. [Repealed]

Investment.(60)

(1) In this section, "authorized short-term money market" means the group of dealer companies that are authorized by the Central Bank to be approved dealers in short-term loans and towards which that Bank acts as lender of last resort.

(2) The Commission may invest any moneys standing to the credit of the bank accounts referred to in Section 15—

(a) in any securities of, or guaranteed by—

(i) the State; or

(ii) Australia, or a State or Territory of Australia; or

(b) in any manner allowed by a law of—

(i) Papua New Guinea; or

(ii) Australia, or a State or Territory of Australia,

for the investment of trust funds; or

(c) on fixed deposit with the Papua New Guinea Banking Corporation or any other prescribed bank; or

(d) in the securities of any authorized short-term money market; or

(e) in any other manner approved by the Minister,

and in such proportions, as between investments or classes of investments, as are approved by the Minister responsible for finance matters.

(3) Moneys held uninvested by the Commission shall be lodged on fixed deposit or at call with the Papua New Guinea Banking Corporation or with any other prescribed bank.

Investment. [Repealed]

Borrowing from approved banks, etc.(61)

(1) In this section— "approved bank" means the Central Bank or any other bank approved by the Minister for the purposes of this section;

"approved institution" means an institution or corporation approved by the Minister for the purposes of this section.

(2) Subject to this Act, the Commission may borrow money at interest from an approved bank or an approved institution, by way of mortgage, bank overdraft or otherwise, for—

(a) the purposes of the Commission under this Act; or

(b) the repayment or partial repayment of an amount previously

borrowed, within such limits and on such conditions as the Minister approves.

(3) The Minister may, for and on behalf of the State, guarantee to any person from whom the Commission borrows money under Subsection (2) the repayment, out of moneys lawfully available for the purpose, of any loan under that subsection, with interest.

17. Borrowing from approved banks, etc. [Repealed]

(62) 18. Application of Part VIII of Public Finances (Management) Act 1995. [Repealed]

18A. Audit.(63)

(1) For the purposes of this section, "subsidiary company of the Commission" shall, in relation to the Commission, have the meaning given to a subsidiary corporation of a public body in Section 49 of the Public Finances (Management) Act 1995.

(2) Subject to this section, the Auditor-General shall—

(a) inspect and audit the accounts and records of the Commission and any subsidiary company of the Commission and records relating to its assets or assets in its custody; and

(b) immediately draw the attention of the Minister to any irregularity disclosed by the inspection and audit that is, in the opinion of the Auditor-General, of sufficient importance to justify his doing so.

(3) The Auditor-General may, in his discretion, dispense with the whole or any part of the detailed inspection and audit of any accounts referred to in Subsection (2).

(4) The Auditor-General may, at his discretion for the purpose of assisting him in an inspection and audit under Subsection (2), employ a registered company auditor who shall act under the direction of the Auditor-General and under the terms and conditions determined by the Auditor-General.

(5) Where—

(a) by 1 April in each year, the Auditor-General or a registered company auditor employed by him under Subsection (4), has not commenced the inspection and audit in respect of the previous financial year; or

(b) by 1 July in each year, in relation to the continuous inspection of the accounts of the Commission, the Auditor-General or a registered company auditor employed by him under Subsection (4), has not commenced the inspection of the books and records of the Commission,

the Commission may employ a registered company auditor specified by the Auditor-General to carry out the inspection and audit.

(6) A person carrying out an inspection or audit under this section or a person authorized by him—

(a) is entitled at all reasonable times to full and free access to all accounts, records, documents and papers of the Commission and of any subsidiary company of the Commission relating directly or indirectly to the receipt, or payment of moneys by it, or to the acquisition, receipt, custody or disposal of assets by it; and

(b) may make copies of, or take extracts from, any such accounts, records, documents or papers; and

(c) may require any person to furnish him with such information in his possession or to which he has access as the person carrying out the inspection or audit, or the person authorized by him, thinks necessary for the purposes of the functions of the Auditor-General under—

(i) the Constitution; and

(ii) this Act; and

(iii) the Public Finances (Management) Act 1995.

(7) A person who contravenes Subsection 6(c) is guilty of an offence.

Penalty: A fine not exceeding K200.00.

18A. Audit. [Repealed]

(64) 19. (Repealed.)

**PART III.—POWERS AND FUNCTIONS OF THE COMMISSION.**

Division 1.—General.

20. Policy directions by N.E.C.(65)

The Commission shall give effect to any direction given to it by the Minister on any matter relating to the performance or exercise of its functions, duties or powers.

20. Policy directions by N.E.C. [Repealed]

(66) 20A. Role of the Commission. [Repealed]

21. General functions of the Commission.(67)

(1) Subject to this Act, the functions of the Commission are—

(a) to plan and to co-ordinate the supply of electricity throughout the country; and

(b) to generate, transmit, distribute, reticulate and sell electricity; and

(c) to provide to the public, to public bodies and to the State, services related to the sale, consumption and use of electricity; and

(d) to provide to the State services for the operation or maintenance of

plant for the generation, distribution and consumption of electricity; and

(e) to promote the sale and use of electricity; and

(f) to sell or hire, and to promote the sale or hiring of, electrical appliances and apparatus and motors and other devices utilizing electrical power; and

(g) to determine standards for and control the registration and licensing of electricians and electrical contractors; and

(h) to control the testing and approval of appliances, apparatus, motors, fittings and things used in connexion with the use or consumption of electricity; and

(i) to determine standards for, and to inspect and control the application of the standards to, wiring, fittings, apparatus, appliances and things used in connexion with the supply of electricity to, or the use of electricity in, consumers' premises connected to the public supply of electricity; and

(j) to determine standards for, and to inspect and control the application of the standards to, electrical machinery, lines and apparatus used in the generation, distribution and use of electricity by persons other than electricity undertakers; and

(k) to determine standards and methods of procedure to be adopted by workers within the electrical industry in order to ensure the safety of such workers, and to control and implement the operation of the standards; and

(l) to require the adoption of such standards of plant, apparatus and equipment and system frequencies as permit the efficient interconnexion of any electrical undertakings in the country as and when required; and

(m) to prescribe the terms of Orders and to issue, control and terminate Orders to electricity undertakers for the supply of electricity to the public; and

(n) generally to do such supplementary, incidental or consequential acts and things as are, in the opinion of the Commission, necessary or convenient for carrying out the functions referred to in the preceding paragraphs of this subsection.

(1A) The Minister may, by direction to the Commission, relieve it of functions, add to its functions or otherwise vary its functions as the Minister considers necessary or expedient.(68)

(2)

The Commission may act as the agent of the State or the Government in relation to any matter within the functions of the Commission.

(3) The Commission may make recommendations to the Minister on any matter in connexion with the generation, supply or use of electricity in the country.

General functions of the Commission. [Repealed]

Special reports to the Government.(69)

Where the Minister requests the Commission to furnish a report or information on the activities or operations, or proposed activities or operations, of the Commission, or on any matter relating to the generation, supply or use of electricity in the country, the Commission shall, to the best of its ability, furnish the report or information requested.

Special reports to the Government. [Repealed]

General powers of the Commission.(70)

(1) The Commission may do all things that are necessary or convenient to be done for or in connexion with the performance of its functions or the discharge of its duties under this Act.

(2) Without limiting the generality of Subsection (1), the Commission has power, subject to this Act—

(a) to receive moneys advanced by the Minister for the purpose of the performance of its functions or the discharge of its duties under this Act; and

(b)

for the purpose of securing any moneys borrowed by the Commission—

(i) to give security over the property of the Commission, or to charge the revenues of the Commission; and

(ii) to execute all mortgages and other instruments of assurance or charge; and

(c) to purchase land, and to purchase or construct buildings, for use in carrying on the operations of the Commission, and to dispose of land or buildings owned by the Commission; and

(d) to take on lease land or buildings for use in carrying on the operations of the Commission, and to dispose of any such lease; and

(e) to negotiate with the Government or any other person for the acquisition by the Commission of any electrical works or undertaking or for the transfer to the Commission of the benefit of or liability under any contract connected with the electrical works or undertaking, on such conditions as are agreed on by the Commission and the State or the other person; and

(f) to purchase, take on hire or otherwise acquire plant, machinery, equipment or other goods necessary for carrying on the operations of the Commission, and to dispose of any plant, machinery, equipment or other goods owned by the Commission; and

(g) to maintain and operate and, where necessary, improve and extend any works for or in connexion with the generation and supply of electricity vested in the Commission, and to construct new, additional or supplementary works or acquire works or property for or in relation to the generation or supply of electricity; and

(71) (h) to supply electricity and other goods and services to any person in the country at such price and on such terms as are agreed between the Commission and that person; and

(i) with the approval of the Minister—

(i) to conduct any business arising out of or ancillary to the generation and supply of electricity; and

(ii) to construct works or acquire works or property; and

(iii) to maintain and operate the works or property for the purposes of conducting any such business; and

(j)

to purchase electricity from any person in the country; and

(72) (k) to devise and operate a Home Ownership Scheme for officers and employees of the Commission; and

(73) (l) to request the Minister to declare under Section 23A Special Categories of houses for sale under the Home Ownership Scheme to which the provisions of Paragraph (c) do not apply; and

(m)

to make a loan to, or guarantee a mortgage on behalf of an officer or employee of the Commission for the purpose of house purchase or construction where such officer or employee of the Commission has been accepted to take part in a Home Ownership Scheme devised and operated by the Commission; and(74)

(n) to do such other things as are required or permitted to be done by the Commission under this Act or any other law; and(75)

(o) to do anything incidental to its powers or functions.(76)

23. General powers of the Commission. [Repealed]

23A. Sale of Special Categories of houses.(77)

(1) The Minister may, on the request of the Commission after receiving the approval of the National Executive Council, declare Special Categories of houses.

(2) A declaration under Subsection (1) shall—

(a) specify the terms and conditions under which the Special Categories of houses are to be sold; and

(b) be published in the National Gazette.

23A. Sale of Special Categories of houses. [Repealed]

23B. Report on Home Ownership Scheme.(78)

The Commission shall, at least once in each fiscal year, furnish to the Minister for presentation to the National Executive Council, a report on any Home Ownership Scheme devised and operated by the Commission.

23B. Report on Home Ownership Scheme. [Repealed]

24. Delegation.(79)

The Commission may delegate to a person all or any of its powers and functions under this Act (except the power to accept tenders and this power of delegation).

24. Delegation. [Repealed]

**PART IIIA.—ADMINISTRATION.(80)**

24A. Functions and Powers of Regulator.(81)

(1) The Regulator has, in addition to its functions under the Independent Consumer and Competition Commission Act 2002, the following functions:—

(a) any function that a regulatory contract issued under the Independent Consumer and Competition Commission Act 2002, being a regulatory contract which relates to the electricity supply industry, contemplates will be performed by the Regulator for the purposes of that regulatory contract; and

(b) the licensing functions conferred by this Act; and

(c) the monitoring and regulation of safety and technical standards in the electricity supply industry; and

(d) the monitoring and regulation of safety and technical standards with respect to works, electrical installations, electrical appliances and apparatus and associated equipment; and

(e) any other function or power conferred by this Act or by regulation under this Act; and

(f) any other function or power conferred by a prescribed contract.

(2)

The Regulator has, in addition to its powers under the Independent Consumer and Competition Commission Act 2002, the power to do all things necessary or convenient to be done for or in connection with or otherwise incidental to the performance of it functions under this Act.

(3)

The Regulator shall perform its functions in a manner consistent with the terms of any regulatory contract issued under the Independent Consumer and Competition Commission Act 2002 which relates to the electricity supply industry.

24B. Delegation.(82)

(1) Subject to Subsection (2), the Regulator may, by unanimous decision of all members of the Regulator and subject to any regulation made under this section, delegate to any member, officer or committee of the Regulator or to any other person any of its functions and powers (other than this power of delegation).

(2) The Regulator shall not delegate any of its functions or powers under— (a) a regulatory contract issued under the Independent Consumer and Competition Commission Act 2002; or

(b) Part IIIB, to a person other than a member or officer of the Regulator.

(3) A delegation under Subsection (1)—

(a) shall be in writing; and
(b) may be subject to such conditions or restrictions as are specified in the instrument of delegation; and
(c) is revocable at will by resolution of the Regulator in writing; and
(d) does not affect or prevent the performance of a function or the exercise of a power by the Regulator.

**PART IIIB.—ELECTRICITY SUPPLY INDUSTRY.(83)**

Division 1.—Declaration.(84)

24C. Declaration.(85)

The electricity supply industry is declared to be a regulated industry for the purposes of the Independent Consumer and Competition Commission Act 2002.

Division 2.—Licensing of Electricity Undertakers.(86)

24D. Requirement for licence.(87)

(1) A person, firm or company shall not carry on operations in the electricity supply industry for which a licence is required unless the person holds a licence under this Part authorizing the relevant operations.

Penalty: A fine not exceeding K10,000,000.00.

Default penalty: A fine not exceeding K1,000,000.00.

(2) The operations in the electricity supply industry for which a licence is required are:—

(a) the generation of electricity; and

(b) the operation of a transmission or distribution network; and

(c) the retailing of electricity; and

(d) other operations for which a licence is required by the regulations.

24E. Application for licence.(88)

(1) An application for the issue of a licence shall—

(a) be made to the Regulator in a form approved by the Regulator; and

(b) contain the information specified in the form.

(2) The applicant shall pay to the Regulator an application fee fixed by the Minister responsible for treasury matters of an amount that he considers appropriate to meet the reasonable costs of determining the application.

(3) The applicant shall give the Regulator further relevant information requested by the Regulator.

24F. Consideration of application.(89)

(1) The Regulator shall consider an application for the issue of a licence and may, subject to this Division, issue, or refuse to issue, the licence.

(2)

In considering an application for a licence, the Regulator shall have regard to the general factors specified in Part II of the Independent Consumer and Competition Commission Act 2002 and, subject to this section, may only issue a licence if it is satisfied that—

(a) the applicant is a suitable person to hold the licence; and

(b) the grant of the licence would be consistent with the criteria (if any) as are prescribed for a licence of that kind.

(3) In deciding whether an applicant is a suitable person to hold a licence, the Regulator may consider—

(a) the applicant's previous commercial and other dealings and the standard of honesty and integrity shown in those dealings; and

(b) the financial, technical and human resources available to the applicant; and

(c) the officers and, if applicable, major shareholders of the applicant and their previous commercial and other dealings and the standard of

honesty and integrity shown in those dealings (including breaches of statutory and other legal obligations); and

(d) such other matters as are prescribed.

24G. Licences may be held jointly.(90)

(1) A licence may be held jointly by two or more persons.

(2) If a licence is held jointly by two or more persons, those persons are jointly and severally liable to meet the requirements imposed under this Act or the Independent Consumer and Competition Commission Act 2002.

24H. Authority conferred by licence.(91)

(1) A licence authorizes the person named in the licence to carry on operations in the electricity supply industry in accordance with the terms and conditions of the licence.

(2) The operations authorized by a licence need not be all of the same character or at the same location but may consist of a number of different operations or operations at different locations.

24I. Term of Licence.(92)

A licence may be issued for an indefinite period or for a term specified in the licence.

24J. Licence Fees and Returns.(93)

(1) Notwithstanding Section 24I, a person is not entitled to the issue of a licence unless he first pays to the Regulator the annual licence fee, or the first installment of the annual licence fee, as the case may require.

(2) The holder of a licence issued for a term of more than one year shall—

(a) in each year lodge with the Regulator, before the date prescribed for that purpose, an annual return containing information required by the Regulator by condition of the licence or by written notice; and

(b) in each year pay to the Regulator, before the date prescribed for that purpose, the annual licence fee, or the first installment of the annual licence fee, as the case may require.

(3) The annual licence fee for a licence is the fee fixed, from time to time, by the Minister responsible for treasury matters in respect of that licence as an amount that he considers to be a reasonable contribution towards administrative costs.

(4)

An annual licence fee may, if the Regulator so determines, be paid in equal installments at intervals fixed by the Regulator.

(5) If the holder of a licence fails to lodge the annual return or to pay the annual licence fee or an installment of the annual licence fee, as the case may be, in accordance with this section, the Regulator may, by written notice, require the holder to make good the default and, in addition, to pay to the Regulator the amount prescribed as a penalty for default.

(6) An annual licence fee (including any installment of an annual licence fee or any penalty for default) payable under this section is recoverable as a debt due

to the Regulator.

(7) In this section— "administrative costs" means—

(a) the costs of administration of this Act; and

(b) any costs of administration of the Independent Consumer and Competition Commission Act 2002 relating to the electricity supply industry; and

(c) such other costs as are prescribed;

"holder" of a licence includes the holder of a licence that has been suspended.

24K. Specially Issued Licences.(94)

(1) The Minister may, by order in writing, require that one or more licences authorizing specified operations be issued under this Division to PNG Power, or to PNG Power's purchaser, in accordance with specified requirements as to the term and conditions of such licence or licences and the rights conferred by such licence or licences.

(2) The requirements of the Minister as to the conditions of a licence shall be consistent with the provisions of this Act as to such conditions.

(3) The Minister may, by order in writing, require that a licence issued to PNG Power in accordance with an order under Subsection (1) be transferred to PNG Power's purchaser.

(4) An order under this section shall be given effect without the need for PNG Power or PNG Power's purchaser to apply for the licence or agreement to the transfer of the licence and notwithstanding the provisions of this Act and Section 23 of the Independent Consumer and Competition Commission Act 2002.

(5) A licence issued to PNG Power in accordance with an order under this section may not be suspended or cancelled under this Act on the ground of any change that has occurred in the officers or shareholders of PNG Power associated with the shares in PNG Power being transferred from a Minister or Ministers to PNG Power's purchaser.

(6) In this section— "PNG Power" means the company incorporated pursuant to Section 3(1) of the Electricity Commission (Privatization) Act 2002;

"PNG Power's purchaser" means the purchaser to whom the shares in PNG Power are transferred in accordance with the Electricity Commission (Privatization) Act 2002.

24L. Licence Conditions.(95)

(1) On the issue of a licence, the Regulator shall make the licence subject to such conditions as it determines—

(a) requiring compliance with applicable codes or rules made under the Independent Consumer and Competition Commission Act 2002 as in force from time to time; and

(b) requiring compliance with applicable technical or safety requirements or standards; and

(c) requiring compliance with any regulatory contract issued under Section 34 or Section 35 of the Independent Consumer and Competition Commission Act 2002 that applies to the electricity undertaker; and

(d) requiring the electricity undertaker to have all or part of the operations authorized by the licence audited and to report the results of the audit to the Regulator; and

(e) requiring the electricity undertaker to notify the Regulator about changes to officers and, if applicable, major shareholders of the electricity undertaker; and

(f) requiring the electricity undertaker to provide, in the manner and form determined by the Regulator, such other information as the Regulator may from time to time require; and

(g) requiring the electricity undertaker to maintain specified accounting records and to prepare accounts according to specified principles; and

(h) requiring the business the operation of which is authorized under the licence or any part of that business to be kept separate from any other business of the electricity undertaker or any other person in the manner and to the extent specified in the conditions; and

(i) requiring the electricity undertaker to inform persons seeking or in receipt of specified services supplied by the electricity undertaker under the licence of the terms on which those services are provided (including the charges for these services) and of any changes in those terms; and

(j) in the case of a licence authorizing the generation of electricity or the operation of a transmission or distribution network, requiring the electricity undertaker—

(i) to prepare and periodically revise a safety and technical management plan dealing with such matters as are prescribed; and

(ii) to obtain the approval of the Regulator to the plan and any revision; and

(iii) to comply with the plan as approved from time to time; and (iv) to audit from time to time the electricity undertaker's compliance with the plan and report the results of those audits to the Regulator; and

(k) in the case of a licence authorizing the generation of electricity, requiring the electricity undertaker not to do anything affecting the compatibility of the electricity undertaker's electricity generating plant with any transmission or distribution network so as to prejudice public safety or the security of the power system of which the generating plant forms a part; and

(l) in the case of a licence authorizing the operation of a transmission or distribution network, requiring the electricity undertaker not to do anything affecting the compatibility of the electricity undertaker's transmission or distribution network with any electricity generating plant or transmission or distribution network so as to prejudice public safety or the security of the power system of which the transmission or distribution network forms a part; and

(m) in the case of a licence authorizing the operation of a transmission or distribution network, requiring the electricity undertaker to comply with—

(i) specified provisions for or relating to the granting to other electricity undertakers of rights to use or have access to the electricity undertaker's transmission or distribution network for the transmission or distribution of electricity by the other electricity undertakers; and

(ii) any scheme that the Regulator may establish by a code made under the Independent Consumer and Competition Commission Act 2002 for the resolution of disputes in relation to such rights; and

(n) in the case of a licence authorizing the operation of a transmission or distribution network, requiring the electricity undertaker to comply with—

(i) specified provisions for or relating to the granting to all electricity undertakers and customers of a class specified in the condition of rights to use or have access to the electricity undertaker's transmission or distribution network to obtain electricity from the network; and

(ii) any scheme that the Regulator may establish by a code made under the Independent Consumer and Competition Commission Act 2002 for the resolution of disputes in relation to such rights; and

(o) in the case of a licence authorizing the operation of a transmission or distribution network, requiring the electricity undertaker to comply with code provisions in force from time to time under the Independent Consumer and Competition Commission Act 2002 establishing a method for sharing of the costs of an augmentation of the network, being an augmentation of a kind specified in the code provisions, between customers who benefit from that augmentation; and

(p) in the case of a licence authorizing the operation of a transmission or distribution network or the retailing of electricity, requiring a specified process to be followed to resolve any dispute between the electricity undertaker and a customer as to the supply or sale of electricity; and

(q) in the case of a licence authorizing the operation of a transmission or distribution network or the retailing of electricity, requiring or relating to standard contractual terms and conditions to apply to the supply or sale of electricity to customers of a prescribed class; and

(r) in the case of a licence authorizing the operation of a transmission or distribution network or the retailing of electricity, requiring the electricity undertaker to comply with code provisions in force from time to time under the Independent Consumer and Competition Commission Act 2002 imposing minimum standards of service for customers and requiring the electricity undertaker to monitor and report on levels of compliance with those minimum standards; and

(s) in the case of a licence authorizing the operation of a transmission or distribution network or the retailing of electricity, requiring the

electricity undertaker to comply with code provisions in force from(96) time to time under the Independent Consumer and Competition Commission Act 2002 limiting the grounds on which the supply or sale of electricity to customers may be disconnected or discontinued and prescribing the process to be followed before the supply or sale of electricity is disconnected or discontinued; and

(t) in the case of a licence authorizing the retailing of electricity which confers an exclusive right to sell electricity pursuant to Section 24M, requiring the electricity undertaker to sell electricity to the relevant customers within the specified area.

(2) On the issue of a licence, the Regulator shall make the licence subject to further conditions that the Regulator is required by regulation to impose on the issue of such a licence.

(3) On the issue of a licence, the Regulator may make the licence subject to further conditions considered appropriate by the Regulator.

(4) A condition of an electricity undertaker's licence imposed under Subsection (1)(m) is not to take effect until the date prescribed for that purpose.

(5)

Nothing in this section permits a condition to be included in a licence where that condition would be inconsistent with the terms of a regulatory contract issued under Section 34 or Section 35 of the Independent Consumer and Competition Commission Act 2002 which applies to the electricity undertaker.

24M. Exclusive retail licences.(97)

A licence authorizing the retailing of electricity may, if the Regulator so determines, confer on the electricity undertaker an exclusive right to sell electricity to customers or classes of customers within a specified area.

24N. Regulatory duplication.(98)

Notwithstanding the preceding provisions of this Division, the Regulator is not to impose a condition on a licence if the Regulator is satisfied that the condition would unnecessarily duplicate, or be inconsistent with, regulatory requirements under any other Act that are binding on the electricity undertaker.

24O. Offence to contravene licence conditions.(99)

(1) An electricity undertaker shall not contravene a condition of its licence.

Penalty: A fine not exceeding K10,000,000.00.

Default penalty: a fine not exceeding K1,000,000.00.

(2) If an electricity undertaker profits from contravention of a condition of its licence, the Regulator may recover an amount equal to the profit from the electricity undertaker—

(a) on application to a court convicting the electricity undertaker of an offence against this section; or

(b) by action in a court of competent jurisdiction.

(3) An amount recovered under Subsection (2) shall be paid into the Consolidated Revenue Fund.

24P. Variation of licence.(100)

(1) The Regulator may vary the terms or conditions of an electricity undertaker's licence by written notice to the electricity undertaker as the Regulator considers appropriate, but not so as to—

(a) remove a condition that the Regulator is required by this Act to impose on such a licence; or

(b) vary or remove a term or condition contained in a licence issued under Section 24K to the extent that, as at the date of issue of the licence, the licence provided that such term or condition is not be varied or removed.

(2) A variation may only be made—

(a) on application by the electricity undertaker or with the electricity undertaker's agreement; or

(b) after giving the electricity undertaker reasonable notice of the proposed variation and allowing the electricity undertaker a reasonable opportunity to make submissions about the proposed variation.

24Q. Transfer of licence.(101)

(1) A licence may only be transferred with the Regulator's agreement.

(2) The Regulator shall not agree to the transfer of a licence if the transferee would not be entitled to the issue of the licence.

(3) An application for agreement to the transfer of a licence shall—

(a) be made by the transferor with the consent of the transferee to the Regulator in a form approved by the Regulator; and

(b) contain the information specified in the form.

(4) The applicant shall pay to the Regulator an application fee fixed by the Minister responsible for treasury matters of an amount that he considers appropriate to meet the reasonable costs of determining the application.

(5) The applicant shall give the Regulator further relevant information requested by the Regulator.

24R. Notice of licence decisions.(102)

(1) The Regulator shall give an applicant for a licence, or for agreement to the transfer of a licence, written notice of the Regulator's decision on the application.

(2) The Regulator shall give the holder of a licence written notice of any decision by the Regulator affecting the terms or conditions of the licence.

24S. Surrender of licence.(103)

(1) An electricity undertaker may, by written notice given to the Regulator, surrender its licence.

(2) A notice given under Subsection (1) shall be given to the Regulator at least six months before the surrender is to take effect or, if the licence requires a longer period of notice, as required by the licence.

(3) The Regulator may, by agreement with the electricity undertaker, shorten the required period of notice.

24T. Register of licences.(104)

(1) The Regulator shall keep a register of the licences issued to electricity undertakers under this Act.

(2)

The register shall include—

(a)

the terms and conditions of each licence; and

(b)

such other information as is required under the regulations.

(3) A person may, without payment of a fee, inspect the register.

Division 3.—Standard Terms and Conditions for Sale or Supply.(105)

24U. Standard terms and conditions for sale or supply.(106)

(1) An electricity undertaker may, from time to time, fix standard terms and conditions governing the sale or supply of electricity (including the service of making connections to a transmission or distribution network) by the electricity undertaker to customers of a prescribed class.

(2) An electricity undertaker shall publish in the National Gazette and in a daily newspaper circulating nationally a notice setting out any standard terms and conditions fixed by the electricity undertaker.

(3) Standard terms and conditions fixed under this section—

(a) shall comply with the conditions of the electricity undertaker's licence; and

(b) shall come into force on the day specified by the electricity undertaker in the notice of the standard terms and conditions published under this section, being a day not earlier than the day on which the notice is published; and

(c) when in force, are contractually binding on the electricity undertaker and the class of customers to which the terms and conditions are expressed to apply.

(4) Subject to the conditions of an electricity undertaker's licence, a standard term or condition fixed under this section may be modified or excluded by express agreement between the electricity undertaker and a customer of the electricity undertaker.

Division 4.—Suspension or Cancellation of Licences.(107)

24V. Suspension or cancellation of licences.(108)

(1) Upon being satisfied that—

(a) the holder of a licence obtained the licence improperly; or

(b) the holder of a licence has been guilty of a material contravention of a condition of a licence or any other requirement imposed by or under this Act or any other Act in connection with the operations authorized by the licence; or

(c) the holder of a licence has ceased to carry on operations authorized by the licence; or

(d) there has been any act or default or change of circumstances such that the holder of a licence would no longer be entitled to the issue of such a licence,

the Regulator may suspend or cancel the licence with effect from a specified date.

(2) A suspension under this section may be for a specified period, or until the fulfillment of specified conditions, or until further order of the Regulator.

(3) Before the Regulator acts under this section, the Regulator shall—

(a) notify the holder of the licence in writing of the proposed action specifying the reasons for the proposed action; and

(b) allow the holder of the licence at least 14 days within which to make submissions to the Regulator in relation to the proposed action.

Division 5.—Regulator's powers to take over operations.(109)

24W.Power to take over operations.(110)

(1) If—

(a)

an electricity undertaker contravenes a condition of its licence or any other requirement of this Act, or an electricity undertaker's licence is suspended, cancelled or surrendered; and

(b) it is necessary, in the Regulator's opinion, to take over the electricity undertaker's operations (or some of them) to ensure an adequate supply of electricity to customers,

the Head of State, acting on advice, may make an order under this section.

(2) Before an order is made under this section, the Regulator shall give the electricity undertaker a reasonable opportunity to make written representations giving reasons why the order should not be made.

(3) An order under this section—

(a) authorizes the Regulator to take over the electricity undertaker's operations or a specified part of the electricity undertaker's operations; and

(b) may contain ancillary directions (and may, in particular, contain directions about how the costs of carrying on the operations, and revenue generated from the operations, are to be dealt with).

(4) A direction under Subsection (3)(b) operates to the exclusion of rights that are inconsistent with it.

24X. Appointment of operator.(111)

(1)

If an order is made under this Division, the Regulator shall appoint a suitable person to take over the relevant operations on agreed terms and conditions.

(2) A person appointed under Subsection (1)—

(a) is referred to in this section as the "operator; and

(b) may, but need not, be an electricity undertaker.

(3) The electricity undertaker shall facilitate the take over of the relevant operations by the operator.

(4) The operator may have access to the employees, and equipment, infrastructure and other property, of the electricity undertaker for the purposes of carrying on the relevant operations.

(5) A person shall not obstruct the operator's access to employees or property or the exercise by the operator of the operator's responsibilities under this Division.

Penalty: A fine not exceeding K10,000,000.00.

(6) A person shall comply with reasonable directions given by the operator in the exercise of the operator's responsibilities under this Division.

Penalty: A fine not exceeding K10,000,000.00.

## PART IIIC.—CONSTRUCTION, ENTRY ON LAND, REGISTRATION OF TITLES.(113)

Division 1.—Construction, Entry on Land, etc.(114)

25. Erection of transmission lines, etc.

(1) In this section, "Government land" means all land other than—

(a) customary land that is not leased by the owners to the State; and

(b) land held by a person other than the State for an estate greater than a term of years; and

(c) land that is the subject of a State lease under the Land Act.

(2) For the purposes of the conveyance, transmission and distribution of electricity, an electricity undertaker, on giving notice of its intention to do so to the owner or occupier of the land, may, subject to Subsection (4), erect, maintain and remove—

(a)

pylons, posts, poles or pillars in, under, through, over, across or on any land to which this subsection applies; and

(b) electric lines (including, without limiting the definition of that expression in Section 1, conduits, substations, transformers and other appliances and things necessary for the works) in, under, through, over, across or on any such land or any building, house or premises on any such land.

(3) The land to which Subsection (2) applies is land, including land under the sea or a river or stream, that—

(a) is outside a town; or

(b) is a street or other Government land within a town, at the time when the pylons, posts, poles, pillars or electric lines are erected.

(4) The exercise of the powers conferred by Subsection (2) is subject to the prior approval of—

(a) the Head of State, acting on advice, in the case of land outside a town; or

(b) the Minister, in the case of land within a town.

(116)

(5) . . . [Repealed]

25A. Ownership of transmission lines, etc.(117)

Notwithstanding anything in any other law, but subject to any agreement in writing to the contrary, the ownership of pylons, posts, poles, pillars and electric lines erected or operated by an electricity undertaker is not affected by their affixation to land.

26. Entry on land, etc.(118)

(119) (1) Notwithstanding anything in any other law, a person authorized by an electricity undertaker may, subject to Subsections (2) and (3), at all reasonable times—

(a) enter on any land on which pylons, posts, poles, pillars and electric lines owned or operated by the electricity undertaker have been or may be erected, or on any adjoining land, with such assistants, vehicles and things as the thinks necessary; and

(b) make surveys, take levels, sink pits, examine the soil and do any other

thing in relation to the land, for the purposes of maintaining, removing or (where otherwise authorized or permitted to do so) erecting or preparing (including through surveying and obtaining other information in relation to the land) for the possible erection of pylons, posts, poles, pillars and electric lines.

(2) Subject to Subsection (3), before entering any land under Subsection (1) the person concerned shall give notice to the owner or occupier of the land of his intention to do so.

(3) Notice in accordance with Subsection (2) need not be given if—

(a) the land, or part of the land, is in a Local Government Council area and written notice has, not less than one week before entry, been given to the Council specifying the area, or the approximate area, affected, together with a request that the Council advise any persons likely to be affected; or

(120)

(b) the name, or the place of abode or business, of the owner or occupier cannot, after the exercise of reasonable diligence, be found and unreasonable delay or expense would otherwise be caused to the electricity undertaker; or

(c) the land is apparently unoccupied, but in any such case the authorized person shall advise any person who asks for

his authority for being on the land that he is on the land for the purposes of this Act.

(4) In addition to the powers conferred by Subsection (1), the authorized person or his assistants, doing as little damage as may be, may—

(a) trim, lop or cut down any trees and bushes that may obstruct the work being carried out; and

(121) (b) place on or below the surface of the soil such pegs, marks, metal pins or other distinguishing marks as are necessary for any of the purposes set out in Subsection (1).

(5) An electricity undertaker shall minimize the impact of things done under this section on activities of others on the relevant land.(122)

(123) 27. Notice of intention to enter under Section 25 or 26.

(1) Notice of intention to enter land under Section 25 or 26 may be given—

(a) orally or in writing to the owner or occupier personally; or

(b) by post addressed to the owner or occupier at his usual or last-known place of abode or business; or

(c) in writing to a person apparently living or employed at that place of

abode or business and apparently not less than 16 years of age, but where notice of intention is given in accordance with Paragraph (b), entry shall not be made before the notice would be delivered in the ordinary course of post.

(2) In an emergency, a person authorized by an electricity undertaker may exercise a power of entry referred to in Section 25 or 26—

(a) at any time and without prior notice if it is not practicable to give such notice; and

(b) if necessary in the circumstances, by the use of reasonable force, but only if the authorized person is accompanied by a member of the police force.

(124) 28. Ancillary powers. [Repealed]

(125) Division 2.—Registration of Titles.(126)

29. Noting of N.E.C. approval to works.

Where— (a) the Head of State, acting on advice, under Section 25(4)(a); or

(b) the Minister, under Section 25(4)(b), approves the erection of electric lines in, under, through, over, across or on any land or on a building, house or premises on any land, that is subject to the Land

Registration Act (127)(Chapter 191), a copy of the approval shall be forwarded by the Clerk of the Executive Council to—

(c) the Registrar of Titles, with a request that the approval be noted on the title or titles affected; and

(d) the registered proprietor of the land.

30. Registration of rights, etc.

(128) (1) As soon as practicable after the erection of electric lines—

(a) under Section 25; or

(b) by agreement between an electricity undertaker and any other person,

the electricity undertaker shall conduct a survey and forward to the Registrar of Titles a copy of the survey plan specifying details of the land affected.

(2) The Registrar of Titles shall—

(a) when requested under Section 29, note the approval on the title or titles affected; and

(129)

(b) on receipt of a survey plan required by Subsection (1) specifying the width of the land affected and the extent of the restrictions imposed, cause the rights conferred by Sections 25 and 26 and any regulations to be registered on any title or titles affected.

(3) Notwithstanding the absence of a dominant tenement, the registration of rights under Subsection (2)(b) shall be deemed to be the registration of an easement, and the Land Registration Act(130) (Chapter 191) shall be read subject to this section.

**PART IV.—ELECTRICITY UNDERTAKERS.**

(131) 31. Authorization to supply electricity. [Repealed]

(132) PART V.—INSPECTION, SAFETY AND TECHNICAL REQUIREMENTS.(133)

Division 1.—Authorized Officers.(134)

31A. Appointment of Authorized Officers.(135)

(1)

The Regulator may appoint suitable persons as Authorized Officers for the purposes of this Act.

(2)

An Authorized Officer holds office on the conditions stated in the instrument of appointment.

31B. Identity Card.(136)

(1) The Regulator shall give each Authorized Officer an identity card.

(2) The identity card shall—

(a) contain a photograph of the Authorized Officer taken for the purpose; and

(b) identify the Authorized Officer as an Authorized Officer appointed by the Regulator.

(3) A person shall, within two days after ceasing to be an Authorized Officer, return the identify card to the Regulator.

Penalty: A fine not exceeding K200.00.

(4) An Authorized Officer shall, before exercising a power in relation to another person, produce his identity card for inspection by that other person.

Division 2.—Powers of Authorized Officers.(137)

31C. Power of Entry.(138)

(1)

An Authorized Officer may, as reasonably required for the purposes of the enforcement of this Act, enter and remain in any place with such assistants, vehicles and things as he thinks necessary.

(2) In an emergency, an Authorized Officer may exercise a power of entry under Subsection (1) at any time and, if necessary in the circumstances, by the use of reasonable force.

(3) An Authorized Officer may not enter a place by force in an emergency unless accompanied by a member of the police force.

31D. General Investigative Powers.(139)

(1) An Authorized Officer who enters a place under this Division may exercise any one or more of the following powers:—

(a) investigate whether the provisions of this Act are being or have been complied with; and

(b) examine and test works, electrical installations or equipment in the place to find out whether the works, electrical installations or equipment are safe and comply with the requirements of this Act; and

(c) investigate a suspected electrical accident; and

(d) investigate a suspected interference with works or an electrical installation; and

(e) investigate a suspected theft or diversion of electricity; and

(f) search for, examine and copy or take an extract from a document or record of any kind as reasonably required for the purposes of the enforcement of this Act; and

(g) take photographs or make films or other records of activities in the place and works, electrical installations or equipment in the place; and

(h) take possession of any object that may be evidence of an offence against this Act.

(2) If an Authorized Officer takes possession of an object that may be evidence of an offence—

(a) the Authorized Officer shall give the occupier of the place a receipt for the object; and

(b) the object shall be returned to its owner—

(i) if proceedings for an offence are not commenced within six months after the Authorized Officer takes possession of the object—at the end of that period; or

(ii) if such proceedings are commenced within that period—on completion of the proceedings, unless the court, on application by the Regulator, orders confiscation of the object.

(3) A court may order the confiscation of an object of which an Authorized Officer has taken possession under Subsection (1) if it is of the opinion that the object has been used for the purpose of committing an offence or there is some other proper reason for ordering its confiscation.

(4) If the court orders the confiscation of an object, the Regulator may dispose of the object.

31E. Disconnection of Electricity Supply.(140)

(1) If an Authorized Officer finds that electricity is being consumed or supplied contrary to this Act, the Authorized Officer may disconnect the

electricity supply.

(2) If an Authorized Officer disconnects an electricity supply under this section, the Authorized Officer shall give written notice to the occupier of the relevant place—

(a) informing the occupier that the electricity supply has been disconnected under this section; and

(b) directing that the electricity supply shall not be reconnected until arrangements have been made to the satisfaction of an Authorized Officer to ensure against future contravention of this Act.

(3) If an electricity supply has been disconnected under this section, no person shall reconnect the electricity supply, or have it reconnected, without the approval of an Authorized Officer.

Penalty: A fine not exceeding K2,000.00.

31F. Power to make works or installation safe.(141)

(1) If an Authorized Officer finds that works or an electrical installation are unsafe, the Authorized Officer may—

(a) disconnect the electricity supply or give a direction requiring the disconnection of the electricity supply; or

(b) give a direction requiring the carrying out of the work necessary to make the works or electrical installation safe before the electricity supply is reconnected.

(2) Subject to this section, a direction under this section shall be given—

(a) in relation to works—to the electricity undertaker or other person that operates the works; or

(b) in relation to an electrical installation—to the person in charge of the electrical installation or the occupier of the place in which the electrical installation is situated.

(3) A direction under this section may be given by written notice or, if the Authorized Officer is of the opinion that immediate action is required, orally but shall subsequently be confirmed in writing.

(4) A person to whom a direction is given under this section—

(a) shall comply with the direction; and

(b) shall not reconnect or permit the reconnection of the electricity supply unless the work required by the direction under this section has been carried out, or an Authorized Officer approves the reconnection of the electricity supply.

Penalty: A fine not exceeding K2,000.00.

31G. Power to require information.(142)

(1) An Authorized Officer may require a person to provide information in the person's possession relevant to the enforcement of this Act.

(2) An Authorized Officer may require a person to produce documents in the person's possession that may be relevant to the enforcement of this Act for inspection by the Authorized Officer.

(3) A person shall not, without reasonable excuse, fail to comply with a requirement under this section.

Penalty: A fine not exceeding K2,000.00.

(4) A person is not required to give information or produce a document under this section if the answer to the question or the contents of the document would tend to incriminate the person of an offence.

Division 3.—Electricity Inspectors.(143)

32. Appointment of Inspectors.(144)

(1) An electricity undertaker may, subject to conditions determined by the Minister, appoint an officer or employee to be an Electricity Inspector for the purposes of this Act.

(2) An Inspector may only exercise powers under this Act subject o his conditions of appointment and any directions given to him by the electricity undertaker.

33. Identity card.(145)

(1) An electricity undertaker shall give each Inspector appointed by the electricity undertaker an identity card.

(2) The identity card shall be in a form approved by the Minister and shall—

(a) contain a photograph of the Inspector taken for the purpose; and

(b) identify the Inspector as an Electricity Inspector appointed by the electricity undertaker.

(3) A person shall, within two days after ceasing to be an Inspector for the relevant electricity undertaker, return the identity card to the electricity undertaker.

Penalty: A fine not exceeding K200.00.

(4) An Inspector shall, before exercising a power in relation to another person, produce his identity card for inspection by that other person.

34. Powers of Inspectors.(146)

(1) An Inspector for an electricity undertaker may—

(a) require the owner or occupier of any land to cut down or lop any trees or undergrowth growing on the land that obstruct or, in the opinion of the electricity undertaker or the Inspector, are likely to interfere with an electric line; and

(b) at all reasonable times enter any premises to which electricity is, or is to be or has been, supplied or sold by the electricity undertaker for the purpose of—

(i) inspecting or testing any electric line or works; or

(ii) ascertaining the quantity of electricity consumed or supplied; or

(iii) installing, repairing or replacing meters and testing their accuracy; or

(iv) removing or disconnecting any electric line or works or electricity supply where—

(A) a supply of electricity to the premises is no longer required; or

(B) the electricity undertaker desires to cut off the supply of electricity to the premises; or

(C) in the opinion of the Inspector, the supply of electricity to the premises is unsafe; or

(v) inspecting electrical installations in the place to ensure that it is safe to connect or reconnect electricity supply; or

(vi)

taking action to prevent or minimize an electrical hazard; or

(vii) investigating a suspected theft or diversion of electricity.

(2)

In an emergency, an Inspector may exercise a power of entry under Subsection (1)(b) at any time and, if necessary in the circumstances, by the use of reasonable force.

(3) An Inspector may enter a place under Subsection (1)(b) with such assistants, vehicles and things as he thinks reasonably necessary.

(4) An Inspector may not enter a place by force in an emergency unless accompanied by a member of the police force.

Division 4.—Safety and Technical Requirements.(147)

35. Safety and Technical Compliance of Works, Electrical Installations and Equipment.(148)

(1) A person who connects an electrical installation to a transmission or distribution network shall ensure that the electrical installation, and the connection, comply with technical and safety requirements imposed under the regulations.

Penalty: A fine not exceeding K2,000.00 and, in addition, a fine not exceeding K200.00 for every day during which the offence continues.

(2) A person who owns or operates works or an electrical installation shall ensure that—

(a) the works or electrical installation comply with, and are operated in accordance with, technical and safety requirements imposed under the regulations; and

(b) the works or electrical installation are safe and are safely operated.

Penalty: A fine not exceeding K2,000.00 and, in addition, a fine not exceeding K200.00 for every day during which the offence continues.

36. Power to require rectification, etc., in relation to works or electrical installations.(149)

(1) If works or an electrical installation are unsafe, or do not comply with this Act, the Regulator may give a direction requiring—

(a) the rectification of the works or electrical installation to the Regulator's satisfaction; or

(b) if appropriate, the temporary disconnection of the electricity supply while the rectification is carried out; or

(c) the disconnection and removal of the works or installation.

(2) Subject to this section, a direction under this section shall be given—

(a) in relation to works—to the electricity undertaker or other person that operates the works; or

(b) in relation to an electrical installation—to the person in charge of the electrical installation or the occupier of the place in which the installation is situated.

(3) A direction may be given by written notice or, if the Regulator is of the opinion that immediate action is required, orally but shall subsequently be confirmed in writing.

(4) A person to whom a direction is given under this section shall comply with the direction.

Penalty: A fine not exceeding K2,000.00 and, in addition, a fine not exceeding K200.00 for every day during which the offence continues.

(5) If a person does not comply with a direction, the Regulator may take any action that is reasonable and necessary to have the direction carried out.

(6) A person, authorized in writing by the Regulator, may do what is reasonable and necessary to carry out the direction.

(7) The costs incurred in carrying out the direction are recoverable as a debt due to the Regulator.

37. Reporting of Accidents.(150)

If an accident happens that involves electric shock caused by the operation or condition of works or an electrical installation—

(a) the accident shall be reported as required under the regulations—

(i) if the accident involves part of an electricity undertaker's works—by the electricity undertaker; or

(ii) if the accident happens while an electrician or an electrical contractor is working on an electrical installation and the electrician or electrical contractor is able to make the report—by the electrician or electrical contractor; or

(iii) in any other case—by the occupier of the place in which the accident happens; and

(b) the works or electrical installation shall not be altered or interfered with unnecessarily by any person so as to prevent a proper investigation of the accident.

Penalty: A fine not exceeding K2,000.00.

## PART VA.—ELECTRICAL CONTRACTORS AND ELECTRICIANS.(151)

38. Licensing of Electrical Contractors and Electricians.(152)

The Regulator may issue electrical contractor's licences and electrician's licences in accordance with the regulations.

39. Electrical wiring work.(153)

(1) Subject to Section 40, a person other than—

(a) the holder of an electrical contractor's or electrician's licence under this Act; or

(b) a person who is in the employment of and carries out the work under

the personal supervision of a person so licensed, who undertakes or carries out any electrical wiring work is guilty of an offence.

Penalty: A fine not exceeding K100.00.

(2) Subject to Section 40, an electrical contractor who undertakes any electrical wiring work shall—

(a) himself, carry out the work whether with or without assistance; or

(b) constantly employ on the work a person who is the holder of an electrician's licence or electrical contractor's licence.

Penalty: A fine not exceeding K100.00 and, in addition, a fine not exceeding K10.00 for every day during which the offence continues.

(3) Subsection (2) does not apply to work that consists of fixing, connecting and maintaining overhead electrical conductors not in conduits, or of other work usually carried out by a linesman, where the work is carried out under the personal supervision of the holder of an electrical contractor's licence or electrician's licence.

(4) The holder of an electrician's licence who undertakes or carries out electrical wiring work otherwise than—

(a) on his own premises; or

(b) as an employee of an electrical contractor; or

(c) in accordance with Section 40(b), is guilty of an offence.

Penalty: A fine not exceeding K100.00.

(5) This section does not prevent the carrying out of electrical wiring work by an apprentice electrician working under the supervision of his master.

40. Exceptions.(154)

Notwithstanding this Division—

(a) an unlicensed person may carry out electrical wiring work as part of a contract for building or construction work if the installation is carried out by or under the personal supervision of a person holding an electrical contractor's licence or electrician's licence; and

(b) a person, or body of persons, corporate or unincorporate, who or that—

(i) is not trading as an electrical contractor; and

(ii) is employing a licensed electrician for the purpose of making or maintaining the installations necessary for the conduct of the business of that person,

is not required to be licensed under this Division, and a licensed electrician so employed may carry out the duties of that employment.

**PART VB.—ELECTRICAL APPLIANCES AND APPARATUS.(155)**

41. Prohibited appliances, etc.(156)

(1) The regulations may prohibit the sale, hiring or exposure or advertisement for sale or hire of any class, description or type of wire, cable, appliance, fitting, meter, insulator, apparatus or material intended, suggested or designed for use in or for the purposes of or for connection to any electrical installation, unless the wire, cable, appliance, fitting, meter, insulator, apparatus or material, as the case may be, has been approved by the Regulator and is stamped or labelled as prescribed.

"(2) Regulations made for the purposes of this section may provide for the approval of the Regulator to be signified by approval of a sample or by some other means.

**PART VC.—REVIEW.(157)**

42. Review of decisions under Act.(158)

(1) An application may be made to the Appeals Panel—

(a)

by an applicant for the issue or variation of the terms or conditions of a licence under Part IIIB, or for agreement to the transfer of such a licence, for review of the decision of the Regulator to refuse the application; or

(b) by an electricity undertaker for review of a decision of the Regulator under Part IIIB to suspend or cancel the electricity undertaker's licence or to vary the terms or conditions of the electricity undertaker's licence; or

(c) by a person to whom a direction has been given under Part V by the Regulator or an Authorized Officer for review of the decision to give the direction; or

(d) by a person affected by the decision for review of the decision of an Authorized Officer or an Inspector to disconnect an electricity supply.

(2) An application for review of a decision referred to in Subsection (1) shall—

(a) be in writing; and

(b) set out the decision to which the application relates; and

(c) set out in detail the grounds on which the applicant seeks review and the decision sought on the review; and

(d) be accompanied by any information that the applicant considers should be taken into account by the Appeals Panel on the review; and

(e) be lodged with the Appeals Panel—

(i) in the case of a decision relating to a licence or application for a licence—within ten days after written notice of the decision is given to the electricity undertaker or applicant; or

(ii) in the case of a decision to give a direction—within ten days after the direction is given; or

(iii) in the case of a decision to disconnect an electricity supply—within ten days after notice of the disconnection is given or, if notice is not given, within ten days after the supply is disconnected,

or, in any of these cases, such longer period as the Appeals Panel may allow.

(3)

The Appeals Panel may stay the operation of the decision to which the application relates.

(4)

A review shall be decided within four weeks of the application being lodged with the Appeals Panel.

(5)

After considering the application, the Appeals Panel may confirm, amend or substitute the decision or return the matter to the original decision maker with directions the Appeal Panel considers appropriate.

(6)

The Appeals Panel shall give the applicant written notice of the decision, and the reasons for the decision, on the review.

43. Minister's power to intervene.(159)

The Minister may intervene, personally or by counsel or other representative, in a review under this Part for the purpose of introducing evidence, or making submissions, on any question relevant to the public interest.

## PART VD.—EXEMPTIONS.(160)

43A. Power of Exemption.(161)

(1) The Regulator may, with the approval of the Minister, grant an exemption from Part IIIB, or specified provisions of Part IIIB, on terms and conditions the Regulator considers appropriate.

(2) If the Regulator exempts a person from the requirement to hold a licence under Part IIIB, the Regulator may, without limiting Subsection (1), by conditions of the exemption require that the person is to be treated as an electricity undertaker for the purposes of specified provisions of this Act.

(3) Except as otherwise provided in the exemption, an exemption under Subsection (1) may be varied or revoked by the Regulator by notice in writing.

43B. Register of exemptions.(162)

(1) The Regulator shall keep a register of exemptions granted under this Act.

(2)

The register shall include—

(a) the terms and conditions of each exemption; and

(b) any other information required under the regulations.

(3) A person may, without payment of a fee, inspect the register.

43C. Obligation to comply with conditions of exemption.(163)

(1) A person in whose favour an exemption is given shall comply with the conditions of the exemption.

Penalty: A fine not exceeding K10,000,000.00.

Default penalty: A fine not exceeding K1,000,000.00.

(2) If a person in whose favour an exemption is given profits from contravention of a condition of its exemption, the Regulator may recover an amount equal to the profit from the person—

(a) on application to a court convicting the person of an offence against this section; or

(b) by action in a court of competent jurisdiction.

(3)

Any amount recovered under Subsection (2) shall be paid into the Consolidated Revenue Fund.

(164) PART VI.—THE BY-LAWS OF THE COMMISSION. [Repealed]

## PART VII.—OFFENCES.

47. Obstruction, etc.

A person who hinders or obstructs a person in the performance of his functions or the exercise of his powers under this Act is guilty of an offence.

Penalty: A fine not exceeding K100.00.

48. Corruption.(165)

(1) In this section, "bribe" includes the giving, conferring or procuring of any property or benefit of any kind in respect of—

(a)

any act done or to be done; or

(b) any forbearance observed or to be observed; or

(c) any favour or disfavour shown or to be shown,

in relation to the affairs or business of the Commission or to any matter under this Act.

(2) A member, officer or employee of the Commission who obtains or attempts to obtain a bribe is guilty of an offence.

(3) A person who bribes or attempts to bribe a member, officer or employee of the Commission is guilty of an offence.

Penalty: Imprisonment for a term not exceeding two years.

Corruption. [Repealed]

Removing, tampering with, etc., electric lines, etc.(166)

(1) A person who—

(167) (a) wilfully and without lawful excuse removes, destroys or damages an electric line, or a pillar, post, lamp, meter, sealing device, fitting, insulator, apparatus or works connected with or relating to the supply of electricity by the State, or an electricity undertaker; or

(168) (b) wilfully and unlawfully extinguishes a public lamp or light maintained by the State, or an electricity undertaker,

is guilty of an offence.

Penalty: A fine not exceeding K100.00 or imprisonment for a term not exceeding 12 months.

(2) A person who—

(a) wilfully, fraudulently or by culpable negligence—

(169)

(i)

injures an electric line or a pillar, post, lamp, meter, sealing device, fitting, insulator, apparatus or works connected with or relating to the supply of electricity by the State, or an electricity undertaker, or permits one to be injured; or

(ii) alters the index of a meter; or

(iii) prevents a meter from duly registering the quantity of electricity supplied; or

(170) (b) fraudulently abstracts, causes to be wasted or diverted, consumes or

uses electricity supplied by the State, or an electricity undertaker, is guilty of an offence.

Penalty: A fine not exceeding K1,000.00 or imprisonment for a term not exceeding three years.

(171) (3) In addition to any damages that may be recovered, a person who is convicted of an offence against Subsection (1) or (2) shall for each offence forfeit and pay to the State, or the electricity undertaker such sum as the court that convicts him thinks reasonable, not exceeding K50.00.

(172)

(4) Subsection (3) does not affect any other right or remedy for the protection of the State, or an electricity undertaker, or the punishment of the offender.

(5) The existence, in connexion with a meter that is in the custody or control of the consumer, of artificial means for—

(a) causing the alteration of the index of the meter; or

(b) preventing the meter from duly registering the quantity of electricity supplied; or

(c) abstracting, wasting, diverting or using electricity supplied by the

State, the Commission or an electricity undertaker, is prima facie evidence that the alteration, prevention, abstraction, waste, diversion, consumption or use, as the case may be, has been fraudulently, knowingly and wilfully caused by the consumer.

(173)

50. Impersonation.

A person shall not impersonate an Authorized Officer, an Electricity Inspector or other person entitled to exercise a power or perform a function under this Act.

Penalty: A fine not exceeding K2,000.00.

Default penalty: A fine not exceeding K200.00.

50A. False or misleading information.(174)

A person shall not make a statement that is false or misleading in a material particular (whether by reason of the inclusion or omission of any particular) in any information furnished under this Act.

Penalty: If the person made the statement knowing that it was false or misleading—a fine not exceeding K2,000.00.

In any other case—a fine not exceeding K200.00.

50B. Offences by corporations or firms.(175)

If a corporation or a firm is guilty or an offence against this Act, a director, manager, secretary, officer or member of the corporation or of the firm, as the case may be, who knowingly and willfully authorizes or permits the commission of the offence is also guilty of the offence.

51. Agreements for re-supply of electricity.

(1) Where—

(a) electricity is supplied to a person; and

(b) he makes electricity available to a second person under an agreement, express or implied, that the second person shall pay to him an amount of money in respect of the electricity,

(176) the first-mentioned person must not, without the consent of the Regulator, demand or receive an amount for the electricity greater than the amount that the second person would be liable to pay if the electricity had been supplied directly to the second person.

Penalty: A fine not exceeding K200.00.

(2) The excess of any amount paid in contravention of Subsection (1) may be recovered by the person who paid it from the person to whom it was paid as a debt.

**PART VIII.—MISCELLANEOUS.**

52. Purposes of the Commission to be public purpose.(177)

The purposes of the Commission are a public purpose within the meaning of any law.

Purposes of the Commission to be public purpose. [Repealed]

Authorization for purposes of the Land Act.(178)

(1) The Commission, or an officer or employee of the Commission authorized by it for the purpose, shall be deemed to be a person authorized by the Minister for the purposes of Sections 79, 80, 81 and 82 of the Land Act.

(2) In the application of Section 83 of the Land Act in relation to the Commission or an officer or employee of the Commission by virtue of this section, a reference to the Minister or to the State shall be read as a reference to the Commission.

Authorization for purposes of the Land Act. [Repealed]

Proof of certain matters.(179)

In any proceedings by or against the Commission, proof is not required, unless evidence is given to the contrary, of—

(a) the constitution of the Commission; or

(b) a resolution of the Commission; or

(c) the appointment of a member, officer, servant or agent of the Commission; or

(d) the presence of a quorum at a meeting at which a determination is made or an act done by the Commission.

Proof of certain matters. [Repealed]

Indemnity.(180)

A member, officer, employee or agent of the Commission is not personally liable for any thing done or omitted to be done in good faith in the course of the operations of the Commission or for the purposes of this Act.

Indemnity. [Repealed]

Service of process.(181)

Any notice, summons, writ or other process required to be served on the Commission may be served by being left at the office of the Commission or, in the case of a notice, by post.

Service of process. [Repealed]

Authentication of documents.(182)

Any document requiring authentication by the Commission is sufficiently authenticated without the seal of the Commission if signed by the Chairman.

Authentication of documents. [Repealed]

Appointment of attorneys.(183)

(1) The Commission may, by instrument under its seal, appoint a person to act as its attorney outside the country for the purpose of doing anything that the Commission itself might lawfully do.

(2) A person appointed under Subsection (1) may, on behalf of and in the name of the Commission, do any act, exercise any power and perform any function that he is authorized by the instrument to do, exercise or perform.

58. Appointment of Attorneys. [Repealed]

(184) 58A. Immunity.(185)

Any person engaged in the administration or enforcement of this Act is not personally liable for any thing done or omitted to be done in good faith in the performance or exercise, or purported performance or exercise, of a function or power under this Act.

58B. Immunity for failure to supply.(186)

An electricity undertaker is not liable in damages to any person for any partial or total failure to supply electricity or any variation in electricity supply to the extent that the failure or variation is due to an event that is beyond the reasonable control of the electricity undertaker.

59. Compensation.(187)

(1) Where loss or damage is suffered by any person by reason of the exercise, by or on behalf of an electricity undertaker, of a power conferred by or under this Act, compensation for the loss or damage is payable to him by the electricity undertaker.

(2) Subject to Subsection (3), the amount of compensation payable under Subsection (1) is as determined by the Minister.

(3) A person aggrieved by a determination of the Minister under Subsection

(2)may appeal to the National Court.

59A. Emergency.(188)

An electricity undertaker may, without incurring any liability, cut off the supply of electricity to any region, area, land or place if it is, in the electricity undertaker's opinion, necessary to do so to avert danger to person or property.

60. Recovery of money due.(189)

Any money due to the Commission under this Act may be recovered by the Commission as a debt.

60. Recovery of money due. [Repealed]

61. Regulations.

(1) The Head of State, acting on advice, may make regulations, not inconsistent with this Act, prescribing all matters that by this Act are required or permitted to be prescribed, or that are necessary or convenient to be prescribed for carrying out or giving effect to this Act.

(2) Without limiting Subsection (1), the regulations may deal with the following matters:—

(a) the construction, installation and positioning of cables, poles, structures, pipes, fittings and other works supplying electricity, the notice to be given of such work, the superintendence of such work, the making good and replacement of ground disturbed in the course of such work and the inspection of such work; and

(b) the method (including the notice (if any) to be given) and means of access to land on or from which any pylon, post, pole, pillar or electric line is or is to be erected, maintained or removed under Subsection 25(2) and the prohibition or restriction of any use of any such land to the extent necessary or desirable for the maintenance of,

or the prevention of damage or interference to, any such pylon, post, pole, pillar or electric line or the conveyance, transmission or distribution of electricity; and

(c) the construction, distribution, installation, inspection and reading of meters, and access to them; and

(d) the lamps, meters, appliances and electricity-consuming devices that a consumer may connect to an electricity supply; and

(e) the licensing of electrical contractors and electricians, the standards required and the fees to be paid for such licences and the conditions on which such licences may be cancelled, suspended or limited in their application; and

(f) standards of safety in the construction, operation, maintenance and use of—

(i) electrical installations, works and equipment for the generation, transmission, distribution, supply and consumption of electricity; and

(ii) electrical apparatus and appliances; and

(g) technical, operational and safety requirements and standards; and

(h) the generation, transmission, distribution, sale and supply of electricity; and

(i) the exemption (conditionally or unconditionally) of persons or operations from the application of this Act or specified provisions of this Act; and

(j) fees to be paid in respect of any matter under this Act and the recovery, refund, waiver or reduction of such fees; and

(k) penalties not exceeding K100.00, or K10.00 for every day during which the offence continues, for contravention of a regulation.

(3) Without limiting Subsection (1), the regulations may contain provisions of a saving or transitional nature consequent on the enactment of this Act or anything done under or for the purposes of this Act.

(4) If the regulations grant an exemption from the requirement to hold a licence under Part IIIB, the regulations may require a person exempted from the requirement to be treated as an electricity undertaker for the purposes of specified provisions of this Act.

(5) The regulations may—

(a) be of general application or limited in application according to the persons, areas, times or circumstances to which they are expressed to apply; or

(b) provide that a matter or thing in respect of which regulations may be made is to be determined, regulated or prohibited according to the discretion of the Minister or the Regulator; or

(c) refer to or incorporate, wholly or partially and subject to such modifications, conditions or restrictions as are prescribed, any standard, code, procedure or other document prepared or laid down by the Standards Association of Australia or any other authority, as in force from time to time or as in force at a particular time.

(191) SCHEDULE. EXCEPTIONS AND MODIFICATIONS TO PART VIII OF THE PUBLIC FINANCES (MANAGEMENT) ACT 1995.

Provision. Modificating etc.

Section 51 Applies as if the requirement of estimates, etc., not later than three months before the end of the fiscal years were a requirement of submission before 30 November in each year.

Section 52 Does not apply. Section 53 Does not apply. Section 56 Does not apply. Section 57 Does not apply. Section 58 Does not apply. Section 59 Applies as if the sum specified is K4,000.00.

# LEGAL NATURE OF THE PAPUA NEW GUINEA PETROLEUM ARRANGEMENT[9]

Petroleum exploration and development in Papua New Guinea (PNG) are carried out under a policy regime that fixes in advance, conditions under which rights to explore for and produce petroleum are granted. The legal regime is set out primarily in the legislation and complemented by petroleum agreements that are entered into in respect of each exploration licence.

Some countries do not use the legislation to set out the terms and conditions of petroleum development. If there is such a law, it is of a general nature. The government grants exploration and production titles on the basis of individually negotiated agreements.

Other countries take the middle ground by using a hybrid system of fixing the terms of petroleum exploration and production, partly by legislation and partly by agreements. In such cases, certain fundamental terms of petroleum exploration and production are set out in the legislation while the specific terms and conditions are negotiated and settled by agreements.

Petroleum agreements are used in many countries as the main policy instruments, to set the scope of, and govern petroleum exploration and production. These agreements are used exclusively or in association with petroleum legislation.

The public and private arrangements under which petroleum exploration and production are authorised and undertaken have gone through a variety of phases since the emergence of petroleum as an internationally traded commodity, from the earliest grants of concessions by various sovereigns in the Middle East to the modern concessions, joint venture agreements, service contracts, production sharing contracts or combination of one or more of these traditional forms of petroleum arrangements.

Petroleum arrangements of some countries have the characteristics of more than one formally recognised legal arrangements. This paper will endeavour to identify and consider the salient features of these legal arrangements and apply them to the Papua New Guinea's (PNG) petroleum arrangement. The object of this exercise will be, firstly, to highlight the fundamental features of PNG's petroleum arrangement and, secondly, to classify the PNG's petroleum arrangement under one or more of the recognised forms of petroleum arrangements that are in use in the petroleum industry, globally.

A. Different Petroleum Arrangements

Whilst various legal arrangements are used by different countries to secure and regulate petroleum exploration and production, they deal with common considerations that are essential for petroleum exploration and production. It is the treatment of these features that distinguish the different legal arrangements under which petroleum development is conducted.

(a) Concessions

The history of petroleum agreements begins with the granting of an oil concession by the Persian Government to William D'Arcy in 1901. The original 1901 D'Arcy concession was granted over the whole of the Persian Empire with the exception of 5 provinces, covering 480,000 square miles. Concessions granted by the rulers of Abu Dhabi and Kuwait covered their entire countries. The concessions were granted for very

[9] Melvin Yalapan Law School, University of Papua New Guinea.

long periods and on modest fiscal terms. Professor Charles Lipton summarised the traditional concession arrangement as follows:

> "It was a long term agreement. 99 years was not untypical. It created enclave and give rise to exception to the general law application. Management 'prerogative' were left to the operating company. There was no government participation in the basic decisions such as the rate of operation or marketing. The investor provided all capital typically, and was entitled to all profits, originally paying the government a per ton royalty."

Thus under the traditional concession, the concessionaire was granted, and had, the exclusive right to explore for, produce and deal with petroleum within the concession area. The oil companies therefore made decisions affecting all aspects of the petroleum operation. In terms of petroleum exploration, it meant that the oil companies decided exclusively how much or how little exploration they wished to undertake. Upon discovery, the oil companies decided the rate, extent and level of production.

The companies also had, in a traditional concession, by the grant of the concession, title to the petroleum *in situ*. The host government, or ruler, normally received an initial consideration, roughly amounting to the modern day signature bonus and only the right to receive financial return from the petroleum operation. Originally, this was in the form of royalty payment, and later royalty and taxes.

The scope of the traditional concession is startling when other aspects of a concession are considered. The 1901 Mexican petroleum law, for example, authorised, granting of liberal tax exemption, the right to import machinery, equipment and materials duty free and other special privileges, which included the right to expropriate land necessary to conduct petroleum operations.

The situation existed until the late 1950's when governments with the aid of progress in technology, considerable discovery of new oil fields and worldwide dependence on oil, broke the shackle that underpinned the traditional concession arrangement. These enabled governments to demand and secure improved terms under which the petroleum resources located within their territories could be developed.

The post 1950's concessions provided significant new terms. The financial return to the host country increased significantly with provisions for equitable profit sharing. The petroleum acreages were reduced, and provisions for relinquishment of the concession areas or part of the concession areas, driven by work program and budget were introduced. It was during this period that governments began to take direct equity participation in petroleum projects. In addition, host governments also enacted legislation that dealt specifically with petroleum exploration and production, thus establishing uniformity the basic terms under which petroleum exploration and production were undertaken within the country.

The increased concerns of governments with regard to ownership and control of the natural resources led to the assertion of permanent sovereignty over the natural resources within the states' territories. The 1962 *UN Resolution on the Permanent Sovereignty over Natural Resources[13]* is the reflection of the assertion of sovereignty, particularly by the newly independent third world governments, to natural resources within their territories.

The *UN Resolution on the Permanent Sovereignty over Natural Resources* also provided further impetus for the creation of alternative legal arrangements for petroleum development. These were structured not only to enable host states to retain ownership of the resources *in situ* in their national boundaries but at the same time, to allow oil companies to conduct petroleum operation in the country. Old concession arrangements were revised and new concession arrangements were established.

The modern concessions differ in important respect from the traditional form of concession. Under the new concession arrangements:

> "...ownership of petroleum in the ground remains with the State, and at best provision is made for 'sharing' of petroleum at the well-head between governments and companies. Power of management and control over operations are vested in the government. Duration is shorter and the size of the area covered by the agreement considerably smaller than under the traditional concession".*[15]*

Provisions for relinquishment of, and reduction in, the concession areas were introduced. Minimum work and expenditure commitments were established. Requirements for training of national work force and procurement of local goods and services were also introduced. In some instances, provisions were made for crude oil to be made available for local consumption and host states also participated in the petroleum development either directly or through a state enterprise. Generally, greater powers of management and control of petroleum development shifted from the oil companies to the host states. One can say that the entire bundle of rights that governed petroleum development changed hands, from the oil companies to the host governments.

New legal arrangements for petroleum development were also developed and introduced. Such arrangements included joint venture agreements, service contracts and production sharing contracts.

(b) Joint Ventures

The oil companies traditionally prefer partnership with the host government in the petroleum exploration and production to be limited to *profit sharing.*[16] As host governments become conscious of the need to actively participate in petroleum development, they began pressing for greater control over the resources in their territories.

Under the traditional concessions, the near total control exercised by the companies was based on its ownership of the petroleum resources. However, the exclusive ownership of the petroleum resources by the concessionaire naturally militated against the desire by governments to own the petroleum resources located in their territory and to develop these resources to pursue national development objectives. The joint venture arrangement was therefore developed to realise these national goals and aspirations.

The joint venture agreement was pioneered as a new form of petroleum arrangement by Italian State Oil Company – ENI. The first of such agreement was entered into between ENI through its subsidiary Agip Mineraria and the National Iranian Oil Company (NIOC). The Agip-NIOC Joint Venture was established under a joint stock company, and a joint Board of Directors managed the company.[17]

Under the joint venture arrangement, the entire petroleum operation is a joint activity. A joint operation company is formed between the host country (more usually the host country's national oil company), and the company to develop the petroleum reserves. The acreage is jointly licensed and the petroleum operation is jointly conducted, consistent with the joint ownership of the venture. However, the entire exploration expenditure is financed solely by the oil company. In the event of a commercial discovery, the oil company is fully reimbursed either in kind or out of revenue earned either directly by the state or through the allocation of part of the state's share of the petroleum produced. *[18]* The joint venture arrangement is therefore a partnership arrangement between the state through its national oil company and the non-state oil company, under an arrangement of share equity, ownership rights and interest in the project. Martin Olisa summarised the arrangement as follows:
"The structure and content of various joint ventures vary considerably...(On) the national side you have private, or government controlled enterprises. The foreign enterprise supplies the risk capital for, and carries out, exploration. Explorations expenses in whole or in part are recoverable from production, if obtained. If commercial production is obtained, an equity joint venture company is established as an operating company. Participation may be on 50:50 basis or one 'partner' may be in a minority position, in which case, a management contract is entered into."*[19]*

The joint venture arrangement was therefore seen as a realisation of host governments' aspirations, not only to take greater management and control over the natural resources within their territories, but also as a realisation of joint ownership of the exploration and production titles.

(c) Production sharing Contract

The "Production Sharing Contract" was pioneered in Indonesia in 1967 and is still used there. Libya, Egypt, India, Ghana, Malaysia and Trinidad and Tobago are some of the countries that also use this contractual arrangement.[20] A. Zen Umar Purba summarised the main features of the Indonesian Production Sharing Contract as follows:

- *management of the oil operations rest with PERTAMINA.[21]*
    - *at the time the contract is signed, the contractor pays a bonus to PERTAMINA, which can be treated as a tax credit.*
    - *exploration expenses are recoverable if oil is discovered by contractor.*

*- after the exploration cost and expenses are deducted from the oil extracted, the balance (after tax) is divided under a certain formula, mainly 85%:15% in favour of PERTAMINA.*
*- the contractor is required to spare 8.5% of its portion (based on the above formula) to supply the domestic market in Indonesia.*
*- after a certain period of time, the contractor has to relinquish areas of its operations, the area must be re-surrendered if oil is not discovered, or if at the end of the exploration stage, the areas are considered not commercially viable.*
*- title to equipment used in the exploration rest with PERTAMINA as soon as the goods enter Indonesian customs."[22]*

Under the production sharing contract arrangement, the exploration and production of petroleum can be undertaken only by the State, and is exclusively carried out by the State enterprises. The oil company has no proprietary interest in the petroleum exploration and production titles. The company is engaged as a contractor for the state enterprise to undertake services that cannot or yet to be undertaken by the state enterprise.[23]

Although, the oil companies are engaged as contractors to undertake petroleum operations, they however bear all the exploration risk so that if no commercial discovery of petroleum is made, the loss is borne by the contractor. In the event of a commercial discovery, the contractor is entitled to be reimbursed by a percentage of the oil produced. This is achieved by applying portions of petroleum produced as *"cost oil,"* to defray the pre-development expenditure. Once all the authorised expenses have been deducted up to the maximum percentage of "cost oil" set out in the agreement, the remaining oil, usually called the *"profit oil,"* (less *"cost oil,"*) is shared between the contractor and the national oil company in accordance with an agreed formula.[24]

Ownership of the petroleum, either in the ground or as produced, rest with the state until it reaches the point of export. This differs from the traditional concession arrangement where title in petroleum rest in the oil company, and under the new concession arrangement where the petroleum companies acquire title to the petroleum at the wellhead.

The legal rational for using the production sharing contract is that from the host government's standpoint, it does not involve surrender of the host country's sovereignty in the title to the resource. In entering into a production sharing contract, the company receives less than title or interest to the oil.[25]

(d) Service Contracts

The final form of petroleum exploration and production arrangement that require specific consideration for the purpose of this paper is the service contract. Under this contractual arrangement, the foreign oil company is engaged by the national oil company to conduct petroleum exploration for a fee or a share of production. The oil company also provides the host country and its national oil company with technical services and information relating to the development of the petroleum resources.

Upon discovery of petroleum in the area, the national oil company engages the foreign oil company as its agent to produce the oil, and if it so agrees, also to market the oil produced on behalf of the national oil company. The feature of a service contract is summarised as follows:
"The national oil company is by law the sole titular holder of the area under the agreement. All petroleum deposit and oil and/or gas produced are the property of the national oil company at the wellhead. The foreign company either directly or through a subsidiary, acts as general contractor for the national oil company and as such carries out, in the name and on behalf the latter, all operations necessary for exploration and development of oil deposits. Thus the contractor is not a concession holder or partner, but merely a hired agent."*[26]*

In a pure service contract, the host country's national oil company would contract the oil company to perform a specified service for a flat fee. However, in view of the difficulties that countries face in obtaining capital to finance the payment of service fees, some agreements provide that the contractor may be paid in kind with a certain specified amount of production from the acreage, the subject of the service contract. Thus service contracts can be arranged as *Risk-Service Contract* or *Service Contract (Non-Risk)*. Under a Risk-Service Contract arrangement, the host government pays for the services of the oil companies in cash and not in kind. On the other hand, under the Service Contract (Non-Risk) arrangement, the oil company is paid a flat rate for its services usually by applying a percentage of the oil produced.[27]

Generally, the oil company provides all the risk capital. If oil is found, the amount spent in exploration is "deemed" as loan to the national oil company to be debited from the national oil company's accounts. The oil company may also sell for the national oil company, if agreed, the oil produced. From the revenue earned by the national oil company, a percentage is applied towards the repayment of the "deemed loan" until the loan is reduced to zero.[28]

The title in the petroleum *in situ* rests in the state and upon production is transferred at the wellhead to the national oil company. The oil company does not acquire exploration or production title nor does it acquire ownership to the petroleum produced at any stage of the production chain. It is engaged simply as an agent to the national oil company and is paid a fee either in cash or in kind from the oil produced, in consideration for the services rendered.

Service contracts are used in countries like Venezuela, Brazil and Iran as a form of legal arrangement for the development of petroleum located within the territories of these countries.[29]

(e) Petroleum Arrangements

Petroleum arrangements developed post 1950's also included contracts under names such as Operations Agreement[30] and Works and Technical Services Agreement.[31]

The post 1950's contractual arrangements have different *"labels"* but they have common objectives and hence share common features. For instance, the production sharing contract petroleum arrangement is similar in terms to the service contract arrangement. The arrangements differ from each other on the consideration as to who bears the exploration risk. In a service contract, the title to petroleum *in situ* rests with the host state through its national oil company and the oil company is engaged by the national oil company as a contractor to conduct petroleum operations for consideration either in cash or in kind from petroleum produced from the petroleum operations. The exploration and production risk rest with the national oil company or the host government. However, under the production sharing contract, the oil company undertakes the petroleum exploration and production at its risk. It then takes the share of production as *"cost oil."* The balance of the production, which is normally termed *"profit oil,"* is shared between the host government or its national oil company and the oil company. On the other hand, under the joint venture structure, title to the licence and the means of production are jointly held between the state and the oil companies, and petroleum is jointly produced and sold. The following features are common in the post-1950 petroleum arrangements.[32]

- (i) The risk of exploration is borne by the oil company and the cost of exploration is not recoverable unless a commercial discovery is made.
- (ii) The exploration phase is distinguished from the production phase. Accordingly, if no significant discovery of petroleum is made within the stipulated period, the company must surrender the acreage.
- (iii) The oil company is subjected to minimum work and expenditure program.
- (iv) The oil company is subject to obligations to provide information and data to the host government.
- (v) Provisions are made for division of revenue generated by the projects which feature increased financial take by governments in the form of income tax and revenue from equity in the projects.
- (vi) Provisions are made for procurement of local goods and services and for the training and employment of nationals.

There are variances in the treatment of different considerations under different petroleum arrangements. Notable among these is the treatment of title in the oil produced, whether title in the oil is acquired by the oil company either at the point of export or at the wellhead. The second consideration relates to exploration and production risk – whether the exploration and production risk is borne by the oil company or the host government. The third consideration relates to the fiscal arrangement under which governments take active participation in the management and control over the project; in essence, equity participation in the project.

The key features of the petroleum titular system, the arrangement for State equity participation under the petroleum arrangements and the fiscal regime applicable to petroleum exploration and development will be considered in some details with particular reference to the PNG's petroleum arrangement.
B. PNG's Petroleum Exploration and Production Licencing Regime

The PNG legal and fiscal regime that governs petroleum development could be described as that which is governed primarily by legislation. The terms for the granting of petroleum exploration and production licences are set out in the legislation[33] and these are supplemented by details set out in the petroleum licence.

The basic considerations in dealing with natural resources development is firstly, the question of who has the title to the resources and secondly, who has right to exclusive use, control or management of the resources. Generally, the owner of the resources would have the right to use, control and manage the exploitation of these resources. Ownership therefore underpins property rights and provides the basis to manage the exploitation of the resources.[34]

The English Common Law presumes that the owner of the land is entitled to all that is located above and below the land*; cujus est solum ejus est usque ad colum et usque ad inferos.* Under common law, minerals naturally occurring form part of the land on which they are situated unless these minerals are specifically severed from the crown land grant. The only exceptions are the royal metals; gold and silver, which remain subject to crown ownership, notwithstanding the crown grant of the land on which minerals are naturally occurring.[35]

PNG's natural resources laws adopted the practice of reserving title to mineral and petroleum *in situ* exclusively to the State.[36] Ownership in resources *in situ* therefore rests with the State. The vesting of ownership of mineral and petroleum resources *in situ* together with the vesting of the prerogative to licence the exploration and production of these resources, and the prerogative to manage the exploration and development of same, provides the foundation of resources law. It underpins the legal arrangement under which the resources are developed. The prerogative to manage the exploitation of these resources is a significant factor that one would need to examine in the quest to identify the contractual arrangement of the PNG's petroleum regime. This is underlined by the fact that despite State ownership of the petroleum naturally occurring, the resources will be developed by private enterprise and hence the petroleum policy regime is geared towards encouraging private sector investment in petroleum development.

The licensing system governing petroleum exploration and production is therefore the ultimate exercise of the host state's ownership of these resources and the exercise of the management prerogative is the ultimate exercise of sovereignty over the exploration and production of the resources that lay within its national boundaries.

(a) Exploration Licence

The PNG's petroleum exploration and development licensing system is primarily a two-tier system. A Petroleum Prospecting Licence (PPL) is an exploration licence issued to an oil company pursuant to which the oil company undertakes petroleum exploration.[37] The Petroleum Development Licence (PDL) is a production licence[38] issued to the holder of a PPL upon commercial discovery of petroleum, to produce and deal with the petroleum produced within the acreage.

The process of granting a PPL commences on application for or upon invitation by the Minister, for a PPL.[39] For the purpose of granting an exploration or a production licence, the earth's surface is divided up into gratucular sections called-blocks, comprising five minutes longitudes and five minutes latitude.[40] An application for a PPL would be made in respect of not more than 60 blocks[41]and in special circumstances the minimum acreage could be increased to 200 blocks.[42]

The conditions under which petroleum exploration and production will be undertaken are prescribed by legislation.[43] A PPL is granted for a term not exceeding 6 years[44]and renewable for a further term of 5 years but for a reduced area,[45] and is also subject to work and expenditure requirements.[46]

A licence sets out the basic terms and conditions under which petroleum exploration will be undertaken.[47]

Where petroleum discovery is made in a exploration acreage, a declaration would be made of a location, within the exploration acreage, of a petroleum discovery. [48] Subsequent to the declaration of a location, the oil company may apply for and be granted a further extension of the exploration licence for a further period of not more than 3 years.[49]

A PPL confers on the licensee the exclusive right to explore for petroleum, to carry out appraisal work in respect of the petroleum discovery, and to undertake such task as are necessary to otherwise explore for, produce and sell or otherwise disposed of petroleum produced. The legislation provides the scope of a PPL as follows:

> "A petroleum prospecting licence, while it remains in force, confers on the licensee, subject to this Act, and to the conditions specified in the licence, the exclusive right to explore for petroleum, and to carry out appraisal of a petroleum discovery, and to carry on such operations and execute such works as are necessary for those purposes, in the licence area, including the construction and operations of water lines, tests for appraisal of a petroleum pool (including the construction in accordance with the authorization and disposal), and the recovery and sale or other disposal of all petroleum so produced."*[50]*

As noted, the legislation gives sufficient scope and rights, in exclusivity, to the holder of an exploration licence to explore for, produce and sell or dispose of petroleum produced within the exploration acreage. The scope of a PPL is therefore as wide as a PDL. The case on point is the Moran Petroleum Project.[51] In September 1996, oil was discovered in Moran IX sidetrack well in PDL 2.[52] In early 1997, the State approved the PDL 2 (Kutubu Joint Venture) to carry out an Extended Well Test Program (EWT)[53] within PDL 2 pursuant to which the PDL 2 licensee produced oil within the block under the EWT program.[54]

Moreover, the State proceeded to approve the licence holders of PPL 138[55] to conduct EWT program using Moran 4 well and the PPL 138 licensees produced oil within the exploration licence area from Moran 4 exploration well under a EWT program. Hence, oil was produced at PPL 138 under the EWT program prior to carving out the area and grant of PDL.[56] The production of petroleum at Moran 4 well within Moran PPL 138 is a case on point to demonstrate that the scope of a PPL - an exploration licence, includes exclusive rights not only to explore for, but also to produce and sell or dispose of, petroleum produced within the exploration acreage. A PPL could also contain incidental features as are necessary to undertake and facilitate production of oil within the PPL, including construction of flow-lines and gathering lines, roads and bridges, and other infrastructure.

Technical justifications can be advanced to justify oil production within the exploration acreage under an EWT program but consideration of the same is not within the scope of this paper. The fact that petroleum production is undertaken within the exploration acreage is, for the purposes of this paper, sufficient endorsement of the view that petroleum production can be undertaken under an exploration licence in the PNG's petroleum arrangement.

(b) Petroleum Retention Licence

An exploration licensee may also exclusively apply for a Petroleum Retention Licence (retention licence) in respect of blocks within the exploration acreage in which petroleum is located.[57] This may be done within 2 years from the date on which the blocks were declared as a location.[58]

A retention licence can be issued over *"... a gas field or, a part of the gas field or, for better administration of petroleum activities."* [59] The provision is designed primarily to allow holders of an exploration licence to retain and hold natural gas discoveries within the acreage pending commercial extraction of the same. However, provisions are also made for retention licence to be issued in respect of oil discoveries within the acreage "... *for better administration of petroleum activities."* The proviso creates scope for retention licences to be issued in respect of marginal oil fields where the reserves cannot be commercially produced.[60] That is, where a discovery is over a marginal field and it is not commercially viable to produce the petroleum discovered within the location, a retention licence may be issued over the respective blocks in the exploration acreage, which would allow the exploration licensee to retain the discovery pending further appraisal, further and additional discovery and commercial production of the petroleum discovered within the acreage.[61]

A retention licence may be granted for 5 years[62]and may be extended for further terms of 5 years at each extension.[63] Accordingly, a retention licence can be further extended over number of 5 years extension periods before commercial production can be realised. It therefore allows a holder of an exploration licence to hold onto the acreage pending commercial production of the discovery.[64]

(c) Petroleum Development Licence

If significant petroleum discovery is made that can sustain commercial production, a PDL, which is the production licence, will be issued to the holder of the PPL.[65] The basic requirement of a PDL is fixed by legislation.[66] A PDL is issued to the holder of an exploration or retention licence for a period not exceeding 25 years, renewable for a term not exceeding 20 years.[67]

A PDL confers on the licensee the exclusive rights to explore for petroleum within the licence area, to produce petroleum within the licence area, to sell or otherwise disposed of petroleum so produced and to carry out such other works in the licence area as are necessary to conduct petroleum operations in accordance with the terms of the licence.[68] The works necessary to carry out petroleum operations include construction of flow lines and gathering lines, roads, bridges and other civil works, airports, seaports and related facilities.[69]

In the case of the Kutubu project, the PDL 2 licensees also own and operate the only oil pipeline in PNG that transport oil from the oil fields to the offshore loading terminal.

The development licensee is therefore licensed not only to produce and sell or disposed of petroleum produced, but also the added right to *"...carry on such operations and execute such work as are necessary for or in connection..."* with carrying out petroleum operations.[70]

C. Charecteristics of Petroleum Agreements

The PNG petroleum agreements deal with matters, which include State equity participation, foreign currency management, local business development and procurement of local goods and services. For the purpose of this paper, particular consideration is given to those provisions dealing with State equity participation.

The State takes its share of the revenue from production and sale of petroleum, primarily from petroleum taxation computed and collected under the *Income Tax Act*,[71] petroleum royalty and from direct equity participation in the project. In computing the State's share of the petroleum produced or the revenue derived from sale of petroleum produced within the acreage, and the oil companies' share of the petroleum produced, the amount taken up by the State pursuant to the exercise of its rights to take equity participation in the petroleum project within a license area is regarded and treated by oil companies as the State's share of the oil or revenue. Accordingly, the State equity participation policy regime is an important element of the State's petroleum policy regime, and that which forms the core of the petroleum agreement.

The terms under which the State may take equity participation in the petroleum project are set out in the petroleum agreements entered into in respect of each PPL. The petroleum agreements are entered into pursuant to the petroleum legislation.[72] The respective petroleum agreements, as a matter of policy, are entered into prior to discovery of petroleum. Therefore the subsequent PDL incorporates provisions of both the negotiated agreement and legislation, which form the conditions of the PDL.[73] Both instruments are therefore needed to undertake petroleum development.

The detailed features of State equity participation in a petroleum project are not covered by the legislation[74] but are set out in the respective petroleum agreements. This is a major feature of the PNG's petroleum arrangement that can be termed as *the heart* of the petroleum agreement. It is therefore the fiscal arrangement and the arrangement for the State's equity participation in the projects that distinguish the PNG's petroleum agreement from other recognised forms of petroleum agreements.

The basis of the State's equity participation in petroleum projects is legislatively framed[75] and forms part and parcel of the State's petroleum policy regime. The genesis of the State equity participation policy can be traced backed to the 1976 petroleum policy white paper which provides that the government's *"total financial take"* from oil produced in any production licence area follows:

> "(I) 11/4 percent royalty on well-head value of production;
> (II) a percentage income tax at a rate of 50 per cent of taxable income;
> (III) an additional profits tax at rate 50 per cent of after tax cash flow after total investment has been recouped with a money returned of 25 per cent;
> (IV) State participation in development of commercial fields on 'carried interest' principles"[76] (My emphasis).

The State's equity participation in petroleum projects is, therefore, on the basis of *"carried interest principles."*

As a matter of practice, the holder of a PPL is advised to enter into a petroleum agreement with the State before any well is drilled in the exploration acreage. The agreement defines, *inter alia,* the State's equity participation in the subsequent petroleum discovery. [77] The agreements state that the State has an option to take equity participation in the project, up to the nominated percentage.[78] It can also elect not to take equity participation in a particular project. For instance, the *PPL 100 (Kutubu) Petroleum Agreement*, provides that:

"...the State may acquire for a Nominee of the State from the Oil Companies constituting the Development Licensee in the Development License Area, an unencumbered ... interest in the venture interest attributable to the Development Licence Area... up to nominated percentage not exceeding twenty – two and one-half percent (22 ½%) and where the State has acquired such a Joint Venture Interest for a Nominee of the State, the Nominee of the State shall have the right to share... production from that Development Licence Area equal to the nominated percentage,..."*[79]*

The provisions of the petroleum agreement[80] set out the terms under which the State will take equity participation in the project.[81] The State upon electing to take equity participation in the project acquires equity through its Nominee,[82] to the value of the nominated percentage.[83] It also enters into joint venture arrangement with the oil companies that are holders of the PDL. In entering into a joint venture agreement with the oil companies, the State's Nominee becomes a joint participant under the joint venture arrangement,[84] effectively a tenant in common of the PDL under the joint venture structure with the other joint participants. In this respect it also subscribes to all licences, permits and authorisations necessary for the conduct of project development as a joint venturer and holds the petroleum titles jointly and severally with the oil companies in the joint venture as a tenant in common.

The State in taking up equity in the project, through its Nominee, also becomes a joint venturer and a joint licensee of the PDL. The non-State joint venturers finance the Nominee's *pro rata* percentage of exploration, development and other cost and expenditures under the *"carried interest"* arrangement. Under the arrangement, the amount owed to the oil companies by the Nominee is "deemed" as a loan from the oil companies to the Nominee at a commercial interest rate, to be debited from the Nominee's revenue from its proportionate share of the petroleum produced within that PDL.[85]

The production titleholders acquire title to the petroleum, upon production, at the wellhead. Similarly, the State, through the Nominee, as joint licensee and tenant in common, acquires title to petroleum produced at the wellhead. However, the Nominee does not lift the petroleum produced and deal with oil produced during the period it has outstanding liability to the oil companies under the *carried interest* arrangement. Instead, the oil companies lift the State's proportionate share of the petroleum produced, sell same and apply the revenue derived to defray the liability of the State under the *carried interest* arrangement. When the aggregate of the exploration, development and operation expenditures, proportionately owed to the respective oil companies, is reduced to zero, the *carried interest* arrangement is discharged and the State, through the Nominee, is able to take petroleum, unencumbered, at the well-head and sell or dispose of same as a joint licensee and a member of the joint venture.

The liability to the oil companies is computed, applying a pre-agreed formula.[86] This is ascertained, at any given time, by deducting from the State's proportionate share of the revenue earned, the *pro rata* share of exploration and capital expenditures, and amount spent by the oil companies attributable to the oil production. The arrangement remains in place for the duration of the period when income from the share of oil produced, attributable to the State's equity participation, is insufficient to discharge its liability to the oil companies.

The legal arrangement under which the State equity participation is accommodated and facilitated by the oil companies constituting the relevant licence is similar to the arrangement under the joint venture agreement.[87]

D. Income Tax Treatment of the "Carried Interest Arrangement"

The treatment of the petroleum exploration and production titles in the petroleum legislation and the petroleum agreements is followed through in the taxation regime.[88] Under the taxation regime, a petroleum project is *"re-fenced"* for taxation purposes and taxed on project basis.[89] That is, each oil company as a taxpayer (taxpayer) is assessed in relation to each project as if the assessable income of the taxpayer from petroleum operations attributable to the petroleum project was the only assessable income derived by that taxpayer, and conversely, all allowable deductions are deducted against future income from the petroleum project.[90]

For petroleum tax purposes, the pre-PDL exploration expenditures incurred by the taxpayer within the relevant exploration licence area in relation to a petroleum project are carried forward and accumulated for 20 years.[91] Upon commencement of petroleum production, the exploration expenditure is deducted from the income derived by the taxpayer from sale of petroleum produced from petroleum operations conducted within the PDL area. The exploration expenditure incurred in relation to the PDL is reduced; firstly in paying for the exploration expenditure incurred by the taxpayer in relation to the PDL in the relevant year of income; and secondly, any excess amount is applied to reduce the exploration expenditure incurred by the taxpayer in relation the PDL against the expenses earliest incurred within the 20 years period to the year of income, until the amount is fully recovered. [92] This has the effect of accelerating the recovery of exploration expenditures by applying all the available income derived from sale of petroleum produced from the petroleum project.

The *Income Tax Act's* treatment of allowable capital expenditures is similar to treatment of allowable exploration expenditure under income tax principles.[93] In substance, the capital expenditures are carried forward and depreciated against future income derived by the taxpayer from sale of petroleum produced from petroleum operations conducted within the PDL area until the amount is fully depreciated by applying the relevant rate of depreciation.[94]

As to the nature of the petroleum titles, the *Income Tax Act* recognises that interest in the petroleum title is proprietary in nature, which can be sold or transferred for valuable consideration by the titleholders. In such transaction, the vendor and the purchaser can agree to treat the exploration expenditures as exploration expenditure *per se*, or capital expenditures, or partly capital and partly exploration expenditures, at their discretion, with minimum requirement to inform the Commissioner General of the Internal Revenue Commission of the arrangement as between the parties.[95] The holder of a petroleum title can therefore deal with the petroleum titles as a property right.[96]

The State, through its Nominee, is also treated as a purchaser of petroleum title, from the oil companies constituting the relevant petroleum title, as a tenant in common. The interest in the petroleum title, acquired by the State through its Nominee, is treated by the *Income Tax Act* as a sale of petroleum interest between oil companies. The tax treatment of the State's equity in the petroleum projects also endorses the proprietary nature of the PDL. The *Income Tax Act* treatment of the petroleum title held by the State, through its Nominee, is also consistent with the treatment of the same under the petroleum legislation and the petroleum agreements.

Upon becoming a joint licensee and a member of the relevant joint venture, the Nominee, as a joint licensee, produces petroleum and acquires title to same at the well-head[97] together with other joint licensees, as tenant in common,[98] and pay royalty, for the petroleum produced, which is also computed and paid using the well head value. The Nominee, for the purpose of petroleum operations, is treated as a joint licensee of the PDL. This is the arrangement under which states or their nominee take an active participation in petroleum operations conducted within the country under the new concession arrangement.

In addition to the concession based tax regime, the petroleum agreements guarantee the holder of a production licence, the right to export petroleum free of export tax.[99] The oil company is also given a degree of comfort in relation to import duties in that the petroleum agreement guarantees non-discriminatory rates, taxes, duties, levies and other impost.[100] The concessions accorded in export duty exemptions for the petroleum exported and the degree of comfort given in relation to rate, taxes, import duties, levies and other impost are incidence of a concession based contract.

The PNG petroleum taxation regime is, without doubt, a concession based taxation regime.

E. Conclusion, The Nature of Petroleum Arrangement

The question to be considered at this juncture is; what is the legal nature of the PNG's petroleum arrangement if one has to classify the arrangement under one or more of the internationally recognised petroleum arrangements.

(a) The Legal Nature of the Licensing Regime

As observed in this paper, there is little doubt that the PNG's petroleum licensing regime is concession based. It can also be noted that the general emphasis in the petroleum licensing or titular system has always been to create and give certainty as to petroleum title. The petroleum titular regime therefore guarantees the holder of an exploration licence the exclusive right to be given a retention licence[101]where an application for such a licence can be sustained. An exploration licence also gives the holder of the licence exclusive right to explore for, produce petroleum and sell or dispose of the petroleum produced within the exploration acreage and to undertake works that are necessary to explore for and produce petroleum within the exploration acreage.[102] The exploration licence is also issued over a relatively large area. These are incidents of a concession-based licensing system.

The introduction of retention licence to the licensing regime underlines the concession nature of the licensing regime.[103] Upon petroleum discovery, the holder of the exploration licence is guaranteed a production licence. In addition, the exploration licensee is guaranteed the right to produce marginal fields in future by utilising the provisions for retention licences, which can be issued exclusively to the holder of a PPL, where the discovery is not sufficient to undertake commercial production of the discovery. Further, the scope of the production licence is such that it guarantees exclusive rights to produce and sell or disposed of petroleum.[104] Upon production of the petroleum, title to the petroleum produced transfers from the State to the holder of the production licence at the wellhead.[105] The holder of a production licence may also undertake such work as are necessary to produce petroleum.[106] These are features of the new concession arrangement.

The terms of the petroleum exploration, retention and production licences are relatively longer compared to petroleum titular regimes where petroleum exploration and production is conducted under the joint venture, service contract and the production sharing contract petroleum arrangements. The comparatively longer terms of the petroleum exploration licences, retention licences and production licences give the PNG petroleum titular regime the nature of a petroleum concession arrangement. Further, the tenants of the PNG's petroleum regime are closely related to the concession arrangement where the concessionaire has the exclusive right to explore for, produce and deal with petroleum produced within the concession for relative long title period.[107]

Title to petroleum *in situ* is vested in the State and passes to the production licensee at the wellhead.[108] This is an incident of the modern concession arrangement as opposed to the traditional oil concession arrangement where title to petroleum *in situ* is granted to and held by the concessionaire. The treatment of title to petroleum *in situ* is consistent with the new concession arrangement, where title to petroleum is owned by the State, but upon production, the title in the petroleum produced shifts from the State to production licensees.

The petroleum titular regime is without doubt a concession-based licensing regime.

(b) Legal Nature of the Petroleum Agreements

Several matters can be considered as distinguishing features of the PNG's petroleum agreements.

Firstly, petroleum title is acquired and exclusively held by the oil companies and not by the State enterprise. In this respect, the oil companies own the petroleum titles and operate the projects as opposed to the production sharing contract, and service contract arrangements where the host state holds the petroleum title, either directly or through its national oil company, and the oil company is engaged as a service provider. Further, under the PNG's petroleum arrangement, title to the petroleum produced passes from the State to the oil company at the wellhead. This is opposed to the production sharing contract and service contract arrangements where title to petroleum always rest with the host state.

Secondly, the State's share of revenue from the project is appropriated, primarily through petroleum taxation and by modest royalty rate of 2%, applied at the wellhead. [109] This can be contrasted with the production sharing contract arrangements where the petroleum produced is apportioned as cost oil and profit oil, and under the service contract arrangement where the oil company is engaged as a contractor and hence the issue of royalty payment for the oil produced is not a relevant consideration. These place the PNG's petroleum arrangement away from the production sharing contract and service contract petroleum arrangements and align the arrangement with the new concession arrangement and joint venture arrangement.

Thirdly, oil companies are granted exploration title, exclusively of the State, with the State retaining the right to participate in petroleum production. Upon successful petroleum exploration and discovery, the State may elect to take up an equity position in the ensuing petroleum project. In such case, the State, through its

Nominee, is assigned a portion of the petroleum production licence and other titles, leases, licences, permits and authorisations proportionate to its participating interest. It also enters into a joint operating agreement with the oil companies, and hold the petroleum title and the project assets and liabilities, jointly and severally with the oil companies as a tenant in common. These are features of joint venture contractual arrangements.

Fourthly, the State's equity participation, as set out under the relevant petroleum agreements, is paid for under a carried interest arrangement. Under this arrangement, the *pro rata* amount on account of exploration, capital and operation expenditure is represented as a debt from the State to the oil companies. The debt is classified as a loan to the State from the oil companies, from the issuance of the production licence. The amount owed to the oil companies accrues interest at a commercial rate and the debt or the "deemed loan" is defrayed by the revenue earned from sale of "oil foregone" in favour of the oil companies during the period the liability remains outstanding. The financial arrangement under which the State pays for its participation in the project reflects features of a service contract and joint venture arrangement. However, the treatment of the title to petroleum produced under the PNG's petroleum arrangement is not analogous to the arrangements under the service contract arrangements[110] but is more aligned with the treatment of title to oil produced and owned under a joint venture agreement, where title to the petroleum passes at the wellhead upon production. The petroleum titles, under the PNG's petroleum arrangement rest with the oil companies, which are granted the same under the petroleum legislation. This is unlike the service contract arrangement or the production sharing contract where the petroleum title rest with the state enterprise, and the oil company is engaged as a contractor and its services are paid for either in cash or from portion of the oil produced. Further, the State equity participation is carried by the oil companies and defrayed through the allocation of the State's share of petroleum produced. This incident is consistent with that of a joint venture petroleum arrangement.

Fifthly, title in the petroleum *in situ* rests with the State and is acquired upon production at the wellhead. Accordingly, it can be argued that the petroleum title is of proprietary nature.[111] This is confirmed by the taxation treatment of the titles, which gives the petroleum titles proprietary nature. The acquisition of title to petroleum by the companies from the State at the wellhead, upon production, is a feature of the concession arrangement.

In summation, the PNG's petroleum arrangement cannot be exclusively classified under one of the established petroleum arrangements. However, it contains basic features, primarily of the joint venture and the new concession arrangements. The bundle of legal incidences governing petroleum exploration and production and the fiscal regime is a concession-based regime. However, the State equity participation arrangement, established under the petroleum agreement, is primarily a joint venture agreement.

Generally, the PNG's petroleum arrangement is a *unique hybrid* with features of different established petroleum arrangements, fixed partly by legislation and partly by agreement. The salient features of the arrangement that distinguish it from other petroleum arrangement are the legal incidences of the petroleum titles set out under the legislation,[112] the arrangement for the State's equity participation in the projects as set out under the petroleum agreements[113] and the tax treatment of title to petroleum produced as set out under the *Income Tax Act*.[114]

The titular regime established by legislation and the income tax regime are concession based, and the petroleum agreement shows elements of arrangements under joint venture agreement. Consistently therefore, the PNG petroleum agreements can be *labeled* as a *Concession Based Joint Venture Agreement.*

---

**AL=SVI (E+D+OC)+S-F-W-Z-R.** Where-

**AL=** total amount owing to the PDL licensee at any time by the State Nominee.

**SVI=** State Nominee's interest expressed in percentage.

**E=** Pre-PDL exploration expenditures.

**D=** PDL Capital Expenditures

**OC=** Any amount spent by the oil companies in the PDL area attributable to the State's equity participation, during the period in which income from pro rata share of the oil production is insufficient to finance project cost that is not specifically included under E&D.

**S=** Amount spent on behalf of the State Nominee during the shortfall period when its pro rata share of the revenue from the petroleum produced an sold is in-sufficient to meet project costs.

**F=** Aggregate revenue from sale of oil attributable to the State Nominee's equity interest.

**W=** Amounts attributable to money spent by the State in funding any project facility or amount spent in connection with project development.

**Z=** **A**mount contributed by the Nominee of the State or the State in reduction of the AL.

**R=** Amounts foregone by the State Nominee (share of insurance proceeds, etc.) that is credited to the oil companies towards payment and discharge of the AL.

**188. PIPELINE LICENCES UNDER FORMER ACT.**

(1) Where, on the commencement date a pipeline licence issued under Division III.5 of the former Act was in force, that pipeline licence shall continue in force and shall be deemed for all purposes under this Act to be a pipeline licence issued under Division III.9 of this Act, commencing on the date on which such licence was issued under the former Act.
(2) A licence referred to in Subsection (1) shall be subject, to the extent consistent with this Act, to the conditions to which it was subject immediately prior to the commencement date.
(3) Where construction or operation of a pipeline has commenced under a pipeline licence issued under the former Act and in force on the commencement date, the pipeline in question shall for the purposes of this Act be a project pipeline, unless converted to a strategic pipeline under Section 81 or 82.

**189. EXISTING OR PROPOSED PETROLEUM PROCESSING FACILITIES.**

(1) Where prior to the commencement date a person has commenced construction of a petroleum processing facility which was not previously required to be licensed under the former Act, or the State has entered into an agreement with a person which provides for the construction of a petroleum processing facility or has granted to a person a licence or pipeline licence under the former Act which provides for the construction of a petroleum processing facility in circumstances where a separate petroleum processing facility licence is required under this Act, the Minister shall, upon request by that person and without the requirement for a formal application or an application fee, grant to that person a petroleum processing facility licence under this Act on terms consistent with any applicable existing agreement with or licence or pipeline licence granted under the former Act which is held by that person.
(2) Where a person referred to in Subsection (1) requests the Minister to grant a petroleum processing facility licence within six months of the commencement date, until that person is granted a petroleum processing facility licence as required by Subsection (1) the petroleum processing facility in question shall be deemed to be licensed under this Act and the person shall not be in breach of this Act only by reason of the fact that he is continuing to construct or is operating a petroleum processing facility without a petroleum processing facility licence in respect thereof.

**190. REFERENCES TO FORMER ACT, ETC.**

A reference in any law or in any instrument made under or in relation to the former Act or a provision of the former Act shall, on and after the commencement date, unless the context otherwise requires, be read and construed as a reference to this Act or to the corresponding provision of this Act.

**SCHEDULE 1 – DETERMINATION OF VALUE OF PETROLEUM UNDER SECTION 158.**

Sec. 158.

**PART 1. – PRELIMINARY.**

**1. INTERPRETATION OF SCHEDULE.**

In this Schedule–

**"adjusted price"** means net realisable price with any appropriate adjustment for sales margins or commissions;
**"appropriate adjustment"**, in relation to any provision of this Schedule, means such adjustment for the purposes of the provision as is agreed on between the Minister and the licensee, or in default of agreement, as is reasonably determined by the Minister;

**"domestic value"** means a value to be determined under Section 158 for petroleum not intended for export;
**"export value"** means a value to be determined under Section 158 for petroleum intended for export;
**"the guidelines"** means the guidelines adopted under Part 3 of this Schedule;
**"the licensee"** means the holder of the licence from which the petroleum which is to be given a value under Section 158 is produced;
**"relevant contract"** means an agreement for the sale at an arms' length price of petroleum for delivery–

(*a*) by more than one shipment; and
(*b*) over a period of more than three months,

that was in force during the relevant period;
**"the relevant period"**, in relation to the determination of a value for any petroleum, means the period of three months, or such longer period as in special circumstances is agreed on between the Minister and the licensee, before the date as at which the value is to be determined.

**2. "SALE AT ARMS' LENGTH".**

For the purposes of this Schedule, a sale is at arms' length where–

(*a*) the consideration expressed in the agreement for the sale is the sole consideration for the sale; and
(*b*) the terms of the sale are not affected by any commercial relationship (other than the relationship created by the agreement or sale) between the seller and the buyer or any person connected with the buyer; and
(*c*) neither the seller nor any person connected with him has any direct or indirect interest in the subsequent re-sale or disposal of the petroleum or of any product of it,

and no other sale shall be taken to be at arms' length.

**3. "ARMS' LENGTH PRICE".**

(1) In this Schedule, **"arms' length price"**, in relation to a sale or an agreement for the sale of any petroleum, means–

(*a*) where the sale was, or was to be, at arms' length–the sale price; and
(*b*) where the sale was not, or was not to be, at arms' length–the price that, in the opinion of the Minister, the petroleum would have brought had the sale been at arms' length.

(2) Subject to Subsection (3), where in the opinion of the Minister it is not practicable in the circumstances of a particular sale that was not at arms' length, or of a particular agreement for such a sale, to determine what would have been the price referred to in Subsection (1)(b), the sale shall be disregarded for the purposes of any provision of this Schedule that relates to arms' length prices.
(3) For the purposes of any provision of this Schedule that refers to an average price based on sales at arms' length or arms' length prices, a sale that is not a sale at arms' length, or a price that is not an arms' length price, may be taken into account where the Minister is satisfied that a series of sales, or a number of related sales, of which the sale concerned was one, was or were such that the total of the prices paid amounted to, or was the equivalent of, an arms' length price for all the petroleum sold.

**4. COMPARISON OF PETROLEUM.**

Where it is necessary for the purposes of this Schedule to compare–

(*a*) petroleum of different qualities or grades; or
(*b*) prices of–

(i) petroleum of different qualities or grades; or
(ii) petroleum sold, or agreed to be sold, in significantly different quantities,

appropriate adjustments shall be made to reconcile or compensate for the difference.

**5. COMPARISON OF PRICES.**

Where it is necessary for the purposes of this Schedule to compare prices, appropriate adjustments shall be made for differences in any relevant costs, including the terms of any credit allowed and transport costs, in addition to any adjustments to be made in accordance with Schedule Section 4 to enable the prices to be related to comparable qualities, grades or quantities of petroleum.

**PART 2. – NORM VALUES.**

**6. DETERMINATION OF VALUE BY REFERENCE TO RELEVANT CONTRACTS.**

If the Minister is satisfied that there has been a sufficient number of relevant contracts for the sale–

(*a*) where the value to be determined is an export value–of locally produced petroleum for export; or
(*b*) where the value to be determined is a domestic value–of locally produced petroleum for refining or processing in Papua New Guinea,

to allow a norm price to be satisfactorily determined, the export value or the domestic value, as the case may be, shall be determined having regard to the weighted average of the comparable adjusted prices per barrel under the contracts to which Paragraph (a) or (b), as the case may be, relates.

**7. DETERMINATION OF VALUE IN OTHER CASES.**

In a case to which Schedule Section 6 does not apply, the Minister shall determine an export value or a domestic value, as the case requires, that in his opinion represents a fair arms' length price for the petroleum concerned, and in so doing he shall have regard to any appropriate marker price adopted under Schedule Section 9.

# IMPORTANT CONTACTS

## CHAMBER OF MINES AND PETROLEUM

The Chamber Secretariat is the administrative arm of the organisation and is headed by an Executive Director.

**Office Location**
Port Moresby, Papua New Guinea

**Courier Address**
First Floor, The Lodge, Bampton Street, Port Moresby, National Capital District, Papua New Guinea

**Postal Address**
PO Box 1032, Port Moresby, National Capital District, 121, Papua New Guinea

**Telephone**
(675+) 321 2988 / 321 3827 / 321 0546

**Facsimile**
(675+) 321 7107

**Email:** info@pngchamberminpet.com.pg

**STAFF**

**Greg Anderson** FAusIMM Executive Director
ga@pngchamberminpet.com.pg

**Jacinta Towamwesi** Admin/Finance Officer
jdt@pngchamberminpet.com.pg

**Leah Warupi** Projects Officer
proj@pngchamberminpet.com.pg

**Women in Mining Project**

**Lesley Bennett** Project Manager
wim@pngchamberminpet.com.pg

# PETROLEUM DIVISION

Department of Petroleum & Energy
PO Box 1993
Port Moresby
Papua New Guinea

Telephone: (+675) 322 4200
Facsimile: (+675) 322 4222
E-mail: Stanley_Pono@petroleum.gov.pg

Department of Petroleum & Energy
PO Box 1993
Port Moresby
Papua New Guinea

Telephone: (+675) 322 4207
Facsimile: (+675) 322 4222
E-mail: Peter_Woyengu@petroleum.gov.pg

Department of Petroleum & Energy
PO Box 1993
Port Moresby
Papua New Guinea

Telephone: (+675) 322 4299
Facsimile: (+675) 322 4222
E-mail: lati_Ai@petroleum.gov.pg

Department of Petroleum & Energy
PO Box 1993
Port Moresby
Papua New Guinea

Telephone: (+675) 322 4245
Facsimile: (+675) 322 4222
E-mail: Rendle_Rimua@petroleum.gov.pg

Department of Petroleum & Energy
PO Box 1993
Port Moresby
Papua New Guinea

Telephone: (+675) 322 4282
Facsimile: (+675) 322 4222
E-mail: Peter_Kogl@petroleum.gov.pg

Department of Petroleum & Energy
PO Box 1993
Port Moresby
Papua New Guinea

Telephone: (+675) 322 4207
Facsimile: (+675) 322 4222
E-mail: Joe_Kuatowa@petroleum.gov.pg

*For general enquiry's, contact us at: enquiry@petroleum.gov.pg or if you wish to send us electronic correspondence, please forward to: registrar@petroleum.gov.pg.*

Mr. Stanley Pono
DIRECTOR

Mr. Peter Woyengu
a/ Assistant Director
Exploration Branch
Mr. Iati Ai
REGISTRAR
Licence Administration Branch
Mr. Rendle Rimua
Assistant Director
Policy Branch
Mr. Peter Kogl
Assistant Director
Engineering Branch
Mr. Joe Kuatowa
Assistant Director
Co-ordination Branch

# PAPUA NEW GUINEA DEPARTMENT OF MINING

The functions of the Department of Mining are:

- Develop the mining industry by actively encouraging socially, environmentally and technically responsible private sector exploration and development of mineral resources
- Expedite rural development by promoting and facilitating small-scale mining
- Provide background data, advice and services in the fields of exploration, geotechnical engineering, hydrogeology, volcanology and seismology aimed at facilitating development and identifying, monitoring and mitigating geological hazards
- Negotiate mining agreements and carry out related research and policy analysis
- Provide services to standing or *ad hoc* organisations relating to the functions of the Department

### DEPARTMENT OF MINES CONTACTS

DEPARTMENT OF MINES
PMB PO,
Port Moresby 121
Konedobu
Port Moresby,
NCD
Papua New Guinea
Fax: (+675) 321 3701
General Enquiries: (+675) 322 7600

### DoM Staff

| | |
|---|---|
| Ms Isabella **Abiari** | Regional Geologist |
| Telephone: | 321 5888 Ext 612 |
| email: | - |
| Mineral District Survey Section | Geol Survey, Headquarters, Newtown |
| Mr Jack **Abrahams** | Engineering Geologist |
| Telephone: | 3224 620 |
| email: | jack_abrahams@mineral.gov.pg |
| Geotechnical & Hydrogeological Survey Branch (GHS) | Geol Survey, Headquarters, Newtown |

| | |
|---|---|
| Ms Janet **Amean** | Director |
| Telephone: | 322 7648 |
| email: | janet_amean@mineral.gov.pg |
| Corporate Services Division | Headquarters, Konedobu |
| Mr Lawrence **Anton** | Chief Seismologist |
| Telephone: | 321 3976 Ext 15 |
| email: | - |
| Geophysical Observatory Branch (GPS) | Geol Survey, Headquarters, Newtown |
| Ms Rori **Arua** | Revenue Officer |
| Telephone: | 322 7652 |
| email: | - |
| Finance & Accounts Branch | Headquarters, Konedobu |
| Mr John **Arumba** | Sysmin Co-ordinator |
| Telephone: | 322 7680 |
| email: | john_arumba@mineral.gov.pg |
| Office Of The Secretary | Headquarters, Konedobu |
| Mr Ken **Aua** | General Labourer |
| Telephone: | - |
| email: | - |
| Reception Section | Headquarters, Konedobu |
| Mr Kuma **Aua, OBE** | Secretary |
| Telephone: | 322 7675 (Direct Line 321 1961) |
| email: | kuma_aua@mineral.gov.pg |
| Office Of The Secretary | Headquarters, Konedobu |
| Ms Sharon **Bagi** | Secretary/KBO |
| Telephone: | 322 7606 |
| email: | - |
| Tenements Administration Branch | Headquarters, Konedobu |
| Mr Malcolm **Baibuni** | Co-ordinator (Porgera) |
| Telephone: | 322 7620 |
| email: | malcolm_baibuni@mineral.gov.pg |
| Mining Co-ordination Branch | Headquarters, Konedobu |
| Mr Daniel **Baine** | Senior Programmer (Hardware) |
| Telephone: | 322 7669 |
| email: | daniel_baine@mineral.gov.pg |
| Information Services Branch | Headquarters, Konedobu |
| Mr Fafaeg **Bibin** | Liaison Officer |
| Telephone: | 852 1706 |
| email: | - |
| Ramu Liaison Office | Headquarters, Konedobu |
| Ms Hedwig **Bob** | Executive Secretary |
| Telephone: | 322 7629 |
| email: | hedwig_bob@mineral.gov.pg |
| Mining Division | Headquarters, Konedobu |

Mr John **Bosco** — Manager, Technical Services
Telephone: 982 1004 Ext 20
email: -
Electronics Section (Technical Support) — Rabaul Volcanological Observatory Branch

Mr Joe **Buleka** — Chief Government Geologist (Director)
Telephone: 321 1973
email: joe_buleka@mineral.gov.pg
GEOLOGICAL SURVEY DIVISION — Geol Survey, Headquarters, Newtown

Mr Tom **Charlton** — Geologist / Database Admnistrator
Telephone: -
email: palunkit@hotmail.com
TerraSearch — Headquarters

Ms Judy **Daniel** — Branch Clerk
Telephone: 322 7608
email: -
Mining Co-ordination Branch — Headquarters, Konedobu

Mr Justin **Edimani** — Mining Engineer
Telephone: 474 6214
email: -
Wau Office — Headquarters, Konedobu

Ms Marisah **Egara** — Secretary/KBO
Telephone: 321 3976 Ext 10
email: -
Geophysical Observatory Branch (GPS) — Geol Survey, Headquarters, Newtown

Mr Simon **Egara** — Hydrogeologist
Telephone: 321 1360 Ext 222
email: -
Geotechnical & Hydrogeological Survey Branch (GHS) — Geol Survey, Headquarters, Newtown

Mr Jason **Elemunop** — Geologist
Telephone: 321 1360 Ext 224
email: -
Geotechnical & Hydrogeological Survey Branch (GHS) — Geol Survey, Headquarters, Newtown

Mr Kawa **Eva** — Security
Telephone: -
email: -
Wau Office — Headquarters, Konedobu

Dr Robert H. **Findlay** — Assistant Director
Telephone: Ext 205
email: gspng@mineral.gov.pg
Geological Mapping and Mineral District Survey Branch (GM — Geol Survey, Headquarters, Newtown

Ms Fresli **Fone** — General Labourer
Telephone: 321 1360 Ext 223
email: -
Geotechnical & Hydrogeological Survey Branch (GHS) — Geol Survey, Headquarters, Newtown

| | |
|---|---|
| Mr Kerry **Gadua** | Assets Manager |
| Telephone: | 322 7653 |
| email: | - |
| Assets Section | Headquarters, Konedobu |

| | |
|---|---|
| Mr Vance **Gaoro** | Lands Officer |
| Telephone: | 986 4100 |
| email: | - |
| Lihir Liaison Office | Headquarters, Konedobu |

| | |
|---|---|
| Mr Boge **Gari** | Senior Examiner |
| Telephone: | 322 7650 |
| email: | - |
| Finance & Accounts Branch | Headquarters, Konedobu |

| | |
|---|---|
| Mr Vele **Gavu** | Mining Warden |
| Telephone: | 322 7635 |
| email: | - |
| Tenements Administration Branch | Headquarters, Konedobu |

| | |
|---|---|
| Mr Ron **Gawi** | Assistant Director |
| Telephone: | 322 7622 |
| email: | ron_gawi@mineral.gov.pg |
| Mining Co-ordination Branch | Headquarters, Konedobu |

| | |
|---|---|
| Mr Lawrie **Giwi** | Technical Officer |
| Telephone: | 321 1360 Ext 215 |
| email: | - |
| Technical Staff | Geol Survey, Headquarters, Newtown |

| | |
|---|---|
| Mr Rausi **Guba** | Driver |
| Telephone: | - |
| email: | - |
| Mining Co-ordination Branch | Headquarters, Konedobu |

| | |
|---|---|
| Mr Ipi **Hailaeavila** | Assistant Director |
| Telephone: | 322 7657 |
| email: | ipi@mineral.gov.pg |
| Human Resources Management Branch | Headquarters, Konedobu |

| | |
|---|---|
| Dr Graeme **Hancock** | Director |
| Telephone: | 321 0466 |
| email: | graeme_hancock@mineral.gov.pg |
| Project Co-ordination & Implementation Unit ? Wbta (pciu) | Headquarters, Konedobu |

| | |
|---|---|
| Ms Margaret **Haoda** | Office Manageress (Executive Secretary) |
| Telephone: | 321 0466 |
| email: | pciu@mineral.gov.pg |
| Project Co-ordination & Implementation Unit ? Wbta (pciu) | Headquarters, Konedobu |

| | |
|---|---|
| Mr Peter **Harou** | Expenditure Manager |
| Telephone: | 322 7659 |
| email: | - |
| Finance & Accounts Branch | Headquarters, Konedobu |

Mr Nagnining **Hawak** | General Labourer
Telephone: | -
email: | -
Wau Office | Headquarters, Konedobu

Miss Rachel **Heaven** | World Bank Consultant
Telephone:
email: | reh@bgs.ac.uk
Geological Survey | Geophysics

Mr Shadrach **Himata** | Snr Co-ordinator (Misima/Simberi)
Telephone: | 322 7623
email: | shadrach_himata@mineral.gov.pg
Mining Co-ordination Branch | Headquarters, Konedobu

Ms Tova **Hou** | Paying Officer
Telephone: | 322 7646
email: | -
Finance & Accounts Branch | Headquarters, Konedobu

Mr Kennis **Ikilik** | Branch Clerk
Telephone: | 982 1004 Ext 12
email: | -
RVO DIVISION | Rabaul Volcanological Observatory Branch

Mr Robert **Imuli** | Security (Back Gate)
Telephone: | 322 7664
email: | -
Reception Section | Headquarters, Konedobu

Mr Ima **Itikarai** | Assistant Director
Telephone: | 982 1699 Ext 11
email: | hgurial@global.net.pg
RVO DIVISION | Rabaul Volcanological Observatory Branch

Mr Valu **Ivoa** | Systems Administration
Telephone: | 322 7649
email: | -
Finance & Accounts Branch | Headquarters, Konedobu

Ms Nellie **James** | Registrar
Telephone: | 322 7615 (Direct Line 321 7981)
email: | nellie_james@mineral.gov.pg
Tenements Administration Branch | Headquarters, Konedobu

Ms Patricia **Japhlom** | Executive Secretary
Telephone: | 322 7660
email: | patsony_japh@mineral.gov.pg
Corporate Services Division | Headquarters, Konedobu

Mr Lasark **Joseph** | Senior Economic Geologist
Telephone: | 322 7634
email: | lasark_joseph@mineral.gov.pg
Mineral Project Assessment Branch | Headquarters, Konedobu

| | |
|---|---|
| Ms Serah **Kais** | Secretary/KBO |
| Telephone: | 474 6214 |
| email: | - |
| Wau Office | Headquarters, Konedobu |

| | |
|---|---|
| Mr Pius **Kami** | Senior Liaison Officer |
| Telephone: | 548 9087 |
| email: | - |
| Tabubil Liaison Office | Headquarters, Konedobu |

| | |
|---|---|
| Mr Walo **Karona** | Chief Accountant |
| Telephone: | 322 7662 |
| email: | - |
| Finance & Accounts Branch | Headquarters, Konedobu |

| | |
|---|---|
| Mr Leo **Kasa** | Senior Mining Engineer |
| Telephone: | 322 7603 |
| email: | leo_kasa@mineral.gov.pg |
| Mineral Project Assessment Branch | Headquarters, Konedobu |

| | |
|---|---|
| Mr Paul **Kia** | Regional Geologist |
| Telephone: | Ext 214 |
| email: | - |
| Geological Mapping and Mineral District Survey Branch (GM | Geol Survey, Headquarters, Newtown |

| | |
|---|---|
| Mr Pokana **Kila** | Training & Staff Development Manager |
| Telephone: | 322 7693 |
| email: | - |
| Personnel Section | Headquarters, Konedobu |

| | |
|---|---|
| Mr Terry Win **Kilya** | Senior Regional Geologist |
| Telephone: | Ext 609 |
| email: | geosurvl@daltron.com.pg |
| Geological Mapping and Mineral District Survey Branch (GM | Geol Survey, Headquarters, Newtown |

| | |
|---|---|
| Mr Kessie **Kimbek** | Personnel Officer (Wages) |
| Telephone: | 322 7642 |
| email: | - |
| Personnel Section | Headquarters, Konedobu |

| | |
|---|---|
| Mr Gwaibo **Kopi** | Senior Exploration Geologist |
| Telephone: | 321 1360 Ext 208 |
| email: | - |
| Mineral District Survey Section | Geol Survey, Headquarters, Newtown |

| | |
|---|---|
| Mr Timonty **Kota** | Chief Mining Warden |
| Telephone: | 322 7635 |
| email: | - |
| Tenements Administration Branch | Headquarters, Konedobu |

| | |
|---|---|
| Mr Gideon **Kouoru** | Senior Registry Clerk |
| Telephone: | 322 7644 |
| email: | - |
| Registry Section | Headquarters, Konedobu |

| | |
|---|---|
| Mr Jonathan **Kuduon** | Senior Technical Officer |
| Telephone: | 982 1004 Ext 18 |
| email: | - |
| Seismology Section | Rabaul Volcanological Observatory Branch |
| Mr Gabriel **Kuna** | Assistant Director |
| Telephone: | 321 1360 Ext 218 |
| email: | ghs@mineral.gov.pg |
| Geotechnical & Hydrogeological Survey Branch (GHS) | Geol Survey, Headquarters, Newtown |
| Mrs Gege **Kwapena** | Executive Secretary |
| Telephone: | 322 7686 |
| email: | gege_kwapena@mineral.gov.pg |
| Office Of The Secretary | Headquarters, Konedobu |
| Mr Kwapena **Kwapena** | Assistant/Driver |
| Telephone: | - |
| email: | - |
| Project Co-ordination & Implementation Unit ? Wbta (pciu) | Headquarters, Konedobu |
| Ms Tania **Kwaragu** | Secretary/KBO |
| Telephone: | Ext 213 |
| email: | - |
| Geological Mapping and Mineral District Survey Branch (GM | Geol Survey, Headquarters, Newtown |
| Ms Maxine **Lahan** | Acting Mining Warden |
| Telephone: | 322 7606 |
| email: | - |
| Tenements Administration Branch | Headquarters, Konedobu |
| Mr Peter **Laka** | Contract Geologist |
| Telephone: | 322 7606 |
| email: | - |
| Tenements Administration Branch | Headquarters, Konedobu |
| Ms Daisy **Lele** | General Labourer |
| Telephone: | - |
| email: | - |
| Mineral Project Assessment Branch | Headquarters, Konedobu |
| Ms Helen **Lohai** | Secretary/KBO |
| Telephone: | 322 7678 |
| email: | - |
| Mineral Project Assessment Branch | Headquarters, Konedobu |
| Mr Howard **Lole** | Senior Mines Inspector |
| Telephone: | 322 7616 |
| email: | min_lole@datec.com.pg |
| Inspection & Engineering Branch | Headquarters, Konedobu |
| Ms Nancy **Lolya** | Secretary/KBO |
| Telephone: | 322 7677 |
| email: | - |
| Human Resources Management Branch | Headquarters, Konedobu |

| | |
|---|---|
| Mr Jim **Lytham** | Chief Hydrogeologist |
| Telephone: | 321 1360 Ext 219 |
| email: | - |
| Geotechnical & Hydrogeological Survey Branch (GHS) | Geol Survey, Headquarters, Newtown |
| Ms Bernadette **Mararan** | Secretary/KBO |
| Telephone: | 982 1004 Ext 26 |
| email: | - |
| RVO DIVISION | Rabaul Volcanological Observatory Branch |
| Mr John **Marcus** | Senior Mines Inspector |
| Telephone: | 322 7614 |
| email: | john_marcus@mineral.gov.pg |
| Inspection & Engineering Branch | Headquarters, Konedobu |
| Mr Chris **McKee** | Assistant Director |
| Telephone: | 321 3976 Ext 12 (Direct Line 321 4500) |
| email: | pmgo@daltron.gov.pg |
| Geophysical Observatory Branch (GPS) | Geol Survey, Headquarters, Newtown |
| Ms Helen **McKenzie** | General Labourer |
| Telephone: | - |
| email: | - |
| Tenements Administration Branch | Headquarters, Konedobu |
| Mr Mathew **Moihoi** | Geophysicist |
| Telephone: | 321 3976 Ext 15 |
| email: | - |
| Geophysical Observatory Branch (GPS) | Geol Survey, Headquarters, Newtown |
| Mr James **Mokepwesi** | Geophysicist |
| Telephone: | 321 1360 Ext 216 |
| email: | james_mokepwesi@mineral.gov.pg |
| Geophysics Section | Geol Survey, Headquarters, Newtown |
| Ms Evelyn **Mopafi** | Resource Scientist |
| Telephone: | 322 7668 |
| email: | emopafi@hotmail.com |
| Mineral Project Assessment Branch | Headquarters, Konedobu |
| Mr Nathan **Mosusu** | Principal Geophysicist |
| Telephone: | 321 1360 Ext 216 |
| email: | nathan_mosusu@mineral.gov.pg |
| Geophysics Section | Geol Survey, Headquarters, Newtown |
| Ms Judy **Muliap** | Assistant Accountant |
| Telephone: | - |
| email: | judy_muliap@mineral.gov.pg |
| Project Co-ordination & Implementation Unit ? Wbta (pciu) | Headquarters, Konedobu |
| Mr Kila **Mulina** | Senior Volcanologist |
| Telephone: | 982 1004 Ext 18 |
| email: | - |
| Volcanology Section | Rabaul Volcanological Observatory Branch |

| | |
|---|---|
| Mr Anselm **Mulungu** | Internal Auditor |
| Telephone: | 322 7661 |
| email: | - |
| Office Of The Secretary | Headquarters, Konedobu |
| Mr Jerry **Naime** | Co-ordinator (Tolukuma/Ramu/H. Valley) |
| Telephone: | 322 7625 |
| email: | jerry_naime@mineral.gov.pg |
| Mining Co-ordination Branch | Headquarters, Konedobu |
| Ms Noelyn **Naisen Lakl** | Executive Secretary |
| Telephone: | Ext 201 |
| email: | noelyn_naisen@mineral.gov.pg |
| GEOLOGICAL SURVEY DIVISION | Geol Survey, Headquarters, Newtown |
| Mr Neka **Nansia** | General Labourer |
| Telephone: | - |
| email: | - |
| Wau Office | Headquarters, Konedobu |
| Mr Steven **Narawen** | Co-ordinator (Kainantu) |
| Telephone: | 322 7630 |
| email: | - |
| Mining Co-ordination Branch | Headquarters, Konedobu |
| Mr Stan **Nekitel** | Deputy Registrar |
| Telephone: | 322 7633 |
| email: | snekitel@mineral.gov.pg |
| Tenements Administration Branch | Headquarters, Konedobu |
| Mr Stevie T.S **Nion** | Deputy Secretary |
| Telephone: | 322 7618 (Direct Line 321 2945) |
| email: | steve_nion@mineral.gov.pg |
| Office Of The Secretary | Headquarters, Konedobu |
| Mr John **Nohou** | Technical Officer |
| Telephone: | 982 1004 Ext 31 |
| email: | - |
| Survey Section | Rabaul Volcanological Observatory Branch |
| Mr James **Passmore** | World Bank Consultant |
| Telephone: | - |
| email: | jpass@bgs.ac.uk |
| British Geological Survey | Geol Survey and DoM HQ |
| Mr Herman **Patia** | Chief Seismologist |
| Telephone: | 982 1004 Ext 17 |
| email: | - |
| Seismology Section | Rabaul Volcanological Observatory Branch |
| Mr Firoz **Patwa** | Chief Mines Inspector |
| Telephone: | 322 7607 |
| email: | firoz_patwa@mineral.gov.pg |
| Inspection & Engineering Branch | Headquarters, Konedobu |

| | |
|---|---|
| Ms Patricia **Pepena** | Senior Resource Scientist |
| Telephone: | 322 7695 |
| email: | pat_pepena@mineral.gov.pg |
| Mineral Project Assessment Branch | Headquarters, Konedobu |
| Mrs Carol **Peter** | Executive Secretary |
| Telephone: | 322 7687 |
| email: | carol_peter@mineral.gov.pg |
| Office Of The Secretary | Headquarters, Konedobu |
| Ms Naomi **Peter** | Secretary/KBO |
| Telephone: | 322 7688 |
| email: | - |
| Mining Co-ordination Branch | Headquarters, Konedobu |
| Ms Mary **Pino?on** | Librarian |
| Telephone: | 321 1360 Ext 217 |
| email: | - |
| Technical Staff | Geol Survey, Headquarters, Newtown |
| Ms Ikanau **Pohu Aumi** | Receptionist (Switchboard Operator) |
| Telephone: | Ext 202/200 |
| email: | - |
| GEOLOGICAL SURVEY DIVISION | Geol Survey, Headquarters, Newtown |
| Ms Kila **Pokana** | Secretary/KBO |
| Telephone: | 322 7604 |
| email: | - |
| Information Services Branch | Headquarters, Konedobu |
| Mr Igua **Robert** | Project Accountant |
| Telephone: | 321 0466 |
| email: | igua_robert@mineral.gov.pg |
| Project Co-ordination & Implementation Unit ? Wbta (pciu) | Headquarters, Konedobu |
| Ms Gepsy **Salala** | General Labourer |
| Telephone: | Ext 202 |
| email: | - |
| GEOLOGICAL SURVEY DIVISION | Geol Survey, Headquarters, Newtown |
| Mr Steve **Saunders** | Chief Geodetic Surveyor |
| Telephone: | 982 1004 Ext 30 |
| email: | - |
| Survey Section | Rabaul Volcanological Observatory Branch |
| Mr Sigu **Sivok** | General Labourer |
| Telephone: | 321 3976 Ext 10 |
| email: | - |
| Geophysical Observatory Branch (GPS) | Geol Survey, Headquarters, Newtown |
| Ms Mary **Soi** | Senior Personnel Officer |
| Telephone: | 322 7643 |
| email: | - |
| Personnel Section | Headquarters, Konedobu |

| | |
|---|---|
| Mr Robin **Suami** | General Labourer |
| Telephone: | 321 1360 Ext 215 |
| email: | - |
| Technical Staff | Geol Survey, Headquarters, Newtown |

| | |
|---|---|
| Mr Douglas **Swalili** | Assistant Librarian (Engineering) |
| Telephone: | 321 1360 Ext 223 |
| email: | - |
| Geotechnical & Hydrogeological Survey Branch (GHS) | Geol Survey, Headquarters, Newtown |

| | |
|---|---|
| Mr Peter **Taboko** | Technical Officer |
| Telephone: | 982 1004 Ext 21 |
| email: | - |
| Electronics Section (Technical Support) | Rabaul Volcanological Observatory Branch |

| | |
|---|---|
| Mr Sonic **Taguse** | Supervising Draftsman |
| Telephone: | 322 7632 |
| email: | - |
| Drafting Section (terra Search Ltd) | Headquarters, Konedobu |

| | |
|---|---|
| Mr Felix **Taranu** | Seismologist |
| Telephone: | 982 1004 Ext 18 |
| email: | - |
| Seismology Section | Rabaul Volcanological Observatory Branch |

| | |
|---|---|
| Mr William **Tau-Vali** | Assistant Director |
| Telephone: | 322 7638 |
| email: | willy_tauvali@mineral.gov.pg |
| Information Services Branch | Headquarters, Konedobu |

| | |
|---|---|
| Mr Husain **Tawakkul** | Deputy Mines Inspector |
| Telephone: | 322 7602 |
| email: | tawakkul_husain@mineral.gov.pg |
| Inspection & Engineering Branch | Headquarters, Konedobu |

| | |
|---|---|
| Mr Graham **Taylor** | Sustainable Development Advisor |
| Telephone: | 321 0466 |
| email: | graham_taylor@mineral.gov.pg |
| Project Co-ordination & Implementation Unit ? Wbta (pciu) | Headquarters, Konedobu |

| | |
|---|---|
| Mr Simon **Tohui** | Chief Technical Officer |
| Telephone: | 982 1004 Ext 20 |
| Electronics Section (Technical Support) | Rabaul Volcanological Observatory Branch |

| | |
|---|---|
| Mr Gideon **Tongo** | Senior Mining Engineer |
| Telephone: | 474 6353 |
| email: | - |
| Wau Office | Headquarters, Konedobu |

| | |
|---|---|
| Ms Ani **Topurua** | Senior Policy Officer |
| Telephone: | 322 7604 |
| email: | atopurua@mineral.gov.pg |
| Mineral Project Assessment Branch | Headquarters, Konedobu |

| | |
|---|---|
| Mr Tony **Torea** | Office Assistant |

| | |
|---|---|
| Telephone: | 322 7600 Ext. 9 |
| email: | - |
| Reception Section | Headquarters, Konedobu |

| | |
|---|---|
| Mr Augustine **Tukas** | Liaison Officer |
| Telephone: | - |
| email: | - |
| Lihir Liaison Office | Headquarters, Konedobu |

| | |
|---|---|
| Mr Gabriel **Tukas** | Senior Liaison Officer |
| Telephone: | 986 4059 |
| email: | - |
| Lihir Liaison Office | Headquarters, Konedobu |

| | |
|---|---|
| Ms Nisal **Turbarat** | Secretary/KBO |
| Telephone: | 322 7692 |
| email: | - |
| Mining Co-ordination Branch | Headquarters, Konedobu |

| | |
|---|---|
| Ms Morea **Varuko** | Secretary/KBO |
| Telephone: | 322 7611 |
| email: | - |
| Mineral Project Assessment Branch | Headquarters, Konedobu |

| | |
|---|---|
| Mr Adrian **Walker** | World Bank Consultant |
| Telephone: | Ext 204 |
| email: | - |
| WBTA Project | Geol Survey, Headquarters, Newtown |

| | |
|---|---|
| Ms Jessie **Wama** | Exploration Geologist |
| Telephone: | 321 5888 x 611 |
| email: | - |
| Mineral District Survey Section | Geol Survey, Headquarters, Newtown |

| | |
|---|---|
| Mr James **Wanjik** | Assistant Director |
| Telephone: | 322 7628 |
| email: | james_wanjik@mineral.gov.pg |
| Mineral Project Assessment Branch | Headquarters, Konedobu |

| | |
|---|---|
| Mr Sylvester **Wapea** | Staff Development Officer |
| Telephone: | 322 7676 |
| email: | - |
| Personnel Section | Headquarters, Konedobu |

| | |
|---|---|
| Mr Aaron **Watan** | Security (Front Gate) |
| Telephone: | 322 7664 |
| email: | - |
| Reception Section | Headquarters, Konedobu |

| | |
|---|---|
| Mr Anthony **Williamson** | Director |
| Telephone: | 322 7624 (Direct Line 321 3093) |
| email: | anthony_williamson@mineral.gov.pg |
| Mining Division | Headquarters, Konedobu |

| | |
|---|---|
| Mr Joseph **Wukawa** | Geodetic Surveyor |

| | |
|---|---|
| Telephone:<br>email:<br>Survey Section | 982 1004 Ext 31<br>-<br>Rabaul Volcanological Observatory Branch |
| Mr James **Yako**<br>Telephone:<br>email:<br>Finance & Accounts Branch | General Labourer<br>322 7660<br>-<br>Headquarters, Konedobu |
| Mr Thomas **Yetuin**<br>Telephone:<br>email:<br>Information Services Branch | Senior Programmer (Software)<br>322 7670<br>yetuin@mineral.gov.pg<br>Headquarters, Konedobu |
| Mrs Columbana **Ziksieh**<br>Lihir Liaison Office | Secretary/KBO<br>Headquarters, Konedobu |

List generated on: Friday 26 March 2004

# ASSOCIATIONS AND REPRESENTATIVE GROUPS

### KEY CONTACTS FOR INVESTORS

The Investment Promotion Authority maintains a comprehensive database of contacts within the Government and the private sector. Contact the IPA for further assistance.

Managing Director
Investment Promotion Authority
PO Box 5053 Tel: +675 3217311
Boroko NCD 111 Fax: +675 3212819
Papua New Guinea

Investment & Export Promotion Fax: +675 3202237
Research & Information Services Fax: +675 3200262
Business Registration Office Fax: +675 3213049

### GOVERNMENT DEPARTMENTS AND AGENCIES

***Industry, Commerce, Manufacturing and Small Business***

The Secretary
Department of Commerce & Industry
PO Box 375 Tel: +675 3011806
Waigani NCD 131 Fax: +675 3252403
Papua New Guinea

Managing Director
Small Business Development Corporation
PO Box 481 Tel: +676 3250100
Port Moresby NCD 121 Fax: +675 3253725
Papua New Guinea

Managing Director
Industrial Centres Development Corporation
PO Box 1571 Tel: +675 3232913 / 3231179
Boroko NCD 111 Fax: +675 3231109
Papua New Guinea

***Immigration & Visas***

The Secretary
Department of Foreign Affairs
PO Box 422 Tel: +675 3001121
Waigani NCD 131 Fax: +675 3254467
Papua New Guinea

The Director General Tel: +675 3271026 / 3001237
Immigration & Citizenship Division Fax: +675 3256644 / 3231022

***Labour, Work Permits and Industrial Relations***

The Secretary
Department of Industrial Relations
PO Box 5644 Tel: +675 3217408
Boroko NCD 111 Fax: +675 3201062

Papua New Guinea

OIC Research & Projects Tel: +675 3213396
Department of Industrial Relations Fax: +675 3214805

***Matters of National Treasury***

The Secretary
Department of Finance
PO Box 710 Tel: +675 3288452 / 3288000
Waigani NCD 131 Fax: +675 3288445 / 3288495
Papua New Guinea

***Agriculture and Livestock***

The Secretary
Department of Agriculture and Livestock
PO Box 417 Tel: +675 3214699 / 3213302
Konedobu NCD 125 Fax: +675 3211387
Papua New Guinea

Chief Quarantine Officer (Plants) Tel: +675 3217405
Department of Agriculture and Livestock Fax: +675 3214630

***Mining***

The Secretary
Department of Mining
Private Mail Box Tel: +675 3211961
Port Moresby NCD 121 Fax: +675 3217958
Papua New Guinea

***Petroleum & Natural Gas***

The Secretary
Department of Petroleum and Energy
PO Box 1993 Tel: +675 3201199
Port Moresby NCD 121 Fax: +675 3201141
Papua New Guinea

***Fisheries Permits and Licences***

Executive Director
PNG National Fisheries Authority
PO Box 165 Tel: +675 3203133
Konedobu NCD 125 Fax: +675 3212662
Papua New Guinea

***Forestry Permits and Licences***

Managing Director
PNG Forest Authority
PO Box 5055 Tel: +675 3277841
Boroko NCD 111 Fax: +675 3254433
Papua New Guinea

***Land Tenure***

The Secretary
Department of Lands and Physical Planning
PO Box 5665 Tel: (675) 3013116
Boroko NCD 111 Fax: (675) 3013139
Papua New Guinea

Chief Land Titles Commissioner
Land Titles Commission
PO Box 815 Tel: (675) 3212366
Port Moresby NCD 121 Fax: (675) 3213922
Papua New Guinea

***Foreign Exchange Controls***

The Governor
The Bank of Papua New Guinea
PO Box 121 Tel: +675 3227200 / 3212999
Port Moresby NCD 121 Fax: +675 3211617
Papua New Guinea

Controller of Foreign Exchange Tel: +675 3227255 / 3227200

***Taxation, Customs and Excise***

Commissioner General
Internal Revenue Commission
PO Box 777
Port Moresby NCD 121 Tel: +675 3226600
Papua New Guinea Fax: +675 3214249 / 3213484

Internal Revenue Commission Tel: +675 3226828
Director (Tariffs) Fax: +675 3214249 / 3213484

Internal Revenue Commission Tel: +675 3226807
Assistant Commissioner (Revenue) Fax: +675 3214249 / 3213484

***Tourism Developments and Promotion***

Chief Executive
Tourism Promotion Authority
PO Box 1291 Tel: +675 3200211
Port Moresby NCD 121 Fax: +675 3200223
Papua New Guinea

***Electricity Supply***

General Manager
PNG Electricity Commission
PO Box 1105 Tel: +675 3243111 / 3243200
Boroko NCD 111 Fax: +675 3253877 / 3250008
Papua New Guinea

Deputy General Manager Tel: +675 3243112 / 3243113

Executive Manager Operations Tel: +675 3243531 / 3243115
Manager Business Development Tel: +675 3243396

***Telecommunications***

Managing Director
Post and Telecommunication Corporation
PO Box 1349 Tel: +675 300 4010
Boroko NCD 111 Fax: +675 3250665
Papua New Guinea

***Urban Water Supply and Sewerage Facilities***

General Manager
Waterboard
PO Box 2779 Tel: +675 3241600
Boroko NCD 111 Fax: +675 3241610
Papua New Guinea

***Water Supply Licences and Fees, Environmental Matters***

General Manager
Bureau of Water Resources
PO Box 6580 Tel: +675 3211747 / 3230166
Boroko NCD 111 Fax: +675 3217025 / 3231240
Papua New Guinea

***Transport Matters***

The Secretary
Department of Transport and Works
PO Box 1489 Tel: +675 3213418
Port Moresby NCD 121 Fax: +675 3200236
Papua New Guinea

**PRIVATE SECTOR ORGANISATIONS**

Industry associations represent economic sectors. There are also bilateral business associations with countries in the region.

The President
Papua New Guinea Chamber of Commerce & Industry
PO Box 1621 Tel: +675 3251192
Port Moresby NCD 121 Fax: +675 3251451
Papua New Guinea

The President
Papua New Guinea National Business Association
PO Box 5523 Tel: +675 3230576
Boroko NCD 111 Fax: +675 323587
Papua New Guinea

The Chairman
Papua New Guinea Council of Manufacturers
PO Box 598 Tel: +675 3259512
Port Moresby NCD 121 Fax: +675 3253080
Papua New Guinea

The President
Papua New Guinea Chamber of Mines & Petroleum
PO Box 1032 Tel: +675 3212988
Port Moresby NCD 121 Fax: +675 3217107
Papua New Guinea

The President
Employers' Federation of Papua New Guinea
PO Box 490 Tel: +675 3214722
Port Moresby NCD 121 Fax: +675 3214070
Papua New Guinea

The Chairman
Rural Industries Council
PO Box 14 Tel: +675 9821377
Rabaul East New Britain Province 611 Fax: +675 9821385
Papua New Guinea

The Chairman
PNG Grower's Association
PO Box 14 Tel: +675 9821377
Rabaul East New Britain Province 611 Fax: +675 9821385
Papua New Guinea

Chief Executive
Coffee Industry Corporation
PO Box 958 Tel: +675 7322466
Goroka Eastern Highlands Province 441 Fax: +675 7321351
Papua New Guinea
The Chairman
Oil Palm Industry Association
PO Box 3216 Tel: +675 3231511 / 3231562
Boroko NCD 111 Fax: +675 3231573
Papua New Guinea

Dami Oil Palm Research Station
PO Box 97 Tel: +675 9835204
Kimbe, West New Britain Province 621 Fax: +675 983 5476
Papua New Guinea

The President
Papua New Guinea Law Society
PO Box 1994 Tel: +675 3258483 / 3253717
Boroko NCD 111 Fax: +675 3256609
Papua New Guinea

The President
Papua New Guinea Trade Union Congress
PO Box 4279 Tel: +675 3257642
Boroko NCD 111
Papua New Guinea

The President
PNG Commercial Worker's Union
PO Box 336 Tel: n/a
Boroko NCD 111
Papua New Guinea

The President
PNG Liklik Bisnis Manmeri Association Inc
PO Box 399 Tel: +675 3251758 / 3251807
Boroko NCD 111
Papua New Guinea

The President
PNG Waterside Workers and Seamen's Union
PO Box 265 Tel: +675 3212132
Port Moresby NCD 121 Fax: +675 3213925
Papua New Guinea

The Director
PNG Institute of Bankers
PO Box 1721 Tel: +675 3212088 / 3212136
Port Moresby NCD 121
Papua New Guinea

The Chairman
PNG Institute of Architects
PO Box 1278 Tel: +675 3212155
Port Moresby NCD 121 Fax: +675 3214660
Papua New Guinea

The President
PNG New Zealand Business Council
C/o The Secretariat
PO Box 47 Tel: +64 9 3096100
AUCKLAND Fax: +64 9 3090081
New Zealand

The President
PNG Malaysia Business Council
C/o The Secretariat Tel: +675 3257677
PO Box 102 Fax: +675 3257972
PORT MORESBY NCD 121
Papua New Guinea

The President
PNG Australia Business Council
C/o The Secretariat
GPO Box 1155 Tel: +61 6 2884553
CANBERRA ACT 2601 Fax: +61 6 2319403
Australia

# BUSINESS TRAVEL

## US STATE DEPARTMENT SUGGESTIONS

**COUNTRY DESCRIPTION:** Papua New Guinea is a parliamentary democracy and a member of the British Commonwealth. The country consists of the eastern half of New Guinea Island, the Bismarck Archipelago, the D'Entrecasteaux Islands, the Louisiade Archipelago, and the islands of Buka and Bougainville. Good tourist facilities exist in the capital of Port Moresby and in major towns such as Lae and Madang. The quality of tourist facilities in other areas varies and may be below U.S. standards, particularly in remote areas. Crime is a serious concern throughout Papua New Guinea (see paragraph on crime below).

**ENTRY REQUIREMENTS:** A valid passport, onward/return ticket, and proof of sufficient funds for the intended visit are required. Tourist visas are required for stays up to 60 days. (Visas are issued upon arrival at Jacksons International Airport in Port Moresby). Business visas require passport validity of at least one year from the date the visa is issued, two application forms, two photos, a company letter, biographic data, a recent annual report of the parent company and a fee for multiple entries. An AIDS test is required for work and residency permits (U.S. test accepted).

American citizens who remain in Papua New Guinea beyond the period authorized by immigration authorities may face fines and penalties. Papua New Guinea collects a departure tax. The departure tax is normally incorporated into airline fares at the time of ticket issuance.

For more information about entry and exit requirements, travelers may contact the Embassy of Papua New Guinea, 1615 New Hampshire Ave., NW, Suite 300, Washington DC 20009, Tel. 202-745-3680, or visit the Embassy's website at http://www.pngembassy.org.

Travelers may also wish to obtain entry permission from the Government of Australia for transit or other purposes (see section on Medical Facilities) before traveling to Papua New Guinea. American citizens no longer need a visa to travel to Australia as tourists but must obtain an Electronic Travel Authority (ETA) through their travel agent. For further information about Australian visas or the ETA, contact the Embassy of Australia in Washington, D.C., at 1-800-242-2878 or at the Embassy of Australia's website at http://www.austemb.org.

**SAFETY AND SECURITY:** Before traveling to Bougainville, the largest island in the North Solomons province, it is recommended that visitors obtain updated security information from the U.S. Embassy in Port Moresby. Despite a peace agreement between the government and dissidents, law enforcement is weak on Bougainville, there are no tourist facilities on the island and transportation facilities are limited.

An Indonesian secessionist group remains active along the largely inaccessible Papua New Guinea/Indonesia border on the island of New Guinea.

The Southern Highlands Province is also an area of instability. Incidents of ethnic violence have occurred near urban centers and tourist sites. American citizens considering travel to the region should consult with their tour operator and the American Embassy prior to doing so.

The town of Rabaul, on the island of New Britain, is located near two active volcanoes that buried half of the town during eruptions in September 1994. Volcanic activity continues, and travelers should be aware of the potential for further eruptions. Persons with respiratory problems may find that airborne ash exacerbates their conditions.

**CRIME:** Papua New Guinea has a high crime rate. Crime and personal security are serious concerns throughout Papua New Guinea. Carjackings, armed robberies, and stoning of vehicles are a problem in Port Moresby, the capital. Pickpockets and bag-snatchers frequent crowded public areas. Hiking in rural areas and visiting isolated public areas such as parks, golf courses, beaches, or cemeteries can be dangerous.

Persons traveling alone are at greater risk for robbery or gang rape than those who are part of an organized tour or under escort. Visitors to Papua New Guinea should avoid using taxis or buses, known as public motor vehicles, and should rely instead on their sponsor or hotel to arrange for taxi service or a rental car.

Travel outside of Port Moresby and other major towns at night can be hazardous, as criminals set up roadblocks. Visitors should consult with the U.S. Embassy or with local law enforcement officials concerning security conditions before driving between towns. Travel to isolated places in Papua New Guinea is possible primarily by small passenger-aircraft; there are many small airstrips throughout the country. Security measures at these airports are rare. Organized tours booked through travel agencies remain the safest means to visit attractions in Papua New Guinea. The Embassy recommends that prospective visitors consult "A Primer on Personal Security for Visitors to Papua New Guinea," available from the Bureau of Consular Affairs homepage at http://travel.state.gov.

The loss or theft abroad of a U.S. passport should be reported immediately to the local police and the nearest U.S. Embassy or Consulate. U.S. citizens may refer to the Department of State's pamphlet *A Safe Trip Abroad* for ways to promote a more trouble-free journey. The pamphlet is available by mail from the Superintendent of Documents, U.S. Government Printing Office, Washington, D.C. 20402, via the Internet at http://www.access.gpo.gov/su_docs, or via the Bureau of Consular Affairs home page at http://travel.state.gov.

**MEDICAL FACILITIES:** Medical facilities in Papua New Guinea vary from hospitals in Port Moresby and the larger towns to aid posts (including some missionary stations) in remote areas. Medical facilities vary in quality, but those in the larger towns are usually adequate for routine problems and some emergencies. Equipment failures and sudden shortages of common medications can mean, however, that even routine treatments and procedures (such as X-rays) may become unavailable. A hyperbaric recompression chamber for diving emergencies is available in Port Moresby. Pharmacies in Papua New Guinea are small and may be inadequately stocked. They are found only in urban centers and at missionary clinics. Doctors and hospitals often expect immediate cash payment for medical services.

Medical conditions arising as a result of diving accidents will almost always require medical evacuation to Australia. More sophisticated medical facilities are located in Australia. The most commonly used facilities are in Brisbane and Cairns, both in the Australian state of Queensland. Travelers who anticipate the need for ongoing medical treatment should obtain entry permission for Australia in advance. Entry permission for Australia can be granted by the Australian Embassy in Port Moresby, but it is easier to obtain prior to leaving the United States.

**MEDICAL INSURANCE:** U.S. medical insurance is not always valid outside the United States. U.S. Medicare and Medicaid programs do not provide payment for medical services outside the United States. Doctors and hospitals often expect immediate cash payment for health services. Uninsured travelers who require medical care overseas may face extreme difficulties.

Check with your own insurance company to confirm whether your policy applies overseas, including provision for medical evacuation, and for adequacy of coverage. Serious medical problems requiring hospitalization and/or medical evacuation to the United States can cost tens of thousands of dollars. Ascertain whether payment will be made to the overseas hospital or doctor or whether you will be reimbursed later for expenses you incur. Some insurance policies also include coverage for psychiatric treatment and for disposition of remains in the event of death.

Useful information on medical emergencies abroad, including overseas insurance programs, is provided in the Department of State's Bureau of Consular Affairs brochure *Medical Information for Americans Traveling Abroad*, available via the Bureau of Consular Affairs home page or autofax: (202) 647-3000.

**OTHER HEALTH INFORMATION:** Information on vaccinations and other health precautions may be obtained from the Centers for Disease Control and Prevention's hotline for international travelers at 1-877-FYI-TRIP (1-877-394-8747); fax 1-888-CDC-FAXX (1-888-232-3299), or via CDC's Internet site at http://www.cdc.gov.

**TRAFFIC SAFETY AND ROAD CONDITIONS:** While in a foreign country, U.S. citizens may encounter road conditions that differ significantly from those in the United States. The information below concerning Papua New Guinea is provided for general reference only, and may not be totally accurate in a particular location or circumstance.

Safety of Public Transportation: Poor
Urban Road Conditions/Maintenance: Poor to Good
Rural Road Conditions/Maintenance: Poor
Availability of Roadside Assistance: Not Available

Traffic in Papua New Guinea moves on the left. Travel on highways outside of major towns can be hazardous. Motor vehicle accidents, especially where passengers are sitting in the open bed of a pickup truck, are one of the more common causes of serious injury in Papua New Guinea. Drivers and passengers are urged to wear seatbelts whenever possible. There is no countrywide road network, roads are generally in poor repair, and flat tires occur routinely as a result of debris on the roadways. Landslides can be a problem on some stretches of the Highlands Highway between Lae and Mount Hagen during the rainy season. Criminal roadblocks have occurred during the day on the Highlands Highway and more widely after dark. Travelers should consult with local authorities or the U.S. Embassy before traveling on the Highlands Highway.

Reactions by crowds after road accidents in Papua New Guinea can be emotional and violent. Crowds form quickly after an accident and may attack those whom they hold responsible, stoning and/or burning their vehicles. Friends and relatives of an injured party may demand immediate compensation from the party they hold responsible for injuries, regardless of legal responsibility. Persons involved in accidents usually find it prudent to proceed directly to the nearest police station rather than stopping at the scene of an accident.

For additional general information about road safety, including links to foreign government sites, see the Department of State, Bureau of Consular Affairs home page at http://travel.state.gov/road_safety.html. For specific information concerning Papua New Guinea driving permits, vehicle inspection, road tax and mandatory insurance, contact the Papua New Guinea Tourism Promotion via the Internet at http://www.paradiselive.org.pg.

**AVIATION SAFETY OVERSIGHT:** As there is no direct commercial air service by local carriers at present, or economic authority to operate such service, between the U.S. and Papua New Guinea, the U.S. Federal Aviation Administration (FAA) has not assessed Papua New Guinea's Civil Aviation Authority for compliance with international aviation safety standards.

For further information, travelers may contact the Department of Transportation within the U.S. at 1-800-322-7873, or visit the FAA's Internet website at http://www.faa.gov/avr/iasa/. The U.S. Department of Defense (DOD) separately assesses some foreign air carriers for suitability as official providers of air services. For information regarding the DOD policy on specific carriers, travelers may contact DOD at (618) 229-4801.

**CUSTOMS REGULATIONS:** Papua New Guinea customs authorities may enforce strict regulations concerning temporary importation into or export from Papua New Guinea of items such as firearms, certain prescription drugs and sexually explicit material. Other products may be subject to quarantine. It is advisable to contact the Embassy of Papua New Guinea in Washington for specific information regarding customs requirements.

**CRIMINAL PENALTIES:** While in a foreign country, a U.S. citizen is subject to that country's laws and regulations, which sometimes differ significantly from those in the United States and may not afford the protections available to the individual under U.S. law. Penalties for breaking the law can be more severe than in the United States for similar offenses. Persons violating the Papua New Guinea law, even unknowingly, may be expelled, arrested or imprisoned. Penalties for possession, use, or trafficking in illegal drugs in Papua New Guinea are strict, and convicted offenders can expect severe jail sentences and fines.

**CONSULAR ACCESS:** U.S. citizens are encouraged to carry a copy of their U.S. passports with them at all times, so that, if questioned by local officials, proof of identity and U.S. citizenship are readily available.

**DISASTER PREPAREDNESS:** Papua New Guinea is located in an area of high seismic activity. Although the probability of a major earthquake occurring during an individual trip is remote, earthquakes can and will continue to happen. In addition, there are two active volcanoes near the town of Rabaul on New Britain. General information regarding disaster preparedness is available via the Internet from the U.S. Federal Emergency Management Agency (FEMA) home page at http://www.fema.gov.

**CHILDREN'S ISSUES:** For information on international adoption of children or international parental child abduction, please refer to our Internet site at http://travel.state.gov/children's_issues.html or telephone (202) 736-7000.

**REGISTRATION/EMBASSY LOCATION:** U.S. citizens are encouraged to register at the Consular Section of the U.S. Embassy in Port Moresby and obtain updated information on travel and security within Papua New Guinea. The U.S. Embassy is located at Douglas Street, Port Moresby, Papua New Guinea. This address should be used for courier service deliveries. The Embassy is located adjacent to the Bank of Papua New Guinea. The mailing address is P.O. Box 1492, Port Moresby, N.C.D. 121, Papua New Guinea. The U.S. Embassy's telephone number is (675) 321-1455; fax (675) 321-1593. Americans may submit consular inquiries via e-mail to: consularportmoresby@state.gov.

# BUSINESS CUSTOMS

The workday is 8:00 a.m. to 4:30 p.m. Monday to Friday for most people. Banks are open from 9:00 a.m. until 2:00 p.m. from Monday to Thursday and from 9:00 a.m. to 5:00 p.m. on Fridays. Most business and government offices do not open on the weekends.

Business dress is moderately casual, befitting PNG's tropical climate. Work attire usually consists of shirt and tie or sport shirt for men, and light business suit or dress for women. In most areas, lightweight clothing is appropriate year round, but warmer clothes may be necessary in the Highlands, especially in the evening.

# IMPORTANT INFO FOR TRAVEL

### TRAVEL ADVISORY AND VISAS

Entry Requirements: Tourists may obtain a 60-day visa for K10 (about US$ 7.50) at a Papua New Guinea diplomatic mission or for K25 (less than US$ 20) upon arrival at Port Moresby International Airport. The visa can only be obtained upon presentation of an onward air ticket and evidence of funds sufficient for the proposed stay. Business travellers must apply at a Papua New Guinea diplomatic mission to obtain a business visa. The one-year visa allows multiple entries not exceeding 60 days per visit and costs K250 (about US$ 190).

Travellers may also wish to obtain a visa for Australia before travelling to PNG. Australia began participating in the Visa Waiver Pilot Program with the U.S. in July 1996. However, depending on the carrier, Australian visas may be required for U.S. citizens whose travel to Australia originates in PNG. Travellers who anticipate the need for on-going, routine, or other forms of medical treatment in Australia are advised to obtain visas for Australia before leaving the United States. Australian visas are issued in Port Moresby, but in a case involving medical treatment the Australian visa authorities will require a referral from a local doctor, proof of acceptance by an Australian doctor, and proof of the patient's ability to pay for treatment. For information on Australian visa requirements, contact an Australian diplomatic mission.

Information on Crime: Crime and personal security are serious concerns in PNG. Armed robberies and carjackings are a problem in Port Moresby and other urban areas. Armed robbery is sometimes accompanied by gratuitous violence. Criminals often target persons who are part of large crowds. There is a danger of rape, including gang rape, in many urban and rural areas of PNG. Women should not walk alone in PNG, especially at night. Travellers to PNG should avoid using taxis or buses and should rely instead on a sponsor or on a rented car for transportation. Travel outside of Port Moresby by car at night can be hazardous. Holdups at roadblocks have been known to occur day or night on the Highlands Highway. Reactions to road accidents involving fatalities or serious injuries can be emotional and violent, regardless of legal responsibility. Persons involved in accidents should proceed to the police station in the provincial capital.

A curfew has been in force in Port Moresby and the Central Province since November 9, 1996. A nationwide curfew, which includes Port Moresby and the Central Province, took effect from June 11 to August 11, 1997 to help ensure a trouble-free election period. It is possible that the curfew will again be extended in the Port Moresby. Travellers to PNG should contact the Embassy for advice on the current curfew status. While the curfew is in effect, all persons are required to remain indoors from 10 p.m. through 4 a.m. The curfew is strictly enforced.

**STATUTORY HOLIDAYS**

**NEW YEAR'S DAY JANUARY 1**
**GOOD FRIDAY VARIABLE**
**EASTER SATURDAY VARIABLE**
**EASTER MONDAY VARIABLE**
**QUEEN'S BIRTHDAY MID-JUNE**
**PROVINCIAL GOVERNMENT DAY JULY 19**
**(OBSERVED 7/18/97)**
**REMEMBRANCE DAY JULY 23**
**(OBSERVED 7/21/97)**
**INDEPENDENCE DAY SEPTEMBER 16**
**CHRISTMAS DAY DECEMBER 25**
**BOXING DAY DECEMBER 26**
**BUSINESS INFRASTRUCTURE**

Language: English is the official language of government and commerce and will be spoken by almost all people with whom the business traveller is likely to deal. However, the language understood by the majority of Papua New Guineans is Melanesian Pidgin.

Currency: No restrictions are placed on bringing U.S. dollars into or out of PNG. Letters of credit, travellers' checks, U.S. currency, and personal checks drawn on U.S banks are freely negotiable. PNG uses a decimal currency system; the units are kina and toea (100 toea = 1 kina).

Health: Most serious endemic diseases are not a problem in PNG. Malaria, however, is endemic to the area and includes coroquine-
resistant strains. Seek medical advice prior to arrival for recommended precautions. There are hospitals in Port Moresby and in the larger towns. Medical facilities vary in quality, but in the larger towns generally are adequate for routine problems and some emergencies. Equipment failures, shortages of common medications, and reductions in services due to lack of government funding can mean, however, that even routine treatments and procedures are sometimes unavailable. The nearest reliable medical facilities are located in the Australian town of Cairns in North Queensland, a 1 1/2 hour flight from Port Moresby. Medevac flight services are available.

Communications: International telephone, telegraph, telex, internet, and facsimile services are available. International telecommunications and postal services are reasonably reliable.

Transportation: PNG is served by an international airport at Port Moresby and over 400 other airports and airstrips throughout the country. Air Niugini, the national carrier, operates scheduled domestic cargo and passenger services within PNG and international services to Australia, Indonesia (Jayapura, Irian Jaya), Solomon Islands, Manila, Singapore and Hong Kong. Several smaller carriers offer scheduled domestic service and charters. Qantas flies regularly to Port Moresby from Sydney, Brisbane and Cairns. Milne Bay Air recently inaugurated a passenger service from Port Moresby to Cairns and Townsville, Australia. Rental cars are available in the major towns. Traffic moves on the left, as in the United Kingdom. Bus service exists in the few areas where there are connecting roads but is not recommended. The longest road is the Highlands Highway from Lae to Mendi. There are no railroads.

Housing: There are hotels of moderate to good quality in Port Moresby and other major towns. Suitable Western-style residential and business premises are available in urban areas. Rental rates are high due to the shortage of land available for lease.

Food: Supermarkets stock a wide variety of fresh foods and groceries. There are several good restaurants in Port Moresby and other major towns.

# IMPORTANT INFORMATION: VISAS

**ENTRY PERMITS (FOR EMPLOYMENT PURPOSES)**

These procedures are a guide to all employers recruiting non-citizens for employment purposes and for prospective employees who wish to obtain an entry permit for employment.

**PNG position Approval and Work Permit Requirement**

The Employment of Non Citizen's Act Chapter 374 and Fourth Edition Work Permit Guidelines prescribe that subject tot he receipt of a satisfactory Training and Localization Programme in the context of a Three Year training plan, approval will be granted to a company or an employer to recruit non-citizens to fill certain positions.

The approval by the Department of Industrial Relations (DIR) of a position to be held by a non-citizen is valid for up to three years.

The non-citizen also must obtain a valid work permit from the DIR before entry to PNG.

**Immigration Requirements for Entry to PNG for Employment**

In addition to DIR requirements the prospective employee must meet immigration requirements. To enter PNG the employee must obtain a valid and appropriate entry permit.

**How to Obtain a Entry Permit for Employment: What the Employer Has to Do**

**The employee must provide:**

a written sponsorship letter to the ICD indicating the job offer to the employee highlighting person's name, position number, position title, period of contract approved by the DIR, salary range and a company guarantee of accommodation and transportation for the employee and dependents.
an original maintenance guarantee bond/s for the employee/applicant and dependents.
copy of the work permit approval letter from the DIR for employment of the applicant in the approved position.
an Immigration Fee for an entry permit for employment purposes and appropriate dependent entry permit fees are to be paid by the employer/agent in PNG. Fees are to be paid tot he Department of Finance Cash Office, Bureau of Management Services or nearest Customs Office and receipts are to be given as evidence of payment to ICD. See Schedule 1 for appropriate fees.
the overseas Mission at which the applicant will apply for the entry permit.
What the Employee Has To Do

The prospective employee is to complete an entry permit application and forward/deliver it to the nearest PNG Overseas Mission or if there is no PNG presence the nearest Australian Overseas Mission.

The Entry Permit Application will require the applicant to provide full personal particulars of the applicant and his/her dependents (if any, whether travelling/not travelling as below:

Full Name
Date of Birth
Marital Status
Citizenship Status during last ten (10) years
What Does It Cost?

A fee of K50 (US$52.00) is also payable to cover facsimile and telephone costs incurred in facilitating issue of the permit.

**Processing of the Application**

Once the employee completes the entry permit application, details of the application will be sent to the Immigration and Citizenship Division (ICD) in Port Moresby who will consider issue of an entry Permit for the non-citizen.

At the same time, the DIR in Port Moresby will consider the employer's application to employ the applicant against the approved position. If the DIR accepts the application, a work permit approval will be sent to the employer and notification to ICD.

Once the overseas Mission has the ICD approval to issue an Entry Permit, an entry permit with work permit number included will be issued. The permit will be issued for a maximum of three (3) years subject to the applicant's passport also being valid for the three year period. Should the passport expire before the three year period, the entry permit will only be issued for the period of validity of the passport. When the applicant obtains a new passport, ICD Port Moresby will issue an entry permit for the balance of the three year period. This new entry permit will be issued without charge.

An extension to a work permit beyond the three year limit is also possible. Please read the procedures for entry permit extension.

**CHANGE OF STATUS**

From/To Dependant's entry Permit (Foreign Employee)

A dependant spouse of a foreign employee ma be allowed to work in PNG after the DIR has assessed the labor market situation and upon receipt of authentic documents in relations o the qualifications and experience of the dependent.

In order to work, a work permit is required from the DIR and the status of the spouse's entry must be changed from "Employment Prohibited" to an employment entry permit. ICD will issue an employment entry permit for the applicant for the period of contract regardless of whether the principal applicant's entry permit expires at an earlier date. It is possible for the principal applicant, at the expiry of his/her contract/entry permit, to seek change of status from "employment" to "dependant" and remain in PNG with his/her spouse.

Persons arriving in PNG on visitor and business entry permits are not permitted to change status to employment.

**How to Apply**

To change entry permit status from dependant to employment the dependant must complete a Request For Entry Permit Extension form with a copy of the DIR work permit. To change entry permit status from employment to dependant, the application must also complete the relevant sections of a Request for Entry permit Extension form, submit details of the employment of his/her spouse and provide his/her passport and also that of the spouse.

**Dependant of Citizen**

A dependant (with foreign nationality) of a PNG citizen may engage in employment in PNG if:

he/she has a DIR work permit and
the appropriate change of status fee and employment entry permitfee are paid (change of status refers to

change of status from dependant to working resident).
Change of Marital Status

A person who whilst in PNG changes marital status detailed on their entry permit is required to apply for change of entry permit status. The applicant must provide ICD with proof of marital status change i.e. marriage or divorce papers and ICD will re-issue the entry permit accordingly.

**What is the fee?**

The cost for a change of marital status is K500 (US$512.50)

**Change of Name/Change of Employer Name**

Where a person changes his/her name by Deed Pole etc or where the name of the company which employs the person changes, the Immigration Regulations require that a change of name be effected on the entry permit. Details of the change of name have to be furnished to ICD and the entry permit will be reissued accordingly.

**What is the fee?**

The cost for a change of name/change of employer name is K500 (US$512.50)

**Change of Contractual Commitment/Status**

Persons in the following categories must seek a change of entry permit status:

who resign from their position and find alternative employment.
whose contract expires and find alternative employment.
People whose contracts expire and are extended in their current position or in another position in the same company do not require a change of status.

The above change of status is usually undertaken in conjunction with an application for an entry permit extension. See entry permit extension guidelines.

**What does it cost?**

The cost for a change of contractual commitment/status is K500 (US$512.50)

**Penalties**

A penalty of K5,000 (US$5,125.00)is payable in respect of failure to obtain an appropriate entry permit for employment and residence purposes and failure to apply for appropriate change of status.

**ENTRY PERMIT EXTENSION FOR EMPLOYMENT PURPOSES**

These procedures are a guide to all employers, agents and/or non-citizen employees requesting entry permit extension for employment or defendants purposes.

**When Does An Entry Permit Need Extension?**

An Entry Permit needs to be extended if the employee is required to continue in the same position beyond the expiry date of his/her initial (entry permits are usually issued for three years) and the DIR issues the necessary work permit.

Entry permits also need to be extended where the employee changes positions in the company or finds alternative employment i.e. changes employers.

**When Can't An Entry Permit Be Extended?**

**Entry permits cannot be extended where:**

the DIR has not issued the appropriate work permit for the position occupied.
for an unmarried child with a dependant entry permit reaches the age of sixteen (6) years. When the child attains sixteen year of age he/she must leave PNG unless he/she is enrolled in academic study in PNG. If the child is enrolled in academic study in PNG, then a student entry permit will be issued. For children over 16 years and not enrolled in study in PNG, future visits would normally occur under sixty day Tourist Entry Permit arrangements.
How To Obtain An Entry Permit Extension

**What The Employer Has To Do**

**The Employer must provide to ICD:**

the job offer to the employee highlighting person's name, position number, position title, period of contract approved by the DIR, salary range and a company guarantee of accommodation and transportation for the employee and defendants.
copy of the DIR work permit approval letter for the person to be employed in the position.
an original maintenance guarantee bond/s for the employee/applicant and defendants.
a copy of the changeof status (if appropriate) and entry permit extension fee receipt is to be attached.

**What the Employee Has To Do**

The applicant must complete a "Request to Extend Period of Validity of an Entry Permit Form" and submit it to ICD together with his/her passport and those of any defendants.

**Rates For Entry Permit Extensions**

The cost for extension of an Entry Permit for Employment is K500 (US$512.50). It should be noted that a fee for change of status is also applicable where the applicant changes employers of class/types e.g. from dependant to working resident.

The fee for each dependant entry permit extended is K20 (US20.50)

**What Penalties Apply?**

A penalty of K500 (US$512.50) applies to late application for entry permit extension. Breaches on the Migration Act attract a penalty of K5,000 (US$5,125.00).

**BUSINESS PERSON/INVESTOR ENTRY PERMIT**

These procedures are a guide to all persons who wish to invest in PNG establish companies and seek an entry permit as an owner/operator or senior executive.

How To Obtain A Entry Permit For Business Person/Investor

**What the Investor Has To Do**

The investor has to invest a minimum of K150,000 (US$153,750) in PNG in a company or business. The K150,000 (US$153,750) must be transferred into PNG and not derived through loans raised with PNG banks. The investment may be by way of cash investment in plant and equipment or a combination of plant/equipment and annual salaries (including annual superannuation) of PNG staff and approved expatriate staff salaries/fees/superannuation paid to the investor or his/her immediate family cannot be included as part of the K150,000 (US$153,750) investment.

The investor also has to seek a position and work permit from the DIR.

**The investor must:**

provide a letter to ICD indicating his/her name, position number, position title, period of contract approved by the DIR and salary range.
documentary evidence that the K150,000 (US$153,750)investment has been transferred into the country and a copy of the Investment Promotion Authority (IPA) approval letter and share/registration certificate.
copy of work permit approval letter in respect of the position from the DIR.
For entry permits for employment purposes and dependant, K250.00 (US$256.25) and K10.00 (US$10.25) are respectively required.
Fees are to be paid to the Department of Finance Cash Office. Bureau of Management Services or nearest Customs Office and receipts are to be given as evidence of payment to ICD.
complete an Entry Permit Application form and forward it to the ICD of the Department of Foreign Affairs and Trade.
Processing of the Application

The ICD in Port Moresby will consider issue of an Entry Permit for the non-citizen. If the applicant meets the criteria and a work permit has been issued by the DIR, any entry permit will be issued.

The applicant need not depart PNG in order to receive the entry permit i.e. a change of status in entry permit category may be effected in PNG at a cost of K500 (US$512.50). An extension of the entry permit beyond an initial three year limit is also possible. Please read the procedures for entry permit extension.

**Dependant Entry Permits**

Entry permits for defendants are also available in the same manner as permits are issued to defendants of applicants for employment entry permits.

**Extension of Entry Permits**

An entry permit extension can be obtained in accordance with the fees and procedures outlined for Entry Permit Extension for Employment purposes.

**BUSINESS ENTRY PERMIT**

These procedures are a guide to all business people and agents requesting business entry permits.

**What is a Business Entry Permit?**

A Business Entry Permit permits a person to enter PNG to conduct business as a distinct from undertaking employment. Business Entry Permits are valid for a maximum of sixty (60) days per entry and are valid for twelve (12) months from date of issue. As such, business entry permits are multiple entry.

**When is a Business Entry Permit Required?**

Business activity encompasses such things as checking on investments, investigating business opportunities, holding meetings with suppliers/buyers, signing contracts, attending board meetings, etc. If a person engages in any of the above activities, a maximum entry business permit is required. A Tourist Entry

Permit is not appropriate if the above activities are undertaken. Heavy penalties apply for engaging in business without having a business entry permit.

**Where To Apply**

Application for permits may be made at PNG Overseas Missions or if there is no PNG presence, the nearest Australian Overseas Mission. Application may also be made on arrival at Jackson's International Airport in Port Moresby.

**How To Apply**

The procedures below are to obtain multiple entry business permits for Papua New Guinea. These procedures apply both to applications lodged overseas and those lodged on arrival in Port Moresby.

The application must complete a "Request for entry Permit" (Form 1).
A covering letter from the sponsor detailing why the applicant is coming to Papua New Guinea and the expected number and length of visits is to be provided. Note that a sponsor letter is required in order to obtain a business entry permit on arrival.
Evidence of return tickets from Papua New Guinea must be supplied.
Payment of the Migration Service Fee of K250 (US$256.25) must be made.
An extension of up to thirty (30) days maybe granted in exceptional cases to the sixty (60) days entry period by application to the Minister of the Department of Foreign Affairs and Trade and payment of K200 (US$205.00). Such applications must provide:
documentary evidence that the applicant still has business to complete in Papua New Guinea.
reasons why it could not be completed within the sixty (60) days period.
A dependant of the applicant may enter PNG under a visitor entry permit upon payment of the fee listed in Schedule 1.
What Penalties Apply?

A penalty of K1,000 (US$1,025.00)applies to any breach of conditions and requirements for business entry permits.

**SHORT TERM ATTACHMENT ENTRY PERMITS**

These procedures are a guide to persons seeking short term attachment entry permits for Papua New Guinea.

**What is a Short Term Attachment?**

A Short Term Attachment refers to situations where a person wishes to enter PNG for a period of not more than three months and undertake a work assignment.

**What are the Restrictions on Such Employment?**

Entry to PNG for short term attachment is only possible in respect of positions approved by the DIR. Short term attachments include, such activities as performing short work assignments (e.g. conduct a company audit, performance reviews, repair/commission equipment, train staff in new systems/procedures, etc) and relief duties.

Entry is only possible where there is a valid reason for the short term attachment. In this respect, employers are not permitted to employ non-citizens on a temporary basis while the permanent occupant is absent on either sick leave or recreation leave without first obtaining the written approval of the DIR. Approval will only be given by DIR where the occupation is classed as professional i.e. doctors, accountants, managers, lawyers, engineers, etc. In all other cases national employees who are qualified and experienced, or understudying non-citizen counterparts, are to assume full responsibilities for such positions during temporary absences of nominal occupants.

**Are Dependant Entry Permits Available?**

Dependant Entry Permits are not issued for short term attachments. Dependants may enter PNG as visitors and receive a 60 day entry permit. Visitor permits are available from PNG Missions overseas or on arrival at Jacksons International Airport in Port Moresby at the cost K25 (US$25.63). A visitor entry permit may be extended for a further 30 days upon application to the Minister of Foreign Affairs and Trade and payment of K50 (US$51.25).

**What are the Procedures for Application?**

The applicant must complete an Application for Entry Permit detailing the reason for requesting a short term entry and have a confirmed return air ticket.
The employer must submit details of the DIR approved position to the Immigration and Citizenship Division in Port Moresby.
Where can Applications be Lodged?

Applications may be lodged at any PNG Overseas Mission or where there is no PNG presence, the nearest Australian Mission.

**How is the Application Processed?**

The PNG Overseas Mission will refer details of the application to ICD for decision. ICD will consider the application and advise the Mission of approval or rejection. The Mission will then issue the necessary entry permit.

**What is the Fee?**

The fee for a short term attachment entry permit is K250 (US$256.25).

**What Penalty Applies for Overstay?**

Heavy penalties apply for overstay of entry permits. It is the responsibility of the permit holder to ensure that he/she leaves the country on or before the date that his/her entry permits expires. If the permit holder is unable to leave on/before the due date it is his/her responsibility to contact the Director of Entries, ICD to explain the circumstances.

If the permit holder fails to contact the ICD and he/she overstays the entry permit, a penalty of K5,000 (US$5,125.00) applies.

**CONSULTANT/SPECIALIST ENTRY PERMIT**

These procedures are a guide for consultants/specifies wishing to enter PNG.

**What is a Consultant/Specialist Entry Permit?**

A Consultant/Specialist Entry Permit allows entry of a person to PNG for consultancy/specialist work for not more than three months.

**What Restrictions Apply on Such Employment?**

Persons entering under this category of entry permit are permitted to enter PNG only once per calendar year. The consultant/specialist must have a PNG sponsor.

**What are the Procedures for Application?**

The applicant must complete an Application for Entry Permit detailing the reason for requesting a permit and have a confirmed return air ticket.
The PNG sponsor must submit details of the requirement for the consultancy/specialist assistance in writing to the ICD in Port Moresby.
Are Dependant Entry permits Available?

Dependant Entry Permits are not issued in respect of this category of entry permit. Dependants may enter PNG as visitors and receive a 60 day entry permit. Visits permits may be obtained overseas or on arrival at Jacksons International Airport in Port Moresby for the costs of K10 (US$10.25). A visitor entry permit may be extended for a further 30 days upon application to the Minister of Foreign Affairs and Trade and payment of K50 (US$51.25).

**Where can Applications be Lodged?**

Applications may be lodged at any PNG Overseas Mission or where thee is no PNG presence, the nearest Australian Mission.

**How is the Application Processed?**

The PNG Overseas Mission will refer details of the application to ICD for decision. ICD will consider the application and advise the Mission of approval or rejection. The Mission will then issue the necessary entry permit.

**What is the Fee?**

The fee for a consultancy/specialist entry permit is K250 (US$256.25).

**What Penalty Applies for Overstay?**

Heavy penalties apply for overstay of entry permits. It is the responsibility of the permit holder to ensure that he/she leaves the country on or before the date that his/her entry permit expires. If the permit holder is unable to leave on/before the due date, it is his/her responsibility to contact the Director of Entries, ICD to explain the circumstances.

If the permit holder fails to contact ICD and he/she overstays the entry permit, a penalty of K5,000 (US$5,125.00).

**DEPENDANTS OF PNG CITIZENS**

Dependants of citizens may enter PNG and reside as non-working or working residents.

**Where to Apply?**

Application for entry permits may be made at PNG Overseas Mission or where there is no PNG presence or the nearest Australian overseas Mission.

**How to Apply**

To reside in PNG as a non working resident, the following information must be provided to ICD or the PNG Mission.

a letter from the applicant's spouse (i.e. the PNG citizen) outlining the personal particulars of the applicant and providing a copy of the marriage certificate (or birth certificate for children).
payment of a landing bond (equivalent tot he cost of return airfare for the dependant/s) and a copy of the receipt.

payment of the appropriate immigration fee of K10 (US$10.25).
To resident in PNG as a working resident, the following information must be provided to ICD or the PNG Mission.

information/receipts as per a non-working resident.
a work permit from the DIR. See procedures for obtaining an employment entry permit. In certain circumstances, a spouse can obtain a letter from the Minister for the DIR exempting him/her from the provisions of the Employment of Non-Citizens Act i.e. exempting the person from the need to obtain a work permit. This letter is accepted by ICD in lieu of a work permit.
payment of an immigration fee for an employment entry permit (instead of a dependant of citizen entry fee). It should be noted that dependants of citizens who initially enter PNG as non working spouses and subsequently seek employment are required to pay not only the fee for an employment entry permit but also pay for a change of status.

**TOURIST ENTRY PERMITS**

These procedures are a guide to all tourist requesting tourist entry permits.

**Where to Apply**

Application for permits may be made a PNG Overseas Missions or where there is no PNG presence, the nearest Australian Overseas Mission or Jacksons International Airport, Port Moresby. Tourist Entry Permits are valid for sixty (60) days.

**How to Apply**

The procedures below are to be followed to obtain tourist entry permits for Papua New Guinea.

The applicant must complete a "Request for Entry Permit" (Form 1).
Evidence of return tickets from Papua New Guinea must be supplied.
Payment of the Migration Service Fee of K10 (US$10.25) must be made if the application is lodged at a PNG or Australian Overseas Mission. where an entry permit application is made on arrival at Jacksons International Airport in Port Moresby, payment of K25 (US$25.63), in local currency, is required. It should be noted that while entry permits for visitors will be issued on arrival, this process obviously takes more time than for passengers with permits. For this reason, it is advisable to obtain entry permits before arrival in PNG.
What is the Fee?

The cost for a Tourist Visa is K10.00 ($ 10.25)

**Tourist Entry Permit Extensions**

The sixty (6) days entry permit may be extended by a maximum of thirty (30) days by application tot he Minister of Foreign Affairs and Trade. The procedure is as follows:

The Applicant must complete a Request to Extend Period of Validity of an Entry Permit, Form 3.
The applicant must provide evidence of payment of the Migration Service Fee of K50 (US$51.25) for Permit Extensions i.e. a copy of the receipt paid to the Department of Finance Cash Office, Bureau of Management Services or nearest Customs Office.

**TOURIST YACHTSMAN ENTRY PERMIT**

Special entry permits are issued for yachtsmen (owner/captain of yacht) and are valid for 60 days. an extension of 30 days is possible upon application tot he Minister for Foreign Affairs and Trade.

The crew of yachts are treated as visitors and are provided with Tourist Entry Permits valid for 60 days. An extension of 30 days is possible upon application to the Minister of Foreign Affairs and Trade.

**Where Can Entry Permits for Yachtsmen be Obtained?**

They can be obtained at PNG Overseas Missions or where there is no PNG presence, the nearest Australian Overseas Mission, on arrival in PNG from any Customs Office or at the ICD in Port Moresby.

**How Much Do they Cost?**

The costs for Entry Permits for Yachtsmen (owner/captain) is K100.00 (US$103.00) whilst the Crew of Yacht is K10.00 (US$10.25)

**What Penalties Apply?**

A penalty of K500 (US$512.50) applies to late application for entry permit renewals and a penalty of K5,000 (US$5,125.00) applies for breaches of the Migration Act.

**ENTRY PERMITS FOR OTHER CATEGORIES**

**JOURNALIST/REPORTERS**

Special entry permits are necessary for journalists/reporters wishing to enter PNG and are valid for 60 days.

**How to Apply**

The applicant must complete an entry permit application and attach a letter of confirmation from the Institute of Papua New Guinea Studies.

**Where to Apply**

Application may be made through a PNG overseas Mission or where thee is no PNG presence, the nearest Australian overseas Mission. Applicants may also be made direct with the ICD of the Department of Foreign Affairs and Trade.

**Are Dependant Entry Permits Available?**

Dependent Entry Permits are not issued in respect of this category of entry permit. Dependants may enter PNG as visitors and receive a 60 day entry permit. Visitor Permit costs K10.00 (US$10.25). A visitor entry permit may be extended for a further 30 days upon submission of application to the Minister of Foreign Affairs and Trade and payment of K50.00 (US$51.25) is applied.

**How Much Do Entry Permits Costs?**

Costs for Entry Permits for journalists/reporters is K100.00 (US$103.00). A thirty day extension will cost K200 (US$205.00).

**ENTERTAINERS**

Entry Permits for commercial entertainers for 60 days are available at a cost listed by category as follows: Comedian (Commercial) K250.00 (US$256.25); Musician (Commercial) K250.00 (US$256.25).

Applicants must complete an entry permit application and have a letter from the event organizer providing details of the event and expected length of stay. Entry Permits for dependants are issued under visitor entry permit provisions.

**FILM MAKERS (COMMERCIAL)**

Entry Permits are available for commercial filmmakers for 60 days at the cost of K500 (US$512.50).

The applicant must complete an entry permit application and produce a letter from the Institute of PNG Studies indicating its approval tot he project and expected length of stay. Entry permits for dependants are issued under visitor entry permit provisions.

**GOSPEL AND CULTURAL EXCHANGE GROUPS**

Entry Permits are available to the above groups at the cost of K10 (US$ 10.25)

for Gospel Group (Charity), K10 (US$ 10.25) for Cultural Exchange (Charity) and K10 (US$ 10.25) for Dependant (considered as tourist)

Gospel groups require a letter from the sponsoring religious organization or performance event organizer providing details of the event and the expected length of stay. Cultural groups require a letter from the Institute of PNG Studies indicating its agreement to the exchange or a letter from the event organizer providing details of the exchange and expected length of stay. In either case, an entry permit application must be completed.

**OCCUPATIONAL TRAINEES**

Entry Permits for foreign cadets and trainees are available at the cost of K10 (US$10.25). Applicants must complete an entry permit application and have a letter from the educational institution or sponsoring organization providing details of the course of study and the expected length of stay. A maintenance guarantee for the costs of repatriating the trainee at the end of their course must also be provided by the sponsoring organization.

**STUDENT/FORMAL EDUCATION**

Entry Permits will be issued to student applicants undertaking full time study in Papua New Guinea. The fee for this type of entry permit is K10 (US$10.25). Student applicants must complete an entry permit application and present a copy of a letter from the educational institution or sponsoring organization providing details of the course of study and the expected length of stay. Confirmation of acceptance into the course must be provided.

**Penalties Applicable to the Above Categories**

A penalty of K5,000 (US$5,125.00) applies to breaches of the Migration Act in respect of the above categories.

**SPECIAL EXEMPTION ENTRY PERMITS**

Multiple Entry Permits for periods of one to five years may be granted to the following categories of persons. The cost of an entry permit is K10 (US$10.25) with the exception of the Melanesian Spearhead Group (MSG) member countries category which is gratis and the diplomatic category which is gratis if the country in question reciprocates for PNG diplomatic staff:

resident or accredited diplomats of foreign governments and international organizations.
nationals of MSG countries (Solomon Islands, Vanuatu, and FLNKS) and Fiji nationals.

church workers engaged in pastoral duties and Mission volunteers not engaged in business activities of a church. Such workers are required to be employed in positions approved by the DIR for foreign occupancy.
volunteers/aid workers from overseas agencies working directly with the PNG community. These volunteers require a sponsor letter detailing work to be performed and the expected length of stay. They are required to be employed in positions approved by the DIR.
Volunteers from overseas on secondment to PNG agencies. These volunteers require a sponsor letter and are required to be employed in positions approved by the DIR. In addition they must obtain a work permit from the DIR.
foreign aid personnel from approved organizations as per the aid Status Act.
personnel from approved research or educational institutions from abroad. Foreign academics working in PNG are required to be employed in positions approved by the DIR for foreign employment.
employees of foreign governments.
researchers/film makers (non commercial).
dependants of the above categories of exempt persons.

**Where to Apply**

Application may be made through any PNG Overseas Mission or where there is no PNG presence, the nearest Australian Overseas Mission. Applications may also be made direct with the ICD of the Department of Foreign Affairs and Trade.

**Papua New Guinea Citizens**

Download Current Immigration Guidelines
Application for New Papua New Guinea Passport
Renewal of Papua New Guinea Passport

**Non-Papua New Guinea Citizens**

Entry Requirements for Business Visa
Requirements for Short-Term Visas (other than tourism and business)
Entry Requirements for Tourist/Visitors Visa
Visa on Arrival
Visa obtained on Post
Long-Term Entry Requirements

**APPLICATION FOR NEW P.N.G PASSPORT**

Please send the following:

Completed new passport application forms (2)
Processing fee of $31.00 per applicant
Three (3) Passport size photographs
Mailing fee to/from Papua New Guinea via Express Mail $44.00
Birth Certificate
Marriage Certificate (if applicable)
Note:
Your application will be sent to the Department of Foreign Affairs Immigration and Citizenship Division.
Your new Papua New Guinea passport will be sent directly to your home address after it is processed.

**RENEWAL OF PAPUA NEW GUINEA PASSPORT**

Please send the following:

Expired Papua New Guinea passport
Completed new passport application forms
Processing fee of $31.00 per applicant

Passport size photographs (3)
Return stamped address envelope (Federal Express, Express Mail or Certified Mail)
Note:

Processing time is 3 - 5 days upon receipt of application.

**ENTRY REQUIREMENTS FOR BUSINESS VISA**

Valid passport (must be valid at least one year from the date visa is issued)
Application form with 1 passport photo.
Brief report on PNG-based company or on-going Business in Papua New Guinea;
Recent annual report of parent company.
Complete bio-data of the applicant.
Self-addressed stamped envelope either certified, express mail or Federal Express (if visa is obtained by mail)
Company letter (endorsing/indicating exact purpose of business).
Travel itinerary or copy of ticket.
Visa Fee: multiple entry - $256.25
(Money order or company check payable to the Embassy of Papua New Guinea)

PERSONAL CHECKS OR CASH NOT ACCEPTABLE

Multiple entry visa is valid for one (1) year, with eight (8) weeks maximum stay each visit.

(*)Extension to period of each visit not exceeding thirty (30) days may be granted upon production of supporting documents and subject to Ministerial approval. Fee: $205.00

Dependent of Business Visitor Fee: $10.25

Extension to period of visit for Dependent of Business visitor may be granted subject to (*) above. Fee: $51.25

Upon receipt of all the required documents your visa will be processed within three (3) to seven (7) working days.

All items on the application form must be completed/signed. Failure to do so will result in return of your visa application.

Revised Migration & Citizenship Policies
Effective March 5, 1996

**REQUIREMENTS FOR SHORT-TERM VISAS OTHER THAN TOURISM AND BUSINESS**

All applicants for Medical Elective, Research, Short Term Consultancy, Volunteer,(see separate section for Journalist & media) are advised to take note of the following important information.

It is very important that approval for all above categories of visas are obtained from Immigration in Port Moresby before visas are issued at this Embassy.

This is necessary to ensure that integration into the rural people of researchers is done with the knowledge of the local authorities to avoid indiscriminate interference with the people's lives.

It is also to ensure that visitors into the country have a genuine interest in the lives and culture of the traditional life of Papua New Guinea in carrying out their programme.

**Journalist and Film Makers**

All applications for the above two (2) categories require the approval of the Secretary of Foreign Affairs, through the Assistant Secretary, Media and Information Branch, Department of Foreign Affairs, P.O. Wards Strip, Waigani.

Telephone: (675) 271260
Fax: 254467
Telex: NE 22136 FOREIGN
NE 22194 FOREIGN

The request for approval to enter Papua New Guinea should be sought in advance of the request for visa being presented at the Embassy.Any tourist writers travelling on the invitation of a tourist agent in Papua New Guinea, or on behalf of a tour agent in the United States or Canada, must submit the letter of invitation and their itinerary for consideration.

**Procedures**

When visas for above are requested, they should be done with a knowledge of an agency in Papua New Guinea. The agency in Papua New Guinea having established where the visit will take place and the purpose of the visit, should formally request for the visa from the Immigration Division, Department of Foreign Affairs, Waigani, PNG. Telex: NE 22377. On the basis of this request from the local authority, approval will then be telexed to the Embassy to issue the visa.

It is also advisable that applications should be accompanied by a copy of their research or programme proposal, as well as a copy of the letter to the Immigration Division from a local authority. This is necessary for the Embassy staff to know if approval for visa requests are delayed.

**Important**

It is therefore important for all interested persons to ensure that a copy of a letter from the Papua New Guinea agency is submitted with the passport and the applications for visa, for speedy processing and to avoid unnecessary delays.

The process of request and approval for visas sometimes takes up to 6 months if members of the public are not familiar with the procedures.

**VISA FEES:**

Entertainer (Commercial) $256.25/passport
Film Maker (Commercial) $512.50/passport
Journalist/Reporter $102.50/passport
(Extension of 30 days) $205.00/passport

**ENTRY REQUIREMENTS FOR TOURIST/VISITORS VISA**

**VISA ON ARRIVAL**

Citizens of the following countries intending to travel to PNG for tourism purposes may be issued with a maximum of 60 days visa on arrival.

Australia Cyprus Japan Portugal
Austria Denmark Netherlands Switzerland
Belgium France Norway Sweden

Canada Germany New Zealand United States
United Kingdom

Entry is subject to the following conditions:

one is not adversely recorded by PNG authorities;
have sufficient funds;
in possession of return/onward tickets to country for which entry rights are assured; (ticket may not be purchased at Jackson Airport)
in possession of 1 completed request for entry permit form
passports bear automatic returnability;
total stay of 60 days;
entry is made at Jacksons Airport, Port Moresby

VISA FEE : K25 = $25.63
VISA OBTAINED ON POST

Following are the short term entry requirements for applicants travelling to Papua New Guinea for the purpose of tourism (maximum of sixty (60) days visa)

Application to be lodged at Embassy of PNG Washington D.C.
Applicant must submit a valid passport at least 6 months from the time application is submitted;)
application form with 1 passport photo;
evidence of return or onward ticket;
self-addressed stamped envelope either certified, express mail or Federal Express (if visa is obtained by mail)
VISA FEE - $10.25 per passport (company check or money order payable to the Embassy)
PERSONAL CHECK OR CASH NOT ACCEPTABLE.

All items on the application form must be completed/signed. Failure to do so will result in return of your visa application)

Upon receipt of all the required documents your visa will be processed within three (3) to seven (7) working days.

Revised Migration & Citizenship Policies
Effective: March 5, 1996

**LONG TERM ENTRY REQUIREMENTS**

Following are the long term entry requirements for applicants travelling to Papua New Guinea (PNG) for the purposes of; Employment and all other applications other than the Tourist/Business/Official Business.

Valid Passport
1 application form
1 passport size photograph
Full medical check
Certificate of AIDS check results from a U.S. Government Health Agency
Chest X-ray results/reports (do NOT send the X-ray film)
Security (police) checks from local place of residence
Character reference from competent authorities
Letter of confirmation from sponsoring organisation or employer
Visa Fee in money order or company check payable to the Embassy of Papua New Guinea.
self-addressed envelope, stamped either certified, Federal express, DHL, UPS, Airborne or Express Mail
PERSONAL CHECKS OR CASH NOT ACCEPTABLE.

**MULTIPLE EMPLOYMENT**

Period of 3 months to 3 years $256.25/passport
Extension to Employment Entry Permit $512.50/passport
Dependents $ 10.25/passport
Volunteer church workers/researchers/missionaries $ 10.25/passport

Children under the age of 16 and accompanying their parent(s) are exempted from requirements 6 to 9.

The medical X-ray reports will be returned to the applicants, who will hand carry together with the X-ray film for presentation to the Immigration Office, Waigani, Port Moresby (PNG)

The Immigration Division of the Department of Foreign Affairs in Papua New Guinea authorises long term entry visas. Employers and sponsoring organisations liaise with Immigration Division to authorise Papua New Guinea Diplomatic Missions and Posts to issue the appropriate visa.

The foregoing are the requirements of the Government of Papua New Guinea.

# SUPPLEMENTS

## IMPORTANT DOCUMENTS

| No. | Title | Year/Author | Country/ Region | Comment |
|---|---|---|---|---|
| COUNTRY SPECIFIC DOCUMENTS – PAPUA NEW GUINEA | | | | |
| 1 | Electricity Industry Policy | 2011 / DPE – Energy Division | PNG | Proposed policy for managing the electricity sector |
| 2 | Electricity Management Committee (EMC) Guideline | 2011 / DPE – Energy Division | PNG | Role and function of the EMC |
| 3 | Development Strategy: 2010 – 2030 | 2010 / Planning | PNG | Long term country strategy including the energy sector |
| 4 | Medium Term Development Plan: 2011-2015 | 2010 / Planning | PNG | Medium term country strategy including the energy sector |
| 5 | Power Sector Development Plan | 2009 / ADB & DPE | PNG | Electricity sector development plan for PNG |
| 6 | Pacific Regional Energy Assessment: PNG | 2004 / SPREP (Johnston) | PNG | Old but still useful review of PNG's energy sector, renewable energy potential & barriers to development |
| 7 | Environmental, Social, and Financing Aspects of Medium and Large Hydropower | 2010 / Paul Cargill | PNG | Interesting analysis of potential hydropower development in PNG |
| 8 | Wabo Dam Proposal | 2010 / Nippon Koei | PNG | Japanese company proposal for Wabo dam development |
| 9 | Opportunities for Hydro Power Development in PNG | 2010 / PNG Power | PNG | Summary of PNG Power's hydro development projects |
| 10 | Petroleum Industry Pricing Review | 2010 / ICCC | PNG | ICCC review of current fuel pricing regulation framework |
| 11 | APEC Energy Overview 2009 | 2010 / APERC | PNG | Chapter giving short PNG energy sector overview |
| 12 | Energy Outlook for Asia and the Pacific | 2009 / ADB | PNG | Chapter giving short PNG energy sector overview |
| 13 | Pacific Islands Greenhouse Gas Abatement through Renewable Energy Project (PIGGAREP) – PNG Interventions | ??? / SREP | PNG | List of PIGGAREP projects in PNG |
| 14 | PNG Power Company Presentation | 2005 / RE Workshop | PNG | Some PNG output / capacity / planning data |
| 15 | Managing Key Landowner Issues within the Context of the Proposed PNG/QLD Hydro project "Wabo Project" | 2011 / Rebecca Ogann Kiage | PNG | Thesis paper examining development issues associated with the Wabo hydro scheme |

# PNG ECONOMIC AND ENERGY OVERVIEW

PNG is by far the largest of the three countries being covered in this study. The recent 2011 Census gives the population as approximately 7 million, compared with 500,000 in the Solomon Islands and 250,000 in Vanuatu. It has also by far the largest population and economy in the South Pacific.

PNG is a very diverse country, with over 600 islands. It is believed that there are about 800 different languages, which is about half the total in the world.

The map below shows the geography of the country. The capital Port Moresby is located in the south. The other largest towns are Lae and Madang further north.

PNG's population was estimated at 7,059,653 in the 2011 Census. That was 1.9 million or 36% higher than the 2000 estimate, implying very high annual growth of about +3.5%.

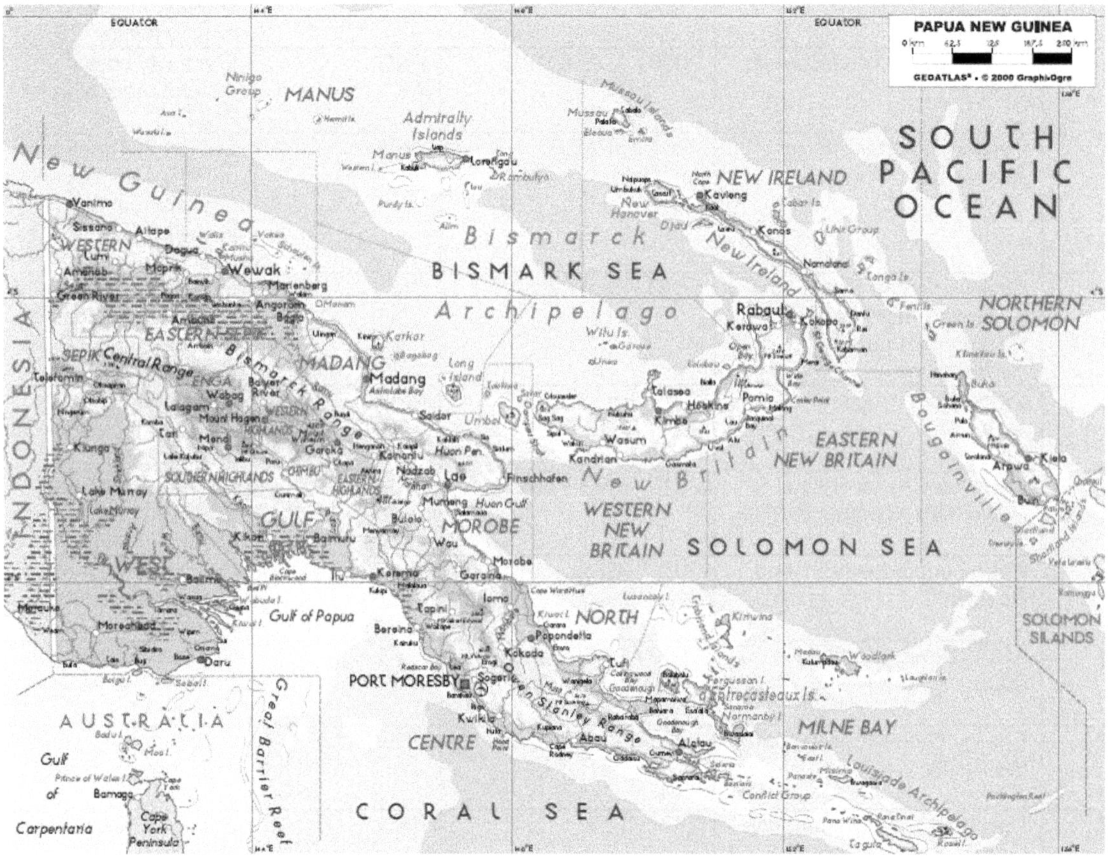


PNG is a classic example of what economists describe as a "dual economy" with two distinct sectors - a traditional subsistence sector dominated by agriculture; and a modern sector dominated by the mining and petroleum industries. The former accounts for about 30% of the country's economic output but about 80% of employment.

The following is a very brief summary of the current state of the PNG economy. More detailed information is available from a range of sources, referenced at the end of this section. They include reports from the Bank of Papua New Guinea (BPNG), ANZ Bank, CIA World Factbook, Australian Government's Department of Foreign Affairs and Trade and the World Bank.

The CIA World Factbook appears to have the most up-to-date information. It gives the country's gross domestic product (GDP) in 2011 as US$ 16.7 billion. That is in purchasing parity prices, which is a common indicator used by the World Bank. At official exchange rates the GDP estimate for 2011 is $11.4 billion, which is significantly lower – by about 32%.

GDP per person/capita grew in real terms (that is taking account of inflation) by an estimated +9% in 2011, +7% in 2010 and +5.5% in 2009. Those are very high rates of growth, well above the world averages, and indicate that the economy has done very well in recent years. PNG was largely unaffected by the global financial crisis.

GDP PPP in 2011 is estimated at $2,500, which was +4% higher than in 2010. PNG ranks 178th in the world (of about 200 countries) on this indicator, so it is still a very poor country despite the recent economic growth.

A key development issue in PNG is clearly the wide disparity in incomes among the local population, which is evident from visiting the capital Port Moresby. As mentioned above, about 80% of the population are dependent on subsistence agriculture, and they have very low incomes as measured in cash. In addition, there has been a significant movement of the rural population into Port Moresby and other cities which has worsened the poverty, crime and related issues there.

According to the CIA Factbook about 30% of PNG's economic output comes from the agricultural sector, 38% from industry and 32% from services. Agriculture's share has been declining slowly and industry's share rising, mainly because of growth in the mining and petroleum industries.

No detailed breakdown of GDP by industry is available but reasonably accurate estimates for the energy industries, notably petroleum and electricity, have been developed during this study.

Most agricultural output is for domestic consumption, although there are some exports. Cash crops ranked by value are coffee, cocoa, copra, tea, rubber and sugar. The fishing industry is also important, not surprisingly because there are so many islands. Vessels from other countries are licensed to fish in PNG waters and shrimps are exported.

There has been substantial growth in timber logging and exports in recent years, although there appear to be many illegal export operations. The most important industries are now mining and petroleum.

PNG is unusual among the South Pacific countries in having significant oil and gas reserves and production. For some years it has been a net exporter of energy through crude oil exports. That has changed in recent years because of declining oil production but the country will soon again become a net exporter of energy when the LNG plant currently under construction becomes operational in 2014.

All the other South Pacific countries are net importers of energy, including the Solomon Islands and Vanuatu, so PNG is unique in that regard.

Accurate energy statistics for PNG are very difficult to obtain. However, some estimates are presented in the next section of this report which are believed to be reasonably accurate.

Oil production in PNG dates back to 1991 when the Kutubu field began production. Peak output was in 1993 since when it has declined, with year-to-year fluctuations.

There have been a few other oil fields discovered but many more gas fields. It seems certain that PNG's gas reserves are many times larger than the oil reserves.

All the crude oil was exported via the Kumul terminal on the Gulf coast. The country continued to import refined oil products such as diesel, petrol (gasoline) and aviation fuel.

InterOil built an oil refinery in Port Moresby, which came on-stream in 2004. It was the first oil refinery in the South Pacific and is still the only one.

The refinery mainly serves the domestic PNG market but exports a few products to other countries in the region. Perhaps surprisingly, it has largely relied on importing crude oil rather than using the oil from Kutubu, for reasons explained later in this report.

Gas production to date has been on a very small scale and largely limited to the Hides gas-to-electricity project, which is discussed later in this report. The main reason for that has been difficulty in finding commercial markets for the gas. In the 1990s a lot of work was done on a proposed Gas-to-Queensland pipeline but that project eventually collapsed and did not go ahead.

However, it was replaced by the LNG project, which is now under construction. That project will pipe gas to a plant near Port Moresby, where it will be liquefied and then exported to markets in Asia.

It is estimated that of the total primary energy consumption in 2011 biomass accounted for 53% of the total, oil products 30% and electricity 17%. Most of the population is dependent on biomass for its energy needs and only 12.4% has access to an electricity service.

The breakdown of consumption by sector in 2011 was residential 59%, industry 34% and transport 7%.

It is also estimated that of PNG's primary energy supply in 2011 crude oil and oil products accounted for 68%, biomass 29% and hydro 3%.

## PNG OIL SECTOR REVIEW

The Kutubu oil field in the Southern Highlands was discovered in 1986 and the first production was in 1992. The oil is piped to a marine terminal at Kumul on the Gulf coast from where it is exported by tankers, as shown on the map below.

Three other oil fields have subsequently been developed – Moran, Gobe and SE Mananda, which are also shown on the map. The oil fields are operated by Oil Search, the main oil company in PNG, in partnership with other companies.

Oil production has been declining slowly since a peak in 1993, as set out in Table 1 and Figure 1. Production in 2011 was just over 10 million barrels, equivalent to just under 1.5 million tonnes. Average daily output was about 30,000 bpd.

Table 1 and Figure 1 also show annual oil consumption in PNG. It appears to have been flat until 2001, averaging about 725,000 tonnes per year or 15,000 bpd but has risen substantially over the last decade to 1.8 million tonnes or 37,000 bpd in 2010.

Because of the large rise in domestic consumption and the decline in production, PNG became a net importer of oil in 2010, as shown in Table 1 and Figure 1. That has obvious implications for the country's balance of payments and energy security.

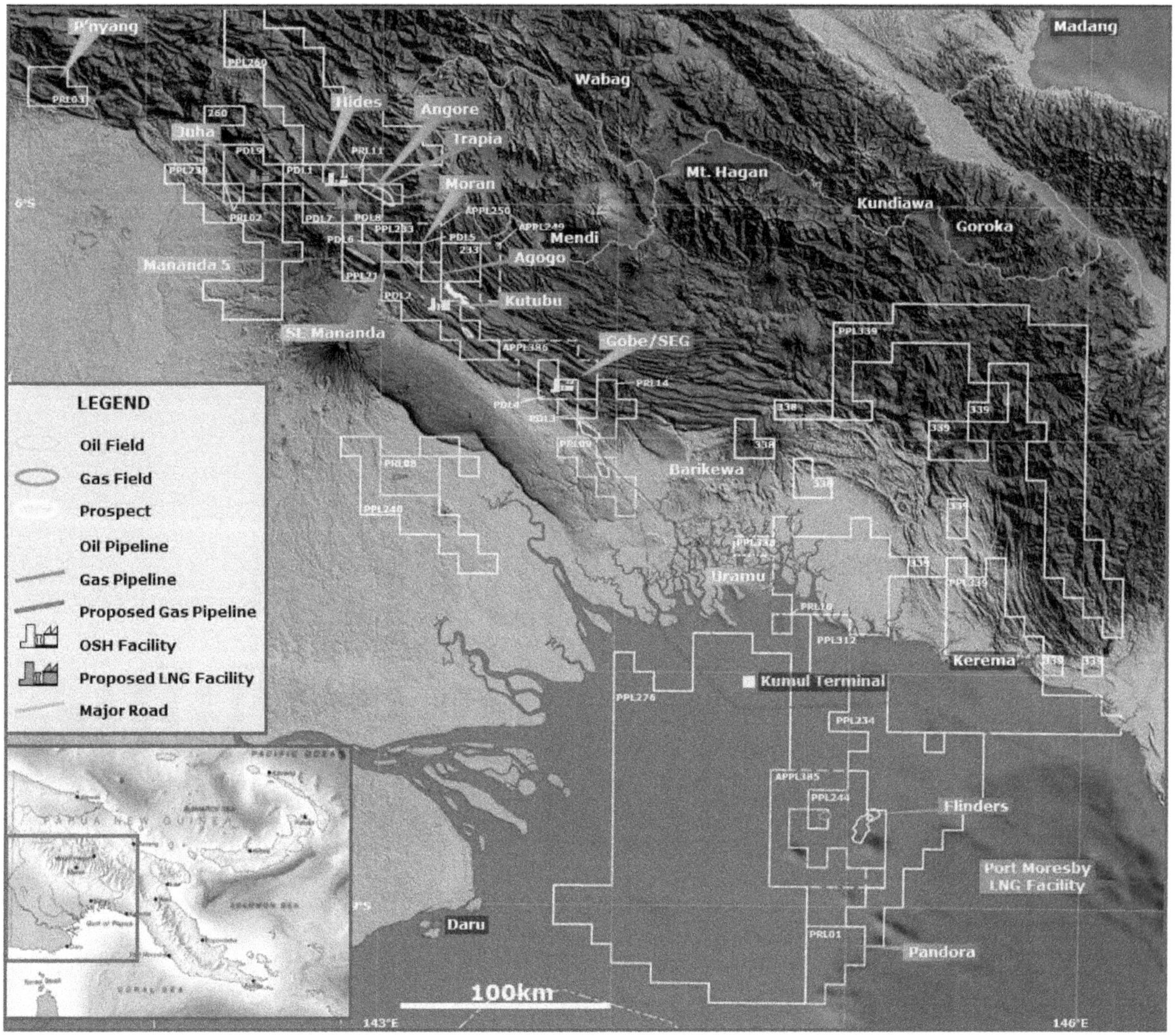


**Table 1: PNG Crude Oil Production and Consumption 1990-2010**

| year | thousands barrels per day | | difference | | year | tonnes per year | | difference |
|---|---|---|---|---|---|---|---|---|
| | production | consumption | | | | production | consumption | |
| 1990 | | 15,600 | -15,600 | | 1990 | | 759,200 | -759,200 |
| 1991 | 200 | 15,470 | -15,270 | | 1991 | | 752,873 | -752,873 |
| 1992 | 53,000 | 15,360 | 37,640 | | 1992 | 2,579,000 | 747,520 | 1,831,480 |
| 1993 | 125,880 | 15,340 | 110,540 | | 1993 | 6,126,160 | 746,547 | 5,379,613 |
| 1994 | 110,000 | 15,000 | 95,000 | | 1994 | 5,353,333 | 730,000 | 4,623,333 |
| 1995 | 100,000 | 15,180 | 84,820 | | 1995 | 4,866,667 | 738,760 | 4,127,907 |
| 1996 | 103,360 | 15,140 | 88,220 | | 1996 | 5,030,187 | 736,813 | 4,293,373 |
| 1997 | 80,000 | 15,450 | 64,550 | | 1997 | 3,893,333 | 751,900 | 3,141,433 |
| 1998 | 79,060 | 14,830 | 64,230 | | 1998 | 3,847,587 | 721,727 | 3,125,860 |
| 1999 | 96,600 | 14,830 | 81,770 | | 1999 | 4,701,200 | 721,727 | 3,979,473 |
| 2000 | 70,060 | 14,940 | 55,120 | | 2000 | 3,409,587 | 727,080 | 2,682,507 |
| 2001 | 67,500 | 14,980 | 52,520 | | 2001 | 3,285,000 | 729,027 | 2,555,973 |
| 2002 | 55,150 | 22,040 | 33,110 | | 2002 | 2,683,967 | 1,072,613 | 1,611,353 |

| | | | | | | | | |
|---|---|---|---|---|---|---|---|---|
| 2003 | 50,490 | 25,180 | 25,310 | | 2003 | 2,457,180 | 1,225,427 | 1,231,753 |
| 2004 | 45,580 | 25,020 | 20,560 | | 2004 | 2,218,227 | 1,217,640 | 1,000,587 |
| 2005 | 40,280 | 25,080 | 15,200 | | 2005 | 1,960,293 | 1,220,560 | 739,733 |
| 2006 | 44,390 | 26,530 | 17,860 | | 2006 | 2,160,313 | 1,291,127 | 869,187 |
| 2007 | 41,990 | 26,440 | 15,550 | | 2007 | 2,043,513 | 1,286,747 | 756,767 |
| 2008 | 38,080 | 31,000 | 7,080 | | 2008 | 1,853,227 | 1,508,667 | 344,560 |
| 2009 | 34,830 | 33,690 | 1,140 | | 2009 | 1,695,060 | 1,639,580 | 55,480 |
| 2010 | 30,360 | 37,280 | -6,920 | | 2010 | 1,477,520 | 1,814,293 | -336,773 |

Source: US Energy Information Administration (EIA)

**Figure 1: PNG Oil Production and Consumption 1980-2010**

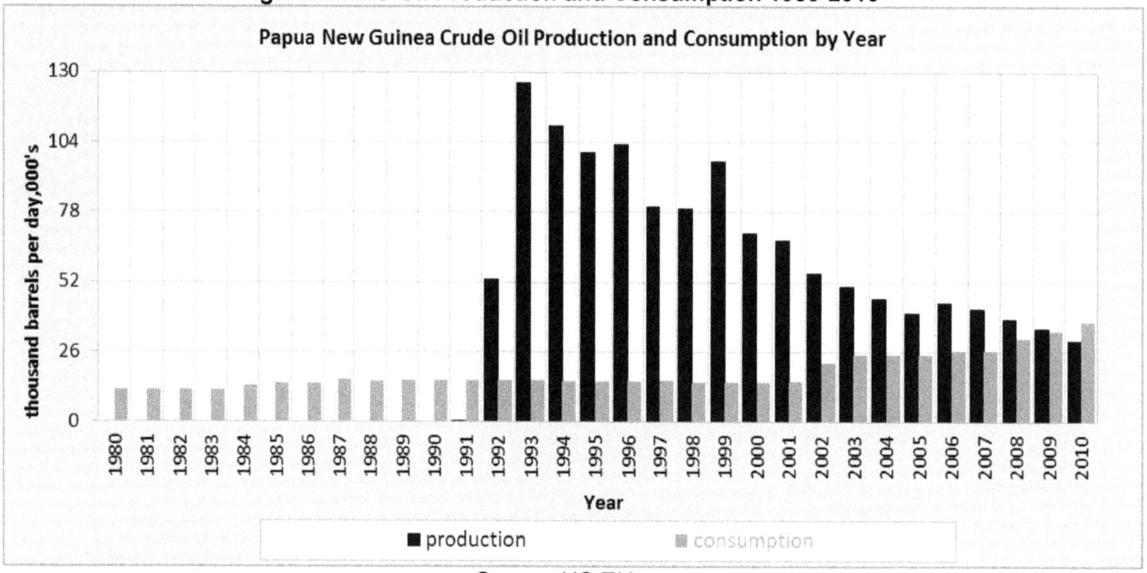


Source: US EIA

According to the EIA crude oil imports since 2007 were as follows:

**Table 2: PNG Crude Oil Imports by Year**

| year | barrels per day |
|---|---|
| 2007 | 15,220 |
| 2008 | 24,680 |
| 2009 | 15,100 |
| 2010 | 19,400 |

Source: US Energy Information Administration (EIA)

The import-export situation is complicated by the InterOil refinery in Port Moresby. It imports virtually all of its crude oil requirements rather than using oil from PNG fields. The company also import various oil products to supplement the refinery's production.

It is very difficult to forecast future oil production and consumption in PNG. As mentioned above, oil production has fallen steadily in recent years and the industry's current efforts are largely focused on the LNG project.

However, Oil Search is reportedly optimistic about finding additional oil reserves in the country. The LNG project will also produce oil liquids, known as condensate, which will be separated from the gas, as described below. They are expected to total about 20,000 bpd. Talisman Energy also has plans to strip liquids from the Stanley gas/condensate field and re-injecting the gas into the reservoir for future use. Those liquids would be used for power generation in the area.

The basic assumption is that PNG's annual oil production will increase from its current level of about 15 million tonnes or 30,000 bpd per year to 25 million tonnes or 50,000 bpd by 2020. Most of that rise will be the condensate from the LNG project.

Oil consumption will undoubtedly continue to increase, albeit with year-to-year fluctuations because of trends in both the national and world economies. In producing the forecast energy balances presented in this Report average annual growth of +5% is assumed during the period to 2020, except for +10% in 2012. On that basis the forecast consumption in 2015 is 2.4 million tonnes or 42,900 bpd and in 2020 2.9 million tonnes or 54,750 bpd.

Table 3 and Figure 2 present these forecasts.

**Table 3: Forecasts of PNG oil production and consumption, 2012-20**

| year | thousands barrels per day | | difference | | year | tonnes per year | | difference |
|---|---|---|---|---|---|---|---|---|
| | production | consumption | | | | production | Consumption | |
| 2011 | 30,000 | 41,010 | -11,010 | | 2011 | 1,460,000 | 2,009,500 | -549,500 |
| 2012 | 30,000 | 45,110 | -15,110 | | 2012 | 1,460,000 | 2,210,400 | -750,400 |
| 2013 | 30,000 | 47,370 | -17,370 | | 2013 | 1,460,000 | 2,321,000 | -861,000 |
| 2014 | 30,000 | 49,730 | -19,730 | | 2014 | 1,460,000 | 2,437,100 | -977,100 |
| 2015 | 40,000 | 52,220 | -12,220 | | 2015 | 1,950,000 | 2,558,900 | -608,900 |
| 2016 | 50,000 | 54,830 | -4,830 | | 2016 | 2,450,000 | 2,686,800 | -236,800 |
| 2017 | 50,000 | 57,570 | -7,570 | | 2017 | 2,450,000 | 2,821,200 | -371,200 |
| 2018 | 50,000 | 60,450 | -10,450 | | 2018 | 2,450,000 | 2,962,200 | -512,200 |
| 2019 | 50,000 | 63,470 | -13,470 | | 2019 | 2,450,000 | 3,110,400 | -660,400 |
| 2020 | 50,000 | 66,650 | -16,650 | | 2020 | 2,450,000 | 3,265,900 | -815,900 |

On the basis of these assumptions the import deficit is forecast to increase to about one third of production in 2014. Once the LNG project begins, PNG could become a net exporter of oil again for a few years. However, it seems more likely that there will continue to be a need for net imports.

# PNG GAS SECTOR REVIEW

PNG has more gas reserves than oil. To date only a tiny proportion of those reserves have been produced but that will change dramatically over the next few years when the LNG project begins production, which is expected in 2014.

The country's proven and probable gas reserves have been estimated to be at least 15 tcf, which is equivalent to approximately 2.7 billion barrels or 360 million tonnes of oil. Thus the gas reserves are probably four times greater than the proven oil reserves and possibly more.

To date only a tiny proportion of those gas reserves have been produced via the Hides gas-to-electricity (GTE) project, which supplies gas for electricity generation at the nearby Porgera gold mine. Some information on that project are presented below

**Figure 2: Forecasts of PNG oil production and consumption, 2012-20**

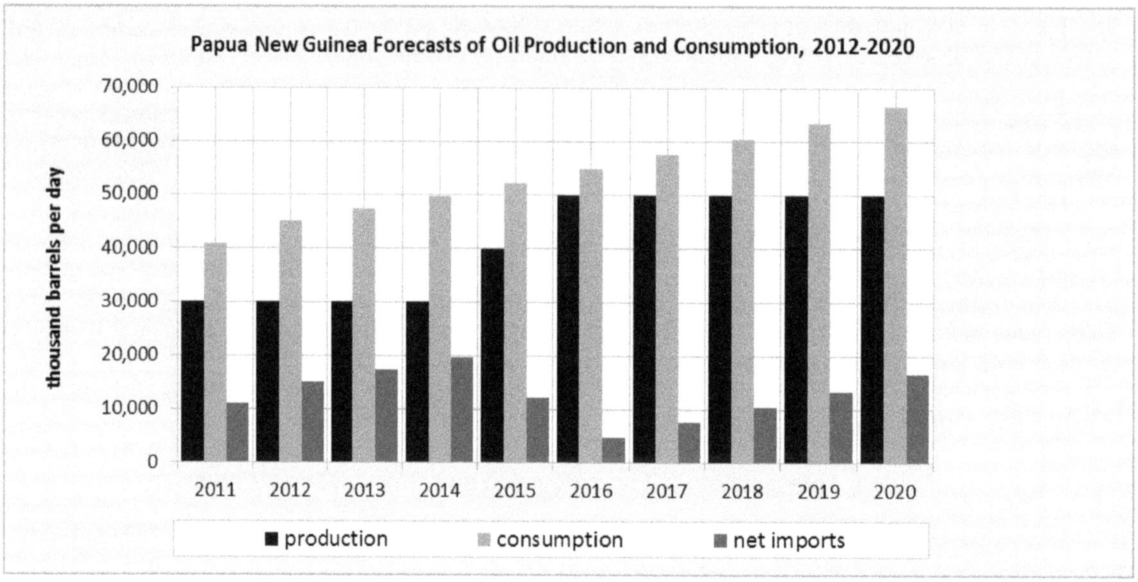


The map shows various other gas discoveries such as Juha and Angore which will be developed as part of the LNG project.

The biggest challenge for the gas industry in PNG has been to find commercial markets for the gas, particularly export markets. In the first half of the last decade attention was concentrated on a proposed gas pipeline to Queensland in Australia but that project eventually collapsed and did not proceed.

Attention then switched to the possibility of exporting the gas in liquefied form. After many studies and lengthy negotiations, one such project is currently under construction, operated by ExxonMobil, the multinational oil major, in partnership with Oil Search and other partners.

InterOil also has plans for a second LNG project and possibly also Talisman Energy. More information on their plans is given below.

There are currently no firm plans for using the gas for domestic consumption, notably to generate electricity to reduce the dependence on imported and expensive diesel, although there have been many proposals in the past. This issue of domestic use is important for the study and is discussed in the Report as well as in the section below.

## PNG LNG PROJECT

Gas from Hides and other field will be exported from PNG as LNG. It will be piped to the Gulf Coast (284 km onshore pipeline) and then under the sea (407 km offshore) to the LNG plant currently under construction near Port Moresby. The estimated cost of the LNG project is US$ 15 billion.

An artist's impression of the project is reproduced below. It is taken from the project's website (www.pnglng.com).

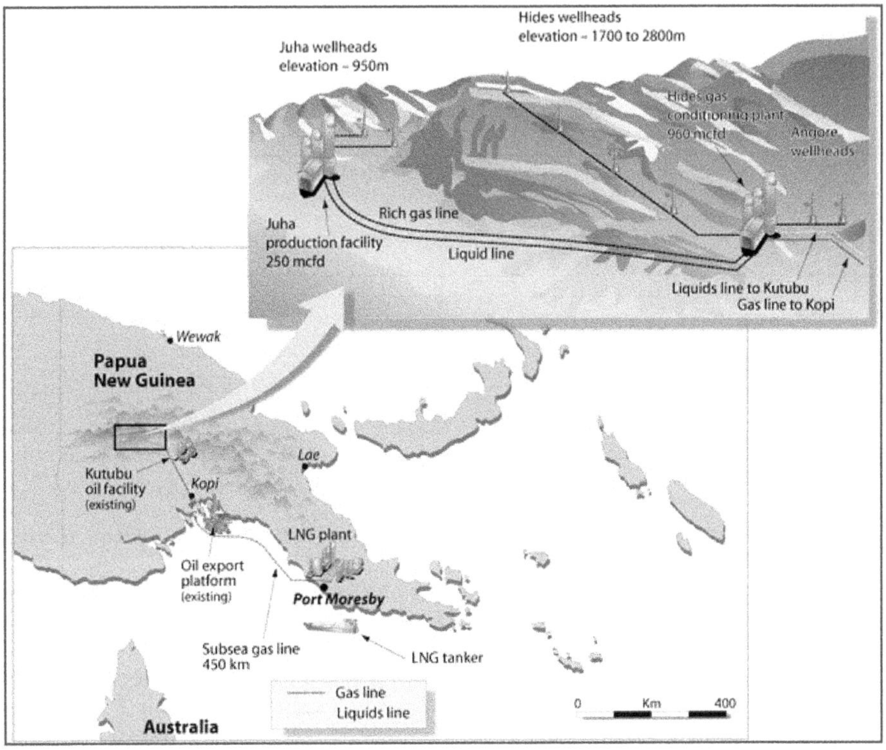


The LNG plant will have two trains with an annual capacity of 6.6 million tonnes per year. That is equivalent to about 8.2 million tonnes of oil per year. First production is expected in 2014.

The country's current oil production is about 1.5 million tonnes per year so the LNG project will result in a very large increase in PNG's petroleum output, as well as economic output and the Government's tax revenues.

There is the possibility of adding a third train at the Port Moresby plant, which would increase the annual production to about 10 million tonnes per year.

Gas from the Hides field should be sufficient to supply the LNG plant for 20 years. Other fields could extend the project's life to at least 30 years.

Table 1 sets out forecasts of LNG production from the project. It is assumed that the first output will be in 2015 rather than 2014 and that in that year it will be 50% of the subsequent annual production. It is also assumed that the third train will come on-stream in 2019, increasing annual production to 10 million tonnes of LNG.

The table also shows the forecasts in million toe using the standard conversion factor of 1 tonne LNG = 1.22 toe. These forecasts are included in the energy balance forecasts presented in the body of this Report.

**Table 1: Forecasts of PNG LNG production**

| year | million tonnes LNG | million tonnes oil equivalent |
|---|---|---|
| 2014 | 0.0 | 0.0 |
| 2015 | 3.3 | 4.0 |
| 2016 | 6.6 | 8.1 |
| 2017 | 6.6 | 8.1 |
| 2018 | 6.6 | 8.1 |
| 2019 | 10.0 | 12.2 |
| 2020 | 10.0 | 12.2 |

*Source: Experts' estimates*

Most of the gas will come from the Hides field. When that begins to decline, gas will be supplied from the Angore field and then Juha. There will also be smaller quantities of gas from the Kutubu and other existing oil fields.

Most of the gas fields in PNG are what are known in the industry as wet fields, which means that they include both gas and liquids such as condensate and liquid petroleum gases (LPG). The PNG LNG project will separate the condensate from the gas and that will be piped via the existing Kutubu oil pipeline to the export terminal on the Gulf Coast. There are also longer term plans to separate the LPG from the gas.

As mentioned earlier, the condensate could average 20,000 bpd during the early years of the LNG project. That compares with the existing oil production of about 30,000 bpd, so it will result in a big increase.

Mention should be made of two other proposed gas projects in PNG by InterOil and Talisman Energy. There could also be others in the future.

InterOil built and operates an oil refinery in Port Moresby, as mentioned in the oil section above, which is the only refinery in the South Pacific. They have also undertaken upstream exploration and discovered two gas fields, Elk and Antelope.

InterOil believes that there are sufficient gas reserves in these fields for a second LNG export plant in PNG. Their plans were approved by the last PNG Government, although the previous Minister of Petroleum and Energy heavily criticised InterOil for lack of progress just before the recent election.

InterOil's LNG plans have not been included in the forecasts to 2020. However, if they go ahead before then they would obviously give another big boost to PNG's energy sector and economy.

Talisman Energy also has gas in the Stanley field and other discoveries. The company have a Gas Aggregation Project (GAP) which is intended "to aggregate significant discoveries and prospective gas resources" with a view to exporting the gas as LNG.

Talisman's short-term plans are to strip the condensate (liquids) from the gas and re-inject the latter for future use. The condensate would be sold as fuel to mines in the region or other customers.

As with InterOil, Talisman's LNG plans have not been included in the gas forecasts to 2020. However, the oil production forecasts include some condensate production from the company's fields.

It is possible that some of the gas could be used for electricity generation in PNG or other domestic uses, if the PNG Government insists on a DMO in any gas agreement for the InterOil and Talisman projects. That possibility is discussed in more detail below.

**HIDES GAS-TO-ELECTRICITY PROJECT**

The existing gas production in PNG is limited to what is known as the Hides GTE project, which supplies electricity to the nearby Porgera gold mine. The project is operated by Oil Search but Hides will soon be the key field in the LNG project. Production has been very small, averaging only about 150,000 tonnes oil equivalent per year.

The Oil Search website states that the "gas is sold under a gas supply contract, which expires in October 2011, but is likely to be extended, in line with the Porgera mine life". That was confirmed by Oil Search officials.

The volume of gas supplied to Porgera in the future is unlikely to change much during the period to 2020. It is very small in comparison with the LNG volumes so this has not been shown separately in the energy balance forecasts.

It is understood that some of the electricity generated is supplied to local people in the Hides and Porgera areas. The quantities involved are very small but a good example of what can be done when there are major industrial developments in the rural parts of the country.

## DOMESTIC MARKET OBLIGATIONS

It is understood that all the gas from the Hides field is committed to the LNG project, except for the Hides/Porgera GTE project. ExxonMobil and Oil Search are also hoping to prove up additional reserves to supply a third LNG train. Thus it is very unlikely that any of the Hides gas will be available for domestic consumption.

Oil Search also indicated that there is no DMO in the LNG project agreement between the state and the companies, except for the possible expansion of Hides GTE.

However, other gas reserves have been found by other companies in PNG so there is the possibility that some of that gas could be used for electricity generation, notably to replace diesel-fired generation in the Port Moresby area. That would presumably require a DMO in future gas project agreements but the Government should be able to ensure that.

A key issue is the difference between the price that the companies would receive for gas used for electricity generation in PNG – and possibly other domestic uses – and the price received for gas exported as LNG. At present it appears that the former would be very much lower and because of that the oil and gas companies have shown little interest in supplying gas to the domestic market.

However, the price of imported diesel is currently very high so an analysis of comparative costs and prices will need to be undertaken to provide an objective assessment of the real differences.

From the work done to date it is believed that using gas for electricity generation, replacing expensive imported diesel, would significantly improve PNG's energy security. This, therefore, should be a high priority for the PNG Government.

The current LNG project, led by ExxonMobil, will also lead to a substantial increase in the PNG Government's annual revenues. Some of those revenues could be used to support renewable energy and energy efficiency projects discussed below.

# PNG ELECTRICITY SECTOR REVIEW

As described in the Report, PPL's operations principally cover three separate systems. These are:

Port Moresby:

Peak demand of 92 MW (peaks in October) in 2009.

Total capacity of 130.5 MW (of which 66 MW is hydro and 64.50 MW is thermal).

Total capacity of 130.5 MW features:

The Rouna system comprising four hydro stations on the Laloki River, controlled water storage in Sirinumu Reservoir and a small generating set at the toe of Sirinumu dam. The total generation capacity from the Rouna Power Stations is 48 MW.

The diesel and gas turbine units at Moitaka have a generation capacity of 36.7 MW.

PPL purchases electricity from a privately owned power station at Kanudi that adds a further 24 MW to the Port Moresby system generation capacity and is utilised as base load.

Demand growth of 6-9% is forecast from 2012 to 2015 but is then expected to slow to approximately 4% per annum until 2020.

Ramu system (Lae-Madang-Mendi):

Peak demand of 70 MW in 2009.

Total capacity of 113 MW all (of which 87 MW is hydro and 26 MW is thermal).

This total capacity features:

The Ramu Hydro Power Station with an installed capacity of 75 MW, comprising of five units of 15 MW each. This station which was previously a run-of-river scheme became a storage scheme when the Yonki dam was commissioned in February, 1991.

The Pauanda run-of-river station in the Western Highlands Province with a capacity of 12 MW.

Power is also purchased (when required) from PNG Forest Products Limited in Morobe Province. This company owns the 5.7 MW Baiune / Bulolo hydro development at Bulolo in Morobe Province. From 1 to 2 MW is accessed by PPL depending on availability.

Peak supply is forecast to reach 100 MW by October 2011 (when Ramu I is fully refurbished).

Demand growth is expected to average 6% per annum from 2012 to 2015 and decline to a steady rate of 3.5% from 2016 to 2020 (excluding mining load).

Gazelle (Rabaul) system:

Peak demand of 10 MW in 2009

Total capacity of 18.2 MW (of which 9.4 MW is hydro and 8.8 MW is thermal).

Total capacity features:

A 9.4MW hydro power system at Warangoi.

The Kerevat Diesel Power Station that has 5.4 MW of capacity.

The Tokubar Disel Power Station has 3.4 MW of capacity.

Demand growth is expected to stay at 2% per annum till 2020.

PNG has many potential sources of RE to be exploited:

With more than 60 active volcanoes, PNG has the potential to generate over 9,000 MW of geothermal power, ranking the country amongst the top five in the world in this regard. The five key volcanic areas (as highlighted by the Ambata Capital Pacific[10]) are Willaumez Peninsula, Rabaul, Kairiru Island, Madilogo and Fergusson Island.[11]

PNG has considerable hydro potential estimated at approximately 15,000 MW[12]

The Port Moresby System will expand to include the Naoro Brown Hydro Scheme Project (expected to be in operation in 2017) located 40 km away from Port Moresby that will offer a potential capacity of 60 MW and produce 270 GWh.[13]

The Port Moresby System will expand to include the Udava Hydro Project which is located 100 km northwest of Port Moresby and will provide potential capacity of 60 MW.[14]

Other areas which have hydro development opportunities include Toriu (40 MW capacity and 244.4 MWh production), Mevelo (24 MW capacity and 91.1 MWh production), Waitavalo (20 MW capacity and 118.26 MWh production) and Begbeg (21 MW capacity and 167.23 MWh production).[15]

Detailed forecasts for RE development are included in the main body of this Report.

There are approximately twenty-five power stations operated by private companies principally for own-supply purposes. These facilities include:

The Ok Tedi mine provides its own electricity from the nearby 58 MW Ok Menga hydroelectric run-of-river scheme and from two 45 MW and 16 MW diesel stations.

10 Ambata is a global investment and advisory firm specializing in clean energy.

11 Reykjavik Geothermal Projects in PNG Briefing for ENG Provincila Government, 2011

12 ADB Power Sector Development Plan, 2009

13 PNG Power Ltd Opportunities for Hydro Power Development in PNG

15 PNG Power Ltd Opportunities for Hydro Power Development in PNG

Lihir Gold Mine, West New Britain Province. The mine is powered with a 52.8 MW geothermal plant.

Tolukuma Mines, Central Province. This mine is actually within 100 km of Port Moresby but it is located in an area unserved by electricity. The mine's power source is a group of hydro and diesel units having capacities of 1.5 MW and 3.2 MW respectively.

Porgera JV Mines, Enga Province. This mine's power supply is from a 62 MW gas-fired plant at the Hides gas field.

Ramu Sugar Limited. The company owns a diesel unit with a capacity of 3 MW.

Kimbe system which is supplied by the Ru Creek Mini hydro system and has a capacity of 0.7 MW.

Bialla system which is supplied by Lake Hargy mini hydro scheme and has a capacity of 1.3MW.

# PNG ELECTRICITY SECTOR – PESSIMISTIC CASE SUMMARY

An alternative – Pessimistic – development scenario has also been run. In this case, demand growth is forecast to increase at an average of just 3.3% for all three existing grid systems as well as for isolated / non-grid locations. Some new capacity development still takes place (existing, planned hydro schemes, one gas plant as well as some limited RE development) but lower growth means the overall capacity development requirement is lower (at approximately 225 MW from 2012 to 2020). Also, no diesel capacity retirements are assumed to take place.

***Pessimistic Case – Key Assumptions***

| Criteria | Assumption |
|---|---|
| Consumption | Pt Moresby: 4% to 2015 and then 3% thereafter<br>Ramu: 2% from 2012 to 2020<br>Gazelle: 2% from 2012 to 2020<br>Other / Western province: 3% from 2012 to 2020 |
| Capacity | Hydro – only ongoing capacity development schemes will materialise by 2020<br>Diesel – no replacement is expected as insufficient other capacity will be developed to meet demand<br>Gas – one plant to be developed by 2020<br>Other – some limited renewable energy capacity development principally to serve demand in off-grid areas |
| Load Factor | No real impact |
| Energy Efficiency | Expected to be negligible across the forecast period |

# US AND COUNTRY CONTACTS

**U.S. GOVERNMENT CONTACTS**

Ambassador: Arma Jane Karaer
Deputy Chief of Mission: Edward J. Michal
Economic/Commercial Officer: Beatrice P. Soila
(September 1997: Edward P. Arrizabalaga)
Commercial Assistant: Crescentia K. Anderson

Consular Officer: Robert Waldrop

Tel: 675-321-1455
Fax: 675-321-3423

International Address:

U.S. Embassy
P.O. Box 1492
Port Moresby, N.C.D. 121
Papua New Guinea

Via U.S. Postal Service:

Port Moresby
Department of State
Washington, DC 20521-4240

U.S. Agricultural Trade Office
541 Orchard Road #08-03
Liat Towers
Singapore 0923

Tel: 65-737-1233
Fax: 65-732-8307

Office of Pacific Island Affairs
EAP/PIA
Room 5317, N.S.
U.S. Department of State
Washington, DC 20520-6310

Tel: 202-647-3546
Fax: 202-647-0118

Office of Pacific Basin
International Trade Administration
U.S. Department of Commerce
Washington, DC 20230

Tel: 202-482-2954
Fax: 202-482-5330

Department of Agriculture
Foreign Agricultural Service
Trade Assistance and Promotion Office
Washington, DC 20250

Tel: 202-720-7420

TPCC Trade Information Center
Tel: 1-800-USA-TRADE

Office of the Coordinator for Business Affairs
U.S. Department of State

Tel: 202-647-1625
Fax: 202-647-3953

**MULTILATERAL DEVELOPMENT BANK CONTACTS**

U.S. Department of Commerce
Liaison to the U.S. Executive Director's Office
International Bank for Reconstruction and Development
Room D-13004
1818 H Street, NW
Washington, DC 20433

Tel: 202-458-0118
Fax: 202-477-2967

Cantwell Walsh
Senior Commercial Officer
ADB Liaison Office
U.S. Embassy, Manila
APO AP 96440

Fax: 632-816-7684
e-mail: cwalsh@doc.gov

Janet Thomas, Acting Director
Multilateral Development Bank Office
U.S. Department of Commerce
14th and Constitution, NW
Washington, DC 20007

Phone: 202-482-3399
Fax: 202-482-5179

**PNG TRADE AND INDUSTRY ASSOCIATIONS**

PNG Chamber of Mines and Petroleum
PO Box 1032
Port Moresby, N.C.D. 121

Tel: 675-321-2988
Fax: 675-321-7107

**PNG GOVERNMENT OFFICES**

Embassy of Papua New Guinea
1615 New Hampshire Ave. NW
Washington, DC 20009

Tel: 202-745-3680
Fax: 202-745-3679

Investment Promotion Authority
PO Box 5053
Boroko, N.C.D. 111

Tel: 675-321-7311
Fax: 675-321-2819

Department of Mining & Petroleum
PO Box 352
Konedobu, N.C.D. 125

Office of the Secretary: Ph 675-321-7600/Fax 321-7958
Mining Division: Ph 675-322-7624/Fax 321-3701

Department of Mining & Petroleum
Petroleum Division
PO Box 778
Port Moresby, N.C.D. 121

Tel: 675-322-4200/321-2422
Fax: 322-4222

Internal Revenue Commission
Customs and Excise Operations
PO Box 777
Port Moresby, N.C.D. 121

Tel: 675-322-6600
Fax: 675-321-4249/321-3484

PNG National Fisheries Authority
PO Box 2016
Port Moresby, N.C.D. 121

Tel: 675-321-2643
Fax: 675-320-2074

Papua New Guinea Forest Authority
PO Box 5055
Boroko, N.C.D. 111

Tel: 675-327-7800
Fax: 675-325-4433

Country Market Research Firms

IMPS Research Pty Ltd
PO Box 986
Port Moresby, N.C.D. 121

Tel: 675-321-3283
Fax: 675-321-7360

Publishes "Petroleum & Minerals Industry Directory" and "The Governments of PNG" (directory of Government Ministries, Departments, etc.)

The CAM Group Pty Ltd
P.O. Box 7312
Cairns, Qld 4870
Australia

Tel: 61-70-521-999
Fax: 61-70-313-661

Publishes "Papua New Guinea Oil and Gas" (monthly report on developments in petroleum industry) and offers mining and petroleum research materials and services

## PAPUA NEW GUINEA BASIC TITLES

***IMPORTANT!***
***All publications are updated annually!***
***Please contact IBP, Inc. at ibpusa3@gmail.com for the latest ISBNs and additional information***
***Global Business and Investment Info Databank: www.ibpus.com***

| title |
|---|
| Papua New Guinea A "Spy" Guide |
| Papua New Guinea A Spy" Guide" |
| Papua New Guinea Banking & Financial Market Handbook |
| Papua New Guinea Banking & Financial Market Handbook |
| Papua New Guinea Business and Investment Opportunities Yearbook |
| Papua New Guinea Business and Investment Opportunities Yearbook |
| Papua New Guinea Business and Investment Opportunities Yearbook Volume 1 Strategic Information and Opportunities |
| Papua New Guinea Business and Investment Opportunities Yearbook Volume 1 Strategic Information and Opportunities |
| Papua New Guinea Business Intelligence Report |
| Papua New Guinea Business Intelligence Report |
| Papua New Guinea Business Law Handbook |
| Papua New Guinea Business Law Handbook |
| Papua New Guinea Business Law Handbook |
| Papua New Guinea Business Law Handbook |
| Papua New Guinea Country Study Guide |
| Papua New Guinea Country Study Guide |

| title |
| --- |
| Papua New Guinea Country Study Guide Volume 1 Strategic Information and Developments |
| Papua New Guinea Diplomatic Handbook |
| Papua New Guinea Diplomatic Handbook |
| Papua New Guinea Ecology & Nature Protection Handbook |
| Papua New Guinea Ecology & Nature Protection Handbook |
| Papua New Guinea Ecology & Nature Protection Laws and Regulation Handbook |
| Papua New Guinea Economic & Development Strategy Handbook |
| Papua New Guinea Economic & Development Strategy Handbook |
| Papua New Guinea Energy Policy, Laws and Regulation Handbook |
| Papua New Guinea Energy Policy, Laws and Regulations Handbook |
| Papua New Guinea Energy Policy, Laws and Regulations Handbook |
| Papua New Guinea Foreign Policy and Government Guide |
| Papua New Guinea Foreign Policy and Government Guide |
| Papua New Guinea Investment and Business Guide |
| Papua New Guinea Investment and Business Guide |
| Papua New Guinea Investment and Business Guide |
| Papua New Guinea Investment and Business Guide |
| Papua New Guinea Mineral & Mining Sector Investment and Business Guide |
| Papua New Guinea Mineral & Mining Sector Investment and Business Guide |
| Papua New Guinea Mining Industry Business Opportunities Handbook |
| Papua New Guinea Mining Industry Business Opportunities Handbook |
| Papua New Guinea Mining Laws and Regulations Handbook |
| Papua New Guinea Oil & Gas Sector Business & Investment Opportunities Yearbook |
| Papua New Guinea Oil & Gas Sector Business & Investment Opportunities Yearbook |
| Papua New Guinea Oil & Gas Sector Business and Investment Opportunities Yearbook Volume 2 |
| Papua New Guinea Oil & Gas Sector Energy Policy, Laws and Regulations Handbook |
| Papua New Guinea Oil & Gas Sector Energy Policy, Laws and Regulations Handbook |
| Papua New Guinea Oil & Gas Sector Oil & Gas Sector Business & Investment Opportunities Yearbook |
| Papua New Guinea Oil & Gas Sector Oil & Gas Sector Business & Investment Opportunities Yearbook |
| Papua New Guinea Oil & Gas Sector Oil and Gas Exploration Laws and Regulation Handbook |
| Papua New Guinea Oil and Gas Exploration Laws and Regulation Handbook |
| Papua New Guinea Recent Economic and Political Developments Yearbook |
| Papua New Guinea Taxation Laws and Regulations Handbook |

# NUCLEAR ENERGY SECTOR POLICY LIBRARY

**(PRICE $149.95 each)**

| |
|---|
| Argentina Nuclear Energy Sector Policy, Laws and Regulations Handbook |
| Armenia Nuclear Energy Sector Policy, Laws and Regulations Handbook |
| Belgium Nuclear Energy Sector Policy, Laws and Regulations Handbook |
| Brazil Nuclear Energy Sector Policy, Laws and Regulations Handbook |
| Bulgaria Nuclear Energy Sector Policy, Laws and Regulations Handbook |
| Bulgaria Nuclear Energy Sector Policy, Laws and Regulations Handbook |
| Bulgaria Nuclear Energy Sector Policy, Laws and Regulations Handbook |
| China Mainland Nuclear Energy Sector Policy, Laws and Regulations Handbook |
| Czech Republic Nuclear Energy Sector Policy, Laws and Regulations Handbook |
| Finland Nuclear Energy Sector Policy, Laws and Regulations Handbook |
| France Nuclear Energy Sector Policy, Laws and Regulations Handbook |
| Germany Nuclear Energy Sector Policy, Laws and Regulations Handbook |
| Hungary Nuclear Energy Sector Policy, Laws and Regulations Handbook |
| India Nuclear Energy Sector Policy, Laws and Regulations Handbook |
| Iran Nuclear Energy Sector Policy, Laws and Regulations Handbook |
| Japan Nuclear Energy Sector Policy, Laws and Regulations Handbook |
| Korea, Democratic People's Republic of Nuclear Energy Sector Policy, Laws and Regulations Handbook |
| Korea, Republic of Nuclear Energy Sector Policy, Laws and Regulations Handbook |
| Mexico Nuclear Energy Sector Policy, Laws and Regulations Handbook |
| Netherlands Nuclear Energy Sector Policy, Laws and Regulations Handbook |
| Pakistan Nuclear Energy Sector Policy, Laws and Regulations Handbook |
| Romania Nuclear Energy Sector Policy, Laws and Regulations Handbook |
| Russia Nuclear Energy Sector Policy, Laws and Regulations Handbook |
| Slovakia Nuclear Energy Sector Policy, Laws and Regulations Handbook |
| Slovenia Nuclear Energy Sector Policy, Laws and Regulations Handbook |
| South Africa Nuclear Energy Sector Policy, Laws and Regulations Handbook |
| Spain Nuclear Energy Sector Policy, Laws and Regulations Handbook |
| Sweden Nuclear Energy Sector Policy, Laws and Regulations Handbook |
| Switzerland Nuclear Energy Sector Policy, Laws and Regulations Handbook |
| Taiwan Nuclear Energy Sector Policy, Laws and Regulations Handbook |
| Ukraine Nuclear Energy Sector Policy, Laws and Regulations Handbook |
| United Kingdom Nuclear Energy Sector Policy, Laws and Regulations Handbook |
| United States Nuclear Energy Sector Policy, Laws and Regulations Handbook |

# WORLD OIL & GAS SECTOR BUSINESS, INVESTMENT OPPORTUNITIES LIBRARY

## Price: $199.95 Each

| Title |
| --- |
| Global Oil & Gas Sector Business & Investment Opportunities Yearbook |
| Algeria Oil & Gas Sector Business & Investment Opportunities Yearbook |
| Angola Oil & Gas Sector Business & Investment Opportunities Yearbook |
| Australia Oil & Gas Sector Business & Investment Opportunities Yearbook |
| Azerbaijan Oil & Gas Sector Business & Investment Opportunities Yearbook |
| Bahrain Oil & Gas Sector Business & Investment Opportunities Yearbook |
| Bangladesh Oil & Gas Sector Business & Investment Opportunities Yearbook |
| Benin Oil & Gas Sector Business & Investment Opportunities Yearbook |
| Brazil Oil & Gas Sector Business & Investment Opportunities Yearbook |
| Brunei Oil & Gas Sector Business & Investment Opportunities Yearbook |
| Cameroon Oil & Gas Sector Business & Investment Opportunities Yearbook |
| Canada Oil & Gas Sector Business & Investment Opportunities Yearbook |
| China Oil & Gas Sector Business & Investment Opportunities Yearbook |
| Colombia Oil & Gas Sector Oil & Gas Sector Business & Investment Opportunities Yearbook |
| Congo Oil & Gas Sector Business & Investment Opportunities Yearbook |
| Congo, Dem. Republic Oil & Gas Sector Business & Investment Opportunities Yearbook |
| Cote d'Ivoire Oil & Gas Sector Business & Investment Opportunities Yearbook |
| Dubai Oil & Gas Sector Business & Investment Opportunities Yearbook |
| Ecuador Oil & Gas Sector Business & Investment Opportunities Yearbook |
| Egypt Oil & Gas Sector Business & Investment Opportunities Yearbook |
| Equatorial Guinea Oil & Gas Sector Business & Investment Opportunities Yearbook |
| Gabon Oil & Gas Sector Business & Investment Opportunities Yearbook |
| India Oil & Gas Sector Business & Investment Opportunities Yearbook |
| Indonesia Oil & Gas Sector Business & Investment Opportunities Yearbook |
| Iran Oil & Gas Sector Business & Investment Opportunities Yearbook |
| Iraq Oil & Gas Sector Business & Investment Opportunities Yearbook |
| Kazakhstan Oil & Gas Sector Business & Investment Opportunities Yearbook |

---

**For additional analytical, business and investment opportunities information, please contact Global Investment & Business Center, USA at (202) 546-2103. Fax: (202) 546-3275. E-mail: rusric@erols.com**

| Title |
|---|
| Kuwait Oil & Gas Sector Business & Investment Opportunities Yearbook |
| Libya Oil & Gas Sector Business & Investment Opportunities Yearbook |
| Malaysia Oil & Gas Sector Business & Investment Opportunities Yearbook |
| Mexico Oil & Gas Sector Business & Investment Opportunities Yearbook |
| Morocco Oil & Gas Sector Business & Investment Opportunities Yearbook |
| Namibia Oil & Gas Sector Business & Investment Opportunities Yearbook |
| New Zealand Oil & Gas Sector Business & Investment Opportunities Yearbook |
| Nigeria Oil & Gas Sector Business & Investment Opportunities Yearbook |
| Norway Oil & Gas Sector Business & Investment Opportunities Yearbook |
| Oman Oil & Gas Sector Business & Investment Opportunities Yearbook |
| Pakistan Oil & Gas Sector Business & Investment Opportunities Yearbook |
| Papua New Guinea Oil & Gas Sector Business & Investment Opportunities Yearbook |
| Papua New Guinea Oil & Gas Sector Oil & Gas Sector Business & Investment Opportunities Yearbook |
| Peru Oil & Gas Sector Business & Investment Opportunities Yearbook |
| Philippines Oil & Gas Sector Business & Investment Opportunities Yearbook |
| Qatar Oil & Gas Sector Business & Investment Opportunities Yearbook |
| Sri Lanka Oil & Gas Sector Business & Investment Opportunities Yearbook |
| Romania Oil & Gas Sector Business & Investment Opportunities Yearbook |
| Russia Oil & Gas Sector Business & Investment Opportunities Yearbook |
| Saudi Arabia Oil & Gas Sector Business & Investment Opportunities Yearbook |
| Sudan Oil & Gas Sector Business & Investment Opportunities Yearbook |
| Suriname Oil & Gas Sector Business & Investment Opportunities Yearbook |
| Syria Oil & Gas Sector Business & Investment Opportunities Yearbook |
| Trinidad and Tobago Oil & Gas Sector Oil & Gas Sector Business & Investment Opportunities Yearbook |
| Tunisia Oil & Gas Sector Business & Investment Opportunities Yearbook |
| Turkey Oil & Gas Sector Business & Investment Opportunities Yearbook |
| Turkmenistan Oil & Gas Sector Business & Investment Opportunities Yearbook |
| Ukraine Oil & Gas Sector Oil & Gas Sector Business & Investment Opportunities Yearbook |
| United Arab Emirates Oil & Gas Sector Business & Investment Opportunities Yearbook |
| United Kingdom Oil & Gas Sector Business & Investment Opportunities Yearbook |
| United Kingdom Oil & Gas Sector Oil & Gas Sector Business & Investment Opportunities Yearbook |
| United States Oil & Gas Sector Business & Investment Opportunities Yearbook |
| Venezuela Oil & Gas Sector Business & Investment Opportunities Yearbook |
| Vietnam Investment Pojects and Joint Ventures Hnadbook |
| Vietnam Oil & Gas Sector Business & Investment Opportunities Yearbook |
| Yemen Oil & Gas Sector Business & Investment Opportunities Yearbook |

www.ingramcontent.com/pod-product-compliance
Ingram Content Group UK Ltd.
Pitfield, Milton Keynes, MK11 3LW, UK
UKHW051456290926
15471UKWH00008B/1242

9 781438 737980